Contents

Acknowledgments

To the folks who responded over the years to my requests for details on specific boats, I give my thanks, especially to Ted Brewer, Richard Byrd, Bob Dailey, Tony Davis, Tony Dubourg, Steve Fisher, Sam Fiske, Bob Foote, John Garfield, Chris Harlan, Garry Hoyt, Bruce Kirby, Nils Lucander, Bill Menger, Giles Morris, Peter Schermerhorn, Bill Shaw, Tim Seibert, Fritz and Lynn Spindler, Jim Taylor, Phil and Vera Williams, Stuart Windley, Charlie Wittholz, and to many, many others. Thanks also to the numerous contributors to the data I found on the Internet, which was very useful, even if some of it turned out to be not entirely accurate. For advice and encouragement on and off during the long period this book took to come to fruition, I thank Jon Eaton and Molly Mulhern of International Marine/McGraw-Hill, Dan Spurr, formerly editor of *Practical Sailor*, Mark Smith, formerly editor of *Yacht Racing/Cruising* and later of *Sailor* magazine, and as always, my loving wife Carol for her patience, understanding, and support.

Preface

This book germinated more than 52 years ago, when my wife Carol and I bought our first fiberglass boat—an 8-foot sailing dinghy, in 1957. At the same time, we started collecting sailboat brochures at boat shows and saving our old and dog-eared boating magazines in a closet, so we could keep track of ads and editorial reports of new fiberglass sailboats being introduced, in anticipation of some day moving up in size.

Every few years we did indeed move up, which resulted in an even greater accumulation of paper. Over the years, the closet became a room full of literature—brochures, ads, books, magazines, plans.

In the 1960s Carol wrote an article for *Yachting* magazine on how she and I had built a fiberglass cruising sailboat (a Carl Alberg–designed South Coast 23) from a kit in our backyard in Darien, Connecticut. Shortly thereafter I wrote my first boating magazine article. Figuring she was ahead of the game with one acceptance and no rejections, Carol retired from writing to pursue other interests (such as bearing and raising two kids in the 1960s, working for a local yacht charter firm in the 1970s, and becoming the first female harbormaster for the town of Darien in the 1980s) while I continued to write (and occasionally illustrate with pen-and-ink drawings) as a sideline to my regular jobs for big corporations doing engineering, financial and corporate planning, business analysis, and consulting in New York City.

Eventually, just as I realized that corporate life was no longer as much fun as it once had been, I found I could make a living as a writer and illustrator. In the mid-1980s I left corporate life and began a career as a freelance writer for boating magazines, among them *Sail, Yachting, Yacht Racing and Cruising* (now *Sailing World*), *Small Boat Journal, WoodenBoat, Practical Sailor*, and others (including some powerboat magazines). I even helped start a new magazine, *Sailor*, which unfortunately folded after a couple of years despite excellent editorial reviews—a victim of bad timing in a "down" sailboat market.

Also in the mid-1980s, Carol and I acquired our first computer and began to tabulate data on our favorite boats. In 1991, we moved from Darien to Sarasota, Florida, bringing a freelance writing business and a roomful of boat records with us. Every once in a while I'd look at the old brochures and magazines to check my memory on the statistics for this boat or that, or just to admire the crisp draftsmanship of a Philip Rhodes or Charlie Wittholz drawing.

One day in 1995, Carol surprised me by asking when I was going to throw out all those old boating files. When I said I had no plans to do so, she asked why I was saving them. I replied that someday I might write a book that summarized the material—maybe a compendium or catalog of some type. (By this time I had already written three successful books, so Carol knew I might be serious.) She asked when I was going to start. Knowing from past experience that I was on shaky ground, I answered: "Now." And so I started.

In looking through the literature to see what "Sailboat Guides"—one-shot books as well as magazine annuals—were already on the market, I realized that none came close to what I had in mind. None covered anywhere near the number of different designs I wanted to include (especially in the under 30-foot range). None provided, for each boat reported, a group of comparable boats—"comps"—that were truly similar in size and performance. In fact, few of these guides applied any kind of penetrating analysis at all to the boats being reported. And few used large-scale drawings with good legibility. I resolved to avoid these problems whenever possible in my book.

So what took me fourteen more years? Among other things, several serious illnesses and other nonwriting activities slowed my continuing research. The job has turned out to be much bigger than I thought it would be. Data on some boats has been elusive. Accommodations plans have not been available on every design. Many letters and e-mails to designers and builders have gone unanswered. Still, it has been an experience I am glad to have had. I hope you will find the results worthwhile.

Introduction

Since the first few fiberglass cruising sailboats popped out of their molds in the late 1950s, well over 2,000 production designs have been built and/or sold in the United States alone. These boats have ranged from around 14 feet to over 70 feet in length, and in type from a few long-running favorites to hoards of run-of-the-mill vessels for which production stopped almost as soon as it started.

Within each size range there has been an incredible number of individual types of vessels—with styles sleek or tubby, traditional or modern, and sometimes just plain weird. One might ask: Why so many different designs? Isn't there a "best" standard of boat for each size range?

The answer is that, regardless of any logic or expert pronouncements to the contrary, as long as individual sailors manifest a variety of tastes, prejudices, budgets, and intended uses, there will be room in the marketplace for a huge variety of different designs. After all, one man's meat is another man's poison.

* * *

Has anybody ever tried to catalog all these designs?

Well, yes and no. Many books and annuals have attempted to keep track of new—and sometimes older—cruising designs. But most of the annuals are merely advertisements for what's currently available, and what is printed is usually paid for by the boatbuilders, giving them editorial license to say only good things about their products, and in some cases to "slant the truth." Reference tomes like the *BUC Book* and the *NADA Guide* (periodicals often available at your local public library and on the Internet), cover approximate pricing but don't include graphics. Some books, like *Field Guide to Sailboats* and *Mauch's Sailboat Guide*, cover some useful details, sail and accommodations plans, and even some analysis of individual designs, but don't cover nearly enough designs or offer detailed statistics or analysis. A few publications cover several hundred boats sketchily, or fifty or a hundred more thoroughly. Graphics tend to be too small, too fuzzy, or missing altogether. Numerous details may be sparse, rife with errors, or both. Commentary may simply parrot a builder's sometimes outlandish claims, without adding honest, objective comment for the benefit of the uninitiated.

The book you are now reading is the result of an attempt to go where no book has gone before—to catalog, list, describe in numbers and words, comment on, and illustrate with sail plans and (whenever possible) accommodations plans virtually every fiberglass production cruising sailboat ever built and sold in the United States—plus some built in Canada, the U.K., and elsewhere and imported for sale in the U.S. market. To limit the huge number of boats to a group that would fit between the covers of a single book, we have chosen to report initially on sailboats between 14 and 25 feet on deck—so-called pocket cruisers.

If the attempt has not fully succeeded, it is not due to lack of effort. It has proven impossible to find sufficient data on some boats. Accommodations plans are not available on every boat. Even sail plans aren't always available. Maybe they are out there somewhere, but despite a valiant effort, we have failed to find a few of them. So this book, too, has defects. Still, we estimate that it covers 80 to 90 percent of all the production boat designs ever brought to the U.S. market.

Consequently, if you are looking for information on cruising sailboats—what types are available, which have what good and bad features, which are considered hot and which are not—you need look no further.

You can learn about what makes some boats better than others, and why some are good for certain sailors and bad for others.

If you're buying a boat, you can examine the details of models you like and compare them with "comps" (comparable vessels in the same range of size and general performance).

If you're thinking of selling your own boat, you may find some positive factoids to advertise.

If you're just window-shopping or even just reminiscing, you can check out what's out there. Examine details of sail plans, special features, layouts, dimensions, performance ratios, and more. You won't find a catalog of new and used boats like this anywhere else.

Happy browsing.

ONE
Guide to the Reviews

WHAT'S COVERED
IN THIS VOLUME

This volume covers 360 cruising sailboats from the smallest feasible size for cruising—about 14' in length on deck (LOD)—up to a nominal 25', that is, up to (but not including) 25' 6" in length. If ever we get around to the next volume, we expect it will cover boats from a nominal 26' (25' 6") through a nominal 31' LOD, and will likewise encompass approximately 360 boats. Part of the reason for this cutoff in size at 25' LOD is to limit each book to a reasonable number of pages, with about 360 boats each, one boat to a page.

Another reason for a 25' cutoff is that above that range, most boats are not conveniently trailerable without heavy commercial trailers, and below it, generally they are. Consequently, by simply eliminating less than 20 percent or so of the heaviest boats included here, this volume could have been named "300 Trailerable Cruising Sailboats."

This is because the main dimension that determines easy trailerability is not a vessel's length or beam, as many people might think; it is her weight. For example, in the 1980s many owners of Hobie 33s (33' long, 8' beam, 4,000 pounds displacement) routinely trailered their boats using ordinary large cars as tow vehicles. Today, of course, almost no ordinary cars would be up to the task, due to reengineering that made cars lighter and weaker. And although beam is a factor, with most states imposing towing restrictions on loads more than 8½' or even 8' wide, many wide-boat owners, including us, have successfully towed their wide boats (such as the J/24, an inch short of 9' in beam), on both interstate highways and back roads without ever receiving a traffic ticket.

Weight, the main practical limit on towability, seldom exceeds 5,000 pounds for boats under 25' LOD. What's magic about 5,000 pounds? Until recently, that was the limit of towing capability of the largest ordinary passenger vehicles. Today many so-called sport utility vehicles (SUVs)—often passenger bodies stuck to truck frames—can sometimes handle more weight, but the SUV owner pays a sizable price in terms of fuel mileage, first cost, and maintenance cost.

Of course, the 5,000-pound limit doesn't refer to what the *boat* weighs. The true limit is the weight of the towed boat *plus* its trailer *plus* its sailing extras: outboard motor, fuel and water tanks, personal gear for the crew, food and ice, and so on. For more on this, see the section on **Trailer towing weight** on page 10.

AN ITEM NOT COVERED: BOAT PRICES

No price ranges are given here. There are several reasons for this.

First and foremost, there's often a wide range of advertised prices for a given make and model, depending on the boat's age, her condition, and what gear goes with her. Note too that pricing for boats—new or used—is not nearly as uniform or consistent as for automobiles. Second, prices fluctuate with the economy. Recessions, for example, create a larger supply and lower demand, forcing prices down, sometimes sharply. Prices also vary considerably with season and geographic area. Any prices we were to quote here would soon be obsolete. The price for a given boat at a given place and time is best estimated by following local ads for similar boats in publications such as *Soundings* or *Latitude 38*, or in online listings (which you can access by Web search engine).

But do exercise caution because quoted prices may vary wildly. For example, actual prices for a Marshall Sanderling 18 (page 40) advertised online in mid-2009 (during an economic recession): for a new boat, $37,000 (plus $11,500 for an inboard diesel and more for other extras); for two boats built in 1981, $12,000 and $15,000; for two boats built in 1975, $10,000 and $17,000; and for a boat built in 1963, $23,000. Is it possible that the condition and gear of the 1963 model justify its seemingly high asking price? Yes, it's possible, but without examining each of the boats you'll have no idea which is the best deal.

You can also consult a free online boat price guide such as www.nadaguides.com, but the prices quoted there may be unrealistically low or occasionally too high. For example, the NADA guide in mid-2009 shows the following Marshall Sanderling 18 prices (rounded to nearest thousand): for a new 2009 boat, $48,000; for a 1999 model, $13,000; for a 1989 model, $7,000; and for a 1979 model, $3,000.

In the end, of course, any boat's market value depends on how much a ready buyer is willing to spend and how little a ready seller is willing to accept. The range of market choices is often so broad that attempting to cite realistic numbers from either ads or NADA is next to useless.

ACCURACY OF THE INFORMATION

The information in this book is taken from many sources, including manufacturers' brochures, sailing magazine articles, information given in books on sailboats and sailing, and interviews and correspondence with designers, builders, owners, and others familiar with the boats concerned. In some cases, information from one source is in conflict with information from another source. For example, different sources may give tabular dimensional information in conflict with what are purported to be drawings made to scale, even when the drawings are from the same source as the tabular data.

It should be obvious to the reader that we have not personally sailed or even set foot on all the vessels reported here. We have sailed in some, however, and even owned a few of them.

In many cases, the boats included here have been out of production for some years (though they continue to be bought and sold on the used-boat market), and verifying questionable information is difficult. Indeed, many of the designers and builders of the boats listed are no longer in business, so contacting them for explanations of anomalies in the data either has not been possible or has resulted in no useful information being received.

This has proven very frustrating for us, since an important objective of this project has been to produce a reference tool with the most accurate data possible. In the end, we used our best judgment in reporting dimensions and other particulars, even when these are in conflict with one or another "official" source. As a consequence, though we hope that errors have been minimized by this approach, some wrong data have almost certainly crept in. Readers are invited to report any errors found, together with suggestions for correction and citation of sources of their information, by writing to the publisher. By this means, correction in a later edition of the book may be possible.

To cite an example: one of the most troublesome dimensions to be dealt with is a sailboat's length. By popular definition, a boat's *Length Overall* (LOA) is her total length including all projections, such as pulpits, pushpits, overhanging booms, boomkins, bowsprits, anchor pulpits, and so on. But this dimension is seldom used by builders, marketers, and sailing publications.

Instead—and despite the fact that their own brochures often inaccurately call it LOA—these folks usually follow the time-honored sailing-industry practice of using *Length On Deck* (LOD) as the fairest measure of a boat's nominal length (i.e., the length by which she is called, such as "Gloucester 19" or "Pearson 22"). This is usually the length from one end of the hull to the other, *omitting* all projections including pulpits, pushpits, booms, boomkins, bowsprits, anchor pulpits, and so on. In the case of reverse transoms, the extensions beyond the after end of the deck are technically not included in LOD (though some marketers may sneak them in anyway, and either call the dimension "hull length" instead of "LOD," or revert to the above LOA definition to get credit for the extra length).

Current industry practice is to round LOD to the nearest whole foot when discussing nominal LOD. Consequently, if a boat is greater than 20.49 feet in length but less than 21.50, most industry folks deem it to be nominally a "21-footer," whereas a boat 21.50 feet LOD is a "22-footer," and a boat 20.49 feet LOD is a "20-footer."

Some builders and marketers, particularly in the early days of fiberglass, didn't seem to be fully aware of this practice (which probably developed in the 1960s). For example, the **Pearson Electra** and **Pearson Ensign**, both with reverse transoms and hull lengths of 22' 6", were sometimes referred to in ads as 22s and sometimes as 23s (though their LOD actually is 22' 3"). In line with the usual industry practice, in this guide they are both called 22s. Similarly, we record the **Cape Dory Typhoon 18** as really 19, and the **J/22** and the **Capri 22** as really 23s.

This lack of uniform industry practice opens up an area for unscrupulous marketers to stretch their boats in words without adding anything to actual length—sometimes resulting in owners thinking they have bought a bigger boat than they actually have.

That is, while *most* designers, builders, and marketers use LOD as the proper measure of length, not all do. And to make matters worse, these days the boating magazines often use the term LOA (Length Overall) in their descriptions of boats when what they really mean is LOD. Unfortunately, this gives a loophole to the few builders, marketers, and others who are not averse to a little "innocent" misrepresentation to ignore industry practice and include bowsprits, boom overhangs, and everything else but the kitchen sink in their "LOD" length.

For example, the **Sovereign 18** is 17' 0" LOD, though the LOA (with a stubby bowsprit) is 18' 0". For another example, the **Herreshoff Eagle 22** is really an "18," having started with the same basic hull as the **Herreshoff America 18** catboat. The **Eagle** folks simply added a sloop rig with a long bowsprit to the 18' hull, and called her a "22."

This guide adds the true size in parentheses after the name to set the record straight. To keep such marketing practices from confusing readers, both the LOA and LOD of every boat are reported here, and each boat name is followed by its nominal length on

Figure One: Dimensions Used in This Guide

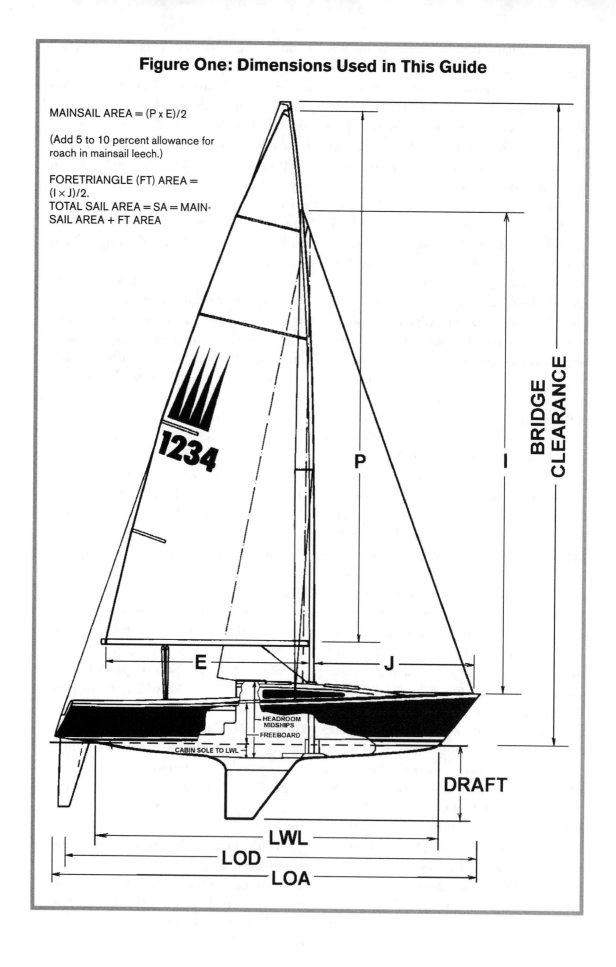

MAINSAIL AREA = (P x E)/2

(Add 5 to 10 percent allowance for roach in mainsail leech.)

FORETRIANGLE (FT) AREA = (I × J)/2.
TOTAL SAIL AREA = SA = MAINSAIL AREA + FT AREA

deck—even when the builder or marketer has intimated that the boat is longer (or, in a few cases, shorter).

Thus the Sovereign 18 (which in one of its permutations was called the Sovereign 5.0) is reported as the **Sovereign 5.0/18 (17)**, and the **Herreshoff Eagle 22** is reported as the **Herreshoff Eagle 22 (18)**. *Caveat emptor.*

At the other end of the spectrum, some builders tend to underplay the issue of length. For example, the **Morgan 24/25** measures 24' 11³/₄" on deck (LOD), so by rights should be called a Morgan 25. But for years Charlie Morgan sold her as a Morgan 24. When I asked Charlie for an explanation of this strange naming practice, he told me that the design was conceived as a 24-footer but gradually grew in length as he fine tuned her. He said he simply never got around to correcting the sales literature. After he sold the company, the new owners promptly began selling her as a Morgan 25, without changing her hull length at all.

Sometimes a boat's length is misrepresented as larger than she is through no fault of the marketer. For example, Pacific Seacraft, an outfit with a well-deserved reputation for good quality, built a boat known as the **Pacific Seacraft Flicka 20**, with an LOD of 20 feet. However, with her outboard rudder, bowsprit, and bow pulpit, she measures 24 feet LOA. In this guide, she is grouped with other 20-footers. But over the years, many annual issues of sailing magazines have mistakenly stuck the Flicka in with the 24-footers, making her harder to find in catalogs, and making comparisons with truly similar boats more difficult.

Sometimes different sources give different data for the same boat, or the data within a single source are inconsistent. For example, the **Elite 25** sales brochure gives the total sail area as 241 square feet, but the E, J, P, and I dimensions (Figure One) are also given, and these result in a total sail area of 252 square feet. Furthermore,

a scale drawing is shown in the boat's sales brochure, but the LOA and LWL dimensions printed in the sales brochure do not match the LOA (or the LOD) and LWL on the drawing. A sailboat annual catalog gives totally different numbers that don't match either, but gives the same scale drawings. Go figure!

THE REVIEWS

While some readers may find the information in the boat reviews presented in the following pages to be self-evident, others may require some guidance in interpreting them. Those who want details are invited to examine the comments below, which refer to specific items on the data sheets.

Arrangement of the Reviews

Chapters are grouped by boat size, as measured by length on deck (LOD), and within each chapter the boats are arranged alphabetically, one boat to a page. There are between 51 and 71 boats in each chapter. For example, Chapter 2 covers 63 boats from 14' to 19' LOD, Chapter 3 covers 71 boats measuring 20' and 21' LOD, Chapter 4 covers 65 boats measuring 22' LOD, and so on.

Boat Name

A few boats are virtually identical to one another except for their names, usually bestowed on identical hulls at different times by different builders or marketers. For example, the Aquarius 23, the Aquarius 7.0, and the Balboa 23 are all different names for virtually the same design, built by successive builders. The same is true of the Gloucester 16 and the Newport 16, the North Star 22 and the Hughes 22, the Starwind 19 and Spindrift 19, and others. Also, sometimes a boat is named for her designer (e.g., the Alberg 22), sometimes for her builder (Pearson 22), and sometimes for some other entity that appeals to the marketer (Sea Sprite 22). Sometimes this free-form naming game can make it difficult to determine exactly which boat is which. To help sort out any confusion, the list at the start of each chapter and the index at the back of this book include all known names for each included boat.

LOD and LOA

As already explained, the LOD is the hull's length on deck, bow to stern with all overhangs omitted. The LOA, as used in this guide, is the overall length of a hull, from outboard tip of bowsprit or other bow overhang to outboard tip of any overhanging boom, boomkin, outboard rudder, or other stern overhang. These definitions of LOA and LOD are not always honored, whether in periodical literature, in compendiums similar to this one, in sales brochures, or even by marketers in naming the boat.

The LOD and the LWL (explained below) are better indicators than the LOA of how much stowage space and elbow-room may be available on board. The LOA, however, is not totally useless, as it is usually employed by boatyards and marinas to figure storage charges and slip fees, and by owners of small trailerable boats to decide if their boats will fit in their garages.

LWL

The LWL is the "load" or "length" (depending on who is doing the defining) of a hull's waterline bow to stern, with the boat upright and equipped for sailing, including crew. It is important to know for several reasons. For one, it is an indicator of speed—the longer the LWL, the greater the maximum theoretical speed. (See *Maximum Speed,*

page 14.) However, it's interesting to observe that the waterline will often become longer when the boat is heeled and when more crew and gear are added. And the waterline is almost always longer in fresh water than in salt water, and the draft is always deeper, since a hull displaces its own weight in water, and fresh water is lighter than salt water (62.4 pounds per cubic foot versus 64 pounds for salt water). In any case, most if not all of the LWLs listed for boats in this guide are calculated assuming the boat is used in salt water.

Draft, Minimum and Maximum

Draft can vary from very shallow to very deep, as defined in **Table One** below. Shallow draft is important for exploring "gunkholes" or for cruising shoal waters such as some of the estuaries along Long Island Sound or the Gulf of Mexico. Also, the shallower the draft, the easier it is to launch and retrieve a trailerable boat at a ramp, and the less top-heavy the load will be while trailering on a highway. Conversely, deep draft is important for efficient sailing close-hauled (with or without centerboard) and (if keel is weighted with ballast) for stability while sailing and comfort in a seaway.

Bridge Clearance

Bridge clearance is the distance from the top of the masthead (or "truck") to the waterline (or from the peak of the gaff in a gaff-rigged boat). It is given with standard rig, and with alternative rigs if known. The number should be taken as approximate, since in some cases we have scaled it from drawings when it is not reported by the builder in

Table One: Two Relative Measures of Draft					
Relative Draft	Very Shallow	Shallow	Moderate	Deep	Very Deep
For cruising	Under 2.5'	2.5' to 3.49'	3.5' to 4.49'	4.5' to 5.5'	Over 5.5'
For easy trailering	Under 0.75'	0.75' to 1.17'	1.18' to 1.99'	2.0' to 3.0'	Over 3.0'

sales brochures or other readily accessible form—and even builders get it wrong sometimes. Moreover, "mast length," when quoted in sales brochures, sometimes refers to the length of the mast from its truck to its heel (or base), rather than truck to waterline, especially when the mast is stepped on deck. Consequently, "mast length" should be checked in each instance to determine whether it is the length from deck to truck, step to truck (when stepped below), or waterline to truck, since "mast length" cannot be relied on to be synonymous with "bridge clearance."

Ballast/Displacement (B/D) Ratio

This is simply the boat's ballast (see page 12), in pounds, divided by the boat's total displacement in pounds. On a given hull design with a given total displacement, increasing the B/D ratio (i.e., increasing ballast while decreasing other weight in the boat) will improve sail-carrying ability, but at the expense of amenities, load-carrying ability, and in the extreme case, even at the expense of hull strength. This is true since, for every pound of ballast added, a pound of utilitarian features must be eliminated, whether it be decorative wood trim or cabinetry, tankage capacity, permissible passenger weight, or stiffening of the hull structure.

In evaluating B/D numbers, we use the following guidelines:

If B/D is. . .	The ballast is said to be relatively. . .
Below 30%	Low (tending to make a boat relatively faster in light air but tender in heavy air)
30% to 40%	Moderate (often the best range for a cruising boat sailed in varying weather conditions)
40% to 50%	High
Above 50%	Very High (tending to make a boat relatively slower in light air but stable in heavy air).

Designer(s)

The designer's name, if known, is given. The best yacht designers usually have a following, similar to their counterparts in other creative fields (sculptors, painters, authors, and others working in the arts). In general, a well-liked designer's boats are recognizable by many sailors, and can be expected to attract a larger, more avid group of potential buyers than boats designed by "the Ajax design team." Some designers are favored for their racing machines, others for their cruisers.

Builder(s)

In some cases, more than one builder utilizes the same or similar molds to build a given boat design. For instance, with some boats in the O'Day line, more than a half dozen different builders, marketers, and/or parent companies can be involved in building a single basic design, at different times and different places. Rather than naming all builders on every data sheet, only the most recognizable builders of each boat (which often is neither the first nor the last to build the boat) are named.

Years Produced

Sometimes the year of introduction and the last year of production are known; sometimes not. Where there is uncertainty, a question mark is used to so indicate.

Sail Area

By and large, the total sail area given here is the total of the mainsail area plus the area of the foretriangle, plus the area of the mizzen sail, if any. (See Figure One.) In some cases, however, the builders or marketers may have calculated total sail area as the sum of the mainsail and a genoa jib, which is larger than the area of a foretriangle—without revealing what they've done. In such cases—if we didn't note and correct the difference—the sail area may be slightly overstated, and resulting ratios, such as SA/D, will also be slightly overstated.

Table Two: Method of Calculating Approximate Trailer Towing Weight (lbs.)

Vessel Displacement	Assumed Additional Gear Weight	Subtotal Boat and Gear	Approximate Trailer Weight	Total Approximate Towing Weight
Under 850	150	Max. 1,000	300	Max 1,300
850–999	180	1,180	325	1,505
1,000–1,199	190	1,390	375	1,765
1,200–1,399	200	1,600	400	2,000
1,400–1,599	210	1,810	450	2,260
1,600–1,799	220	2,020	500	2,520
1,800–1,999	230	2,230	550	2,780
2,000–2,199	240	2,440	650	3,090
2,200–2,399	250	2,650	700	3,350
2,400–2,599	260	2,860	900	3,760
2,600–2,999	300	3,300	1,050	4,350
3,000–3,499	400	3,900	1,200	5,100
3,500–3,999	500	4,500	1,350	5,850
4,000–4,999	600	5,600	1,500	7,100
5,000 & up	10% of displ. plus 100 lbs.	Sum of boat and gear	27% of weight of boat and gear	Sum of boat, gear, and trailer

Fuel Tankage

Where permanent tankage is standard, and is given in the boat's sales or marketing brochures, the stated capacity is given in gallons. Otherwise tankage is noted as "portable."

Water Tankage

Where permanent tankage is standard, and is given in the boat's sales or marketing brochures, the stated capacity is given in gallons. Otherwise tankage is noted as "portable."

Approximate Trailering Weight

This is a combination of displacement as given by the manufacturer or marketer, plus an assumed "additional gear weight" (such as outboard engine, portable fuel tank topped up, and a personal effects allowance for each crew member), plus the weight of the empty trailer, according to the guidelines in **Table Two**. But these data give only an approximate trailering weight. Exact weight depends on how much gear is loaded on board a particular boat, the exact weight of the trailer, and the accuracy of the displacement figure given by the manufacturer.

When considering what vehicle might be used to tow a particular loaded trailer, it is useful to consult the vehicle manufacturer's specifications. These may be obtained at various vehicle dealerships or at various Web sites on the Internet, such as www.campinglife.com/towratings.

For a general idea of what type of vehicle might be required for a given towing service, some 2008 cars and trucks rate as follows:

2008 Ford Focus sedan—1,000 lbs.
maximum

2008 Ford Mustang coupe—1,000 lbs.
maximum

2008 Ford Taurus sedan—1,250 lbs.
maximum

2008 Ford Crown Victoria wagon—1,500
lbs. maximum

2008 Ford Escape sedan—1,000 to 3,500
lbs. depending on engine power

2008 Ford Explorer SUV—3,500 lbs.
except Sefi V8—7,100 lbs.
maximum

2008 Ford Expedition truck—6,000 to
9,000 lbs., depending on engine and
axle type

2008 Ford F-150 truck, 5.4L—9,200 lbs.
maximum

Earlier model years may have significantly different towing ratings. For example,
for the year 1991:

1991 Ford Escort, 1.9 liter 4-cyl.
engine—1,000 lbs. maximum

1991 Toyota Corolla sedan, 1.6 liter 4-cyl.
engine—1,500 lbs. maximum

1991 Toyota Camry sedan, 2.0 liter 4-cyl.
engine—2,000 lbs. maximum

1991 Chevrolet Caprice Wagon,
5.0 V-8—5,000 lbs. maximum

1991 Ford Explorer SUV, 4.0 liter—
5,700 lbs. maximum

1991 Chevy Blazer full sized SUV, 4 × 4,
5.7 liter—6,000 lbs. maximum

1991 Chevrolet S-10 compact pickup,
4.3 liter—6,000 lbs. maximum

1991 Ford F-250, HD 4 × 2, 7.5
liter—10,000 lbs. maximum

The moral of the story: check your owner's
manual before towing a boat or trailer.

Comparable Designs or "Comps"

A small group of comparable designs, total-
ing three to five boats, is shown for every
boat reported. Such information should be
useful for anyone who is interested in buying a specific design, but who doesn't want to
overlook other boats with very similar characteristics. This is the same concept used
in the real estate business to lead potential
home buyers to properties that are likely
to be of higher than average interest to the
prospect. Using real estate lingo, we call
these relatively close competitors "comps."

To identify these comps, the following
method has been used:

1. A "short list" was made of boats of similar LOD, displacement, and ballast.
2. Any boats on the short list were
   removed as comps if they were too dis-
   similar in appearance or sail plan. By the
   same token, boats grouped together as
   "comps" had certain distinctive characteristics in common, such as gaff-rigged
   catboats. The remaining boats were then
   split into groups of three to five.

Note that boats of widely different ages
are not necessarily separated, nor did we
presume (as do some sailing magazines)
to determine intended use (cruiser, racer/
cruiser, or racer) for purposes of separating
categories. In our opinion, the boundaries
between these categories are generally too
fuzzy to make hard-and-fast judgments.

Beam

Beam is the extreme width of the hull
("extreme beam") measured from outside
rail to outside rail. This is as distinguished
from the "waterline beam," which is often
much less, and which sometimes has a much
more pronounced effect on the boat's stability. Unfortunately, waterline beam is seldom given in boat brochures and ads, so the
information is not readily available, and consequently is not reported here.

Displacement

There are three main types of displacement.
Which one is used in stating specifications is

frequently a mystery, since designers and/or builders and marketers seldom identify which type they are reporting. Hence, unfortunately, the type of displacement quoted in sales brochures and boat magazines varies, and this can cause confusion and hinder calculation of some performance parameters such as the D/L ratio (see next page).

Dry displacement, sometimes called **light displacement**, is the hull and rig weight *excluding* weight of crew, equipment, fuel and water, stores, outboard engine if any, and so on. This number is helpful in determining trailer-towing weight. However, "dry" displacement, if shown in brochures, may or may not include water ballast on boats that use that type of ballast.

Loaded or **sailing displacement** is the weight as equipped for sailing, *including* crew, equipment, fuel and water, stores, outboard engine if any, and so on.

Half-load displacement is a variation on **loaded displacement**, being the weight with normal crew and equipment, but with half-filled fuel and water tanks. In theory, either loaded or half-load displacement should be used for calculating various performance ratios such as **B/D, SA/D,** and **D/L** (see pages 9, 12, and 13).

Differences between displacement types can be substantial, particularly in small cruisers. For example, designer Charlie Wittholz specifies that the **loaded displacement** of the Cape Cod Cat 17 is 2,800 lbs. However, he suggests taking off two or three people and their gear, weighing approximately 600 lbs. in total, to obtain the boat's trailering, or **dry displacement**. Thus he estimates dry displacement at around 2,200 lbs.

But in reality, we believe most sales brochures use dry displacement as the measure of displacement for all purposes—and for lack of a better method of determining half-load or full displacement using our vast collection of sales brochures, we are stuck with using whatever displacement the sales brochures declare. Consequently, in this guide, the number reported is usually **dry displacement**. Typically, sailing magazines and books also use this same dry displacement to calculate SA/D and D/L ratios. Technically, this is incorrect, but for comparing one boat to another, if done consistently, no great injustice is done.

Even if displacement reported in sales brochures uses the correct definitions, the number can still be grossly in error. For example, in the original C&C Bluejacket 23 sales brochure, the displacement was erroneously listed as 6,000 pounds—much too high for a sleek racer-cruiser of that size. Later the number was amended, without explanation, to 4,000 pounds.

Ballast

This is the weight, in pounds, of lead, iron, steel punchings, cement, water, or other relatively high-density materials located in or on the hull, somewhere below the waterline, generally as low as possible. The purpose of ballast is to add stability to the hull in large waves, and to counteract the force of the wind on the sails tending to heel the boat over on its side. For more on ballast, see **Ballast/Displacement ratio** on page 9.

Sail Area/Displacement Ratio (SA/D)

This is a nondimensional ratio, devised to compare sail power with a vessel's weight. The higher a boat's SA/D ratio, the faster she will accelerate in a breeze, and (usually) the faster she will be in light air. On the other hand, the higher the ratio, the more tender and tippy she is apt to be.

SA/D is not just sail area divided by displacement, but instead is adjusted to eliminate dimensional elements (i.e., square feet and pounds). This is done by converting pounds to displacement in cubic feet of water, and using exponents to move from volume to area. That is:

SA/D ratio

$$= \frac{\text{Sail area}}{(\text{Pounds of displacement} \div 64.0\,\text{lbs./cu.ft.})}$$

Therefore, for example, for a boat with 260 square feet of sail area and 2,750 lbs. displacement:

$$\text{SA/D ratio} = \frac{260}{(2,750/64.0)} = \frac{260}{(42.97)} = \mathbf{21.2}$$

In evaluating SA/D numbers, we use the following guidelines, which are appropriate for sailboats 14' to 25' LOD:

If SA/D is...	The boat's SA/D is said to be...
Below 16	Very Low (tending to make a boat relatively slower in light air but more stable in heavy air)
16 to 18	Low
18 to 21	Moderate (often the best range for a cruising boat sailed in varying weather conditions)
21 to 25	High
Above 25	Very High (tending to make a boat relatively faster in light air but more tender in heavy air).

Displacement/Length Ratio (D/L)

The displacement/length ratio is another nondimensional figure, in this case one that gives a measure of wave-making resistance. Again, it is not a simple ratio, but instead is adjusted to eliminate dimensional elements (i.e., pounds and feet). The lower a boat's D/L, the smaller the waves she makes as she moves through the water, and the lower the wave-making resistance. Also, the lower a boat's D/L, the faster she will accelerate in a breeze—and (on the negative side) the more likely it is that she will be relatively tender and jumpy in a seaway. Conversely, the higher the D/L, the more likely it is that she will be slower, but more comfortable and

stable—all other things being equal, which they seldom are.

$$\text{D/L ratio} = \frac{\text{Displacement}/2,240}{(0.01 \times \text{LWL})^3}$$

Therefore, for example, for a boat displacing 2,750 pounds and having a load waterline length of 20.25 feet, the D/L is:

$$\text{D/L ratio} = \frac{2,750/2,240}{(0.01 \times 20.25)^3} = \frac{1.2277}{0.0083} = \mathbf{148}$$

In evaluating D/L numbers, we use the following guidelines, which are appropriate for sailboats 14' to 25' LOD:

If D/L is...	it is said to be...	and the boat's hull is termed to be of...
Below 100	Very Low	Ultralight Displacement (tending to make a boat relatively faster in light air but more tender in heavy air)
100 to 140	Low	Light Displacement
140 to 200	Moderate	Medium Displacement (often the best range for a cruising boat sailed in varying weather conditions)
200 to 300	High	Heavy Displacement
Above 300	Very High	Very Heavy Displacement (tending to make a boat relatively slower in light air but more stable in heavy air).

Average PHRF Rating

Average ratings are taken from data compiled by the United States Sailing Association, published annually. PHRF stands for "Performance Handicap Racing Fleet," and its ratings are used to determine the relative speed potential of any given class of yacht.

An initial handicap rating for a new class design is assigned based on the boat's critical dimensions, its similarities to other rated yachts, the designer's speed predictions, and other such theoretical data. Observations of actual racing performance are then used to adjust the design's rating from time to time. What is rated is the boat itself, not the skill of its crew or its gear. Thus, a skilled crew using new sails and gear may be able to sail, say, a J/24 faster than its rating would indicate.

The handicaps are given in seconds per nautical mile around a race course. For example, a J/24 (page 294, average PHRF 174 seconds per mile), racing on a ten-nautical-mile course against a Dufour 24 (page 287, average PHRF 240 seconds per mile), would give the Dufour a handicap of 66 seconds per mile, or 660 seconds for the ten miles. Thus, even if the Dufour finished the race as much as 660 seconds (11 minutes) after the J/24, the Dufour would still tie the race.

For more on the PHRF system, see http://www.ussailing.org/phrf.

Not every sailboat has a PHRF rating; where none has been found, the expression "NA" (for "Not Available") is used in this guide.

Maximum Speed (also known as *hull speed*)

This is calculated using the formula: $\text{Speed}_{max} = 1.34 \times \sqrt{\text{LWL}}$.

That is, the theoretical maximum speed of a displacement hull (as opposed to a planing hull, which obeys different hydrodynamic rules) is approximately $1\frac{1}{3}$ times the square root of its waterline length. Above that speed, the waves a displacement hull makes, which are induced by the boat dragging a hole in the water along with it as it plows forward, become so large that the boat expends all additional increments of motive power trying to climb out of its hole. Planing hulls can escape that fate by climbing out of their holes and skimming the water's surface.

Hull shape and wave conditions sometimes alter the 1.34 factor a bit, but basically 1.34 is the applicable factor in most cases.

Motion Index

This index is borrowed from Ted Brewer's very useful book, *Ted Brewer Explains Sailboat Design* (International Marine/McGraw-Hill). Those who are familiar with the book will recognize the index as a renamed "Comfort Ratio." We changed the name to "Motion Index" since many other factors reported here also influence overall comfort, such as amount of headroom, interior elbow room and storage space, cockpit space, ease of going forward on deck, height and slope of cockpit coamings, and other factors sometimes seen as minor or inconsequential, such as ease of operating engine controls from a comfortable position at the helm.

As Ted puts it in his book, "the comfort ratio is based on the fact that motion comfort depends on the rapidity of the motion; the faster the motion, the more upsetting it is to our human gyroscopes . . . Greater weight [of the boat] or lesser area [surface acted upon, represented by LWL] means a slower motion, and thus more comfort."

Motion Index (A.K.A. Ted Brewer's "Comfort Ratio")

$$= \frac{\text{Displacement in pounds}}{0.65 \times (0.7\ \text{LWL} + 0.3\ \text{LOA}) \times (\text{Beam})^{1.333}}$$

The higher the Motion Index, the greater the comfort due to motion—or more precisely, the lack of it.

Space Index

We devised the Space Index specifically for this guide in order to compare relative elbow room below between one boat and another of generally similar size. It is a rough measure of the number of cubic feet of cabin space available for elbow room and stowage as given by the formula:

Space index = LWL × Beam × [(distance midcabin sole to LWL) + (midships freeboard)]

Naturally, the bigger the resulting number, the more space available for moving around and for stowage, at least in theory.

Headroom

This is the height at the centerline of the cabin, which we measure under the cabin-top amidships, usually located just forward of the companionway hatch. If headroom is less than 5' 0", it is sometimes given in brochures or ads as "sitting," whether it is 4' 11" or 3' 6". However, what counts as "sitting" for one observer may be "standing" for another. For example, designer Bob Perry, who is over six-feet tall, asserts that any headroom less than six feet is "sitting." But to the average person (men = 5' 9", women = 5' 4"), anything 5' 10" or more would be "standing." We attempt to ascertain headroom whenever we can, even if approximate, by measuring from plans or by quoting specifications in sales brochures.

TWO
Sixty-Three Boats 14'–19'

Alacrity 19 (18)
Early twin-keel cruiser imported from England

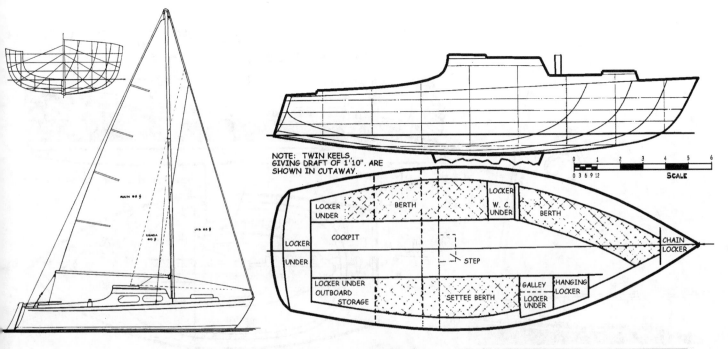

NOTE: TWIN KEELS, GIVING DRAFT OF 1'10", ARE SHOWN IN CUTAWAY.

LOD:	18' 0"
LOA:	19' 9"
LWL:	17' 0"
Min./max. draft:	1' 10"
Bridge clearance:	25' 6"
Power:	outboard 3 to 5 hp
B/D ratio:	33%

Designer:	Peter Stevenson
Builder:	Wells Yachts (importer)
Years produced:	1961–1967?
Sail area:	150 sq. ft.
Fuel tankage:	portable
Water tankage:	portable
Approx. trailering wgt.:	2,100 lbs.

Over 700 Alacritys were sold in the U.S. and in England, where she was made by Russell Marine Ltd. We have not found a good cutaway side view (inboard profile), so her outboard line drawing is substituted here. It indicates a nice shape for fast sailing, except for her pair of stubby keels (not shown in full), the relatively large wetted surface of which would deter from good performance. It appears that this boat's marketers used hull length (18' 6") rather than LOD (18' 0") to describe length. That's why we designate this boat as an "18" rather than a "19." ***Best features:*** About the best

we can say is that the Alacrity is a nice boat for her vintage, but in this case her comps, which are more up-to-date designs, are better. ***Worst features:*** Her two comps, with their shallower board-up drafts, would be easier to launch and retrieve at a ramp. With her shallow twin keels of iron, which rusts, each weighing a mere 240 pounds, she is probably least weatherly, most tender, and slowest in light air compared to her lighter comps with their deeper centerboards, beamier hulls, bigger sail areas, etc.—all in all not the boat to seek if performance is at all important to you.

Comps	LOD	Beam	MinDr	Displ	Bllst	SA/D	D/L	Avg. PHRF	Max. Speed	Motion Index	Space Index	No. of Berths	Head-room
Alacrity 19 (18)	18' 0"	6' 11"	1' 10"	1,450	480	18.7	132	378	5.5	9.5	223	2 or 3	3' 11"
Windrose 18	18' 5"	7' 0"	1' 0"	1,500	400	18.4	169	288	5.3	10.4	201	4	3' 9"
Hunter 18.5	18' 5"	7' 1"	2' 0"	1,600	520	20.8	141	288	5.6	10.3	253	3	4' 0"

Alerion Express Cat 19
Modernized classic catboat by Garry Hoyt

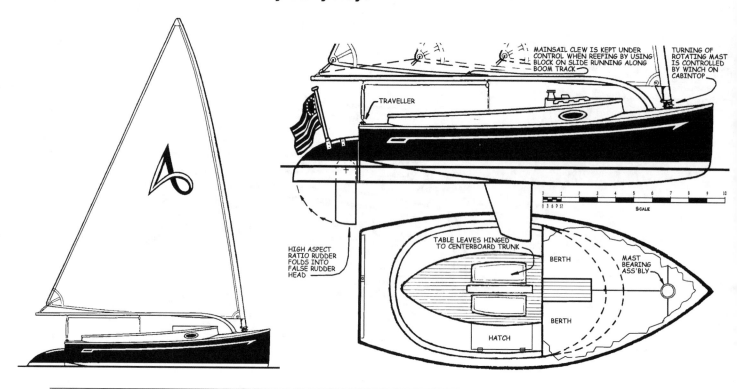

LOD:	19' 2"	**Designer:**	Garry Hoyt
LOA:	23' 2"	**Builder:**	TPI Corp.
LWL:	17' 6"	**Years produced:**	1998–2002?
Min./max. draft:	1' 2"/3' 0"	**Sail area:**	272 sq. ft.
Bridge clearance:	32' 0"	**Fuel tankage:**	portable
Power:	outboard 4 to 6 hp	**Water tankage:**	portable
B/D ratio:	31%	**Approx. trailering wgt.:**	2,150 lbs.

Designer Hoyt decided to try to minimize some chronic catboat weaknesses, including sluggish windward performance, bothersome weather helm, difficulties in reefing, and excessive sailing and trailering weight. The Express Cat is the result. ***Best features:*** Compared to other cats (as opposed to the comps below), this design is much lighter and has a higher SA/D ratio, and hence is likely to be faster in light air. Her comparatively narrow, foil-shaped centerboard is more efficient, adding more speed. A lightweight aluminum or optional carbon fiber, free-standing, rotating mast and Hoyt-patented self-vanging boom solves several problems at once: less windage, advantages of a vang (seldom available in traditional cats due to their low booms), and easier reefing (sail rolls up around the mast). The boat is significantly simpler than her comps to sail, as well as to launch and retrieve at a ramp. Moreover, she is beamier and therefore has more stowage room below. Construction quality is high, perhaps justifying generally high resale market prices. ***Worst features:*** Compared to comps, cabin amenities and headroom are somewhat less generous.

Comps	LOD	Beam	MinDr	Displ	Bllst	SA/D	D/L	Avg. PHRF	Max. Speed	Motion Index	Space Index	No. of Berths	Head-room
Alerion Express Cat 19	19' 2"	8' 6"	1' 2"	1,450	450	34.0	121	NA	5.6	7.1	313	2	3' 6"
Capri 18	18' 0"	7' 7"	2' 0"	1,500	425	18.9	149	NA	5.4	9.0	248	2	3' 6"
ETAP 20	19' 10"	7' 6"	1' 6"	1,500	441	21.4	136	NA	5.5	8.8	278	4	4' 0"
Windrose 5.5 (18)	18' 0"	8' 0"	2' 3"	1,500	500	18.6	163	288	5.4	8.7	228	4	3' 9"

Blue Water Blackwatch 19

Cute but tiny cutter from Texas

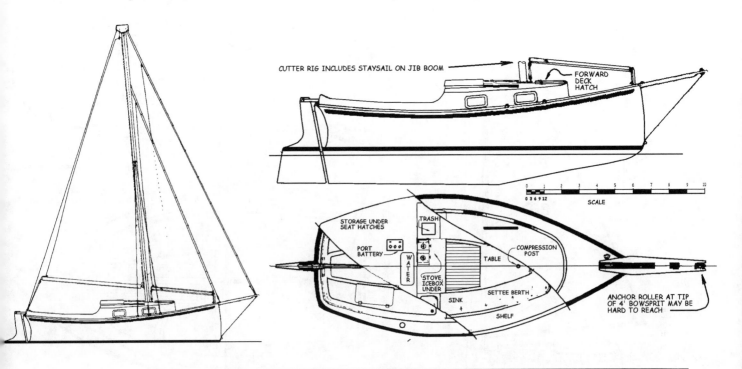

LOD:	18' 6"		**Designer:**	Dave Autry
LOA:	23' 6"		**Builder:**	Blue Water Boat Works
LWL:	17' 6"		**Years produced:**	1979–1981?
Min./max. draft:	2' 0"		**Sail area:**	212 sq. ft.
Bridge clearance:	30' 0"		**Fuel tankage:**	portable
Power:	outboard 4 to 6 hp		**Water tankage:**	15 gal.
B/D ratio:	36%		**Approx. trailering wgt.:**	3,200 lbs.

This offering from Blue Water Boat Works in Amarillo, TX, was only on the market for a short time; only 82 hulls were produced. We don't know why; we have seen worse boats which stayed on the market for a lot longer. Perhaps selling a New England-style boat in Amarillo, TX, proved harder than the builders thought. We would have liked to have tried her. *Best features:* The sales literature indicates a high level of finish—though we have never seen a sample of this boat, so we can't verify the accuracy of the advertising.

Four opening bronze ports with screens and a forward deck hatch supplement the wide main hatch for ventilation. The cabin (says the brochure) packs in a two-burner stove, stainless steel sink (with water tank of undisclosed size), built-in ice chest, and enclosed trash bin. *Worst features:* The two-foot draft is borderline in terms of easy trailering and launching—but the 800 pounds of ballast isn't very deep, so some tenderness should be expected in a breeze (a problem shared by two of the Blackwatch's three comps).

Comps	LOD	Beam	MinDr	Displ	Bllst	SA/D	D/L	Avg. PHRF	Max. Speed	Motion Index	Space Index	No. of Berths	Head-room
Skipper 20 (18)	18' 4"	6' 7"	2' 0"	2,000	800	14.4	265	NA	5.2	14.6	223	2	4' 6"
Blue Water Blackwatch 19	18' 6"	7' 11"	2' 0"	2,500	800	19.8	187	231	5.6	11.3	255	2	4' 4"
Cornish Shrimper 19	19' 3"	7' 2"	1' 6"	2,350	700	17.6	193	390	5.6	13.2	251	2	3' 4"
Cape Cod Goldeneye 18	18' 3"	6' 4"	3' 0"	2,500	1,300	16.8	281	NA	5.3	19.8	199	2	3' 6"

Cape Cod Cat 17

The author owned and loved one of these cats

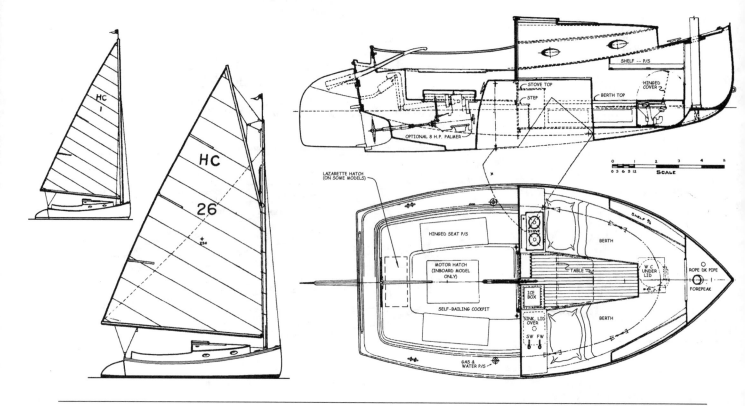

LOD:	17' 0"
LOA:	19' 4"
LWL:	16' 5"
Min./max. draft:	1' 11"/6' 3"
Bridge clearance:	30' 3"
Power:	4 to 6 hp outboard optional inbd.
B/D ratio:	23%

Designer:	Charlie Wittholz
Builder:	Hermann, Cape Cod Shipbuilding
Years produced:	1968–present
Sail area:	250 sq. ft.
Fuel tankage:	portable (17 gal. opt.)
Water tankage:	17 gal.
Approx. trailering wgt.:	3,150 lbs.

First built as the Hermann Cat by Ted Hermann's Boat Shop, this design was eventually taken over by Cape Cod Shipbuilding and became the "Cape Cod Cat." The "CCC" is traditional and salty looking, with ample ability to cruise two for a week or more. The author owned *Pipit*, Hermann Cat hull #18, for several years, and sailed and trailered her all over New England. Two rigs are available as shown (with the Marconi rig giving 240 sq. ft. of area and 33' bridge clearance). The builder offers her either as a centerboarder (as shown), or as a very shoal draft (1' 11") keel cat—not deep enough to give

her satisfactory performance to windward. ***Best features:*** A big sail and low wetted surface make her quicker than her comps in light air. Layout below is perfect for two—especially if a forward hatch is added over the head, as the author did on *Pipit*. ***Worst features:*** Partly due to her hourglass hull form, she can become overpowered and hard to steer upwind under full sail at about 12 knots of breeze, until a reef is tucked in—a chore which is not difficult if jiffy reefing is used. Also, her cockpit footwell is too wide to provide a good footrest for some folks when she's heeled in a breeze.

Comps	LOD	Beam	MinDr	Displ	Bllst	SA/D	D/L	Avg. PHRF	Max. Speed	Motion Index	Space Index	No. of Berths	Head-room
Lynx 16	16' 6"	7' 11"	1' 2"	2,000	200	20.2	218	NA	5.4	11.4	179	2	3' 4"
Menger Cat 17	17' 0"	8' 0"	1' 8"	2,200	500	23.6	219	351	5.4	12.4	194	2	4' 3"
Cape Cod Cat 17	17' 0"	7' 11"	1' 8"	2,200	500	23.6	222	372	5.4	12.4	222	2	4' 6"
Marshall Sanderling 18	18' 2"	8' 6"	1' 7"	2,200	500	23.9	178	315	5.6	10.5	281	2	3' 7"
Molly Catboat 17	17' 0"	7' 6"	2' 2"	3,000	1,000	15.4	317	NA	5.4	19.2	194	2	4' 0"

Cape Dory Typhoon 18 (19)

A little gem by Carl Alberg

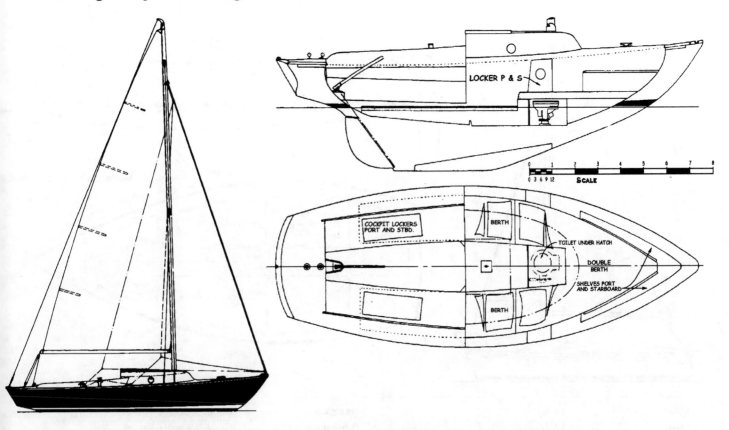

LOD:	18' 6"		**Designer:**	Carl Alberg
LOA:	18' 6"		**Builder:**	Cape Dory Yachts
LWL:	13' 11"		**Years produced:**	1967–1986
Min./max. draft:	2' 7"		**Sail area:**	160 sq. ft.
Bridge clearance:	27' 3"		**Fuel tankage:**	portable
Power:	outboard 3 to 6 hp		**Water tankage:**	portable
B/D ratio:	51%		**Approx. trailering wgt.:**	2,470 lbs.

Of all the boats in this comp group of four, the CD Typhoon 18 is the design we'd feel most comfortable with in iffy weather—despite the fact that her cockpit sole is too close to the waterline to be fully self-bailing, though you could probably leave her at a mooring and expect the rain that falls into her to drain successfully. ***Best features:*** She has enough ballast to keep her stiff when sailing short-handed in a blow. Her motion in a chop will be relatively comfortable. She looks competent and pretty in a traditional way, and is well-built with quality bronze fittings and wood trim. She was made over a span of 25 years, so you can probably find used boats in a wide range of prices that might suit your budget. ***Worst features:*** Since she was built by several builders before Cape Dory began production, through hard times as well as good, the construction quality may vary widely among the old boats available today. Buyer beware!

Comps	LOD	Beam	MinDr	Displ	Bllst	SA/D	D/L	Avg. PHRF	Max. Speed	Motion Index	Space Index	No. of Berths	Head-room
Gloucester 19	19' 3"	7' 6"	1' 0"	1,600	550	20.3	159	NA	5.4	9.7	241	2	3' 8"
Cape Dory Typhoon 18	18' 6"	6' 6"	2' 7"	1,750	900	17.6	290	306	5.0	15.0	176	2 or 4	3' 11"
Quickstep 19	19' 4"	7' 9"	2' 2"	1,800	750	18.3	164	NA	5.5	10.2	236	2	3' 8"
Vivacity 20 (19)	18' 6"	7' 0"	2' 4"	1,800	785	18.9	127	288	5.6	10.6	215	4	3' 0"

Capri 16 (17)
Catalina's smallest cruising sailboat

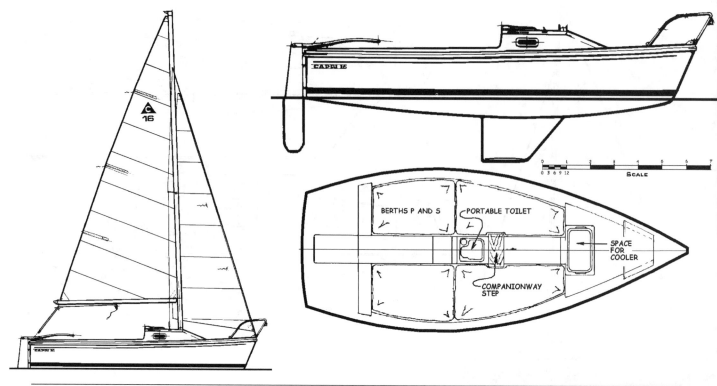

BERTHS P AND S   PORTABLE TOILET

SPACE FOR COOLER

COMPANIONWAY STEP

SCALE

LOD:	16' 6"	**Designer:**	Catalina Design Team
LOA:	18' 0"	**Builder:**	Catalina Yachts
LWL:	15' 6"	**Years produced:**	1987–present
Min./max. draft:	2' 5"	**Sail area:**	138 sq. ft.
Bridge clearance:	25' 0"	**Fuel tankage:**	portable
Power:	outboard 3 to 6 hp	**Water tankage:**	portable
B/D ratio:	31%	**Approx. trailering wgt.:**	1,950 lbs.

Production of the popular and affordable Catalina-built Capri 16 is now in the 500-plus range. As sailboats of this size go, the cockpit is larger and the cabin is smaller than average. The 425-pound wing keel is intended to combine shallow (2' 5") draft for gunkholing with reasonable windward performance—although this puts draft near the upper limit for convenient trailering. This might make a good first boat for a young couple. ***Best features:*** If you are looking for other owners of Capris to socialize with or to compare notes, you can probably find them in almost any place there's

sailing water. (Check Google under "Catalina Capri.") Construction is simple but neat, and adequate for this size and type of craft. The boat seems well designed and the sail-plan looks manageable and efficient, though perhaps on the small side for really spritely performance. ***Worst features:*** Compared with her comps, the Capri 16 has a low Motion Index, and has less headroom (though her storage space below is about at the average of her comps). On the other hand, after all, she's only intended to be a weekender; and her two berths are long enough for the tallest sailors.

Comps	LOD	Beam	MinDr	Displ	Bllst	SA/D	D/L	Avg. PHRF	Max. Speed	Motion Index	Space Index	No. of Berths	Head- room
Capri 16 (17)	16' 6"	6' 11"	2' 5"	1,350	425	18.1	162	NA	5.3	9.7	198	2	3' 6"
Sovereign 5.0/18 (17)	17' 0"	7' 0"	1' 10"	1,350	540	18.1	198	NA	5.1	10.0	197	4	4' 0"
Cornish Crabber 17	17' 0"	6' 9"	1' 7"	1,450	50	22.2	158	NA	5.4	10.2	211	2	4' 3"
Silhouette 17	17' 3"	6' 7"	2' 1"	1,500	550	20.1	244	NA	5.0	12.5	167	2 to 4	3' 8"

Capri 18
One step up from her little sister

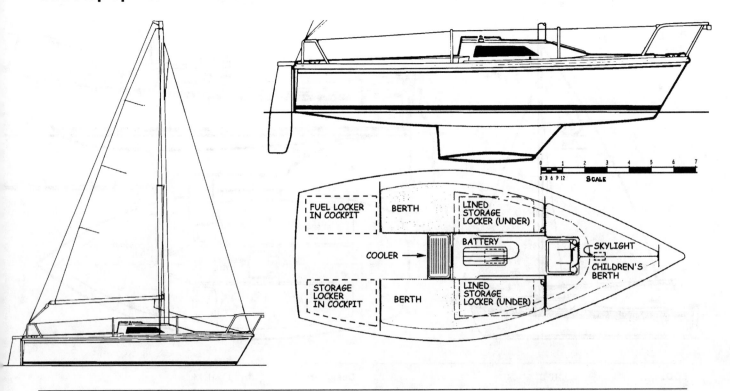

LOD:	18' 0"	**Designer:**	Catalina Design Team
LOA:	19' 0"	**Builder:**	Catalina Yachts
LWL:	16' 6"	**Years produced:**	1985–present
Min./max. draft:	2' 0" or 2' 3"	**Sail area:**	155 sq. ft.
Bridge clearance:	26' 5"	**Fuel tankage:**	portable
Power:	outboard 3 to 6 hp	**Water tankage:**	portable
B/D ratio:	28%	**Approx. trailering wgt.:**	2,300 lbs.

The Capri 18 is one step up from her little sister, the Capri 16. Whether it is worth spending roughly 40% more (new) to gain two feet of length and 150 more pounds of displacement is up to the customer. *Best features:* She sleeps only two—perhaps a plus on a boat this small—and on a very big double berth, when the two filler cushions are in place. Foam flotation is standard. *Worst features:* Low headroom, and the fact that she sleeps only two adults (plus two children forward),

may deter some potential buyers (but the "children's berth" is an ideal place to store personal gear when two are cruising). The lead ballast wing keel with a 2' 3" draft, which was an option early in the boat's production history but later was made standard, will make retrieving at a ramp more difficult than with the wingless 2' 0" fin keel, but won't much improve her so-so performance to weather. The mainsheet lead is poor, and there's no provision for a boom vang.

Comps	LOD	Beam	MinDr	Displ	Bllst	SA/D	D/L	Avg. PHRF	Max. Speed	Motion Index	Space Index	No. of Berths	Head-room
Alerion Express Cat 19	19' 2"	8' 6"	1' 2"	1,450	450	34.3	121	NA	5.6	7.1	313	2	3' 6"
Capri 18	18' 0"	7' 7"	2' 0"	1,500	425	18.9	149	NA	5.4	9.0	248	2	3' 6"
ETAP 20	19' 10"	7' 6"	1' 6"	1,500	441	21.4	136	NA	5.5	8.8	278	4	4' 0"
Windrose 5.5 (1.8)	18' 0"	8' 0"	2' 3"	1,500	500	18.6	163	288	5.4	8.7	228	4	3' 9"

Com-Pac 16

Hutchins produced this tiny boat for many years

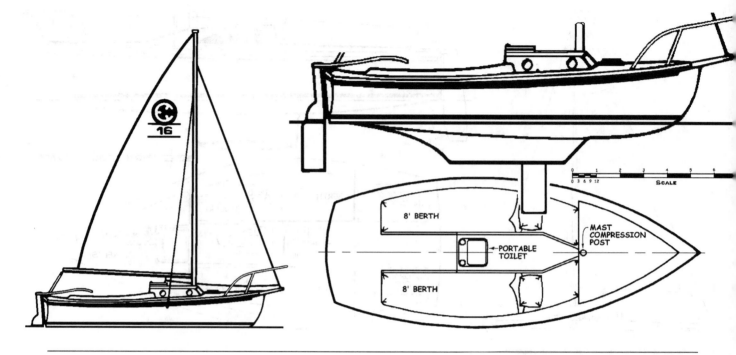

LOD:	16' 0"		**Designer:**	Clark Mills
LOA:	18' 0"		**Builder:**	Hutchins Company
LWL:	14' 0"		**Years produced:**	1974–2002
Min./max. draft:	1' 6"/ 3' 6"		**Sail area:**	120 sq. ft.
Bridge clearance:	20' 6"		**Fuel tankage:**	portable
Power:	outboard 3 to 6 hp		**Water tankage:**	portable
B/D ratio:	41%		**Approx. trailering wgt.:**	1,650 lbs.

The builders say they focus on seaworthiness and value for money. If customer acceptance is an indicator, their claim seems to have held true; the Hutchins Company is well over 30 years old and their boats are still selling well (though their prices compared to comps have risen considerably over the years). The 16 was offered at various times as either a fixed-keel or centerboard boat, and was quite popular as a "starter boat." ***Best features:*** High ballast and D/L ratio, plus small sail area, help to give good heavy-air performance and relatively easy motion in a seaway for a boat this size. Narrow beam gives walkaround room in a standard 10' × 20' garage. Although nothing fancy, construction is relatively above average. ***Worst features:*** Compared with comps, shallow-draft keel of older models restricts performance upwind; small sail area and high D/L make light-air performance relatively poor, as indicated by high PHRF rating. However, in 1996, a centerboard (as well as a mid-boom traveller) were added, improving upwind performance somewhat in newer boats. Narrow beam (lowest in this book next to the West Wight Potter) reduces usable cabin space versus comps.

Comps	LOD	Beam	MinDr	Displ	Bllst	SA/D	D/L	Avg. PHRF	Max. Speed	Motion Index	Space Index	No. of Berths	Head-room
Gloucester 16	15' 7"	6' 3"	0' 9"	900	350	23.5	157	NA	5.0	8.2	122	2	4' 0"
Neptune 16	15' 9"	6' 2"	0' 10"	900	350	25.5	163	NA	4.9	8.5	111	2	3' 6"
Balboa 16	16' 0"	7' 5"	2' 5"	1,000	400	18.7	141	NA	5.1	6.9	171	2	3' 6"
Com-Pac Legacy 17	16' 6"	6' 0"	1' 2"	1,000	400	20.8	154	NA	5.1	9.1	139	2	3' 3"
Com-Pac 16	16' 0"	6' 0"	1' 6"	1,100	450	18.0	179	355	5.0	10.5	136	2	3' 3"

Com-Pac 19
More boat than the Com-Pac 16

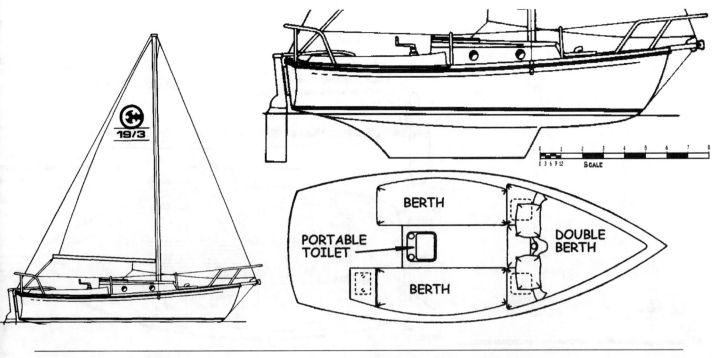

LOD:	18' 8"	**Designer:**	Bob Johnson
LOA:	20' 1"	**Builder:**	Hutchins Company
LWL:	16' 4"	**Years produced:**	1979–2002
Min./max. draft:	2' 0"	**Sail area:**	196 sq. ft.
Bridge clearance:	25' 5"	**Fuel tankage:**	portable
Power:	outboard 3 to 6 hp	**Water tankage:**	portable
B/D ratio:	31%	**Approx. trailering wgt.:**	2,890 lbs.

This design, originally drawn by Island Packet builder/designer Bob Johnson, was gradually changed over her more than 20-year life, but the basics remained the same. Like her little sister, the Com-Pac 16, she was designed to provide easy handling for novice sailors. **Best features:** Very simple rig and fittings, suitable for first-time sailors. Deep cockpit gives feeling of security. **Worst features:** The long keel tends to keep her sailing straight ahead, a plus when cruising in gusty weather but a minus when you want to make a quick turn. New price was a bit above most of her comps, and her Space Index is lowest. The keel is not deep enough for efficient upwind sailing. All comps have only sitting headroom, but the Com-Pac has the least of the bunch. A portable galley was available as an option (shown here abaft the starboard berth), though in the latest model the galley was moved forward and enlarged to include sink (with a small water supply) and ice chest. Otherwise, there's not much below.

Comps	LOD	Beam	MinDr	Displ	Bllst	SA/D	D/L	Avg. PHRF	Max. Speed	Motion Index	Space Index	No. of Berths	Head-room
Com-Pac 19	18' 8"	7' 0"	2' 0"	2,000	800	19.8	205	285	5.4	13.2	212	4	3' 9"
MacGregor PowerSailer 19	18' 10"	7' 5"	0' 9"	2,050	800	18.7	204	NA	5.4	12.7	241	4	4' 0"
Hunter 19	19' 0"	7' 9"	1' 2"	2,100	600	16.1	194	282	5.5	12.0	279	2	4' 5"
Montego 19	19' 3"	7' 2"	1' 2"	2,150	450	18.2	174	288	5.6	13.2	259	4	4' 0"
Com-Pac Eclipse 18	18' 5"	7' 4"	1' 6"	2,200	700	18.9	166	NA	5.7	12.6	254	4	4' 0"

Com-Pac Eclipse 18
A small cruiser that resembles a bigger boat

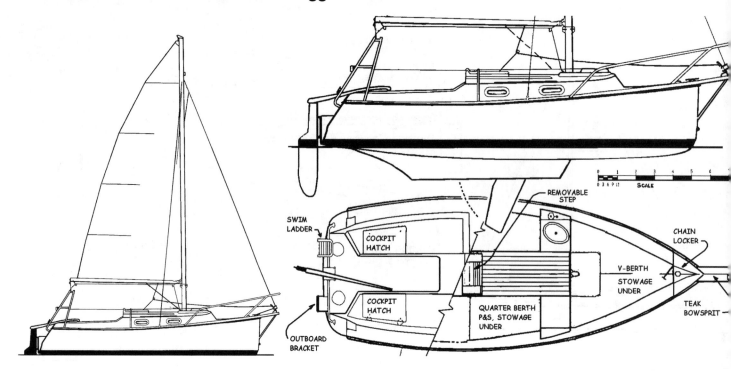

LOD:	18' 5"	**Designer:**	Hutchins Design Team
LOA:	20' 10"	**Builder:**	Hutchins Company
LWL:	18' 1"	**Years produced:**	2005–present
Min./max. draft:	1' 6"/4' 6"	**Sail area:**	200 sq. ft.
Bridge clearance:	27' 0"	**Fuel tankage:**	portable
Power:	outboard 3 to 6 hp	**Water tankage:**	portable
B/D ratio:	41%	**Approx. trailering wgt.:**	3,100 lbs.

Despite being less than 19 feet on deck (without the outboard rudder and bow pulpit included in the measurement), the Eclipse 18 looks to us like a bigger boat. In fact in profile she is reminiscent of the much larger Island Packets designed by Bob Johnson, one of the early designers used by Hutchins for their Com-Pac series of boats. ***Best features:*** Compared with her comps, the Eclipse can be said to be slightly faster due to her long waterline length and relatively high SA/D ratio (though the windage or "top hamper" of the high boom gallows may give back some of that small speed advantage). For neophytes the gallows may be convenient, although a traditional topping lift or a hard vang might serve just as well. The advertising indicates that the gallows is part of the mast raising and lowering scheme, which helps to justify its existence. The open transom gives better than average access to the outboard engine controls and serves as a swim platform. ***Worst features:*** The boat only sleeps four if two of the occupants are small children consigned to the short V-berth forward.

Comps	LOD	Beam	MinDr	Displ	Bllst	SA/D	D/L	Avg. PHRF	Max. Speed	Motion Index	Space Index	No. of Berths	Head-room
Com-Pac 19	18' 8"	7' 0"	2' 0"	2,000	800	19.8	205	285	5.4	13.2	212	4	3' 9"
MacGregor PowerSailer 19	18' 10"	7' 5"	0' 9"	2,050	800	18.7	204	NA	5.4	12.7	241	4	4' 0"
Hunter 19	19' 0"	7' 9"	1' 2"	2,100	600	16.1	194	282	5.5	12.0	279	2	4' 5"
Montego 19	19' 3"	7' 2"	1' 2"	2,150	450	18.2	174	288	5.6	13.2	259	4	4' 0"
Com-Pac Eclipse 18	18' 5"	7' 4"	1' 6"	2,200	700	18.9	166	NA	5.7	12.6	254	4	4' 0"

Com-Pac Horizon 18
Rebuild of a Herreshoff America

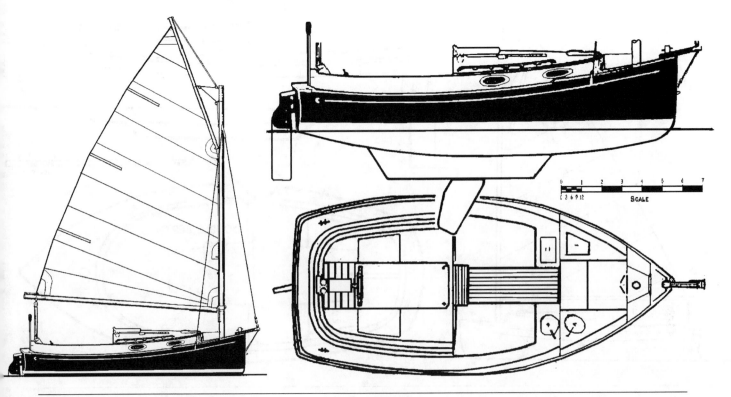

LOD:	18' 2"	**Designer:**	Hutchins Design Team
LOA:	20' 0"	**Builder:**	Hutchins Company
LWL:	17' 9"	**Years produced:**	2002–present
Min./max. draft:	2' 2"/4' 11"	**Sail area:**	205 sq. ft.
Bridge clearance:	28' 0"	**Fuel tankage:**	portable
Power:	outboard 3 to 6 hp	**Water tankage:**	10 gal.
B/D ratio:	24%	**Approx. trailering wgt.:**	3,500 lbs.

The Com-Pac Horizon 18 is a reconstruction of the Herreshoff America (page 35), pursued after builder Hutchins bought the tooling from the last of many molders of the original vessel, first built in 1971. In the comparison below, it is easy to see that many small changes were made in the design—for instance, adding two inches to the beam, and 100 pounds to the ballast (but without increasing the overall weight? hmmmm . . .). **Best features:** Reduced sail area (note lower SA/D versus comps) may slow the Horizon down a little in light air, but advantages more than compensate, e.g., reefing can be delayed a bit versus her comps, and less area results in a lighter mast and boom, making it easier to raise and lower the spars at a launching ramp. The modern deep and high-aspect rudder combined with the keel-centerboard combination should give the Horizon the ability to point higher. The four opening ports and cabintop hatch are a big plus, especially in summer heat. **Worst features:** With the new underbody, the ability to remain comfortably upright "on the hard" is lost. As for the steering wheel shown, let it suffice to say a tiller would be better.

Comps	LOD	Beam	MinDr	Displ	Bllst	SA/D	D/L	Avg. PHRF	Max. Speed	Motion Index	Space Index	No. of Berths	Head-room
Mystic Catboat 20	20' 0"	8' 0"	1' 10"	2,300	700	23.1	184	315	5.6	11.8	270	2	3' 11"
Herreshoff America 18	18' 2"	8' 0"	1' 10"	2,500	500	22.4	200	324	5.6	13.5	257	2	4' 0"
Com-Pac Horizon Cat 18	18' 2"	8' 4"	2' 2"	2,500	600	17.8	200	NA	5.6	12.4	284	2	4' 6"
Herreshoff Eagle 21	18' 2"	8' 2"	1' 10"	2,700	700	26.4	207	NA	5.7	12.4	264	2	4' 0"
Menger Cat 19	19' 0"	8' 0"	1' 10"	2,900	600	21.2	207	NA	5.8	15.0	267	2	4' 10"

Com-Pac Sun Cat 17
Little overnighter from Hutchins

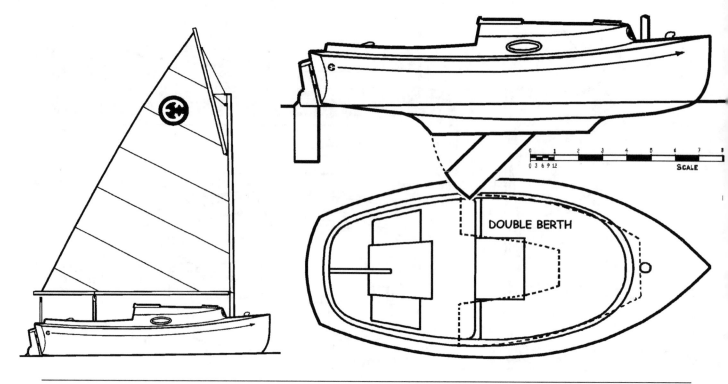

DOUBLE BERTH

SCALE

LOD:	16' 8"	
LOA:	17' 4"	
LWL:	15' 0"	
Min./max. draft:	1' 2"/4' 6"	
Bridge clearance:	22' 3"	
Power:	outboard 3 to 6 hp	
B/D ratio:	15%	

Designer:	Hutchins Company
Builder:	Hutchins Company
Years produced:	1999–present
Sail area:	150 sq. ft.
Fuel tankage:	portable
Water tankage:	portable
Approx. trailering wgt.:	1,950 lbs.

The Sun Cat was designed as a shoal-draft daysailer and overnighter that could be rigged, launched, and sailed easily. She features a stainless steel centerboard and trunk, similar to one installed earlier on her little sister, the Picnic Cat. **Best features:** The Hutchins Company generally does a good job on finishing their boats, even the small ones. The Sun Cat's hull is configured to make trailering and handling at a ramp easy; short spars make striking her rig easier, and give good clearance under low bridges. Considering her small size, her motion index is surprisingly good. **Worst features:** Low SA/D restricts performance under sail. Space below is limited by her relatively narrow beam, low cabin height, and short waterline length. Her stern is narrow compared with her comps, making it likely that she will sail somewhat down by the stern with more than a pair of light-weight people sitting at the forward end of the cockpit. Her melon-seed hull shape and low ballast tend to limit her use to the light-air end of weather conditions.

Comps	LOD	Beam	MinDr	Displ	Bllst	SA/D	D/L	Avg. PHRF	Max. Speed	Motion Index	Space Index	No. of Berths	Head-room
Solo II (16)	16' 2"	7' 4"	1' 9"	1,100	400	24.0	167	NA	5.1	7.9	150	2	3' 6"
Slipper Deckhouse 17	16' 10"	8' 0"	1' 7"	1,250	425	20.7	171	NA	5.2	7.7	238	4	4' 3"
Com-Pac Sun Cat 17	16' 8"	7' 3"	1' 2"	1,350	200	19.6	179	NA	5.2	9.4	147	2	3' 2"
Seaward Fox II (17)	17' 4"	8' 0"	1' 7"	1,350	450	22.3	145	NA	5.4	7.8	247	4	4' 3"

Cornish Crabber 17

Fiberglass version of a West Country work boat

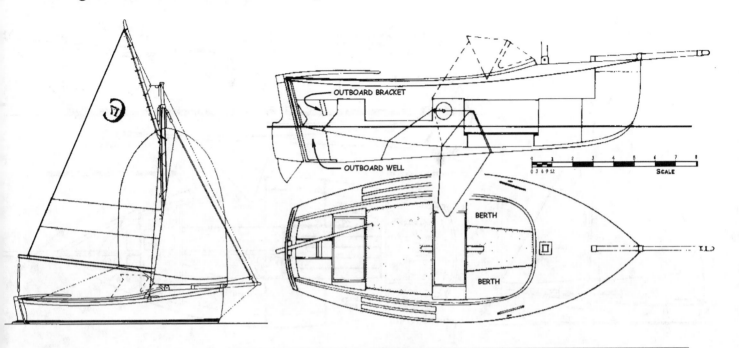

LOD:	17' 0"		**Designer:**	Roger Dongray
LOA:	20' 0"		**Builder:**	Britannia Boats (Import)
LWL:	16' 0"		**Years produced:**	1990–present
Min./max. draft:	1' 7"/4' 0"		**Sail area:**	178 sq. ft.
Bridge clearance:	19' 0" (see note)		**Fuel tankage:**	portable
Power:	outboard 2 to 6 hp		**Water tankage:**	portable
B/D ratio:	26%		**Approx. trailering wgt.:**	2,100 lbs.

The Crabber is part of a line of traditional West Cornwall (England) watercraft recreated in fiberglass and elegantly finished. She's intended mainly as a daysailer but has camping space for two overnight under the fold-down "spray hood" (dodger) with a zip-in back panel. ***Best features:*** Workmanship is outstanding for a boat this size. Foam flotation gives positive buoyancy. Intelligent organization of the very limited space includes a place for a portable head as well as basic overnighting gear (sleeping bags, camp stove, etc). Position of the outboard, in a well amidships and forward of the rudder, provides good steering control in both forward and reverse, and the engine can be removed and stowed in a locker meant for the purpose to eliminate prop drag. With her gaff rig and tanbark sails, she's pretty as a picture underway. ***Worst features:*** Spars are varnished wood, beautiful to look at but a time-consuming maintenance chore. Price of both new and used boats, well above her comps, may not fit everyone's budget. **Note:** Bridge clearance shown above is with gaff scandalized (i.e., dropped temporarily). With gaff fully hoisted, clearance is 24' 0". Headroom as shown below is under dodger.

Comps	LOD	Beam	MinDr	Displ	Bllst	SA/D	D/L	Avg. PHRF	Max. Speed	Motion Index	Space Index	No. of Berths	Head-room
Capri 16 (17)	16' 6"	6' 11"	2' 5"	1,350	425	18.1	162	NA	5.3	9.7	198	2	3' 6"
Sovereign 5.0/18 (17)	17' 0"	7' 0"	1' 10"	1,350	540	18.1	198	NA	5.1	10.7	197	4	4' 0"
Cornish Crabber 17	17' 0"	6' 9"	1' 7"	1,450	380	22.2	158	NA	5.4	10.2	211	2	4' 3"
Silhouette 17	17' 3"	6' 7"	2' 1"	1,500	550	20.1	244	NA	5.0	12.5	167	2 to 4	3' 8"

Cornish Shrimper 19
The Crabber, plus two feet

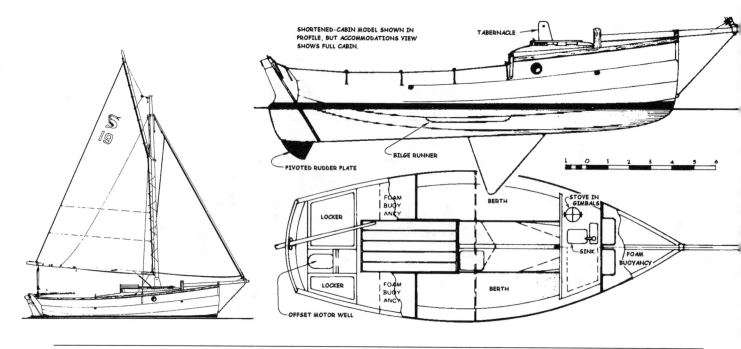

SHORTENED-CABIN MODEL SHOWN IN PROFILE, BUT ACCOMMODATIONS VIEW SHOWS FULL CABIN.

TABERNACLE

BILGE RUNNER

PIVOTED RUDDER PLATE

LOCKER

FOAM BUOYANCY

BERTH

STOVE IN GIMBALS

SINK

FOAM BUOYANCY

LOCKER

FOAM BUOYANCY

BERTH

OFFSET MOTOR WELL

LOD:	19' 3"		**Designer:**	Roger Dongray
LOA:	25' 0"		**Builder:**	Britannia Boats Ltd.
LWL:	17' 6"		**Years produced:**	1978–present
Min./max. draft:	1' 6"/4' 0"		**Sail area:**	194 sq. ft.
Bridge clearance:	26' 3"		**Fuel tankage:**	portable
Power:	outboard 4 to 6 hp		**Water tankage:**	portable
B/D ratio:	31%		**Approx. trailering wgt.:**	3,300 lbs.

This is a character boat with concomitant grace, and with a good measure of performance and practicality, too. What she lacks in headroom, she makes up in charm. In England, she has cult-boat status. **Best features:** The outboard well, placed inside the cockpit, gives easy access to engine controls and helps maintain vessel's good looks. Extensive use of varnished wood below lends a touch of elegance. Short bilge runners allow the boat to take the ground nearly upright. Foam buoyancy for safety is built in under cockpit seats and under foredeck. Handy self-draining bow well in the foredeck gives secure stowage for ground tackle. Ramp launching is easier than comps due to shallow draft. Sturdy tabernacle is judged easier to use than a mere hinge on deck when raising and lowering mast. **Worst features:** New and resale prices are high, and headroom is low, compared to comps. Cockpit footwell is non-self-bailing. Substantial use of varnished wood looks great, but means more than ordinary maintenance is needed.

Comps	LOD	Beam	MinDr	Displ	Bllst	SA/D	D/L	Avg. PHRF	Max. Speed	Motion Index	Space Index	No. of Berths	Head- room
Skipper 20 (18)	18' 4"	6' 7"	2' 0"	2,000	800	14.4	265	NA	5.2	14.6	223	2	4' 6"
Blue Water Blackwatch 19	18' 6"	7' 11"	2' 0"	2,250	800	19.8	187	231	5.6	11.3	255	2	4' 4"
Cornish Shrimper 19	19' 3"	7' 2"	1' 6"	2,350	700	17.6	193	390	5.6	13.2	251	2	3' 4"
Cape Cod Goldeneye	18' 3"	6' 4"	3' 0"	2,500	1,300	16.8	281	NA	5.3	19.8	199	2	3' 6"

Gloucester 16
Names may change, but here the face is the same

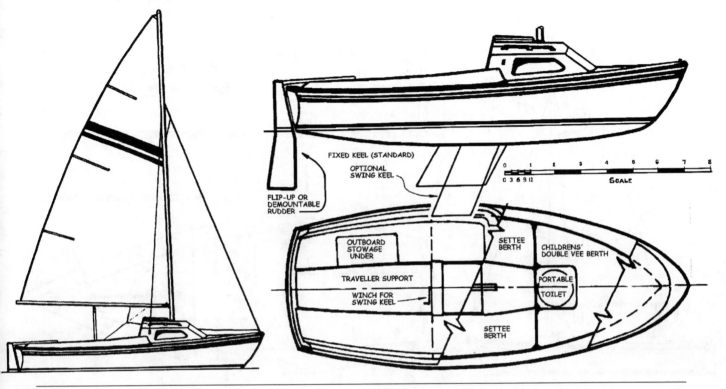

LOD:	15' 7"		**Designer:**	C. William Lapworth
LOA:	16' 11"		**Builder:**	Gloucester Yachts et al.
LWL:	13' 8"		**Years produced:**	1967–1986
Min./max. draft:	0' 9"/3' 9" swing, 2' 6" fixed		**Sail area:**	137 sq. ft.
Bridge clearance:	21' 3"		**Fuel tankage:**	portable
Power:	outboard 2 to 4 hp		**Water tankage:**	portable
B/D ratio:	39%		**Approx. trailering wgt.:**	1,245 lbs.

At various times, this boat was built by different companies and given different names. She was called the Newport 16, the Lockley Newport 16, and the Gloucester 16—and maybe additional names as well. Depending on the manufacturer of the moment, she was available with a swing keel (200-lb. board) or a fixed keel (2' 6" draft), or at times, a choice of either. She has a relatively large cockpit and small cabin, with two quarter berths, a small footwell, and storage space forward, with a central notch molded in for a portable toilet. The Neptune 16 (page 47) is so similar in appearance, weight, and dimensions, despite her two-step raised cabintop, as to indicate a virtually identical hull and rig. **Best features:** Big cockpit and fair-sized sailplan make her a sprightly daysailer. Long waterline and relatively heavy ballast give her good stability. **Worst features:** The fixed-keel model would be relatively difficult to launch and retrieve on a trailer. Caution: On some versions, the mast section is so small ($2^1/_4$" $\times$ $2^1/_4$") and light (0.776 lbs. per foot) that it will bend in a stiff breeze to the point where it may take a permanent set. The absence of a permanent backstay doesn't help this condition.

Comps	LOD	Beam	MinDr	Displ	Bllst	SA/D	D/L	Avg. PHRF	Max. Speed	Motion Index	Space Index	No. of Berths	Head-room
Gloucester 16	15' 7"	6' 3"	0' 9"	900	350	23.5	157	NA	5.0	8.2	122	2	4' 0"
Neptune 16	15' 9"	6' 2"	0' 10"	900	350	23.5	163	NA	4.9	8.5	111	2	3' 6"
Balboa 16	16' 0"	7' 5"	2' 5"	1,000	400	18.7	141	NA	5.1	6.9	171	2	3' 6"
Com-Pac Legacy 17	16' 6"	6' 0"	1' 2"	1,000	400	20.8	154	NA	5.1	9.1	139	2	3' 3"
Com-Pac 16	16' 0"	6' 0"	1' 6"	1,100	450	18.0	179	355	5.0	10.2	136	2	3' 3"

Gloucester 19
Child of LN19, parent of Gloucester 20 et al.

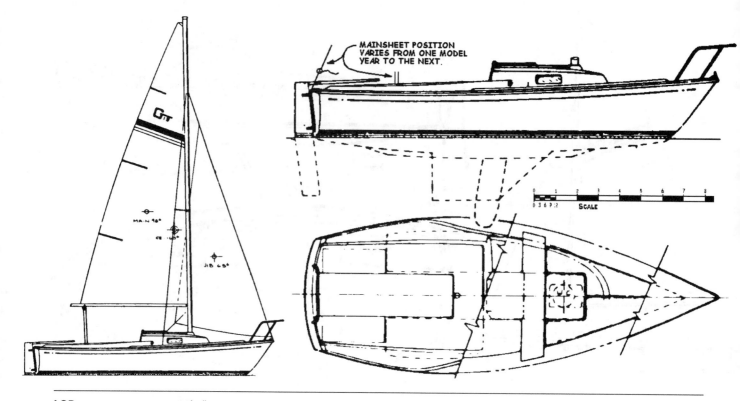

MAINSHEET POSITION VARIES FROM ONE MODEL YEAR TO THE NEXT.

SCALE

LOD:	19' 3"	**Designer:**	Stuart Windley
LOA:	19' 11"	**Builder:**	Gloucester Yachts
LWL:	16' 6"	**Years produced:**	1981–1986
Min./max. draft:	1' 0"/4' 6"	**Sail area:**	174 sq. ft.
Bridge clearance:	28' 3"	**Fuel tankage:**	portable
Power:	outboard 3 to 6 hp	**Water tankage:**	portable
B/D ratio:	34%	**Approx. trailering wgt.:**	2,320 lbs.

This boat started life as the Lockley Newport 19 (LN19), and under new owner-builders, with three inches added to LOD, on paper at least, she became the Gloucester 20 by early 1984. However, by late 1984, with a smaller sail area and a length once again 19' 3", she became the Gloucester 19 . . . and 16 years later, with some construction quality improvements, she was cloned into the Quickstep 19 (see page 72). She was available with either centerboard (draft above) or fixed keel (3' 3" draft). *Best features:* The Gloucester version of this boat is at the lower end of the price scale (but part of this may be tied in with an only so-so level of construction quality). *Worst features:* Although the Space Index indicates a large available volume for stowage, in fact space is limited to bins under berths and two tiny counters separating the V-berth from quarter berths. The V-berth is short. For some reason there was no permanent backstay on some models (as there is on every one of her comps), resulting in a relatively loose rig and insufficient jib stay tension for best efficiency upwind. Construction quality is so-so at best. Critics point out a poorly finished hull-deck joint and misaligned chainplates, among other problems.

Comps	LOD	Beam	MinDr	Displ	Bllst	SA/D	D/L	Avg. PHRF	Max. Speed	Motion Index	Space Index	No. of Berths	Head- room
Gloucester 19	19' 3"	7' 6"	1' 0"	1,600	550	20.3	159	NA	5.4	9.7	241	2	3' 8"
Cape Dory Typhoon 18	18' 6"	6' 6"	2' 7"	1,750	900	17.6	290	306	5.0	15.0	176	2 to 4	3' 11"
Quickstep 19	19' 4"	7' 9"	2' 2"	1,800	750	18.3	164	NA	5.5	10.2	236	2	3' 8"
Vivacity 20 (19)	18' 6"	7' 0"	2' 4"	1,800	785	18.9	127	288	5.6	10.6	215	4	3' 0"

Herreshoff America 18
Several builders have taken a shot at this one

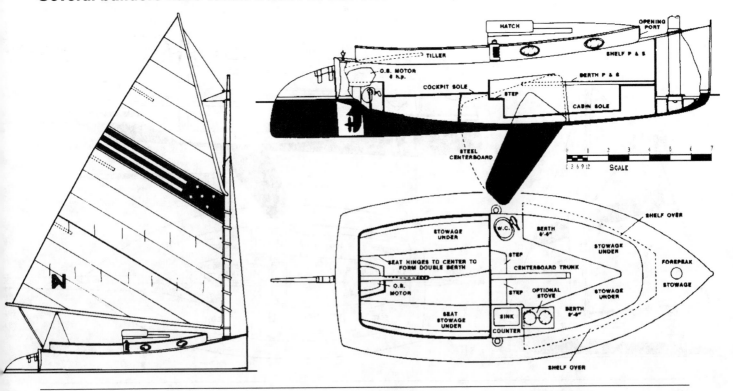

LOD:	18' 2"	**Designer:**	Halsey Herreshoff
LOA:	21' 4"	**Builder:**	N&W and others
LWL:	17' 9"	**Years produced:**	1971–2002
Min./max. draft:	1' 10"/5' 0"	**Sail area:**	258 sq. ft.
Bridge clearance:	29' 6"	**Fuel tankage:**	portable
Power:	outboard 4 to 6 hp	**Water tankage:**	not specified
B/D ratio:	20%	**Approx. trailering wgt.:**	3,450 lbs.

Introduced in 1971 as a direct competitor to the perennially successful Marshall 18 (page 40), the Halsey (not Nat) Herreshoff 18 was successively sold by Nowak & Williams (N&W), Nauset Marine, and, for a while, NOA. Eventually the molds were acquired by Hutchins and morphed into their Horizon Cat (page 29). When N&W were in business they also offered a bowsprited sloop version (the Eagle 21; see page 36) and a daysailing cat ketch on the same hull. *Best features:* The outboard, mounted in the cockpit, is more convenient to operate than one hung on a transom bracket would have been. The centerboard has a relatively high aspect ratio, which adds efficiency upwind. Some sailors may prefer sacrificing privacy for an aft head position, which gives unlimited headroom with the hatch open. Price on the used market compared with the generally better finished comps tends to be at the low end of the scale. *Worst features:* The prop of the outboard, mounted in a cockpit well, can't be tilted out of the water, making for extra drag and possible fouling if the motor is left in place between voyages. The centerboard is steel, requiring extra maintenance to prevent rust.

Comps	LOD	Beam	MinDr	Displ	Bllst	SA/D	D/L	Avg. PHRF	Max. Speed	Motion Index	Space Index	No. of Berths	Head-room
Mystic Catboat 20	20' 0"	8' 0"	1' 10"	2,300	700	23.1	184	315	5.6	11.8	270	2	3' 11"
Herreshoff Amercia 18	18' 2"	8' 0"	1' 10"	2,500	500	22.4	200	324	5.6	13.5	257	2	4' 0"
Com-Pac Horizon 18	18' 2"	8' 4"	2' 2"	2,500	600	17.8	200	NA	5.6	12.4	284	2	4' 6"
Herreshoff Eagle 21	18' 2"	8' 2"	1' 10"	2,700	700	26.4	207	NA	5.7	12.4	264	2	4' 0"
Menger Cat 19	19' 0"	8' 0"	1' 10"	2,900	600	21.2	207	NA	5.8	15.0	267	2	4' 10"

Herreshoff Eagle 21 (18)

Is it an 18, a 21, or a 22?

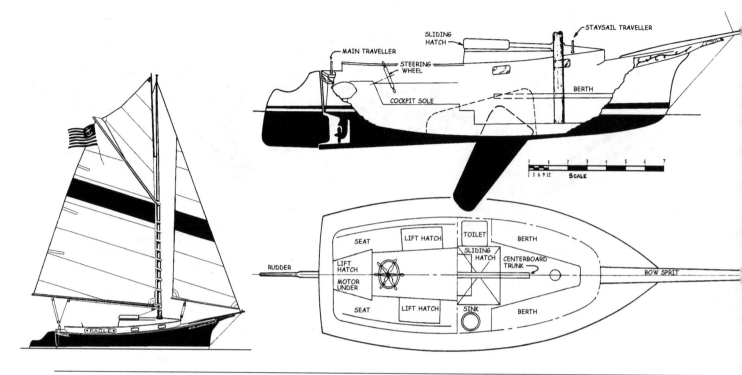

LOD:	18' 2"
LOA:	25' 9"
LWL:	18' 0"
Min./max. draft:	1' 10"/5' 0"
Bridge clearance:	31' 4"
Power:	outboard 4 to 6 hp
B/D ratio:	26%

Designer:	Halsey Herreshoff
Builder:	Nowak & Williams
Years produced:	1971–1980?
Sail area:	320 sq. ft.
Fuel tankage:	portable
Water tankage:	not specified
Approx. trailering wgt.:	3,650 lbs.

Although the ads didn't say so, this boat appears to be the Herreshoff America 18 dressed up in an old-timey costume with a bowsprit, topsail, and jib added. Strangely, the ads at first called her a "21" and later she became a "22," though by scaling off her LOD from the plans, we measure her as an "18." We wonder why the builders, no longer around to ask, advertised her with such a major discrepancy in size. ***Best features:*** To some she may appear to be a pretty replica of a 19th century vessel, though we doubt that she has a close resemblance to any real boat of the past. Her good features generally match the Herreshoff America 18 (page 35). ***Worst features:*** The rather long bowsprit and small forward deck with no lifelines or rails make dousing the jib a precarious and chancy affair. The "clipper bow" appears to us to be inappropriate to use with the fat hull and the blunt stern, though some might feel it looks okay. Wheel rather than tiller on a boat this size is a bad idea, reducing control rather than improving it.

Comps	LOD	Beam	MinDr	Displ	Bllst	SA/D	D/L	Avg. PHRF	Max. Speed	Motion Index	Space Index	No. of Berths	Head-room
Mystic Catboat 20	20' 0"	8' 0"	1' 10"	2,300	700	23.1	184	315	5.6	11.8	270	2	3' 11"
Herreshoff America 18	18' 2"	8' 0"	1' 10"	2,500	500	22.4	200	324	5.6	13.5	257	2	4' 0"
Com-Pac Horizon 18	18' 2"	8' 4"	2' 0"	2,500	600	17.8	200	NA	5.6	12.4	284	2	4' 6"
Herreshoff Eagle 21	18' 2"	8' 2"	1' 10"	2,700	700	26.4	207	NA	5.7	12.4	264	2	4' 0"
Menger Cat 19	19' 0"	8' 0"	1' 10"	2,900	600	21.2	207	NA	5.8	15.0	267	2	4' 10"

Hunter 18.5

Streamlined design by the Hunter Design Team

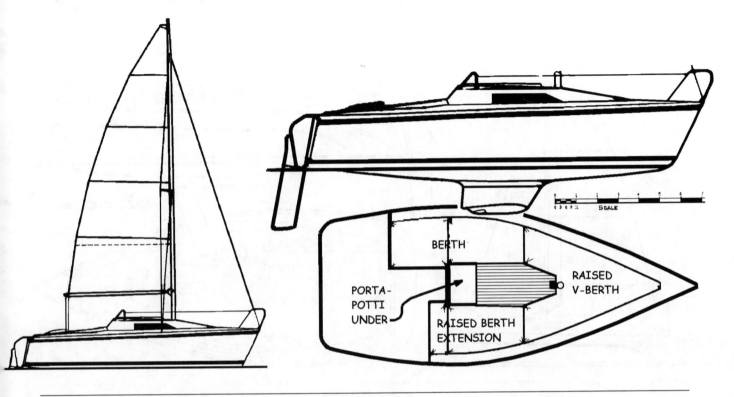

LOD:	18' 5"	**Designer:**	Hunter Design Team
LOA:	20' 2"	**Builder:**	Hunter Marine
LWL:	17' 2"	**Years produced:**	1987–1992
Min./max. draft:	2' 0"	**Sail area:**	178 sq. ft.
Bridge clearance:	27' 5"	**Fuel tankage:**	portable
Power:	outboard 3 to 6 hp	**Water tankage:**	portable
B/D ratio:	33%	**Approx. trailering wgt.:**	2,300 lbs.

In the late 1980s, Hunter Marine expanded their cruising boat line into smaller sizes. They also redesigned the line with a more "modern" look. The Hunter 18.5 was one of the first of Hunter's minicruisers to be introduced. Unique features include a very shallow (two-foot draft) keel with both a bulb and "winglets." ***Best features:*** Headroom of four feet is exceptional for a boat of this size. It helps to make her Space Index best of the comps shown below. Ballast is also highest for the group, improving her Motion Index. ***Worst features:*** The keel is too shallow, and has too small a lateral area, to expect even so-so upwind sailing performance, with or without the winglets (which we suspect are too small to serve any real purpose). The full-length battens make it difficult to "read" the trim of the mainsail. The flip-up rudder, being deeper than the keel, is thus unprotected and therefore subject to damage or loss if a sudden shoal water situation is encountered and the flip-up mechanism isn't ready for it.

Comps	LOD	Beam	MinDr	Displ	Bllst	SA/D	D/L	Avg. PHRF	Max. Speed	Motion Index	Space Index	No. of Berths	Head-room
Alacrity 19 (18)	18' 0"	6' 11"	1' 10"	1,450	480	18.7	132	378	5.5	9.5	223	2 or 3	3' 11"
Windrose 18	18' 5"	7' 0"	1' 0"	1,500	400	18.4	169	288	5.3	10.4	201	4	3' 9"
Hunter 18.5	18' 5"	7' 1"	2' 0"	1,600	520	20.8	141	288	5.6	10.3	253	3	4' 0"

Hunter 19

A "new look" from Hunter in the early 1990s

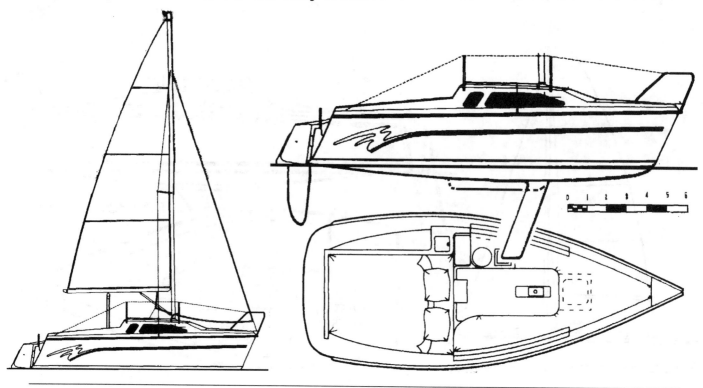

LOD:	19' 0"	**Designer:**	Hunter Design Team
LOA:	20' 6"	**Builder:**	Hunter Marine
LWL:	16' 11"	**Years produced:**	1993–1996
Min./max. draft:	1' 2"/4' 9"	**Sail area:**	165 sq. ft.
Bridge clearance:	29' 6"	**Fuel tankage:**	portable
Power:	outboard 3 to 6 hp	**Water tankage:**	portable
B/D ratio:	29%	**Approx. trailering wgt.:**	2,400 lbs.

Here is a boat that focuses on the relatively inexperienced sailor who seeks a vessel with certain characteristics: room down below; a modern streamlined look; easy trailerability; good affordability; and inclusion of all equipment and instruction required to go sailing so there's no need for endless trips to a marine store. **Best features:** Hunter hit their target market dead center. The boat is roomy (best Space Index among comps); has splashy hull decorations to lend a streamlined look; uses water ballast that can be drained before trailering, saving 600 pounds compared to comps; is priced for the budget-minded; and includes a "Cruise Pac" with all gear needed, including a copy of *Chapman's*. **Worst features:** What the new sailor may not know is that he or she is getting a boat that is slow (lowest SA/D in the comp group) due to small sail area; tender (i.e., tips easily) due to water ballast high up rather than lead or iron ballast down low (poorest Motion Index in the group); and has a tendency to be blown sideways when the wind is abeam, limiting manueverablity under power, due to unusually high freeboard. The pity is that many of these owners think all sailboats have the faults they encounter, and just learn to live with them or quit sailing altogether.

Comps	LOD	Beam	MinDr	Displ	Bllst	SA/D	D/L	Avg. PHRF	Max. Speed	Motion Index	Space Index	No. of Berths	Head-room
Com-Pac 19	18' 8"	7' 0"	2' 0"	2,000	800	19.8	205	285	5.4	13.2	212	4	3' 9"
MacGregor PowerSailer 19	18' 10"	7' 5"	0' 9"	2,050	800	18.7	204	NA	5.4	12.7	241	4	4' 0"
Hunter 19	19' 0"	7' 9"	1' 2"	2,100	600	16.1	194	282	5.5	12.0	279	2	4' 5"
Montego 19	19' 3"	7' 2"	1' 2"	2,150	450	18.2	174	288	5.6	13.2	259	4	4' 0"
Com-Pac Eclipse 18	18' 5"	7' 4"	1' 6"	2,200	700	18.9	166	NA	5.7	12.6	254	4	4' 0"

MacGregor PowerSailer 19
20 knots with a 40 hp outboard

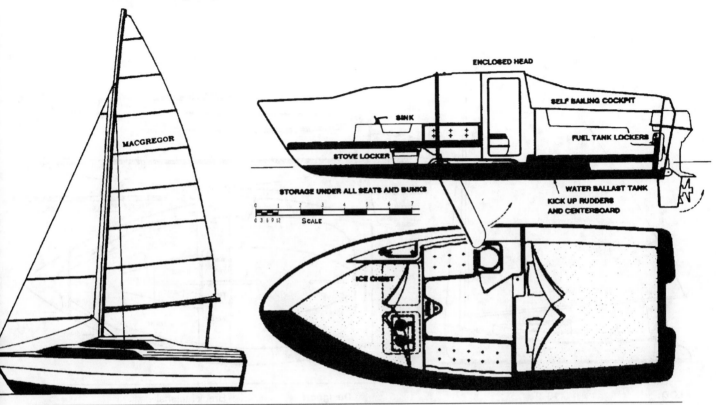

LOD:	18' 10"	**Designer:**	Roger MacGregor
LOA:	19' 10"	**Builder:**	MacGregor Yachts
LWL:	16' 7"	**Years produced:**	1991–1998
Min./max. draft:	0' 9"/5' 1"	**Sail area:**	166 sq. ft.
Bridge clearance:	27' 10"	**Fuel tankage:**	portable
Power:	outboard 8 to 40 hp	**Water tankage:**	portable
B/D ratio:	39%	**Approx. trailering wgt.:**	2,150 lbs.

Not too many sailboats can go 20 knots under power. Only one other boat in this book of 360 designs qualifies: the Picnic 17 (page 52). In the case of both the PowerSailer and the Picnic, the necessary sacrifices of sailing qualities (sailing speed, stability, manueverability, aesthetics) to attain speed under power will be unacceptable to many, if not most, sailors. ***Best features:*** Speed under power, of course, is the main selling feature. In addition, very shallow draft is good for exploring beaches. Her self-bailing cockpit is deep and comfortable.

A sizable double berth extending all the way across the boat under the cockpit is about as roomy as you'll get on a 19-foot sailboat—but it's not for folks with claustrophobia. ***Worst features:*** Steering the PowerSailer 19 under sail can be very frustrating, especially when attempting to make sharp turns. This is partly because the twin rudders are too small for the job. Excessive side-slip when steering under power can also be a problem unless the centerboard is dropped. Water ballast provides inadequate stability in breezy wind conditions.

Comps	LOD	Beam	MinDr	Displ	Bllst	SA/D	D/L	Avg. PHRF	Max. Speed	Motion Index	Space Index	No. of Berths	Head-room
Com-Pac 19	18' 8"	7' 0"	2' 0"	2,000	800	19.8	205	285	5.4	13.2	212	4	3' 9"
MacGregor PowerSailer 19	18' 10"	7' 5"	0' 9"	2,050	800	18.7	204	NA	5.4	12.7	241	4	4' 0"
Hunter 19	19' 0"	7' 9"	1' 2"	2,100	600	16.1	194	282	5.5	12.0	279	2	4' 5"
Montego 19	19' 3"	7' 2"	1' 2"	2,150	450	18.2	174	288	5.6	13.2	259	4	4' 0"
Com-Pac Eclipse 18	18' 5"	7' 4"	1' 6"	2,200	700	18.9	166	NA	5.7	12.6	254	4	4' 0"

Marshall Sanderling 18
First production glass catboat is still popular

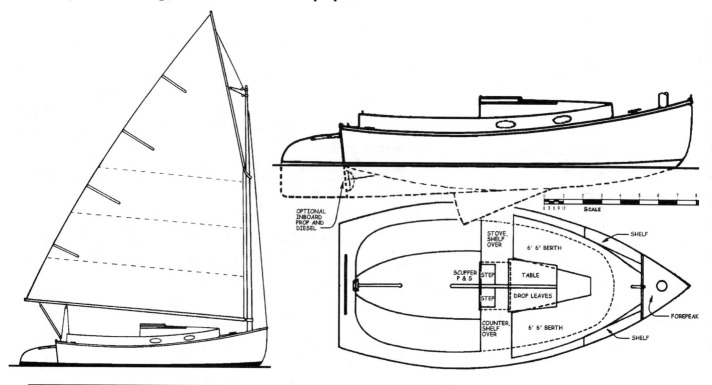

LOD:	18' 2"		**Designer:**	Breck Marshall
LOA:	20' 7"		**Builder:**	Marshall Marine
LWL:	17' 8"		**Years produced:**	1963–present
Min./max. draft:	1' 7"/4' 4"		**Sail area:**	253 sq. ft.
Bridge clearance:	32' 0"		**Fuel tankage:**	portable, inbd. 10 gal.
Power:	outboard 4 to 6 hp		**Water tankage:**	portable
B/D ratio:	23%		**Approx. trailering wgt.:**	3,000 lbs.

This salty-looking vessel is one of the longest running fiberglass designs around. It is still selling well after almost 50 years on the market. ***Best features:*** The basic design is virtually unchanged from the earliest production boats, which means that there are many used boats to choose from. You may be able to pick up an older boat for only a few thousand dollars—or pay mid-five-figures or more for a new boat loaded with extras. Under sail the Sanderling is relatively fast, stiff, well-balanced, and forgiving. Construction is solid if somewhat plain, at least on older boats. Surprisingly for such a small boat, you have a choice of outboard or Yanmar 1GM inboard. There are quite a few one-design racing and cruising fleets of these boats, mostly in New England and New Jersey. ***Worst features:*** Painted wood cockpit seats are open underneath, making stowage of gear easy but leaving it open to the weather. Shelves along the berths below can catch your shoulders when you are lying down and try to turn over. Galley facilities are minimal, and there's no good spot below for a portable cooler. Headroom is only barely adequate for moving around the cabin, and storage below is below average. A forward hatch for better ventilation would be a good idea.

Comps	LOD	Beam	MinDr	Displ	Bllst	SA/D	D/L	Avg. PHRF	Max. Speed	Motion Index	Space Index	No. of Berths	Head-room
Lynx 16 (17)	16' 6"	7' 11"	1' 2"	2,000	200	20.0	218	NA	5.4	11.4	179	2	3' 4"
Menger Cat 17	17' 0"	8' 0"	1' 8"	2,200	500	23.6	219	351	5.4	12.4	194	2	4' 3"
Cape Cod Cat 17	17' 0"	7' 11"	1' 8"	2,200	500	23.6	222	372	5.4	12.4	222	2	4' 6"
Marshall Sanderling 18	18' 2"	8' 6"	1' 7"	2,200	500	23.9	178	315	5.6	10.5	281	2	3' 7"
Molly Catboat 17	17' 0"	7' 6"	2' 2"	3,000	1,000	15.4	317	NA	5.4	19.2	194	2	4' 0"

Maxi-Peep 19
Reuben Trane's ultimate macro-mini-micro

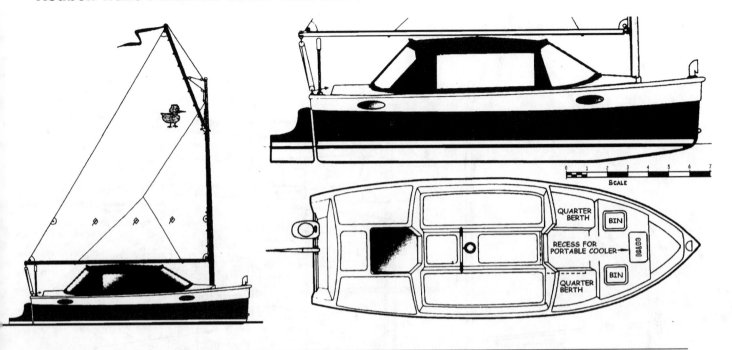

LOD:	19' 2"		**Designer:**	Reuben Trane
LOA:	21' 0"		**Builder:**	Nimble Boats
LWL:	18' 3"		**Years produced:**	1997–1999
Min./max. draft:	0' 9"/ 3' 0"		**Sail area:**	165 sq. ft.
Bridge clearance:	25' 6"		**Fuel tankage:**	portable
Power:	outboard 3 to 6 hp		**Water tankage:**	portable
B/D ratio:	31%		**Approx. trailering wgt.:**	1,500 lbs.

A flyer issued in 1997 by the Florida Bay Boat Company on its then-new Maxi-Peep explains that the forward end of the boat "is identical to the 14' Peep [Hen; see page 51] with a galley, two 6' 3" berths and room for stowage and a porta-potti under the cockpit sole. The center cockpit is 6' 6" long with even wider, more comfortable seats than the 14-footer. Then there is the after cabin (or master stateroom if you will), with sitting headroom, double berth 6' 6" long, and even room for its own porta-potti and stowage of personal gear. Forward of the transom is room for fuel tanks and wet gear." **Best features:** Like the 14-foot Peep Hen, the Maxi-Peep features very shallow draft with centerboard up, and is easily trailerable (approximate towing weight only 1,500 lbs). She has a deep, comfortable self-bailing cockpit, and has a relatively spacious interior for her size. The boom gallows is a handy feature, as is an optional bimini and cockpit enclosure that zips to the bimini. **Worst features:** She has a funky look, but we like her despite it—or because of it? Too bad the boat was never produced in any significant numbers.

Comps	LOD	Beam	MinDr	Displ	Bllst	SA/D	D/L	Avg. PHRF	Max. Speed	Motion Index	Space Index	No. of Berths	Head-room
Maxi-Peep 19	19' 2"	6' 4"	0' 9"	975	300	26.8	72	NA	5.7	6.9	228	4	3' 3"
Pierce Arrow 18	17' 6"	8' 0"	0' 9"	1,100	400	27.8	106	NA	5.5	6.1	283	2	3' 10"
Hermann 19	18' 8"	6' 5"	0' 9"	1,200	200	24.2	92	312	5.7	8.5	184	2	3' 6"
West Wight Potter 19	18' 9"	7' 6"	0' 6"	1,225	370	18.9	116	NA	5.5	7.4	230	4	4' 7"

Menger Cat 17
A worthy competitor to the Marshall 18

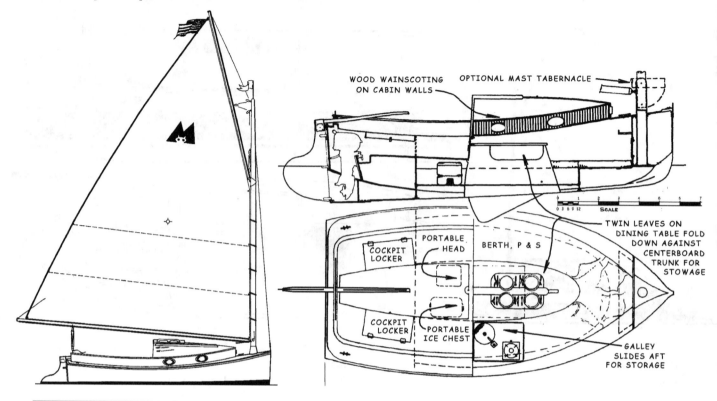

WOOD WAINSCOTING ON CABIN WALLS

OPTIONAL MAST TABERNACLE

COCKPIT LOCKER

PORTABLE HEAD

BERTH, P & S

TWIN LEAVES ON DINING TABLE FOLD DOWN AGAINST CENTERBOARD TRUNK FOR STOWAGE

COCKPIT LOCKER

PORTABLE ICE CHEST

GALLEY SLIDES AFT FOR STORAGE

SCALE

LOD:	17' 0"	**Designer:**	Andrew Menger
LOA:	18' 6"	**Builder:**	Menger Boatworks
LWL:	16' 6"	**Years produced:**	1976–1990
Min./max. draft:	1' 8" / 4' 6"	**Sail area:**	250 sq. ft.
Bridge clearance:	23' 0"	**Fuel tankage:**	portable, inbd. 12 gal.
Power:	outboard 3 to 6 hp, opt. inbd.	**Water tankage:**	portable
B/D ratio:	23%	**Approx. trailering wgt.:**	3,250 lbs.

This design started as the hull lines from an old catboat designed in 1905 by William Goeller. She is an easily trailerable, readily cruisable boat loaded with character. ***Best features:*** She responds to her helm nicely in all but the strongest (25–30 knots) gusts. The cabin arrangement is outstanding, made possible by moving the lower portion of the companionway bulkhead aft. That means a portable ice chest, portable head, even a galley unit can be slid out of the way under the cockpit. The cabin finish also wins high marks for its neat white fiberglass cabin liner, varnished pine

wainscotting on cabin sides, teak and holly sole, and maple drop-leaf table hinged off the centerboard trunk. The cabin arrangement permits extra-long berths: the starboard berth measures 7' 10" end to end; the port berth extends 10' 6". ***Worst features:*** The fiberglass gaff saddle on some boats is unlined and may tend to scrape away the mast paint. Also, the outboard gas tank is kept in the port cockpit locker, so that although the open shelf where it sits is vented to the cockpit, gasoline fumes still might find their way into the bilge, a potentially dangerous situation.

Comps	LOD	Beam	MinDr	Displ	Bllst	SA/D	D/L	Avg. PHRF	Max. Speed	Motion Index	Space Index	No. of Berths	Head-room
Lynx 16	16' 6"	7' 11"	1' 2"	2,000	200	20.2	218	NA	5.4	11.4	179	2	3' 4"
Menger Cat 17	17' 0"	8' 0"	1' 8"	2,200	500	23.6	219	351	5.4	12.4	194	2	4' 3"
Cape Cod Cat 17	17' 0"	7' 11"	1' 8"	2,200	500	23.6	222	372	5.4	12.4	222	2	4' 6"
Marshall Sanderling 18	18' 2"	8' 6"	1' 7"	2,200	500	23.9	178	315	5.6	10.5	281	2	3' 7"
Molly Catboat 17	17' 0"	7' 6"	2' 2"	3,000	1,000	15.4	317	NA	5.4	19.2	194	2	4' 0"

Menger Cat 19
Expanded version of the Menger 17

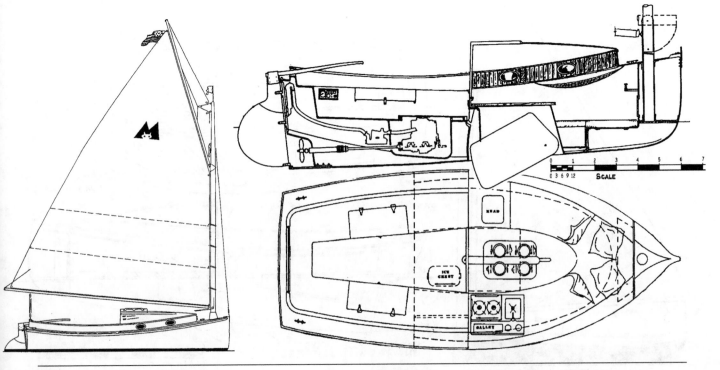

LOD:	19' 0"	**Designer:**	Bill and Andrew Menger
LOA:	21' 0"	**Builder:**	Menger Enterprises and others
LWL:	18' 5"	**Years produced:**	1990–present
Min./max. draft:	1' 10" / 4' 6"	**Sail area:**	270 sq. ft.
Bridge clearance:	33' 6"	**Fuel tankage:**	portable, inbd 12 gal.
Power:	outboard 4 to 6 hp, optional inbd.	**Water tankage:**	portable
B/D ratio:	21%	**Approx. trailering wgt.:**	3,850 lbs.

After a lightning fire destroyed the molds for the successful Menger 17 catboat (page 42), Bill Menger and his son designed the Menger Cat 19, an "expanded and improved" version of the 17, two feet longer, two inches deeper, and 700 pounds heavier (including 100 pounds more ballast). Obvious visual differences include the addition of an extra cabin port for more light, and a longer cockpit. Most of the extra two feet of length is in the aft end of the cockpit. (Compare the two boats' inboard profiles aft of the cockpit hatch for where most of the space went.) The same "best" and "worst"

features apply to the 19 as apply to the 17, but because of the longer LOD and heavier displacement, we now have a different set of boats to compare. ***Best features:*** The Menger 19 has more headroom than any of her comps, plus a better Motion Index (no doubt due to her combination of heavier displacement and longer length). The optional mast tabernacle works well, and is highly recommended for trailer-sailors. Note: When last noticed, this boat was being made by Wagner Boatworks of Oyster Bay, NY, and was called the Thom Cat 19 Catboat. ***Worst features:*** Price is high.

Comps	LOD	Beam	MinDr	Displ	Bllst	SA/D	D/L	Avg. PHRF	Max. Speed	Motion Index	Space Index	No. of Berths	Head-room
Mystic Catboat 20	20' 0"	8' 0"	1' 10"	2,300	700	23.1	184	315	5.6	11.8	270	2	3' 11"
Herreshoff America 18	18' 2"	8' 0"	1' 10"	2,500	500	22.4	200	324	5.6	13.5	257	2	4' 0"
Com-Pac Horizon 18	18' 2"	8' 4"	2' 2"	2,500	600	17.8	200	NA	5.6	12.4	284	2	4' 6"
Herreshoff Eagle 21	18' 2"	8' 2"	1' 10"	2,700	700	26.4	207	NA	5.7	12.4	264	2	4' 0"
Menger Cat 19	19' 0"	8' 0"	1' 10"	2,900	600	21.2	207	369	5.8	15.0	267	2	4' 10"

Molly Catboat 17
West Coast entry in the catboat sweepstakes

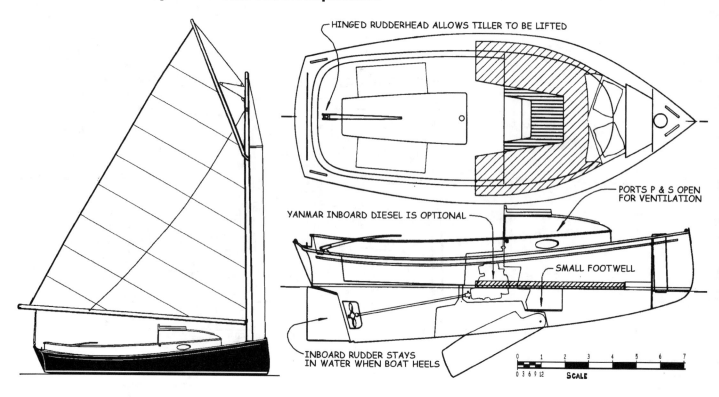

HINGED RUDDERHEAD ALLOWS TILLER TO BE LIFTED

PORTS P & S OPEN FOR VENTILATION

YANMAR INBOARD DIESEL IS OPTIONAL

SMALL FOOTWELL

INBOARD RUDDER STAYS IN WATER WHEN BOAT HEELS

SCALE

LOD:	17' 0"	**Designer:**	Gerard De Witt
LOA:	17' 0"	**Builder:**	Fernandes Boatworks
LWL:	16' 2"	**Years produced:**	1987–1988?
Min./max. draft:	2' 2"/4' 0"	**Sail area:**	200 sq. ft.
Bridge clearance:	25' 0"	**Fuel tankage:**	portable
Power:	outboard 3 to 6 hp, inbd. optional	**Water tankage:**	portable
B/D ratio:	33%	**Approx. trailering wgt.:**	4,000 lbs.

The California-built Molly Cat is different from her eastern-built cousins in a number of respects, e.g., her stem has a jaunty tumblehome, and the use of wood is more lavish (lignum vitae deck cleats, ash sheet blocks, extensive teak deck trim) compared to her comps. She is beautifully built. *Best features:* The rudder is inboard, so it stays in the water when the boat heels. The tiller also can be tilted up and out of the way, making it easier to move about the cockpit in comfort. On all the other comps except the Lynx, the tillers are fixed to the rudderheads. *Worst features:* Her gigantic cockpit reduces her cabin space to pup tent proportions (though the centerboard trunk is buried beneath the cabin sole, mitigating the claustrophobic space a bit). Her cockpit is self-draining until four or five people load it down, at which point water sloshes in through the scuppers instead of out. Compared to her comps, the Molly has the lowest sail area and the highest displacement, as well as the narrowest beam, limiting her light-air performance. In heavy air, the comps just reef.

Comps	LOD	Beam	MinDr	Displ	Bllst	SA/D	D/L	Avg. PHRF	Max. Speed	Motion Index	Space Index	No. of Berths	Head-room
Lynx 16	16' 6"	7' 11"	1' 2"	2,000	200	20.2	218	NA	5.4	11.4	179	2	3' 4"
Menger Cat 17	17' 0"	8' 0"	1' 8"	2,200	500	23.6	219	351	5.4	12.4	194	2	4' 3"
Cape Cod Cat 17	17' 0"	7' 11"	1' 8"	2,200	500	23.6	222	372	5.4	12.4	222	2	4' 6"
Marshall Sanderling 18	18' 2"	8' 6"	1' 7"	2,200	500	23.9	178	315	5.6	10.5	281	2	3' 7"
Molly Catboat 17	17' 0"	7' 6"	2' 2"	3,000	1,000	15.4	317	NA	5.4	19.2	194	2	4' 0"

Montego 19
Simple cruiser for a young family

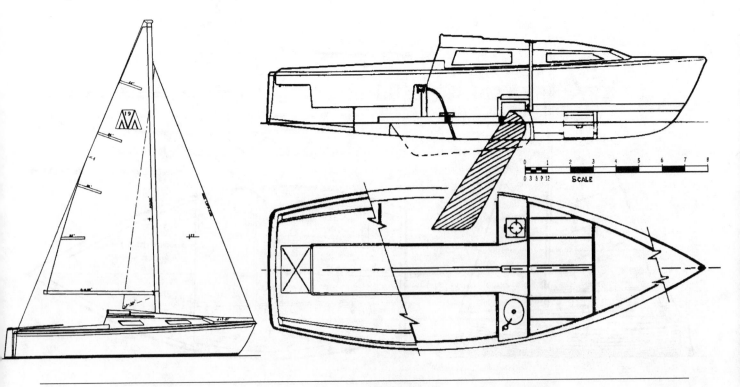

LOD:	19' 3"		**Designer:**	Jopie Helsen
LOA:	20' 0"		**Builder:**	Universal Marine Corp.
LWL:	17' 8"		**Years produced:**	1976–1985
Min./max. draft:	1' 2"/ 4' 6"		**Sail area:**	166 sq. ft.
Bridge clearance:	27' 3"		**Fuel tankage:**	portable
Power:	outboard 3 to 6 hp		**Water tankage:**	portable
B/D ratio:	21%		**Approx. trailering wgt.:**	3,000 lbs.

This is a boat designed for the weekend sailor who wants to trailer-sail alone or with a companion, plus perhaps a couple of small children. She is relatively easy to sail, though her lack of controls (no vang, Cunningham, reef points, etc.) limits performance, and so limits the fun of attaining maximum speed in any wind conditions by easing this string and tightening that one. The Montego 19 was superseded in 1985 by the Montego 20 (see page 110), which uses the same basic hull and rig and has identical sail dimensions, but adds some ballast weight in a fixed keel, thus eliminating the cumbersome 450-pound swing keel. *Best features:* The boat is relatively heavily built, judging by her notably higher "bare" weight compared to comps when ballast weight is subtracted. That could make her less subject to damage, say, in a collision. *Worst features:* Her heavy iron keel is exposed to submerged hazards even when in the raised position. When lowered, the keel can damage its fiberglass housing, perhaps causing a serious leak, if struck a blow to the side.

Comps	LOD	Beam	MinDr	Displ	Bllst	SA/D	D/L	Avg. PHRF	Max. Speed	Motion Index	Space Index	No. of Berths	Head-room
Com-Pac 19	18' 8"	7' 0"	2' 0"	2,000	800	19.8	205	285	5.4	13.2	212	4	3' 9"
MacGregor PowerSailer 19	18' 10"	7' 5"	0' 9"	2,050	800	18.7	204	NA	5.4	12.7	241	4	4' 0"
Hunter 19	19' 0"	7' 9"	1' 2"	2,100	600	16.1	194	282	5.5	12.0	279	2	4' 5"
Montego 19	19' 3"	7' 2"	1' 2"	2,150	450	18.2	174	288	5.6	13.2	259	4	4' 0"
Com-Pac Eclipse 18	18' 5"	7' 4"	1' 6"	2,200	700	18.9	166	NA	5.7	12.6	254	4	4' 0"

Montgomery 17
Lapstrake beauty from Lyle Hess

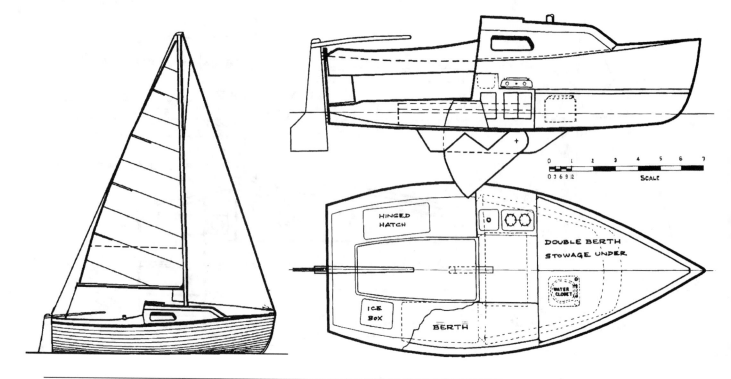

LOD:	17' 1"		Designer:	Lyle Hess
LOA:	18' 6"		Builder:	Montgomery Marine et al.
LWL:	15' 10"		Years produced:	1973–present
Min./max. draft:	1' 9"/3' 6"		Sail area:	154 sq. ft.
Bridge clearance:	25' 6"		Fuel tankage:	portable
Power:	outboard 3 to 6 hp		Water tankage:	portable
B/D ratio:	31%		Approx. trailering wgt.:	1,900 lbs.

As with her 15-foot sistership (page 71), the Montgomery 17 was built starting in 1973 by Montgomery Marine. In 1999, Nor'Sea took over production; now Montgomery Boats builds them. Over the years many changes have been made. Different rigs were offered for a time, notably a tall rig. In the late 1970s, a fourth berth was added as an option. The berth took the place of the galley area and reduced storage space, but improved sitting comfort below. The first boats had a choice of fixed cast iron keels or keel-centerboards with 400-pound cast iron boards. Later the board weight was increased to

550 pounds, and finally to a fiberglass board of 600 pounds with a lead insert. Stated displacement grew from 1,280 to 1550 pounds. The stats shown here are as reported for early boats. ***Best features:*** As with her little 15-foot sister, we like her looks. She displays a good level of attention to detail in her construction. ***Worst features:*** With the same underbody design as the Montgomery 15, compared to her comps she will have the same penalties. That is, she'll be harder to handle at the launching ramp and give poorer performance upwind.

Comps	LOD	Beam	MinDr	Displ	Bllst	SA/D	D/L	Avg. PHRF	Max. Speed	Motion Index	Space Index	No. of Berths	Head-room
Skippers Mate 17	17' 2"	7' 2"	1' 0"	1,100	250	22.4	146	NA	5.2	7.7	193	3	4' 6"
Precision 18 (17)	17' 5"	7' 5"	1' 6"	1,100	350	21.8	134	275	5.3	7.1	197	4	4' 0"
Montgomery 17	17' 1"	7' 4"	1' 9"	1,280	400	20.9	144	294	5.3	8.3	229	3	4' 8"

Neptune 16
Near-clone of Gloucester/Newport 16

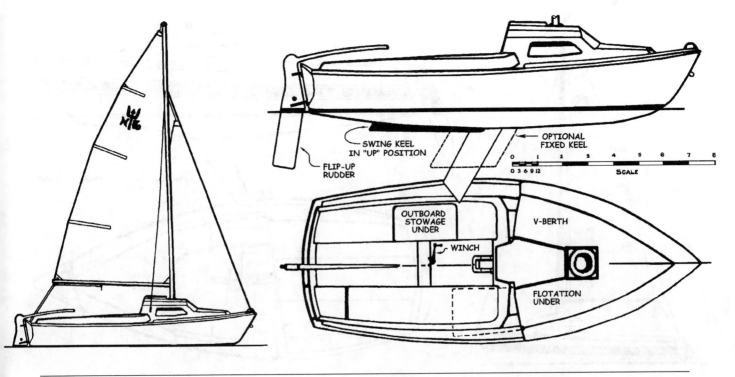

LOD:	15' 9"	**Designer:**	C. William Lapworth
LOA:	16' 9"	**Builder:**	Capital Yachts
LWL:	13' 6"	**Years produced:**	1974–1987
Min./max. draft:	0' 10"/4' 0"	**Sail area:**	137 sq. ft.
Bridge clearance:	21' 3"	**Fuel tankage:**	portable
Power:	outboard 2 to 6 hp	**Water tankage:**	portable
B/D ratio:	46%	**Approx. trailering wgt.:**	1,400 lbs.

The Neptune 16's dimensions and appearance are only slightly different from the Gloucester 16/Newport 16's; the cabintop is slightly raised in the Neptune to provide more headroom, but performance can be expected to be about the same. However, the boat came in a choice of swing-keel or fixed-keel underbody, and the fixed-keel version (900 pound displacement, 2' 9" draft) is probably slightly stiffer than the swing keel model (750 pounds), while the swing keel, being deeper with keel down, will probably give better windward performance. *Best features:* This boat

is low cost and easy to trailer (in the swing-keel version). Her extra-shallow draft (on the swing-keel model only) is especially good for ramp launching and retrieving. Her big cockpit is good for daysailing, and the fixed-keel model (though less handy on the launch ramp) is relatively stable. *Worst features:* Construction was focused on economy (e.g., iron rather than lead ballast), so maintenance on used models must be carried out diligently to prevent disastrous deterioration. Space below is relatively cramped. Raised forward deck makes foredeck footing precarious.

Comps	LOD	Beam	MinDr	Displ	Bllst	SA/D	D/L	Avg. PHRF	Max. Speed	Motion Index	Space Index	No. of Berths	Head-room
Gloucester 16	15' 7"	6' 3"	0' 9"	900	350	23.5	157	NA	5.0	8.2	122	2	4' 0"
Neptune 16	15' 9"	6' 2"	0' 10"	900	350	23.5	163	NA	4.9	8.5	111	2	3' 6"
Balboa 16	16' 0"	7' 5"	2' 5"	1,000	400	18.7	141	NA	5.1	6.9	171	2	3' 6"
Com-Pac Legacy 17	16' 6"	6' 0"	1' 2"	1,000	400	20.8	154	NA	5.1	9.1	139	2	3' 3"
Com-Pac 16	16' 0"	6' 0"	1' 6"	1,100	450	18.0	179	355	5.0	10.2	136	2	3' 3"

O'Day 19
Little trailerable cruiser by C. Raymond Hunt

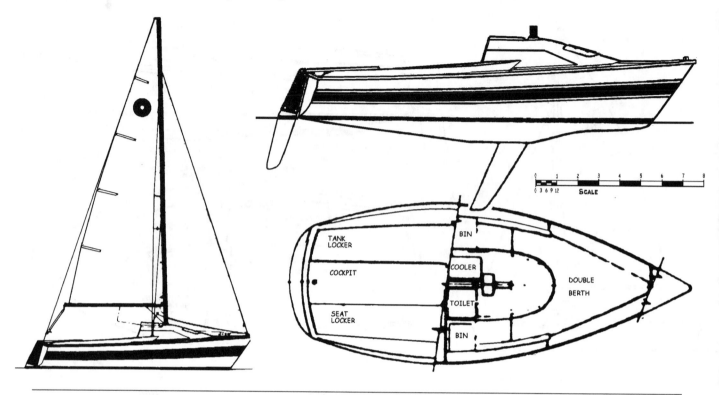

LOD:	19' 0"	**Designer:**	C. Raymond Hunt Assoc.
LOA:	20' 8"	**Builder:**	O'Day Div., Bangor Punta
LWL:	16' 8"	**Years produced:**	1979–1982
Min./max. draft:	1' 0"/4' 4"	**Sail area:**	165 sq. ft.
Bridge clearance:	29' 6"	**Fuel tankage:**	portable
Power:	outboard 3 to 5 hp	**Water tankage:**	portable
B/D ratio:	21%	**Approx. trailering wgt.:**	2,060 lbs.

Over 400 of these little shallow-draft racer-cruisers were built in the three years ending in 1982. O'Day may have hoped that they could start some fleets for one-design club racing, but the boat is probably a bit too small for that purpose, given her relatively short cockpit and lack of buoyancy aft (insufficient to support much crew weight). ***Best features:*** The O'Day 19's high-aspect-ratio rig and centerboard, low wetted surface, and light weight should make her fast in light air—assuming a small crew. ***Worst features:*** The O'Day's average PHRF of around 218 compared to

much higher numbers for her comps would indicate that she is a faster boat. This might be the case in light air with a small crew, or in heavy air if the skipper piles plenty of beef along the rail. Otherwise her relatively light ballast (300 lbs. compared with up to 400 for her comps) installed high in the boat would cause her to be too tender to be fast in all conditions. Other faults include an awkward mainsheet lead (with no traveler to keep the boom in close in a breeze) and a rudder whose bottom is lower than the keel with board up (asking for trouble in shoal waters).

Comps	LOD	Beam	MinDr	Displ	Bllst	SA/D	D/L	Avg. PHRF	Max. Speed	Motion Index	Space Index	No. of Berths	Head-room
Rhodes Mariner 19	19' 2"	7' 0"	0' 10"	1,305	320	24.8	104	285	5.6	8.1	188	2	3' 8"
Starwind 19	18' 7"	7' 6"	1' 6"	1,350	395	20.0	159	288	5.5	8.6	215	4	3' 2"
O'Day 19	19' 0"	7' 9"	1' 0"	1,400	300	21.1	135	218	5.5	8.1	232	2	3' 10"
O'Day 192 (19)	18' 7"	7' 1"	1' 5"	1,400	400	19.2	135	270	5.5	9.2	223	4	4' 0"
O'Day 20 (19)	18' 11"	7' 0"	1' 2"	1,600	400	20.3	139	276	5.6	10.1	206	4	3' 10"

O'Day 192
The O'Day 19 updated

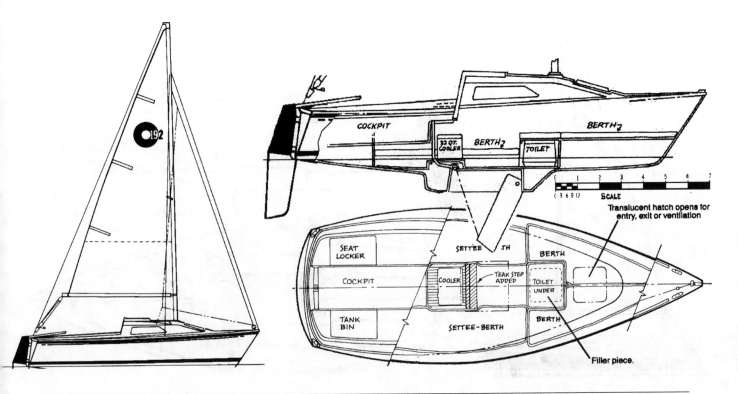

LOD:	18' 7"
LOA:	19' 9"
LWL:	16' 8"
Min./max. draft:	1' 5"/4' 2"
Bridge clearance:	27' 8"
Power:	outboard 3 to 6 hp
B/D ratio:	29%

Designer:	C. Raymond Hunt Assoc.
Builder:	O'Day Div., Bangor Punta
Years produced:	1985–1987?
Sail area:	150 sq. ft.
Fuel tankage:	portable
Water tankage:	portable
Approx. trailering wgt.:	2,100 lbs.

The O'Day 192 is a nicely finished update of the O'Day 19. With limited interior space (just room for a child-sized V-berth and two adult-sized quarter berths), the designers decided against including room for a galley, though they did find space for a chemical head beneath the V-berth and an ice chest in the companionway. The low quarter berths have 4' 0" sitting headroom, reduced to 3' 4" over the cushion atop the toilet. **Best features:** The finish and construction is very good, above and below decks. The comfortable, angled seating in the cockpit and the effective, no-slip non-skid in the cockpit and on deck are also big pluses. Schaefer roller furling is standard, which is a plus, but the jib is sheeted through fixed jib blocks, which limits control of the size and shape of the sail. **Worst features:** Sail controls are too few and too simple. The 3-to-1 mainsheet attached to the backstay is awkward to release in moderate or strong winds. We'd add a vang, rerig the mainsheet to a block on the cockpit sole, and install jibsheet tracks along the rail.

Comps	LOD	Beam	MinDr	Displ	Bllst	SA/D	D/L	Avg. PHRF	Max. Speed	Motion Index	Space Index	No. of Berths	Head-room
Rhodes Mariner 19	19' 2"	7' 0"	0' 10"	1,305	320	24.8	104	285	5.6	8.1	188	2	3' 8"
Starwind 19	18' 7"	7' 6"	1' 6"	1,350	395	20.0	159	288	5.5	8.6	215	4	3' 2"
O'Day 19	19' 0"	7' 9"	1' 0"	1,400	300	21.1	135	218	5.5	8.1	232	2	3' 10"
O'Day 192	18' 7"	7' 1"	1' 5"	1,400	400	19.2	135	270	5.5	9.2	223	4	4' 0"
O'Day 20 (19)	18' 11"	7' 0"	1' 2"	1,600	400	20.3	139	276	5.6	10.1	206	4	3' 10"

O'Day 20 (19)
A replacement for the O'Day 22?

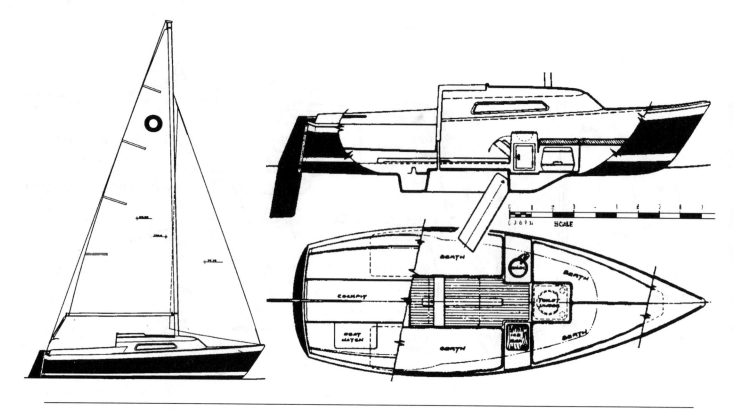

LOD:	18' 11"
LOA:	20' 9"
LWL:	17' 3"
Min./max. draft:	1' 2"/4' 5"
Bridge clearance:	26' 6"
Power:	outboard 3 to 6 hp
B/D ratio:	25%

Designer:	C. Raymond Hunt Assoc.
Builder:	O'Day Div., Bangor Punta
Years produced:	1973–1979
Sail area:	174 sq. ft.
Fuel tankage:	portable
Water tankage:	portable
Approx. trailering wgt.:	2,300 lbs.

The O'Day 22 (page 118) was introduced in 1972, and a year later the O'Day 20 came along. According to the yachting press of the time, the smaller O'Day 20 was a lower-priced follow-up to the similar O'Day 22. In reality, the O'Day 20 was misnamed, as she is only 18' 11" on deck. (As with the O'Day 22, the marketers threw in the added length of the reverse transom, thus reporting "hull length" instead of "length on deck" as standard convention would have called for.) Caveat emptor! **Best features:** It is interesting to compare the O'Day

20 with her near sisterships, the O'Day 19 and 192, one longer and one shorter in LOD. For example, both these comps have more internal space than the O'Day 20. But the O'Day 20 has a slightly better Motion Index resulting from her extra 200 pounds of ballast, and slightly more speed due to her longer LWL. **Worst features:** Other than the above, we don't see much difference. Maybe the only really bad feature was in the higher new price extracted from innocent buyers by adding a phantom foot to her announced length.

Comps	LOD	Beam	MinDr	Displ	Bllst	SA/D	D/L	Avg. PHRF	Max. Speed	Motion Index	Space Index	No. of Berths	Head-room
Rhodes Mariner 19	19' 2"	7' 0"	0' 10"	1,305	320	24.8	104	285	5.6	8.1	188	2	3' 8"
Starwind 19	18' 7"	7' 6"	1' 6"	1,350	395	20.0	159	288	5.5	8.6	215	4	3' 2"
O'Day 19	19' 0"	7' 9"	1' 0"	1,400	300	21.1	135	218	5.5	8.1	232	2	3' 10"
O'Day 192	18' 7"	7' 1"	1' 5"	1,400	400	19.2	135	270	5.5	9.2	223	4	4' 0"
O'Day 20 (19)	18' 11"	7' 0"	1' 2"	1,600	400	20.3	139	276	5.6	10.1	206	4	3' 10"

Peep Hen 14
Reuben Trane's ultimate micro

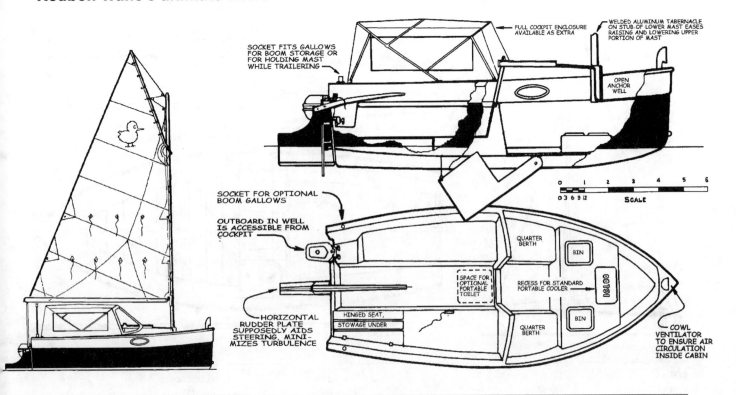

SOCKET FITS GALLOWS FOR BOOM STORAGE OR FOR HOLDING MAST WHILE TRAILERING

FULL COCKPIT ENCLOSURE AVAILABLE AS EXTRA

WELDED ALUMINUM TABERNACLE ON STUB OF LOWER MAST EASES RAISING AND LOWERING UPPER PORTION OF MAST

OPEN ANCHOR WELL

SOCKET FOR OPTIONAL BOOM GALLOWS

OUTBOARD IN WELL IS ACCESSIBLE FROM COCKPIT

HORIZONTAL RUDDER PLATE SUPPOSEDLY AIDS STEERING, MINI-MIZES TURBULENCE

HINGED SEAT, STOWAGE UNDER

SPACE FOR OPTIONAL PORTABLE TOILET

QUARTER BERTH

BIN

RECESS FOR STANDARD PORTABLE COOLER

IGLOO

QUARTER BERTH

BIN

COWL VENTILATOR TO ENSURE AIR CIRCULATION INSIDE CABIN

LOD:	14' 2"	**Designer:**	Reuben Trane
LOA:	16' 2"	**Builder:**	Fla. Bay Boats; Nimble Boats
LWL:	13' 3"	**Years produced:**	1985–2003
Min./max. draft:	0' 9"/3' 0"	**Sail area:**	115 sq. ft.
Bridge clearance:	24' 0"	**Fuel tankage:**	portable
Power:	outboard 3 to 6 hp	**Water tankage:**	portable
B/D ratio:	31%	**Approx. trailering wgt.:**	1,100 lbs.

Designer Trane says he conceived this boat "after a good New Year's Eve party" as a small, beachable, easy-to-use microcruiser. The "Peep" has the smallest LOD in this book, though she's far from smallest in usable space. In fact, her big freeboard and beam give her second-best space versus the comps shown here. **Best features:** Very shallow draft with centerboard up is good for exploring shoal waters. She's easily trailerable (approximate towing weight 1,100 pounds), and short enough to fit into a standard sized garage.

Self-bailing cockpit is deep and comfortable. She has a relatively spacious interior for her size—though 14 feet is about the absolute minimum for living aboard, even for a weekend and in protected waters. Boom gallows is a handy feature, as is an optional bimini and cockpit enclosure that zips to the bimini. **Worst features:** Price new was high, headroom low compared to comps. Tanbark sails and a high, boxy hull with a wide sheer stripe may make her look cute, but few would call her graceful.

Comps	LOD	Beam	MinDr	Displ	Bllst	SA/D	D/L	Avg. PHRF	Max. Speed	Motion Index	Space Index	No. of Berths	Head-room
West Wight Potter 15	15' 0"	5' 6"	0' 7"	475	85	18.1	161	NA	4.5	5.8	103	2	3' 9"
Peep Hen 14	14' 2"	6' 4"	0' 9"	650	200	24.5	125	NA	4.9	6.3	167	2	3' 3"
Precision 165 (16)	15' 8"	7' 2"	1' 9"	750	250	28.1	94	NA	5.2	5.4	173	2	3' 6"
Montgomery 15	15' 0"	6' 4"	1' 3"	750	275	23.6	144	NA	4.9	7.2	125	2	4' 0"

Picnic 17

Sail, plane with a 40 hp motor, or waterski?

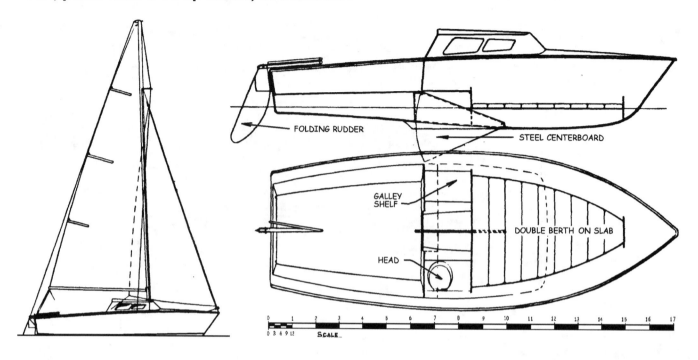

LOD:	17' 0"	Designer:	Nils Lucander
LOA:	18' 8"	Builder:	General Boats
LWL:	15' 4"	Years produced:	1959–1972
Min./max. draft:	0' 10"/2' 2"	Sail area:	204 sq. ft.
Bridge clearance:	29' 0"	Fuel tankage:	portable
Power:	outboard 4 to 6 hp	Water tankage:	portable
B/D ratio:	42%	Approx. trailering wgt.:	1,200 lbs.

This is one of the first fiberglass sailboats, sold beginning around 1959, and was claimed by the marketer to do "everything." Even though she's only 17 feet long, she supposedly sleeps five (though we don't see where). Even though she weighs only 700 pounds all up (i.e., with spars and sails), she supposedly can handle a 40-horse outboard, plane, and tow waterskiers. The flared hull shape supposedly deflects spray so the cockpit stays bone dry. But she never caught on, though available new for thirteen years—perhaps because she didn't live up to her advertised capabilities. **Best features:** If you really want to waterski behind your sailboat, this is one of the few sailboats specifically designed to do that—though we'd rather opt for a ski boat to tow skiers, plus a separate sailboat to go sailing. **Worst features:** Her narrow waterline beam combined with big rig (compared to her comps, the Picnic has the highest SA/D) tends to make her a bit tippy in a breeze.

Comps	LOD	Beam	MinDr	Displ	Bllst	SA/D	D/L	Avg. PHRF	Max. Speed	Motion Index	Space Index	No. of Berths	Head-room
Newport 17 (18)	17' 8"	6' 4"	0' 9"	600	150	34.2	63	NA	5.4	4.6	191	2	3' 4"
Picnic 17	17' 0"	6' 6"	0' 10"	700	0	41.4	87	NA	5.2	5.4	200	2	3' 10"
Siren 17	17' 2"	6' 8"	0' 8"	750	130	22.7	99	NA	5.2	5.8	144	4	3' 8"
Baymaster 18	17' 8"	6' 11"	0' 9"	750	150	28.3	99	NA	5.2	5.5	171	2	3' 3"
Holder 17	17' 0"	7' 3"	1' 8"	950	345	24.3	126	NA	5.2	6.6	207	2	4' 0"

Pierce Arrow 18
Has this boat disappeared without a trace?

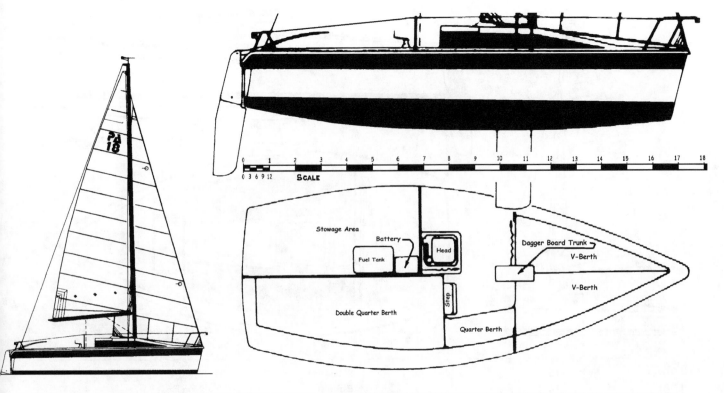

LOD:	17' 6"	Designer:	Mark Leonard
LOA:	18' 7"	Builder:	Pierce Arrow Marine
LWL:	16' 8"	Years produced:	1982–1984?
Min./max. draft:	0' 9"/ 4' 0"	Sail area:	185 sq. ft.
Bridge clearance:	30' 10"	Fuel tankage:	portable
Power:	outboard 3 to 6 hp	Water tankage:	portable
B/D ratio:	36%	Approx. trailering wgt.:	1,700 lbs.

The PA18 is unusual in several ways. For one thing, she weighs only 1,100 pounds, ready to sail. Also, with her wide beam, she has a bigger Space Index than any of her comps. For still another thing, she has a heavy (400 pound) daggerboard, which must be mechanically lifted via a winch into a trunk just aft of the mast. *Best features:* With an SA/D over 25 and thus in the "very high" range, and a D/L nearly in the ultralight category, this boat should be quite fast in light air. The only other boats in this size range with comparable SA/D and D/L ratios are the Picnic 17 and the Newport 17, but neither of these boats have anywhere near the PA18's 400 pounds of ballast. *Worst features:* Cranking that heavy daggerboard up and down must be a nuisance, and hitting a rock with the board down is likely to be a cause for alarm, if not of damage to the trunk and hull. We searched the Internet for any trace of information on this boat, or her designer or owners, and found none. R.I.P.

Comps	LOD	Beam	MinDr	Displ	Bllst	SA/D	D/L	Avg. PHRF	Max. Speed	Motion Index	Space Index	No. of Berths	Head-room
Maxi-Peep 19	19' 2"	6' 4"	0' 9"	975	300	26.8	72	NA	5.7	6.9	228	4	3' 3"
Pierce Arrow 18	17' 6"	8' 0"	0' 9"	1,100	400	27.8	106	NA	5.5	6.1	283	2	4' 10"
Hermann 19	18' 8"	6' 5"	0' 9"	1,200	200	24.2	92	312	5.7	8.5	184	2	3' 6"
West Wight Potter 19	18' 9"	7' 6"	0' 6"	1,225	370	18.9	116	NA	5.5	7.4	230	4	4' 7"

Precision 165 (16)

Little gem by a notable designer

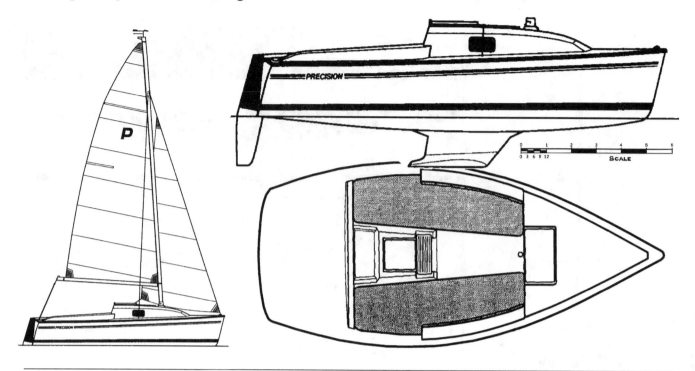

LOD:	15' 8"		**Designer:**	Jim Taylor
LOA:	16' 5"		**Builder:**	Precision Boatworks
LWL:	15' 3"		**Years produced:**	1995–present
Min./max. draft:	1' 9"		**Sail area:**	145 sq. ft.
Bridge clearance:	25' 4"		**Fuel tankage:**	portable
Power:	outboard 4 to 6 hp		**Water tankage:**	portable
B/D ratio:	33%		**Approx. trailering wgt.:**	1,250 lbs.

Designer Jim Taylor was one of the leading designers of America's Cup boats in the 1990s. He has plenty of technical expertise, a good eye for what looks right in a small boat design, and has drawn a number of successful pocket cruisers. For some time he has been the designer of record for Precision Boatworks. The Precision 165 is the smallest cruising boat in the company's line. **Best features:** The P165 has a bigger beam, heavier ballast, and a fixed lead keel with "end-plate effect" bulb compared with her peers' centerboards, plus the largest SA/D and lowest D/L in the comp group. These differences help to make this boat relatively stiff and fast in a breeze. A simple three-stay rig (with no spreaders) makes rigging at the ramp easier and faster. Relatively short overhangs contribute to more manageable storage, especially in a one-car garage. Quality Harken blocks, vang sheeting arrangement, and a forward hatch are all nice features. **Worst features:** Fixed keel is less convenient at the launching ramp.

Comps	LOD	Beam	MinDr	Displ	Bllst	SA/D	D/L	Avg. PHRF	Max. Speed	Motion Index	Space Index	No. of Berths	Head-room
West Wight Potter 15	15' 0"	5' 6"	0' 7"	475	85	18.1	161	NA	4.5	5.8	103	2	3' 9"
Peep Hen 14	14' 2"	6' 4"	0' 9"	650	200	24.5	125	NA	4.9	6.3	167	2	3' 3"
Precision 165 (16)	15' 8"	7' 2"	1' 9"	750	250	28.1	94	NA	5.2	5.4	173	2	3' 6"
Montgomery 15	15' 0"	6' 4"	1' 3"	750	275	23.6	144	NA	4.9	7.2	125	2	4' 0"

Precision 18 (17)

A wholesome microcruiser

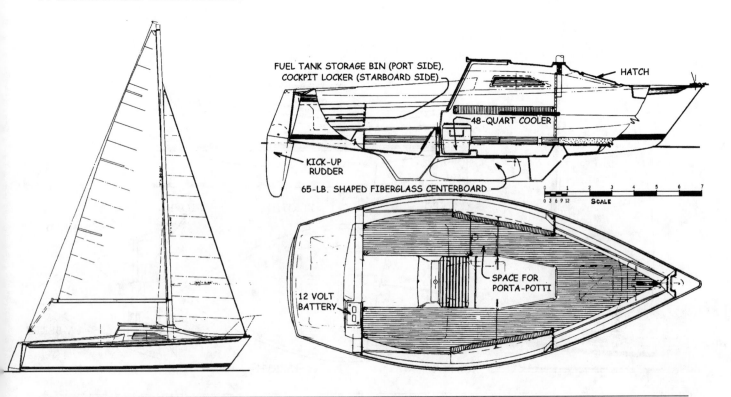

FUEL TANK STORAGE BIN (PORT SIDE),
COCKPIT LOCKER (STARBOARD SIDE)

HATCH

48-QUART COOLER

KICK-UP RUDDER

65-LB. SHAPED FIBERGLASS CENTERBOARD

SCALE

12 VOLT BATTERY

SPACE FOR PORTA-POTTI

LOD:	17' 5"	**Designer:**	Jim Taylor
LOA:	18' 7"	**Builder:**	Precision Boatworks
LWL:	15' 5"	**Years produced:**	1984–present
Min./max. draft:	1' 6"/4' 3"	**Sail area:**	145 sq. ft.
Bridge clearance:	27' 0"	**Fuel tankage:**	portable
Power:	3 to 6 hp	**Water tankage:**	portable
B/D ratio:	32%	**Approx. trailering wgt.:**	1,700 lbs.

This is an attractive, well built modern trailer-sailer with a keel-housed centerboard—what used to be called a "wholesome" boat. Below is a 40-quart cooler, and a space for a porta-pottie, but no sink, stove, or table. At some point after the boat was introduced in 1984, the side windows were changed from single non-opening to four opening ports, changing the appearance somewhat. **Best features:** Solid, neatly laid-up construction, good attention to detail (e.g., nicely faired NACA-profile fiberglass centerboard). **Worst features:** The basic boat comes without boom vang, backstay tensioner, reefing lines led back to the cockpit for easy singlehanding, and other small conveniences. For example, the end-boom mainsheet tackle is attached to a fitting on the backstay, an awkward reach for a singlehander sitting forward in the cockpit to balance the boat. Some owners complain that the cockpit scuppers are too small for proper draining.

Comps	LOD	Beam	MinDr	Displ	Bllst	SA/D	D/L	Avg. PHRF	Max. Speed	Motion Index	Space Index	No. of Berths	Head-room
Skippers Mate 17	17' 2"	7' 2"	1' 0"	1,100	250	22.4	146	NA	5.2	7.7	193	3	4' 6"
Precision 18 (17)	17' 5"	7' 5"	1' 6"	1,100	350	21.8	134	275	5.3	7.1	197	4	4' 0"
Montgomery 17	17' 1"	7' 4"	1' 9"	1,280	400	20.9	144	294	5.3	8.3	229	3	4' 8"

Seaward Fox II (17)

Nick Hake's entry in the microcruiser range

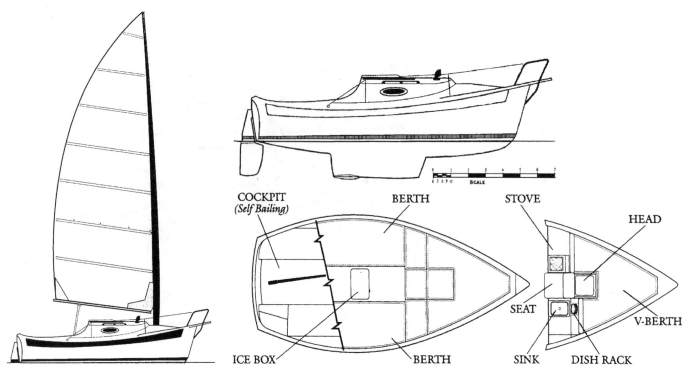

COCKPIT (Self Bailing)   BERTH   STOVE   HEAD

ICE BOX   BERTH   SEAT   SINK   DISH RACK   V-BERTH

LOD:	16' 6"	**Designer:**	Nick Hake
LOA:	17' 11"	**Builder:**	Hake Yachts Inc.
LWL:	16' 1"	**Years produced:**	2001–2007
Min./max. draft:	1' 9"	**Sail area:**	170 sq. ft.
Bridge clearance:	33' 0"	**Fuel tankage:**	portable
Power:	3 to 6 hp	**Water tankage:**	portable
B/D ratio:	35%	**Approx. trailering wgt.:**	1,900 lbs.

Designer Hake has taken the same basic beamy hull that he created in 1979 with the Slipper Deckhouse 17 (page 59), spruced her up with fancier oval ports and other gear, increased some of her dimensions slightly, and changed her name. For a while she was available with either a sloop rig or a very tall cat rig (bridge clearance 33' for the cat, 8' less for the sloop). The cat rig is shown here. ***Best features:*** We think she's relatively good-looking, with springy sheer, pronounced tumblehome, molded bulwarks, and nice fittings such as shiny stainless opening oval ports and cowl vent on the cabintop. Her self-bailing cockpit is deep and comfortable for two people, and her interior is relatively spacious considering her modest LOD; her Space Index is highest of her comps. The rotating, freestanding carbon-fiber mast is 28' 6" long, weighs only 33 pounds, and is secured by a two-foot-long sliding aluminum tube inside the mast, which couples the upper mast to a rotating mast bearing on the deck. It is claimed that the vessel takes less than five minutes to rig at a boat ramp. ***Worst features:*** Her shallow fixed keel, despite the small wings, prevents pointing as high as her comps, especially in light air.

Comps	LOD	Beam	MinDr	Displ	Bllst	SA/D	D/L	Avg. PHRF	Max. Speed	Motion Index	Space Index	No. of Berths	Head-room
Solo II (16)	16' 2"	7' 4"	1' 9"	1,100	400	24.0	167	NA	5.1	7.9	150	2	3' 6"
Slipper Deckhouse 17	16' 10"	8' 0"	1' 7"	1,250	425	20.7	171	NA	5.2	7.7	238	4	4' 3"
Com-Pac Sun Cat 17	16' 8"	7' 3"	1' 2"	1,350	200	19.6	179	NA	5.2	9.4	147	2	3' 2"
Seaward Fox II (17)	16' 6"	8' 0"	1' 9"	1,350	450	22.3	145	NA	5.4	7.8	247	4	4' 3"

Skipper 20 (18)
Lapstrake lifeboat-type double-ender

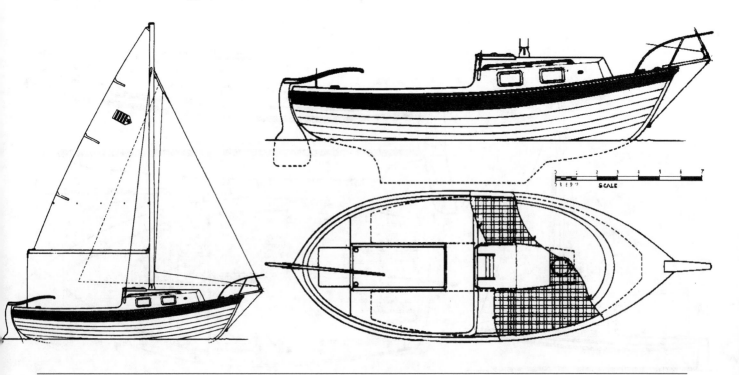

LOD:	18' 4"	**Designer:**	not specified
LOA:	20' 10"	**Builder:**	Southern Sails
LWL:	15' 0"	**Years produced:**	1978?–1982?
Min./max. draft:	2' 0"	**Sail area:**	143 sq. ft.
Bridge clearance:	25' 0"	**Fuel tankage:**	portable
Power:	3 to 6 hp	**Water tankage:**	portable
B/D ratio:	40%	**Approx. trailering wgt.:**	2,900 lbs.

This is a character boat of a type attractive to people who think that a sailboat hull shaped like a lifeboat is safer than a hull with a normal transom. In reality, it isn't, at least in a vessel this small. *Best features:* Compared with her comps, the Skipper 20 has a larger cockpit, with a convenient outboard engine in a well under a hatch just ahead of the rudder, and her simulated lapstrake topsides give her a jaunty antique look. *Worst features:* Perhaps the designer (who is unidentified in the literature we've seen)

expected all skippers to spend most of their time under power. That seems a likely possibility considering the boat's pitifully short mast and tiny sails—exacerbated by a main boom which is needlessly high on the mast. Moreover, the stubby keel is too shallow to keep the boat from side-slipping under sail, and for reasons we can't fathom, the rudder is much too small for effective steering while sailing. For an indication of this, compare its size to the rudder areas on the profile drawings of her comps.

Comps	LOD	Beam	MinDr	Displ	Bllst	SA/D	D/L	Avg. PHRF	Max. Speed	Motion Index	Space Index	No. of Berths	Head-room
Skipper 20 (18)	18' 4"	6' 7"	2' 0"	2,000	800	14.4	265	NA	5.2	14.6	223	2	4' 6"
Blue Water Blackwatch 19	18' 6"	7' 11"	2' 0"	2,250	800	19.8	187	231	5.6	11.3	255	2	4' 4"
Cornish Shrimper 19	19' 3"	7' 2"	1' 6"	2,350	700	17.6	193	390	5.6	13.2	251	2	3' 4"
Cape Cod Goldeneye 18	18' 3"	6' 4"	3' 0"	2,500	1,300	16.8	281	NA	5.3	19.8	199	2	3' 6"

Skippers Mate 17
Look-alike to the Snug Harbor 17, Sanibel 18, etc.

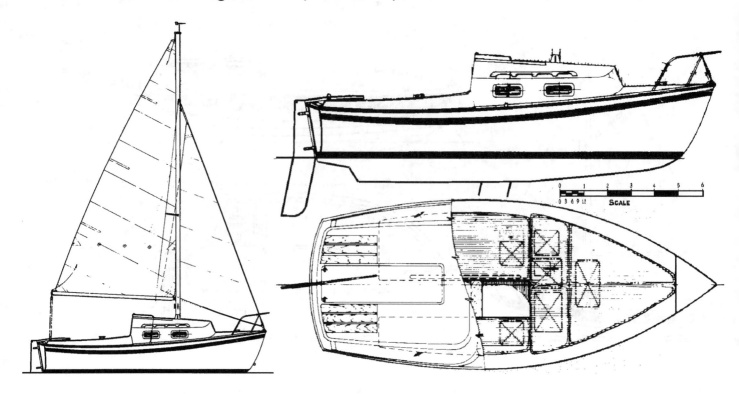

LOD:	17' 2"	**Designer:**	Charles Ludwig
LOA:	18' 2"	**Builder:**	Southern Sails and others
LWL:	15' 0"	**Years produced:**	1982–present
Min./max. draft:	1' 0"/3' 6"	**Sail area:**	160 sq. ft.
Bridge clearance:	29' 0"	**Fuel tankage:**	portable
Power:	outboard 2 to 5 hp	**Water tankage:**	portable
B/D ratio:	23%	**Approx. trailering wgt.:**	1,550 lbs.

In 1982, Southern Sails built this boat as the Skippers Mate 17. In 1984, Commodore Yacht Corp. built the same design as the Commodore 17. In 1985 Captiva Yachts built her, first as the Sanibel 17, and starting in August 1986 as the Sanibel 18 (without any change in her 17' 2" length on deck). Captiva's production ceased in late 1988, but in 1990 Leisure-Time Fiberglass Products began turning out the boat, calling her the Snug Harbor 18. International Marine, builders of the West Wight Potter line, acquired a set of molds and began production of the Sanibel 18, with dimensions slightly different from those shown here. The West Wight Potter 16 has been selling well since 1960, and the WWP 19 since 1976, so this 17-footer fits nicely into their line. It's a design that refuses to die! *Best features:* The Skippers Mate is generally less expensive on the used market than her comps. *Worst features:* Compared to her comps, she has less space below, is not as pretty, and, in past years at least, displayed less attention to detail in her construction. Perhaps International Marine will fix at least some of these shortcomings as time goes on.

Comps	LOD	Beam	MinDr	Displ	Bllst	SA/D	D/L	Avg. PHRF	Max. Speed	Motion Index	Space Index	No. of Berths	Head-room
Skippers Mate 17	17' 2"	7' 2"	1' 0"	1,100	250	22.4	146	NA	5.2	7.7	193	3	4' 6"
Precision 18 (17)	17' 5"	7' 5"	1' 6"	1,100	350	21.8	134	275	5.3	7.1	197	4	4' 0"
Montgomery 17	17' 1"	7' 4"	1' 9"	1,280	400	20.9	144	294	5.3	8.3	229	3	4' 8"

Slipper Deckhouse 17
Early forerunner of the Seaward Fox

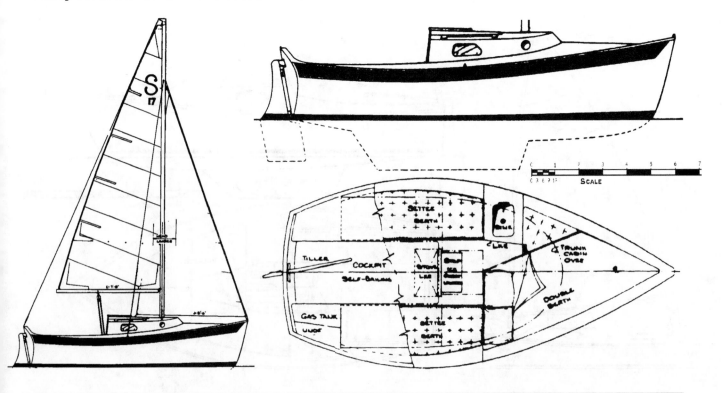

LOD:	16' 6"	**Designer:**	Nick Hake	
LOA:	17' 4"	**Builder:**	Starboard Yacht Co.	
LWL:	14' 10"	**Years produced:**	1979–1985	
Min./max. draft:	1' 7"/2' 7"	**Sail area:**	150 sq. ft.	
Bridge clearance:	25' 0"	**Fuel tankage:**	portable	
Power:	outboard 3 to 6 hp	**Water tankage:**	portable	
B/D ratio:	34%	**Approx. trailering wgt.:**	1,850 lbs.	

Nick Hake started Starboard Yacht Company in 1979 with the cute little Slipper 17. Over the years the dimensions varied a bit, and so did the rig (cat or sloop), the deck configuration (deckhouse or flush deck) and the name of the builder (Starboard, Seaward, Hake Yachts) but with Nick Hake always in control. See the Seaward Fox II on page 56 for more. **Best features:** Relatively wide beam gives her more space inside compared to her comps. She was available over the years in several different layouts, including two-berth, three-berth, and the four-berth model shown. (Two berths is probably the maximum most sailors would want to try, except for those with very small children.) **Worst features:** The early models had a rudder with too little area for quick manueverability (note the deeper rudder on page 56). Shallow draft, whether in the plain keel model (1' 7" draft, shown here) or the centerboarder, is insufficient for good upwind performance. Sail area is on the low side (later corrected by adding 20 square feet on the Seaward Fox II).

Comps	LOD	Beam	MinDr	Displ	Bllst	SA/D	D/L	Avg. PHRF	Max. Speed	Motion Index	Space Index	No. of Berths	Head-room
Solo II (16)	16' 2"	7' 4"	1' 9"	1,100	400	24.0	167	NA	5.1	7.9	150	2	3' 6"
Slipper Deckhouse 17	16' 6"	8' 0"	1' 7"	1,250	425	20.7	171	NA	5.2	7.7	238	4	4' 3"
Com-Pac Sun Cat 17	16' 8"	7' 3"	1' 2"	1,350	200	19.6	179	NA	5.2	9.4	147	2	3' 2"
Seaward Fox II (17)	17' 4"	8' 0"	1' 9"	1,350	450	22.3	145	NA	5.4	7.8	247	4	4' 3"

Solo II (16)

Unusual cat-rigged microcruiser

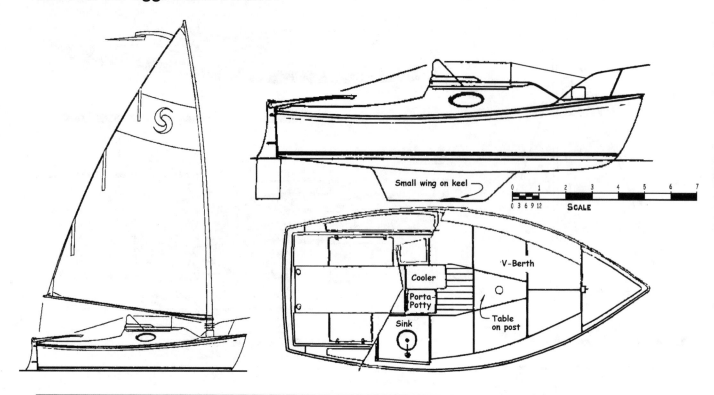

LOD:	16' 2"	**Designer:**	Wm. C. "Buddy" Helton Jr.
LOA:	16' 11"	**Builder:**	Helton Marine
LWL:	14' 4"	**Years produced:**	1992–1994
Min./max. draft:	1' 9"	**Sail area:**	160 sq. ft.
Bridge clearance:	26' 0"	**Fuel tankage:**	portable
Power:	outboard 2 to 5 hp	**Water tankage:**	portable
B/D ratio:	36%	**Approx. trailering wgt.:**	1,700 lbs.

This is a good-looking small catboat with a shoal-draft winged keel. Below there is just enough space for a tiny galley, portable head, portable 40-quart cooler, and a table which converts to part of a double berth. In 1992 the boat had a bendy, stayless kevlar-and-fiberglass mast (as shown here), with vertical battens so the sail could be rolled around the mast. **Best features:** Simple rig with rotating mast, according to the builder, "allows one person to raise and lower the mast with ease"—if it worked. However . . .

Worst features: By 1993 she had acquired a three-stay conventional cat rig with full-length horizontal battens, raising the question of whether the freestanding mast was in some way inadequate. The vertical battens seem especially unlikely to have been successful, if their purpose was to prevent leech curl. Her fixed keel with wings might hinder easy trailer loading and unloading. An underbody more similar to the Com-Pac Sun Cat 17 (page 30), a comp, might have been a better choice.

Comps	LOD	Beam	MinDr	Displ	Bllst	SA/D	D/L	Avg. PHRF	Max. Speed	Motion Index	Space Index	No. of Berths	Head-room
Solo II (16)	16' 2"	7' 4"	1' 9"	1,100	400	24.0	167	NA	5.1	7.9	150	2	3' 6"
Slipper Deckhouse 17	16' 10"	8' 0"	1' 7"	1,250	425	20.7	171	NA	5.2	7.7	238	4	4' 3"
Com-Pac Sun Cat 17	16' 8"	7' 3"	1' 2"	1,350	200	19.6	179	NA	5.2	9.4	147	2	3' 2"
Seaward Fox II (17)	17' 4"	8' 0"	1' 9"	1,350	450	22.3	145	NA	5.4	7.8	247	4	4' 3"

Sovereign 5.0/18 (17)

A product of a company that has left no trace

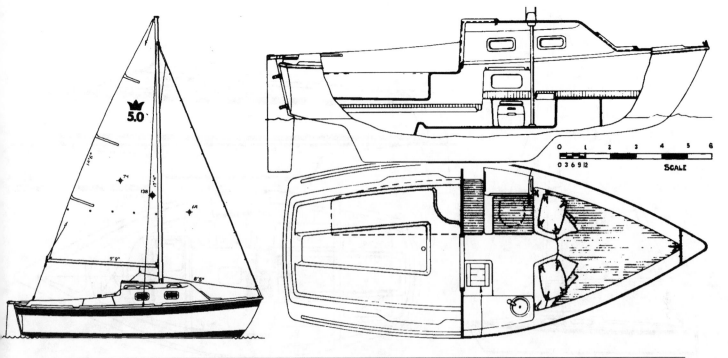

LOD:	17' 0"		**Designer:**	not specified
LOA:	18' 0"		**Builder:**	Sovereign America, Inc.
LWL:	14' 6"		**Years produced:**	1980–1994?
Min./max. draft:	1' 10"		**Sail area:**	138 sq. ft.
Bridge clearance:	24' 6"		**Fuel tankage:**	portable
Power:	outboard 3 to 6 hp		**Water tankage:**	portable
B/D ratio:	40%		**Approx. trailering wgt.:**	1,950 lbs.

I still remember meeting Sovereign's sales rep at a boat show in the 1980s, and getting a complete brush-off for asking questions like "Who designed her?" I'm still puzzled by that salesman's unhelpful responses, but even today, the company's secrets, if any, are safe; the firm seems to have disappeared without a trace. This model started out as the "17" with an LOA of 17' 0", a small V-berth, and two quarter berths. Then without changing the hull, the builders added a plank anchor sprit, removed one of the quarter berths, and called her an "18." ***Best features:*** Shallow draft is good for exploring shoal waters. She's trailerable (approximate towing weight is just under 2,000 lbs.), and short enough to fit into a standard sized garage. Self-bailing cockpit is deep and comfortable. ***Worst features:*** The Sovereign 5.0's V-berth has less than six feet of usable length because of its narrow foot end—good for small kids but not adults. There's only one quarter berth in most versions, so we suppose that makes her a boat for single moms or dads. Her rig is undersized for winds below about eight knots, so she'll need a small outboard to get her home in most typical harbor conditions. When the wind does pipe up, she will slide off considerably on close reaches and beats to windward due to her very shallow keel and absence of a centerboard. The shorter Capri 16, a comp, could sail rings around her.

Comps	LOD	Beam	MinDr	Displ	Bllst	SA/D	D/L	Avg. PHRF	Max. Speed	Motion Index	Space Index	No. of Berths	Head-room
Capri 16 (17)	16' 6"	6' 11"	2' 5"	1,350	425	18.1	162	NA	5.3	9.7	198	2	3' 6"
Sovereign 5.0/18 (17)	17' 0"	7' 0"	1' 10"	1,350	540	18.1	198	NA	5.1	10.0	197	1 + kids	4' 0"
Cornish Crabber 17	17' 0"	6' 9"	1' 7"	1,450	50	22.2	158	NA	5.4	10.2	211	2	4' 3"
Silhouette 17	17' 3"	6' 7"	2' 1"	1,500	550	20.1	244	NA	5.0	12.5	167	2 to 4	3' 8"

Starwind 19/Spindrift 19
Nice design by Jim Taylor

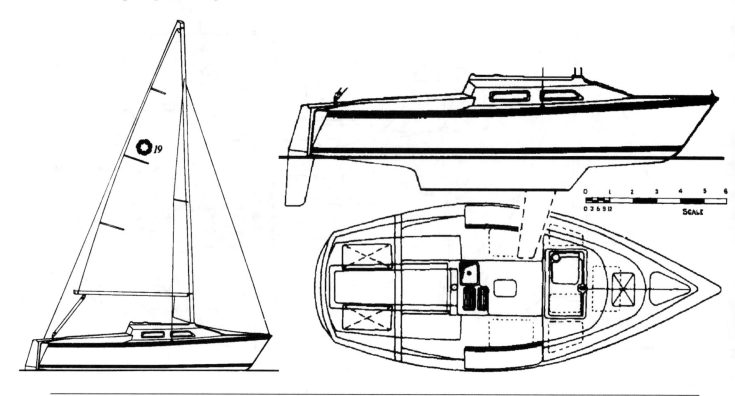

LOD:	18' 7"		**Designer:**	Jim Taylor
LOA:	19' 7"		**Builder:**	Starwind Div., Wellcraft
LWL:	15' 7"		**Years produced:**	1982–1992?
Min./max. draft:	1' 6"/4' 6"		**Sail area:**	153 sq. ft.
Bridge clearance:	27' 0"		**Fuel tankage:**	portable
Power:	outboard 3 to 6 hp		**Water tankage:**	2.5 gal.
B/D ratio:	29%		**Approx. trailering wgt.:**	1,950 lbs.

"An innovatively detailed trailerable mini-cruiser," says designer Jim Taylor's website. "Flattered by immediate imitation by the O'Day 192. Well known for lively, reliable performance and for an active owners' group." Over 600 of these nice-looking boats were built. No wonder one of designer Taylor's competitors, Raymond Hunt Associates, used the Starwind as the starting point in designing the O'Day 192 (page 49). **Best features:** The Starwind is a nicely conceived and well-made boat for her size and era.

A good-sized opening hatch forward, rare in a boat this size, is good for ventilation and escape in an emergency. An on-deck anchor locker is also a plus. The Starwind, with a PHRF of 288, may have a small advantage on the race course; even the smaller Precision 18, more than a foot shorter on deck, but with a waterline length only four inches less, and with eight square feet less sail area, has a handicap of only 282. **Worst features:** We could find none significant enough to mention.

Comps	LOD	Beam	MinDr	Displ	Bllst	SA/D	D/L	Avg. PHRF	Max. Speed	Motion Index	Space Index	No. of Berths	Head-room
Rhodes Mariner 19	19' 2"	7' 0"	0' 10"	1,305	320	24.8	104	285	5.6	8.1	188	2	3' 8"
Starwind 19	18' 7"	7' 6"	1' 6"	1,350	395	20.0	159	288	5.5	8.6	215	4	3' 2"
O'Day 19	19' 0"	7' 9"	1' 0"	1,400	300	21.1	135	218	5.5	8.1	232	2	3' 10"
O'Day 192	18' 7"	7' 1"	1' 5"	1,400	400	19.2	135	270	5.5	9.2	223	4	4' 0"
O'Day 20 (19)	18' 11"	7' 0"	1' 2"	1,600	400	20.3	139	276	5.6	10.1	206	4	3' 10"

Vivacity 20 (19)
Early British entry in the "glass" sweepstakes

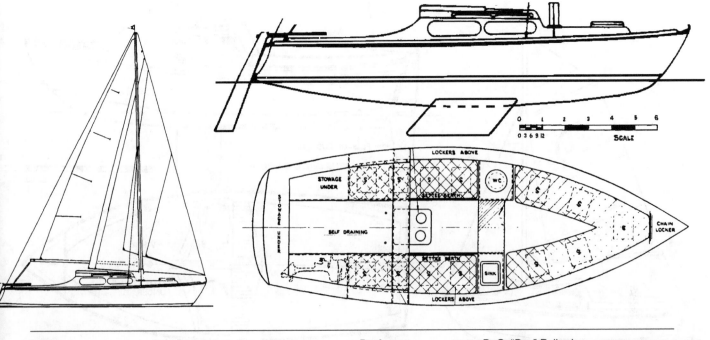

LOD:	18' 6"		**Designer:**	D. C. "Des" Pollard
LOA:	20' 9"		**Builder:**	Wells Yachts (importer)
LWL:	18' 4"		**Years produced:**	1962–1973
Min./max. draft:	2' 4"		**Sail area:**	175 sq. ft.
Bridge clearance:	25' 0"		**Fuel tankage:**	portable
Power:	outboard 2 to 4 hp		**Water tankage:**	portable
B/D ratio:	44%		**Approx. trailering wgt.:**	2,600 lbs.

Built by Hurley Marine and later by Russell Marine in Essex, England, and imported by Wells Yachts starting in the early 1960s, the Vivacity 20 was a popular early fiberglass microcruiser. Like her predecessor, the Alacrity 19 (page 19), she features twin bilge keels and a low profile doghouse. About 600 Alacritys and Vivacitys were imported into the United States, and over 1,200 Vivacitys were sold in total throughout the world. The boat was available as a kit, so there are numerous variations in finish and details. Note: based on measurement of the boat's drawings, it appears that this boat's marketers used hull length (20' 0") rather than LOD (18' 6") to describe length. That's why we designate this boat as a "19" rather than a "20." It should also be noted that apart from six inches more on the waterline and 350 pounds more ballast, the Vivacity is thought by many to be almost indistinguishable from the Alacrity. *Best features:* About the best we can say for the Vivacity is that, like her near-sister Alacrity, she's a nice boat for her vintage, but her generally more up-to-date comps are better. *Worst features:* With her shallow twin keels—of iron, which rusts—each weighing a mere 240 pounds, she is probably less weatherly, more tender, and slower in light air than the comps shown below.

Comps	LOD	Beam	MinDr	Displ	Bllst	SA/D	D/L	Avg. PHRF	Max. Speed	Motion Index	Space Index	No. of Berths	Head-room
Gloucester 19	19' 3"	7' 6"	1' 0"	1,600	550	20.3	159	NA	5.4	9.7	241	2	3' 8"
Cape Dory Typhoon 18	18' 6"	6' 6"	2' 7"	1,750	900	17.6	290	306	5.0	15.0	176	2 or 4	3' 11"
Quickstep 19	19' 4"	7' 9"	2' 2"	1,800	750	18.3	164	NA	5.5	10.2	236	2	3' 8"
Vivacity 20 (19)	18' 6"	7' 0"	2' 4"	1,800	785	18.9	127	288	5.6	10.6	215	4	3' 0"

West Wight Potter 15
A long-lived and popular English design

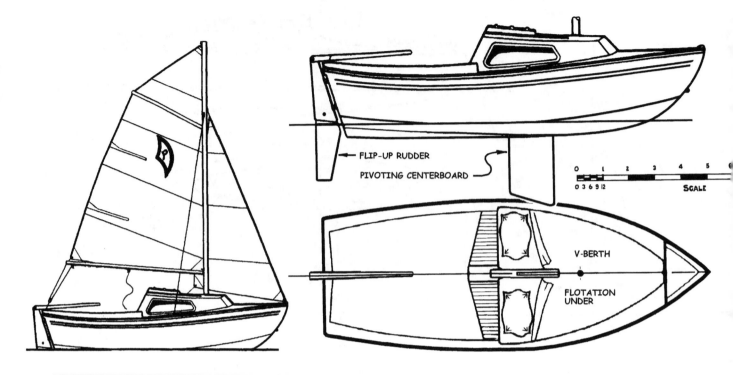

FLIP-UP RUDDER

PIVOTING CENTERBOARD

V-BERTH

FLOTATION UNDER

SCALE

LOD:	15' 0"		Designer:	Stanley T. Smith
LOA:	15' 6"		Builder:	International Marine
LWL:	12' 0"		Years produced:	1977–present
Min./max. draft:	0' 7"/3' 0"		Sail area:	91 sq. ft.
Bridge clearance:	17' 11"		Fuel tankage:	portable
Power:	outboard 2 to 3 hp		Water tankage:	portable
B/D ratio:	14%		Approx. trailering wgt.:	975 lbs.

She's the lightest boat with the smallest rig of all the boats listed in this book. She was produced as a 14' hull from 1960 until about 1977, at which time the current 15' version was introduced. **Best features:** Long-distance cruisers have taken modified versions from California to Hawaii, and from Seattle to Alaska, indicating relatively good stability and ease of handling, despite her tiny lightweight hull and narrow beam. With very shallow draft and a relatively flat V-bottom, she is beachable and easy to launch; her "unsinkable" hull has positive foam flotation. **Worst features:** She has very little space below (ignoring the hard-to-access space under the cockpit). A centerboard fills the central space in the cabin, so there's no footwell; you must sit cross-legged on the berthtop, and finding a convenient place to use a portable toilet is problematical. Using the head in the cockpit, under a boom tent for privacy, seems to be the most practical alternative. Light-air performance is below average.

Comps	LOD	Beam	MinDr	Displ	Bllst	SA/D	D/L	Avg. PHRF	Max. Speed	Motion Index	Space Index	No. of Berths	Head-room
West Wight Potter 15	15' 0"	5' 6"	0' 7"	475	85	18.1	161	NA	4.5	5.8	103	2	3' 9"
Peep Hen 14	14' 2"	6' 4"	0' 9"	650	200	24.5	125	NA	4.9	6.3	167	2	3' 3"
Precision 165	15' 8"	7' 2"	1' 9"	750	250	28.1	94	NA	5.2	5.4	173	2	3' 6"
Montgomery 15	15' 0"	6' 4"	1' 3"	750	275	23.6	144	NA	4.9	7.2	125	2	4' 0"

West Wight Potter 19

A "classic" micro yacht

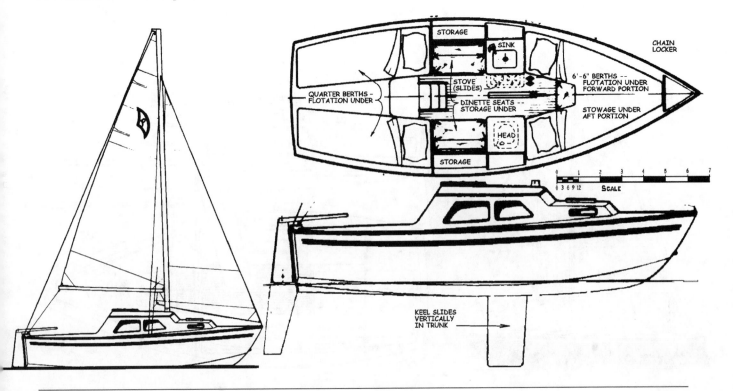

LOD:	18' 9"
LOA:	19' 9"
LWL:	16' 9"
Min./max. draft:	0' 6"/3' 7"
Bridge clearance:	27' 0"
Power:	outboard 3 to 6 hp
B/D ratio:	30%

Designer:	Herb Stewart
Builder:	International Marine
Years produced:	1976–present
Sail area:	135 sq. ft.
Fuel tankage:	portable
Water tankage:	2 gal.
Approx. trailering wgt.:	1,800 lbs.

The history of this boat, like her little sister the WWP 15, goes way back. An earlier version, the HMS 18, was introduced in 1970. That version had slightly different dimensions (shorter, beamier, deeper draft, more ballast) and sold for $2,600 in 1973. Thirty five years later, the 2008 version had a number of modern improvements and sold for $15,245 including sails, trailer, and other extras. **Best features:** The WWP 19 shares many of the positive features listed for the WWP 15 (page 64), including the ability to sail in adverse conditions (up to a point). Her longer LOD, higher headroom, and two feet of extra beam relieve some (but perhaps not all) of the claustrophobic feeling of the WWP 15 (and of some of her comps; only the even beamier Pierce Arrow, a boat with less headroom, is more commodious). **Worst features:** The WWP 19's high, slab-sided hull—which of course give her a lot more than her share of cabin space—detract from her looks. And we wonder what the damage would be to her keel trunk if her vertically sliding keel collided with a rock ledge at five or six knots.

Comps	LOD	Beam	MinDr	Displ	Bllst	SA/D	D/L	Avg. PHRF	Max. Speed	Motion Index	Space Index	No. of Berths	Head- room
Maxi-Peep 19	19' 2"	6' 4"	0' 9"	975	300	26.8	72	NA	5.7	6.9	228	4	3' 3"
Pierce Arrow 18	17' 6"	8' 0"	0' 9"	1,100	400	27.8	106	NA	5.5	6.1	283	2	3' 10"
Hermann 19	18' 8"	6' 5"	0' 9"	1,200	200	24.2	92	312	5.7	8.5	184	2	3' 6"
West Wight Potter 19	18' 9"	7' 6"	0' 6"	1,225	370	18.9	116	NA	5.5	7.4	230	4	4' 7"

Windrose 18
Evolution of a West Coast cruiser

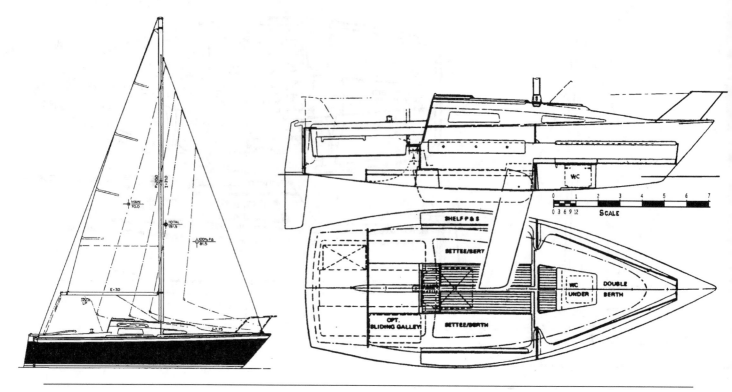

LOD:	18' 5"	**Designer:**	W. Shad Turner
LOA:	19' 5"	**Builder:**	Laguna Yachts
LWL:	15' 10"	**Years produced:**	1974–1980
Min./max. draft:	1' 0"/4' 0"	**Sail area:**	151 sq. ft.
Bridge clearance:	26' 6"	**Fuel tankage:**	portable
Power:	outboard 3 to 6 hp	**Water tankage:**	portable
B/D ratio:	27%	**Approx. trailering wgt.:**	2,150 lbs.

In the late 1950s and throughout the 1960s and 1970s, the basic concepts of fiberglass sailboat design and construction were gestating and developing, sometimes by mere luck and intuition. Designs in California were often quite different from those of the eastern states—and were apt to be more modern and daring. It wasn't until the late 1980s that eastern boats began to "go modern," as typified by the streamlined Hunter 18.5 (page 37), a comp of the Windrose 18 shown here. Shad Turner was among the dozen or so designers of California's avant garde small sailboats during the 1970s, and the Windrose 18 is a good example of the very latest in California thinking at that time. **Best features:** The boat is a showpiece for some of the design features Turner contributed—for example, light and shallow-draft hull for easy trailering, modest-sized sails and a relatively short mast so as not to frighten neophyte sailors. **Worst features:** The steel centerboard pivot point is so close to the bottom of its trunk that there is very little "bury" when the board is in the down position, putting the trunk in danger of being pried wide open if the board tip meets an immovable object to one side, creating a lever with a very long fulcrum arm. Also, the narrow forward V-berth is likely to be useful only for small children.

Comps	LOD	Beam	MinDr	Displ	Bllst	SA/D	D/L	Avg. PHRF	Max. Speed	Motion Index	Space Index	No. of Berths	Head-room
Alacrity 19 (18)	18' 0"	6' 11"	1' 10"	1,450	480	18.7	132	378	5.5	9.5	223	2 or 3	3' 11"
Windrose 18	18' 5"	7' 0"	1' 0"	1,500	400	18.4	169	288	5.3	10.4	201	4	3' 9"
Hunter 18.5	18' 5"	7' 1"	2' 0"	1,600	520	20.8	141	288	5.6	10.3	253	3	4' 0"

Windrose 5.5 (18)

Evolution of a small cruiser, stage two

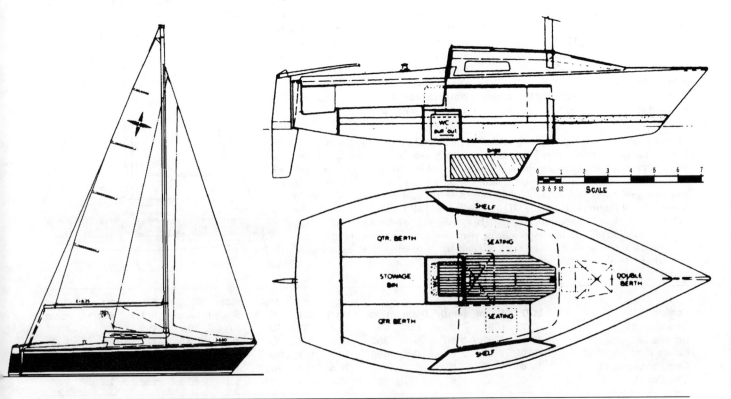

LOD:	18' 0"	Designer:	W. Shad Turner
LOA:	19' 0"	Builder:	Laguna Yachts
LWL:	16' 0"	Years produced:	1980–1983?
Min./max. draft:	2' 3"	Sail area:	152 sq. ft.
Bridge clearance:	26' 6"	Fuel tankage:	portable
Power:	outboard 3 to 6 hp	Water tankage:	portable
B/D ratio:	33%	Approx. trailering wgt.:	2,150 lbs.

By 1980 the design trend was toward wider boats, for extra stability as well as cabin space. Laguna Yachts and Shad Turner responded by widening the six-year-old Windrose 18 (previous page) from seven feet to eight feet, and introducing a number of other changes. Principal among these were (a) eliminating the potentially troublesome steel centerboard and substituting instead a shallow iron-filled fixed keel, and (b) rearranging the cabin space for more elbow room. For example, the portable head was moved aft where its use wouldn't interfere with V-berth sleepers;

the settee berths in the "18" were replaced by wider quarter berths and a central seating area. **Best features:** The new design eliminates worry over centerboard difficulties, and provides more elbow room. **Worst features:** The fixed keel is too shallow to give good sailing performance compared to the Windrose 18's (despite the fact that PHRF rating for both the 18 and the 5.5 is—unfairly—identical at 288), and the keel makes launching and retrieving at a launching ramp considerably more difficult than with her comps or with the shallower-draft "18."

Comps	LOD	Beam	MinDr	Displ	Bllst	SA/D	D/L	Avg. PHRF	Max. Speed	Motion Index	Space Index	No. of Berths	Head-room
Alerion Express Cat 19	19' 2"	8' 6"	1' 2"	1,450	450	34.0	121	NA	5.6	7.1	313	2	3' 6"
Capri 18	18' 0"	7' 7"	2' 0"	1,500	425	18.9	149	NA	5.4	9.0	248	2	3' 6"
ETAP 20	19' 10"	7' 6"	1' 6"	1,500	441	21.4	136	NA	5.5	8.8	278	4	4' 0"
Windrose 5.5 (18)	18' 0"	8' 0"	2' 3"	1,500	500	18.6	163	288	5.4	8.7	228	4	3' 9"

Balboa 16 (Laguna 16)

A Southern California trailer sailer circa 1981

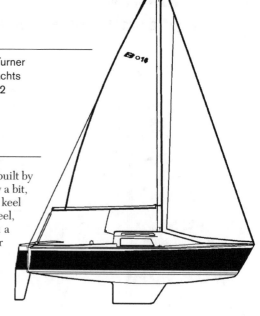

LOD:	16' 0"
LOA:	17' 0"
LWL:	14' 8"
Min./max. draft:	2' 5"
Bridge clearance:	22' 0"
Power:	outboard 2 to 5 hp
B/D ratio:	40%

Designer:	W. Shad Turner
Builder:	Laguna Yachts
Years produced:	1981–1982
Sail area:	117 sq. ft.
Fuel tankage:	portable
Water tankage:	portable
Approx. trailering wgt.:	1,530 lbs.

This little cruiser was originally built by Balboa Yachts and later (as the Laguna 16) built by Laguna Yachts. **Best features:** The Balboa's relatively wide beam may help stability a bit, and also provides extra stowage space below, highest of her comp group. Her fixed keel may appeal to novice sailors who don't want to fuss with a centerboard or swing keel, and with a relatively high B/D ratio and low SA/D, she may be relatively stable in a breeze. **Worst features:** Her low SA/D and shallow keel also make her a poor bet for sailing fast or close to the wind in light air. Her shallow (2' 5") fixed keel will make it harder to slide off a trailer, especially on shallow-sloped launching ramps. And because the keel is steel, it will be more difficult and time-consuming to maintain properly, particularly in salt water.

Comps	LOD	Beam	MinDr	Displ	Bllst	SA/D	D/L	Avg. PHRF	Max. Speed	Motion Index	Space Index	No. of Berths	Head-room
Gloucester 16	15' 7"	6' 3"	0' 9"	900	350	23.5	157	NA	5.0	8.2	122	2	4' 0"
Neptune 16	15' 9"	6' 2"	0' 10"	900	350	25.5	163	NA	4.9	8.5	111	2	3' 6"
Balboa 16	16' 0"	7' 5"	2' 5"	1,000	400	18.7	141	NA	5.1	6.9	171	2	3' 6"
Com-Pac Legacy 17	16' 6"	6' 0"	1' 2"	1,000	400	20.8	154	NA	5.1	9.1	139	2	3' 3"
Com-Pac 16	16' 0"	6' 0"	1' 6"	1,100	450	18.0	179	355	5.0	10.2	136	2	3' 3"

Baymaster 18

Rare fiberglass design from a wood boat architect

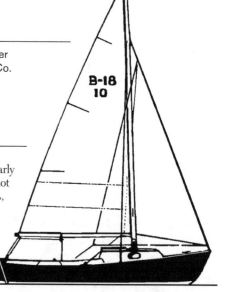

LOD:	17' 8"
LOA:	18' 1"
LWL:	15' 0"
Min./max. draft:	0' 9"/4' 0"
Bridge clearance:	23' 6"
Power:	outboard 2 to 5 hp
B/D ratio:	20%

Designer:	Winthrop L. Warner
Builder:	Regatta Plastics Co.
Years produced:	1969–1972
Sail area:	146 sq. ft.
Fuel tankage:	portable
Water tankage:	portable
Approx. trailering wgt.:	1,200 lbs.

The Baymaster 18 was designed by master cruising yacht designer Winthrop L. Warner in the early days of fiberglass. The designer's intent was to place emphasis on safety and stabilty. Perhaps not surprisingly considering this, he has kept the main performance parameters (displacement, D/L, SA/D,) in the middle of the comp group. **Best features:** The large self-bailing cockpit has room enough to sleep two under a boom-tent, adding space for the other two crew in the cabin, though we think having four crew aboard overnight would be like sleeping four in a closet. That's not necessarily bad; we have met people who like to sleep four in a closet. In any case, she has the look of a classic little sailer and we suspect sails well, though we have never seen one sailing. **Worst features:** The Baymaster has the lowest headroom among her comps.

Comps	LOD	Beam	MinDr	Displ	Bllst	SA/D	D/L	Avg. PHRF	Max. Speed	Motion Index	Space Index	No. of Berths	Head-room
Newport 17 (18)	17' 8"	6' 4"	0' 9"	600	150	34.2	63	NA	5.4	4.6	191	2	3' 4"
Picnic 17	17' 0"	6' 6"	0' 10"	700	0	41.4	87	NA	5.2	5.4	200	2	3' 10"
Siren 17	17' 2"	6' 8"	0' 8"	750	130	22.7	99	NA	5.2	5.8	144	4	3' 8"
Baymaster 18	17' 8"	6' 11"	0' 9"	750	150	28.3	99	NA	5.2	5.5	171	2	3' 3"
Holder 17	17' 0"	7' 3"	1' 8"	950	345	24.3	126	NA	5.2	6.6	207	2	4' 0"

Cape Cod Goldeneye 18

An old Nat Herreshoff design revisited

LOD:	18' 3"	**Designer:**	Nat/Sidney Herreshoff
LOA:	19' 0"	**Builder:**	Cape Cod Shipbuilding
LWL:	15' 10"	**Years produced:**	1963–present
Min./max. draft:	3' 0"	**Sail area:**	193 sq. ft.
Bridge clearance:	27' 3"	**Fuel tankage:**	portable
Power:	outboard 3 to 6 hp	**Water tankage:**	portable
B/D ratio:	54%	**Approx. trailering wgt.:**	3,500 lbs.

The Goldeneye was adapted from an old design of Captain Nat Herreshoff (1848–1938), the "Wizard of Bristol," who was by far the most revered of the several Herreshoff boat designers. Nat's son Sidney (brother of L. Francis and father of Halsey) drew the sailplan for this fiberglass version. ***Best features:*** This is a sturdy (and heavy) overnighter, with a large, comfortable, deep, but still self-bailing cockpit. Her heavy ballast (B/D ratio 54%) and high Motion Index help to indicate she will be more comfortable than her comps in a seaway, and her low SA/D and heavy ballast, bolted to a keel deeper than her comps, should provide relatively good heavy-air performance, though slowing her down a bit in light air. ***Worst features:*** Her draft is relatively deep (beyond the range of easy retrieving at shallow ramps) and she is also the heaviest (trailering weight 3,500 lbs.), which might give prospective trailer sailors second thoughts about owning this model. Her large cockpit precludes all but the most rudimentary accommodations below (namely a pair of 6' 6" berths and an optional toilet). Space Index is below that of all her comps, and her headroom is near the low end too. Big and tall cruisers beware!

Comps	LOD	Beam	MinDr	Displ	Bllst	SA/D	D/L	Avg. PHRF	Max. Speed	Motion Index	Space Index	No. of Berths	Head-room
Skipper 20 (18)	18' 4"	6' 7"	2' 0"	2,000	800	14.4	265	NA	5.2	14.6	223	2	4' 6"
Blue Water Blackwatch 19	18' 6"	7' 11"	2' 0"	2,500	800	19.8	187	231	5.6	11.3	255	2	4' 4"
Cornish Shrimper 19	19' 3"	7' 2"	1' 6"	2,350	700	17.6	193	390	5.6	13.2	251	2	3' 4"
Cape Cod Goldeneye 18	18' 3"	6' 4"	3' 0"	2,500	1,300	16.8	281	NA	5.3	19.8	199	2	3' 6"

Com-Pac Legacy 17

Hutchins creates yet another new tiny cruiser

LOD:	16' 6"	**Designer:**	Hutchins Company
LOA:	18' 6"	**Builder:**	Hutchins Company
LWL:	14' 3"	**Years produced:**	2007–present
Min./max. draft:	1' 2"/3' 6"	**Sail area:**	130 sq. ft.
Bridge clearance:	22' 0"	**Fuel tankage:**	portable
Power:	outboard 2 to 4 hp	**Water tankage:**	portable
B/D ratio:	40%	**Approx. trailering wgt.:**	1,600 lbs.

The Com-Pac Legacy 17 is the successor to the Com-Pac 16, the first sailboat the Hutchins Company built, back in 1975. The new (2007) boat has gained three inches on the waterline compared to her older sister, adding a theoretical half a knot to her maximum speed. She is also 100 pounds lighter, with 50 of those pounds coming out her lead ballast. Most other dimensions remain the same as the original Com-Pac 16. ***Best features:*** The new boat's trailerability has been improved by a special system to hoist and drop the mast quickly at the launching ramp. It's called the MasTendr and BoomTendr Quick Rig Sailing System, and with it, the boom and sail never leave the mast. The skipper simply unsnaps the mainsheet and folds the boom up to the mast, then folds everything down for trailering. The flip-up rudder also adds to trailering convenience. While sailing, a slightly taller rig should make her faster in light air compared to her older sister. ***Worst features:*** Compared with her comps, relatively low headroom and narrow beam somewhat restrict cabin space.

Comps	LOD	Beam	MinDr	Displ	Bllst	SA/D	D/L	Avg. PHRF	Max. Speed	Motion Index	Space Index	No. of Berths	Head-room
Gloucester 16	15' 7"	6' 3"	0' 9"	900	350	23.5	157	NA	5.0	8.2	122	2	4' 0"
Neptune 16	15' 9"	6' 2"	0' 10"	900	350	25.5	163	NA	4.9	8.5	111	2	3' 6"
Balboa 16	16' 0"	7' 5"	2' 5"	1,000	400	18.7	141	NA	5.1	6.9	171	2	3' 6"
Com-Pac Legacy 17	16' 6"	6' 0"	1' 2"	1,000	400	20.8	154	NA	5.1	9.1	139	2	3' 3"
Com-Pac 16	16' 0"	6' 0"	1' 6"	1,100	450	18.0	179	355	5.0	10.2	136	2	3' 3"

Hermann 19

Little overnighter designed by Dick Ketcham

LOD:	18' 8"	**Designer:**	Richard P. Ketcham, Jr.
LOA:	18' 8"	**Builder:**	Ted Hermann's Boat Shop
LWL:	18' 0"	**Years produced:**	1963–1967?
Min./max. draft:	0' 9"/1' 8"	**Sail area:**	171 sq. ft.
Bridge clearance:	28' 6"	**Fuel tankage:**	portable
Power:	outboard 3 to 6 hp	**Water tankage:**	portable
B/D ratio:	17%	**Approx. trailering wgt.:**	1,800 lbs.

We don't know much about this boat, and so far haven't been able to find out more. About the only information we have is an old ad in *Yachting* magazine (with the sailplan as shown to right), and some photos found on the Internet (which indicate she has a hard-chined hull, similar to a Snipe). Perhaps someone reading this will drop us a note, care of the publisher, to help with more data and an accommodations plan. *Best features:* Compared with other boats of her approximate size, weight, and draft, the Hermann 19 has less ballast but more weight in the fiberglass, perhaps making her skin tougher (which is true of other Ted Hermann Boat Shop productions, like the Hermann Cat 17). Very shallow draft with centerboard up, as with her comps, makes her suitable for exploring shoal waters. *Worst features:* Headroom is relatively low—though a small collapsible dodger in the companionway, as shown in the sailplan, may give some relief to those crouching below.

Comps	LOD	Beam	MinDr	Displ	Bllst	SA/D	D/L	Avg. PHRF	Max. Speed	Motion Index	Space Index	No. of Berths	Head- room
Maxi-Peep 19	19' 2"	6' 4"	0' 9"	975	300	26.8	72	NA	5.7	6.9	228	4	3' 3"
Pierce Arrow 18	17' 6"	8' 0"	0' 9"	1,100	400	27.8	106	NA	5.5	6.1	283	2	3' 10"
Hermann 19	18' 8"	6' 5"	0' 9"	1,200	200	24.2	92	312	5.7	8.5	184	2	3' 6"
West Wight Potter 19	18' 9"	7' 6"	0' 6"	1,225	370	18.9	116	NA	5.5	7.4	230	4	4' 7"

Holder 17

A sloop from the land of catamarans

LOD:	17' 0"	**Designer:**	Ron Holder
LOA:	18' 0"	**Builder:**	Hobie Cat
LWL:	15' 0"	**Years produced:**	1981–1984
Min./max. draft:	1' 8"/4' 2"	**Sail area:**	147 sq. ft.
Bridge clearance:	24' 3"	**Fuel tankage:**	portable
Power:	outboard 2 to 5 hp	**Water tankage:**	portable
B/D ratio:	36%	**Approx. trailering wgt.:**	1,450 lbs.

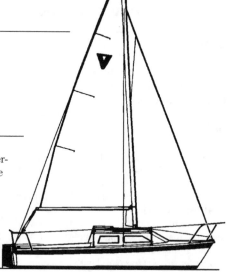

Unlike most of Hobie Cat's boats, the Holder 17 is neither a catamaran nor a product of the fertile mind of Hobie Alter, the multihull firm's namesake. It is instead a "monomaran" from the drawing board of businessman and designer Ron Holder. First came the cabin sloop, in 1981; the next year, a daysailer version was introduced. *Best features:* The Holder has good sitting headroom compared to her comps. Foam flotation is intended to make her more or less sinkproof. Her relatively heavy swing keel keeps her minimum draft low for easy launching and retrieval at a ramp, while offering good stability with the keel in the "down" position. With a relatively high D/L and low SA/D compared with her comps, she should be stable in heavy air. *Worst features:* The steel swing keel can be a pain in the neck to keep from rusting.

Comps	LOD	Beam	MinDr	Displ	Bllst	SA/D	D/L	Avg. PHRF	Max. Speed	Motion Index	Space Index	No. of Berths	Head- room
Newport 17 (18)	17' 8"	6' 4"	0' 9"	600	150	34.2	63	NA	5.4	4.6	191	2	3' 4"
Picnic 17	17' 0"	6' 6"	0' 10"	700	0	41.4	87	NA	5.2	5.4	200	2	3' 10"
Siren 17	17' 2"	6' 8"	0' 8"	750	130	22.7	99	NA	5.2	5.8	144	4	3' 8"
Baymaster 18	17' 8"	6' 11"	0' 9"	750	150	28.3	99	NA	5.2	5.5	171	2	3' 3"
Holder 17	17' 0"	7' 3"	1' 8"	950	345	24.3	126	NA	5.2	6.6	207	2	4' 0"

Lynx 16 (17)
Expensive little cruiser from a small builder

LOD:	16' 6"	**Designer:**	Tony Davis
LOA:	20' 0"	**Builder:**	Arey's Pond Boat Yard
LWL:	16' 0"	**Years produced:**	1997–present
Min./max. draft:	1' 2"/4' 6"	**Sail area:**	200 sq. ft.
Bridge clearance:	26' 8"	**Fuel tankage:**	portable
Power:	outboard 2 to 6 hp	**Water tankage:**	portable
B/D ratio:	11%	**Approx. trailering wgt.:**	2,700 lbs.

This small catboat is from the board of Tony Davis, a relatively new designer who also happens to be owner and operator of Arey's Pond Boat Yard in South Orleans on Cape Cod. Arey's Pond builds the boat—but only a few have been built so far, so the jury is still out on how she stacks up against the competition. ***Best features:*** This is a good-looking catboat, particularly if she is dolled up with the optional (but, alas, extravagantly expensive) mahogany or oak trim, tanbark sail, nine coats of varnish on the wood (the varnish being a thousand-dollar-plus extra all by itself), teak centerboard enclosure with louvered doors (another $1,000), etc. She does have foam flotation. ***Worst features:*** Compared with her comps, her lower displacement will make her less stable and bouncier. She has less space below, and is relatively expensive. Our guess is that she won't perform as well as the huskier Marshall Sanderling or Menger Cat, particularly in heavy air, and may not do as well in light air either, due to her 20% smaller mainsail. But she sure is pretty.

Comps	LOD	Beam	MinDr	Displ	Bllst	SA/D	D/L	Avg. PHRF	Max. Speed	Motion Index	Space Index	No. of Berths	Head-room
Lynx 16	16' 6"	7' 11"	1' 2"	2,000	200	20.2	218	NA	5.4	11.4	179	2	3' 4"
Menger Cat 17	17' 0"	8' 0"	1' 8"	2,200	500	23.6	219	351	5.4	12.4	194	2	4' 3"
Cape Cod Cat 17	17' 0"	7' 11"	1' 8"	2,200	500	23.6	222	372	5.4	12.4	222	2	4' 6"
Marshall Sanderling 18	18' 2"	8' 6"	1' 7"	2,200	500	23.9	178	315	5.6	10.5	281	2	3' 7"
Molly Catboat 17	17' 0"	7' 6"	2' 2"	3,000	1,000	15.4	317	NA	5.4	19.2	194	2	4' 0"

Montgomery 15
Little lapstrake cruiser from California

LOD:	15' 0"	**Designer:**	Jerry Montgomery
LOA:	15' 6"	**Builder:**	Montgomery Marine and Nor'Sea
LWL:	13' 3"	**Years produced:**	1980–present
Min./max. draft:	1' 3"/2' 6"	**Sail area:**	122 sq. ft.
Bridge clearance:	22' 3"	**Fuel tankage:**	portable
Power:	outboard 2 to 5 hp	**Water tankage:**	portable
B/D ratio:	37%	**Approx. trailering wgt.:**	1,250 lbs.

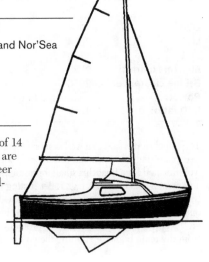

Several hundred of these little boats were built and sold by Montgomery Marine over a period of 14 years, and in 1999 production recommenced, under the wing of Nor'Sea Yachts. Now the boats are being built under yet another name, Montgomery Boats. ***Best features:*** With her springy sheer and simulated lapstrake hull, she looks very graceful despite the relatively high freeboard. Headroom and Motion Index is better than her comps. Attention to detail in her construction is above average. Her ballast and displacement are high enough to give her good stability for a 15-footer. ***Worst features:*** She has the shallowest maximum draft (2' 6" with board down), making for somewhat poorer upwind performance compared to other comps, which all have drafts in the 3' to 4' range.

Comps	LOD	Beam	MinDr	Displ	Bllst	SA/D	D/L	Avg. PHRF	Max. Speed	Motion Index	Space Index	No. of Berths	Head-room
West Wight Potter 15	15' 0"	5' 6"	0' 7"	475	85	18.1	161	NA	4.5	5.8	103	2	3' 9"
Peep Hen 14	14' 2"	6' 4"	0' 9"	650	200	24.5	125	NA	4.9	6.3	167	2	3' 3"
Precision 165 (16)	15' 8"	7' 2"	1' 9"	750	250	28.1	94	NA	5.2	5.4	173	2	3' 6"
Montgomery 15	15' 0"	6' 4"	1' 3"	750	275	23.6	144	NA	4.9	7.2	125	2	4' 0"

Newport 17 (18)
Lightweight cruiser by Harry Sindle

LOD:	17' 8"	**Designer:**	Harry Sindle
LOA:	19' 0"	**Builder:**	Lockley-Newport Boats
LWL:	16' 2"	**Years produced:**	1977–1980
Min./max. draft:	0' 9"/4' 9"	**Sail area:**	152 sq. ft.
Bridge clearance:	26' 0"	**Fuel tankage:**	portable
Power:	outboard 2 to 5 hp	**Water tankage:**	portable
B/D ratio:	25%	**Approx. trailering wgt.:**	1,100 lbs.

This Harry Sindle design is a daysailer with basic overnight accommodations (double berth, a place for a head, and some storage space). *Best features:* Sindle specialized in designing lightweight race boats, so perhaps not surprisingly, this design's sailing performance in light air is good compared to her comps—though her speed is also helped simply by her light weight and relatively high SA/D ratio. Storage space extending under cockpit seats is large enough to serve as quarterberths for two small children. Shallow draft with board up makes trailer launching easier. *Worst features:* Narrow beam and light weight compared to comps help to make her relatively tender, and high "top hamper" (i.e., freeboard and cabin height) combined with her lightness could make control quirky in gusty wind conditions. Thus even though ads say she is "an ideal boat for novices" and "easy to handle," we think this would be true perhaps only in light air and settled weather conditions.

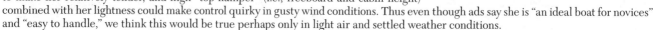

Comps	LOD	Beam	MinDr	Displ	Bllst	SA/D	D/L	Avg. PHRF	Max. Speed	Motion Index	Space Index	No. of Berths	Head-room
Newport 17 (18)	17' 8"	6' 4"	0' 9"	600	150	34.2	63	NA	5.4	4.6	191	2	3' 4"
Picnic 17	17' 0"	6' 6"	0' 10"	700	0	41.4	87	NA	5.2	5.4	200	2	3' 10"
Siren 17	17' 2"	6' 8"	0' 8"	750	130	22.7	99	NA	5.2	5.8	144	4	3' 8"
Baymaster 18	17' 8"	6' 11"	0' 9"	750	150	28.3	99	NA	5.2	5.5	171	2	3' 3"
Holder 17	17' 0"	7' 3"	1' 8"	950	345	24.3	126	NA	5.2	6.6	207	2	4' 0"

Quickstep 19
A near-clone of the Gloucester 19

LOD:	19' 4"	**Designer:**	Stuart Windley
LOA:	20' 4"	**Builder:**	Quickstep Boats
LWL:	17' 0"	**Years produced:**	1990–1995?
Min./max. draft:	2' 2"	**Sail area:**	169 sq. ft.
Bridge clearance:	29' 0"	**Fuel tankage:**	portable
Power:	outboard 3 to 6 hp	**Water tankage:**	portable
B/D ratio:	42%	**Approx. trailering wgt.:**	2,600 lbs.

The Quickstep is said to have been produced from the Gloucester 19 molds (though if true, it's then hard to explain slight dimensional differences). *Best features:* Unlike the Gloucester, the Quickstep is quite well-finished for a boat this small (opening ports, teak trim below, including teak and holly cabin sole), and came well equipped, e.g., roller furling jib was standard. *Worst features:* The rudder is deeper than the fixed keel when extended, a risk when sailing in shoal waters. The mainsheet is cleated at one side of the transom—awkward when the helmsman is trying to uncleat the sheet while sitting on the opposite side. However, this problem should be easy to solve by either hanging a cam cleat from the main boom or running the control forward to a cleat on the cabintop.

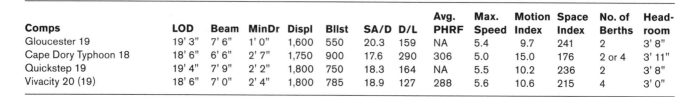

Comps	LOD	Beam	MinDr	Displ	Bllst	SA/D	D/L	Avg. PHRF	Max. Speed	Motion Index	Space Index	No. of Berths	Head-room
Gloucester 19	19' 3"	7' 6"	1' 0"	1,600	550	20.3	159	NA	5.4	9.7	241	2	3' 8"
Cape Dory Typhoon 18	18' 6"	6' 6"	2' 7"	1,750	900	17.6	290	306	5.0	15.0	176	2 or 4	3' 11"
Quickstep 19	19' 4"	7' 9"	2' 2"	1,800	750	18.3	164	NA	5.5	10.2	236	2	3' 8"
Vivacity 20 (19)	18' 6"	7' 0"	2' 4"	1,800	785	18.9	127	288	5.6	10.6	215	4	3' 0"

Rhodes Mariner 19

A popular Phil Rhodes design originated in 1945

LOD:	19' 2"	**Designer:**	Philip Rhodes
LOA:	20' 0"	**Builder:**	O'Day, Stuart Marine
LWL:	17' 9"	**Years produced:**	1962–present
Min./max. draft:	0' 10"/4' 11"	**Sail area:**	185 sq. ft.
Bridge clearance:	29' 0"	**Fuel tankage:**	portable
Power:	outboard 3 to 6 hp	**Water tankage:**	portable
B/D ratio:	25%	**Approx. trailering wgt.:**	2,000 lbs.

Originally a centerboard racer-daysailer designed in 1945 and known as the Rhodes 19, in the 1950s O'Day switched from molded plywood to fiberglass, added a cabin and—voila!—the fiberglass Mariner was conceived. After O'Day left the scene, Stuart took over production, which it has continued. The boat is available in both centerboard and iron keel versions, and as a two-sleeper (V-berth) or four-sleeper (V-berth plus quarterberth). Drawings in the Stuart sales brochures appear to have a narrower entry than the original Rhodes design, but Stuart tells us it's their drawings that are slightly inaccurate, not the boats. We'd ask around before buying to determine if the newest Mariners can be raced as a one-design class against the older O'Day boats, if that's what you have in mind. Since Mariners have been around a long time, you can find them in all age groups and price ranges. **Best features:** Mast tabernacle and shallow draft in the centerboard version makes launching relatively easy— but the keel version has more stability. Take your choice. **Worst features:** The design, being close to 50 years old, is a bit old-fashioned, particularly in her underbody.

Comps	LOD	Beam	MinDr	Displ	Bllst	SA/D	D/L	Avg. PHRF	Max. Speed	Motion Index	Space Index	No. of Berths	Head- room
Rhodes Mariner 19	19' 2"	7' 0"	0' 10"	1,305	320	24.8	104	285	5.6	8.1	188	2	3' 8"
Starwind 19	18' 7"	7' 6"	1' 6"	1,350	395	20.0	159	288	5.5	8.6	215	4	3' 2"
O'Day 19	19' 0"	7' 9"	1' 0"	1,400	300	21.1	135	218	5.5	8.1	232	2	3' 10"
O'Day 192 (19)	18' 7"	7' 1"	1' 5"	1,400	400	19.2	135	270	5.5	9.2	223	4	4' 0"
O'Day 20 (19)	18' 11"	7' 0"	1' 2"	1,600	400	20.3	139	276	5.6	10.1	206	4	3' 10"

Silhouette 17

Early pocket cruiser, first in plywood, then fiberglass

LOD:	17' 3"	**Designer:**	Robert Tucker
LOA:	17' 3"	**Builder:**	Bamford, Ferrier, et al.
LWL:	14' 0"	**Years produced:**	1958–1969?
Min./max. draft:	2' 8"	**Sail area:**	165 sq. ft.
Bridge clearance:	22' 3"	**Fuel tankage:**	portable
Power:	outboard 3 to 5 hp	**Water tankage:**	portable
B/D ratio:	37%	**Approx. trailering wgt.:**	2,160 lbs.

This little cruiser, first built of plywood in 1958, became available in fiberglass in the mid-1960s. At various times she was available either with twin or single fin keel, and with either a two-berth or four-berth layout. **Best features:** She probably would be among the least expensive sailboats to buy on the used market, if you could find one in reasonable condition. **Worst features:** Her shallow keel and relatively high wetted surface keep her from being fast or weatherly, though her comps are probably not much better. She has the shortest waterline (slow under power), the smallest cockpit, and the least space below among her comps. Her old-fashioned hard-chine, tortured hull shape, originally dictated by the fact that she was to be built of flat sheets of plywood, give her a strange look that some would call ugly.

Comps	LOD	Beam	MinDr	Displ	Bllst	SA/D	D/L	Avg. PHRF	Max. Speed	Motion Index	Space Index	No. of Berths	Head- room
Capri 16 (17)	16' 6"	6' 11"	2' 5"	1,350	425	18.1	162	NA	5.3	9.7	198	2	3' 6"
Sovereign 5.0/18 (17)	17' 0"	7' 0"	1' 10"	1,350	540	18.1	198	NA	5.1	10.0	197	4	4' 0"
Cornish Crabber 17	17' 0"	6' 9"	1' 7"	1,450	50	22.2	158	NA	5.4	10.2	211	2	4' 3"
Silhouette 17	17' 3"	6' 7"	2' 1"	1,500	550	20.1	244	NA	5.0	12.5	167	2 to 4	3' 8"

Siren 17
Canadian microcruiser for a family

LOD:	17' 2"	**Designer:**	Vandestadt & McGruer
LOA:	17' 9"	**Builder:**	Vandestadt & McGruer
LWL:	15' 0"	**Years produced:**	1974–1990?
Min./max. draft:	0' 8"/4' 3"	**Sail area:**	117 sq. ft.
Bridge clearance:	22' 0"	**Fuel tankage:**	portable
Power:	outboard 2 to 5 hp	**Water tankage:**	portable
B/D ratio:	17%	**Approx. trailering wgt.:**	1,200 lbs.

Siren is a good design for an overnight cruiser for two adults and two small children. Versus her comps, she has the lowest SA/D, making for relatively good stability, but at the expense of light-air performance. And she has the lowest draft, meaning relatively easy launching and retreiving from a trailer. **Best features:** Below she has foam flotation, a molded-in icebox, space for a stove and a toilet. Space is allocated in the cockpit for a gas tank and storage battery—though its aft location may not be optimal for proper hull trim. Construction and finish are above average. **Worst features:** Among her comps, she has the lowest Space Index, although for any 17-footer space is going to be tight. A steel centerboard, even though galvanized, may cause maintenance problems, particularly in salt water. Her outboard well doesn't permit an engine to be tilted, causing drag unless engine is removed and stowed—a good reason to choose a small, lightweight engine.

Comps	LOD	Beam	MinDr	Displ	Bllst	SA/D	D/L	Avg. PHRF	Max. Speed	Motion Index	Space Index	No. of Berths	Head- room
Newport 17 (18)	17' 8"	6' 4"	0' 9"	600	150	34.2	63	NA	5.4	4.6	191	2	3' 4"
Picnic 17	17' 0"	6' 6"	0' 10"	700	0	41.4	87	NA	5.2	5.4	200	2	3' 10"
Siren 17	17' 2"	6' 8"	0' 8"	750	130	22.7	99	NA	5.2	5.8	144	4	3' 8"
Baymaster 18	17' 8"	6' 11"	0' 9"	750	150	28.3	99	NA	5.2	5.5	171	2	3' 3"
Holder 17	17' 0"	7' 3"	1' 8"	950	345	24.3	126	NA	5.2	6.6	207	2	4' 0"

What Size Boat?

What length boat you choose mainly depends on end use, the size of your pocketbook, where you plan to keep her, and how comfortable you feel about running a big boat vs. a little boat.

Incidentally, a boat isn't necessarily easier to handle just because she's small. In fact, very often the opposite is true for boats up to around 30 feet in length.

A well-designed boat in the 18- to 26-foot range makes an ideal adult beginner's training vessel. For kids, a smaller first boat, in the range of 8 feet (for a 7- or 8-year-old) to 14 feet (for a 12- to 14-year-old) is better.

For singlehanding by an experienced boater, any well-designed boat up to about 30 feet is a comfortable maximum size. Beyond that, the gear (such as the anchor and the sails) get heavier and more awkward to lug about, and the deck is long enough from end to end to make it harder to singlehand into a pier and tie up without rushing around in an unseemly manner, particularly if maneuvering room is limited or when the wind is blowing the boat off the pier.

—*from* Boating for Less, *Second Edition, 1991, by Steve Henkel,*
published by International Marine, Camden, Maine

THREE
Seventy Boats 20'–21'

*2 vessels without accommodations plans are grouped together at end of chapter

AMF 2100
Ted Hood designs a little cruiser/racer

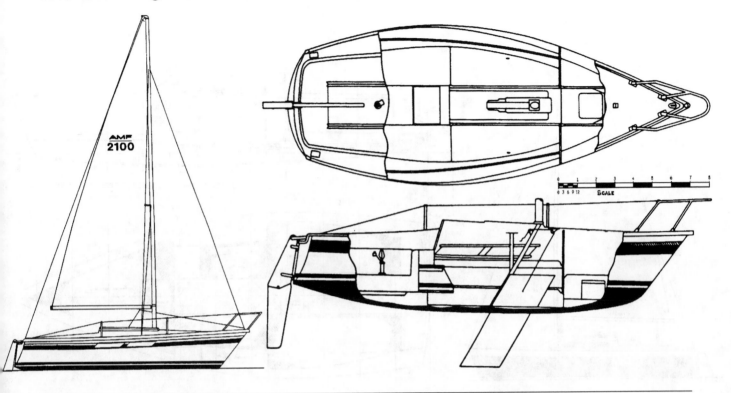

LOD:	21' 1"	**Designer:**	Ted Hood
LOA:	22' 6"	**Builder:**	AMF Alcort
LWL:	17' 7"	**Years produced:**	1981–1983
Min./max. draft:	1' 0"/4' 0"	**Sail area:**	209 sq. ft.
Bridge clearance:	31' 0"	**Fuel tankage:**	portable
Power:	outboard 3 to 6 hp	**Water tankage:**	portable
B/D ratio:	39%	**Approx. trailering wgt.:**	3,200 lbs.

Ted Hood was good at designing fast cruisers and elegant racers, and it looks like he succeeded with the 2100. Still, the boat did not sell in any great numbers, perhaps because AMF Alcort was a little late in coming to market, and had to contend with boats like the popular J/24 (page 294), conceived by a couple of ex-Alcort employees in 1979. By 1981 the J/24 had already seized a strong market position targeting roughly the same customer base as the 2100. **Best features:** Here is a boat intended to race and also to cruise, with a tremendous amount of usable space for

her LOD. In fact, her big freeboard and beam give her best space by a good margin relative to her comps. Also note her unusually shallow draft with keel raised, making trailering relatively easy. **Worst features:** The lifting keel, weighing over 800 pounds and controlled by a winch down below, must be somewhat of a nuisance to operate while underway, particularly during tight racing maneuvers when speed is of the essence. Also the keel trunk sits squarely in the middle of the cabin, making passage forward to the head awkward.

Comps	LOD	Beam	MinDr	Displ	Bllst	SA/D	D/L	Avg. PHRF	Max. Speed	Motion Index	Space Index	No. of Berths	Head-room
O'Day 222 (21)	21' 5"	7' 11"	1' 8"	2,200	800	19.6	131	258	5.9	10.4	290	4	4' 1"
AMF 2100	21' 1"	8' 0"	1' 0"	2,200	850	19.8	181	228	5.6	11.4	363	4	4' 3"
O'Day 22 (21)	20' 10"	7' 2"	1' 3"	2,283	800	18.1	150	288	5.8	12.4	294	4	4' 6"
Rhodes Continental 22	21' 6"	8' 0"	1' 8"	2,500	700	18.2	140	334	6.0	11.6	334	4	4' 6"

Antrim 20

Small racer with some cruising possibilities

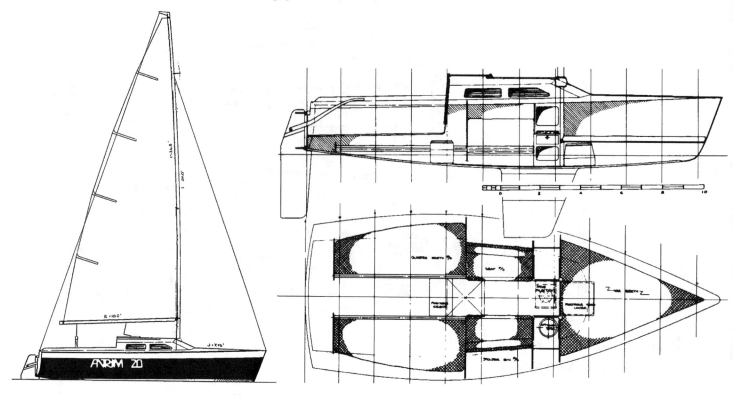

LOD:	20' 5"		**Designer:**	Jim Antrim
LOA:	21' 8"		**Builder:**	Antrim Marine
LWL:	17' 6"		**Years produced:**	1981–1982
Min./max. draft:	4' 0"		**Sail area:**	280 sq. ft.
Bridge clearance:	32' 7"		**Fuel tankage:**	portable
Power:	outboard 2 to 5 hp		**Water tankage:**	portable
B/D ratio:	41%		**Approx. trailering wgt.:**	2,700 lbs.

Designer Jim Antrim conceived this nice-looking vessel to be "the smallest boat with a workable interior, attractive appearance and eight-foot trailerable beam, and . . . to provide the performance and feeling of spaciousness one might expect in a larger boat." ***Best features:*** She is probably the best sailer in light and medium air in her comp group, combining a deep fin, big sail area and SA/D ratio, and broad waterplane aft. She is also tied with the Harpoon 6.2 and the Jeanneau Bahia 23 for spaciousness, and (except for the Jeanneau) has headroom as good as or better than her comps. ***Worst features:*** The same factors that make her a good sailer, particularly in light air, also work against her to some extent in heavy air. She needs a big crew to keep her on her feet in a blow, or if short-handed, she needs to be reefed early. Being deep draft, she is relatively difficult to trailer and launch. Still, overall, we like this design a lot, and are sorry that she was produced for such a short time.

Comps	LOD	Beam	MinDr	Displ	Bllst	SA/D	D/L	Avg. PHRF	Max. Speed	Motion Index	Space Index	No. of Berths	Head-room
Harpoon 6.2 (20)	20' 4"	8' 0"	3' 6"	1,700	550	24.7	191	234	5.3	9.5	339	2	4' 3"
Jeanneau Bahia 23 (20)	20' 4"	7' 11"	1' 5"	1,850	620	22.3	140	177	5.7	9.4	339	4	4' 11"
Mystic Miniton 21 (20)	20' 3"	7' 11"	4' 0"	1,850	700	22.6	168	219	5.5	9.9	313	4	4' 0"
Antrim 20	20' 5"	8' 0"	4' 0"	1,850	750	29.7	154	NA	5.6	9.7	339	4	4' 4"
Precision 21	20' 9"	8' 3"	1' 9"	1,875	600	21.4	156	270	5.6	9.4	317	4	4' 4"

Aquarius 21
Rub-a-dub-dub . . .

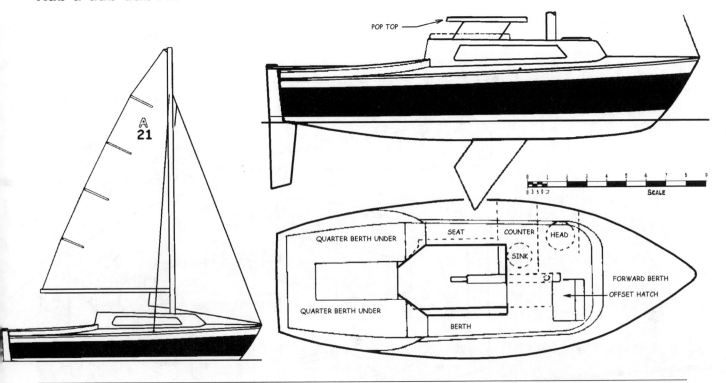

LOD:	21' 0"	Designer:	Peter Barrett
LOA:	22' 0"	Builder:	Coastal Recreation
LWL:	18' 3"	Years produced:	1969–1981
Min./max. draft:	1' 0"/ 4' 7"	Sail area:	181 sq. ft.
Bridge clearance:	25' 8"	Fuel tankage:	portable
Power:	outboard 3 to 6 hp	Water tankage:	portable
B/D ratio:	35%	Approx. trailering wgt.:	2,700 lbs.

Olympic medal-winner Peter Barrett designed this little boat. We found it hard to keep from calling her a "tub" until we realized that she looks better in real life than in the crude drawings that were used to market her, from which the diagrams you see here were taken. She began in 1969 as an Aquarius 21, then (with very minor changes) became the Aquarius Pelican about 1978, and still later was called the Balboa 21. **Best features:** A pop top gives 5' 9" headroom, which together with a galley area (sizable for this size boat; not shown on the plan of this early version), good storage space, and a folding table, make this boat quite a livable weekender. Ballast is highest of the comps and beam next highest, helping to improve her stability versus her comps. (However, her centerboard weighs only 165 pounds, and the rest of her 665 pounds of ballast is all contained near or at the waterline, and that reduces her stability compared to her comps.) Minimum draft of one foot with no centerboard projection makes launching from a trailer relatively easy. **Worst features:** She is billed as a four-sleeper, but we wouldn't try sleeping more than two.

Comps	LOD	Beam	MinDr	Displ	Bllst	SA/D	D/L	Avg. PHRF	Max. Speed	Motion Index	Space Index	No. of Berths	Head- room
Hunter 20	19' 8"	7' 6"	1' 3"	1,700	400	19.1	204	276	5.3	10.5	258	5	4' 2"
Sovereign 20	20' 0"	7' 2"	2' 0"	1,700	600	21.2	154	NA	5.5	10.6	237	4	4' 2"
Hunter 212 (21)	21' 0"	8' 2"	0' 10"	1,800	135	23.0	138	216	5.7	8.7	329	4	4' 4"
Aquarius 21	21' 0"	7' 10"	1' 0"	1,900	665	18.9	140	273	5.7	9.9	300	4	4' 6"
Spirit 6.5 (21)	21' 3"	7' 10"	1' 8"	2,100	550	19.1	142	261	5.8	10.7	334	4 to 5	4' 4"

Arey's Pond Catboat 21
A Cape Cod Cat built on Cape Cod

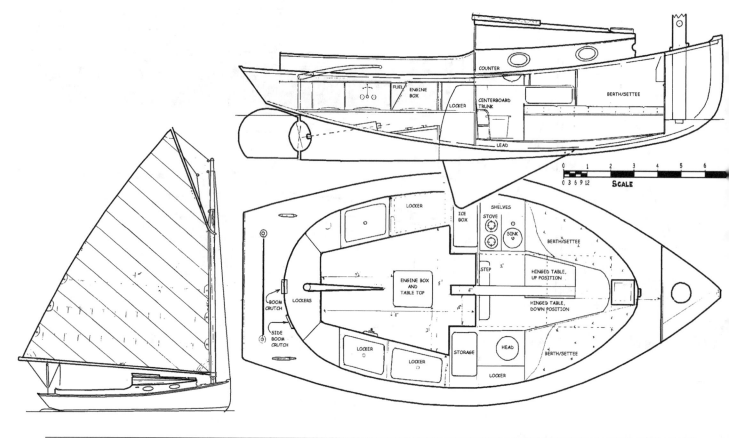

LOD:	20' 10"		**Designer:**	G. Anthony Davis
LOA:	22' 8"		**Builder:**	Arey's Pond Boat Yard
LWL:	17' 6"		**Years produced:**	1998–present
Min./max. draft:	1' 9"/4' 1"		**Sail area:**	320 sq. ft.
Bridge clearance:	32' 0"		**Fuel tankage:**	NA
Power:	10 hp inboard		**Water tankage:**	NA
B/D ratio:	12%		**Approx. trailering wgt.:**	5,200 lbs.

This version of the traditional "Cape Cod Cat" was designed in the late 1990s by Tony Davis to be built of strip-planked Southern cedar sheathed in fiberglass and epoxy. Therefore it's questionable whether we should have included this "non-pure" fiberglass boat in our assemblage of vessels for this book. Our excuse is that without the APC there would be nothing to compare relative to the other two comps listed in the box below. **Best features:** The cockpit appears to be the largest of the three comps, making the APC a candidate for daysailing with large parties. With lower freeboard, she is also the sleekest looking. **Worst features:** On the other hand, lower freeboard means lower headroom and a lower Space Index. Her ballast seems to be on the low side, her forward hatch seems a bit small, and her centerboard trunk, while traditional, intrudes into the cabin more than the trunk of either of her comps.

Comps	LOD	Beam	MinDr	Displ	Bllst	SA/D	D/L	Avg. PHRF	Max. Speed	Motion Index	Space Index	No. of Berths	Head- room
Arey's Pond Cat 21	20' 10"	10' 0"	1' 9"	3,444	400	22.4	287	NA	5.6	13.3	342	2	5' 0"
Coquina Cat 22	21' 9"	10' 4"	2' 3"	3,800	1,200	21.3	202	NA	6.0	12.5	473	2	5' 8"
Atlantic City Kitty 21	21' 3"	9' 6"	2' 0"	5,300	1,800	18.4	417	281	5.7	21.5	404	2	5' 3"

Atlantic City Kitty 21

New Jersey designer tries his hand at sail

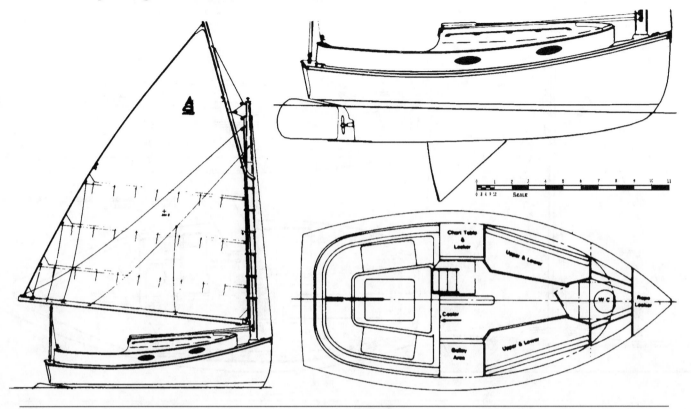

LOD:	21' 3"
LOA:	22' 9"
LWL:	17' 10"
Min./max. draft:	2' 0"/5' 0"
Bridge clearance:	33' 6"
Power:	outboard or inboard 4 to 10 hp
B/D ratio:	34%

Designer:	Bob O'Donnell
Builder:	Mark-O Custom
Years produced:	1982–1989
Sail area:	350 sq. ft.
Fuel tankage:	portable (opt inbd)
Water tankage:	15 gal.
Approx. trailering wgt.:	7,500 lbs.

Like her comps, the Arey's Pond Cat 21 and the Coquina Cat 21, the Atlantic City Kitty 21 or ACK can be distinguished from other more traditional cats, such as the Marshall 22 (page 182) and Menger Cat (page 183) by her rudder. Both of the ACK's comps have so-called inboard rudders, tucked under the stern in contrast with the so-called barn-door rudders of traditional catboats. There are advantages and disadvantages of each alternative. ***Best and worst features:*** Despite being narrower and in the same length range, the ACK is much heavier than her comps. The reason appears to be in her tremendous ballast of 1,800 pounds, 34% of her total weight (compared to 10% to 15% for most cats of this size and type) which, if subtracted from the total, leaves 3,500 lbs. for everything else—hull, deck, engine, spars, sail, hardware, etc. If the same mathematical exercise is performed on her comps, the Arey's Pond Cat ex-ballast weighs 3,044 lbs., and the Coquina Cat weighs 2,600 lbs. Quite a difference for three boats within a foot of each other in length. It makes one wonder if the reported ballast figure might be misreported—or (unlike the other boats in this book) might be calculated to include crew, stores, etc.

Comps	LOD	Beam	MinDr	Displ	Bllst	SA/D	D/L	Avg. PHRF	Max. Speed	Motion Index	Space Index	No. of Berths	Head-room
Arey's Pond Cat 21	20' 10"	10' 0"	1' 9"	3,444	400	22.4	287	NA	5.6	13.3	342	2	5' 0"
Coquina Cat 22	21' 9"	10' 4"	2' 3"	3,800	1,200	21.3	202	NA	6.0	12.5	473	2	5' 8"
Atlantic City Kitty 21	21' 3"	9' 6"	2' 0"	5,300	1,800	18.4	417	281	5.7	21.5	404	2	5' 3"

Balboa 20
The boat that got Lyle Hess involved full-time

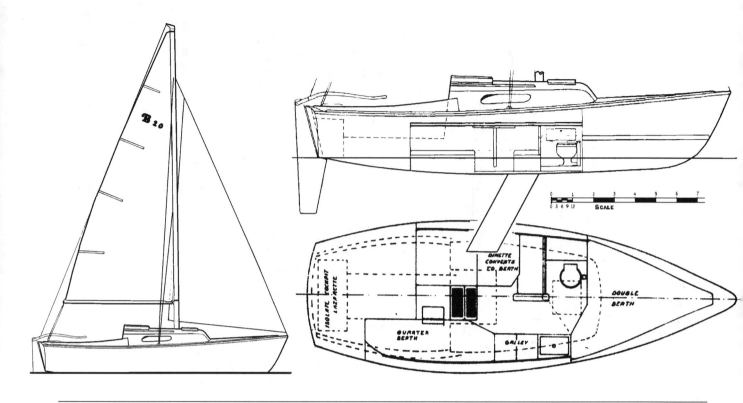

LOD:	20' 0"	**Designer:**	Lyle Hess
LOA:	20' 5"	**Builder:**	Coastal Recreation
LWL:	17' 5"	**Years produced:**	1968–1977
Min./max. draft:	1' 9"/4' 0"	**Sail area:**	182 sq. ft.
Bridge clearance:	27' 6"	**Fuel tankage:**	portable
Power:	outboard 3 to 6 hp	**Water tankage:**	portable
B/D ratio:	26%	**Approx. trailering wgt.:**	2,400 lbs.

The three comps listed below are all Lyle Hess designs. The Balboa was Hess's first fiberglass design (1968). The Ensenada 20, with the Balboa hull but a different house (see page 97), came four years later, in 1972. The RK20 (see page 126), which was introduced in the late 1970s, appears to be a virtually identical hull but with somewhat different layouts, dimensions, and weights. A production run of over 10 years, albeit under different names, indicates that the hull design was a success. **Best features:** All three of the comps listed below are so close in statistical data that it's difficult to find a distinction among them, except perhaps in aesthetic appeal—which is of course in the eye of the beholder. Lyle Hess's designs are usually thought to be prettier (or handsomer?) than most, but in this early design it is hard to see a clear distinction from many other trailer-sailers of the era. **Worst features:** The cast iron swing keel, weighing more than a quarter of the total boat and controlled by a winch in the cabin, is at best a maintenance headache and at worst could cause serious leakage in the hull due to strain.

Comps	LOD	Beam	MinDr	Displ	Bllst	SA/D	D/L	Avg. PHRF	Max. Speed	Motion Index	Space Index	No. of Berths	Head-room
Ensenada 20	20' 0"	7' 1"	1' 0"	1,600	550	20.3	133	288	5.6	9.9	238	4	4' 2"
Balboa 20	20' 0"	7' 1"	1' 9"	1,700	450	20.4	142	276	5.6	10.5	252	4	4' 0"
RK20	20' 0"	7' 1"	1' 9"	1,700	550	21.8	142	264	5.6	10.5	222	4	3' 9"

Bay Hen 21
A design from Bob Johnson of Island Packet fame

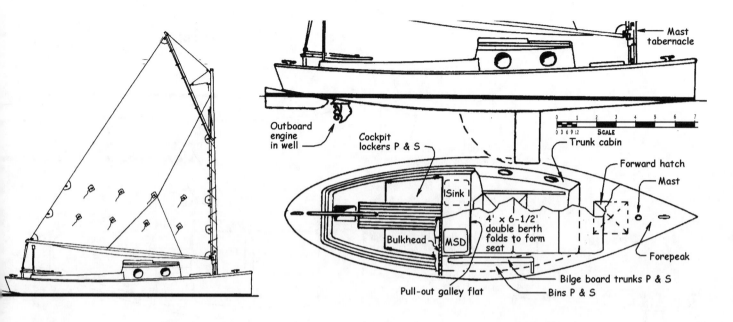

LOD:	21' 0"	Designer:	Bob Johnson
LOA:	21' 6"	Builder:	Nimble Boats and others
LWL:	18' 3"	Years produced:	1984?–1990?
Min./max. draft:	0' 9"/3' 6"	Sail area:	175 sq. ft.
Bridge clearance:	22' 0"	Fuel tankage:	portable
Power:	outboard 2 to 5 hp	Water tankage:	portable
B/D ratio:	0%	Approx. trailering wgt.:	1,400 lbs.

Bob Johnson, designer of the popular Island Packet series, created a daysailer called the Lightfoot Sharpie. Florida Bay Boat Company acquired the molds to this design, then added a deck and cuddy. The last we heard, Nimble Boats had the molds. **Best features:** She has a big, deep cockpit with stowage under the seats, and a nice motor well which allows a small outboard to be tipped up while sailing. An offset centerboard trunk keeps the cabin sole clear, though space below is meager, as with the Bay Hen's comps. Cushions are fitted to the cabin sole, and they may be laid against the sides of the boat to use as seatbacks as well. She has a mast tabernacle which permits fast rigging and unrigging. **Worst features:** The boat handles like a typical flat-bottomed sharpie, pounding a bit going upwind, and her shallow sharpie rudder can result in considerable weather helm in a breeze. Construction quality may vary from one model year to another, since several different builders came and went.

Comps	LOD	Beam	MinDr	Displ	Bllst	SA/D	D/L	Avg. PHRF	Max. Speed	Motion Index	Space Index	No. of Berths	Head-room
Sea Pearl 21	21' 0"	5' 6"	0' 6"	550	0	32.9	36	NA	5.8	4.4	147	2	3' 6"
Dovekie 21	21' 5"	6' 8"	0' 4"	600	0	32.2	39	NA	5.8	3.7	181	2	3' 0"
Bay Hen 21	21' 0"	6' 3"	0' 9"	900	0	30.0	66	NA	5.7	6.3	158	2	3' 3"

Beneteau First 210 (21)
Smallest boat in the Beneteau line

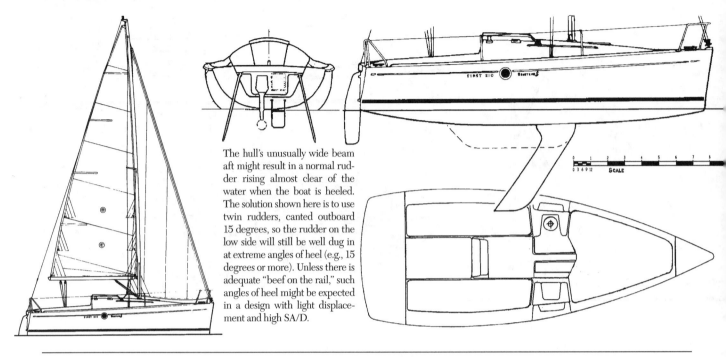

The hull's unusually wide beam aft might result in a normal rudder rising almost clear of the water when the boat is heeled. The solution shown here is to use twin rudders, canted outboard 15 degrees, so the rudder on the low side will still be well dug in at extreme angles of heel (e.g., 15 degrees or more). Unless there is adequate "beef on the rail," such angles of heel might be expected in a design with light displacement and high SA/D.

LOD:	21' 0"	**Designer:**	J. M. Finot
LOA:	21' 10"	**Builder:**	Beneteau
LWL:	19' 8"	**Years produced:**	1992–1996
Min./max. draft:	2' 4"/5' 10"	**Sail area:**	243 sq. ft.
Bridge clearance:	34' 6"	**Fuel tankage:**	portable
Power:	outboard 3 to 6 hp	**Water tankage:**	portable
B/D ratio:	35%	**Approx. trailering wgt.:**	3,200 lbs.

This is a boat that looks good on paper—and pretty good even in real life. In 1993 she was chosen as the Daysailer/Weekender Boat of the Year by *Sailing World*, the magazine for sailboat racing fans. **Best features:** She has positive flotation ("unsinkability is ensured"), and a neat and quite adequate open-plan cabin. And we do like her sleek looks, though that's a matter of individual taste. **Worst features:** Not enough ballast down low enough, a hull shape that looks as if it needs a lot of beef on the rail in any kind of breeze, and a big sail area in relation to her weight all work against her popularity as anything except a pure racer. Her rather low PHRF (average 195) is only 21 seconds per mile higher than a J/24, which is a much bigger—and more purpose-built—boat. The judges in the *Sailing World* Boat of the Year competition were "not unanimously taken with the novel aesthetics of the design, and questioned how well this aspect would be received in the United States market." Indeed, she was withdrawn from the United States market after only five years, leading us to think that perhaps she was not much of a commercial success. We wonder if the board-down draft of 5' 10" might have contributed to mediocre sales, along with her unconventional twin rudders, which, according to the ads, "ensure good steerage no matter what the angle of heel." "Oh, she heels a lot?" could well have been the reaction of potential buyers.

Comps	LOD	Beam	MinDr	Displ	Bllst	SA/D	D/L	Avg. PHRF	Max. Speed	Motion Index	Space Index	No. of Berths	Head-room
Newport 214	21' 2"	7' 7"	0' 9"	2,000	450	23.1	130	NA	5.8	10.4	318	4	4' 0"
Beneteau First 210 (21)	21' 0"	8' 2"	2' 4"	2,200	770	23.0	129	195	5.9	10.3	371	4	4' 6"
S2 6.9 (21)	21' 0"	8' 0"	0' 9"	2,200	770	22.3	149	205	5.8	10.7	328	4	4' 0"
S2 6.7 (21)	21' 0"	8' 0"	0' 10"	2,200	775	21.3	149	205	5.8	10.7	320	4	4' 0"

Buccaneer 200 (20)

Bayliner tries the sailboat business

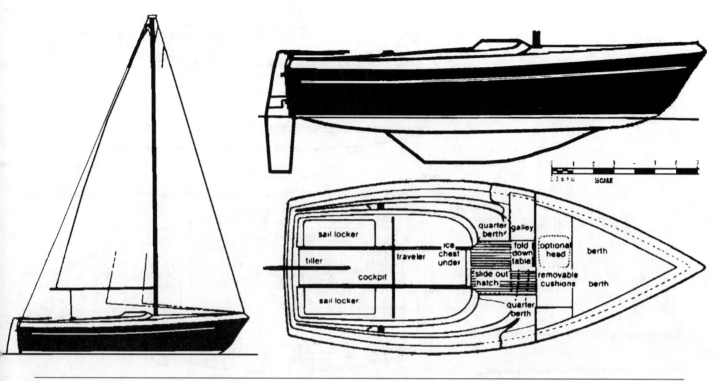

LOD:	20' 5"		Designer:	Buccaneer Design Team
LOA:	21' 4"		Builder:	Bayliner Yachts
LWL:	17' 3"		Years produced:	1977–1981
Min./max. draft:	2' 0"		Sail area:	191 sq. ft.
Bridge clearance:	32' 0"		Fuel tankage:	portable
Power:	outboard 3 to 6 hp		Water tankage:	portable
B/D ratio:	36%		Approx. trailering wgt.:	2,900 lbs.

The Buccaneer 200 represents one of Bayliner's entries in the "hot market" for fiberglass sailboats that took place in the late 1970s and early 1980s. But the line wasn't as popular as the company had anticipated, and soon Bayliner withdrew back to selling just the powerboat line that they were originally known for. *Best features:* The competition in this size and weight range was fierce in the 1970s, and to clearly differentiate their product, Bayliner went for low price, a wide beam for plenty of space below, and a simple-to-use boat. Then, as now, this attracted the non-sailing public as buyers.

Neophyte sailors found a vessel with a low first cost, and a shallow keel for easy launching and retrieving on a trailer ramp. The long keel also enables the hull to track well under power or when going downwind. Space is best among the comps. *Worst features:* The new sailors would also find eventually that a boat with a shallow keel tends to side-slip when sailing upwind in a light to moderate breeze. A long, narrow centerboard housed within the keel (such as on the Chrysler 20) would have eliminated that shortcoming, but would raise the price and complicate sailing.

Comps	LOD	Beam	MinDr	Displ	Bllst	SA/D	D/L	Avg. PHRF	Max. Speed	Motion Index	Space Index	No. of Berths	Head-room
Chrysler 20	20' 0"	7' 11"	1' 11"	1,950	500	18.3	149	264	5.7	10.1	311	4	3' 9"
Buccaneer 200 (20)	20' 5"	8' 0"	2' 0"	2,100	750	18.6	183	276	5.6	10.9	336	4	3' 6"
Signet 20	19' 10"	6' 8"	2' 0"	2,146	800	18.5	234	NA	5.4	15.4	200	4	4' 0"
Wild Wind 20	20' 0"	7' 11"	2' 0"	2,200	800	18.3	168	NA	5.7	11.5	302	6	4' 3"
Montego 20	19' 6"	7' 2"	2' 0"	2,300	600	17.4	184	282	5.6	14.0	246	4	4' 0"

Buccaneer 210 (21)

One of the first of the "wedding cake" designs

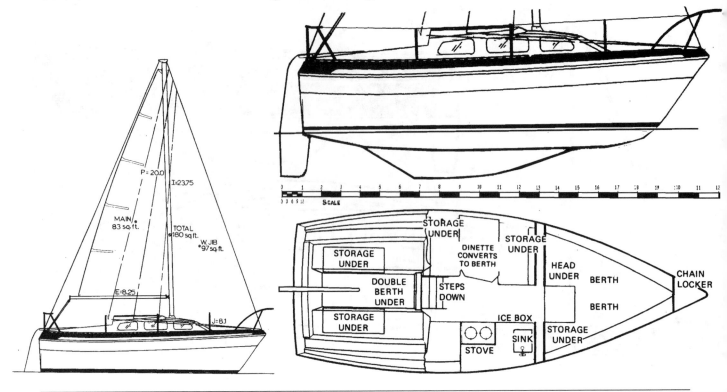

LOD:	20' 10"		**Designer:**	Buccaneer Design Team
LOA:	21' 6"		**Builder:**	Bayliner Marine
LWL:	18' 4"		**Years produced:**	1975–1978?
Min./max. draft:	2' 0"		**Sail area:**	179 sq. ft.
Bridge clearance:	29' 6"		**Fuel tankage:**	portable
Power:	outboard 3 to 6 hp		**Water tankage:**	20 gal.
B/D ratio:	30%		**Approx. trailering wgt.:**	4,600 lbs.

In the 1970s, sailboat marketers perceived a public outcry for more space below, more creature comforts, and more features which would appeal to women. Many yacht designers couldn't face the prospect of ruining the graceful appearance of their creations by raising the deck of a small sailboat beyond what looked good. But Bayliner Marine, used to designing powerboats which already were boxy enough to have more or less the same silhouette as a wedding cake, had no such compunctions. Ignoring conventional aesthetic considerations, Bayliner came up with the high-topped but roomy design shown here.

Best features: What? A 21-foot boat that sleeps six, has 5' 8" headroom, a dinette, and a full galley including a built-in icebox? Feast your eyes. Oh, and she's got positive foam flotation. **Worst features:** All the design considerations that allow the "best features" listed above also mean a high, boxy look and excessive windage, that can cause poor upwind performance from sideways slippage (accentuated by a too-shallow fixed keel). The Buccaneer 210 also has a very low SA/D ratio and a high D/L ratio, both tending to make her slow in light air. And the cabin sole and sides of the hull are covered with plush pile carpeting. Ugh!

Comps	LOD	Beam	MinDr	Displ	Bllst	SA/D	D/L	Avg. PHRF	Max. Speed	Motion Index	Space Index	No. of Berths	Head-room
Mistral T-21	21' 0"	8' 2"	1' 2"	2,800	750	19.5	192	234	5.8	13.3	371	5	4' 8"
Golif 21	21' 0"	7' 5"	3' 2"	2,860	1,056	18.2	174	264	5.9	15.0	333	4	5' 0"
Chrysler 22 (21)	21' 2"	7' 9"	1' 11"	2,900	725	17.3	189	270	5.8	14.7	313	5	4' 4"
Buccaneer 210 (21)	20' 10"	8' 0"	2' 0"	3,000	900	13.8	217	300	5.7	15.0	398	6	5' 8"

Cal 20

Bill Lapworth designs another winner

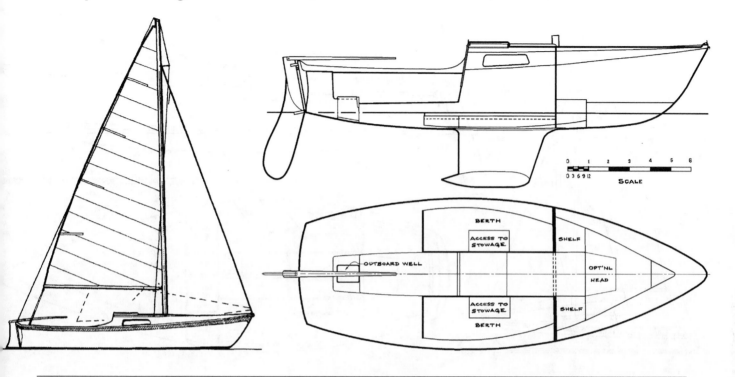

LOD:	20' 0"		**Designer:**	C. William Lapworth
LOA:	21' 6"		**Builder:**	Cal Boats
LWL:	18' 0"		**Years produced:**	1961–1977
Min./max. draft:	3' 4"		**Sail area:**	196 sq. ft.
Bridge clearance:	26' 9"		**Fuel tankage:**	portable
Power:	outboard 3 to 6 hp		**Water tankage:**	portable
B/D ratio:	46%		**Approx. trailering wgt.:**	3,000 lbs.

Bill Lapworth, whose Cal 40 made history as a fast design in the early days of fiberglass, also created the Cal 20. A popular club racer and weekend cruiser right from the start, and serially produced until 1977, she is durable enough to still warrant several active class fleets (mostly in California) and a national association with a presence on the Internet. ***Best features:*** She is fast and easy to sail. A 46% B/D ratio, with a bulb keel concentrating her ballast low, gives her good stability. An outboard well located in the cockpit keeps the engine under the helmsman's control. And for those looking for camaraderie, the big network of Cal 20 fleets (largely on the West Coast) will be attractive. ***Worst features:*** Fin keel with bulb makes the boat a chore to launch at shallow ramps. Also, the boats are among the oldest fiberglass boats around, and most will require more strenuous than ordinary maintenance to keep in top condition. The keel (made of iron, which rusts), keel bolts, and surrounding fiberglass are common causes of concern.

Comps	LOD	Beam	MinDr	Displ	Bllst	SA/D	D/L	Avg. PHRF	Max. Speed	Motion Index	Space Index	No. of Berths	Head-room
Cal 20	20' 0"	7' 0"	3' 4"	1,950	900	20.1	149	276	5.7	11.8	244	4	3' 11"
Islander 21	20' 10"	7' 10"	3' 4"	1,950	1,000	21.3	149	282	5.7	10.2	280	4	3' 9"
Ranger 22 (21)	21' 4"	7' 10"	4' 3"	2,182	900	19.8	182	222	5.6	11.4	306	4	4' 0"

Cal 21

Jensen Marine and Bill Lapworth team up again

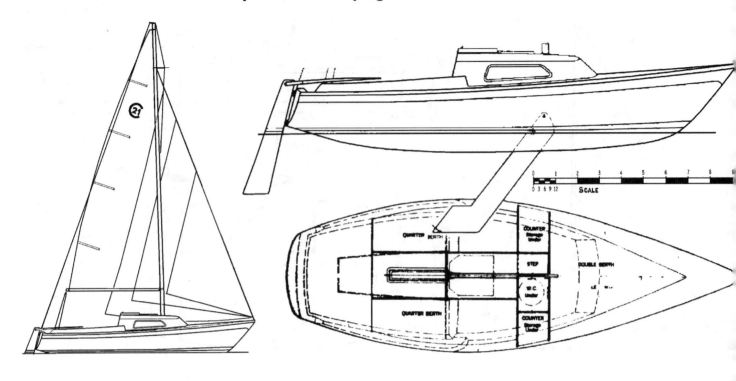

LOD:	20' 6"	**Designer:**	Bill Lapworth
LOA:	21' 6"	**Builder:**	Jensen Marine & others
LWL:	16' 8"	**Years produced:**	1969–1976
Min./max. draft:	0' 9"/4' 3"	**Sail area:**	196 sq. ft.
Bridge clearance:	28' 0"	**Fuel tankage:**	portable
Power:	outboard 3 to 6 hp	**Water tankage:**	portable
B/D ratio:	33%	**Approx. trailering wgt.:**	1,700 lbs.

This design, a near lookalike to MacGregor's Venture 21 (page 145; shown as a comp here), was introduced four years after the Venture and in the same year (1969) as the San Juan 21 Mk I (page 129), another comp. All three of these West Coast designs helped pioneer the retractable-keel type of vessel that is easily trailered and can be rigged and launched in a jiffy. ***Best features:*** Relative to her comps, the Cal 21 is a bit narrower and shallower (good for storage and ramp launching), and lighter (good for light-air performance). Her PHRF rating appears to be generous, since her comps all have to give her six seconds per mile despite her probable better performance in light stuff. She also has better headroom than her comps. In good weather a pair of sleepers can be accommodated on her unusually spacious (eight feet long) cockpit seats. ***Worst features:*** The mahogany rudder is detachable but not folding, a potential problem in shallows. The iron keel is subject to pitting and rust. The keel hoisting system is said by some owners to be a weakness.

Comps	LOD	Beam	MinDr	Displ	Bllst	SA/D	D/L	Avg. PHRF	Max. Speed	Motion Index	Space Index	No. of Berths	Head-room
Cal 21	20' 6"	6' 8"	0' 9"	1,100	360	29.4	106	258	5.5	7.6	221	4	4' 1"
Venture 21	21' 0"	6' 10"	1' 0"	1,200	400	24.8	85	252	5.8	7.4	203	4	3' 3"
San Juan 21 Mk I	20' 6"	7' 0"	1' 0"	1,250	400	26.2	114	252	5.5	8.0	227	4	3' 6"
San Juan 21 Mk II	20' 6"	7' 0"	1' 0"	1,250	400	26.2	114	252	5.5	8.0	227	4	3' 6"

Chrysler 20

An automaker enters the sailing market

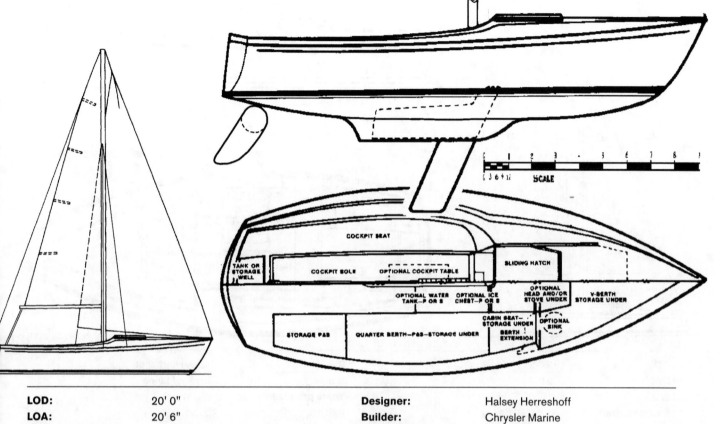

LOD:	20' 0"
LOA:	20' 6"
LWL:	18' 0"
Min./max. draft:	1' 11"/5' 7"
Bridge clearance:	28' 6"
Power:	outboard 3 to 6 hp
B/D ratio:	26%

Designer:	Halsey Herreshoff
Builder:	Chrysler Marine
Years produced:	1977–1980
Sail area:	179 sq. ft.
Fuel tankage:	portable
Water tankage:	portable
Approx. trailering wgt.:	2,700 lbs.

Halsey Herreshoff, son of Sidney DeW. Herreshoff, and not to be confused with Cap'n Nat Herreshoff, the so-called Wizard of Bristol (although he happens to be the old man's grandson), has been a yacht designer most of his life. He worked with Chrysler Marine as a consultant to design the 20-footer shown here. Chrysler had been in the outboard engine business for some years; then in 1965, the company purchased Lone Star Boats in Plano, TX, and began producing small powerboats and (eventually) some small sailboats, including this one. **Best features:**

The boat is nicely constructed, with good finish, smooth fiberglass cabin liner, and quality hardware (e.g., Harken blocks). She doesn't look bad on the water either. **Worst features:** Probably the most unusual (and least attractive) feature of the Chrysler 20 is her inboard pivoting rudder. Very seldom is this type of rudder design used, since it is complicated (and therefore hard to repair), and subject to collecting weed and plastic bags on its leading edge. A flip-up outboard rudder hung on the transom would have been a better choice.

Comps	LOD	Beam	MinDr	Displ	Bllst	SA/D	D/L	Avg. PHRF	Max. Speed	Motion Index	Space Index	No. of Berths	Head-room
Chrysler 20	20' 0"	7' 11"	1' 11"	1,950	500	18.3	149	264	5.7	10.1	311	4	3' 9"
Buccaneer 200 (20)	20' 5"	8' 0"	2' 0"	2,100	750	18.6	183	276	5.6	10.9	336	4	3' 6"
Signet 20	19' 10"	6' 8"	2' 0"	2,146	800	18.5	234	NA	5.4	15.4	200	4	4' 0"
Wild Wind 20	20' 0"	7' 11"	2' 0"	2,200	800	18.3	168	NA	5.7	11.5	302	6	4' 3"
Montego 20	19' 6"	7' 2"	2' 0"	2,300	600	17.4	184	282	5.6	14.0	246	4	4' 0"

Chrysler 22 (21)

How long is this boat?

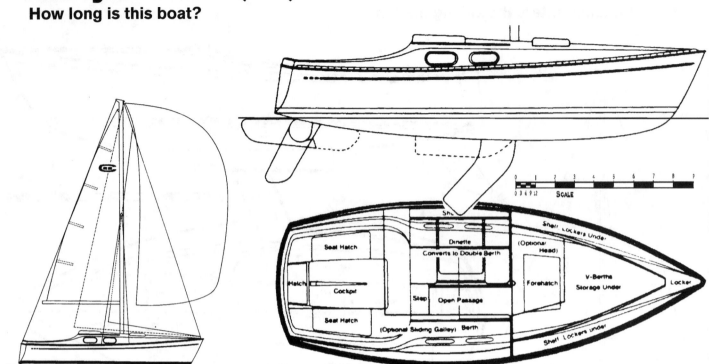

LOD:	21' 2"	**Designer:**	Halsey Herreshoff
LOA:	21' 7"	**Builder:**	Chrysler Marine
LWL:	19' 0"	**Years produced:**	1975–1980
Min./max. draft:	1' 11"/4' 6"	**Sail area:**	220 sq. ft.
Bridge clearance:	29' 10"	**Fuel tankage:**	portable
Power:	outboard 3 to 6 hp	**Water tankage:**	4 gal.
B/D ratio:	29%	**Approx. trailering wgt.:**	4,100 lbs.

This boat came with the standard rig shown here or with an optional tall rig 1' 6" higher. She also was available with a fixed fin keel weighing 1,010 pounds, in place of the swing keel shown here, which weighed 725 pounds (increased to 825 pounds in later production). Displacement is given in sales documents as 3,000 pounds with either keel, despite the 285-pound ballast difference, indicating a certain casualness in bandying about specs. (We use 2,900 pounds as the displacement, though it may be considerably less.) Furthermore, the manufacturer called this a 22-foot boat (although in a few places we've seen 21' 7" as the LOA) with a 19-foot waterline. Just by glancing at the drawings, one can see that the LOD is only a little longer than the waterline length. We measured LOD on the drawing and got 21' 2", so we're calling the boat by the length most marketers would: a 21-footer. By the way, some literature says it's the predecessor to the TMI (Texas Marine International) 22, and to the Starwind 22, also designed by Halsey Herreshoff. It looks similar, and both boats have 19-foot waterlines, but the Starwind 22 has a more angular stem and a different transom shape, which brings her LOD to just about 22 feet. ***Best features:*** We noticed no special features worth mentioning. ***Worst features:*** The inboard pivoting rudder has the same problems as described for the Chrysler 20 (page 91), a similar design. Headroom is lowest among the comps.

Comps	LOD	Beam	MinDr	Displ	Bllst	SA/D	D/L	Avg. PHRF	Max. Speed	Motion Index	Space Index	No. of Berths	Head-room
Mistral T-21	21' 0"	8' 2"	1' 2"	2,800	750	19.5	192	234	5.8	13.3	371	5	4' 8"
Golif 21	21' 0"	7' 5"	3' 2"	2,860	1,056	18.2	174	264	5.9	15.0	333	4	5' 0"
Chrysler 22 (21)	21' 2"	7' 9"	1' 11"	2,900	725	17.3	189	270	5.8	14.7	313	5	4' 4"
Buccaneer 210 (21)	20' 10"	8' 0"	2' 0"	3,000	900	13.8	217	300	5.7	15.0	398	6	5' 8"

Clipper 21
Another West Coast swing-keel lightweight

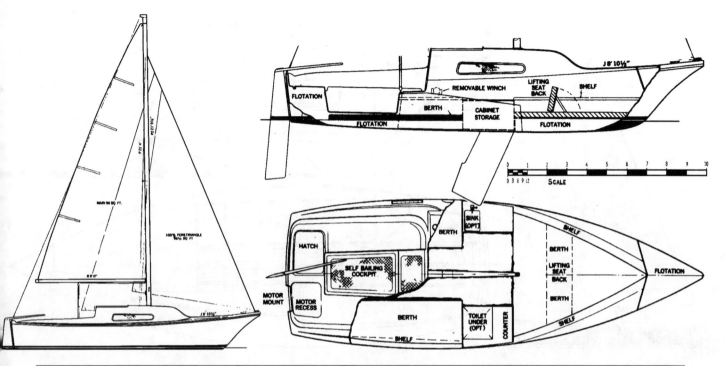

LOD:	20' 11"	**Designer:**	William Crealock
LOA:	21' 11"	**Builder:**	Clipper Marine Corp.
LWL:	17' 10"	**Years produced:**	1970–1977
Min./max. draft:	0' 7"/4' 4"	**Sail area:**	193 sq. ft.
Bridge clearance:	27' 0"	**Fuel tankage:**	portable
Power:	outboard 3 to 6 hp	**Water tankage:**	portable
B/D ratio:	23%	**Approx. trailering wgt.:**	2,600 lbs.

This vessel from the board of the well-known West Coast yacht designer William Crealock has a long, distinctive (and, to us, a somewhat weird-looking) clipper bow, a "trademark look" of Clipper, the company that built her. ***Best features:*** The Clipper 21's draft of only seven inches should make her relatively easy to launch and retrieve. Down below, a 'thwartships lifting seatback eases the problem of low headroom. The ads proclaim that she has enough foam flotation to be unsinkable, even with her interior full of water. ***Worst features:*** Construction quality is nothing to rave about on this lightly built boat, which was made to sell at a low target price—only $2,800 brand new in 1971. Headroom is lowest of her comps, and her Space Index is also lowest. Her cast iron swing keel

could be a maintenance problem, and the winch to raise and lower it is located inconveniently down in the cabin. A relatively narrow beam combined with below-average ballast weight will make her tender relative to her comps. On the deck just forward of her transom is a recess in the deck for clamping an outboard engine, but the placement of the recess appears to be too close to the centerline, so that the outboard rudder may be damaged by the engine's prop when turning hard to starboard. In addition, the ads say that the transom will accept a 25 hp engine which will drive the boat at 15 mph. Given the light structure of the boat, we would not attempt anything more than 5 or 6 hp if the boat were ours, and be content to make 5 or 6 knots maximum speed.

Comps	LOD	Beam	MinDr	Displ	Bllst	SA/D	D/L	Avg. PHRF	Max. Speed	Motion Index	Space Index	No. of Berths	Head-room
Clipper 21	20' 11"	7' 3"	0' 7"	1,800	410	20.9	142	270	5.7	10.5	275	4	3' 9"
Parker Dawson Poacher 21	21' 1"	7' 6"	1' 0"	1,800	550	24.7	144	201	5.6	10.1	358	4	4' 0"
Nautica Flamingo 21	20' 8"	7' 5"	2' 0"	1,870	550	21.5	125	267	5.8	10.3	360	4	4' 1"

Companion 21
Traditional design by Aborn Smith

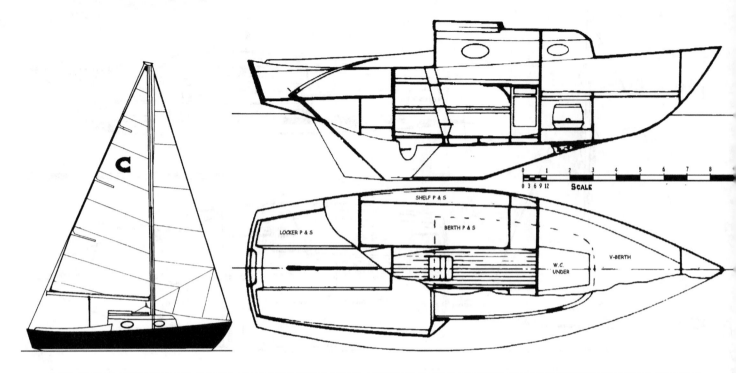

LOD:	20' 6"	**Designer:**	Aborn D. Smith
LOA:	20' 6"	**Builder:**	Trump Yachts
LWL:	16' 0"	**Years produced:**	1982–1983
Min./max. draft:	2' 9"	**Sail area:**	218 sq. ft.
Bridge clearance:	28' 9"	**Fuel tankage:**	portable
Power:	outboard 3 to 6 hp	**Water tankage:**	portable
B/D ratio:	33%	**Approx. trailering wgt.:**	4,600 lbs.

Aborn "Denny" Smith (1929–2007) for most of his life was not a yacht designer. At the age of 15 he was a tugboat deckhand. At 16 he joined the army and served in Japan; eventually he became the owner of Smitty's Auto Body in Stonington, CT. After retiring from the auto industry he was an active sailboat racer, and on the side designed and built sailboats under the name of Trump Yachts in Stonington. As far as we know, however, the Companion 20 is the only sailboat he designed and sold commercially. **Best features:** Built of quality materials (cast lead ballast, solid bronze rudder post, solid teak trim and jointerwork), this is the kind of small yacht a proud owner might like to just sit in and polish. At sea she will behave herself, and if you need to go somewhere fast, there's always the outboard engine, conveniently located in a notch in the middle of the transom. **Worst features:** Under sail she will be slow, like her comps, since she—and her comps—are heavy, have low SA/D ratios and high D/L ratios. All have drafts of under three feet, so none should be expected to point very high either. As one owner aptly wrote when advertising his Companion 20 for sale, "Great boat for beginner or retired person." Sailors with more experience will want something faster.

Comps	LOD	Beam	MinDr	Displ	Bllst	SA/D	D/L	Avg. PHRF	Max. Speed	Motion Index	Space Index	No. of Berths	Head-room
Companion 21	20' 6"	7' 1"	2' 9"	3,000	1,000	16.8	327	303	5.4	19.6	245	4	4' 7"
Heritage 20	20' 0"	6' 6"	2' 9"	3,100	1,000	18.1	410	NA	5.2	23.8	235	4	4' 7"
Sea Islander 20	20' 0"	7' 6"	2' 2"	3,180	886	14.9	289	NA	5.5	18.6	294	4	4' 4"
Seaforth Coastal Cruiser 21	20' 6"	7' 4"	2' 6"	4,000	1,600	13.8	363	NA	5.5	22.6	276	2	4' 4"

Corinthian 19 (20)
Popular design from Carl Alberg

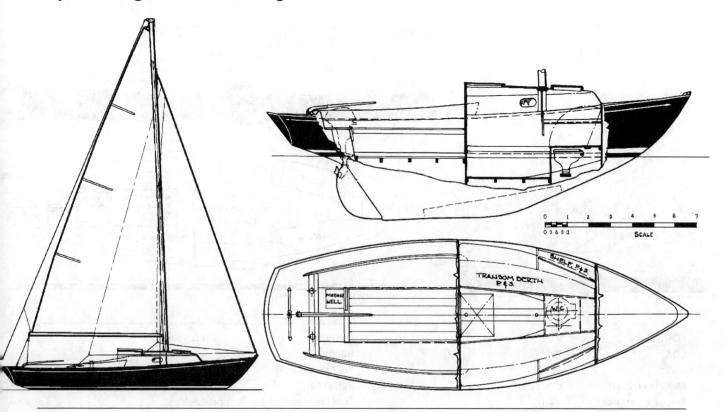

LOD:	19' 6"
LOA:	19' 6"
LWL:	14' 6"
Min./max. draft:	2' 9"
Bridge clearance:	26' 6"
Power:	outboard 3 to 6 hp
B/D ratio:	45%

Designer:	Carl Alberg
Builder:	Sailstar Boats, Bristol Yachts
Years produced:	1965–1981?
Sail area:	186 sq. ft.
Fuel tankage:	portable
Water tankage:	portable
Approx. trailering wgt.:	4,000 lbs.

Over 700 of these shippy-looking little sloops were built between 1965 and the early 1980s. Alberg's designs are so distinctive that his trademark look is hard to miss. For example, compare this boat with a near lookalike, the Cape Dory Typhoon 18 (19) on page 23. The resemblance is striking, at least until one realizes that the smaller boat is not only a foot shorter but also almost 1,000 lbs. lighter. In any case, while not usually seen on the racing circuit, like most Alberg designs, this one is a solid, wholesome, forgiving, and easy-to-sail vessel, great for daysailing and overnighting in

that harbor a few miles away from your home base. **Best features:** The Corinthian's springy sheer, extended overhangs fore and aft, and reasonably good finish make her a pleasure to behold. Her in-the-cockpit engine well (an optional extra when new) offers convenience to the helmsperson, and because of her hull shape, keeps propeller cavitation in waves to a minimum. **Worst features:** Her SA/D of 15.3 is in the "very low" category, and her D/L of 399 is considered very high, making her relatively slow in light air (but relatively stable in heavy air).

Comps	LOD	Beam	MinDr	Displ	Bllst	SA/D	D/L	Avg. PHRF	Max. Speed	Motion Index	Space Index	No. of Berths	Head-room
Quickstep 21	20' 10"	8' 0"	1' 11"	2,500	950	17.5	176	279	5.8	12.3	316	4	4' 4"
Halman 20	19' 6"	7' 9"	2' 10"	2,500	1,000	15.8	248	276	5.4	14.0	295	4	5' 0"
Nordica 20	19' 6"	7' 8"	3' 3"	2,520	1,020	15.7	250	276	5.4	14.7	292	4	5' 0"
Corinthian 19 (20)	19' 6"	6' 6"	2' 9"	2,724	1,100	15.3	399	292	5.1	21.6	216	2	4' 2"

Dovekie 21
A truly unique design from Phil Bolger

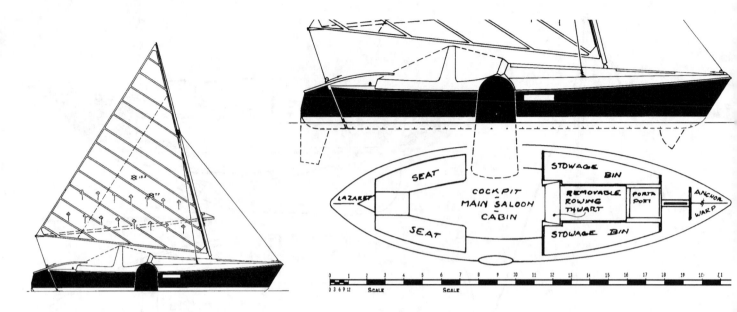

LOD:	21' 5"	**Designer:**	Philip Bolger
LOA:	21' 5"	**Builder:**	Edy & Duff
LWL:	19' 0"	**Years produced:**	1976–1983
Min./max. draft:	0' 4"/2' 6"	**Sail area:**	143 sq. ft.
Bridge clearance:	24' 0"	**Fuel tankage:**	portable
Power:	outboard 2 hp	**Water tankage:**	portable
B/D ratio:	0%	**Approx. trailering wgt.:**	1,100 lbs.

Like her comps, Dovekie is basically a decked-over open boat. Bolger's design is unusual (some would say radical) with a dead-flat bottom (no rocker, no deadrise), leeboards, a tiny bow centerboard for working to weather in shallows, and oar ports so she can be used without resorting to outboard power (though a side-mounted outboard bracket is a popular option). ***Best features:*** Dovekie feels like a big skiff under sail, and is fairly stable both underway and at anchor, especially considering her light, unballasted hull. But her best features are (A) ease of towing behind a small car, (B) ease of launching and hauling at ramps, (C) ease of striking the mast (six-foot clearance under bridges), (D) ease of rigging and unrigging, and (E) the ability to cruise camper-style in very shallow water. With a boards-up draft of four inches, she can easily be beached for lunch and a swim. ***Worst features:*** Rowing power or a 2-hp outboard will only move her at about 2 to 3 knots. Accommodations are minimal, though no worse than her comps. Be prepared to rough it.

Comps	LOD	Beam	MinDr	Displ	Bllst	SA/D	D/L	Avg. PHRF	Max. Speed	Motion Index	Space Index	No. of Berths	Head-room
Sea Pearl 21	21' 0"	5' 6"	0' 6"	550	0	32.9	36	NA	5.8	4.4	147	2	3' 6"
Dovekie 21	21' 5"	6' 8"	0' 4"	600	0	32.9	39	NA	5.8	3.7	181	2	3' 0"
Bay Hen 21	21' 0"	6' 3"	0' 9"	900	0	30.0	66	NA	5.7	6.3	158	2	3' 3"

Ensenada 20

The Balboa 20 with a different cabin house

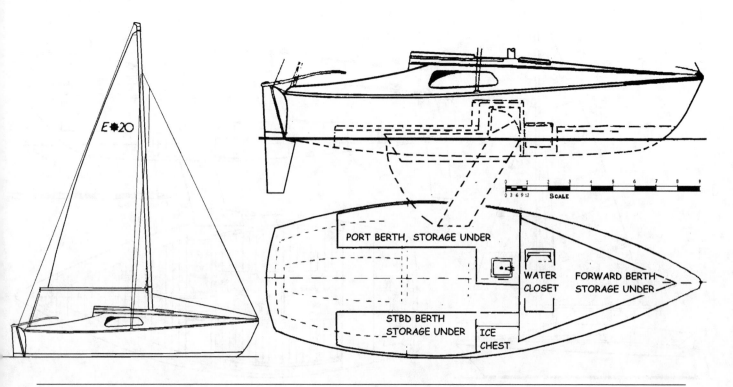

PORT BERTH, STORAGE UNDER

WATER CLOSET

FORWARD BERTH STORAGE UNDER

STBD BERTH STORAGE UNDER

ICE CHEST

SCALE

LOD:	20' 0"
LOA:	20' 0"
LWL:	17' 6"
Min./max. draft:	1' 0"/4' 0"
Bridge clearance:	27' 0"
Power:	outboard 3 to 6 hp
B/D ratio:	34%

Designer:	Lyle Hess
Builder:	Coastal Recreation Inc.
Years produced:	1972–1981?
Sail area:	174 sq. ft.
Fuel tankage:	portable
Water tankage:	portable
Approx. trailering wgt.:	2,300 lbs.

This vessel has a hull that is virtually identical to the earlier Balboa 20 (page 84) and the later RK20 (page 126) but has a different deck mold and slightly different layout, headroom and other dimensions, ballast weight, etc. *Best features:* Optional poptop increases headroom significantly but can be a nuisance underway, as owners report that visibility is affected and the jibsheets can catch. The big foredeck is good for sunbathing. *Worst features:* As with the Balboa 20 and RK20, the heavy swing keel can be a nuisance and even dangerous if it is not locked and pinned. (See Class notes on the Internet for details.) Most boats produced included kickup rudders, but some were fixed, and those could be damaged going aground. Deck winches as furnished are too small for yeoman duty. Starboard-mounted mainsheet cam cleat is an inconvenience when on starboard tack. Owner must add his own topping lift. There's no good place to store a portable gas tank.

Comps	LOD	Beam	MinDr	Displ	Bllst	SA/D	D/L	Avg. PHRF	Max. Speed	Motion Index	Space Index	No. of Berths	Head-room
Ensenada 20	20' 0"	7' 1"	1' 0"	1,600	550	20.3	133	288	5.6	9.9	238	4	4' 2"
Balboa 20	20' 0"	7' 1"	1' 9"	1,700	450	20.4	142	276	5.6	10.5	252	4	4' 0"
RK20	20' 0"	7' 1"	1' 9"	1,700	550	21.8	142	264	5.6	10.5	222	4	3' 9"

ETAP 20
Unsinkable sloop from Belgium

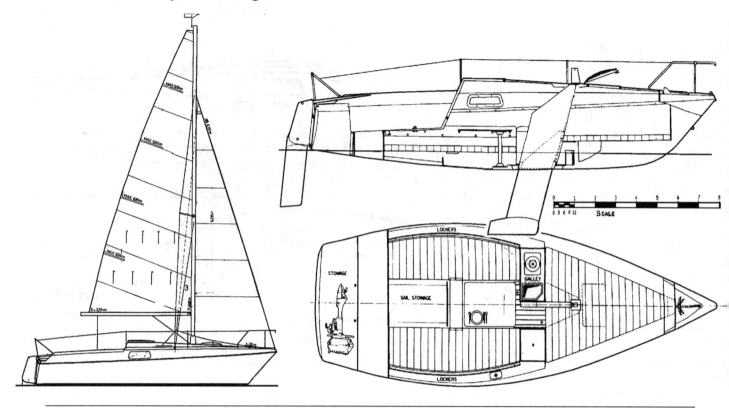

LOD:	19' 10"	**Designer:**	E. G. Van de Stadt
LOA:	21' 4"	**Builder:**	ETAP (Belgium)
LWL:	17' 0"	**Years produced:**	1985–1995?
Min./max. draft:	1' 6"/3' 9"	**Sail area:**	175 sq. ft.
Bridge clearance:	29' 0"	**Fuel tankage:**	portable
Power:	outboard 3 to 6 hp	**Water tankage:**	portable
B/D ratio:	29%	**Approx. trailering wgt.:**	2,200 lbs.

This nicely conceived 20-footer was introduced in Europe in 1980 and in the U.S. in 1985, by Belgian builder ETAP (acronym for Electro Technical Apparatus, a diversified manufacturer of lighting, aluminum, and fiberglass products, which entered the boatbuilding business in 1970). *Best features:* Like the firm's other small sailboats (including the ETAP 22i and ETAP 23), the ETAP 20 is built to a very high standard, and is unsinkable. The boats have double-skinned closed-cell foam-filled compartments similar to the old Boston Whaler, which not only provide flotation but also stiffness and insulation. Space Index is good, and headroom is highest compared to comps. Designated stowage space for sails and outboard engine, and a stowable dining-and-chart table, are nice touches. The foam flotation is precisely distributed so when the hull is filled with water, the boat still floats level. The lifting keel with bulb at bottom keeps center of gravity low when lowered and gives easy trailering when raised using self-locking worm drive, operated from on deck. *Worst features:* None to speak of.

Comps	LOD	Beam	MinDr	Displ	Bllst	SA/D	D/L	Avg. PHRF	Max. Speed	Motion Index	Space Index	No. of Berths	Head-room
Alerion Express Cat 19	19' 2"	8' 6"	1' 2"	1,450	450	34.0	121	NA	5.6	7.1	313	2	3' 6"
Capri 18	18' 0"	7' 7"	2' 0"	1,500	425	18.9	149	NA	5.4	9.0	248	2	3' 6"
ETAP 20	19' 10"	7' 6"	1' 6"	1,500	441	21.4	136	NA	5.5	8.8	278	4	4' 0"
Windrose 5.5 (18)	18' 0"	8' 0"	2' 3"	1,500	500	18.6	163	288	5.4	8.7	228	4	3' 9"

Golif 21

Early pocket cruiser from Jouet & Co. in France

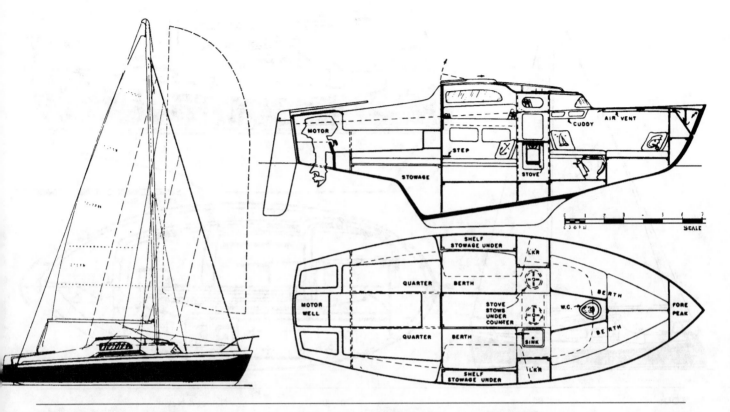

LOD:	21' 0"	**Designer:**	Jouet & Co.
LOA:	22' 6"	**Builder:**	Jouet & Co.
LWL:	19' 5"	**Years produced:**	1963–1970?
Min./max. draft:	3' 2"	**Sail area:**	229 sq. ft.
Bridge clearance:	30' 6"	**Fuel tankage:**	portable
Power:	outboard 3 to 6 hp	**Water tankage:**	portable
B/D ratio:	37%	**Approx. trailering wgt.:**	4,200 lbs.

This interesting French design, imported to the United States by Ersco Boats from Sartouville, France, appeared early in the era of molded fiberglass. Among the many unusual ideas incorporated in the design is (A) a wraparound "windshield" at the forward end of the cabin, and (B) the ventilating system, which takes in air through small holes at the bow into a watertight space built into the forepeak, as shown in the profile view. There the incoming air, along with whatever spray or solid water splashes in, are separated. The air flows aft through a duct into the cabin, and

the water drains by gravity back to the sea through a hole at the bottom of the compartment. ***Best features:*** The motor well, built into the aft end of the cockpit directly ahead of the outboard rudder, helps make steering under power more responsive. The heavy keel, relatively narrow beam and long waterline, and high-aspect sailplan all add up to a comfortable sea boat (if there can be such a thing in only 21 feet of length). The unusually long quarter berths are also admirable. ***Worst features:*** The forward berths are too short and narrow at the foot for two adults.

Comps	LOD	Beam	MinDr	Displ	Bllst	SA/D	D/L	Avg. PHRF	Max. Speed	Motion Index	Space Index	No. of Berths	Head-room
Mistral T-21	21' 0"	8' 2"	1' 2"	2,800	750	19.5	192	234	5.8	13.3	371	5	4' 8"
Golif 21	21' 0"	7' 5"	3' 2"	2,860	1,056	18.2	174	264	5.9	15.0	333	4	5' 0"
Chrysler 22 (21)	21' 2"	7' 9"	1' 11"	2,900	725	17.3	189	270	5.8	14.7	313	5	4' 4"
Buccaneer 210 (21)	20' 10"	8' 0"	2' 0"	3,000	900	13.8	217	300	5.7	15.0	398	6	5' 8"

Halman 20
Lookalike: Halman or Nordica?

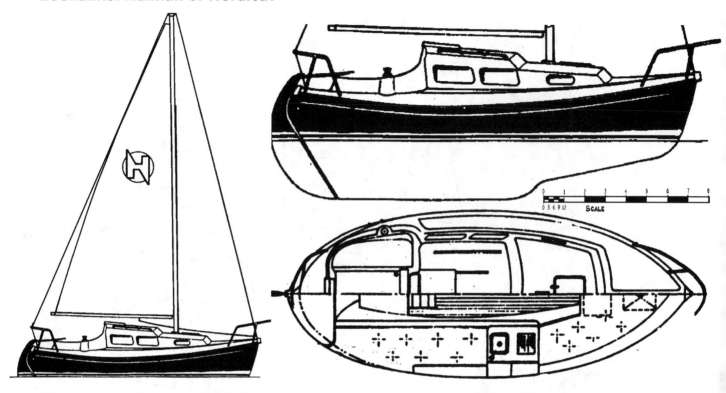

LOD:	19' 6"		**Designer:**	Nisket & Navin
LOA:	21' 2"		**Builder:**	Halman Mfg. Co.
LWL:	16' 6"		**Years produced:**	1977?–1989?
Min./max. draft:	2' 10"		**Sail area:**	182 sq. ft.
Bridge clearance:	29' 0"		**Fuel tankage:**	portable
Power:	outboard 3 to 6 hp		**Water tankage:**	portable
B/D ratio:	40%		**Approx. trailering wgt.:**	3,600 lbs.

For comments on the similarities and differences between the Nordica 20 and the Halman 20, see the sheet on the Nordica (page 117). The Halman Manufacturing Company of Beamsville, Ontario, built this boat, and also at one time or another built (among other boats) the Bluejacket 23 (page 222) and the Shark 24 (page 312). After a few years of selling the Halman 20, the builders added a bowsprit, and without otherwise lengthening the boat, began calling her the Halman 21. (They also increased the sail area somewhat, added bronze port lights, led halyards aft to the cockpit, and—surprise!—increased the price.) ***Best features:***

Comments on the Nordica 20 also apply to the Halman. Also: the doghouse is raised a bit more than on the Nordica, giving an extra six inches of headroom on the Halman. The beamy hulls give good space below. ***Worst features:*** Compared to the heavier, narrower Corinthian, a comp, both the Halman and the Nordica can be expected to be slower, especially in light air, due to their higher wetted surface. And neither the Halman nor the Nordica can match the sailing performance of the other comp, the centerboarder Quickstep 21, with her two-foot longer waterline, bigger sail area, and deeper draft with her board down.

Comps	LOD	Beam	MinDr	Displ	Bllst	SA/D	D/L	Avg. PHRF	Max. Speed	Motion Index	Space Index	No. of Berths	Head-room
Quickstep 21	20' 10"	8' 0"	1' 11"	2,500	950	17.5	176	NA	5.8	12.3	316	4	4' 3"
Halman 20	19' 6"	7' 9"	2' 10"	2,500	1,000	15.8	248	276	5.4	14.0	295	4	5' 0"
Nordica 20	19' 6"	7' 8"	3' 3"	2,520	1,020	15.7	250	276	5.4	14.7	292	4	5' 0"
Corinthian (20)	19' 6"	6' 6"	2' 9"	2,724	1,100	15.3	399	292	5.1	21.6	216	2	4' 2"

Harpoon 6.2 (20)

Boston Whaler's brief venture into sailboats

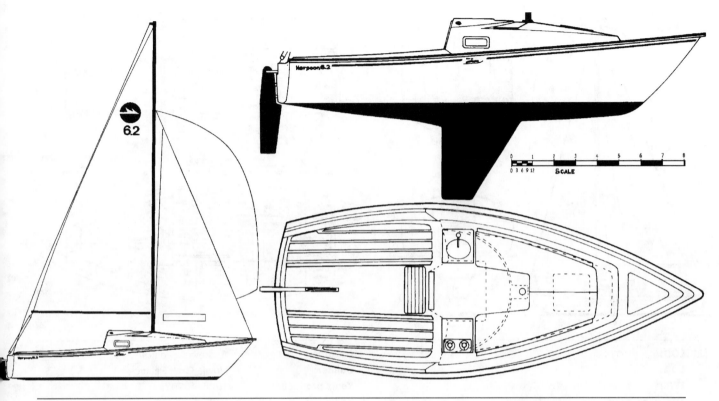

LOD:	20' 4"	**Designer:**	C&C Design Group
LOA:	21' 4"	**Builder:**	Boston Whaler
LWL:	15' 10"	**Years produced:**	1981–1984
Min./max. draft:	3' 6"	**Sail area:**	220 sq. ft.
Bridge clearance:	28' 6"	**Fuel tankage:**	portable
Power:	outboard 2 to 4 hp	**Water tankage:**	portable
B/D ratio:	32%	**Approx. trailering wgt.:**	2,400 lbs.

For a few years in the early 1980s, Boston Whaler went into the sailboat business, producing a "5.2" (17 feet long) and a "6.2" as shown here. Both boats were thickly cored with foam to make them stiff and unsinkable. Some fleets still exist today, as indicated on Internet sites. **Best features:** The Harpoon 6.2 comes close to the best racing sailers among her comps, the Antrim 20 and the Mystic Mini-Ton 21, but we don't think she makes the grade in terms of beauty or grace. **Worst features:** A short waterline and relatively shallower and lighter ballast keeps her racing performance from equalling the Antrim or the Mini-Ton. Space below is equal to the roomy Antrim, but is not laid out as well—and includes only two berths, not four as with all her comps. Prices for used boats may be higher than what may seem rational, based on the hypnotic drawing power of the Boston Whaler name.

Comps	LOD	Beam	MinDr	Displ	Bllst	SA/D	D/L	Avg. PHRF	Max. Speed	Motion Index	Space Index	No. of Berths	Head- room
Harpoon 6.2 (20)	20' 4"	8' 0"	3' 6"	1,700	550	24.7	191	234	5.3	9.5	339	2	4' 3"
Jeanneau Bahia 23 (20)	20' 4"	7' 11"	1' 5"	1,850	620	22.3	140	177	5.7	9.4	339	4	4' 11"
Mystic Mini-Ton 21 (20)	20' 3"	7' 11"	4' 0"	1,850	700	22.6	168	219	5.5	9.9	313	4	4' 0"
Antrim 20	20' 5"	8' 0"	4' 0"	1,850	750	29.7	154	NA	5.6	9.7	339	4	4' 4"
Precision 21	20' 9"	8' 3"	1' 9"	1,875	600	21.4	156	270	5.6	9.4	317	4	4' 4"

Heritage 20
Clever design with her head in her bilge

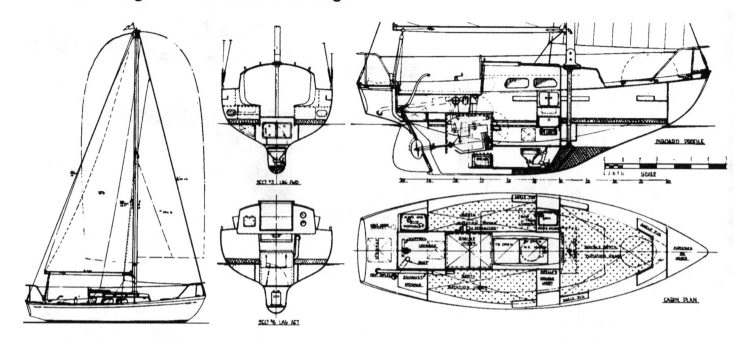

LOD:	20' 0"	**Designer:**	Andrew Davidhazy
LOA:	20' 0"	**Builder:**	Howie Craft Plastics
LWL:	15' 0"	**Years produced:**	1966–1970?
Min./max. draft:	2' 9"	**Sail area:**	240 sq. ft.
Bridge clearance:	31' 0"	**Fuel tankage:**	portable of 15 gal.
Power:	outboard or inboard dsl. 4 to 10 hp	**Water tankage:**	15 gal.
B/D ratio:	32%	**Approx. trailering wgt.:**	4,700 lbs.

Hungarian naval architect Andrew Davidhazy (1911–2003) graduated as an engineer, and then worked in shipyards and as a ship's captain, was a draftsman for the well-known yacht design firm of John G. Alden in Boston, and later designed tankers, tugs, and hydrofoil ships. The most unusual feature of the Heritage 20 is her extra-wide keel, big enough to contain a marine toilet (though we wonder how the waste is pumped uphill to a seacock without backflow, in the good old days before the advent of holding tanks). ***Best features:*** Perhaps it is no accident that the Heritage's shape bears a strong resemblance to the beauteous profiles of John Alden's designs, since her designer worked in the Alden office. Her curved stem and stern counter could be right out of an Alden style book. Pretty! Despite her shallow draft and tall rig, Heritage will probably sail better than her comps, none of which is deeper; her high SA/D will make her relatively faster in light air. ***Worst features:*** Even with the trick cabin sole, there's not much room below. Big and tall people beware!

Comps	LOD	Beam	MinDr	Displ	Bllst	SA/D	D/L	Avg. PHRF	Max. Speed	Motion Index	Space Index	No. of Berths	Head-room
Companion 21	20' 6"	7' 1"	2' 9"	3,000	1,000	16.8	327	303	5.4	19.6	245	4	4' 7"
Heritage 20	20' 0"	6' 6"	2' 9"	3,100	1,000	18.1	410	NA	5.2	23.8	235	4	4' 7"
Sea Islander 20	20' 0"	7' 6"	2' 2"	3,180	886	14.9	289	NA	5.5	18.6	294	4	4' 4"
Seaforth Coastal Cruiser 21	20' 6"	7' 4"	2' 6"	4,000	1,600	13.8	363	NA	5.5	22.6	276	2	4' 4"

Holder 20

High-performance keelboat by Hobie Cat

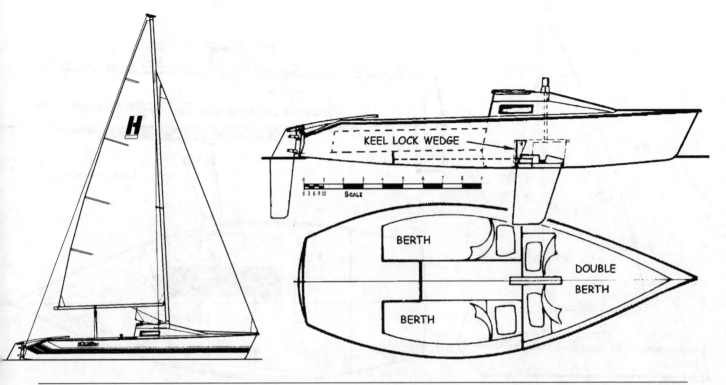

KEEL LOCK WEDGE

BERTH

DOUBLE BERTH

BERTH

SCALE

LOD:	20' 4"
LOA:	21' 10"
LWL:	18' 5"
Min./max. draft:	fixed keel 3' 7"
Bridge clearance:	29' 0"
Power:	outboard 2 to 4 hp
B/D ratio:	29%

Designer:	Ron Holder
Builder:	Hobie Cat
Years produced:	1980–1987
Sail area:	198 sq. ft.
Fuel tankage:	portable
Water tankage:	portable
Approx. trailering wgt.:	1,725 lbs.

The Holder 20 was designed by Ron Holder in the early 1980s, in collaboration with Olympic racer and sailmaker Dave Ullman. The boat is typically raced in one-design fleets, with a crew of three. **Best features:** The Holder 20 is light enough to plane in a modest breeze. A long, wide cockpit offers plenty of room for crew in optimizing weight position and sail handling. A "drop" keel (fixed but retractable for trailering) makes launching relatively easy. The boat has an active class association with a presence on the Internet. We can't fully explain the big divergence of average PHRF ratings amongst her comps, though the Hotfoot certainly has

the edge on SA/D and D/L ratios. Perhaps the Hotfoot's rating is too low and the Mirage's rating is too high? **Worst features:** Crew weight is crucial for stability on a boat this small and light. Hence the Holder 20 is not recommended for carefree family daysailing. The hull can't deal with rough water; owners say you can feel the hull flex and the drop keel begin to move around in a chop. The boat can be—and has been—capsized when sailed aggressively. Despite the pretense of cruising accommodations, we'd shy away from spending even one night aboard such a confined space. As one owner put it: "The cabin is strictly for storage."

Comps	LOD	Beam	MinDr	Displ	Bllst	SA/D	D/L	Avg. PHRF	Max. Speed	Motion Index	Space Index	No. of Berths	Head-room
Hotfoot 20	20' 0"	8' 6"	1' 6"	1,000	400	36.0	77	159	5.7	4.8	216	4	2' 7"
Holder 20	20' 4"	7' 10"	1' 2"	1,160	335	28.7	83	185	5.8	6.0	220	4	3' 5"
Mirage 5.5 (20)	20' 0"	8' 0"	1' 6"	1,200	320	26.9	103	231	5.6	6.4	240	4	3' 0"

Hunter 20
20-footer with a dinette

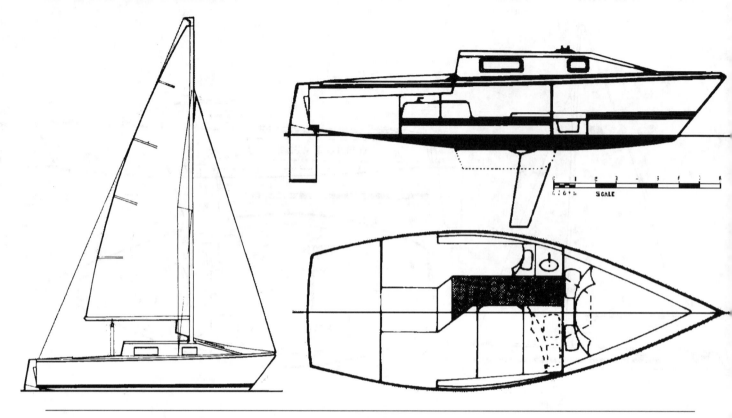

LOD:	19' 8"	**Designer:**	Cortland Steck
LOA:	20' 8"	**Builder:**	Hunter Marine
LWL:	15' 6"	**Years produced:**	1982–1984
Min./max. draft:	1' 3"/4' 0"	**Sail area:**	170 sq. ft.
Bridge clearance:	29' 6"	**Fuel tankage:**	portable
Power:	outboard 3 to 6 hp	**Water tankage:**	5 gal.
B/D ratio:	24%	**Approx. trailering wgt.:**	2,400 lbs.

The Luhrs family originally built powerboats on the New Jersey coast, until 1973, when young Warren Luhrs created Hunter Marine and started making sailboats, targeting the lower priced market. Since then Hunter (not to be confused with the British builder Hunter Boats a.k.a. British Hunter) has evolved into one of the largest, if not the largest, volume producer of low- and mid-priced sailing yachts, in direct competition with Catalina Yachts and Beneteau. The Hunter 25 was introduced in 1973, and the 22 and 20 in 1982. **Best features:** Compared to her comps, the Hunter 20 is small. She is shortest on LOD, has the lowest ballast and the highest D/L (with by far the shortest waterline), and ties for lowest displacement. Nevertheless the accommodations, while not spacious, are cleverly arranged to include a dinette, complete with table and facing seats. A galley slides forward from under the cockpit when needed. **Worst features:** The forward V-berth does not provide adequate room for two adults to share.

Comps	LOD	Beam	MinDr	Displ	Bllst	SA/D	D/L	Avg. PHRF	Max. Speed	Motion Index	Space Index	No. of Berths	Head-room
Hunter 20	19' 8"	7' 6"	1' 3"	1,700	400	19.1	204	276	5.3	10.5	258	5	4' 2"
Sovereign 20	20' 0"	7' 2"	2' 0"	1,700	600	21.2	154	NA	5.5	11.6	237	4	4' 2"
Hunter 212 (21)	21' 0"	8' 2"	0' 10"	1,800	135	23.0	138	216	5.7	8.7	329	4	4' 4"
Aquarius 21	21' 0"	7' 10"	1' 0"	1,900	665	18.9	140	273	5.7	9.9	300	4	4' 6"
Spirit 6.5 (21)	21' 3"	7' 10"	1' 8"	2,100	550	19.1	142	261	5.8	10.7	334	4 to 5	4' 4"

Hunter 212 (21)
An experiment in new materials

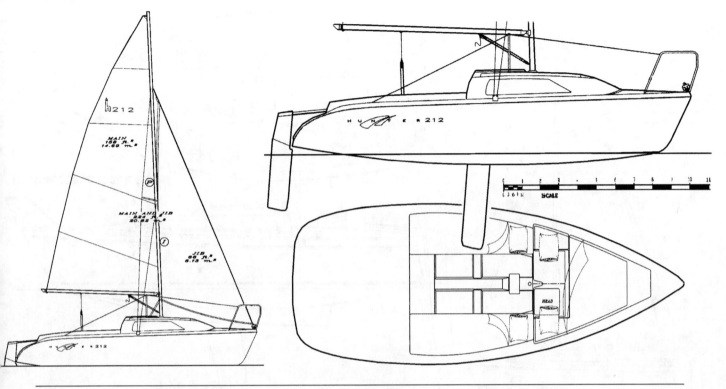

LOD:	21' 0"
LOA:	22' 5"
LWL:	18' 0"
Min./max. draft:	0' 10"/5' 0"
Bridge clearance:	31' 0"
Power:	outboard 3 to 6 hp
B/D ratio:	8%

Designer:	Glenn Henderson
Builder:	Hunter Marine
Years produced:	1998–2002
Sail area:	213 sq. ft.
Fuel tankage:	portable
Water tankage:	portable
Approx. trailering wgt.:	2,600 lbs.

The Hunter 212 shares the same bulbous "modern" look with several other Hunter boats, but is different in that she is made with a non-fiberglass plastic material Hunter ads identified only as ACP, or Advanced Composite Process—"five times more impact resistant than fiberglass"—and the hulls were molded by JY Sailboats in a joint venture arrangement. The construction involves a sandwich with a 1/8" thick sheet of ABS plastic, and an inch or more of closed cell foam with a fiberglass mat backing. *Best features:* With a board-up draft of ten inches and an optional mast raising device that is designed for one person to use, the Hunter 212 should be easier than most of her comps to launch at a ramp. *Worst features:* The only ballast is the 135-pound weighted centerboard, so practically all the vessel's stability is derived from the form of the hull plus the crew's weight. From this we would guess her stability in a breeze would be considerably worse than any of her comps. As for the "ACP" material, it requires special adhesives to bond repairs. Plain resins, epoxy, or marine fillers won't stick and hold.

Comps	LOD	Beam	MinDr	Displ	Bllst	SA/D	D/L	Avg. PHRF	Max. Speed	Motion Index	Space Index	No. of Berths	Head-room
Hunter 20	19' 8"	7' 6"	1' 3"	1,700	400	19.1	204	276	5.3	10.5	258	5	4' 2"
Sovereign 20	20' 0"	7' 2"	2' 0"	1,700	600	21.2	154	NA	5.5	10.6	237	4	4' 2"
Hunter 212 (21)	21' 0"	8' 2"	0' 10"	1,800	135	23.0	138	216	5.7	8.7	329	4	4' 4"
Aquarius 21	21' 0"	7' 10"	1' 0"	1,900	665	18.9	140	273	5.7	9.9	300	4	4' 6"
Spirit 6.5 (21)	21' 3"	7' 10"	1' 8"	2,100	550	19.1	142	261	5.8	10.7	334	4 to 5	4' 4"

Jeanneau Bahia 23 (20)

French entry in the microcruiser sweepstakes

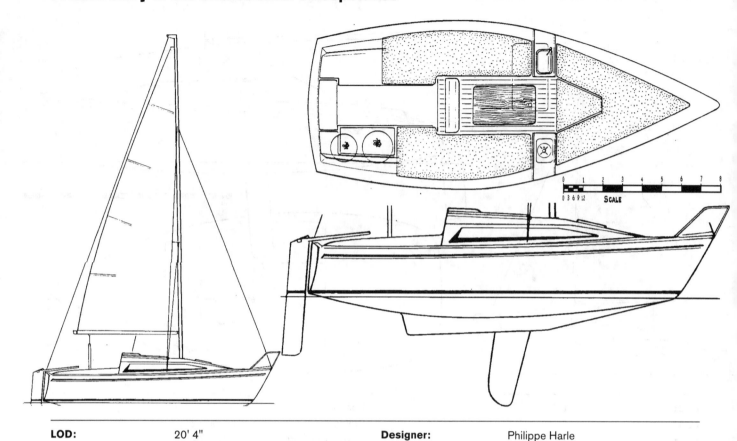

LOD:	20' 4"	**Designer:**	Philippe Harle
LOA:	21' 11"	**Builder:**	Jeanneau
LWL:	18' 1"	**Years produced:**	1984–1987
Min./max. draft:	1' 5"/4' 9"	**Sail area:**	210 sq. ft.
Bridge clearance:	31' 0"	**Fuel tankage:**	portable
Power:	outboard 3 to 6 hp	**Water tankage:**	portable
B/D ratio:	34%	**Approx. trailering wgt.:**	2,700 lbs.

The Bahia 23 (22' 9" LOA if you include both the outboard rudder and the bow pulpit in the length, but only 20' 4" LOD and 21' 11" LOA measured the conventional way) was built in France, and some few hulls were imported to the United States. As with many other French designs, a lot of thought has gone into the execution. ***Best features:*** The cabin arrangement is better than the average 20-footer's. Headroom is almost five feet, best of the comp group. Settee berths are both in the range of 7' 0" to 7' 6" long.

A central table folds down, and also swings to one side for ingress and egress, or fore and aft for dining or other social activity. A companionway step can also serve as a bench at the table. On deck, lifeline stanchions have fixing points for beaching legs to hold the hull upright, in case you get caught on a falling tide. ***Worst features:*** The main hatch is hinged at the forward end, rather than sliding fore and aft, which limits headroom as well as visibility for those who like to stand in the companionway to look around.

Comps	LOD	Beam	MinDr	Displ	Bllst	SA/D	D/L	Avg. PHRF	Max. Speed	Motion Index	Space Index	No. of Berths	Head-room
Harpoon 6.2 (20)	20' 4"	8' 0"	3' 6"	1,700	550	24.7	191	234	5.3	9.5	339	2	4' 3"
Jeanneau Bahia 23 (20)	20' 4"	7' 11"	1' 5"	1,850	620	22.3	140	177	5.7	9.4	339	4	4' 11"
Mystic Mini-Ton 21 (20)	20' 3"	7' 11"	4' 0"	1,850	700	22.6	168	219	5.5	9.9	313	4	4' 0"
Antrim 20	20' 5"	8' 0"	4' 0"	1,850	750	29.7	154	NA	5.6	9.7	339	4	4' 4"
Precision 21	20' 9"	8' 3"	1' 9"	1,875	600	21.4	156	270	5.6	9.4	317	4	4' 4"

Matilda 20
Trailerable import from Canada

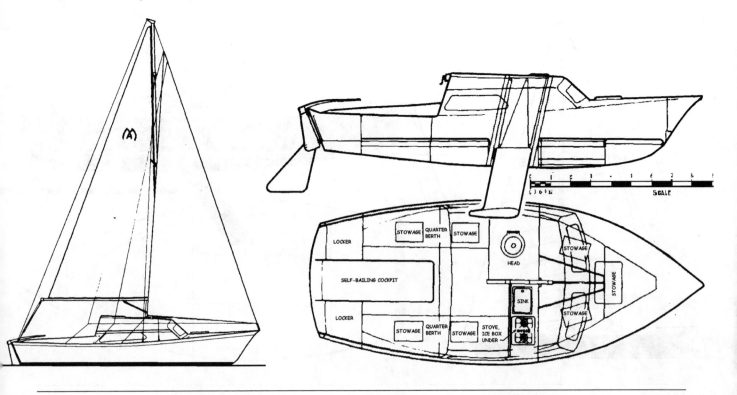

LOD:	19' 6"	**Designer:**	Robert Tucker
LOA:	19' 9"	**Builder:**	Ouyang Boatworks
LWL:	16' 4"	**Years produced:**	1970–1979?
Min./max. draft:	0' 9"/4' 2"	**Sail area:**	195 sq. ft.
Bridge clearance:	27' 0"	**Fuel tankage:**	portable
Power:	outboard 3 to 6 hp	**Water tankage:**	portable
B/D ratio:	19%	**Approx. trailering wgt.:**	2,150 lbs.

The Matilda 20 was created by British designer Robert Tucker and imported to the U.S. from Ouyang Boatworks in Whitby, Ontario. Other manufacturers supplied fractionally rigged, hard-chine, plywood versions of the boat to other markets from plants in the United Kingdom, South Africa, and Australia, but all the Matilda 20s produced by Ouyang have round-bilge fiberglass hulls and a masthead rig with a relatively larger foretriangle. The design features a relatively wide beam for her length (a characteristic shared by both of her comps). That, combined with her full-width cabin house (no side decks), makes her relatively roomy,

but also results in a somewhat awkward appearance—and ironically, compared to her higher-topside comps, the Matilda ends up with a lower Space Index. **Best features:** The lifting keel has a bulb at the bottom, helping (along with a high D/L) to give good stability under sail, as well as a motion index higher than her comps. The keel height is controlled by a cockpit mounted winch. Unlike some lifting-keel designs, the Matilda 20 can be sailed with the keel in any position as the occasion demands. **Worst features:** Access to the forward V-berth is through the curtain-enclosed head area, a minor inconvenience.

Comps	LOD	Beam	MinDr	Displ	Bllst	SA/D	D/L	Avg. PHRF	Max. Speed	Motion Index	Space Index	No. of Berths	Head-room
Santana 20	20' 3"	8' 0"	4' 0"	1,350	550	24.4	147	222	5.4	7.5	259	4	3' 4"
Matilda 20	19' 6"	7' 10"	0' 9"	1,550	300	23.3	159	276	5.4	8.9	219	4	4' 2"
MX 20	19' 7"	8' 0"	3' 11"	1,560	635	27.4	119	189	5.7	8.1	227	4	4' 6"

Mirage 5.5 (20)
Successful lightweight from Ken Fickett

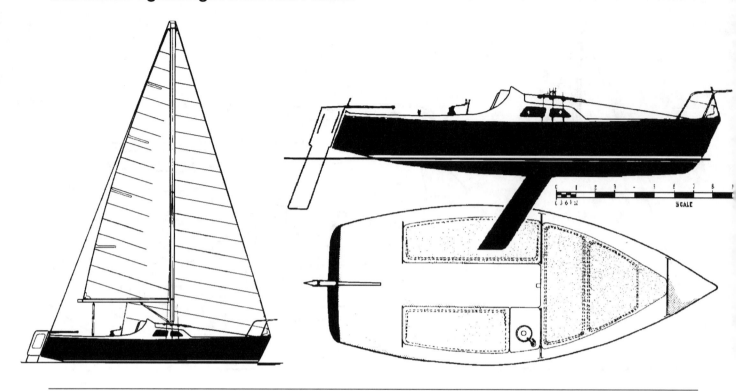

LOD:	20' 0"	**Designer:**	Ken Fickett
LOA:	21' 6"	**Builder:**	Mirage Manufacturing
LWL:	17' 4"	**Years produced:**	1975–1989?
Min./max. draft:	1' 6"/5' 4"	**Sail area:**	190 sq. ft.
Bridge clearance:	29' 6"	**Fuel tankage:**	portable
Power:	outboard 2 to 4 hp	**Water tankage:**	portable
B/D ratio:	27%	**Approx. trailering wgt.:**	1,800 lbs.

The ad copy (in 1987) said that this is "a roomy small cruiser that can be easily trailerered and rigged . . . should perform well in light wind . . . built and equipped with the best materials available and modestly priced." We would argue with the word "roomy" and perhaps the word "cruiser," but the rest sounds plausible; we see her as a pure racer. She is named the "5.5," presumably in meters, but that's eighteen feet, which is neither the waterline length nor the LOD nor the LOA. Go figure. ***Best features:*** The swing keel on the "5.5" seems to us to be more manageable than the lifting keels on both her comps. She features a galley and sink in a cabin with more elbow room (Space Index of 240)—but with headroom of only three feet, who would want to stay below to cook? Her fittings (Harken, Barient, North) are all top-of-the-line, and she comes as standard with internal halyards, boom vang, 3:1 outhaul, cunningham, jiffy reefing, and a perforated toerail. ***Worst features:*** With performance numbers so close to her comps, we question why her PHRF would be 240 versus 168 and 183 for the other two comps. That could be considered as a "plus" to some, but for those who don't want their race course buddies to shun them, maybe it should be counted as a "minus."

Comps	LOD	Beam	MinDr	Displ	Bllst	SA/D	D/L	Avg. PHRF	Max. Speed	Motion Index	Space Index	No. of Berths	Head-room
Hotfoot 20	20' 0"	8' 6"	1' 6"	1,000	400	36.0	77	168	5.7	4.8	216	4	2' 7"
Holder 20	20' 4"	7' 10"	1' 2"	1,160	335	28.7	83	183	5.8	6.0	220	4	3' 5"
Mirage 5.5 (20)	20' 0"	8' 0"	1' 6"	1,200	320	26.9	103	240	5.6	6.4	240	4	3' 0"

Mistral T-21

Canadian entry in the racer/cruiser game

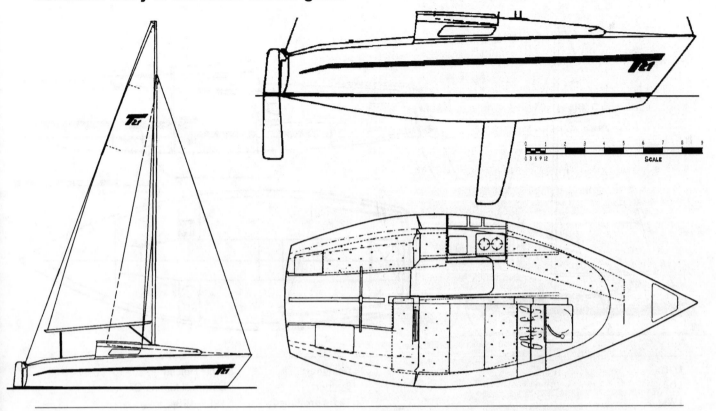

LOD:	21' 0"	Designer:	Mistral Sailboats Inc.
LOA:	21' 11"	Builder:	Mistral Sailboats Inc.
LWL:	18' 8"	Years produced:	1982–1986
Min./max. draft:	1' 2"/5' 1"	Sail area:	280 sq. ft.
Bridge clearance:	33' 0"	Fuel tankage:	portable
Power:	outboard 3 to 6 hp	Water tankage:	portable
B/D ratio:	27%	Approx. trailering wgt.:	4,100 lbs.

Mistral Sailboats Inc. of Longueuil, Quebec, built this beamy vessel in the 1980s. We haven't been able to find much information on her other than what you see here, so our comments are mainly guesses based on a side-by-side comparison with what we deem to be comparable designs. We have no information, for example, on how good the quality of her construction was, or how well she sails in real life as opposed to "on paper." **Best features:** Her layout is very intriguing for a mere 21-footer, encompassing at least two single berths and a double, a dinette, a hanging locker, and a head that, though lacking a door, is virtually "enclosed" in the forepeak. (The literature we have says she has berths for five, but we can't find the fifth one.) With her fully retracting high-aspect centerboard, and drawing only 1' 2" with the board up, she should be easy to launch and retrieve from a trailer. **Worst features:** The drawings seem to indicate that the centerboard is relatively light, perhaps 100 to 200 pounds at most. If so, the ballast, which is reported to be 750 pounds, must be located not far below the waterline, which would seem to make it relatively ineffective.

Comps	LOD	Beam	MinDr	Displ	Bllst	SA/D	D/L	Avg. PHRF	Max. Speed	Motion Index	Space Index	No. of Berths	Head- room
Mistral T-21	21' 0"	8' 2"	1' 2"	2,800	750	22.5	234	234	5.8	13.5	371	5	4' 8"
Golif 21	21' 0"	7' 5"	3' 2"	2,860	1,056	18.2	174	264	5.9	15.0	333	4	4' 9"
Chrysler 22 (21)	21' 2"	7' 9"	1' 11"	2,900	725	17.3	189	270	5.8	14.7	313	5	4' 4"
Buccaneer 210 (21)	20' 10"	8' 0"	2' 0"	3,000	900	15.3	300	285	5.7	15.1	359	6	5' 3"

Montego 20
The Montego 19's slightly bigger sister

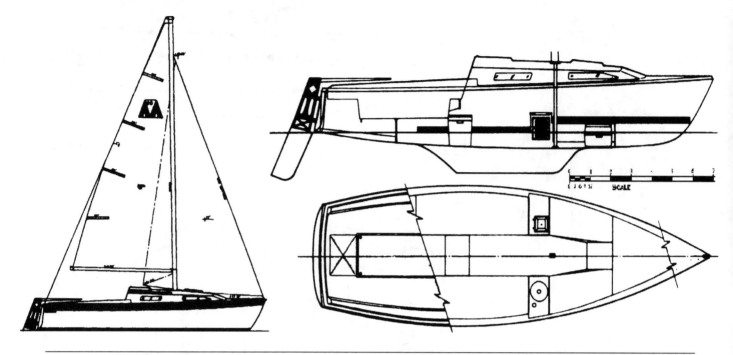

LOD:	19' 6"		**Designer:**	Jopie Helsen
LOA:	20' 3"		**Builder:**	Universal Marine Corp.
LWL:	17' 0"		**Years produced:**	1982–1984
Min./max. draft:	fixed keel 2' 0"		**Sail area:**	166 sq. ft.
Bridge clearance:	27' 3"		**Fuel tankage:**	portable
Power:	outboard 3 to 6 hp		**Water tankage:**	portable
B/D ratio:	26%		**Approx. trailering wgt.:**	3,300 lbs.

The Montego 20 is based on the Montego 19 (page 45) with slightly expanded dimensions and weight. She also has a two-foot deep stub keel in place of a swing keel, which adds 10" to her minimum draft. That in combination with her 2,300 lb. weight (versus 2,150 for the Montego 19) makes her less easily trailered than the Montego 19. A single-burner alcohol stove and a sink came as standard, and a 50-quart ice chest doubles as the companionway step. The mast is deck-stepped above a compression strut. The porta-potti is under the V-berth. **Best features:** She is said to track well, no doubt mainly because of her long stub keel. The seven-foot cockpit is roomy and has high coamings for good back support. Ventilation includes four opening ports in addition to a forward hatch and companionway hatch—great for summer climates. Her average PHRF of 282 seems a bit high, particularly against other similarly shallow fixed-keelers with more top hamper (above-the-water superstructure) like the Buccaneer 200 (page 87). **Worst features:** Her very shallow keel can sideslip, especially in heavy air, reducing speed and pointing ability. The hardware as shipped is minimal; missing are a vang, cunningham, and quick-release jibsheet cleats, along with a better system for cleating the mainsheet. Her particular non-skid deck pattern can be slippery when wet.

Comps	LOD	Beam	MinDr	Displ	Bllst	SA/D	D/L	Avg. PHRF	Max. Speed	Motion Index	Space Index	No. of Berths	Head-room
Chrysler 20	20' 0"	7' 11"	1' 11"	1,950	500	18.3	149	264	5.7	10.1	311	4	3' 9"
Buccaneer 200 (20)	20' 5"	8' 0"	2' 0"	2,100	750	18.6	183	276	5.6	10.9	336	4	3' 6"
Signet 20	19' 10"	6' 8"	2' 0"	2,146	800	18.5	234	NA	5.4	15.4	200	4	4' 0"
Wild Wind 20	20' 0"	7' 11"	2' 0"	2,200	800	18.3	168	NA	5.7	11.5	302	6	4' 3"
Montego 20	19' 6"	7' 2"	2' 0"	2,300	600	17.4	184	282	5.6	14.0	246	4	4' 0"

MX 20
Where does this racer fit in?

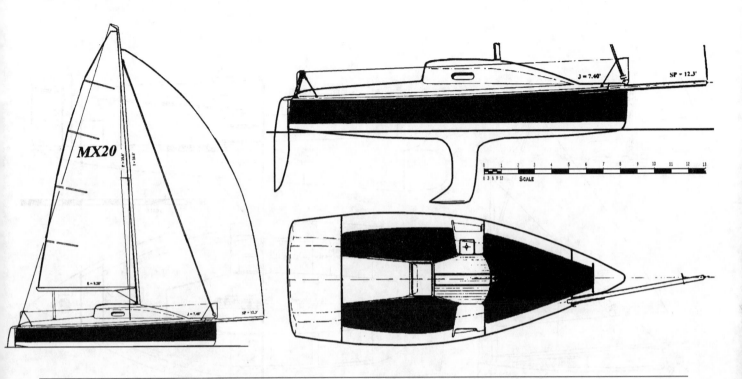

LOD:	19' 9"	**Designer:**	Vladislav Murnikov
LOA:	20' 6"	**Builder:**	Holby Marine
LWL:	18' 9"	**Years produced:**	1994–1996?
Min./max. draft:	fixed keel 3' 11"	**Sail area:**	240 sq. ft.
Bridge clearance:	32' 0"	**Fuel tankage:**	portable
Power:	outboard 3 to 6 hp	**Water tankage:**	portable
B/D ratio:	42%	**Approx. trailering wgt.:**	2,160 lbs.

In 1995 the MX 20 won the *Sailing World* magazine Boat of the Year award for the best daysailer/weekender category. (A different boat, a daysailer, won the PHRF/sportboat category.) With her retractable sprit, huge spinnaker, and streamlined looks, we would have thought the judges might have put her in the sportboat category, but it seems we were mistaken. We can't explain why; her SA/D and D/L certainly point her in that direction—and we can't visualize taking the pre-teen kids on an overnight cruise and dropping the hook in a choppy anchorage in this lightweight streaker. ***Best features:*** Holby Marine is a high-end builder who used balsa core construction and Hall spars. With her round-topped cabin she has a bit more headroom than her comps, at least amidships. ***Worst features:*** Her deep, narrow fin keel and sword-thin rudder look a little fragile for knockabout cruising, and also might attract weed with their vertical leading edges.

Comps	LOD	Beam	MinDr	Displ	Bllst	SA/D	D/L	Avg. PHRF	Max. Speed	Motion Index	Space Index	No. of Berths	Head-room
Santana 20	20' 3"	8' 0"	4' 0"	1,350	550	24.4	147	222	5.4	7.5	259	4	3' 4"
Matilda 20	19' 6"	7' 10"	0' 9"	1,550	300	23.3	159	276	5.4	8.9	219	4	4' 2"
MX 20	19' 7"	8' 0"	3' 11"	1,560	635	27.4	119	189	5.7	8.1	227	4	4' 6"

Mystic Catboat 20
Traditional catboat with a difference

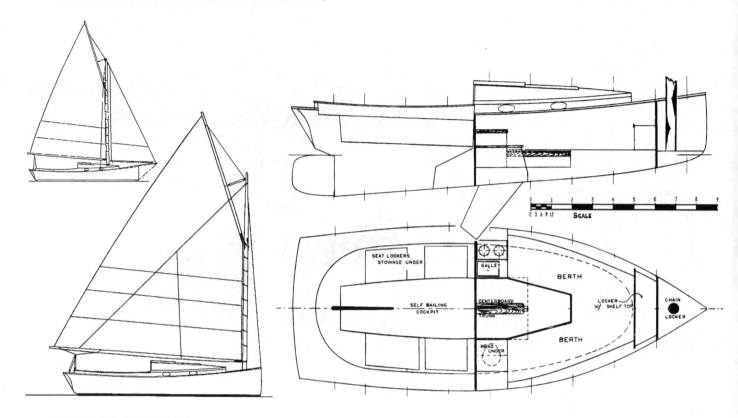

LOD:	20' 0"	**Designer:**	Peter J. Legnos
LOA:	21' 4"	**Builder:**	Legnos Boatbldg. Co.
LWL:	17' 9"	**Years produced:**	1974–1986
Min./max. draft:	1' 10"/4' 3"	**Sail area:**	258 sq. ft.
Bridge clearance:	29' 6"	**Fuel tankage:**	portable or 20 gal.
Power:	outboard or inboard 4 to 8 hp	**Water tankage:**	portable
B/D ratio:	20%	**Approx. trailering wgt.:**	3,450 lbs.

Unlike most of her comps, the Mystic Catboat 20 was designed to resemble a 19th century gentleman's cruising cat rather than a traditional working cat. To a large extent this sealed her fate as a catboat judged to be less seakindly—and therefore less popular—than the "working" cat designs. She was offered with either gasoline or diesel inboard as options, and also was offered as a sloop (see illustration) which may have lessened some of her worst features under sail as enumerated below. ***Best features:*** With her raked, wineglass transom, she is as a pretty as a picture. ***Worst features:*** She lacks many of the salutary features of a typical working cat, such as a big beam-to-length ratio, D/L of at least 200, outboard "barn door" rudder hung on a vertical (not raked) transom, larger rudder and centerboard areas for better control, and big "shoulders" aft to minimize broaching in heavy air and choppy seas.

Comps	LOD	Beam	MinDr	Displ	Bllst	SA/D	D/L	Avg. PHRF	Max. Speed	Motion Index	Space Index	No. of Berths	Head-room
Mystic Catboat 20	20' 0"	8' 0"	1' 10"	2,300	700	23.1	184	315	5.6	11.8	270	2	3' 11"
Herreshoff America 18	18' 2"	8' 0"	1' 10"	2,500	500	22.4	200	324	5.6	13.5	257	2	4' 0"
Com-Pac Horizon Cat 18	18' 2"	8' 4"	2' 2"	2,500	600	17.8	200	NA	5.6	12.4	284	2	4' 6"
Herreshoff Eagle 21	18' 2"	8' 2"	1' 10"	2,700	700	26.4	207	NA	5.7	12.4	264	2	4' 0"
Menger Cat 19	19' 0"	8' 0"	1' 10"	2,900	600	21.2	207	NA	5.8	15.0	267	2	4' 10"

Nautica Flamingo 21
French import by Nautica Corp.

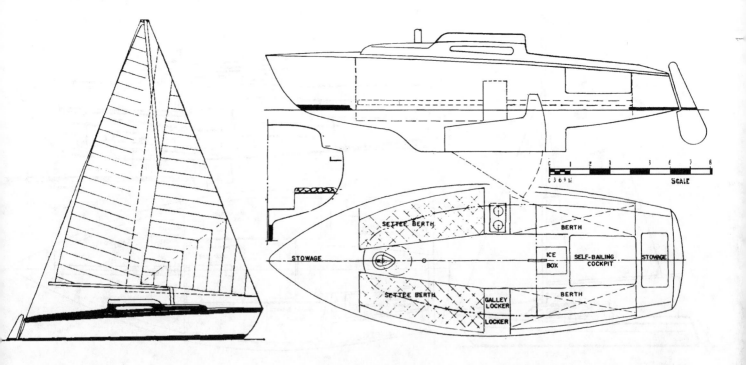

LOD:	20' 8"
LOA:	22' 2"
LWL:	18' 10"
Min./max. draft:	2' 0"/4' 3"
Bridge clearance:	26' 3"
Power:	outboard 3 to 6 hp
B/D ratio:	29%

Designer:	Francois Sergent
Builder:	Lanaverre/Nautica
Years produced:	1971–1973
Sail area:	204 sq. ft.
Fuel tankage:	portable
Water tankage:	portable
Approx. trailering wgt.:	2,650 lbs.

This import was built in France by M. Lanaverre, using the same high-pressure plastic molding technique he did in his successful racing 5-0-5 dinghies (world champion in 1958 through 1960). She comes with a galley area for stove and stowage and an icebox but no sink. ***Best features:*** The boat has foam flotation for safety, and a well (not shown in plans) for an outboard. The layout below, despite the absence of a sink, is well thought out and comfortable-looking. (You can always wash your hands in a plastic bucket.) ***Worst features:*** The reverse sheer on the hull, meant to increase headroom and buoyancy when heeled, may not appeal aesthetically to everyone. The boat's racing pedigree in the 1970s was good, but her relatively high wetted surface, narrow beam, and shallow rudder are no match for more modern designs. The rudder, especially, seems too small to be effective in difficult conditions such as beating in high wind and a severe chop or flying a spinnaker in broaching conditions.

Comps	LOD	Beam	MinDr	Displ	Bllst	SA/D	D/L	Avg. PHRF	Max. Speed	Motion Index	Space Index	No. of Berths	Head-room
Clipper 21	20' 11"	7' 3"	0' 7"	1,800	410	20.9	142	270	5.7	10.5	275	4	3' 9"
Parker Dawson Poacher 21	21' 1"	7' 6"	1' 0"	1,800	550	24.7	144	201	5.6	10.1	358	4	4' 0"
Nautica Flamingo 21	20' 8"	7' 5"	2' 0"	1,870	550	21.5	125	267	5.8	10.3	360	4	4' 1"

Newport 212 (21)

Harry Sindle's unusual centerboard idea

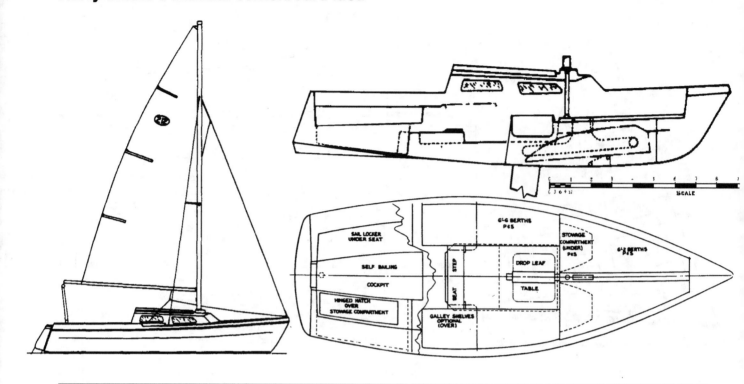

LOD:	21' 2"	**Designer:**	Harry R. Sindle
LOA:	22' 2"	**Builder:**	Newport Boats
LWL:	19' 0"	**Years produced:**	1972–1977
Min./max. draft:	0' 10"/5' 0"	**Sail area:**	177 sq. ft.
Bridge clearance:	28' 0"	**Fuel tankage:**	portable
Power:	outboard 3 to 6 hp	**Water tankage:**	portable
B/D ratio:	27%	**Approx. trailering wgt.:**	2,200 lbs.

Harry Sindle, designer and builder of the Newport 212, first started racing in the mid 1940s in a Lightning. Later he became class champion in several classes, and felt that light weight was a very important advantage in attaining boat speed. "Except in keel boats," said Harry, quoting fellow designer Uffa Fox, "weight is only good in a steamroller." Sindle designed several boats featured in this book, namely the Newport 17, Newport 212, and Newport 214. **Best features:** The biggest advantage of the 212 over her comps is her higher Space Index, a result of comparatively generous freeboard. We also like her spacious cabin layout, complete with dropleaf table, and her shallow draft and smooth bottom with board up, intimating an easy trip on and off a trailer. And her specs make her look faster than her PHRF rating of 267 would indicate, in spite of a somewhat lower S/D, and an extra 100 pounds of displacement compared to her comps. **Worst features:** Immediately noticeable in her inboard profile drawing is her unusual centerboard lifting gear and storage position. All we can say is that it looks complicated, and when it comes to centerboard arrangements, after some bad experiences, we have come to prefer simple.

Comps	LOD	Beam	MinDr	Displ	Bllst	SA/D	D/L	Avg. PHRF	Max. Speed	Motion Index	Space Index	No. of Berths	Head-room
U.S. 21/Triton 21	21' 3"	8' 0"	1' 4"	1,400	200	28.6	107	201	5.7	7.1	299	4	4' 0"
Santana 21	21' 3"	7' 6"	1' 6"	1,400	550	24.2	86	267	5.9	7.4	238	4	3' 10"
Newport 212 (21)	21' 2"	7' 8"	0' 10"	1,500	400	21.6	98	267	5.8	7.6	318	4	4' 2"

Newport 214

Boat with an interesting centerboard configuration

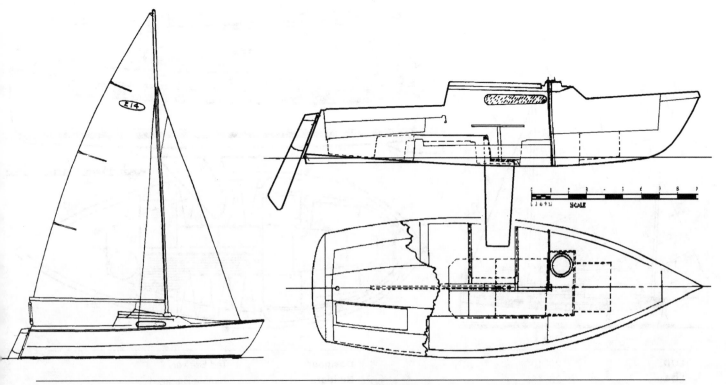

LOD:	21' 2"	**Designer:**	Harry R. Sindle	
LOA:	23' 2"	**Builder:**	Newport Boats	
LWL:	19' 0"	**Years produced:**	1977?–1978?	
Min./max. draft:	0' 9"/5' 0"	**Sail area:**	229 sq. ft.	
Bridge clearance:	30' 0"	**Fuel tankage:**	portable	
Power:	outboard 3 to 6 hp	**Water tankage:**	portable	
B/D ratio:	23%	**Approx. trailering wgt.:**	2,900 lbs.	

The "214" came from the drawing board of Olympic sailor Harry R. Sindle, but we are not sure what to make of her racing ability. The ads say she "will qualify for MORC competition, and performs well in such competition"— but we have not found her handicap listed in our copy of the complete U.S. Sailing PHRF compilation. ***Best features:*** The cabin arrangement seems efficient, with the centerboard trunk forming one wall of the aft dinette seat (but see below for possible problems as a result). Foam flotation is a plus. ***Worst features:*** In the inboard profile view, you can see how the pivot point of the heavy steel centerboard is at the top of the trunk, and the board is cut away to a mere sliver on the aft end to permit the person sitting in the dinette to get in and out without too many contortions. Although we haven't heard of any specific instances of problems, we wouldn't be surprised if the thin section on the board led to trouble with the board bending or trunk crushing at the bottom of the boat. The drawings show a relatively slender mast section with no backstay and a total of only three shrouds— another common source of trouble (such as masts bending in a breeze).

Comps	LOD	Beam	MinDr	Displ	Bllst	SA/D	D/L	Avg. PHRF	Max. Speed	Motion Index	Space Index	No. of Berths	Head-room
Newport 214	21' 2"	7' 7"	0' 9"	2,000	450	23.1	130	NA	5.8	10.4	318	4	4' 0"
Beneteau First 210 (21)	21' 0"	8' 2"	2' 4"	2,200	770	23.0	129	195	5.9	10.3	371	4	4' 6"
S2 6.9 (21)	21' 0"	8' 0"	0' 9"	2,200	770	22.3	149	205	5.8	10.7	328	4	4' 0"
S2 6.7 (21)	21' 0"	8' 0"	0' 10"	2,200	775	21.3	149	205	5.8	10.7	320	4	4' 0"

Nimble 20 (21)
Cute yawl by Ted Brewer

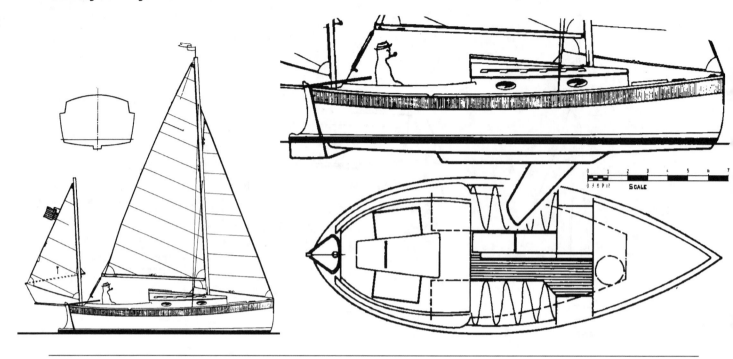

LOD:	20' 10"		**Designer:**	Ted Brewer	
LOA:	25' 4"		**Builder:**	Nimble Boats	
LWL:	19' 9"		**Years produced:**	1986–1991?	
Min./max. draft:	1' 1"/4' 1"		**Sail area:**	207 sq. ft.	
Bridge clearance:	28' 0"		**Fuel tankage:**	portable	
Power:	outboard 3 to 6 hp		**Water tankage:**	14 gal.	
B/D ratio:	36%		**Approx. trailering wgt.:**	3,150 lbs.	

One doesn't see many yawls this small—yet the yawl rig is both practical and fun to deal with. You can sail in strong winds without the main, under jib and "jigger" (i.e., the mizzen). You can control any tendency of the boat to dance around her mooring by hoisting the mizzen alone. You can sometimes balance the helm of an otherwise finicky boat by fine-tuning the mizzen sheet along with the centerboard. And—in the case of the Nimble 20 anyway—we think the yawl rig looks good. Note on displacement: An early sales brochure gives her displacement as 1,650 pounds and her ballast as 400 pounds. A later brochure says she weighs 2,200 pounds and does not mention ballast. Her designer

told us that she was designed to displace 1,800 pounds, including 400 pounds of lead ballast. But lead weighs 708 pounds per cubic foot; we figure there's at least 800 pounds in her, and that's what we report. ***Best features:*** Her traditional looks appeal to us. And the yawl rig suits our taste to a T. ***Worst features:*** Her PHRF is at the high end, indicating that her overall speed potential is below that of her comps, despite her high-end "maximum speed" due to her long waterline. Her speed performance under sail compared to comps is probably a result of a combination of small sail area, split rig, and her hard chine hull shape, which tends to pound a bit in a chop.

Comps	LOD	Beam	MinDr	Displ	Bllst	SA/D	D/L	Avg. PHRF	Max. Speed	Motion Index	Space Index	No. of Berths	Head-room
Sirius 21	21' 2"	7' 11"	1' 4"	2,000	525	20.5	135	258	5.8	10.0	344	5	4' 9"
South Coast 21	21' 4"	6' 11"	3' 0"	2,000	625	19.2	303	252	5.1	14.2	165	2	3' 3"
Sirius 22	21' 2"	7' 11"	1' 4"	2,100	525	19.8	123	243	5.9	9.7	352	5	4' 9"
Nimble 20 (21)	20' 10"	7' 9"	1' 1"	2,200	800	19.6	127	288	6.0	11.0	316	4	4' 3"
Triangle 20 (21)	20' 6"	7' 1"	2' 2"	2,300	800	16.3	222	NA	5.5	14.6	250	2	4' 6"

Nordica 20
Lookalike: Nordica or Halman?

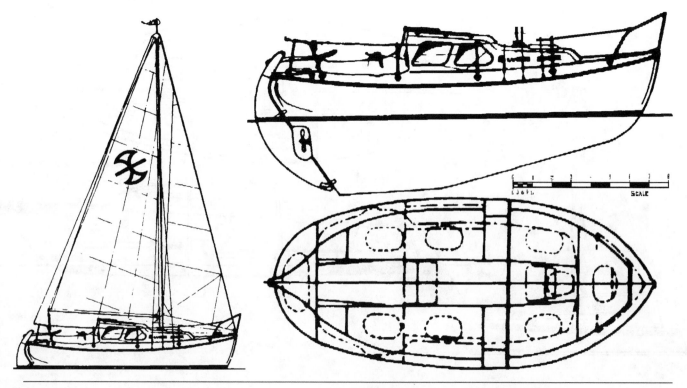

LOD:	19' 6"	**Designer:**	B. Malta-Muller
LOA:	21' 2"	**Builder:**	Exe Fibercraft
LWL:	16' 6"	**Years produced:**	1976?–1983?
Min./max. draft:	fixed keel 3' 3"	**Sail area:**	182 sq. ft.
Bridge clearance:	30' 0"	**Fuel tankage:**	7 gal (inbd only)
Power:	7 hp inboard dsl. or outboard	**Water tankage:**	portable
B/D ratio:	41%	**Approx. trailering wgt.:**	3,700 lbs.

The Nordica 20 is close enough in appearance to the Halman 20 (page 100) that even some owners wonder which brand they have. Still, there are differences, small though they might be. For example, the keel on the Nordica is swept back more than the Halman, is 5" deeper, and the Halman features a small knuckle at the front end, which the Nordica does not. The windows in the Nordica's doghouse are bigger, and the doghouse itself is about six inches lower, decreasing headroom a bit. The Nordica offered an optional inboard engine of about 7 hp, whereas the Halman did not, and the interior layouts were also different. But by and large the boats were very similar. **Best features:** The springy sheer and rounded stern on both the Nordica and Halman give them a salty look. **Worst features:** Both brands have relatively small cockpits; more than two occupants would constitute a crowd. Perhaps that is just as well, since buoyancy aft is limited by the pinched stern; more than two occupants would push the stern down, upsetting the natural trim of the hull. Consequently the extra two berths are pretty much usable only for stowage or in harbor.

Comps	LOD	Beam	MinDr	Displ	Bllst	SA/D	D/L	Avg. PHRF	Max. Speed	Motion Index	Space Index	No. of Berths	Head-room
Quickstep 21	20' 10"	8' 0"	1' 11"	2,500	950	17.5	176	279	5.8	12.3	316	4	4' 4"
Halman 20	19' 6"	7' 9"	2' 10"	2,500	1,000	15.8	248	276	5.4	14.0	295	4	5' 0"
Nordica 20	19' 6"	7' 8"	3' 3"	2,520	1,020	15.7	250	276	5.4	14.7	292	4	5' 0"
Corinthian 19 (20)	19' 6"	6' 6"	2' 9"	2,724	1,100	15.3	399	292	5.1	21.6	216	2	4' 2"

O'Day 22 (21)
This one came in a number of configurations

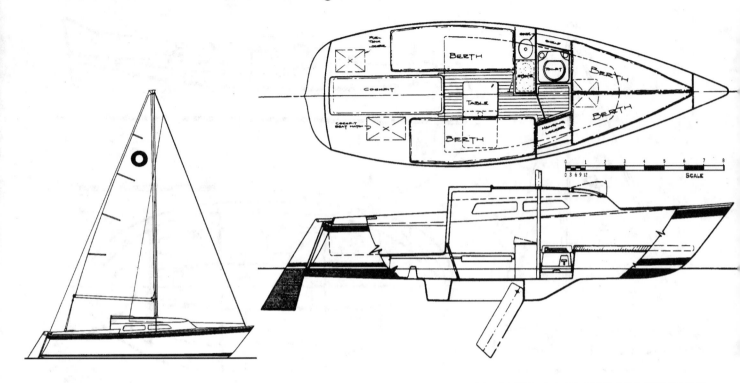

LOD:	20' 10"
LOA:	24' 0"
LWL:	18' 11"
Min./max. draft:	1' 3"/4' 3"
Bridge clearance:	27' 0"
Power:	outboard 3 to 6 hp
B/D ratio:	35%

Designer:	C. Raymond Hunt Assoc.
Builder:	O'Day
Years produced:	1972–1983
Sail area:	196 sq. ft.
Fuel tankage:	portable
Water tankage:	portable
Approx. trailering wgt.:	3,100 lbs.

You could buy an O'Day 22 in a number of configurations: Shoal keel (1' 11" draft) or centerboard (shown here); masthead or ¾ fractional rig; standard or tall rig; settee berths in the cabin or a dinette arrangement. Nowhere in the sales literature does it say that the "22" in the boat's name comes from the overall length of the hull, rather than the length on deck, as is the usual convention. Unfortunately most O'Day boats are named this way. Small and not-so-small changes over the 11 years this boat was produced also add to the confusion; ballast was 600 pounds in early production, then

went to 700, and finally became 800 pounds, strangely with no other changes to the overall weight of the vessel. **Best features:** O'Day produced the 22 with a nice exterior finish. **Worst features:** The rudder is immersed further than the keel on the keel-centerboard model, a no-no when the rudder is fixed in place as this one is. When the keel skims close to a rock but misses it, the rudder may hit and carry away. Also, the position of the mainsheet can interfere with control of the outboard motor, which is not within easy reach of the helmsperson.

Comps	LOD	Beam	MinDr	Displ	Bllst	SA/D	D/L	Avg. PHRF	Max. Speed	Motion Index	Space Index	No. of Berths	Head-room
O'Day 222 (21)	21' 5"	7' 11"	1' 8"	2,200	800	19.6	131	258	5.9	10.4	290	4	4' 1"
AMF 2100	21' 1"	8' 0"	1' 0"	2,200	850	19.8	181	228	5.6	11.4	363	4	4' 3"
O'Day 22 (21)	20' 10"	7' 2"	1' 3"	2,283	800	18.1	150	288	5.8	12.4	294	4	4' 6"
Rhodes Continental 22	21' 6"	8' 0"	2' 8"	2,500	700	18.2	140	334	6.0	11.6	334	4	4' 6"

O'Day 222 (21)
Update of the O'Day 22

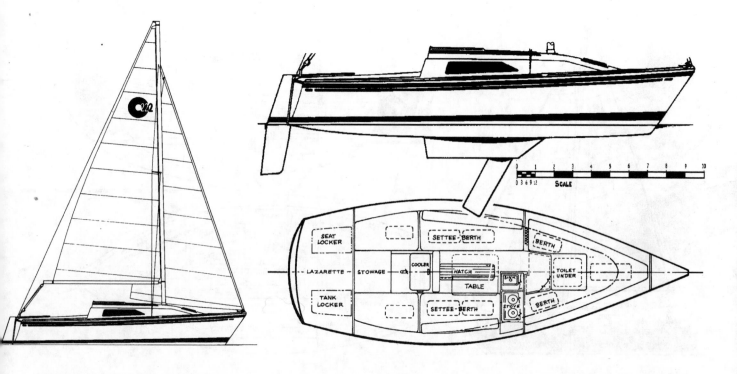

LOD:	21' 5"	**Designer:**	C. Raymond Hunt Assoc.
LOA:	23' 0"	**Builder:**	O'Day Div. of Lear Siegler
LWL:	19' 7"	**Years produced:**	1984–1988
Min./max. draft:	1' 8"/4' 8"	**Sail area:**	207 sq. ft.
Bridge clearance:	29' 6"	**Fuel tankage:**	portable
Power:	outboard 3 to 6 hp	**Water tankage:**	5 gal.
B/D ratio:	36%	**Approx. trailering wgt.:**	3,200 lbs.

The 21- and 22-foot size range is a good length of boat for newish sailors starting out or those moving up from a beach boat or small daysailer. All four boats in this comp group fit that category. The O'Day 222 shown here is a follow-on to the popular O'Day 22 (page 118). The 222 has a deeper board-up draft, but also a deeper board-down draft, which improves upwind performance. ***Best features:*** The O'Day 222's size and modest sailplan and masthead rig make her relatively simple to sail. ***Worst features:*** Her Space Index is lowest of the comp group, as is her headroom. Beware, big and tall people. Her outboard is mounted on her transom, a long way from the helmsman's control. The mainsheet, led aft to the transom, can become entangled with the outboard under certain conditions; some owners have installed a traveler in the forward end of the cockpit to eliminate this problem. The O'Day 222's rudder was made in a sandwich of two fiberglass skins with foam in between. Owners report their rudders are easily broken (e.g., carried away for the same reason as the O'Day 22's rudder). Chainplates also seem to be a weak point, and bear frequent inspection.

Comps	LOD	Beam	MinDr	Displ	Bllst	SA/D	D/L	Avg. PHRF	Max. Speed	Motion Index	Space Index	No. of Berths	Head- room
O'Day 222 (21)	21' 5"	7' 11"	1' 8"	2,200	800	19.6	131	258	5.9	10.4	290	4	4' 1"
AMF 2100	21' 1"	8' 0"	1' 0"	2,200	850	19.8	181	228	5.6	11.4	363	4	4' 3"
O'Day 22 (21)	20' 10"	7' 2"	1' 3"	2,283	800	18.1	150	288	5.8	12.4	294	4	4' 6"
Rhodes Continental 22	21' 6"	8' 0"	2' 8"	2,500	700	18.2	140	334	6.0	11.6	334	4	4' 6"

Pacific Seacraft Flicka 20

Cute and elegant pocket cruiser

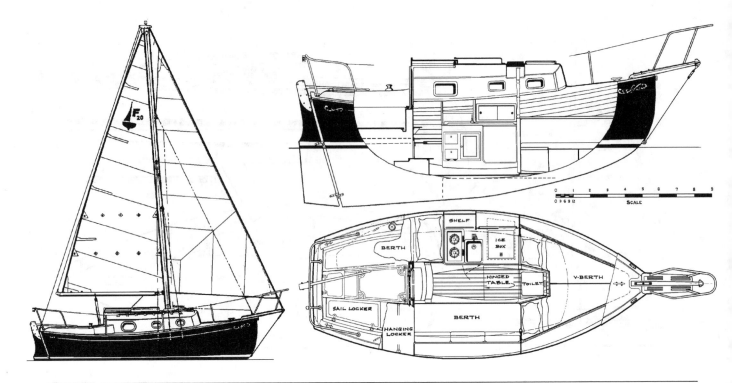

LOD:	20' 0"	Designer:	Bruce Bingham
LOA:	24' 0"	Builder:	(mainly) Pacific Seacraft
LWL:	18' 2"	Years produced:	1975–1998
Min./max. draft:	fixed keel 3' 3"	Sail area:	252 sq. ft.
Bridge clearance:	30' 11"	Fuel tankage:	12 gal.
Power:	Yanmar 9 hp or outboard	Water tankage:	20 gal.
B/D ratio:	33%	Approx. trailering wgt.:	7,800 lbs.

The Flicka ("happy little girl" in Swedish) is a stiff and stable midget cruise-maker, originally built in wood. Nor'star on the United States west coast began fiberglass production in 1975, selling both kits and completed boats. Home-built versions have included cutters, yawls, sloops, schooners, and even junk-rigged. In 1978 Pacific Seacraft bought the tooling and built over 400 Flicka sloops and cutters, ceasing production in 1998. Flickas are considered a very high-quality product, and generally command a premium price in the used market. ***Best features:*** Small size but heavy construction make Flicka a very seaworthy and comfortable singlehander, with adequate space for a couple. (Layouts over the years have included two, three, and four berths.) Headroom is excellent for a 20-footer. The design is pretty, and attracts admiring attention wherever she goes. ***Worst features:*** Being very heavy for her length, she won't reach hull speed under sail until the wind pipes up.

Comps	LOD	Beam	MinDr	Displ	Bllst	SA/D	D/L	Avg. PHRF	Max. Speed	Motion Index	Space Index	No. of Berths	Head-room
Pacific Seacraft Flicka 20	20' 0"	8' 0"	3' 3"	5,500	1,800	12.9	410	288	5.7	26.6	443	3 or 4	5' 11"
Bluejacket 23	23' 0"	10' 0"	2' 3"	6,000	700	9.5	300	NA	6.1	20.0	403	2	6' 2"
Herreshoff Prudence 23	22' 9"	8' 0"	3' 0"	6,800	1,600	16.4	394	NA	6.0	31.7	408	2	4' 9"
Falmouth Cutter (22)	22' 0"	8' 0"	3' 6"	7,400	2,500	15.0	365	NA	6.1	30.0	651	3	5' 11"

Parker Dawson Poacher 21

An unusual cat ketch with wishbone booms

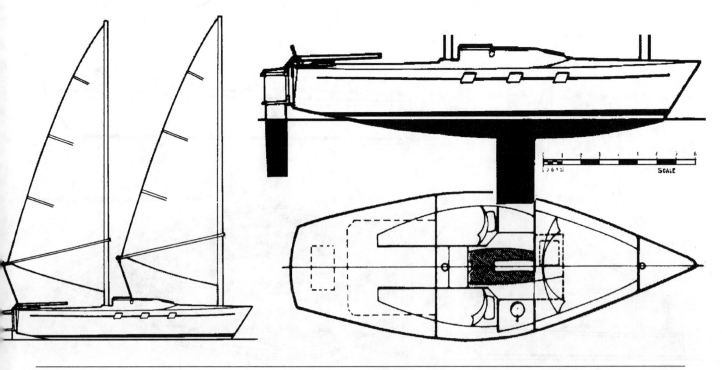

LOD:	21' 1"	**Designer:**	W. Richardson
LOA:	22' 4"	**Builder:**	Parker Dawson Yachts
LWL:	17' 9"	**Years produced:**	1979–1984
Min./max. draft:	1' 0"/4' 6"	**Sail area:**	228 sq. ft.
Bridge clearance:	27' 7"	**Fuel tankage:**	portable
Power:	outboard 3 to 6 hp	**Water tankage:**	15 gal.
B/D ratio:	31%	**Approx. trailering wgt.:**	2,600 lbs.

Parker Dawson Yachts of Hingham, MA, produced this out-of-the-ordinary craft, of which 50 or so were built from 1979 into the early 1980s. The split rig is unusual in a boat this small, since the configuration often means less total sail area. But in this case, the Poacher's total area is higher than any of her comps. The sleeved sails are identical (so a single third sail can be carried as a spare), and both masts are also identical. The aft mast is buried a scant few inches deeper than the forward mast, making the rig a cat ketch; without the extra bury, the masthead heights would be reversed, and the rig would be a cat schooner. **Best features:**

The Poacher's shallow draft with board up gives her a good capability to explore beaches. She also has foam flotation. **Worst features:** Unlike the fin keels or centerboards of her comps, the Poacher has a daggerboard, and a rather deep one (4' 6") at that. The rudder is also the vertical-lifting type. We don't like vertically lifting blades, on the theory that in rocky shallows the system could result in severe damage to the daggerboard trunk and/or rudder assembly. Also, in addition to limiting total sail area, split rigs can be harder to trim properly, and therefore may be harder to sail, especially when going downwind.

Comps	LOD	Beam	MinDr	Displ	Bllst	SA/D	D/L	Avg. PHRF	Max. Speed	Motion Index	Space Index	No. of Berths	Head-room
Clipper 21	20' 11"	7' 3"	0' 7"	1,800	410	20.9	142	270	5.7	10.5	275	4	3' 9"
Parker Dawson Poacher 21	21' 1"	7' 6"	1' 0"	1,800	550	24.7	144	201	5.6	10.1	358	4	4' 0"
Nautica Flamingo 21	20' 8"	7' 5"	2' 0"	1,870	550	21.5	125	267	5.8	10.3	360	4	4' 1"

Precision 21
Jim Taylor draws another nice boat

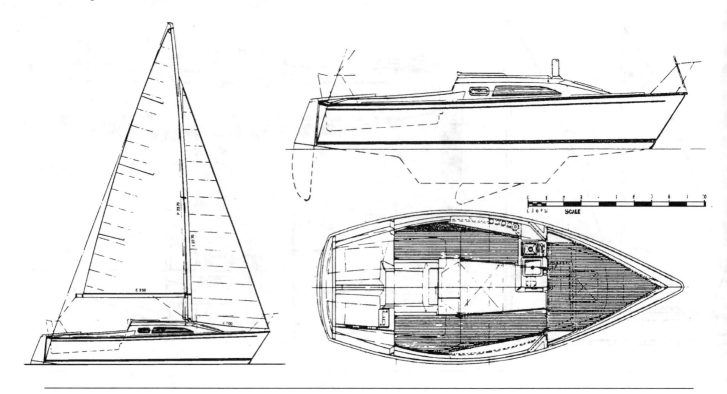

LOD:	20' 9"	**Designer:**	Jim Taylor
LOA:	22' 3"	**Builder:**	Precision Boatworks
LWL:	17' 6"	**Years produced:**	1986–present
Min./max. draft:	1' 9"/4' 8"	**Sail area:**	203 sq. ft.
Bridge clearance:	30' 0"	**Fuel tankage:**	portable
Power:	outboard 3 to 6 hp	**Water tankage:**	portable
B/D ratio:	32%	**Approx. trailering wgt.:**	2,700 lbs.

Designer Jim Taylor (Precision 165, 18, 23, and 27/28; Starwind 19 and 27; Colgate 26, America's Cup designs, among others) draws a nice boat, and the Precision 21 is no exception. Furthermore, Precision Boatworks in Palmetto, FL, does a good job of molding and finishing these boats. ***Best features:*** With her big beam, 4' 4" headroom, and well-designed layout, she seems to have plenty of space below, even though her Space Index is slightly below three out of four of her comps. We think this makes her, more than her comps, what used to be called a "wholesome" weekend boat for a family of two adults and one or two children. Her draft, while not as shallow as the Bahia, beats most of her comps by a wide margin when it comes to easy ramp launching. Workmanship on her hull, on the boats we've seen, is well above average. ***Worst features:*** At one time owners had trouble with the centerboard and leaking windows, but these problems were eventually recognized at the factory and, as we understand it, the board and leak problems were corrected in succeeding production.

Comps	LOD	Beam	MinDr	Displ	Bllst	SA/D	D/L	Avg. PHRF	Max. Speed	Motion Index	Space Index	No. of Berths	Head-room
Harpoon 6.2 (20)	20' 4"	8' 0"	3' 6"	1,700	550	24.7	191	234	5.3	9.5	339	2	4' 3"
Jeanneau Bahia 23 (20)	20' 4"	7' 11"	1' 5"	1,850	620	22.3	140	177	5.7	9.4	339	4	4' 11"
Mystic Mini-Ton 21 (20)	20' 3"	7' 11"	4' 0"	1,850	700	22.6	168	219	5.5	9.9	313	4	4' 0"
Antrim 20	20' 5"	8' 0"	4' 0"	1,850	750	29.7	154	NA	5.6	9.7	339	4	4' 4"
Precision 21	20' 9"	8' 3"	1' 9"	1,875	600	21.4	156	270	5.6	9.4	317	4	4' 4"

Quickstep 21
Short-lived New England design

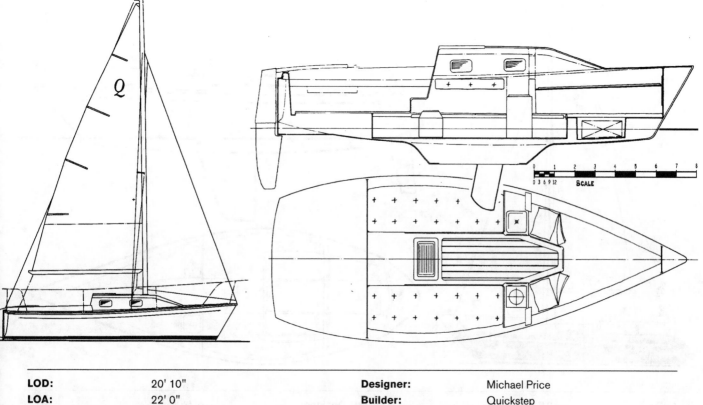

LOD:	20' 10"	**Designer:**	Michael Price
LOA:	22' 0"	**Builder:**	Quickstep
LWL:	18' 6"	**Years produced:**	1987–1988
Min./max. draft:	1' 11"/4' 4"	**Sail area:**	201 sq. ft.
Bridge clearance:	29' 6"	**Fuel tankage:**	portable
Power:	outboard 3 to 6 hp	**Water tankage:**	portable
B/D ratio:	38%	**Approx. trailering wgt.:**	3,700 lbs.

The Quickstep 21 is a pretty boat that was nicely conceived and well made near Newport, RI. Unfortunately she did not sell well in the economic recession of the late 1980s, and like other good products of the time, disappeared from the map too quickly. ***Best features:*** She has a deep forefoot (i.e., her bow is not cut away, as for example is the Corinthian's, one of her comps), which may partly explain why owners say she is easy on the helm and wants to track in a straight line. That's a plus if you are cruising from A to B, but not so good coming in to a pier. (See below.) Along with her comps, her weight is on the heavy side for her length, and that should make her comfortable in a seaway. Her relatively high SA/D should help to make her livelier than her comps in light air. Her Space Index is also high compared to her comps, indicating relatively good stowage space. ***Worst features:*** Docking could be challenging due to her tendency to want to keep moving in a straight line. One owner mentioned that to turn sharply, you have to use the outboard to steer as well as the tiller.

Comps	LOD	Beam	MinDr	Displ	Bllst	SA/D	D/L	Avg. PHRF	Max. Speed	Motion Index	Space Index	No. of Berths	Head-room
Quickstep 21	20' 10"	8' 0"	1' 11"	2,500	950	17.5	176	NA	5.8	12.3	316	4	4' 3"
Halman 20	19' 6"	7' 9"	2' 10"	2,500	1,000	15.8	248	276	5.4	14.0	295	4	5' 0"
Nordica 20	19' 6"	7' 8"	3' 3"	2,520	1,020	15.7	250	276	5.4	14.7	292	4	4' 6"
Corinthian 19 (20)	19' 6"	6' 6"	2' 9"	2,724	1,100	15.3	399	292	5.1	21.6	216	2	4' 2"

Ranger 22 (21)
Speedster by Gary Mull

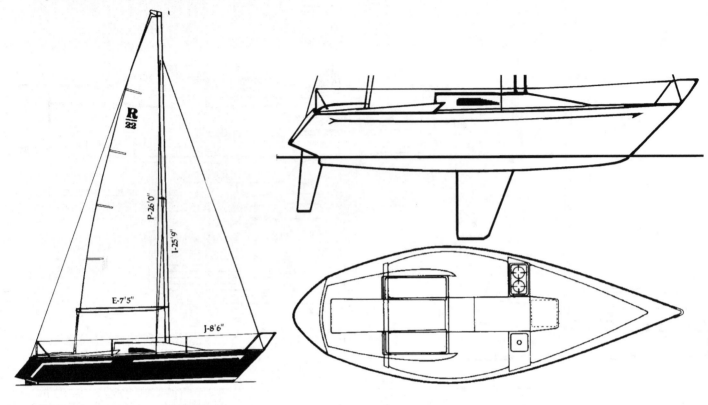

LOD:	21' 4"		**Designer:**	Gary Mull
LOA:	22' 6"		**Builder:**	Ranger Division of Jensen Marine
LWL:	17' 6"		**Years produced:**	1977–1980?
Min./max. draft:	fixed keel 4' 3"		**Sail area:**	206 sq. ft.
Bridge clearance:	33' 3"		**Fuel tankage:**	portable
Power:	outboard 3 to 6 hp		**Water tankage:**	portable
B/D ratio:	41%		**Approx. trailering wgt.:**	3,100 lbs.

This boat, conceived by Gary Mull, a talented designer of fast sailboats, started out as the "Mull 22" and later became the Ranger 22, with the "22" based on the hull length (including reverse transom) of 22' 6". The length on deck is 21' 4" or thereabouts, so we compare her with other speedy boats of the period with similar LOD, displacement, ballast, and sail area. ***Best features:*** The Ranger's draft of 4' 3" and her slightly higher sail area, as well as tweaks such as a mainmast cross-section that reduces weight aloft while its turbulence stimulators (small bumps on the mast to help keep wind flow "attached" to the mainsail) help make the rig's aerodynamics more efficient, will make her closer-winded and faster upwind in light air compared to her comps. Unfortunately for racers, the handicappers have noticed this and have penalized the Ranger for these appealing qualities by reducing her PHRF by about a minute per mile. ***Worst features:*** Her small cockpit is good for racing but too small for a crowd lounging with beer and sandwiches when the racing is done.

Comps	LOD	Beam	MinDr	Displ	Bllst	SA/D	D/L	Avg. PHRF	Max. Speed	Motion Index	Space Index	No. of Berths	Head-room
Cal 20	20' 0"	7' 0"	3' 4"	1,950	900	20.1	149	276	5.7	11.8	244	4	3' 11"
Islander 21	20' 10"	7' 10"	3' 4"	1,950	1,000	21.3	149	282	5.7	10.2	280	4	3' 9"
Ranger 22 (21)	21' 4"	7' 10"	4' 3"	2,182	900	19.8	182	222	5.6	11.4	306	4	4' 0"

Ranger 23 (21) "Fun"
Fast for a 21-footer but slow versus her comps

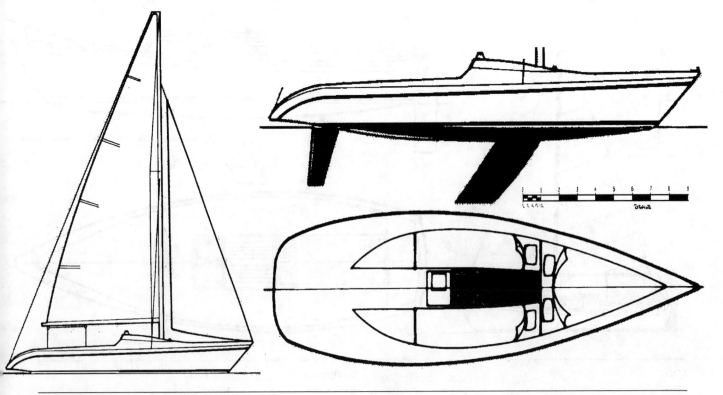

LOD:	21' 4"		**Designer:**	Joubert & Nivelt
LOA:	23' 4"		**Builder:**	Ranger Yachts
LWL:	17' 11"		**Years produced:**	1982–1985
Min./max. draft:	2' 4"/5' 4"		**Sail area:**	243 sq. ft.
Bridge clearance:	33' 0"		**Fuel tankage:**	portable
Power:	outboard 2 to 4 hp		**Water tankage:**	portable
B/D ratio:	41%		**Approx. trailering wgt.:**	2,600 lbs.

Ranger Yachts built about 100 Fun 23's (sometimes called Fun 24's but actually only 21' 4" on deck and 23' 4" overall). The French team of Joubert & Nivelt designed her; she is not to be confused with the Gary Mull-designed Ranger 22 (page 124). Jeanneau in France also built a few, and an Italian firm, Lillia, also has been a builder. Although the Fun is said to have the same sailplan as a Soling (a 27-foot one-design racing sailboat), actually the mainsails have the same dimensions but the foretriangle on the Fun is much smaller than the Soling's. There are two rigs, a short rig and a "regular" rig. The short rig is shown here; the

regular rig has a taller but still less-than-masthead jib. ***Best features:*** In a way it seems unfair to compare the Fun with the two comps we've chosen, since both are at least a foot longer on deck and both have a lower D/L ratio—the Wabbit's being substantially lower. But between the Fun's higher D/L and her bigger beam, maybe she'll be a bit more stable. ***Worst features:*** She may be fast for a 21-footer, but against her comps the Fun is probably slowest, based on the stats in the table below. Like her comps, she is strictly a bare-bones overnighter when it comes to accommodations.

Comps	LOD	Beam	MinDr	Displ	Bllst	SA/D	D/L	Avg. PHRF	Max. Speed	Motion Index	Space Index	No. of Berths	Head-room
Wabbit 24 (23)	23' 1"	5' 7"	3' 6"	875	400	32.5	49	150	6.0	6.4	188	2	2' 8"
Ranger 23 (21) "Fun"	21' 4"	8' 0"	2' 4"	1,875	760	25.6	145	180	5.7	9.2	289	4	3' 10"
Moore 24 (23)	22' 9"	7' 2"	4' 1"	2,050	1,025	24.5	89	156	6.2	10.2	285	2	3' 6"

RK20

Balboa 20 and Ensenada 20 revisited

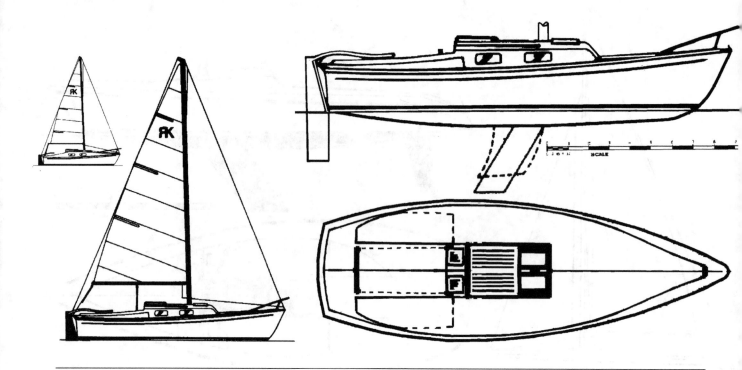

LOD:	20' 0"	**Designer:**	Lyle Hess
LOA:	20' 4"	**Builder:**	RK Industries
LWL:	17' 6"	**Years produced:**	1977–1981?
Min./max. draft:	1' 9"/4' 0"*	**Sail area:**	194 sq. ft.
Bridge clearance:	27' 6"	**Fuel tankage:**	portable
Power:	outboard 3 to 6 hp	**Water tankage:**	7 gal.
B/D ratio:	28%	**Approx. trailering wgt.:**	2,500 lbs.*

Dimensions shown above and below are for the swing keel version. The RK20 was also offered with a fixed 820 lbs. iron keel, which has a 3' 3" draft and a displacement of 1,970 lbs.

RK Industries of Strasburg, VA, at one time associated with Coastal Recreation Inc. of Costa Mesa, CA, built the RK20, an updated version of the Ensenada 20 (see page 97). The hull for the Ensenada 20 was identical to the RK20, but the deck configurations were different. Also the RK20 was available with either a trunk cabin or a flush deck similar to the Ensenada 20, as shown on the small sailplan here. The RK20 fixed-keel version (see fin keel shown as dashed line in the profile drawing) would seem preferable, since it eliminates the mechanical problems some owners have experienced with the swing keel. Otherwise, the **Best features** and **Worst features** are pretty much the same as those as outlined in the write-ups for the Ensenada 20 (page 97) and the Balboa 20 (page 84).

Comps	LOD	Beam	MinDr	Displ	Bllst	SA/D	D/L	Avg. PHRF	Max. Speed	Motion Index	Space Index	No. of Berths	Head-room
Ensenada 20	20' 0"	7' 1"	1' 0"	1,600	550	20.3	133	288	5.6	9.9	238	4	4' 2"
Balboa 20	20' 0"	7' 1"	1' 9"	1,700	450	20.4	142	276	5.6	10.5	252	4	4' 0"
RK20	20' 0"	7' 1"	1' 9"	1,700	550	21.8	142	264	5.6	10.5	222	4	3' 9"

S2 6.7 Grand Slam (21)

Predecessor to the S2 6.9

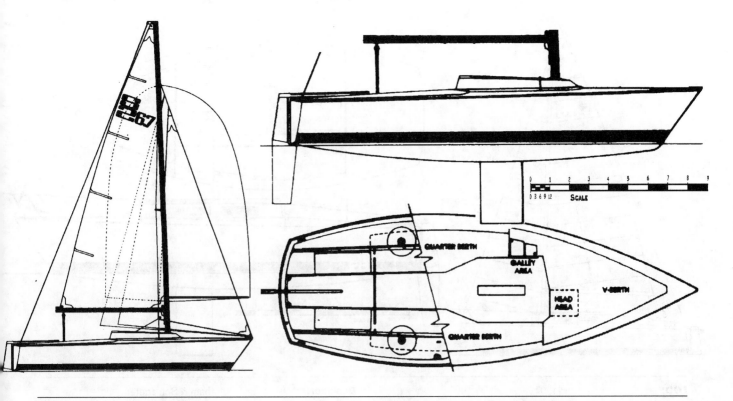

LOD:	21' 0"	**Designer:**	Don Wennersten
LOA:	22' 0"	**Builder:**	S2 Yachts
LWL:	18' 9"	**Years produced:**	1980–1983
Min./max. draft:	0' 10"/4' 3"	**Sail area:**	225 sq. ft.
Bridge clearance:	32' 6"	**Fuel tankage:**	portable
Power:	outboard 3 to 6 hp	**Water tankage:**	portable
B/D ratio:	35%	**Approx. trailering wgt.:**	3,200 lbs.

It is interesting to note what happens when a builder calls in an outside racing design team (in this case the designers Graham & Schlageter) to tweak the performance of an existing boat (the S2 6.7) drawn by an inside designer (in this case Don Wennersten). That's what happened when S2 apparently decided that the 6.7 wasn't fast enough on the race course, and redesigned her, naming her the S2 6.9. You can see what difference it made in the comparison of comp stats below: virtually no difference at all. See the S2 6.9 (next page) for more. In all, S2 produced 160 hulls in four years before moving on to the S2 6.9. ***Best features:*** Like the Newport 214, the S2 6.7 and 6.9 hulls have practically nothing below the waterline with the lifting keel in the up position, making launching and retrieving on a trailer a comparatively easy job. The PHRF seems a bit high (or is the Beneteau First 210 too low?) for boats of this type. It makes us wonder if calling in G&S was necessary. ***Worst features:*** As with the S2 6.9, the heavy lifting keel and its attendant winch is bound to cause problems sooner or later, just by the nature of the beast.

Comps	LOD	Beam	MinDr	Displ	Bllst	SA/D	D/L	Avg. PHRF	Max. Speed	Motion Index	Space Index	No. of Berths	Head- room
Newport 214	21' 2"	7' 7"	0' 9"	2,000	450	23.1	130	NA	5.8	10.4	318	4	4' 0"
Beneteau First 210 (21)	21' 0"	8' 2"	2' 4"	2,200	770	23.0	129	195	5.9	10.3	371	4	4' 6"
S2 6.9 (21)	21' 0"	8' 0"	0' 9"	2,200	770	22.3	149	205	5.8	10.7	328	4	4' 0"
S2 6.7 (21)	21' 0"	8' 0"	0' 10"	2,200	775	21.3	149	205	5.8	10.7	320	4	4' 0"

S2 6.9 (21)
Easy trailerability for the mini-boat racing circuit

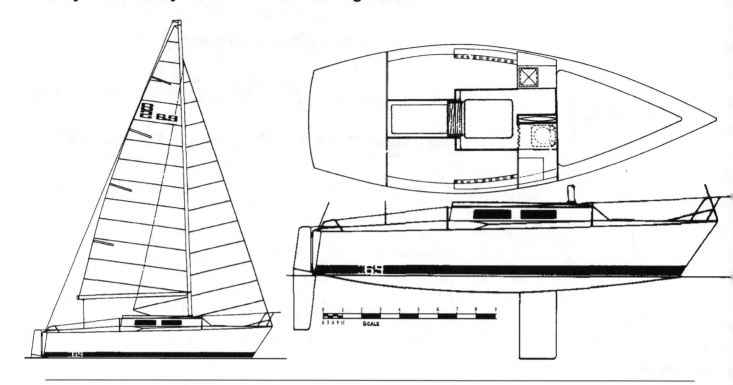

LOD:	21' 0"		**Designer:**	Graham & Schlageter
LOA:	22' 0"		**Builder:**	S2 Yachts
LWL:	18' 9"		**Years produced:**	1985–1986
Min./max. draft:	0' 9"/4' 6"		**Sail area:**	236 sq. ft.
Bridge clearance:	32' 0"		**Fuel tankage:**	portable
Power:	outboard 3 to 6 hp		**Water tankage:**	5 gal.
B/D ratio:	35%		**Approx. trailering wgt.:**	3,200 lbs.

When they wanted an entry-level high-performance sailboat, fast enough to race competitively, stable enough for family daysailing, roomy enough for overnighting, and trailerable, S2 turned to their inside naval architect, Don Wennersten, and their inside industrial engineer Dave Fry. They called the result an S2 6.7, and produced her from 1980 to early 1983. At that point, racing boat designers Graham & Schlageter were asked to tweak details of the cabin, cockpit, and lifting keel, and the result was the S2 6.9 shown here. It has very close to the same dimensions and weights as the original design, and rates the same PHRF numbers, averaging 205. Later, in 1987, the same design was offered with a winged keel, and was called simply the S2-22. The "22" label is misleading, as it is based on LOA rather than the conventional LOD. ***Best features:*** The ten-inch draft and smooth bottom with keel up makes her easy to launch and retrieve to a trailer. ***Worst features:*** The lifting keel takes a winch to lift its 430 pounds straight up. (The other 340 pounds of ballast is in the hull.)

Comps	LOD	Beam	MinDr	Displ	Bllst	SA/D	D/L	Avg. PHRF	Max. Speed	Motion Index	Space Index	No. of Berths	Head-room
Newport 214	21' 2"	7' 7"	0' 9"	2,000	450	23.1	130	NA	5.8	10.4	318	4	4' 0"
Beneteau First 210 (21)	21' 0"	8' 2"	2' 4"	2,200	770	23.0	129	195	5.9	10.3	371	4	4' 6"
S2 6.9 (21)	21' 0"	8' 0"	0' 9"	2,200	770	22.3	149	205	5.8	10.7	328	4	4' 0"
S2 6.7 (21)	21' 0"	8' 0"	0' 10"	2,200	775	21.3	149	205	5.8	10.7	320	4	4' 0"

San Juan 21 Mk I

An old design with an active class association

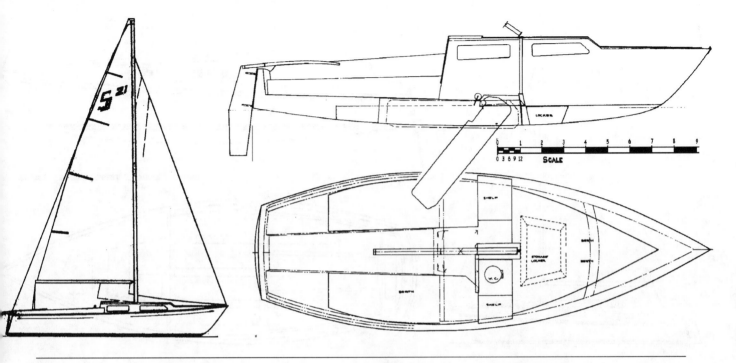

LOD:	20' 6"	**Designer:**	Don Clark
LOA:	21' 6"	**Builder:**	Clark Boat Co.
LWL:	17' 0"	**Years produced:**	1969–1974
Min./max. draft:	1' 0"/4' 0"	**Sail area:**	190 sq. ft.
Bridge clearance:	28' 8"	**Fuel tankage:**	portable
Power:	outboard 3 to 6 hp	**Water tankage:**	portable
B/D ratio:	32%	**Approx. trailering wgt.:**	2,000 lbs.

The San Juan 21, like her comp the Cal 21 and several other boats (Santana 21 and Catalina 22, for example) was designed to capitalize on the success of boats like the Venture 21, designed by MacGregor in 1965. All these vessels are inexpensive trailer-sailers and have the same type of weighted swing keel. These features give the hull good stability and at the same time make trailering and launching at ramps easier. Although the Clark Boat Company is no longer in business, an active class association owns the boat's molds, and may begin building new boats at some point in the future. *Best features:* Unlike the Venture 21 and Cal 21 comps, the SJ21 has a very active racing class association, unusual for a boat designed 30-plus years ago. An efficient foil-shaped rudder and swing keel, plus a sailcloth slot gasket, offer superior hydrodynamics compared with her comps. *Worst features:* The slot gasket, made of sailcloth (which bridges the gap across the trunk slot to prevent turbulence when sailing downwind with the keel raised), requires special maintenance (trimming of frayed edges and periodic replacement) to keep it smooth and effective. The advertised weight of 1,250 pounds may be low; some owners claim weights of 1,500 to 1,750 pounds. For more on this boat, see notes under San Juan 21 Mk II on the next page.

Comps	LOD	Beam	MinDr	Displ	Bllst	SA/D	D/L	Avg. PHRF	Max. Speed	Motion Index	Space Index	No. of Berths	Head-room
Cal 21	20' 6"	6' 8"	0' 9"	1,100	360	29.4	106	258	5.5	7.6	221	4	4' 1"
Venture 21	21' 0"	6' 10"	1' 0"	1,200	400	24.8	85	252	5.8	7.4	203	4	3' 3"
San Juan 21 Mk I	20' 6"	7' 0"	1' 0"	1,250	400	26.2	114	252	5.5	8.0	227	4	3' 6"
San Juan 21 Mk II	20' 6"	7' 0"	1' 0"	1,250	400	26.2	114	252	5.5	8.0	227	4	3' 6"

San Juan 21 Mk II
The second version–with subtle changes

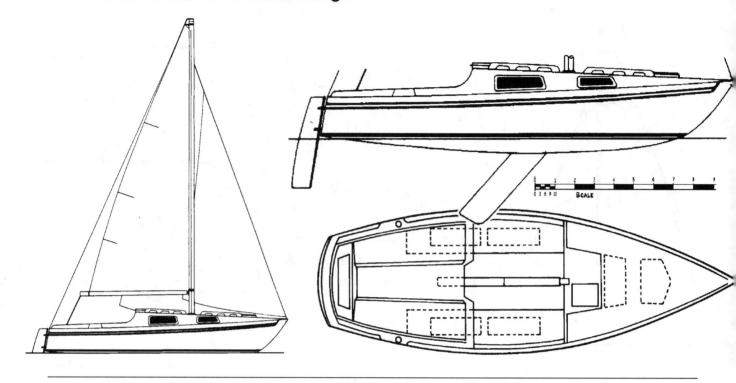

LOD:	20' 6"	**Designer:**	Don Clark
LOA:	21' 6"	**Builder:**	Clark Boat Co.
LWL:	17' 0"	**Years produced:**	1975–1986
Min./max. draft:	1' 0"/4' 0"	**Sail area:**	190 sq. ft.
Bridge clearance:	28' 8"	**Fuel tankage:**	portable
Power:	outboard 3 to 6 hp	**Water tankage:**	portable
B/D ratio:	32%	**Approx. trailering wgt.:**	2,000 lbs.

The comments given under San Juan 21 Mk I on the previous page also apply here. The Mk II version of the SJ21 changed the deck molding (shorter cockpit, longer cabin, no step in roof) and altered the interior as shown. A Mk III version made further minor changes to interior layout. *Best features:* See Mk I comments. *Worst features:* To be race-competitive, the trunk gasket (mentioned on previous page) must be replaced before every regatta. Class rules permit only cloth gaskets, not Mylar. The boat's rudder and swing keel are not always fair, so may need putty to fill in hollows and sanding to get rid of bumps. A kick-up rudder is not standard, though we think it is an essential option. Failures in the lower rudder gudgeon are common. There may be crushing of the deck under the mast step on older models, which used a plywood sandwich rather than solid fiberglass. Failure of the undersized gooseneck is common. Lifelines and pulpits are not allowed by class rules. Forward hatch on newer boats may leak. There's a tendency toward hull dimpling near trailer supports.

Comps	LOD	Beam	MinDr	Displ	Bllst	SA/D	D/L	Avg. PHRF	Max. Speed	Motion Index	Space Index	No. of Berths	Head-room
Cal 21	20' 6"	6' 8"	0' 9"	1,100	360	29.4	106	258	5.5	7.6	221	4	4' 1"
San Juan 21 Mk I	20' 6"	7' 0"	1' 0"	1,250	400	26.2	114	252	5.5	8.0	227	4	3' 6"
San Juan 21 Mk II	20' 6"	7' 0"	1' 0"	1,250	400	26.2	114	252	5.5	8.0	227	4	3' 6"
Venture 21	21' 0"	6' 10"	1' 0"	1,200	400	24.8	85	252	5.8	7.4	203	4	3' 3"

Santana 20

Popular one-design, early sport boat

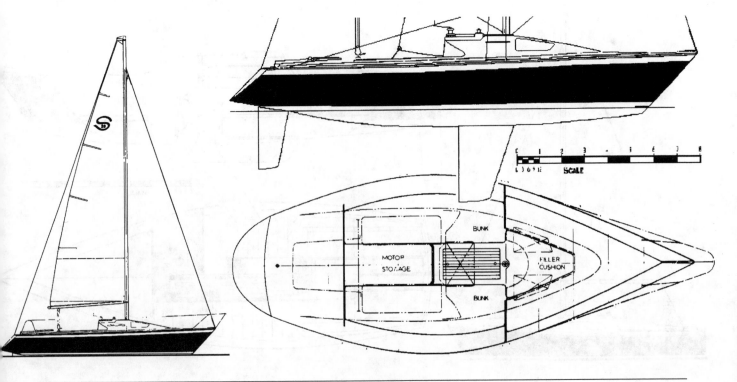

LOD:	20' 3"		**Designer:**	Shad Turner	
LOA:	21' 5"		**Builder:**	W. D. Schock	
LWL:	16' 0"		**Years produced:**	1976–present	
Min./max. draft:	fixed keel 4' 0"		**Sail area:**	186 sq. ft.	
Bridge clearance:	29' 6"		**Fuel tankage:**	portable	
Power:	outboard 3 to 6 hp		**Water tankage:**	portable	
B/D ratio:	41%		**Approx. trailering wgt.:**	2,300 lbs.	

This one-design racer was a very early entry—nine full years before the similar MX 20—in what eventually became known as the "sport boat" category—speedy and light, easy to trailer, with minimum accommodations adequate for weekend regattas. It turned out to be extremely popular, with something like 900 boats being sold. Tom Schock redesigned the boat in 1996. The design changes included the introduction of an open transom, with the decks rolled down to the cockpit floor for better crew comfort; changes in jib track and traveler locations; and some interior redesign. In addition to the standard 550-pound fin keel, a 600-pound wing keel was offered, with a 2' 8" draft (unfortunately not competitive on the race course). **Best features:** There is an extensive Class Association, mainly centered along the United States west coast, for those seeking companionship on the race circuit. **Worst features:** With a four-foot draft, a hoist is the best bet when launching from a trailer. Headroom is lowest compared with comps.

Comps	LOD	Beam	MinDr	Displ	Bllst	SA/D	D/L	Avg. PHRF	Max. Speed	Motion Index	Space Index	No. of Berths	Head-room
Santana 20	20' 3"	8' 0"	4' 0"	1,350	550	24.4	147	222	5.4	7.5	259	4	3' 4"
Matilda 20	19' 6"	7' 10"	0' 9"	1,550	300	23.3	159	276	5.4	8.9	219	4	4' 2"
MX 20	19' 7"	8' 0"	3' 11"	1,560	635	27.4	119	189	5.7	8.1	227	4	4' 6"

Santana 21
Another entry in the swing-keel sweepstakes

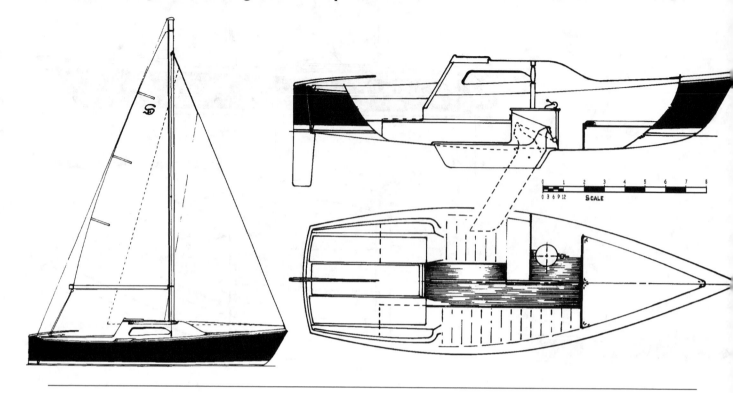

LOD:	21' 3"	Designer:	Seymour Paul
LOA:	21' 11"	Builder:	W.D. Schock
LWL:	19' 4"	Years produced:	1970–1977
Min./max. draft:	1' 6"/5' 0"	Sail area:	189 sq. ft.
Bridge clearance:	28' 6"	Fuel tankage:	portable
Power:	outboard 3 to 6 hp	Water tankage:	portable
B/D ratio:	39%	Approx. trailering wgt.:	2,100 lbs.

As were her comps, the Santana 21 was conceived as a lightweight racer-cruiser, with the emphasis on racing. In fact, with a D/L ratio of 86, she is technically classified as an ultralight. Her major distinction is her unique 550-pound hinged cast-iron keel, mounted in a one-foot-deep fixed stub keel. The swinging part reaches five feet below the waterline in the down position, providing considerable righting moment. The swing-keel trunk has a massive cast-iron hinge weighing approximately 100 pounds, which is said in the builder's literature to give the swinging part "superior lateral support and protects it during beaching manuevers." **Best features:** She looks fast to

us, and we'd give odds she'd beat both her comps in a no-handicap race, even considering the U.S. 21's considerably lower PHRF rating. **Worst features:** The rudder is detachable but not hinged, limiting navigation to waters deeper than three feet (or slightly less in absolutely calm protected water) despite the announced eighteen inch minimum draft. The depth of the keel is controlled by a winch mounted down below, just forward of the mast (see inboard profile), not easy to get to in an emergency. With 3' 10" headroom, cruising of any significant duration would best be done by shorter than average sailors or those with flexible backs.

Comps	LOD	Beam	MinDr	Displ	Bllst	SA/D	D/L	Avg. PHRF	Max. Speed	Motion Index	Space Index	No. of Berths	Head-room
U.S. 21/Triton 21	21' 3"	8' 0"	1' 4"	1,400	200	28.6	107	201	5.7	7.1	299	4	4' 0"
Santana 21	21' 3"	7' 6"	1' 6"	1,400	550	24.2	86	267	5.9	7.4	238	4	3' 10"
Newport 212 (21)	21' 2"	7' 8"	0' 10"	1,500	400	21.6	98	267	5.8	7.6	318	4	4' 2"

Seafarer 22 (21)
One boat, two deck designs, two keels

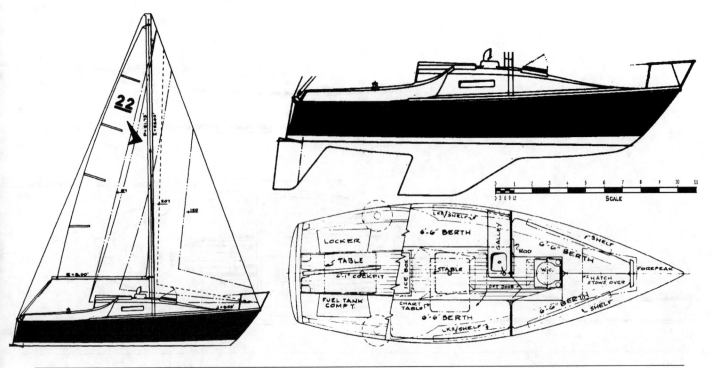

LOD:	21' 4"	**Designer:**	McCurdy & Rhodes
LOA:	22' 6"	**Builder:**	Seafarer Fiberglass
LWL:	18' 4"	**Years produced:**	1975–1985?
Min./max. draft:	keel 2' 10" shoal, 3' 5" deep	**Sail area:**	207 sq. ft.
Bridge clearance:	28' 9"	**Fuel tankage:**	portable
Power:	outboard 3 to 6 hp	**Water tankage:**	12 gal.
B/D ratio:	42%	**Approx. trailering wgt.:**	3,600 lbs.

The first of a long line of McCurdy & Rhodes designs for Seafarer Fiberglass Yachts of Huntington, NY, is shown here. This model featured a streamlined forward deck and only one portlight on each side. Later versions of the "22" used a new deck molding, with extra ports that give more light below, and also offered a choice of two keels, either the 2' 10" so-called "high performance" keel shown here, designed primarily for better stability and speed, or a 2' 1" keel for easier launching and retrieving from a trailer. *Best features:* The coaming on the early boats (as shown here) curled up over the cabin-top to ease attachment of a weather-tight dodger, a great

convenience when cruising in rainy weather. *Worst features:* The shoal-keel version's performance will not satisfy most sailors, and the smaller, shallower rudder that is needed to match the shoal keel will not perform as well either. We recommend sticking with the "high performance" version—which can't be expected to match her comps' upwind pointing ability, since she's just not deep enough. The skeg-mounted rudder in both early and late versions has been known to develop problems at the gudgeons. In the early one-port-per-side boats, some owners have sawn holes for new ports to secure additional light below.

Comps	LOD	Beam	MinDr	Displ	Bllst	SA/D	D/L	Avg. PHRF	Max. Speed	Motion Index	Space Index	No. of Berths	Head-room
Gloucester 22	21' 8"	8' 0"	1' 8"	2,400	800	19.3	165	186	5.8	11.8	324	4	4' 4"
Seafarer 22 (21)	21' 4"	7' 5"	2' 1"	2,400	1,010	18.5	174	270	5.7	13.1	289	4	4' 9"
Starwind 223	22' 3"	8' 6"	1' 10"	2,435	700	19.4	150	237	5.9	10.7	414	4	4' 10"
U.S. 22/Triton 22	21' 6"	7' 10"	2' 5"	2,450	950	17.8	138	279	6.0	11.6	321	5	4' 0"

Seaforth Coastal Cruiser 24 (21)
Traditional cruiser in a small package

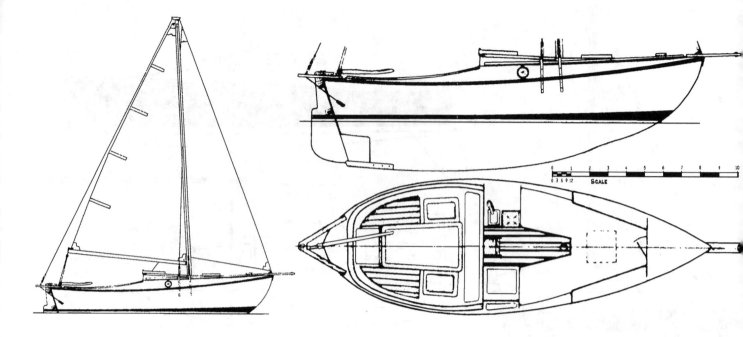

LOD:	20' 6"		**Designer:**	Steve Seaton
LOA:	24' 0"		**Builder:**	Precision Boatworks
LWL:	17' 0"		**Years produced:**	1978–1985
Min./max. draft:	fixed keel 2' 6"		**Sail area:**	217 sq. ft.
Bridge clearance:	30' 0"		**Fuel tankage:**	portable
Power:	6 hp outboard or 8 hp inboard dsl.		**Water tankage:**	portable
B/D ratio:	40%		**Approx. trailering wgt.:**	6,100 lbs.

Steve Seaton, the naval architect behind this little packet, has since been a designer of large power yachts. The craft he drew here is a well-made, pretty vessel that is capable of cruising along coasts—say passages from Long Island Sound to Block Island Sound to Narragansett Bay to Buzzards Bay to Vineyard Sound to Nantucket Sound—despite her modest LOD. By the way, her LOD is 20' 6", despite the sales pitch identifying her as 24 feet. The 24 refers to the LOA, which includes an anchor pulpit and a boomkin, and is a number that's useless as an indicator of size except when paying yard storage bills. Marketers realize that, but nevertheless some continue to use the misleading term LOA instead of the more honest LOD to advertise size. **Best features:** Sturdy, reasonably fast (we hear), and easy on the eyes if you enjoy traditional designs. **Worst features:** Trailering 6,100 pounds on the highway (including all the stuff you'll need for the two-week cruise you'll be starting when you get to your trailer-ramp destination) requires a big truck or SUV to tow the load safely and without incident.

Comps	LOD	Beam	MinDr	Displ	Bllst	SA/D	D/L	Avg. PHRF	Max. Speed	Motion Index	Space Index	No. of Berths	Head-room
Companion 21	20' 6"	7' 1"	2' 9"	3,000	1,000	16.8	327	303	5.4	19.6	245	4	4' 7"
Heritage 20	20' 0"	6' 6"	2' 9"	3,100	1,000	18.1	410	NA	5.2	23.8	235	4	4' 7"
Sea Islander 20	20' 0"	7' 6"	2' 2"	3,180	886	14.9	289	NA	5.5	18.6	294	4	4' 4"
Seaforth Coastal Cruiser 21	20' 6"	7' 4"	2' 6"	4,000	1,600	13.8	363	NA	5.5	22.6	276	2	4' 4"

Sea Islander 20
Basic microcruiser from the '60s

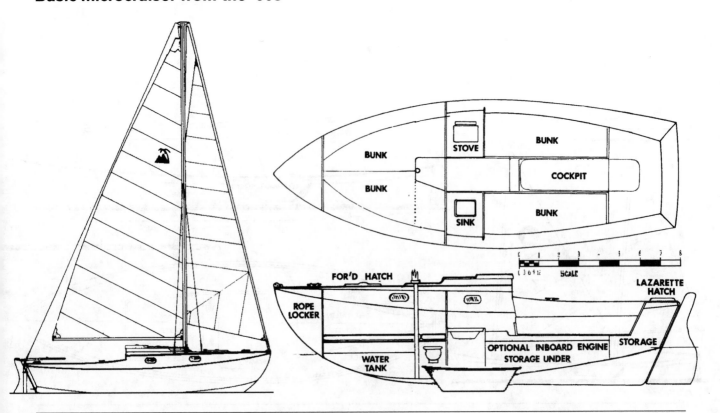

LOD:	20' 0"
LOA:	21' 0"
LWL:	17' 0"
Min./max. draft:	fixed keel 2' 2"
Bridge clearance:	31' 0"
Power:	4 to 8 hp outboard, optional inboard
B/D ratio:	28%

Designer:	Not specified by builder
Builder:	Ed Douthit & Sons Boatworks
Years produced:	1966?–1969?
Sail area:	202 sq. ft.
Fuel tankage:	portable
Water tankage:	portable
Approx. trailering wgt.:	4,800 lbs.

The ad copy from Ed Douthit and Sons Boatworks in Santa Rosa, CA, in 1966 reads: "Roomy! Live aboard, sailing and road traveling. Four berths, full headroom in galley, area for head. Safe! Non-capsizable, self-righting and cockpit self-draining. Capable of extended cruising. Trailerable! You can launch at any boat ramp. Sail waters of only two foot depth. Rigging and sailaway time 20 minutes. Remains upright when beached." Yep, that just about says it all, in a nutshell. ***Best features:*** Shallower draft than comps. Space index is better than comps due

to wider beam. ***Worst features:*** The ad copy above says "Full headroom in galley," but it turns out that's only in the companionway with the hatch open. Otherwise headroom is 4' 4"—three inches less than two-thirds of its comps. The twin keels, weighing 886 pounds in total, do keep the boat upright when grounded on level flats, but don't do much for upwind performance, which is likely to be worse than any of her comps. We assume that the ad suggesting that the reader "Live aboard" means more like "Spend one night."

Comps	LOD	Beam	MinDr	Displ	Bllst	SA/D	D/L	Avg. PHRF	Max. Speed	Motion Index	Space Index	No. of Berths	Head-room
Companion 21	20' 6"	7' 1"	2' 9"	3,000	1,000	16.8	327	303	5.4	19.6	245	4	4' 7"
Heritage 20	20' 0"	6' 6"	2' 9"	3,100	1,000	18.1	410	NA	5.2	23.8	235	4	4' 7"
Sea Islander 20	20' 0"	7' 6"	2' 2"	3,180	886	14.9	289	NA	5.5	18.6	294	4	4' 4"
Seaforth Coastal Cruiser 21	20' 6"	7' 4"	2' 6"	4,000	1,600	13.8	363	NA	5.5	22.6	276	2	4' 4"

Sea Pearl 21

A cat ketch daysailer with a canvas cabin

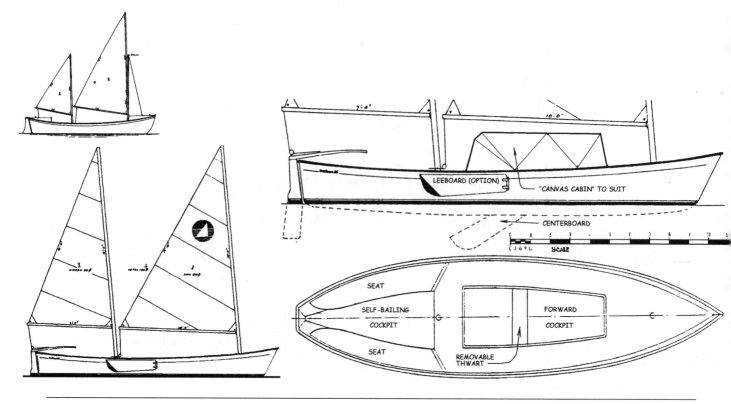

LOD:	21' 0"	**Designer:**	Ron Johnson
LOA:	22' 0"	**Builder:**	Marine Concepts
LWL:	19' 0"	**Years produced:**	1982–present
Min./max. draft:	0' 6"/2' 6"	**Sail area:**	136 sq. ft.
Bridge clearance:	19' 6"	**Fuel tankage:**	portable
Power:	outboard 3 to 6 hp	**Water tankage:**	portable
B/D ratio:	0%	**Approx. trailering wgt.:**	1,450 lbs.

This little decked-over double-ended cat ketch is said to have its design origins in L. Francis Herreshoff's "Carpenter," designed in 1929 (see sailplan inset)—though we see only a minor resemblance. The Sea Pearl comes with a tonneau cover for the forward cockpit, which is non-self-bailing, but also can be rigged with an optional "canvas cabin." A small steering cockpit aft of the mizzen is self-bailing. The base boat has a centerboard, but optional leeboards are available, as are twin lug rigs and water ballast tanks carrying 360 pounds (not shown in stats). ***Best features:*** Foam flotation makes her unsinkable. Split rig

(main and mizzen) permit playing with trim, such as flying the sails wing and wing downwind. Being considerably lighter than her comps, she is easier to rig, launch, and retrieve on a ramp. ***Worst features:*** Narrow and dory-like, the hull has little initial stability—big crew may be necessary in heavy air to keep her on her feet. Boom vangs, an option, should have been made standard, as they are essential to enjoyable sailing. Though it would be fairly simple, no provision has been made for a third mast position where either the main or the mizzen could be stepped, giving her additional versatility.

Comps	LOD	Beam	MinDr	Displ	Bllst	SA/D	D/L	Avg. PHRF	Max. Speed	Motion Index	Space Index	No. of Berths	Head-room
Sea Pearl 21	21' 0"	5' 6"	0' 6"	550	0	32.9	36	NA	5.8	4.4	147	2	3' 6"
Dovekie 21	21' 5"	6' 8"	0' 4"	600	0	32.9	39	NA	5.8	3.7	181	2	3' 0"
Bay Hen 21	21' 0"	6' 3"	0' 9"	900	0	30.0	66	NA	5.7	6.3	158	2	3' 3"

Signet 20
Mini twin-keeler imported from England

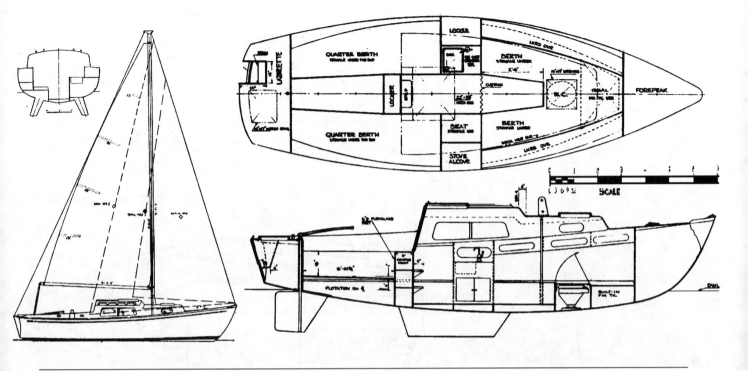

LOD:	19' 10"		**Designer:**	Ray Kaufman	
LOA:	19' 10"		**Builder:**	Signet Marine	
LWL:	16' 0"		**Years produced:**	1960–1979?	
Min./max. draft:	2' 0"/3' 0"		**Sail area:**	181 sq. ft.	
Bridge clearance:	27' 0"		**Fuel tankage:**	portable	
Power:	inboard 4 to 10 hp, or outboard		**Water tankage:**	portable	
B/D ratio:	37%		**Approx. trailering wgt.:**	3,100 lbs.	

Hurley Marine in England, which also produced the Alacrity 19 (page 19), made the Signet 20 and sold them in several countries, including the U.S., through marketer Signet Marine. Most boats coming to the U.S. were twin-keelers with a draft of 2' 0" and a keel skeg, though a later version with a single fin drawing 3' 0" and no skeg probably sold some units here. **Best features:** The twin keels, which have a hydrofoil section, each contain 400 pounds of iron ballast, and permit easy beaching for bottom cleaning and when hauling out. An outboard can be clamped to a built-in fixture on the port side of the transom, making engine access easier from the cockpit than if it were on an external bracket. The head area is hidden from the cockpit by a privacy curtain, not always found on sailboats of this small size. **Worst features:** The shallow twin keels don't provide much lateral resistance when sailing upwind. To be fair, two of her four comps also have shallow draft keels with the same lack of lateral resistance.

Comps	LOD	Beam	MinDr	Displ	Bllst	SA/D	D/L	Avg. PHRF	Max. Speed	Motion Index	Space Index	No. of Berths	Head-room
Chrysler 20	20' 0"	7' 11"	1' 11"	1,950	500	18.3	149	264	5.7	10.1	311	4	3' 9"
Buccaneer 200 (20)	20' 5"	8' 0"	2' 0"	2,100	750	18.6	183	276	5.6	10.9	336	4	3' 6"
Signet 20	19' 10"	6' 8"	2' 0"	2,146	800	18.5	234	NA	5.4	15.4	193	4	4' 0"
Wild Wind 20	20' 0"	7' 11"	2' 0"	2,200	800	18.3	168	NA	5.7	11.5	302	6	4' 3"
Montego 20	19' 6"	7' 2"	2' 0"	2,300	600	17.4	184	282	5.6	14.0	246	4	4' 0"

Sirius 21
Poptop swing-keeler from Canada

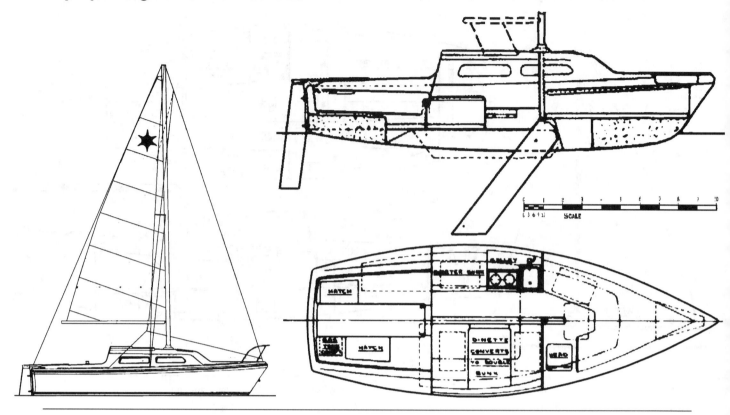

LOD:	21' 2"	**Designer:**	Hubert Vandestadt
LOA:	22' 2"	**Builder:**	Vandestadt & McGruer
LWL:	18' 9"	**Years produced:**	1976–1985
Min./max. draft:	1' 4"/5' 0"	**Sail area:**	203 sq. ft.
Bridge clearance:	29' 0"	**Fuel tankage:**	portable
Power:	outboard 3 to 6 hp	**Water tankage:**	portable
B/D ratio:	26%	**Approx. trailering wgt.:**	2,900 lbs.

This is a wholesome and respectable-looking trailerable sailboat for short cruises, practically identical in the accommodations plan to the Sirius 22 (page 139). She was built from 1976 until 1985 in Ontario, and was succeeded by the Sirius 22, which used the same hull design but tacked on a reverse transom, which increased the hull length (not the LOD) from 21' 2" to 22' 1". **Best features:** Construction quality is above average and overall design is good. Foam flotation is said to make her unsinkable. She can sleep five, including a big V-berth forward and with the dinette converted to a narrow double, but all five (or even four) having breakfast together down below on a rainy day might not appeal to claustrophobes. Hull and deck liners help to make the interior look neat and tidy. A poptop with canvas sides is standard. **Worst features:** As with other cast-iron swing-keel boats, maintenance of the keel surface and lift mechanism eventually may get to be a nuisance. Addition of a babystay on later 21s suggests a problem with mast "tramping" on early production.

Comps	LOD	Beam	MinDr	Displ	Bllst	SA/D	D/L	Avg. PHRF	Max. Speed	Motion Index	Space Index	No. of Berths	Head-room
Sirius 21	21' 2"	7' 11"	1' 4"	2,000	525	20.5	135	258	5.8	10.0	344	5	4' 9"
South Coast 21	21' 4"	6' 11"	3' 0"	2,000	625	19.2	303	252	5.1	14.2	165	2	3' 3"
Sirius 22	21' 2"	7' 11"	1' 4"	2,100	525	19.8	123	243	5.9	9.7	352	5	4' 9"
Nimble 20 (21)	20' 10"	7' 9"	1' 1"	2,200	800	19.6	127	288	6.0	11.0	316	4	4' 3"
Triangle 20 (21)	20' 6"	7' 1"	2' 2"	2,300	800	16.3	222	NA	5.5	14.6	250	2	4' 6"

Sirius 22 (21)

A Canadian trailer-sailer popular in the U.S.

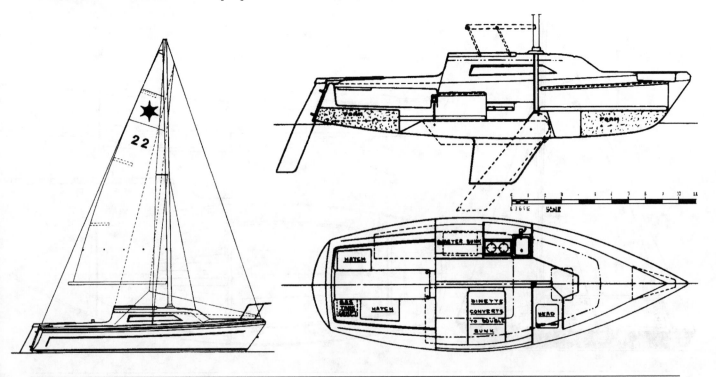

LOD:	21' 2"		**Designer:**	Hubert Vandestadt
LOA:	24' 10"		**Builder:**	Vandestadt & McGruer
LWL:	19' 8"		**Years produced:**	1985–1988
Min./max. draft:	1' 4"/5' 0"		**Sail area:**	203 sq. ft.
Bridge clearance:	29' 0"		**Fuel tankage:**	portable
Power:	outboard 3 to 6 hp		**Water tankage:**	portable
B/D ratio:	25%		**Approx. trailering wgt.:**	3,000 lbs.

The Sirius 22 is a restyling of the Sirius 21 (see page 138), which includes reversing the slope of the transom, which adds 11 inches to the waterline. The interior, poptop, foam flotation, and rig appear to be identical for both boats, and though 100 pounds has been added to her displacement, her ballast and most other dimensions are the same for both models. In the 22, an optional 3' 6" fixed lead keel (shown in solid lines) adds an extra 425 pounds to ballast (making total ballast 950 pounds and displacement a nom-inal 2,500 pounds), and should make the fin-keel version much stiffer than the swing-keel version. ***Best features:*** This good-looking vessel and her near sistership both have more space down below than her narrower peers. Her PHRF may be higher than her speed potential indicates from her stats, given her low D/L. Her draft (in the swing-keel version) should make her fairly easy to launch and retrieve at a ramp. ***Worst features:*** A cast-iron keel can be a maintenance nuisance.

Comps	LOD	Beam	MinDr	Displ	Bllst	SA/D	D/L	Avg. PHRF	Max. Speed	Motion Index	Space Index	No. of Berths	Head-room
Sirius 21	21' 2"	7' 11"	1' 4"	2,000	525	20.5	135	258	5.8	10.0	344	5	4' 9"
South Coast 21	21' 4"	6' 11"	3' 0"	2,000	625	19.2	303	252	5.1	14.2	165	2	3' 3"
Sirius 22	21' 2"	7' 11"	1' 4"	2,100	525	19.8	123	243	5.9	9.7	352	5	4' 9"
Nimble 20 (21)	20' 10"	7' 9"	1' 1"	2,200	800	19.6	127	288	6.0	11.0	316	4	4' 3"
Triangle 20 (21)	20' 6"	7' 1"	2' 2"	2,300	800	16.3	222	NA	5.5	14.6	250	2	4' 6"

South Coast 21
Classic design, reminiscent of a Star Boat

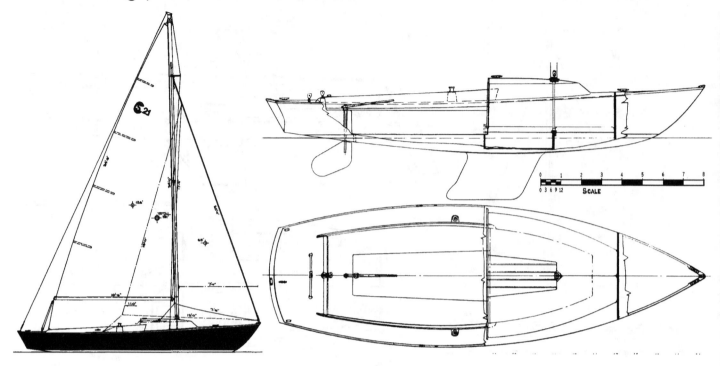

LOD:	21' 4"		**Designer:**	Carl A. Alberg
LOA:	21' 4"		**Builder:**	South Coast Seacraft
LWL:	14' 4"		**Years produced:**	1966–1979
Min./max. draft:	fixed keel 3' 0"		**Sail area:**	191 sq. ft.
Bridge clearance:	29' 0"		**Fuel tankage:**	portable
Power:	outboard 3 to 6 hp		**Water tankage:**	portable
B/D ratio:	31%		**Approx. trailering wgt.:**	2,900 lbs.

The classic low freeboard, narrow beam, and Star Boat-like underbody appeal to us as being a great combination for daysailing and club one-design racing. But somehow the SC21 never caught on in any big way on the club racing circuit. Too bad. ***Best features:*** We imagine the hull configuration gives a good combination of speed and comfort. Note the relatively high Motion Index compared to comps. ***Worst features:*** There is not much space below, even for overnighting—basically a pair of settee berths with almost non-existent (3' 3") headroom, and that's it. No space for a galley or even to store a porta-potti. We'd worry slightly about that rudder tucked away under the counter. Does it have weed dragging us down? If so, we couldn't see it without hanging way over the side, and then only if the water was clear. Launching and retrieving at a ramp might give some trouble because of the relatively deep fin keel. The one cockpit drain is aft on the centerline, rather than the more preferable two drains in the corners, to remove water when the vessel is heeled. And the plan shows a flat cockpit sole; it should be angled downwind aft for drainage.

Comps	LOD	Beam	MinDr	Displ	Bllst	SA/D	D/L	Avg. PHRF	Max. Speed	Motion Index	Space Index	No. of Berths	Head-room
Sirius 21	21' 2"	7' 11"	1' 4"	2,000	525	20.5	135	258	5.8	10.0	344	5	4' 9"
South Coast 21	21' 4"	6' 11"	3' 0"	2,000	625	19.2	303	252	5.1	14.2	165	2	3' 3"
Sirius 22	21' 2"	7' 11"	1' 4"	2,100	525	19.8	123	243	5.9	9.7	352	5	4' 9"
Nimble 20 (21)	20' 10"	7' 9"	1' 1"	2,200	800	19.6	127	288	6.0	11.0	316	4	4' 3"
Triangle 20 (21)	20' 6"	7' 1"	2' 2"	2,300	800	16.3	222	NA	5.5	14.6	250	2	4' 6"

Sovereign 20

There's not much to like about this vessel

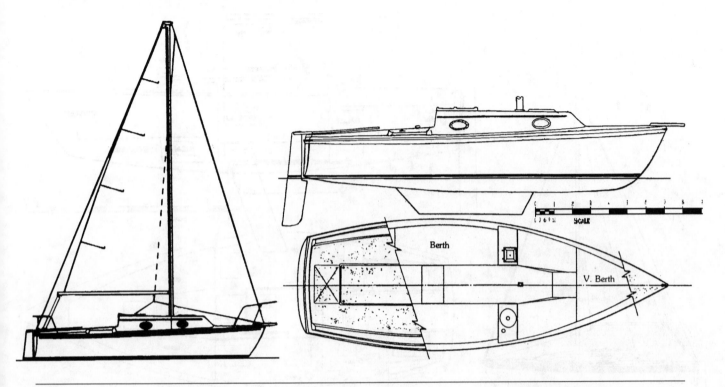

LOD:	20' 0"
LOA:	22' 6"
LWL:	17' 0"
Min./max. draft:	fixed keel 2' 0"
Bridge clearance:	27' 3"
Power:	outboard 3 to 6 hp
B/D ratio:	35%

Designer:	not specified by marketer
Builder:	Coastline Marine and others
Years produced:	1990–1997
Sail area:	189 sq. ft.
Fuel tankage:	portable
Water tankage:	5 gal.
Approx. trailering wgt.:	2,500 lbs.

We have never liked the Sovereign series of boats. We think that as new boats they were grossly overpriced (particularly near the end of their production runs); they were poor sailers relative to their comps; and their marketers made wild claims. Example from a brochure on the Sovereign 20 Mk II in 1997, when the company was about to close: "The 20 Mk II is . . . probably the best mini-cruiser available today." A quick look at the specs below shows that except for her two-foot fixed keel, which effectively ruins whatever upwind sailing performance she might otherwise have had, she is very similar in size and weight to her comps—all of which sail better than she does, are easier to handle at a launching ramp, and cost a lot less to buy when new. ***Best features:*** When new, the Sovereign topsides finish was usually above average in smoothness and gloss. ***Worst features:*** Her 1997 price was a whopping $24,995 FOB Port Richey, FL. A fair price for that year's market? We'd say $11,000 new, sailaway. Her Space Index is lowest in her group. And her rudder hangs below the protection of her shallow keel.

Comps	LOD	Beam	MinDr	Displ	Bllst	SA/D	D/L	Avg. PHRF	Max. Speed	Motion Index	Space Index	No. of Berths	Head-room
Hunter 20	19' 8"	7' 6"	1' 3"	1,700	400	19.1	204	276	5.3	10.5	258	5	4' 2"
Sovereign 20	20' 0"	7' 2"	2' 0"	1,700	600	21.2	154	NA	5.5	10.6	237	4	4' 2"
Hunter 212 (21)	21' 0"	8' 2"	0' 10"	1,800	135	23.0	138	216	5.7	8.7	329	4	4' 4"
Aquarius 21	21' 0"	7' 10"	1' 0"	1,900	665	18.9	140	273	5.7	9.9	300	4	4' 6"
Spirit 6.5 (21)	21' 3"	7' 10"	1' 8"	2,100	550	19.1	142	261	5.8	10.7	334	4 to 5	4' 4"

Spirit 6.5 (21)
Small swing-keeler from a Down East designer

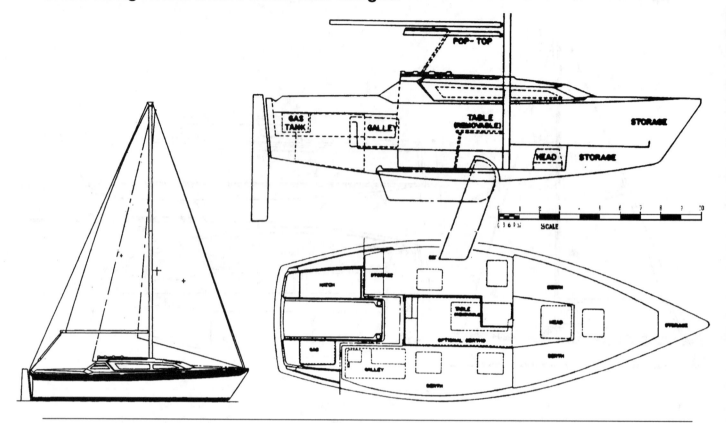

LOD:	21' 3"	**Designer:**	Hank Hinckley
LOA:	22' 3"	**Builder:**	Spirit Yachts and others
LWL:	18' 9"	**Years produced:**	1977–1982
Min./max. draft:	1' 8"/5' 0"	**Sail area:**	196 sq. ft.
Bridge clearance:	28' 8"	**Fuel tankage:**	portable
Power:	outboard 3 to 6 hp	**Water tankage:**	portable
B/D ratio:	26%	**Approx. trailering wgt.:**	3,000 lbs.

Generally speaking, Hank Hinckley, of the Southwest Harbor, Maine, Hinckleys of boatbuilding fame, did a good job designing the Spirit 6.5. The ads for her say that she has "probably the best designed, most spacious, most clearly thought-out interior on any sailboat her size." Indeed, her Space Index is higher than most of her comps by around 10%. But her headroom (poptop down) isn't as good as the Aquarius (though it's 6' 2" with the poptop raised), and her draft is not as ramp-friendly as some of her comps (because her weighted swing keel is positioned lower in the hull to keep the cabin free of a trunk). **Best features:** For the same reason that her ramp draft is deeper than some of her comps, her cabin has more leg room, since there is no above-the-sole trunk housing the swing keel. And as mentioned above, her Space Index is the highest in her group. **Worst features:** The freeboard, which adds to her space below, is noticeably higher than her comps, giving her a boxy look.

Comps	LOD	Beam	MinDr	Displ	Bllst	SA/D	D/L	Avg. PHRF	Max. Speed	Motion Index	Space Index	No. of Berths	Head-room
Hunter 20	19' 8"	7' 6"	1' 3"	1,700	400	19.6	204	276	5.3	10.5	258	5	4' 2"
Sovereign 20	20' 0"	7' 2"	2' 0"	1,700	600	21.2	154	NA	5.5	11.6	237	4	4' 2"
Hunter 212 (21)	21' 0"	8' 2"	0' 10"	1,800	135	23.0	138	216	5.7	8.7	329	4	4' 4"
Aquarius 21	21' 0"	7' 10"	1' 0"	1,900	665	18.9	140	273	5.7	9.9	300	4	4' 6"
Spirit 6.5 (21)	21' 3"	7' 10"	1' 8"	2,100	550	19.1	142	261	5.8	10.7	334	4 to 5	4' 4"

Triangle 20 (21)
Early small cruiser with some nice features

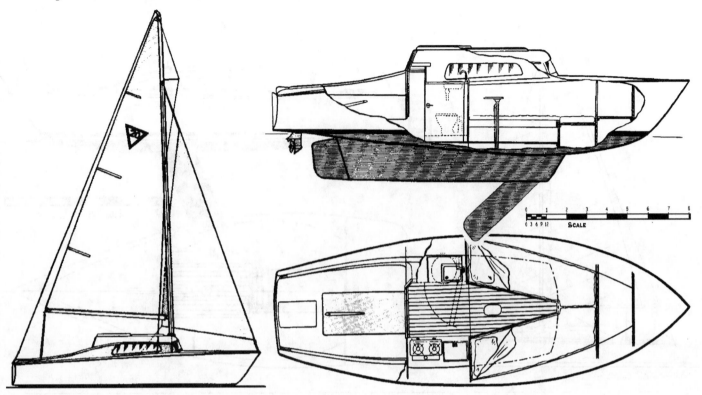

LOD:	20' 6"
LOA:	20' 6"
LWL:	16' 8"
Min./max. draft:	2' 2"/4' 9"
Bridge clearance:	30' 0"
Power:	outboard 3 to 6 hp
B/D ratio:	35%

Designer:	Chuck Angle
Builder:	Grampian/Triangle Marine
Years produced:	1961–1963
Sail area:	177 sq. ft.
Fuel tankage:	portable
Water tankage:	unknown
Approx. trailering wgt.:	3,300 lbs.

An early entry in the fiberglass sweepstakes, this small cruiser was built by Grampian Marine of Ontario, for Chuck Angle, the proprietor of Triangle Marine of Rochester, NY. An ad notes that, among other things, the boat features "bronze hardware; steel keel and centerboard; two 6' 3" berths . . . 6' 3" cockpit seats . . . large built-in icebox; concealed head; sink; water tank; hanging locker; outboard in well; enclosed motor compartment; canvas dodger provides full headroom in galley." The company offered the boat ready to go or in several different stages of completion, for finishing by the buyer. ***Best features:*** Many of the features listed here are quite unusual for a boat so small. A big companionway hatch lets in plenty of air and gives standing headroom under the optional canvas dodger (not shown in drawings). The toilet arrangement, in the way of the hatch, provides good headroom. Note that the sink drains into the toilet. ***Worst features:*** The Triangle 20's SA/D ratio is quite low, suggesting less speed than her comps in light air.

Comps	LOD	Beam	MinDr	Displ	Bllst	SA/D	D/L	Avg. PHRF	Max. Speed	Motion Index	Space Index	No. of Berths	Head-room
Sirius 21	21' 2"	7' 11"	1' 4"	2,000	525	20.5	135	258	5.8	10.0	344	5	4' 9"
South Coast 21	21' 4"	6' 11"	3' 0"	2,000	625	19.2	303	252	5.1	14.2	165	2	3' 3"
Sirius 22	21' 2"	7' 11"	1' 4"	2,100	525	19.8	123	243	5.9	9.7	352	5	4' 9"
Nimble 20 (21)	20' 10"	7' 9"	1' 1"	2,200	800	19.6	127	288	6.0	11.0	316	4	4' 3"
Triangle 20 (21)	20' 6"	7' 1"	2' 2"	2,300	800	16.3	222	NA	5.5	14.6	250	2	4' 6"

U.S. 21/Triton 21
A brief appearance in the Pearson Yachts line

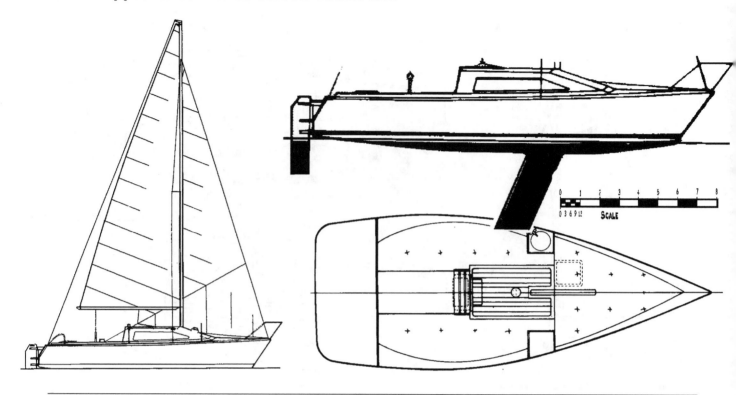

LOD:	20' 6"	**Designer:**	Clark Scarborough
LOA:	21' 0"	**Builder:**	U.S. Yachts and others
LWL:	18' 0"	**Years produced:**	1983–1985
Min./max. draft:	1' 4"/4' 7"	**Sail area:**	244 sq. ft.
Bridge clearance:	31' 8"	**Fuel tankage:**	portable
Power:	outboard 3 to 6 hp	**Water tankage:**	portable
B/D ratio:	14%	**Approx. trailering wgt.:**	2,100 lbs.

This boat was first launched in 1983, just before the Buccaneer Division of Bayliner Marine sold its U.S. Yachts product line (a.k.a. United Sailing Yachts, not "United States Yachts" as one might think) to Pearson Yachts in 1984. Pearson bought the U.S. 21 along with several other models (including the U.S. 22 and the U.S. 25) and called them its Triton line. But the company was in financial trouble even before it took on the new line, which didn't fit their customer base well, and soon Pearson discontinued the Tritons. Unfortunately the whole sailboat market was in a severe economic downturn at the time, and discontinu-

ing the Triton line wasn't enough to stem the company's dwindling cash reserves. Pearson, one of the industry's most respected fiberglass yacht builders, sadly filed for bankruptcy in 1991. ***Best features:*** The U.S. 21's light weight should make her relatively easy to trailer, launch, and retrieve, though perhaps not as easily as the Newport 212. Her PHRF rating, well below that of her comps, intimates that she is fast. ***Worst features:*** Her high SA/D, wide beam, and low ballast compared to her comps may mean she needs more beef on the rail in heavy air to keep her upright.

Comps	LOD	Beam	MinDr	Displ	Bllst	SA/D	D/L	Avg. PHRF	Max. Speed	Motion Index	Space Index	No. of Berths	Head-room
U.S. 21/Triton 21	21' 3"	8' 0"	1' 4"	1,400	200	28.6	107	201	5.7	7.1	299	4	4' 0"
Santana 21	21' 3"	7' 6"	1' 6"	1,400	550	24.2	86	267	5.9	7.4	238	4	3' 10"
Newport 212 (21)	21' 2"	7' 8"	0' 10"	1,500	400	21.6	98	267	5.8	7.6	318	4	4' 2"

Venture 21
Forerunner of lightweight retractable keel boats

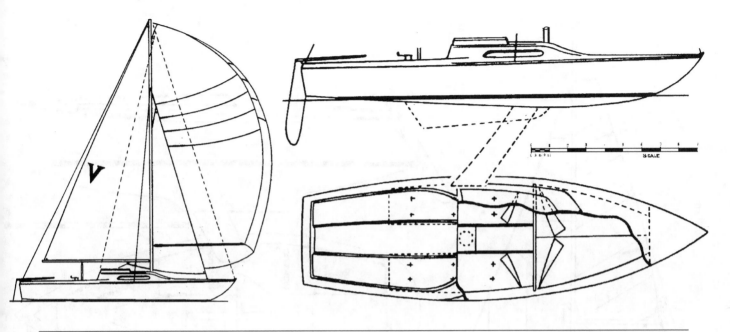

LOD:	21' 0"	**Designer:**	Roger MacGregor
LOA:	22' 0"	**Builder:**	MacGregor Yachts
LWL:	18' 6"	**Years produced:**	1965–1986
Min./max. draft:	1' 0"/5' 6"	**Sail area:**	175 sq. ft.
Bridge clearance:	28' 0"	**Fuel tankage:**	portable
Power:	outboard 3 to 6 hp	**Water tankage:**	portable
B/D ratio:	33%	**Approx. trailering wgt.:**	1,800 lbs.

This design (also known as the MacGregor 21) spawned a variety of similar lightweight retractable-keel boats—easy to launch, easy to sail, and low in cost. Eventually MacGregor produced a whole bevy of similar designs, including the MacGregor 22, 25, and 26, and the Venture 222, 23, and 25. ***Best features:*** Price (on the used market, of course, since this design is no longer made) is below her comps, reflecting an ultra-low price when she was new—and perhaps some perceptions of the level of construction quality. ***Worst features:*** Headroom is lowest of the group of comps. Motion Index is worst of the group (though all her comps are so low it doesn't make much difference). Her Space Index is also at the bottom of the list. Her cast-iron keel, like that on her comps, is a maintenance chore, since it eventually begins to need frequent attention to keep rust at bay. Hardware is not as high quality as her comps.

Comps	LOD	Beam	MinDr	Displ	Bllst	SA/D	D/L	Avg. PHRF	Max. Speed	Motion Index	Space Index	No. of Berths	Head-room
Cal 21	20' 6"	6' 8"	0' 9"	1,100	360	29.4	106	258	5.5	7.6	221	4	4' 1"
Venture 21	21' 0"	6' 10"	1' 0"	1,200	400	24.8	85	252	5.8	7.4	203	4	3' 3"
San Juan 21 Mk I	20' 6"	7' 0"	1' 0"	1,250	400	26.2	114	252	5.5	8.0	227	4	3' 6"
San Juan 21 Mk II	20' 6"	7' 0"	1' 0"	1,250	400	26.2	114	252	5.5	8.0	227	4	3' 6"

Wild Wind 20
A powerboat builder ventures briefly into sailing

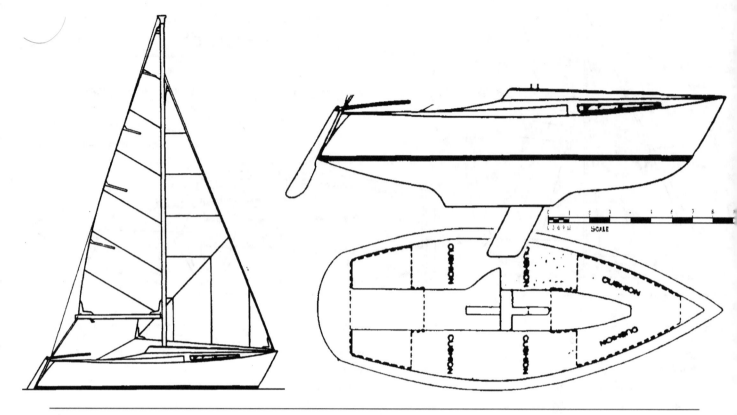

LOD:	20' 0"
LOA:	21' 0"
LWL:	18' 0"
Min./max. draft:	2' 0"/5' 8"
Bridge clearance:	30' 0"
Power:	outboard 3 to 6 hp
B/D ratio:	36%

Designer:	not indicated by builder
Builder:	Rinkerbuilt Co.
Years produced:	1982–1983?
Sail area:	193 sq. ft.
Fuel tankage:	portable
Water tankage:	portable
Approx. trailering wgt.:	3,200 lbs.

In the early 1980s, a Syracuse, IN, powerboat builder named Lossie Rinker decided to take a chance producing sailboats. The Wild Wind (apparently also called the Gale Force 20, if our meager information on this boat is accurate) was the result. It didn't last very long. In a year or so, Rinkerbuilt was back making just powerboats again, and when last contacted were still at it. ***Best features:*** Offhand, we are hard pressed to find anything salutary worth mentioning. ***Worst features:*** The hull seems to

be particularly ungainly, though in fairness, we haven't seen this boat in real life, only on paper. The layout is apparently a series of cushions laid end to end, and very little else—not our idea of a clever arrangement. The rudder appears to be a draftsman's mistake, or a computer-graphics glitch: way too narrow, way too shallow to maintain full steering control in heavy wind and sea (or even in light wind and sea). In all, it isn't hard to see why Rinker decided against continuing production.

Comps	LOD	Beam	MinDr	Displ	Bllst	SA/D	D/L	Avg. PHRF	Max. Speed	Motion Index	Space Index	No. of Berths	Head-room
Chrysler 20	20' 0"	7' 11"	1' 11"	1,950	500	18.3	149	264	5.7	10.1	311	4	3' 9"
Buccaneer 200 (20)	20' 5"	8' 0"	2' 0"	2,100	750	18.6	183	276	5.6	10.9	336	4	3' 6"
Signet 20	19' 10"	6' 8"	2' 0"	2,146	800	18.5	234	NA	5.4	15.4	193	4	4' 0"
Wild Wind 20	20' 0"	7' 11"	2' 0"	2,200	800	18.3	168	NA	5.7	11.5	302	6	4' 3"
Montego 20	19' 6"	7' 2"	2' 0"	2,300	600	17.4	184	282	5.6	14.0	246	4	4' 0"

Islander 21
Early minicruiser from J. H. McGlasson

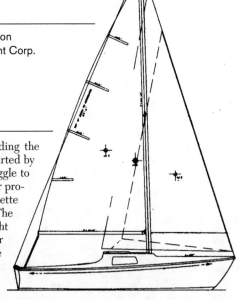

LOD:	20' 10"	**Designer:**	J. H. McGlasson
LOA:	20' 10"	**Builder:**	Wayfarer Yacht Corp.
LWL:	18' 0"	**Years produced:**	1965–1969
Min./max. draft:	3' 4"	**Sail area:**	208 sq. ft.
Bridge clearance:	28' 0"	**Fuel tankage:**	portable
Power:	outboard 3 to 6 hp	**Water tankage:**	portable
B/D ratio:	51%	**Approx. trailering wgt.:**	3,000 lbs.

Wayfarer Yacht Corporation of Costa Mesa, CA, produced the Islander line (including the Islander 21 shown here), the Bahama 24 (page 316), and others. The company was started by Buster Hammond, owned for a while by Cosmodyne and by Radion, and after a struggle to save it, went bankrupt in 1987. We have no accommodations plan to show here, but her promotional literature says she "is equipped with four full-length berths, galley, unusual dinette arrangement, modern head, and plenty of storage lockers." That sounds good to us. The purported 1,000 pounds of ballast seems unusually large—more than half the total weight of the boat—leaving only 950 pounds for the hull, deck, rig, etc. That makes us wonder whether the numbers given in ads are incorrect. (For comparison, this boat's comps have weights excluding ballast as follows: Cal 20, 1,050 pounds; Ranger 22, 1,282 pounds.)
Best and worst features: Not enough information available to comment.

Comps	LOD	Beam	MinDr	Displ	Bllst	SA/D	D/L	Avg. PHRF	Max. Speed	Motion Index	Space Index	No. of Berths	Head-room
Cal 20	20' 0"	7' 0"	3' 4"	1,950	900	20.1	149	276	5.7	11.8	244	4	3' 11"
Islander 21	20' 10"	7' 10"	3' 4"	1,950	1,000	21.3	149	282	5.7	10.2	280	4	3' 9"
Ranger 22 (21)	21' 4"	7' 10"	4' 3"	2,182	900	19.8	182	222	5.6	11.4	306	4	4' 0"

Mystic Mini-Ton 21 (20)
Bruce Kirby's smallest racer/cruiser

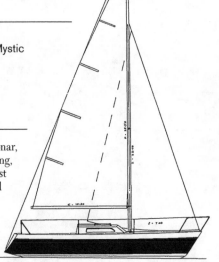

LOD:	20' 3"	**Designer:**	Bruce Kirby
LOA:	21' 3"	**Builder:**	Boat Company of Mystic
LWL:	17' 0"	**Years produced:**	1978–1979
Min./max. draft:	4' 0"	**Sail area:**	213 sq. ft.
Bridge clearance:	31' 0"	**Fuel tankage:**	portable
Power:	outboard 3 to 6 hp	**Water tankage:**	portable
B/D ratio:	38%	**Approx. trailering wgt.:**	2,600 lbs.

This sleek-looking boat was designed by the well-known Bruce Kirby (Laser, Nightwind 35, Sonar, etc.). The sales brochure says she is intended "for MORC competition, IOR Mini-Ton level racing, and as a yacht club one-design." She had some racing successes in Long Island Sound in her first year, but for some reason not many units were sold, perhaps because the marketers appeared not to push the boat's possibilities as a pocket cruiser. In fact, neither her ads nor her brochure shows her layout below—so we don't, either, having no details to pass on. But personally, we think she's very good-looking, and knowing that other Kirby designs are almost always good sailors' boats, we have a warm feeling about this one. Too bad they never really caught on.
Best and worst features: Not enough information available to comment.

Comps	LOD	Beam	MinDr	Displ	Bllst	SA/D	D/L	Avg. PHRF	Max. Speed	Motion Index	Space Index	No. of Berths	Head-room
Harpoon 6.2 (20)	20' 4"	8' 0"	3' 6"	1,700	550	24.7	191	234	5.3	9.5	339	2	4' 3"
Jeanneau Bahia 23 (20)	20' 4"	7' 11"	1' 5"	1,850	620	22.3	140	177	5.7	9.4	339	4	4' 11"
Mystic Mini-Ton 21 (20)	20' 3"	7' 11"	4' 0"	1,850	700	22.6	168	219	5.5	9.9	313	4	4' 0"
Antrim 20	20' 5"	8' 0"	4' 0"	1,850	750	29.7	154	NA	5.6	9.7	339	4	4' 4"
Precision 21	20' 9"	8' 3"	1' 9"	1,875	600	21.4	156	270	5.6	9.4	317	4	4' 4"

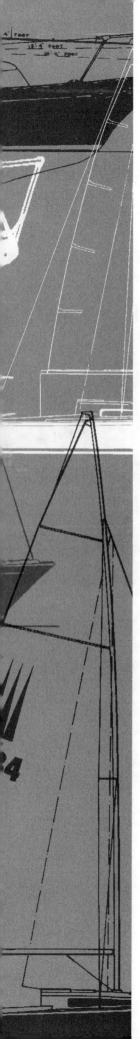

FOUR
Sixty-Five Boats 22'

*2 vessels without accommodations plans are grouped together at end of chapter

Alberg 22

One of a dozen Alberg small sloops in this guide

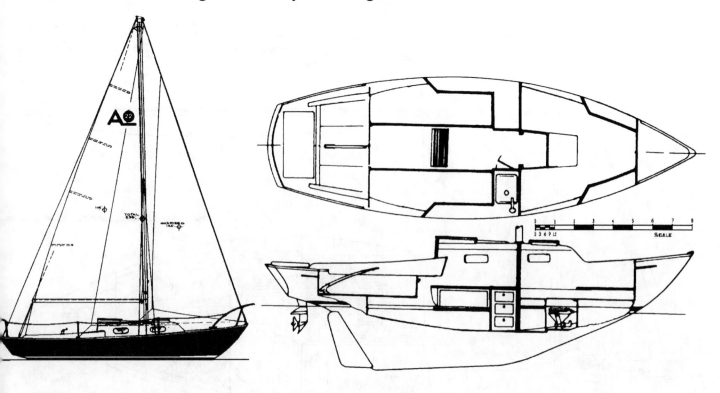

LOD:	22' 0"	**Designer:**	Carl Alberg	
LOA:	22' 0"	**Builder:**	Douglas Marine Craft, Nye Yachts	
LWL:	16' 0"	**Years produced:**	1967?–1987?	
Min./max. draft:	3' 1"	**Sail area:**	263 sq. ft.	
Bridge clearance:	29' 0"	**Fuel tankage:**	portable	
Power:	outboard 3 to 6 hp	**Water tankage:**	portable	
B/D ratio:	47%	**Approx. trailering wgt.:**	4,800 lbs.	

This shippy little craft is almost indistinguishable from a number of similar Alberg designs. For example, the South Coast 23, a foot longer on deck but pretty much the same in her proportions, comes to mind. (We owned a South Coast 23 for nine years; see page 255 for details.) There are a dozen Alberg designs represented in this book, and at least half of them have close to the same silhouette as the "22" shown here. The boat is very good for weekend cruising, though you may find she will get a bit crowded if you bring the kids along. She was built in Canada, first, from about 1967 to 1969, by Douglas Marine Craft of Port Stanley, Ontario. When that firm closed shop, Nye Yachts, also in Ontario, acquired the molds and continued production from about 1970 to 1987. ***Best features:*** The high B/D ratio and long keel provide easy steering and relatively good comfort in cruising mode. The outboard well in the lazarette makes engine access easier and avoids prop cavitation in all but the choppiest seas. ***Worst features:*** Unless you are planning to challenge other Albergs of similar size, forget racing. The keel isn't deep enough to take a big enough bite for good close-hauled performance.

Comps	LOD	Beam	MinDr	Displ	Bllst	SA/D	D/L	Avg. PHRF	Max. Speed	Motion Index	Space Index	No. of Berths	Head-room
Alberg 22	22' 0"	7' 0"	3' 1"	3,200	1,500	17.4	349	282	5.4	20.7	274	4	4' 4"
Cape Dory Typhoon Sr 22	22' 5"	7' 5"	3' 1"	3,300	1,700	17.7	328	273	5.4	19.2	322	4	4' 8"
Ranger 23 (22)	22' 3"	7' 11"	3' 9"	3,400	1,500	18.7	190	216	6.0	15.8	318	4	4' 3"
Westerly Nomad 22	22' 3"	7' 5"	2' 3"	3,600	950	15.5	261	300	5.7	19.6	277	4	4' 7"

Beneteau First 235 (22)
Interesting French racer/cruiser

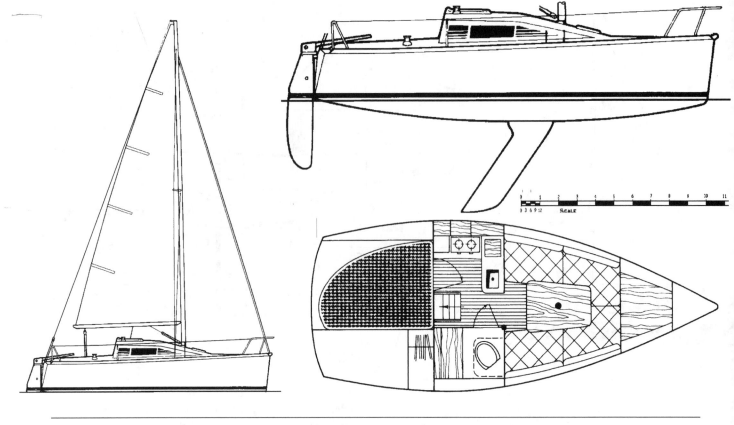

LOD:	21' 8"	**Designer:**	Group Finot
LOA:	23' 4"	**Builder:**	Beneteau
LWL:	20' 4"	**Years produced:**	1986–1992
Min./max. draft:	2' 2"/5' 9"	**Sail area:**	264 sq. ft.
Bridge clearance:	33' 0"	**Fuel tankage:**	portable
Power:	outboard 3 to 6 hp	**Water tankage:**	13 gal.
B/D ratio:	35%	**Approx. trailering wgt.:**	3,300 lbs.

Here is a boat you might call elegant, if you like the French approach to design—all rounded corners and brushed aluminum. It may take time to get over the idea that she's not 23½ feet long. (She's really only 21' 8" on deck, without the rudder, and even her official LOA is only 23' 4" . . . so where does the "235" come from? Marketing!) You can buy the boat three ways. She came with a swing keel (5' 9" full down, 810 lbs. ballast, as shown here) or a fin keel (3' 9" fixed, 950 lbs. ballast). Both rate about 189 PHRF. Or you could opt for a winged keel (less draft than the fin keel, about 195 PHRF, not best for racing). If you want to race against other classes, you may want to try for the swing-keel model—or you may find a local Beneteau one-design fleet to go against. The marketers have a good Internet "club" for owners to stay in touch. *Best features:* Roomy cabin with good headroom and enclosed head. Very pretty, very sleek, very . . . French. *Worst features:* That aft berth under the cockpit is a bear to climb into or out of.

Comps	LOD	Beam	MinDr	Displ	Bllst	SA/D	D/L	Avg. PHRF	Max. Speed	Motion Index	Space Index	No. of Berths	Head-room
Capri 22	22' 0"	8' 0"	2' 8"	2,150	800	22.0	120	201	6.0	10.0	301	4	3' 9"
Cal 22	22' 0"	7' 9"	2' 10"	2,275	950	20.6	135	234	5.9	11.3	314	4	4' 6"
Beneteau First 235 (22)	21' 8"	8' 2"	2' 2"	2,310	810	24.2	123	192	6.0	10.2	393	4	5' 4"

Bristol Caravel 22

Halsey Herreshoff designs a boat for Bristol

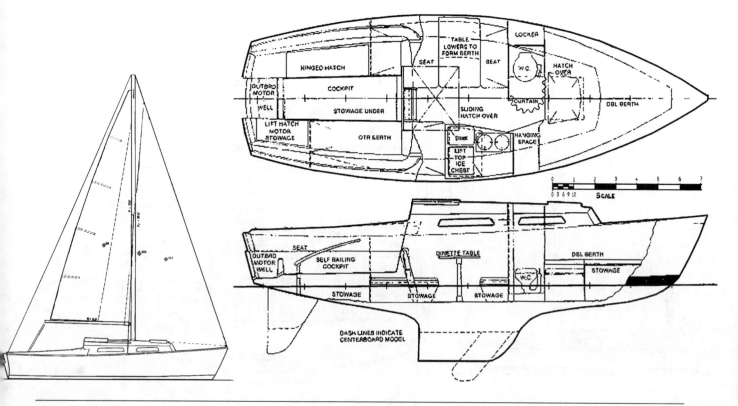

LOD:	22' 0"	**Designer:**	Halsey Herreshoff
LOA:	22' 0"	**Builder:**	Bristol Yachts
LWL:	19' 6"	**Years produced:**	1968–1978
Min./max. draft:	2' 6"/4' 4"	**Sail area:**	206 sq. ft.
Bridge clearance:	33' 6"	**Fuel tankage:**	portable
Power:	outboard 3 to 6 hp	**Water tankage:**	portable
B/D ratio:	40%	**Approx. trailering wgt.:**	4,100 lbs.

In 1964 Clint Pearson bought troubled Sailstar Boats. He renamed the company Bristol Yachts, and in 1968 introduced the Bristol Caravel. The boat could be purchased either with a standard layout with settee berths port and starboard, or with the dinette arrangement shown here, which supposedly will sleep five (though we wouldn't want to try sleeping in the "double" formed by the table lowered flush with the dinette seats, which is barely three feet wide). Another choice for new buyers was either a centerboarder (shown in phantom lines on the plan), or a fin-keel boat with a draft of 3' 6". **Best features:** The outboard well in the cockpit makes life easier for the helmsman when maneuvering in tight quarters. **Worst features:** A peculiarity of the centerboarder is her shallow rudder, necessary to keep it out of harm's way when negotiating shoal waters with board up. It raises the question of whether the rudder has enough area to provide good steering control. If so, why is the area enlarged for the fin-keel version? Why not, instead, cut wetted surface on the fin-keel version's rudder to improve performance?

Comps	LOD	Beam	MinDr	Displ	Bllst	SA/D	D/L	Avg. PHRF	Max. Speed	Motion Index	Space Index	No. of Berths	Head-room
Starwind 22	22' 0"	7' 9"	1' 11"	2,600	775	17.6	169	273	5.8	12.8	346	5	4' 9"
Pearson 22	22' 0"	7' 9"	3' 5"	2,600	1,000	18.4	183	246	5.8	13.3	298	4	4' 2"
Seaward 23 (22)	21' 9"	8' 4"	2' 1"	2,700	900	19.8	138	285	5.8	11.3	325	4	4' 8"
Bristol Caravel 22	22' 0"	7' 9"	2' 6"	2,850	1,150	16.4	172	288	5.8	14.1	322	4	4' 0"

Cal 22
Does this boat resemble the O'Day 222?

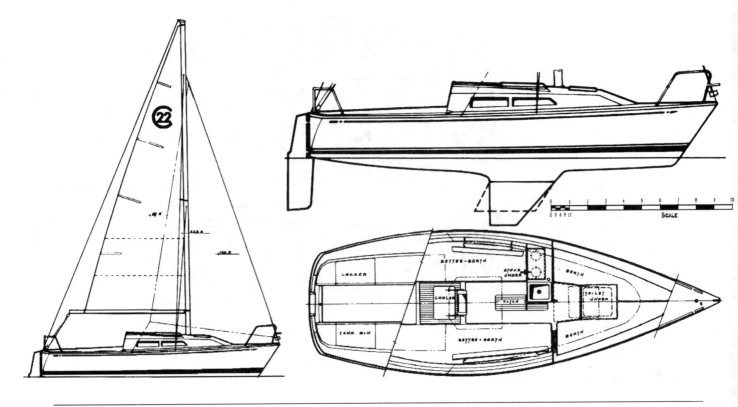

LOD:	22' 0"	**Designer:**	Hunt Associates
LOA:	23' 3"	**Builder:**	Cal Boats
LWL:	19' 7"	**Years produced:**	1985–1989
Min./max. draft:	keel 2' 10" shoal/3' 5" deep	**Sail area:**	223 sq. ft.
Bridge clearance:	32' 7"	**Fuel tankage:**	portable
Power:	outboard 3 to 6 hp	**Water tankage:**	5 gal.
B/D ratio:	42%	**Approx. trailering wgt.:**	3,300 lbs.

C. Raymond Hunt Associates may have tried to draw boats for Cal that would not look too much like boats of another one of the designer's clients, O'Day—but seems to have had only partial success. A case in point is the O'Day 222 (page 119), designed a year earlier than the Cal 22, which appears to be a disguised Cal 22 despite some significant differences: more ballast, slightly reversed transom vs. vertical transom, keel/centerboard vs. fixed keel, and an inch or two difference in various key dimensions. But still, the resemblance, particularly in the accommodations, is remarkable. **Best features:** The deck layout is admirably simple, with all lines led to cockpit. **Worst features:** The Cal 22 came with either a deep (3' 5") or shoal (2' 10") fin keel. The deep keel doesn't match the performance of the Capri, a comp, as is evidenced in the PHRF ratings. The shoal-draft version is too shallow to sail adequately upwind, and too deep to make launching as easy as, say, the swing keel Beneteau First 235. Headroom and space are better in the Beneteau, too. Altogether, judged against her comps, the Cal does not shine.

Comps	LOD	Beam	MinDr	Displ	Bllst	SA/D	D/L	Avg. PHRF	Max. Speed	Motion Index	Space Index	No. of Berths	Head-room
Capri 22	22' 0"	8' 0"	2' 8"	2,150	800	22.0	120	201	6.0	10.0	301	4	3' 9"
Cal 22	22' 0"	7' 9"	2' 10"	2,275	950	20.6	135	234	5.9	11.3	314	4	4' 6"
Beneteau First 235 (22)	21' 8"	8' 2"	2' 2"	2,310	810	24.2	123	192	6.0	10.2	393	4	5' 4"

Cape Dory Typhoon Sr. 22

A Typhoon 18 with extra oomph?

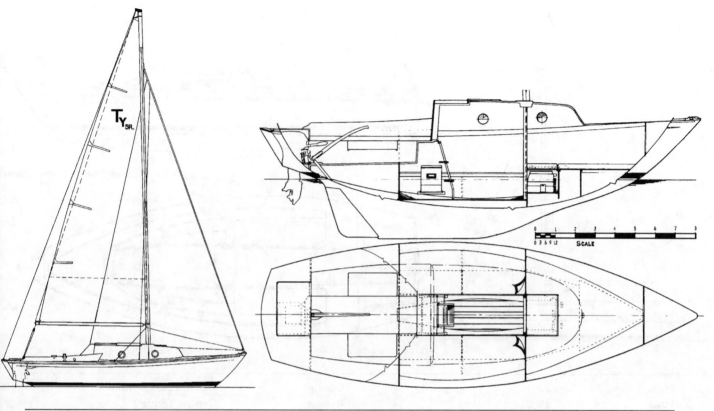

LOD:	22' 5"
LOA:	22' 5"
LWL:	16' 6"
Min./max. draft:	3' 1"
Bridge clearance:	34' 0"
Power:	outboard 3 to 6 hp
B/D ratio:	52%

Designer:	Carl Alberg
Builder:	Cape Dory Yachts
Years produced:	1981–1988
Sail area:	245 sq. ft.
Fuel tankage:	portable
Water tankage:	portable
Approx. trailering wgt.:	4,900 lbs.

The smaller Cape Dory Typhoon 18 (page 23) was introduced in about 1971, when the company was offering only two boats, but it wasn't until 1981 that the 22-foot Typhoon "Senior" came along. The 22 sold well until the late 1980s, when many boatbuilders recognized that better profitability would be gained by the sale of larger boats. ***Best features:*** She's got that Alberg look, with springy sheer and gracefully drawn ends. And though this boat is close in most dimensions to her comps, she has the feel of a bigger boat, with more space and greater headroom below than her comps. ***Worst features:*** Why the quaint little portholes instead of oval or rectangular portlights? Others must have asked the same question; rectangular ports were substituted on a later version. The outboard well amidships, covered with a full hatch, may look good, but we recall that ventilation in the engine compartment was poor, and to keep the engine from starving from lack of fresh air, the crew would have to prop open the hatch.

Comps	LOD	Beam	MinDr	Displ	Bllst	SA/D	D/L	Avg. PHRF	Max. Speed	Motion Index	Space Index	No. of Berths	Head-room
Alberg 22	22' 0"	7' 0"	3' 1"	3,200	1,500	17.4	349	282	5.4	20.7	274	4	4' 4"
Cape Dory Typhoon Sr 22	22' 5"	7' 5"	3' 1"	3,300	1,700	17.7	328	273	5.4	19.2	322	4	4' 8"
Ranger 23 (22)	22' 3"	7' 11"	3' 9"	3,400	1,500	18.7	190	216	6.0	15.8	318	4	4' 3"
Westerly Nomad 22	22' 3"	7' 5"	2' 3"	3,600	950	15.5	261	300	5.7	19.6	277	4	4' 7"

Capri 22
Sleek, fast, and fun

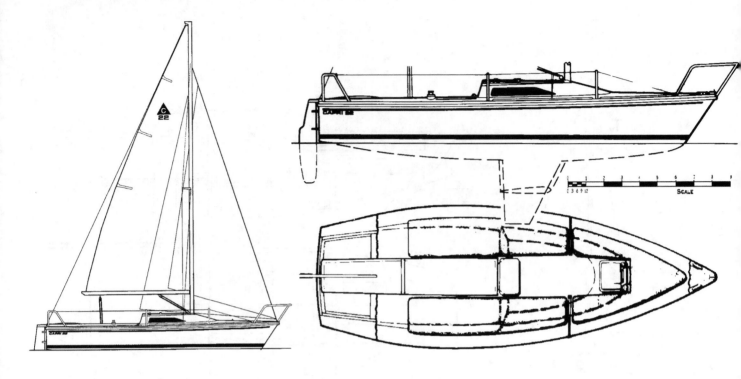

LOD:	22' 0"	**Designer:**	Catalina Design Team
LOA:	23' 0"	**Builder:**	Catalina Yachts
LWL:	20' 0"	**Years produced:**	1985–present
Min./max. draft:	2' 8" wing keel/4' 0" fin	**Sail area:**	229 sq. ft.
Bridge clearance:	30' 0"	**Fuel tankage:**	portable
Power:	outboard 3 to 6 hp	**Water tankage:**	portable
B/D ratio:	37%	**Approx. trailering wgt.:**	3,100 lbs.

The Capri 22 was designed to be a light, fast family boat with an emphasis on daysailing and fleet local racing. One main parameter in conceiving the Capri line was to produce a very well-finished boat for a reasonable price. One result is that both hull and deck have neat and easy-to-clean fiberglass liners. Another result is that when the boat first came off the line in 1985, the base price was a mere $6,000. The company must have done something right; now, more than 25 years later, the boat is still selling—last time we looked, at a base price under $17,000, including some major design updates (new deck profile flared across the stern, wider cockpit curves for crew comfort during and after sailing). Two keel configurations are available: a fin of 650 pounds and 4' 0" draft, or a wing of 700 pounds and 2' 8" draft. (Note ballast was 800 pounds on earlier boats, but less on later production.)

Best features: Her PHRF of 201 puts her in the "fast" category along with the Beneteau, a comp. Active fleets in most parts of the United States can make life more fun and interesting for owners who seek camaraderie. **Worst features:** Accommodations are very basic, and headroom is low vs. comps.

Comps	LOD	Beam	MinDr	Displ	Bllst	SA/D	D/L	Avg. PHRF	Max. Speed	Motion Index	Space Index	No. of Berths	Head-room
Capri 22	22' 0"	8' 0"	2' 8"	2,150	800	22.0	120	201	6.0	10.0	301	4	3' 9"
Cal 22	22' 0"	7' 9"	2' 10"	2,275	950	20.6	135	234	5.9	11.3	314	4	4' 6"
Beneteau First 235 (22)	21' 8"	8' 2"	2' 2"	2,310	810	24.2	123	192	6.0	10.2	393	4	5' 4"

Catalina 22 Mk I
Ultrapopular 22-footer

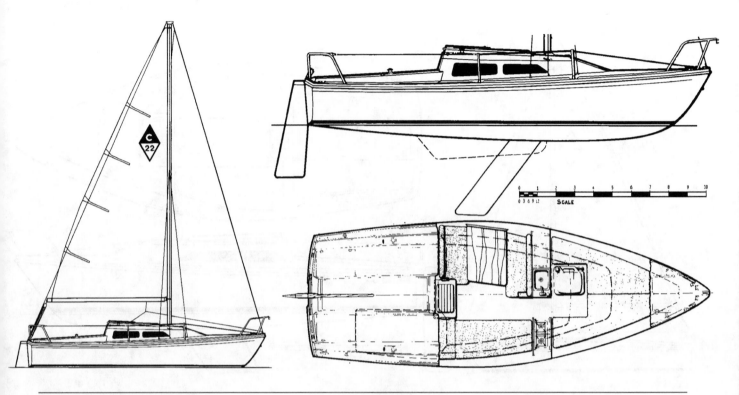

LOD:	21' 6"
LOA:	23' 0"
LWL:	19' 4"
Min./max. draft:	2' 0"/5' 0"
Bridge clearance:	29' 1"
Power:	outboard 3 to 6 hp
B/D ratio:	24%

Designer:	Frank Butler
Builder:	Catalina Yachts
Years produced:	1969–1999
Sail area:	212 sq. ft.
Fuel tankage:	portable
Water tankage:	portable
Approx. trailering wgt.:	3,300 lbs.

This boat wins the grand prize for all-time highest cruising-boat popularity over the 30 years she was offered. She was the first boat marketed by Catalina, and in total well over 10,000 were sold, with sail numbers reaching past 13,000; a Catalina 22 Mk II (page 158) replaced her in the year 2000 and continues in production to this day. Over the years many changes have been made to the original boat; for example, in the mid-1980s options for either a winged keel or a fin were added to the basic swing keel, which continued to be the choice of most new-boat buyers.

A poptop option was also introduced, and has been the choice for 90% of buyers. **Best features:** An active owner's group, the Catalina 22 National Sailing Organization, is easily accessible on the Internet. This can be a useful source of information and advice for owners repairing their decades-old boats. **Worst features:** Maintenance can be time-consuming as these boats age beyond 10 or 20 years. Loose swing keels, broken wire pendants, and chainplate difficulties seem to be among the top problems.

Comps	LOD	Beam	MinDr	Displ	Bllst	SA/D	D/L	Avg. PHRF	Max. Speed	Motion Index	Space Index	No. of Berths	Head-room
Catalina 22 Mk I	21' 6"	7' 8"	2' 0"	2,250	550	19.1	139	270	5.9	11.2	262	5	4' 4"
Catalina 22 Mk II	21' 6"	8' 4"	2' 0"	2,290	550	18.9	141	270	5.9	10.2	370	4	4' 6"
Columbia T23 (22)	21' 10"	7' 11"	1' 11"	2,300	810	20.0	128	264	6.0	10.5	314	4	4' 3"
Catalina 22 Sport	21' 6"	7' 8"	1' 8"	2,380	550	19.7	139	270	5.9	11.9	289	4	4' 2"

Catalina 22 Mk II
Redesign with more elbow room in mind

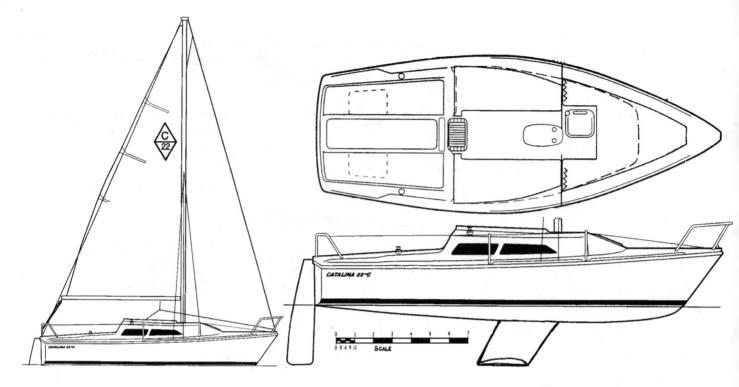

LOD:	21' 6"	**Designer:**	Catalina Design Team
LOA:	22' 10"	**Builder:**	Catalina Yachts
LWL:	19' 4"	**Years produced:**	2000–present
Min./max. draft:	2' 0"/5' 0"	**Sail area:**	205 sq. ft.
Bridge clearance:	29' 1"	**Fuel tankage:**	portable
Power:	outboard 3 to 6 hp	**Water tankage:**	portable
B/D ratio:	24%	**Approx. trailering wgt.:**	3,300 lbs.

This Mk II is an update of the Mk I Catalina 22 (page 157) marketed for the previous 30 years. The new version simplified the layout, eliminating a fifth berth and a dinette table. The midships beam was increased by eight inches, opening up cabin space and increasing the Space Index considerably, but the sailplan and rig dimensions, LOD, LWL, and most other main parameters were preserved from the previous design. A winged keel is shown in the plan, but a fin and swing keel are also available. ***Best features:*** An active class association helps owners meet and sail together. See previous page for particulars. A poptop and fiberglass-jacketed swing keel are standard. The jacket is designed to reduce maintenance on the keel. ***Worst features:*** The storage space of the Mk I version has been truncated, and the sink and stove have been relegated to a platform that slides aft when not in use. This may give the boat a "cleaner" look, but I think I'd miss the little dinette of the Mk I, where in a cozy harbor I could sit with a glass of chardonnay while my mate prepared a feast of canned hash and beans.

Comps	LOD	Beam	MinDr	Displ	Bllst	SA/D	D/L	Avg. PHRF	Max. Speed	Motion Index	Space Index	No. of Berths	Head-room
Catalina 22 Mk I	21' 6"	7' 8"	2' 0"	2,250	550	19.1	139	270	5.9	11.2	262	5	4' 4"
Catalina 22 Mk II	21' 6"	8' 4"	2' 0"	2,290	550	18.9	141	270	5.9	10.2	370	4	4' 6"
Columbia T23 (22)	21' 10"	7' 11"	1' 11"	2,300	810	20.0	128	264	6.0	10.5	314	4	4' 3"
Catalina 22 Sport	21' 6"	7' 8"	1' 8"	2,380	550	19.7	139	270	5.9	11.9	289	4	4' 2"

Catalina 22 Sport
Racing replacement for the Catalina 22

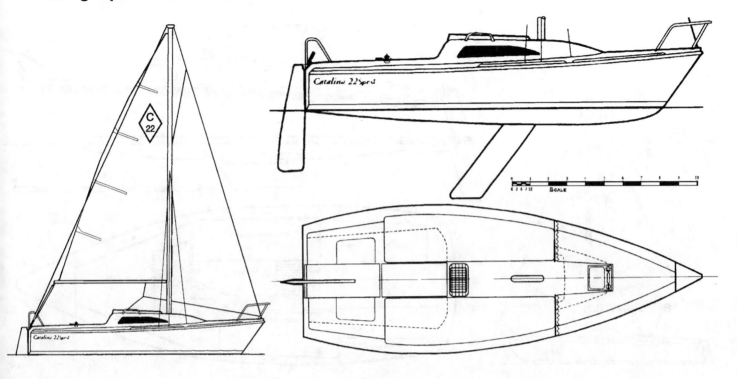

LOD:	21' 6"		**Designer:**	Catalina Design Team
LOA:	22' 10"		**Builder:**	Catalina Yachts
LWL:	19' 4"		**Years produced:**	2000–present
Min./max. draft:	1' 8"/5' 0"		**Sail area:**	205 sq. ft.
Bridge clearance:	28' 6"		**Fuel tankage:**	portable
Power:	outboard 3 to 6 hp		**Water tankage:**	portable
B/D ratio:	24%		**Approx. trailering wgt.:**	3,300 lbs.

The Catalina sales brochure says: "In response to Catalina 22 owners' requests for a production boat that more accurately reflects the original dimensions and weight of this popular one-design boat, Catalina Yachts is now building the Catalina 22 Sport. Catalina Yachts aims to encourage more family racing with the thousands of first generation 22s by offering an alternative to finding an older boat, and restoring it just to be competitive in the dozens of established Catalina 22 fleets. Like the first Catalina 22, the 22 Sport is easy to trailer, and a great boat to step up from dinghy sailing to a pocket cruiser/racer. . . ." ***Best features:*** Despite the effort to "reflect the original dimensions and weight" of the original C22, the Sport weighs 130 pounds more and is four inches shallower than the design it is claimed to emulate. Still, the PHRF rating appears to be at least nominally equal. ***Worst features:*** Headroom is lower than all four comps. A portable ice chest is included, but you'll have to devise your own galley arrangements.

Comps	LOD	Beam	MinDr	Displ	Bllst	SA/D	D/L	Avg. PHRF	Max. Speed	Motion Index	Space Index	No. of Berths	Head-room
Catalina 22 Mk I	21' 6"	7' 8"	2' 0"	2,250	550	19.1	139	270	5.9	11.2	262	5	4' 4"
Catalina 22 Mk II	21' 6"	8' 4"	2' 0"	2,290	550	18.9	141	270	5.9	10.2	370	4	4' 6"
Columbia T23 (22)	21' 10"	7' 11"	1' 11"	2,300	810	20.0	128	264	6.0	10.5	314	4	4' 3"
Catalina 22 Sport	21' 6"	7' 8"	1' 8"	2,380	550	19.7	139	270	5.9	11.9	289	4	4' 2"

Clipper 23 (22)
Bigger sister to the Clipper 21

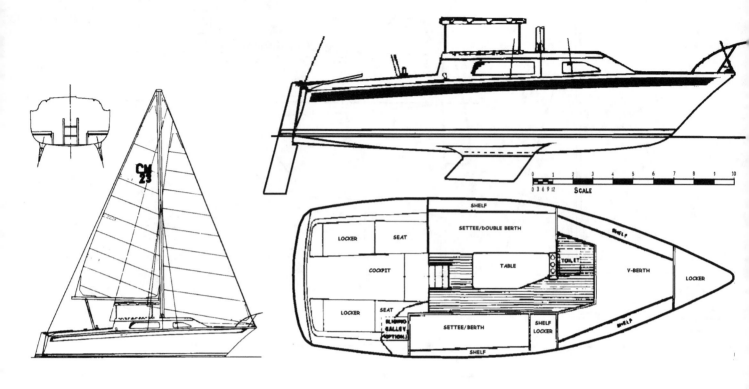

LOD:	22' 4"		**Designer:**	William Crealock
LOA:	23' 5"		**Builder:**	Clipper Marine Corp.
LWL:	18' 9"		**Years produced:**	1973–1976
Min./max. draft:	2' 2"		**Sail area:**	221 sq. ft.
Bridge clearance:	29' 6"		**Fuel tankage:**	portable
Power:	outboard 3 to 6 hp		**Water tankage:**	portable
B/D ratio:	26%		**Approx. trailering wgt.:**	3,000 lbs.

The Clipper 23, a boat with flare at the bow that gives it a pinched look, came in two flavors: (1) twin keels 2' 2" deep, as shown here, or (2) a swing keel (draft 8" keel up, and 4' 6" keel down). In addition, the boat came in at least two cabin layouts, the traditional settee arrangement shown here or a dinette configuration. Also included was a pop-top, which could be raised horizontally, as shown here, or hinged at the front and angled for more air circulation.

Best features: These boats were constructed cheaply to sell cheaply, for those who wanted a plaything but didn't want to invest much. Today their price on the used market continues to be near the bottom of the range for this size and type of vessel. **Worst features:** If the brochure plans are accurate, the rudder, which is deeper than the keel and apparently has no retracting device when in shallow water, may be damaged if the boat goes aground.

Comps	LOD	Beam	MinDr	Displ	Bllst	SA/D	D/L	Avg. PHRF	Max. Speed	Motion Index	Space Index	No. of Berths	Head-room
Venture of Newport (23)	22' 7"	7' 2"	1' 6"	2,000	600	21.5	120	255	5.9	10.2	312	5	4' 0"
Gillmer 23	22' 7"	7' 6"	1' 8"	2,068	500	23.9	100	NA	6.1	9.7	365	2	5' 0"
Clipper 23 (22)	22' 4"	7' 8"	2' 2"	2,100	550	21.6	142	258	5.8	10.6	351	5	4' 6"
Menger Oysterman 23	22' 6"	8' 0"	1' 8"	2,600	700	30.0	124	NA	6.2	10.4	312	4	4' 9"

Columbia 22
Early (and popular) fiberglass sailboat

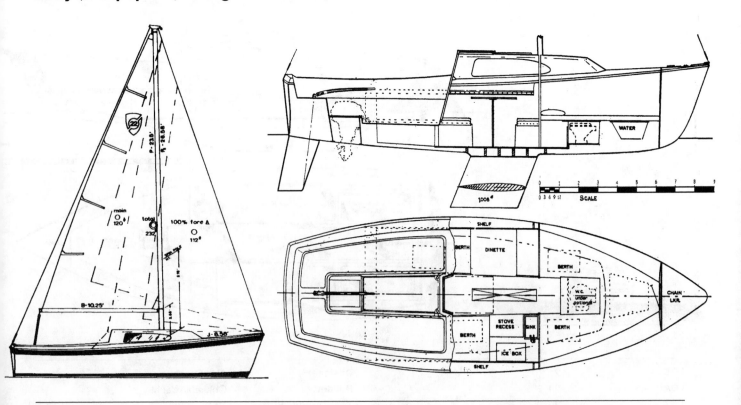

LOD:	22' 0"	**Designer:**	William Crealock	
LOA:	22' 0"	**Builder:**	Columbia Yacht Corp.	
LWL:	20' 1"	**Years produced:**	1965–1972	
Min./max. draft:	3' 2"	**Sail area:**	234 sq. ft.	
Bridge clearance:	30' 4"	**Fuel tankage:**	portable	
Power:	outboard 3 to 6 hp	**Water tankage:**	12 gal.	
B/D ratio:	46%	**Approx. trailering wgt.:**	3,200 lbs.	

Over 1,500 of these boats were made over a seven-year period. They were available either in the 3' 2" fixed-keel version shown here, or as a keel/centerboarder (draft board up 2' 6", down 4' 10"). At some point during Columbia Yacht Corporation's life (between 1961 and 1978), in addition to their regular finished boats, the company sold a line of kit boats under the name Sailcrafter Custom Yachts. As a result, some Columbia 22s on the used market may include such aberrations as no sliding main hatch or no outboard well, the result of a home builder deciding it was too much trouble to complete that part of the kit. **Best features:** The cast iron keel, if shaped as shown in the inboard profile and properly faired, will add measurably to performance on the race course. The boat's PHRF rating suggests that, with her long waterline and low wetted surface, she will be fast relative to her comps. **Worst features:** The dinette is less than 30 inches wide, good for seating two but impossible for four. The fin keel and draft of over three feet might give problems at the launch ramp.

Comps	LOD	Beam	MinDr	Displ	Bllst	SA/D	D/L	Avg. PHRF	Max. Speed	Motion Index	Space Index	No. of Berths	Head-room
Seaward 22	21' 9"	8' 4"	1' 11"	2,200	750	20.3	113	285	6.1	9.5	325	4	4' 6"
Hughes 22	21' 9"	7' 7"	1' 8"	2,200	825	20.8	132	282	5.9	11.2	314	6	5' 0"
Columbia 22	22' 0"	7' 9"	3' 2"	2,200	1,000	22.1	121	186	6.0	10.7	337	4	4' 7"

Columbia T23 (22)
Small boat from the board of Alan Payne

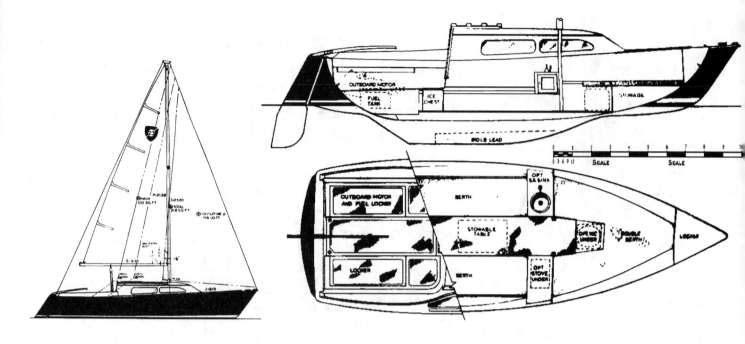

LOD:	21' 10"	**Designer:**	Alan Payne
LOA:	24' 9"	**Builder:**	Columbia Yacht
LWL:	20' 0"	**Years produced:**	1973–1978
Min./max. draft:	1' 11"	**Sail area:**	218 sq. ft.
Bridge clearance:	28' 2"	**Fuel tankage:**	portable
Power:	3 to 6 hp	**Water tankage:**	6 gal.
B/D ratio:	35%	**Approx. trailering wgt.:**	3,300 lbs.

Here's another boat with a reverse transom in which the marketer has added in the "rump" to come up with boat length—which should be LOD, but is given as hull length. And so once again we cut this boat down to size, in this case 21' 10" instead of the claimed 22' 7". The Columbia T23 is said to be identical to the Coronado 23 Mk II, except for the gelcoat colors and cabin windows. This is understandable since in the 1970s the Whittaker Corporation owned both the Columbia and Coronado brands, and deemed that they could be intermingled. ***Best features:*** No notable features perceived by us. ***Worst features:*** Compared to her comps, the T23 has about the same shallow draft, but is the only vessel without a centerboard option. Consequently her upwind performance predictably will be the worst of the group—notwithstanding her PHRF rating. At least one owner reports that two drains in the aft end of the cockpit are plumbed through the transom, but are close enough to the waterline so that when the boat heels with any significant weight in the cockpit, water will drain into the cockpit rather than out of it.

Comps	LOD	Beam	MinDr	Displ	Bllst	SA/D	D/L	Avg. PHRF	Max. Speed	Motion Index	Space Index	No. of Berths	Head-room
Catalina 22 Mk I	21' 6"	7' 8"	2' 0"	2,250	650	19.1	139	270	5.9	11.2	262	5	4' 4"
Catalina 22 Mk II	21' 6"	8' 4"	2' 0"	2,290	550	18.9	141	270	5.9	10.2	370	4	4' 6"
Columbia T23 (22)	21' 10"	7' 11"	1' 11"	2,300	810	20.0	128	264	6.0	10.5	314	4	4' 3"
Catalina 22 Sport	21' 6"	7' 8"	1' 8"	2,380	550	19.7	139	270	5.9	11.9	289	4	4' 2"

Coquina Cat 22
A cat with lots of room

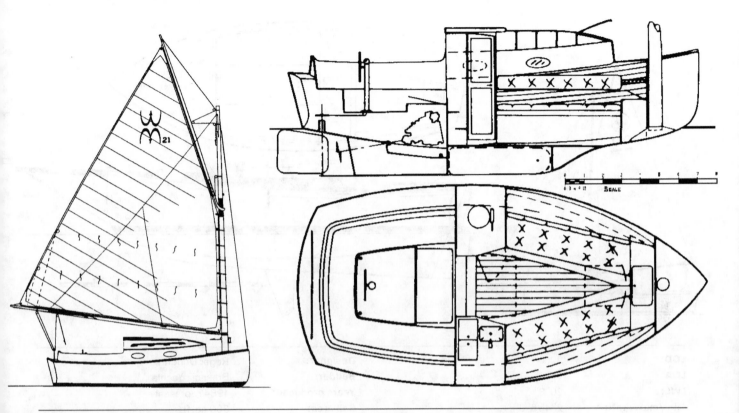

LOD:	21' 9"	Designer:	Dan Wilkinson
LOA:	25' 9"	Builder:	Wilkinson Marine
LWL:	20' 4"	Years produced:	1977?–1983?
Min./max. draft:	2' 3"/5' 6"	Sail area:	324 sq. ft.
Bridge clearance:	36' 6"	Fuel tankage:	10 gal.
Power:	inboard 5 to 9 hp	Water tankage:	30 gal.
B/D ratio:	32%	Approx. trailering wgt.:	5,600 lbs.

Dan Wilkinson designed and built a dozen or so of these compact but roomy boats in the late 1970s and early 1980s in Sarasota, FL. Like her comps, the Coquina Cat is designed with some nontraditional twists. One such twist *not* shared with her comps is her keel-centerboard arrangement, using a long, narrow board that is housed totally below the cabin sole. (Her comps both have traditional centerboard trunks splitting the cabin more or less in two.) **Best features:** The high-aspect board should help with upwind performance, and her long waterline should give her a bit more speed than her comps. Her high, crowned cabin provides more headroom, and her wider beam gives her extra elbow room, revealed in her relatively high Space Index. **Worst features:** We worry that her small rudder might lead to control problems in heavy weather. Her small-diameter wheel on a pedestal might accentuate such problems. We'd rather see a traditional tiller in a boat this small, though it may take careful adjustment of her board, and early reefing, to avoid excessive weather helm and the danger of inadvertent broaching.

Comps	LOD	Beam	MinDr	Displ	Bllst	SA/D	D/L	Avg. PHRF	Max. Speed	Motion Index	Space Index	No. of Berths	Head-room
Arey's Pond Cat 21	20' 10"	10' 0"	1' 9"	3,444	400	22.4	287	NA	5.6	13.3	342	2	5' 0"
Coquina Cat 22	21' 9"	10' 4"	2' 3"	3,800	1,200	21.3	202	NA	6.0	12.5	473	2	5' 8"
Atlantic City Kitty 21	21' 3"	9' 6"	2' 0"	5,300	1,800	18.4	417	281	5.7	21.5	404	2	5' 3"

Cornish Crabber 22
Elegant gaff cutter from England

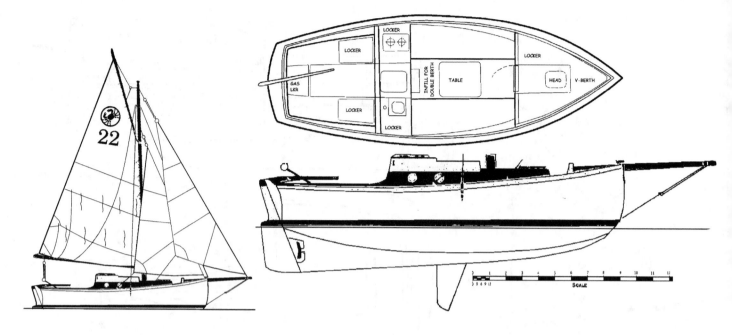

LOD:	22' 0"	**Designer:**	Roger Dongray
LOA:	27' 0"	**Builder:**	Britannia Yachts
LWL:	20' 8"	**Years produced:**	1984?–present
Min./max. draft:	2' 4"/5' 0"	**Sail area:**	300 sq. ft.
Bridge clearance:	31' 6"	**Fuel tankage:**	10 gal.
Power:	Yanmar diesel 9 hp	**Water tankage:**	portable
B/D ratio:	31%	**Approx. trailering wgt.:**	6,600 lbs.

This pretty, traditional 22-footer is reminiscent of the Cornish Shrimper 19 (page 32), with the same nice attention to fit and finish but with a lot more space and apparent size than her smaller sister. *Best features:* There is plenty of stowage in lockers in cockpit and down below. A table with folding leaves, mounted atop the centerboard trunk, is one of many cleverly designed amenities below. The control pendant for the weighted centerboard is routed up the mast support in the cabin, through the coachroof to a four-part purchase on a track on the roof, within easy reach of the cockpit. A 9 hp

Yanmar diesel engine comes with the boat as standard, as does Schaefer roller-furling gear for both staysail and jib. *Worst features:* Her trailer towing weight of over 6,000 pounds (including gear and the weight of a sizable trailer) is above the limit for most passenger vehicles. There's lots of wood, including the mast, boom, gaff, and bowsprit, plus wood lining the bulkheads and cabin down below, all beautifully varnished when new—which eventually will require frequent maintenance. And then there's relative speed. Note the PHRF: a high, high 360 seconds per mile.

Comps	LOD	Beam	MinDr	Displ	Bllst	SA/D	D/L	Avg. PHRF	Max. Speed	Motion Index	Space Index	No. of Berths	Head-room
D&M 22	22' 0"	8' 5"	2' 9"	4,000	1,800	16.1	271	279	5.8	18.2	393	4	4' 10"
Cornish Crabber 22	22' 0"	8' 3"	2' 4"	4,480	500	17.7	227	360	6.1	18.3	393	4	5' 0"
Hermann 22	22' 0"	9' 6"	2' 0"	4,500	300	15.8	251	NA	6.0	16.7	368	4	4' 4"

CS 22

Canadian trailer-sailer with some unusual features

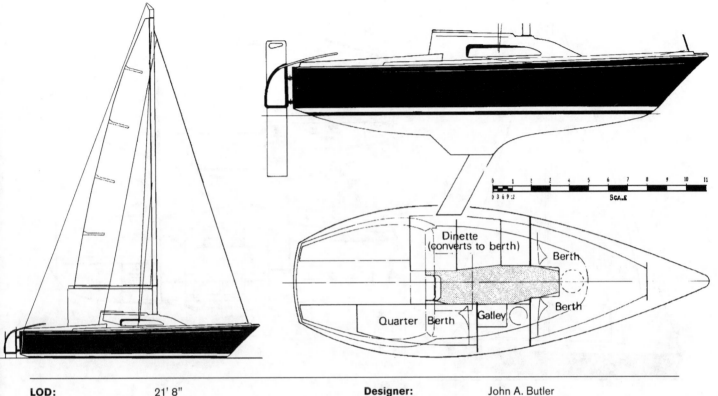

LOD:	21' 8"
LOA:	22' 9"
LWL:	17' 6"
Min./max. draft:	2' 0"/5' 0"
Bridge clearance:	31' 6"
Power:	outboard 3 to 6 hp
B/D ratio:	47%

Designer:	John A. Butler
Builder:	CS Yachts
Years produced:	1970–1979
Sail area:	194 sq. ft.
Fuel tankage:	portable
Water tankage:	portable
Approx. trailering wgt.:	3,600 lbs.

British naval architect John Butler was asked by Canadian Sailcraft Co. (CS) to draw a small trailerable sailboat "suitable for light-weather performance." The centerboard is pivoted in a slot in an unusually stubby external ballast iron keel, which lowers the center of gravity for added stability, keeps the board from encroaching on cabin space, and, it is said, takes the weight of the boat when she is trailered or stored. But we wonder whether the boat can be balanced on her stub keel when grounded by a falling tide. *Best features:* Except for the rudderhead rising above the deck aft, her sleek looks seem better than average to us. *Worst features:* The boat has shallow ballast and slack bilges, which may provide low wetted surface for light-air speed but will also make her more tender than average. The centerboard slot in the keel, open on the aft edge to house the board when up, may cause eddies, which will tend to slow the boat down. The vertical lifting rudder slides up and down in an aluminum frame. It is supposed to shear a retaining pin and swing aft if it hits an underwater object. Like many complicated designs at sea, it may or may not work when you need it most. Why not just a conventional swivel?

Comps	LOD	Beam	MinDr	Displ	Bllst	SA/D	D/L	Avg. PHRF	Max. Speed	Motion Index	Space Index	No. of Berths	Head-room
CS 22	21' 8"	8' 0"	2' 0"	2,460	1,150	17.0	205	249	5.6	12.4	341	4	4' 8"
Watkins 23XL	22' 3"	8' 0"	1' 3"	2,500	900	19.7	147	276	5.9	11.6	365	5	4' 10"
Seafarer 23 (22)	22' 0"	7' 7"	2' 4"	2,550	845	17.7	180	261	5.8	13.4	309	4	5' 1"

D&M 22

S&S designs a Quarter-Tonner

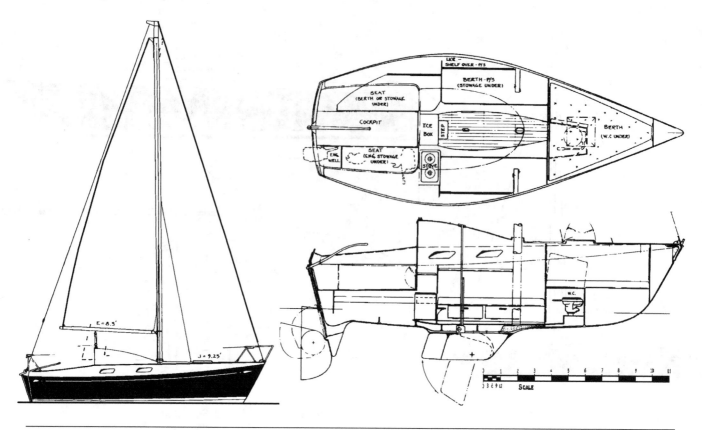

LOD:	22' 0"	Designer:	Sparkman & Stephens
LOA:	22' 6"	Builder:	Douglass & MacLeod
LWL:	18' 9"	Years produced:	1972–1973
Min./max. draft:	2' 9"/5' 3"	Sail area:	254 sq. ft.
Bridge clearance:	30' 6"	Fuel tankage:	portable
Power:	outboard 4 to 6 hp	Water tankage:	10 gal.
B/D ratio:	45%	Approx. trailering wgt.:	6,100 lbs.

The peculiarly shaped D&M 22 was designed by Sparkman & Stephens in 1971 to the then-new IOR (International Offshore Rule). S&S gave her a wide beam, a bubble cabin, a raised deck, and an IOR rating of less than 18, the Rule's maximum for quarter-ton racers at the time. (The Rule has been modified several times since.) S&S's customer for this new boat was Douglass & MacLeod (D&M), a partnership originally interested mainly in small one-design racing boats. However, they had previously commissioned S&S to design the Tartan 27, a successful racer, but wanted to build something a little smaller. They offered the 22 as either a fin-keeler or a keel-centerboarder. **Best features:** The boat's big interior (note Space Index of 393) might be considered an advantage to cruisers; however we suspect that most customers were racers looking for a rating advantage. **Worst features:** It isn't totally clear why the boat was produced for only two years, but her peculiar look and her lack of big wins on the racing circuit may have been factors.

Comps	LOD	Beam	MinDr	Displ	Bllst	SA/D	D/L	Avg. PHRF	Max. Speed	Motion Index	Space Index	No. of Berths	Head-room
D&M 22	22' 0"	8' 5"	2' 9"	4,000	1,800	16.1	271	279	5.8	18.2	393	4	4' 10"
Cornish Crabber 22	22' 0"	8' 3"	2' 4"	4,480	500	17.7	227	360	6.1	18.3	393	4	5' 0"
Hermann 22	22' 0"	9' 6"	2' 0"	4,500	300	15.8	251	NA	6.0	16.7	368	4	4' 4"

Dehler 22
German import designed by Hubert Vandestadt

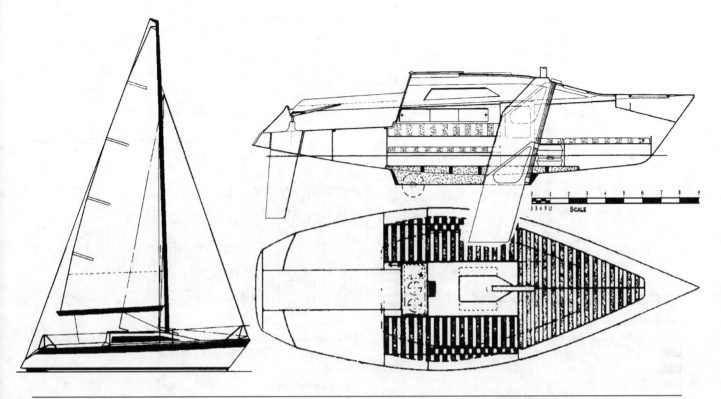

LOD:	22' 0"	**Designer:**	Hubert Vandestadt
LOA:	24' 0"	**Builder:**	Dehler America (importer)
LWL:	18' 6"	**Years produced:**	1985–1987
Min./max. draft:	1' 3"/4' 0"	**Sail area:**	274 sq. ft.
Bridge clearance:	33' 0"	**Fuel tankage:**	portable
Power:	outboard 4 to 6 hp	**Water tankage:**	portable
B/D ratio:	44%	**Approx. trailering wgt.:**	2,360 lbs.

Compare this design to the Sirius 21 and 22 (21) (pages 138 and 139) by the same designer. All have a number of high-quality features. All are well-finished and good-looking, and are among our favorites in this size range. ***Best features:*** Clever and unusual features (of which some were optional) include an outboard motor which slides up and down the transom to reduce drag under sail; a combination of lifting keel and water ballast tank (440 pounds of water, 440 pounds of lead shot in the lifting keel) to keep towing weight low; a worm-drive operated on deck with a standard winch handle to raise and lower the keel; easily removable rudder; floating slipway trolley that rides piggyback on a roll-on, roll-off road trailer; extra stays to prevent mast sway at the launching site and to allow singlehanded rigging and unrigging; slide-out galley unit; opening transom gate for swimming; and availability of kits for finishing at home. ***Worst features:*** Price new was high, and remains high on resale.

Comps	LOD	Beam	MinDr	Displ	Bllst	SA/D	D/L	Avg. PHRF	Max. Speed	Motion Index	Space Index	No. of Berths	Head-room
Balboa 22	21' 7"	8' 0"	1' 3"	1,980	600	20.9	129	246	5.8	9.5	326	4	4' 4"
Dehler 22	22' 0"	8' 0"	1' 3"	1,980	880	25.1	140	225	5.8	9.7	344	4	4' 9"
Spindrift 22	21' 6"	8' 0"	1' 8"	1,990	600	19.6	128	252	5.9	9.5	345	4	4' 8"
Windrose 22/Laguna 22	21' 7"	8' 8"	2' 11"	2,280	900	19.0	148	246	5.8	10.9	337	4	4' 4"

ETAP 22i
Little gem from Belgium

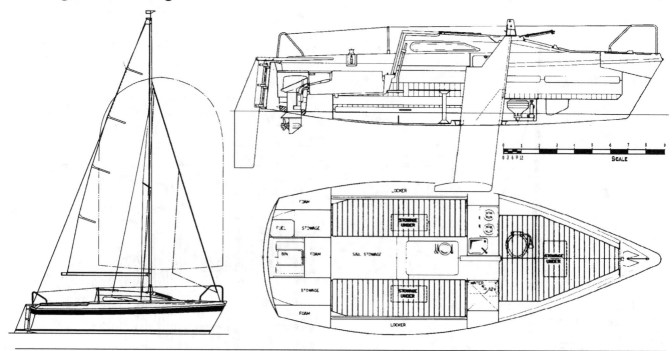

LOD:	22' 3"	**Designer:**	Jac de Ridder
LOA:	23' 11"	**Builder:**	ETAP (Belgium)
LWL:	19' 8"	**Years produced:**	1985–present
Min./max. draft:	1' 4"/5' 0"	**Sail area:**	209 sq. ft.
Bridge clearance:	29' 0"	**Fuel tankage:**	portable
Power:	outboard 3 to 6 hp	**Water tankage:**	portable
B/D ratio:	25%	**Approx. trailering wgt.:**	3,100 lbs.

Imported by an Annapolis firm in the mid-1980s, this boat was popular with high-end small boaters, but there weren't enough of them willing to pay the relatively high price, which included overseas shipping. As this is written, there is no United States representation; you'll have to make your own import arrangements with ETAP if you buy new. This is an elegant and well-thought-out boat we'd consider buying if we were in the market for something in this size range. She has lots going for her. *Best features:* She has a very good fit and finish; maximum speed and headroom are at the top of her peer group; and her trailer towing weight is within striking distance of 3,000 pounds. She has niceties like a double hull sandwich with closed-cell polyurethane

in the middle, which gives added stiffness and makes her virtually unsinkable. (The double skin also keeps the boat cool in direct sunlight, and warm on cold nights.) Add good-quality hardware including clutches and winches, and an outboard motor well as standard, plus optional "legs" for drying out on the hard, and you've got quite a boat. *Worst features:* Lifting keels are not my favorite configuration. In the 22i's case, all is well as long as the 518-pound cast iron keel slides easily on its nylon guides, and no knocking of the keel against its casing is perceived. If something is heard, the boat may require major fixing. See ETAP Owners' Association on the Internet for details of this problem and how it can be fixed.

Comps	LOD	Beam	MinDr	Displ	Bllst	SA/D	D/L	Avg. PHRF	Max. Speed	Motion Index	Space Index	No. of Berths	Head-room
Freedom 21 (22)	21' 8"	8' 0"	2' 0"	2,000	500	16.5	162	260	5.6	10.2	272	4	4' 6"
Merit 22	22' 0"	8' 0"	2' 0"	2,000	600	22.7	153	219	5.7	10.0	303	5	3' 9"
Plas Trend Mustang 22	22' 0"	7' 0"	2' 4"	2,000	750	18.8	182	225	5.5	12.3	221	4	3' 8"
Paceship Bluejacket 23	22' 1"	7' 0"	3' 9"	2,000	900	20.3	167	240	5.6	12.0	186	2	3' 1"
ETAP 22i	22' 3"	8' 1"	1' 4"	2,149	518	20.1	126	NA	5.9	9.7	227	4	4' 6"

ETAP 23 (22)
Innovative design imported from Belgium

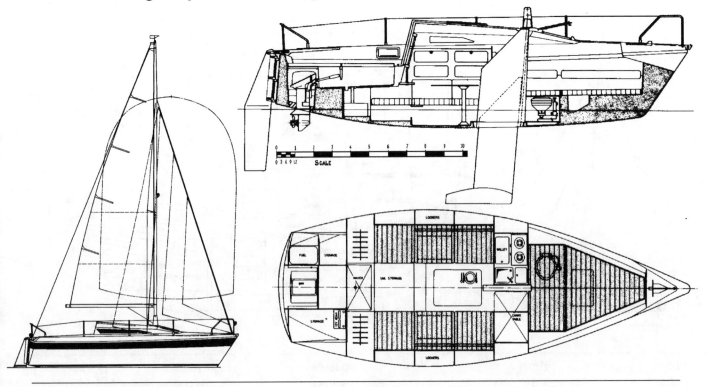

LOD:	22' 0"	**Designer:**	Jac de Ridder
LOA:	24' 0"	**Builder:**	ETAP
LWL:	19' 0"	**Years produced:**	1985–1987?
Min./max. draft:	2' 3"/4' 9"	**Sail area:**	241 sq. ft.
Bridge clearance:	34' 1"	**Fuel tankage:**	portable
Power:	outboard 3 to 6 hp	**Water tankage:**	12 gal.
B/D ratio:	31%	**Approx. trailering wgt.:**	4,900 lbs.

Like other small ETAP sailboats, the Belgian-made 23 (actually 22' on deck and 24' including the outboard rudder) is double skinned, with foam between outside and inside layers of fiberglass. ***Best features:*** The foam sandwich construction helps keep the cabin dry and condensation free, as well as muffling noise. It also stiffens the hull structure and makes the boat unsinkable even when filled with water. (We watched at the Annapolis Sailboat Show in 1986 while the ETAP's seacocks were opened and the boat gradually settled until water was knee-high over the cabin sole, at which point equilibrium was reached and any added water bailed in from outside simply ran out through the seacocks. Then the boat was keeled over to 65 degrees of heel, but popped right up when the hauling lines were released.) The whole boat is extremely well-finished in mahogany and/or teak with polished brass hardware. The wide beam helps to create more usable space than in all but one of her comps; note her Space Index of 384. A ballasted vertical-retracting keel keeps minimum draft low while providing good lowered depth for going upwind. An outboard well is conveniently located in the cockpit near the helm station. ***Worst features:*** Price even of well-used boats is high. In this case, you may get what you pay for.

Comps	LOD	Beam	MinDr	Displ	Bllst	SA/D	D/L	Avg. PHRF	Max. Speed	Motion Index	Space Index	No. of Berths	Head-room
ETAP 23 (22)	22' 0"	8' 2"	2' 3"	3,320	1,035	17.3	216	240	5.8	15.2	384	4	4' 5"
O'Day 23 Mk II (22)	22' 1"	8' 0"	2' 0"	3,500	900	16.3	211	240	6.0	16.1	390	5	5' 0"
S/2 7.0 Meter (22)	22' 3"	8' 0"	2' 2"	3,600	1,300	16.3	261	261	6.0	17.6	344	4	5' 0"
Sailmaster 22	22' 0"	7' 1"	2' 4"	3,650	1,600	15.5	263	288	5.4	22.8	297	2	4' 5"

Falmouth Cutter (22)
A Lyle Hess packet on a small scale

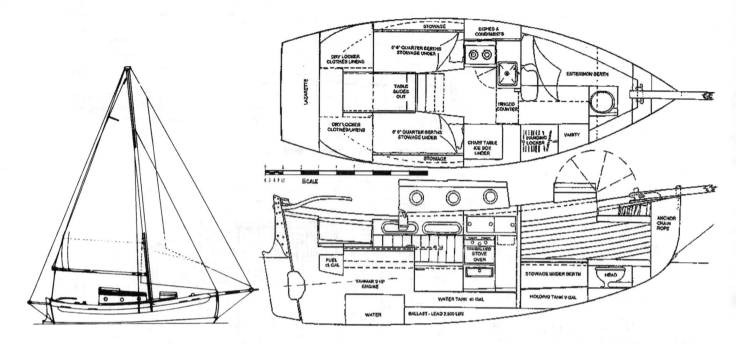

LOD:	22' 0"		Designer:	Lyle Hess
LOA:	30' 6"		Builder:	Cape George Marine Wks.
LWL:	20' 10"		Years produced:	1980−present
Min./max. draft:	3' 6"		Sail area:	357 sq. ft.
Bridge clearance:	33' 6"		Fuel tankage:	23 gal.
Power:	inboard dsl. 10 to 12 hp		Water tankage:	19 gal.
B/D ratio:	34%		Approx. trailering wgt.:	10,800 lbs.

The FC22 was originally built by Sam Morse in CA, but recently her molds and tooling were purchased by Cape George Marine Works of Port Townsend, WA. They, like Morse, offer the boat in various stages of completion from bare hull to finished vessel. Over the years, almost all FC22s have been built to order. The hull is fiberglass, but beyond the bare hull, most of the construction is wood, including the deck frames and house. One feature seen as a plus by owners is the boat's trailerability, but with a towing package of 10,800 pounds a big truck is needed, which may not fit everyone's concept of feasibility. **Best features:** Compared to comps, the FC22 has the biggest space below (about 50% greater than her comps on average), has the deepest draft (indicating possibly better performance to windward), is heaviest (indicating good comfort in heavy seas), and ties with the Bluejacket 23 for greatest theoretical speed (though the Bluejacket's low SA/D ratio probably makes her slower boat-for-boat). **Worst features:** All that wood, mostly varnished, will take a heap of loving care to maintain in the style most owners desire.

Comps	LOD	Beam	MinDr	Displ	Bllst	SA/D	D/L	Avg. PHRF	Max. Speed	Motion Index	Space Index	No. of Berths	Head-room
Pacific Seacraft Flicka 20	20' 0"	8' 0"	3' 3"	5,500	1,800	12.9	410	288	5.7	26.6	443	3 or 4	5' 11"
Bluejacket 23	23' 0"	10' 0"	2' 3"	6,000	700	9.5	300	NA	6.1	20.0	403	2	6' 2"
Herreshoff Prudence 23	22' 9"	8' 0"	3' 0"	6,800	1,600	16.4	394	NA	6.0	31.7	408	2	4' 9"
Falmouth Cutter (22)	22' 0"	8' 0"	3' 6"	7,400	2,500	15.0	365	NA	6.1	30.0	651	3	5' 11"

Freedom 21 (22)
Unusual–and typical–Garry Hoyt design

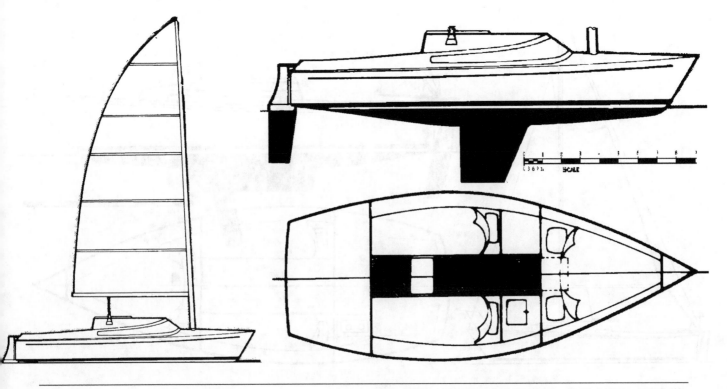

LOD:	21' 8"	**Designer:**	Garry Hoyt
LOA:	22' 8"	**Builder:**	Freedom Yachts/TPI
LWL:	17' 8"	**Years produced:**	1982–1987
Min./max. draft:	keel 2' 0" shoal/3' 9" deep	**Sail area:**	190 sq. ft.
Bridge clearance:	32' 0"	**Fuel tankage:**	portable
Power:	outboard 3 to 6 hp	**Water tankage:**	portable
B/D ratio:	25%	**Approx. trailering wgt.:**	2,900 lbs.

Here's a catboat with a modern flavor. She has a tall, full-battened main with a big roach, a stayless carbon-fiber mast, and a patented "gunmount" spinnaker arrangement. The latest thing in 1982, but perhaps no longer on the leading edge of design. She came either as a shoal-draft fin-keeler (2' 0", 750-pound keel) or with a deep draft (3' 9", 500-pound keel). The deep fin is a better performer, but hard to get off a trailer without a crane. *Best features:* Deep cockpit coamings and a cockpit well proportioned for good foot-bracing help make the Freedom 21 a pleasure to sail. So does the easy-to-control gunmount spinnaker arrangement, which allows you to douse the chute by just popping the halyard and lowering the chute into its launching tube by hauling on a retrieving line. *Worst features:* Going forward isn't always easy, since the port side is taken over by the chute launching tube. She's not fast upwind, especially as a catboat. (A staysail can be rigged.) And her unusual appearance, with dark, wraparound "windshield," may not appeal to everyone.

Comps	LOD	Beam	MinDr	Displ	Bllst	SA/D	D/L	Avg. PHRF	Max. Speed	Motion Index	Space Index	No. of Berths	Head-room
Freedom 21 (22)	21' 8"	8' 0"	2' 0"	2,000	500	16.5	162	260	5.6	10.2	272	4	4' 6"
Merit 22	22' 0"	8' 0"	2' 0"	2,000	600	22.7	153	219	5.7	10.0	303	5	3' 9"
Plas Trend Mustang 22	22' 0"	7' 0"	2' 4"	2,000	750	18.8	182	225	5.5	12.3	221	4	3' 8"
Paceship Bluejacket 23	22' 1"	7' 0"	3' 9"	2,000	900	20.3	167	240	5.6	12.0	186	2	3' 1"
ETAP 22i	22' 3"	8' 1"	1' 4"	2,149	518	20.1	126	NA	5.9	9.7	227	4	4' 6"

Gloucester 22
Simple boat for thrifty sailors

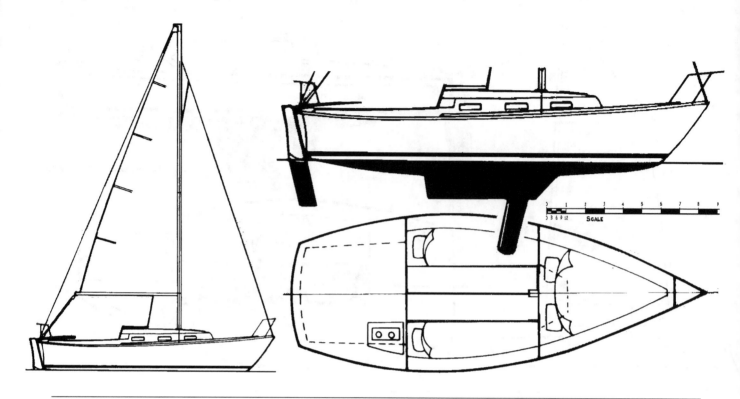

LOD:	21' 8"
LOA:	22' 2"
LWL:	18' 8"
Min./max. draft:	1' 8"/4' 10"
Bridge clearance:	31' 9"
Power:	outboard 3 to 6 hp
B/D ratio:	33%

Designer:	Stuart Windley
Builder:	Gloucester Yachts, later Classic Yachts
Years produced:	1983–2000
Sail area:	216 sq. ft.
Fuel tankage:	portable
Water tankage:	portable
Approx. trailering wgt.:	3,600 lbs.

This vessel was built by Gloucester Yachts from 1983 until that builder closed its doors in 1988. In 1990 Classic Yachts of Chanute, Kansas, picked up the design and offered it for the next ten years. It represents a genre of relatively lightweight and bare-bones designs that can be produced and sold relatively cheaply. ***Best features:*** She has the lowest minimum draft with board up compared with her comps, good for exploring shoal waters under power—though like her comps, her stub keel keeps her from being in the easiest group for trailer launching and

retrieving. Her high-aspect centerboard drops down to give her a draft of almost five feet, giving good performance to windward. She has six opening ports plus a small ventilation hatch forward, an advantage in sultry weather. ***Worst features:*** Construction is only so-so, as the boat is targeted to a thrifty audience. The low cost is obtained partly by offering what is usually standard equipment as optional. A pivoting rudder is optional, but should have been standard; there is danger of clipping it off as it extends below the board-up keel draft.

Comps	LOD	Beam	MinDr	Displ	Bllst	SA/D	D/L	Avg. PHRF	Max. Speed	Motion Index	Space Index	No. of Berths	Head-room
Gloucester 22	21' 8"	8' 0"	1' 8"	2,400	800	19.3	165	186	5.8	11.8	324	4	4' 4"
Seafarer 22 (21)	21' 4"	7' 5"	2' 1"	2,400	1,010	18.5	174	270	5.7	13.1	289	4	4' 9"
Starwind 223	22' 3"	8' 6"	1' 10"	2,435	700	19.4	150	237	5.9	10.7	414	4	4' 10"
U.S. 22/Triton 22	21' 6"	7' 10"	2' 5"	2,450	950	17.8	138	279	6.0	11.6	321	5	4' 0"

Grampian Classic 22
Early George Cuthbertson design

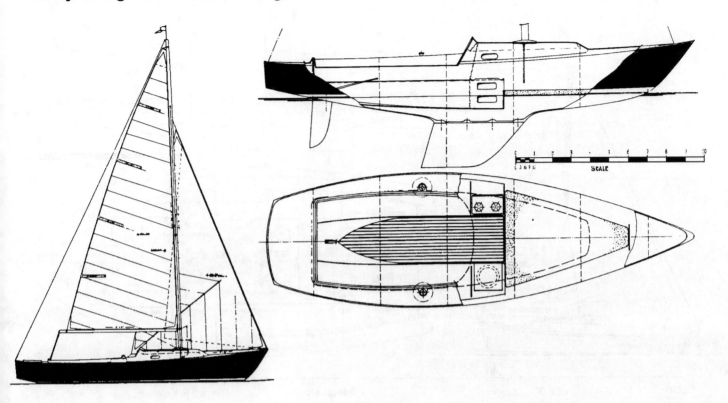

LOD:	22' 4"	**Designer:**	George Cuthbertson
LOA:	22' 4"	**Builder:**	Grampian Marine
LWL:	17' 5"	**Years produced:**	1962–1970?
Min./max. draft:	3' 9"	**Sail area:**	198 sq. ft.
Bridge clearance:	30' 0"	**Fuel tankage:**	portable
Power:	outboard 3 to 6 hp	**Water tankage:**	portable
B/D ratio:	37%	**Approx. trailering wgt.:**	2,700 lbs.

George Cuthbertson (who teamed up with George Cassian to form C&C Yachts in 1961) designed the Grampian Classic 22. Even in 1962, the C&C "look" was apparent in this Grampian model. In her first year, she came in first in the keelboat class in the annual One-of-a-Kind regatta on Lake Ontario against more than ten other competitors, many with larger sail areas. **Best features:** A tall rig, high B/D ratio, ballast centered well below the waterline, and narrow hull all lead to good racing performance, similar to the J/22, a comp. The headroom may be low, but a big cockpit for daysailing and a single V-berth for two are the ingredients of a good overnighter for folks who appreciate a boat that "drinks six, eats four, and sleeps two." And with her long overhangs and low silhouette, she looks quite graceful in a "classic" way, we think. **Worst features:** Headroom is low and accommodation space minimal compared to her comps. She's also harder to launch and retrieve at a ramp, due to her fixed keel—as is the J/22.

Comps	LOD	Beam	MinDr	Displ	Bllst	SA/D	D/L	Avg. PHRF	Max. Speed	Motion Index	Space Index	No. of Berths	Head-room
J/22	21' 6"	8' 0"	3' 9"	1,790	700	24.7	117	180	5.8	8.4	389	4	4' 0"
South Coast 22	22' 0"	7' 1"	0' 10"	1,800	505	20.4	150	276	5.6	10.8	273	5	4' 3"
Grampian Classic 22	22' 4"	7' 0"	3' 9"	1,892	700	20.7	160	234	5.6	11.5	225	2	3' 5"

Hermann 22
First cruiser built at Ted Hermann's Boat Shop

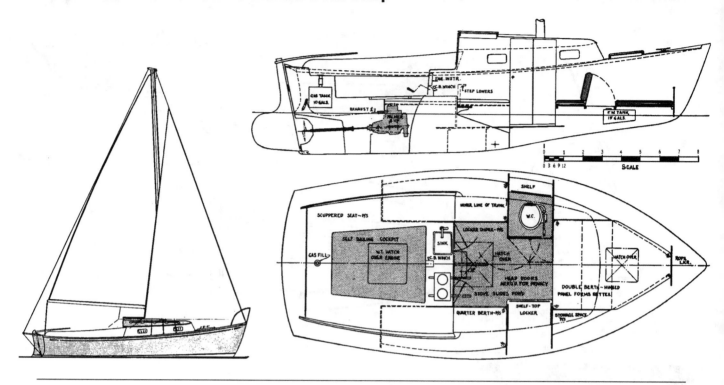

LOD:	22' 0"	**Designer:**	Richard P. Ketcham, Jr.
LOA:	23' 6"	**Builder:**	Ted Hermann's Boat Shop
LWL:	20' 0"	**Years produced:**	1961–1967?
Min./max. draft:	2' 0"/4' 0"	**Sail area:**	270 sq. ft.
Bridge clearance:	29' 0"	**Fuel tankage:**	10 gal.
Power:	8 hp Palmer gasoline	**Water tankage:**	15 gal.
B/D ratio:	7%	**Approx. trailering wgt.:**	6,600 lbs.

Here is a masthead sloop with a hull almost as wide (9½ feet) and as heavy as a typical Cape Cod Catboat. She was the first fiberglass cruising sailboat built by Ted Hermann at his Seaford Harbor, Long Island Boat Shop, way back at the beginning of the fiberglass era. *Best features:* She looks like a trim, prim, and wholesome product of the early 1960s, which is exactly what she is—and among her comps may take the Beauty Prize (though the Cornish Crabber is likely to give her a run for her money in the beauty department). Her large cockpit can handle a sizable crowd for daysailing. And with her shallow draft and smooth bottom, we can see her skipper dropping off the crowd and then putt-putting up to some tranquil gunkhole to anchor for the night. *Worst features:* Her rudder looks more like one sized for a powerboat than a sailboat, and maybe that's how she'd end up being used most of the time, since a sail area of only 270 square feet isn't going to move her wide, heavy hull very fast, at least in light air. My old 17-foot Hermann Cat (page 22), which weighed only 2,200 pounds, had a rudder with more surface area than this 22-footer.

Comps	LOD	Beam	MinDr	Displ	Bllst	SA/D	D/L	Avg. PHRF	Max. Speed	Motion Index	Space Index	No. of Berths	Head-room
D&M 22	22' 0"	8' 5"	2' 9"	4,000	1,800	16.1	271	279	5.8	18.2	393	4	4' 10"
Cornish Crabber 22	22' 0"	8' 3"	2' 4"	4,480	500	17.7	227	360	6.1	18.3	393	4	5' 0"
Hermann 22	22' 0"	9' 6"	2' 0"	4,500	300	15.8	251	NA	6.0	16.7	368	4	4' 4"

Hughes 22/Northstar 22
Canadian boat by a firm involved in two buyouts

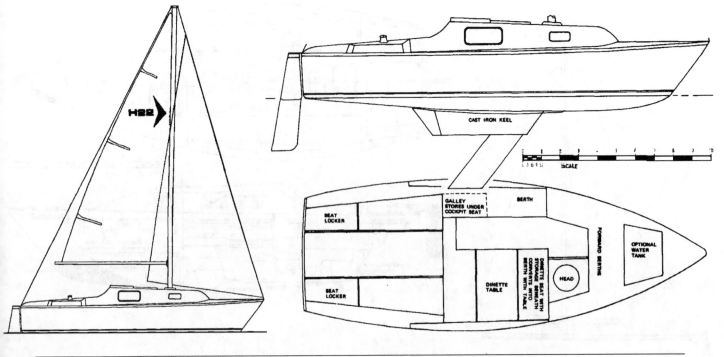

LOD:	21' 9"	Designer:	Howard Hughes
LOA:	23' 3"	Builder:	Hughes Boatworks
LWL:	19' 6"	Years produced:	1967–1977?
Min./max. draft:	1' 8"/6' 0"	Sail area:	220 sq. ft.
Bridge clearance:	27' 6"	Fuel tankage:	portable
Power:	outboard 3 to 6 hp	Water tankage:	portable
B/D ratio:	38%	Approx. trailering wgt.:	3,200 lbs.

Howard Hughes (no relation to the ultra-rich one) started building boats in 1963, and in 1967 designed the Hughes 22. In 1969 Hughes sold his company to U.S. Steel, which changed the name to Northstar Yachts. Most of the Hughes production became named for their new owner (e.g., Northstar 22). Before long Big Steel changed its mind about being in the boat business, and in 1977 Hughes bought back Northstar's assets. Somewhere around that time, production of the Hughes 22 aka Northstar 22 was discontinued. *Best features:* Built for entry-level sailors at a price low enough to attract them, the Hughes 22 has little else to recommend it. *Worst features:* Of the three comps listed together here, the Hughes 22 is to our taste the least salty looking, with her mismatched portlights and featureless, slab-sided hull. She lacks a forward hatch, carries a cast iron keel rather than a molded lead one, and her accommodations plan shows a portside berth only 18 inches wide (versus the accepted industry absolute minimum of 21 inches). In addition, her offset cabin sole is inappropriate for a boat this small.

Comps	LOD	Beam	MinDr	Displ	Bllst	SA/D	D/L	Avg. PHRF	Max. Speed	Motion Index	Space Index	No. of Berths	Head-room
Seaward 22	21' 9"	8' 4"	1' 11"	2,200	750	20.3	113	285	6.1	9.5	325	4	4' 6"
Hughes 22	21' 9"	7' 7"	1' 8"	2,200	825	20.8	132	282	5.9	11.2	314	6	5' 0"
Columbia 22	22' 0"	7' 9"	3' 2"	2,200	1,000	22.1	121	186	6.0	10.7	337	4	4' 7"

Hunter 22
Early design by Cortland Steck

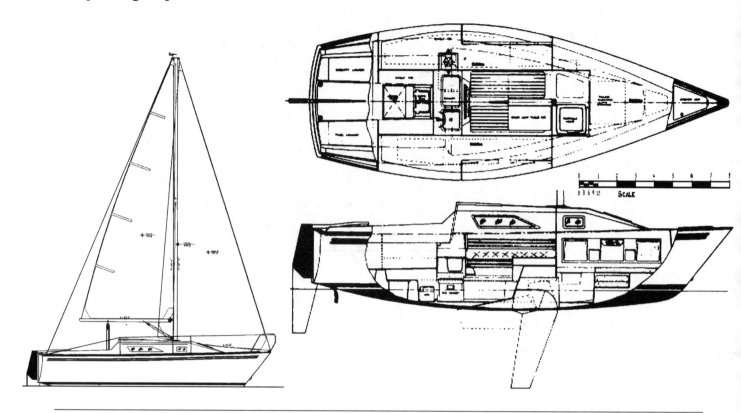

LOD:	21' 10"	**Designer:**	Cortland Steck
LOA:	23' 3"	**Builder:**	Hunter Marine
LWL:	18' 4"	**Years produced:**	1981–1985
Min./max. draft:	1' 11"/5' 0" (fin keel: 3' 2")	**Sail area:**	220 sq. ft.
Bridge clearance:	30' 3"	**Fuel tankage:**	portable
Power:	outboard 3 to 6 hp	**Water tankage:**	portable
B/D ratio:	41%	**Approx. trailering wgt.:**	4,800 lbs.

This model, eventually superseded by the Hunter 23 in 1985, came in two keel configurations—a lead fin keel or an iron keel-centerboard. The fixed fin gives a draft of 3' 2", and the more easily trailerable centerboard version gives a draft of 1' 11" with the board up and 5' 0" with the board down. Construction was on the light side, featuring plastic hatch hinges and low-end hardware. ***Best features:*** With her big beam, the boat has good space for weekend cruising. Theoretical speed is highest among comps as a result of a relatively long waterline, though low SA/D ratio indicates she will not be fast in light air, at least against the comps listed below. ***Worst features:*** Compared to comps, the Motion Index is lowest, due to a relatively low D/L ratio and wide beam. Owners complain that weather helm can be annoying in winds over ten knots. In reality this may be a result of not reefing the main when the breeze pipes up. Owners also complain that, in waves, the outboard prop tends to come out of the water and cavitate.

Comps	LOD	Beam	MinDr	Displ	Bllst	SA/D	D/L	Avg. PHRF	Max. Speed	Motion Index	Space Index	No. of Berths	Head-room
Pearson Electra 22	22' 3"	7' 0"	3' 0"	3,000	1,200	17.5	285	264	5.5	18.7	274	4	3' 6"
Pearson Ensign 22	22' 3"	7' 0"	3' 0"	3,000	1,200	18.0	285	258	5.5	18.7	274	2	3' 0"
Hunter 22	21' 10"	7' 11"	1' 11"	3,200	1,300	16.2	232	253	5.7	15.8	364	4	4' 3"

Hunter 23.5 (22)

Here's an early water-ballasted sailboat

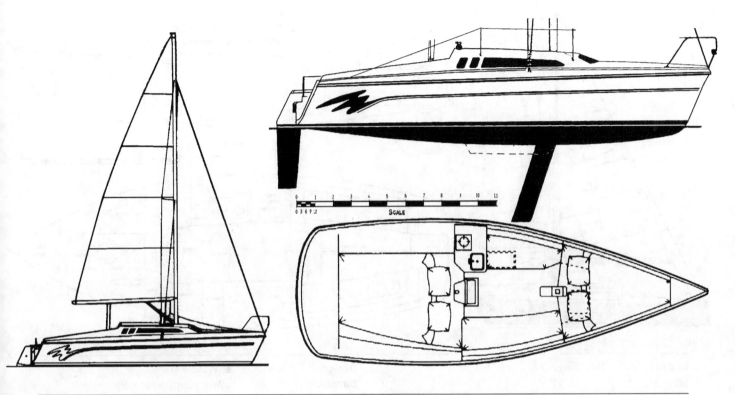

LOD:	21' 8"
LOA:	24' 0"
LWL:	21' 5"
Min./max. draft:	1' 11"/5' 6"
Bridge clearance:	32' 11"
Power:	outboard 3 to 6 hp
B/D ratio:	33%

Designer:	Hunter Design Team
Builder:	Hunter Marine
Years produced:	1992–1997
Sail area:	236 sq. ft.
Fuel tankage:	portable
Water tankage:	5 gal.
Approx. trailering wgt.:	2,950 lbs.

All the comps shown here except the Hunter 23.5 have something in common. What is it? All use lead or iron ballast. The Hunter, on the other hand, uses water ballast, which automatically pours in as the boat is launched and drains out when the boat is pulled from the water and placed on its trailer. The water is supposed to lighten the hull for easier trailering (which it does), while preserving the boat's stiffness under sail (which it doesn't, at least not very well). The water ballast just isn't heavy enough.

Best features: There's lots of space compared to comps.
Worst features: One disillusioned owner said it all: "I love Hunter sailboats, but this model heels so rapidly [a result of the water ballast design] that it scared my wife right out of sailing, so I'm out of this sport altogether now." The same owner pointed out that the handrails were "weak and easily broken." One may wonder, after his bad experience with the 23.5, why he "loves" Hunters. He didn't tell us.

Comps	LOD	Beam	MinDr	Displ	Bllst	SA/D	D/L	Avg. PHRF	Max. Speed	Motion Index	Space Index	No. of Berths	Head-room
Spirit 23 (22)	22' 2"	7' 11"	2' 0"	2,800	835	17.3	156	240	6.0	12.7	391	4	4' 10"
Rob Roy 23	22' 8"	6' 11"	1' 7"	2,800	900	20.7	135	201	6.1	14.3	228	2 or 3	4' 0"
Jeanneau Tonic 23 (22)	22' 5"	8' 2"	2' 3"	2,945	1,086	18.9	156	225	6.0	12.9	429	4	5' 7"
Hunter 23.5 (22)	21' 8"	8' 4"	1' 11"	3,000	1,000	18.2	136	240	6.2	12.3	471	6	4' 6"

Imperial 23 (22)
Import from England is slow but practical

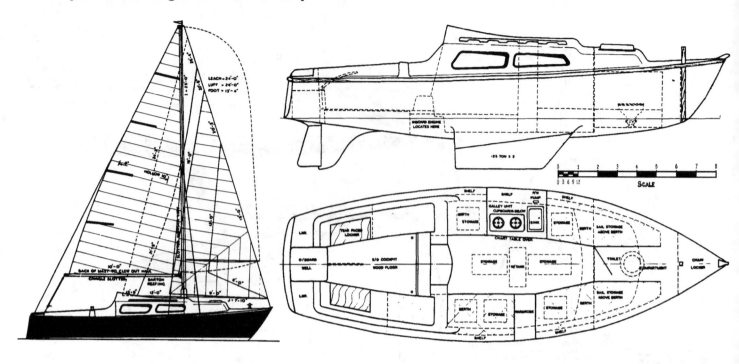

LOD:	22' 2"	**Designer:**	L. Wakefield
LOA:	22' 6"	**Builder:**	Wells Yachts (marketer)
LWL:	20' 0"	**Years produced:**	1966?–1970?
Min./max. draft:	2' 9"	**Sail area:**	210 sq. ft.
Bridge clearance:	30' 6"	**Fuel tankage:**	portable
Power:	optional inboard or outboard 6 hp	**Water tankage:**	6 gal.
B/D ratio:	42%	**Approx. trailering wgt.:**	4,000 lbs.

Here is a typical British import of the 1960s: Twin iron keels and a sturdy rudder skeg for lying upright on the English tidal flats without risk of damage; heavy, sturdy hull and relatively small sail area for dealing with brisk English Channel winds; tabernacle for easier mast lowering; provision for an inboard engine despite the boat's relatively small size. (Re size: The boat measures 22' 6" from the lower tip of her reverse transom to the forward tip of her galvanized steel anchor roller, thus claiming to be a "23-footer." On deck she's only 22' 2".)

Best features: Forward quarter berths instead of the usual V-berths provide easier access to the head, complete with hinged door for privacy. A unique (but optional) "Autohoist" permits vertical storage of an outboard engine; the skipper winds the motor out of the water with a worm-gear driven winch. *Worst features:* The jutting samson post on the small foredeck may make picking up and securing a mooring easier, but might worry the foredeck crew who, when in a hurry, could easily trip on the upward-sticking prong.

Comps	LOD	Beam	MinDr	Displ	Bllst	SA/D	D/L	Avg. PHRF	Max. Speed	Motion Index	Space Index	No. of Berths	Head-room
Santana 22	22' 3"	7' 6"	3' 6"	2,600	1,220	18.4	142	246	5.8	13.8	266	4	3' 10"
Imperial 23 (22)	22' 2"	7' 6"	2' 9"	2,688	1,120	17.4	150	NA	6.0	13.6	301	4	4' 6"
Schock 23 (22)	22' 0"	8' 6"	2' 9"	2,800	1,100	21.5	142	198	6.1	11.6	394	4	4' 6"
Santana 2023 (22)	22' 0"	8' 6"	1' 2"	2,880	1,300	19.0	142	95	6.1	11.9	395	4	4' 8"
S2 6.8 (22)	21' 9"	8' 0"	2' 0"	2,900	1,100	16.5	213	240	5.7	14.3	375	4	4' 3"

J/22

Still a hot one-design class after 25 years

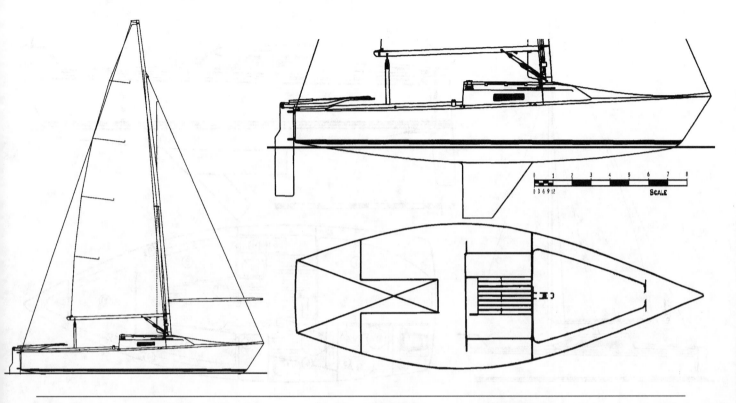

LOD:	21' 6"		**Designer:**	Rod Johnstone
LOA:	22' 6"		**Builder:**	J/Boats
LWL:	19' 0"		**Years produced:**	1983–present
Min./max. draft:	3' 9"		**Sail area:**	223 sq. ft.
Bridge clearance:	31' 0"		**Fuel tankage:**	portable
Power:	outboard 3 to 6 hp		**Water tankage:**	portable
B/D ratio:	40%		**Approx. trailering wgt.:**	2,500 lbs.

The J/22 is the smallest of the well-known J/boat fleet of one-design racer-cruisers. ***Best features:*** Like the other J/boats, the J/22 is well built and well fitted out (Baltek-cored laminates, Harken deck fittings, Hall spars, etc.). Responsive, fast, and early-planing, built for safety with buoyancy tanks and offshore hatches, she is a very popular round-the-buoys racing class (over 1,200 boats sailing in 61 active fleets in eight countries on three continents). There is a strong class association, with a website on the Internet. Strict one-design rules help reduce the cost of

racing. There is a wide choice of used boats in all parts of the U.S. ***Worst features:*** Comfort is limited with no cockpit coamings; crew position is generally forward of the cockpit, hanging along the weather rail in anything but very light winds. A hoist (one ton or more) is almost a necessity to launch and retrieve the J/22 from the water. This boat is mainly a day-racer, but can be overnighted successfully. There are berths for four, but if privacy is an issue, we'd recommend one very friendly couple at most.

Comps	LOD	Beam	MinDr	Displ	Bllst	SA/D	D/L	Avg. PHRF	Max. Speed	Motion Index	Space Index	No. of Berths	Head-room
J/22	21' 6"	8' 0"	3' 9"	1,790	700	24.7	117	180	5.8	8.4	389	4	4' 0"
South Coast 22	22' 0"	7' 1"	0' 10"	1,800	505	20.4	150	276	5.6	10.8	273	5	4' 3"
Grampian Classic 22	21' 4"	7' 0"	3' 9"	1,892	700	18.7	160	234	5.6	11.5	225	2	3' 5"

Jeanneau Tonic 23 (22)

French import with lots of headroom

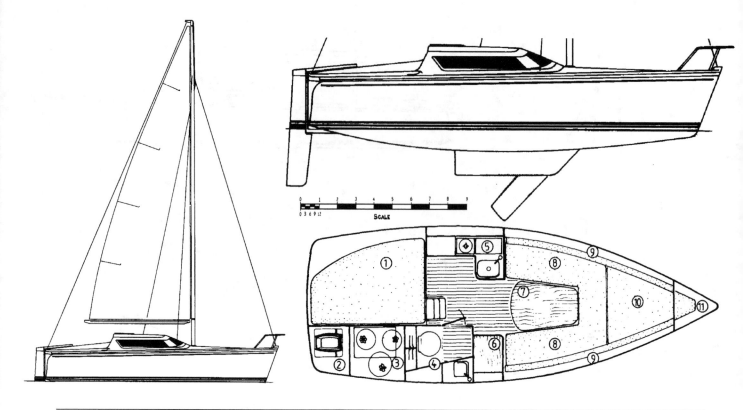

LOD:	22' 5"	**Designer:**	Philippe Harle
LOA:	23' 8"	**Builder:**	Jeanneau
LWL:	20' 4"	**Years produced:**	1985–1995
Min./max. draft:	2' 3"/4' 6"	**Sail area:**	243 sq. ft.
Bridge clearance:	35' 0"	**Fuel tankage:**	portable
Power:	outboard 3 to 6 hp	**Water tankage:**	5 gal.
B/D ratio:	37%	**Approx. trailering wgt.:**	4,300 lbs.

This French boat came in two versions: a keel-centerboarder, the statistics of which are shown above, and a fin-keeler, which draws 3' 7" and has a little less displacement (2,875 lbs., with 990 lbs. of iron ballast in the keel). At one point she was called the Tonic 24, based, we suppose, on the LOA of 23' 8", but then she became the Tonic 23; we are left to guess why this occurred. We call her the Tonic 22 since her length on deck is an inch less than 22½ feet, and LOD is our criteria for size, not LOA or hull length.

Best features: Comparing statistics among the comps, the 5' 7" headroom featured in the Tonic pops right out. Also a plus is her beam, which helps to put her Space Index close to that of the very commodious Hunter 23.5. To our knowledge, the Tonic is not known for her speed, so her average PHRF rating of 225 seems low to us (or is the Spirit 23's and the Hunter 23.5's rating too high?). **Worst features:** The Tonic's iron keel will require regular maintenance to keep from weeping rust.

Comps	LOD	Beam	MinDr	Displ	Bllst	SA/D	D/L	Avg. PHRF	Max. Speed	Motion Index	Space Index	No. of Berths	Head-room
Spirit 23 (22)	22' 2"	7' 11"	2' 0"	2,800	835	17.3	156	240	6.0	12.7	391	4	4' 10"
Rob Roy 23	22' 8"	6' 11"	1' 7"	2,800	900	20.7	135	201	6.1	14.3	228	2 or 3	4' 0"
Jeanneau Tonic 23 (22)	22' 5"	8' 2"	2' 3"	2,945	1,086	18.9	156	225	6.0	12.9	429	4	5' 7"
Hunter 23.5 (22)	21' 8"	8' 4"	1' 11"	3,000	1,000	18.2	136	240	6.2	12.3	471	6	4' 6"

MacGregor 22

Venture 222 on mild steroids

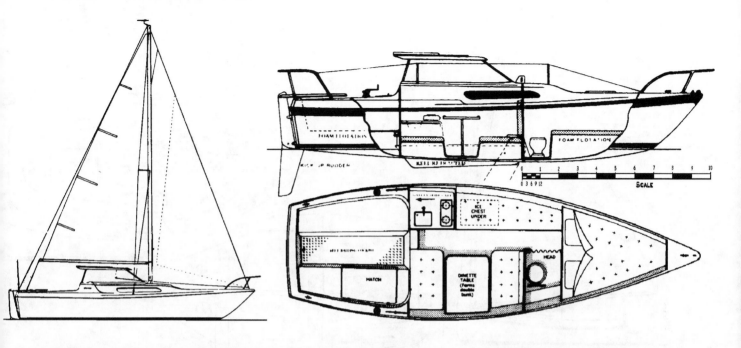

LOD:	22' 0"	**Designer:**	Roger MacGregor
LOA:	22' 11"	**Builder:**	MacGregor Yachts
LWL:	19' 6"	**Years produced:**	1981–1986
Min./max. draft:	1' 0"/5' 6"	**Sail area:**	178 sq. ft.
Bridge clearance:	26' 6"	**Fuel tankage:**	portable
Power:	outboard 3 to 6 hp	**Water tankage:**	portable
B/D ratio:	28%	**Approx. trailering wgt.:**	2,600 lbs.

If you compare the drawings of the Venture 222 (page 210), made by MacGregor between 1970 and 1980, with those of the MacGregor 22, made by the same company from 1981 to 1986, you will not find very many differences. Headroom with poptop not erected appears to be the same. Displacement remains the same, though ballast has increased 25 pounds. Waterline length has increased from 18' 2" to 19' 6", at least in the sales brochure. (With what looks like identical hulls with identical displacements,

how can the draft increase by one inch and the waterline increase by more than a foot? It's a mystery we leave to buyers to figure out.) *Best features:* All the comments we make about the Venture 222 seem to apply to the MacGregor 22 as well. *Worst features:* Could it be that the marketing department just changed a few of the figures (like waterline length and minimum draft) and called the same boat by a different name? Would that be a bad feature? We will ponder the matter.

Comps	LOD	Beam	MinDr	Displ	Bllst	SA/D	D/L	Avg. PHRF	Max. Speed	Motion Index	Space Index	No. of Berths	Head- room
Venture 222	22' 0"	7' 4"	0' 11"	1,800	475	20.2	134	258	5.7	10.1	279	5	4' 0"
MacGregor 22	22' 0"	7' 4"	1' 0"	1,800	500	19.2	108	258	5.9	9.6	263	5	4' 0"
Kells 22	22' 2"	7' 7"	0' 11"	1,890	525	19.2	142	NA	5.7	9.9	306	5	4' 6"

Marshall 22
Take your choice: catboat or sloop

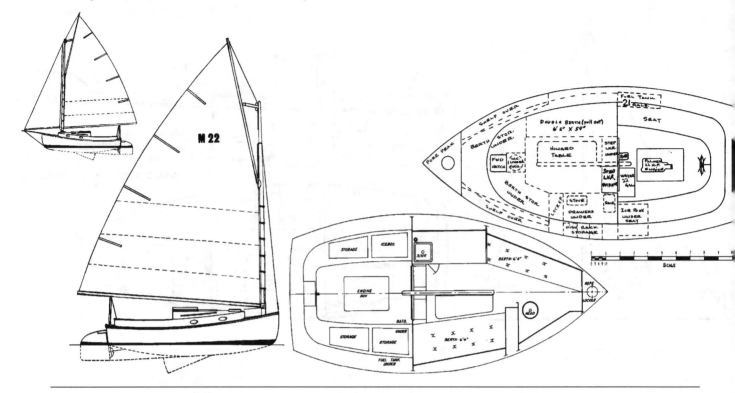

LOD:	22' 2"	**Designer:**	Breck Marshall
LOA:	25' 8" (cat), 31' 8" (sloop)	**Builder:**	Marshall Marine Corp.
LWL:	21' 4"	**Years produced:**	1965–present
Min./max. draft:	2' 0"/5' 5"	**Sail area:**	388 sq. ft. (cat)
Bridge clearance:	38' 6"	**Fuel tankage:**	12 to 21 gal.
Power:	Yanmar 16 to 22 hp	**Water tankage:**	22 gal.
B/D ratio:	15%	**Approx. trailering wgt.:**	8,000 lbs.

The Marshall 22 catboat and her sloop-rigged sister have been in production for over 40 years—one of the longest running continuously produced cruising sailboat designs ever. During the period, understandably, the builder has made many changes. Gasoline engines have been replaced with diesels, horsepower ratings have crept up, interior layout has been modified (the bottom layout shown being the current version), and fit and finish have gone through several iterations (generally toward fancier wood trim). Still, the Marshall 22 remains essentially the same boat it was in 1965, featuring shallow draft (two feet with board up) for gunkholing or lying on the bottom at low tide, and a

good length on deck for a catboat. (Hoisting the sail on a bigger cat can be a pain for a singlehander—and a smaller cat has a lot less space below.) **Best features:** She looks like the pretty Cape Cod cat she is; skippers are likely to get frequent compliments while cruising. There's a good network of other catboaters, especially in the northeastern states, for those seeking nautical camaraderie. **Worst features:** Compared to her comps, headroom is low. Also: the Marshall 22 cat has a reputation for being a bit sluggish in light air; well-sailed Marshall 18s can beat her handily. The sloop rig (338 sq. ft. main, 100 sq. ft. jib) is even slower. Both rigs are better when it breezes up.

Comps	LOD	Beam	MinDr	Displ	Bllst	SA/D	D/L	Avg. PHRF	Max. Speed	Motion Index	Space Index	No. of Berths	Head-room
Nonsuch 22	22' 0"	8' 5"	3' 8"	5,000	1,880	16.3	258	245	6.1	21.3	454	2	6' 0"
Marshall 22	22' 2"	10' 2"	2' 0"	5,660	850	19.3	260	264	6.2	18.3	495	2 or 4	5' 2"
Menger Cat 23	22' 6"	10' 0"	2' 6"	6,500	850	20.0	299	NA	6.2	21.4	526	3	6' 0"
Atlantic City Catboat 24	24' 0"	11' 2"	2' 0"	8,000	2,200	18.1	335	264	6.3	21.7	636	6	6' 2"

Menger Cat 23 (22)

Is this boat really a 22-footer?

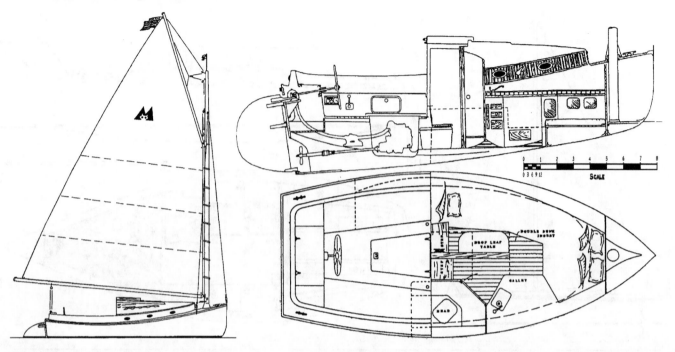

LOD:	22' 6"		**Designer:**	Francis Sweiguth/Andrew Menger
LOA:	24' 9"		**Builder:**	Menger Boatworks, Wagner Boats
LWL:	21' 4"		**Years produced:**	1990–present
Min./max. draft:	2' 6"/5' 0"		**Sail area:**	435 sq. ft.
Bridge clearance:	34' 0"		**Fuel tankage:**	12 gal.
Power:	Yanmar 2GM 20 18 hp		**Water tankage:**	22 gal.
B/D ratio:	13%		**Approx. trailering wgt.:**	9,500 lbs.

The Menger Cat 23 is a very close relative of a design by Francis Sweiguth (1882–1970) built on Long Island, NY, in fiberglass in the late 1960s and early 1970s and called the Americat 22. Bill Menger and his son, Andrew, took the lines off the Americat, and may even have acquired the molds. If so, they never publicized it, though in fact the Menger 23 was so close to the Americat that the first sales brochure Menger put out was a duplicate of the Americat brochure, complete with an A22 emblem on the photos of the boat under sail and identical dimensions. The original Menger brochure claimed 5,500 pounds, about equal to the Marshall 22. But soon the father and son team had fudged a little here and there, raised the cockpit coaming,

added an extra couple of portlights, and rewrote the brochure dimensions, and somehow the result became the Menger 23 (no longer the 22)—now with a whopping 1,000 lbs. more weight, at 6,500 pounds. For now we're call her a "23", though we have our suspicions from measuring her drawings that she's really 22' 4" LOD. ***Best features:*** Compared with the Marshall 22, which is reported to weigh 740 pounds less than the Menger 23, the Menger should be slower to accelerate but have an easier motion in waves. She appears to have considerably more space below than the Marshall, and has more headroom. Her layout below, with an enclosed head, also looks more appealing. ***Worst features:*** We don't see any significant problems so far.

Comps	LOD	Beam	MinDr	Displ	Bllst	SA/D	D/L	Avg. PHRF	Max. Speed	Motion Index	Space Index	No. of Berths	Head-room
Nonsuch 22	22' 0"	8' 5"	3' 8"	5,000	1,880	16.7	258	245	6.1	21.2	454	2	6' 0"
Marshall 22	22' 2"	10' 2"	2' 0"	5,660	850	19.5	260	264	6.2	18.3	495	2 or 4	5' 2"
Menger Cat 23	22' 6"	10' 0"	2' 6"	6,500	850	20.0	299	NA	6.2	21.4	526	3	6' 0"
Atlantic City Catboat 24	24' 0"	11' 2"	2' 0"	8,000	2,200	18.1	335	264	6.3	21.7	636	6	6' 2"

Merit 22

Pocket rocket from California

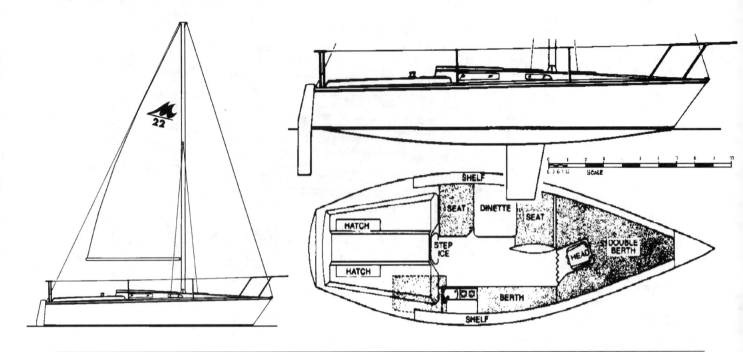

LOD:	22' 0"	**Designer:**	Paul M. Yates
LOA:	22' 11"	**Builder:**	Merit Marine
LWL:	18' 0"	**Years produced:**	1982–1986
Min./max. draft:	2' 0"/4' 0"	**Sail area:**	225 sq. ft.
Bridge clearance:	28' 6"	**Fuel tankage:**	portable
Power:	outboard 3 to 6 hp	**Water tankage:**	portable
B/D ratio:	30%	**Approx. trailering wgt.:**	2,900 lbs.

The Merit 22 (launched 1982), a racer-cruiser, followed the successful look-alike Merit 25 (launched 1979) which won the MORC national championships twice. **Best features:** She looks sleek, and although she suffers in the headroom department a little with the hatch closed, with her poptop erected, she is said to have six-foot headroom. Her vertically lifting keel is lead, not the usual iron, which improves her stability because of the greater density of lead, and avoids the maintenance chores associated with the rust that inevitably goes with iron or steel. The keel is out of the way in the up position and locks in the down position so it doesn't slide up in the event of a capsize. She has enough foam flotation to keep her from sinking. **Worst features:** Try as we might, we came up with only minor negatives. For example, her interior is very plain—designed for racing lightness rather than opulent luxury. Someone complained that her perforated aluminum rail (handy for attaching snatch blocks and fenders) was sharp enough on its top edge to chafe any docking lines that might pass over it. And one sailor suggested bigger mooring chocks and cleats than came standard.

Comps	LOD	Beam	MinDr	Displ	Bllst	SA/D	D/L	Avg. PHRF	Max. Speed	Motion Index	Space Index	No. of Berths	Head-room
Freedom 21 (22)	21' 8"	8' 0"	2' 0"	2,000	500	16.5	162	260	5.6	10.2	272	4	4' 6"
Merit 22	22' 0"	8' 0"	2' 0"	2,000	600	22.7	153	219	5.7	10.0	303	5	3' 9"
Plas Trend Mustang 22	22' 0"	7' 0"	2' 4"	2,000	750	18.8	182	225	5.5	12.3	221	4	3' 8"
Paceship Bluejacket 23	22' 1"	7' 0"	3' 9"	2,000	900	20.3	167	240	5.6	12.0	186	2	3' 1"
ETAP 22i	22' 3"	8' 1"	1' 4"	2,149	518	20.1	126	NA	5.9	9.7	227	4	4' 6"

Nonsuch 22

A simple cruiser with a bit of catboat tradition

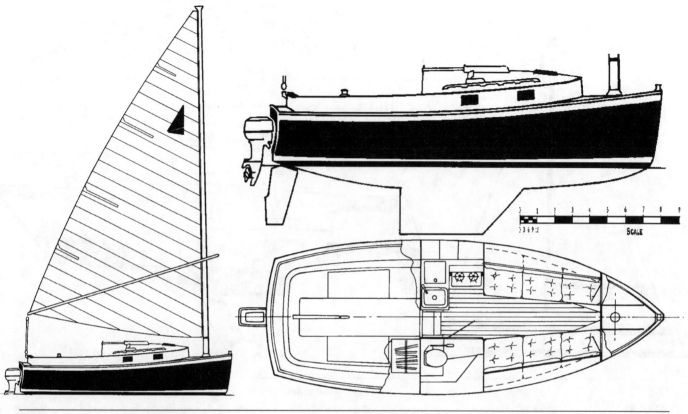

LOD:	22' 0"	**Designer:**	Mark Ellis
LOA:	22' 3"	**Builder:**	Hinterhoeller Yachts
LWL:	20' 6"	**Years produced:**	1982–1988
Min./max. draft:	3' 8"	**Sail area:**	306 sq. ft.
Bridge clearance:	39' 6"	**Fuel tankage:**	6 to 10 gal.
Power:	10 hp outboard or 8 hp dsl.	**Water tankage:**	15 to 26 gal.
B/D ratio:	31%	**Approx. trailering wgt.:**	7,100 lbs.

The Nonsuch 22 was designed for easy daysailing or cruising for a couple. It's not exactly a full-fledged traditional catboat; the beam is not quite as wide, the hull has a fin keel rather than a centerboard, and the sail is not gaff-rigged. In fact the wishbone rig, with its "cradle lines" to contain the lowered sail, is the boat's most unique feature. The whole idea is elegant simplicity, and the rig helps to make the boat quick to get underway and easy to put to bed. **Best features:** With the fin keel and spade rudder, helm response is instantaneous, and the boat will turn in her own length. (This is good for manuevering around slips, but not so good when trying to hold a straight course at sea.) Finish is excellent, with all interior teak satin varnished, and cedar ceiling over the settee. The port settee can be extended to make a king-sized double if desired. Opening ports and forward hatch provide plenty of fresh air. The enclosed head has full headroom for an average sized male, rare in a 22-foot sailing vessel. **Worst features:** The unusual design appeals to a certain group of individualists, but not to everybody.

Comps	LOD	Beam	MinDr	Displ	Bllst	SA/D	D/L	Avg. PHRF	Max. Speed	Motion Index	Space Index	No. of Berths	Head-room
Nonsuch 22	22' 0"	8' 5"	3' 8"	5,000	1,880	16.7	258	245	6.1	21.2	454	2	6' 0"
Marshall 22	22' 2"	10' 2"	2' 0"	5,660	850	19.5	260	264	6.2	18.3	495	2 or 4	5' 2"
Menger Cat 23	22' 6"	10' 0"	2' 6"	6,500	850	20.0	299	NA	6.2	21.4	526	3	6' 0"
Atlantic City Catboat 24	24' 0"	11' 2"	2' 0"	8,000	2,200	18.1	335	264	6.3	21.7	636	6	6' 2"

O'Day 23 Mk II (22)
One of O'Day's entries in one of its key markets

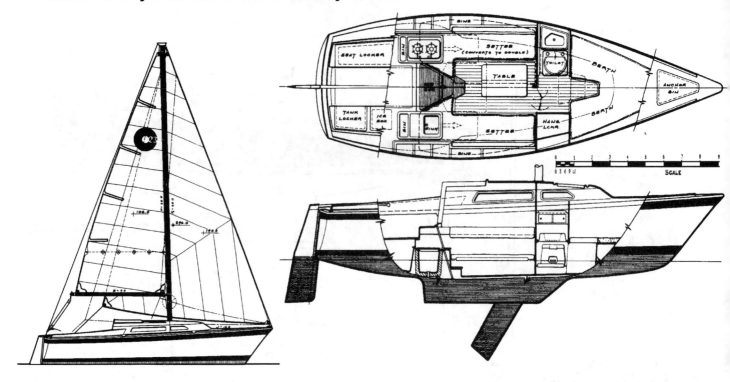

LOD:	22' 1"	**Designer:**	C. Raymond Hunt Assoc.
LOA:	24' 2"	**Builder:**	O'Day/Bangor Punta
LWL:	19' 6"	**Years produced:**	1977–1985
Min./max. draft:	2' 0"/5' 0"	**Sail area:**	235 sq. ft.
Bridge clearance:	32' 0"	**Fuel tankage:**	portable
Power:	3 to 6 hp, or optional inboard	**Water tankage:**	10 gal.
B/D ratio:	26%	**Approx. trailering wgt.:**	5,300 lbs.

The O'Day 23 Mk II (22) follows a series of 21-, 22-, and 23-footers by C. Raymond Hunt Associates and various other designers, all targeted at the same market: The O'Day Tempest 23 (1964–1973, page 242), the O'Day 23 Mk I (22) (1970–1974, page 240), and the O'Day 22 (21) (1972–1983, page 118). It precedes the O'Day 222 (21) (1984–1988, page 119) and the O'Day 240 (23) (page 241). Until the O'Day company ceased operations in 1989, they were a potent force in the small sailboat market in the eastern U.S., particularly in the 21- to 23-foot size range, of which this design is representative.

Best features: Compared to her comps, which are all heavy centerboarders, the O'Day 23 Mk II (22) has the highest (that is, best) Space Index and the lowest minimum draft, is tied for the greatest headroom and the lowest average PHRF, and has the heaviest construction (calculated by subtracting ballast from displacement).
Worst features: The mainsheet traveler, led to a bridle attached to the split backstay, is not one of our favorite rigging arrangements, as the helmsman has to look aft to find the mainsheet bitter end, undesirable when racing in tight quarters.

Comps	LOD	Beam	MinDr	Displ	Bllst	SA/D	D/L	Avg. PHRF	Max. Speed	Motion Index	Space Index	No. of Berths	Head- room
ETAP 23 (22)	22' 0"	8' 2"	2' 3"	3,320	1,035	17.3	216	240	5.8	15.2	384	4	4' 5"
O'Day 23 Mk II (22)	22' 1"	8' 0"	2' 0"	3,500	900	16.3	211	240	6.0	16.1	390	5	5' 0"
S/2 7.0 Meter (22)	22' 3"	8' 0"	2' 2"	3,600	1,300	16.3	261	261	6.0	17.6	344	4	5' 0"
Sailmaster 22	22' 0"	7' 1"	2' 4"	3,650	1,600	15.5	263	288	5.4	22.8	297	2	4' 5"

Paceship Bluejacket 23 (22)
Early Cuthbertson-designed racer-cruiser

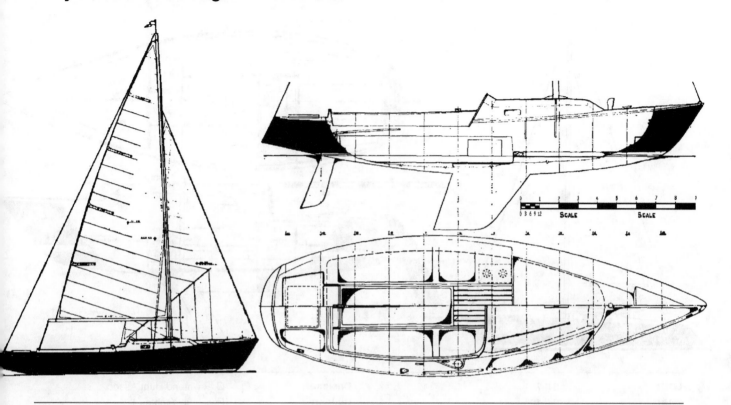

LOD:	22' 1"	**Designer:**	George Cuthbertson
LOA:	22' 10"	**Builder:**	Paceship Yachts
LWL:	17' 6"	**Years produced:**	1967–1973
Min./max. draft:	3' 9"	**Sail area:**	201 sq. ft.
Bridge clearance:	29' 0"	**Fuel tankage:**	portable
Power:	outboard 3 to 6 hp	**Water tankage:**	portable
B/D ratio:	45%	**Approx. trailering wgt.:**	2,900 lbs.

This early design, only 22' 1" on deck but 22' 10" if the extended reverse transom is counted, is by George Cuthbertson, later a partner in the famed C&C design firm. She is remarkable for her sleek looks, rare as early as the year 1967. The Grampian Classic 22 (page 173) is virtually the same design, except for elimination of the Paceship's reverse transom. Our comments recorded there also apply to the Paceship shown here. **Best features:** The Paceship Bluejacket (not to be confused with the totally different

Bluejacket 23 Motorsailer reported on page 222) has positive flotation for safety. A big lazarette hatch has a well inside for an outboard. To our eye she appears to be sleek and graceful. **Worst features:** While all the comps listed here offer weekending accommodations, the Paceship's are most spartan. The cockpit is not self-bailing, requiring the use of canvas covers to keep rain from swamping the boat when left at a mooring or slip for any length of time. Sitting headroom, at a bare 3' 1", is lowest of all her comps.

Comps	LOD	Beam	MinDr	Displ	Bllst	SA/D	D/L	Avg. PHRF	Max. Speed	Motion Index	Space Index	No. of Berths	Head-room
Freedom 21 (22)	21' 8"	8' 0"	2' 0"	2,000	500	16.5	162	260	5.6	10.2	272	4	4' 6"
Merit 22	22' 0"	8' 0"	2' 0"	2,000	600	22.7	153	219	5.7	10.0	303	5	3' 9"
Plas Trend Mustang 22	22' 0"	7' 0"	2' 4"	2,000	750	18.8	182	225	5.5	12.3	221	4	3' 8"
Paceship Bluejacket 23	22' 1"	7' 0"	3' 9"	2,000	900	20.3	167	240	5.6	12.0	186	2	3' 1"
ETAP 22i	22' 3"	8' 1"	1' 4"	2,149	518	20.1	126	NA	5.9	9.7	227	4	4' 6"

Paceship PY23 (22)
Hunt design for a Canadian firm

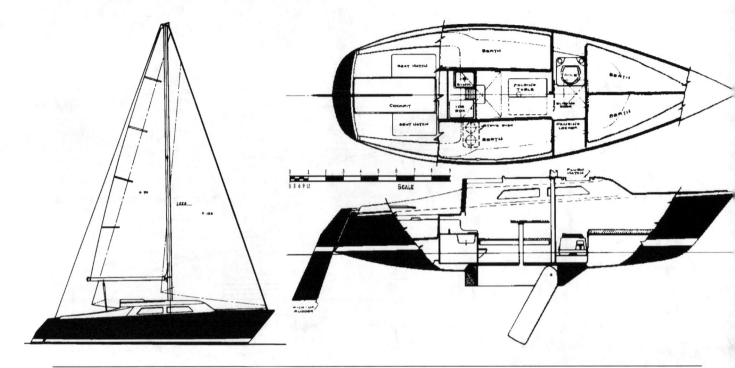

LOD:	21' 7"	**Designer:**	C. Raymond Hunt Assoc.
LOA:	24' 10"	**Builder:**	Paceship Yachts
LWL:	19' 4.5"	**Years produced:**	1972–1980
Min./max. draft:	1' 9"/4' 9"	**Sail area:**	223 sq. ft.
Bridge clearance:	31' 0"	**Fuel tankage:**	portable
Power:	outboard 3 to 6 hp	**Water tankage:**	portable
B/D ratio:	38%	**Approx. trailering wgt.:**	3,600 lbs.

It is interesting to compare this vessel with the slightly smaller O'Day 22 (21) on page 118, designed by the same firm, Raymond Hunt Associates, at around the same time. The PY23, like her little sister, has a reverse transom, which adds a foot to the hull length, justifying the "23" designation, at least in the minds of her marketers. Both boats were offered with either keel or shoal-draft keel-centerboard configuration. The layouts below are also similar, except for the galley location; the bigger boat puts the galley under the main hatch, where the cook, if he wants, can stand up straight to make dinner. *Best features:*

The coamings are unusually high forward, giving good back support to the PY23's crew. The helmsperson, however, has to suffer with a coaming no higher than the O'Day 22 (21)'s. Down below, a sliding door affords privacy in the head compartment, and the head is well positioned under the forward hatch to give good ventilation and good headroom and knee room. *Worst features:* While the PY23's cabin space is certainly greater than the Kirby Blazer's (see Space Indexes below), it's a great deal less than the Precision 23's (which is almost a foot longer and half a foot wider).

Comps	LOD	Beam	MinDr	Displ	Bllst	SA/D	D/L	Avg. PHRF	Max. Speed	Motion Index	Space Index	No. of Berths	Head-room
Blazer 23	22' 6"	7' 10"	3' 11"	2,200	900	25.5	143	180	5.8	10.7	291	4	3' 8"
Aquarius/Balboa 23	22' 8"	7' 11"	1' 1"	2,280	815	19.7	107	282	6.2	10.3	416	5	4' 11"
Hunter 23	22' 9"	8' 0"	2' 3"	2,450	800	20.7	146	237	5.9	11.4	359	4	4' 7"
Precision 23	23' 5"	8' 6"	1' 11"	2,450	850	21.8	137	228	6.0	10.3	464	4	4' 6"
Paceship PY23 (22)	21' 7"	8' 0"	1' 9"	2,460	945	19.6	151	240	5.9	11.6	348	4	4' 6"

Pearson 22
Early (and smallest) Pearson racer-cruiser

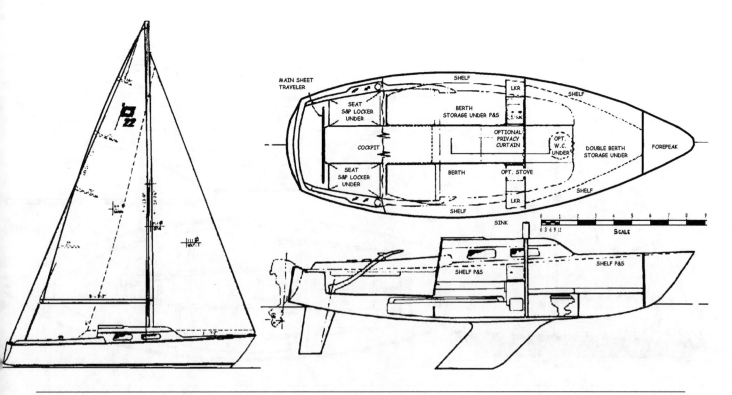

LOD:	22' 0"	**Designer:**	Bill Shaw
LOA:	22' 3"	**Builder:**	Pearson Yachts
LWL:	18' 6"	**Years produced:**	1968–1972
Min./max. draft:	3' 5"	**Sail area:**	217 sq. ft.
Bridge clearance:	29' 7"	**Fuel tankage:**	portable
Power:	outboard 3 to 6 hp	**Water tankage:**	portable
B/D ratio:	38%	**Approx. trailering wgt.:**	3,800 lbs.

Pearson's literature bills this boat as "to sailing what a sports car is to driving—a high performance . . . beautifully balanced design that puts fun into getting there . . . took the season championship although she was the smallest boat in her fleet . . . headed for one-design racing in many areas." In hindsight, it appears that reality did not match the brochure writer's dreams. She was discontinued after four years, superseded by slightly larger cruisers like the Pearson 26. **Best features:** With more ballast, lower center of gravity, and the highest D/L ratio versus her otherwise very similar comps, the Pearson 22 is probably the stiffest boat in the group. That may make her fastest too, sailing without handicap, at least in a moderate breeze. (Her PHRF rating indicates she's fastest, too.) **Worst features:** She's neither wide nor tall down below, giving her relatively low points on the Space Index scale. The outboard engine controls are far aft of the cockpit, and the prop is beyond the counter stern, which would make us worry about prop cavitation when hobby horsing in a seaway.

Comps	LOD	Beam	MinDr	Displ	Bllst	SA/D	D/L	Avg. PHRF	Max. Speed	Motion Index	Space Index	No. of Berths	Head-room
Starwind 22	22' 0"	7' 9"	1' 11"	2,600	775	17.6	169	273	5.8	12.8	346	5	4' 9"
Pearson 22	22' 0"	7' 9"	3' 5"	2,600	1,000	18.4	183	246	5.8	13.3	298	4	4' 2"
Seaward 23 (22)	21' 9"	8' 4"	2' 1"	2,700	900	19.8	138	285	5.8	11.3	325	4	4' 8"
Bristol Caravel 22	22' 0"	7' 9"	2' 6"	2,850	1,150	16.4	172	288	5.8	14.1	322	4	4' 0"

Pearson Electra 22
Cruising version of the Pearson Ensign

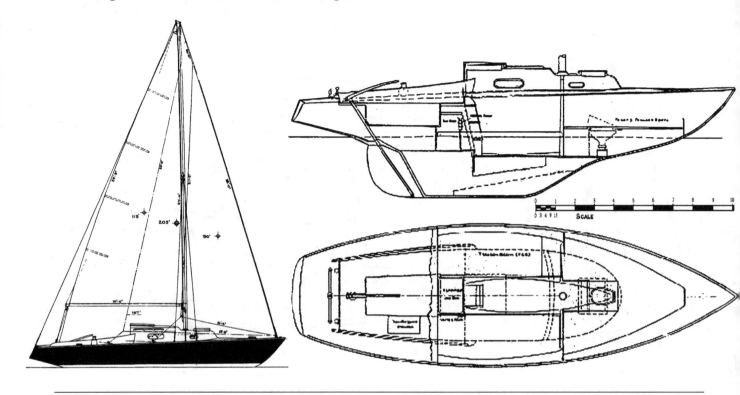

LOD:	22' 3"	**Designer:**	Carl Alberg
LOA:	22' 6"	**Builder:**	Pearson Yachts
LWL:	16' 9"	**Years produced:**	1960–1965
Min./max. draft:	3' 0"	**Sail area:**	227 sq. ft.
Bridge clearance:	29' 9"	**Fuel tankage:**	portable
Power:	outboard 3 to 6 hp	**Water tankage:**	portable
B/D ratio:	40%	**Approx. trailering wgt.:**	4,600 lbs.

This early fiberglass Alberg design was introduced the year after the ground-breaking 29-foot Pearson Triton hit the ways in 1959, and was one of the very first small fiberglass cruising sailboats. In those days the marketers weren't always sure what the market would bear, so the Electra at first was sold as a basic two-berth overnighter, with extra-cost options that would make her a full-fledged cruiser (forward berths, galley, icebox, toilet, etc.). The Pearson Ensign 22 (page 191), a weekend version using the same hull but featuring a larger cockpit and smaller cabin, followed in 1962, and turned out to be much more popular than the Electra. **Best features:** The Electra, being a near clone of the Ensign, has many of the same stats, which make her relatively fast for her day (though definitely not faster relative to more recent designs). Some say she is better looking than many of the cruisers in her size range. **Worst features:** Compared to the Hunter 22, her comp other than the Ensign, she generally has less headroom. Her draft is deep enough for casual racing, but wouldn't stand up to many deeper-draft keelboats or shallower boats with centerboards (unless her extremely high PHRF rating could be brought to bear).

Comps	LOD	Beam	MinDr	Displ	Bllst	SA/D	D/L	Avg. PHRF	Max. Speed	Motion Index	Space Index	No. of Berths	Head-room
Pearson Electra 22	22' 3"	7' 0"	3' 0"	3,000	1,200	17.5	285	264	5.5	18.7	274	4	3' 6"
Pearson Ensign 22	22' 3"	7' 0"	3' 0"	3,000	1,200	18.0	285	258	5.5	18.7	274	2	3' 0"
Hunter 22	21' 10"	7' 11"	1' 11"	3,200	1,300	16.2	232	253	5.7	15.8	364	4	4' 3"

Pearson Ensign 22
Overnighter version of the Pearson Electra 22

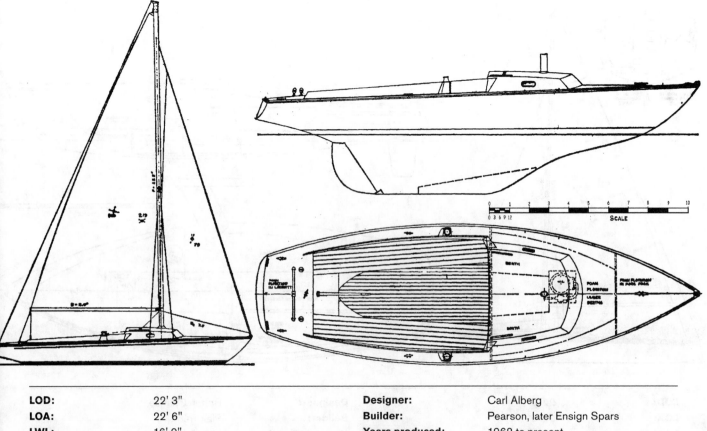

LOD:	22' 3"	**Designer:**	Carl Alberg
LOA:	22' 6"	**Builder:**	Pearson, later Ensign Spars
LWL:	16' 9"	**Years produced:**	1962 to present
Min./max. draft:	3' 0"	**Sail area:**	234 sq. ft.
Bridge clearance:	30' 0"	**Fuel tankage:**	portable
Power:	outboard 3 to 5 hp	**Water tankage:**	portable
B/D ratio:	40%	**Approx. trailering wgt.:**	4,600 lbs.

The Ensign is a daysailer-overnighter and one-design racing version of the Pearson Electra cruiser (page 190). Compared to the Electra, she has the same hull, but a tiny cuddy cabin with two bunks, and a much larger cockpit that can hold 8 (or 3 or 4 while racing). Since the year 2000, Ensigns have been built by Ensign Spars of Dunedin, FL. **Best features:** She is a competent, forgiving, stable, and easy-to-sail one-design class racer. Over the years a strong class organization has developed. Foam flotation is built in. A deep cockpit gives the Ensign above-average crew comfort. With an optional toilet, cushions for the

bunks, and perhaps air mattresses for extra sleeping space in the cockpit under a boom tent if desired, she can be made into a plain-jane but reasonably comfortable weekender. Used boat prices can be quite attractive. **Worst features:** This boat was once considered fast, but that's no longer true compared to modern racing designs—and many of the boats are getting quite old and less competitive, though you can still find fleets to race with here and there. The cockpit is not self-bailing, so a boom tent is required to keep rain from filling her when her crew is not in attendance.

Comps	LOD	Beam	MinDr	Displ	Bllst	SA/D	D/L	Avg. PHRF	Max. Speed	Motion Index	Space Index	No. of Berths	Head-room
Pearson Electra 22	22' 3"	7' 0"	3' 0"	3,000	1,200	17.5	285	264	5.5	18.7	274	4	3' 6"
Pearson Ensign 22	22' 3"	7' 0"	3' 0"	3,000	1,200	18.0	285	258	5.5	18.7	274	2	3' 0"
Hunter 22	21' 10"	7' 11"	1' 11"	3,200	1,300	16.2	232	253	5.7	15.8	364	4	4' 3"

Plas Trend Mustang 22
Texas racer with an unusual keel

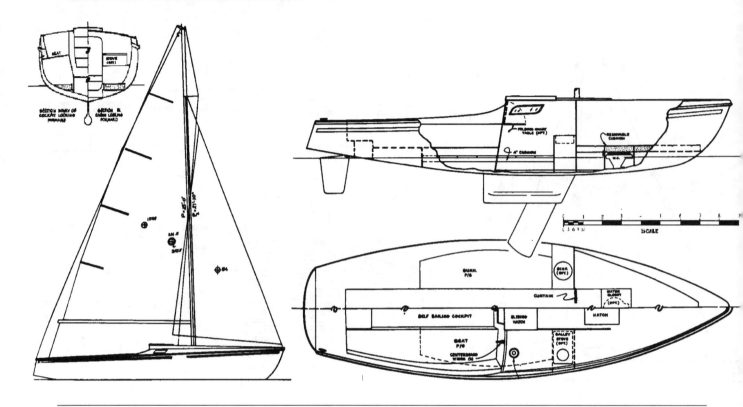

LOD:	22' 0"	**Designer:**	Britton Chance
LOA:	22' 5"	**Builder:**	Plas Trend
LWL:	17' 0"	**Years produced:**	1965?–1973
Min./max. draft:	2' 4"/5' 3"	**Sail area:**	187 sq. ft.
Bridge clearance:	30' 0"	**Fuel tankage:**	portable
Power:	outboard 3 to 6 hp	**Water tankage:**	portable
B/D ratio:	31%	**Approx. trailering wgt.:**	2,900 lbs.

The PT 22, a.k.a. Plas Trend 22 or Mustang 22, was a brand name used by Composite Technology, Inc. of Fort Worth, TX. She has an unusual keel-centerboard arrangement, which includes a bulb on the keel (see inset in sailplan) combined with a centerboad slot splitting the keel in two. The centerboard, weighing 150 pounds, is cranked up and down using a winch mounted on the aft cabin bulkhead on the starboard side of the cockpit. A small inboard was optional, though we don't see where it would fit in such a shallow hull. **Best features:** She looks sleek and fast, with her long cockpit and low profile. **Worst features:** Her buoyancy aft is low, due to her extended counter and pinched aft end, thereby limiting weight at the back end, so her long cockpit is mostly unusable while racing. Her relatively narrow beam and low sitting headroom keep her from being a very comfortable cruiser—not that many owners would have cruising in mind, anyway. Finally, her diamond strut and ¾ fractional rig give her an old-fashioned, outmoded look.

Comps	LOD	Beam	MinDr	Displ	Bllst	SA/D	D/L	Avg. PHRF	Max. Speed	Motion Index	Space Index	No. of Berths	Head-room
Freedom 21 (22)	21' 8"	8' 0"	2' 0"	2,000	500	16.5	162	260	5.6	10.2	272	4	4' 6"
Merit 22	22' 0"	8' 0"	2' 0"	2,000	600	22.7	153	219	5.7	10.0	303	5	3' 9"
Plas Trend Mustang 22	22' 0"	7' 0"	2' 4"	2,000	750	18.8	182	225	5.5	12.3	221	4	3' 8"
Paceship Bluejacket 23	22' 1"	7' 0"	3' 9"	2,000	900	20.3	167	240	5.6	12.0	186	2	3' 1"
ETAP 22i	22' 3"	8' 1"	1' 4"	2,149	518	20.1	126	NA	5.9	9.7	227	4	4' 6"

Ranger 23 (22)
Small Gary Mull speedster

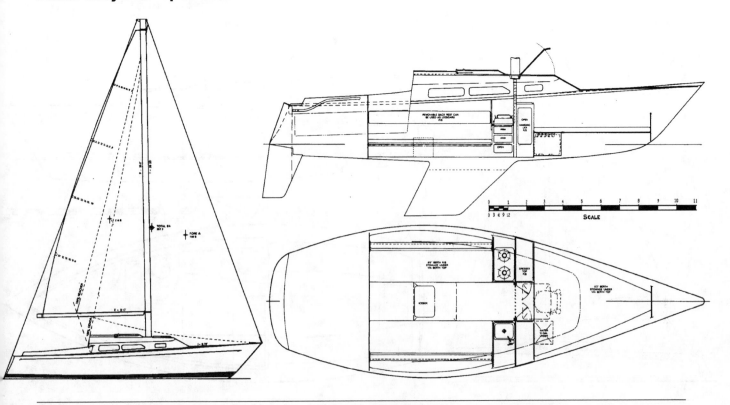

LOD:	22' 3"	**Designer:**	Gary Mull
LOA:	23' 4"	**Builder:**	Ranger Yachts
LWL:	20' 0"	**Years produced:**	1971–1978
Min./max. draft:	3' 9"	**Sail area:**	264 sq. ft.
Bridge clearance:	31' 6"	**Fuel tankage:**	portable
Power:	outboard 3 to 6 hp	**Water tankage:**	12 gal.
B/D ratio:	44%	**Approx. trailering wgt.:**	5,000 lbs.

The Ranger 23 was one in a long series of designs Gary Mull produced for Ranger Yachts, then a division of Jensen Marine, builder of the Cal line of sailboats. In an interview we did with Mull in 1986, he maintained that each of his designs "has to be good looking, and has to sail well. It has to have good balance, and it has to have an airy, bright, pleasant interior so you don't feel like you are going to jail when you go down below. It's got to have a comfortable cockpit where you can work the boat without bashing your elbows or tipping over or whatever. It's a boat that, if you want to cruise it for a while, you can do it by simply loading aboard the stores and some clothes, and just do it. If you want to race it, you can do that by off-loading some of the stores and gear and going racing. And, of course, it's not going to be a successful IOR boat, because it's not an IOR boat, but it's probably going to be a better cruising boat than 99 percent of the cruising boats on the market, which are caricatures of cruising boats." The Ranger 23 appears to fit that description. ***Best*** and ***worst features:*** We think designer Mull summed it all up adequately. Case closed.

Comps	LOD	Beam	MinDr	Displ	Bllst	SA/D	D/L	Avg. PHRF	Max. Speed	Motion Index	Space Index	No. of Berths	Head-room
Alberg 22	22' 0"	7' 0"	3' 1"	3,200	1,500	17.4	349	282	5.4	20.7	274	4	4' 4"
Cape Dory Senior 22	22' 5"	7' 5"	3' 1"	3,300	1,700	17.7	328	273	5.4	19.2	322	4	4' 8"
Ranger 23 (22)	22' 3"	7' 11"	3' 9"	3,400	1,500	18.7	190	216	6.0	15.9	318	4	4' 3"
Westerly Nomad 22	22' 2"	7' 5"	2' 3"	3,600	950	15.5	261	300	5.7	19.6	277	4	4' 7"

Rhodes 22
"Different" Philip Rhodes design

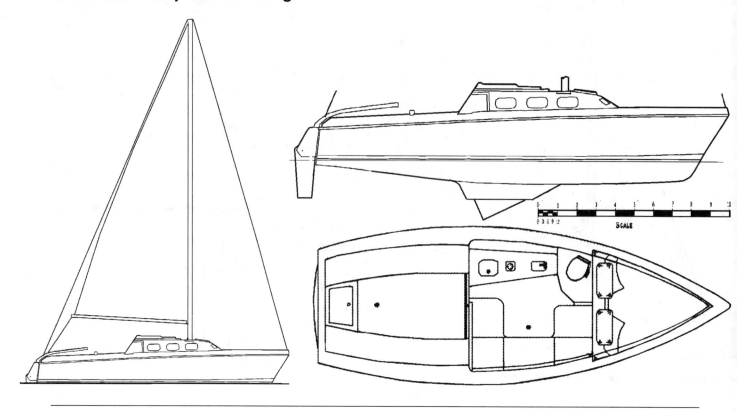

LOD:	21' 6"	**Designer:**	Philip Rhodes
LOA:	22' 9"	**Builder:**	General Boats Corp.
LWL:	20' 0"	**Years produced:**	1970–present
Min./max. draft:	1' 8"/4' 6"	**Sail area:**	210 sq. ft.
Bridge clearance:	30' 0"	**Fuel tankage:**	portable
Power:	outboard 3 to 6 hp	**Water tankage:**	15 gal.
B/D ratio:	28%	**Approx. trailering wgt.:**	3,700 lbs.

Philip Rhodes, who designed many gorgeous if sometimes slow sailboats, was asked in 1968 by General Boats to design a vessel for its owner, Stan Spitzer, to incorporate the builder's ideas. Two years later, after the company's previous craft, the flare-sided 17-foot Picnic (page 52) designed by Nils Lucander was discontinued, the "Rhodes Continental 22" (actually 21' 6" on deck) went into production. How much of the boat was actually designed by Rhodes is a question, since her style is nothing like Rhodes's other very recognizable boats, and Spitzer says he no longer has any drawings

from Rhodes. The Picnic's reverse sheer hull, flared from stem to stern, is repeated in this boat. Spitzer has a voluminous website aimed primarily at customers new to sailing. ***Best features:*** Compared to two of her three comps, the Rhodes 22 has slightly more headroom (though to get standing headroom, the poptop must be raised). ***Worst features:*** Draft with board up is at the high end among comps, making launching relatively harder. Price new (they are still sold) is very high for what is offered. Check out the competition before you buy.

Comps	LOD	Beam	MinDr	Displ	Bllst	SA/D	D/L	Avg. PHRF	Max. Speed	Motion Index	Space Index	No. of Berths	Head- room
O'Day 222 (21)	21' 5"	7' 11"	1' 8"	2,200	800	19.6	131	258	5.9	10.4	290	4	4' 1"
AMF 2100	21' 1"	8' 0"	1' 0"	2,200	850	19.8	181	228	5.6	11.4	363	4	4' 3"
O'Day 22 (21)	20' 10"	7' 2"	1' 3"	2,283	800	18.1	150	288	5.8	12.4	294	4	4' 6"
Rhodes 22	21' 6"	8' 0"	1' 8"	2,500	700	18.2	140	334	6.0	11.6	334	4	4' 6"

S2 6.8 (22)
S2, the powerboat folks, build a sailboat

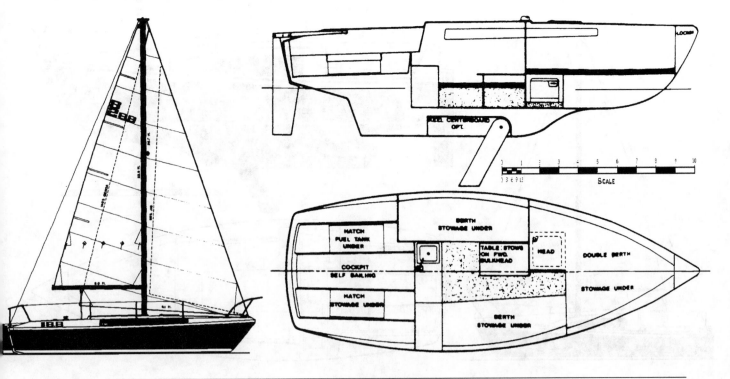

LOD:	21' 9"		**Designer:**	Ed Wennersten
LOA:	22' 4"		**Builder:**	S2 Yachts
LWL:	18' 3"		**Years produced:**	1975–1979
Min./max. draft:	2' 0"/4' 6"		**Sail area:**	210 sq. ft.
Bridge clearance:	30' 0"		**Fuel tankage:**	portable
Power:	outboard 3 to 6 hp		**Water tankage:**	portable
B/D ratio:	38%		**Approx. trailering wgt.:**	4,200 lbs.

Here is a 1970s-style flush-deck offering from S2, the Slikkers family boat business in Holland, MI (started by Leon Slikkers, and eventually run by sons David, Robert, and Tom). The company is still around, but no longer builds sailboats. Now it's just powerboats (Tiara, Pursuit, and Slickcraft Divisions). The S2 6.8 was offered with either a keel-centerboard arrangement (shown) or as a plain shoal-draft keel (same hull without the centerboard). *Best features:* Her big, flat forward deck is ideal for sunbathing, assuming you're not short-tacking upwind with a 150% decksweeper jib. Her cockpit looks big and comfortable, with high coamings for good back support. *Worst features:* To our eyes she's not a pretty boat; we think the flush deck and lack of springy sheer give her a tubby look. With the lowest SA/D ratio, the highest D/L ratio, and the highest Motion Index among her comps, she is apt to be slower (note the relatively high PHRF rating) though more stable and comfortable in a seaway. With only one small forward hatch and no opening ports for ventilation, she wouldn't be a good choice for extended cruising in hot climates.

Comps	LOD	Beam	MinDr	Displ	Bllst	SA/D	D/L	Avg. PHRF	Max. Speed	Motion Index	Space Index	No. of Berths	Head-room
Santana 22	22' 3"	7' 6"	3' 6"	2,600	1,220	18.4	142	246	5.8	13.8	266	4	3' 10"
Imperial 23 (22)	22' 2"	7' 6"	2' 9"	2,688	1,120	17.4	150	NA	6.0	13.6	301	4	4' 6"
Schock 23 (22)	22' 0"	8' 6"	2' 9"	2,800	1,100	21.5	142	198	6.1	11.6	394	4	4' 6"
Santana 2023 (22)	22' 0"	8' 6"	1' 2"	2,880	1,300	19.0	142	see text	6.1	11.9	395	4	4' 8"
S2 6.8 (22)	21' 9"	8' 0"	2' 0"	2,900	1,100	16.5	213	240	5.7	14.3	375	4	4' 3"

S2 7.0 (22)
Early design by Arthur Edmunds

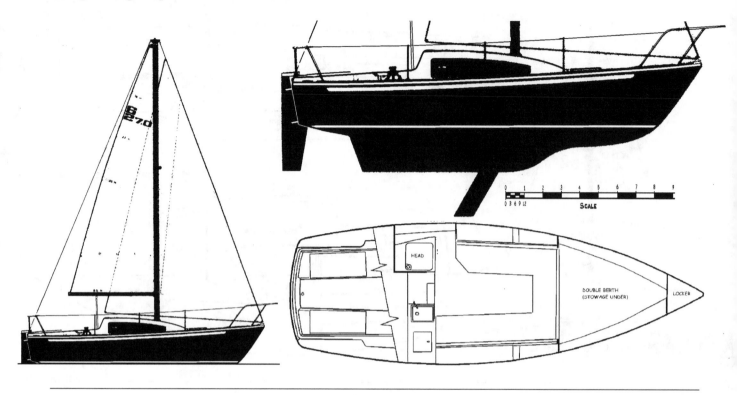

LOD:	22' 3"
LOA:	22' 9"
LWL:	18' 4"
Min./max. draft:	2' 2"/4' 8"
Bridge clearance:	31' 8"
Power:	outboard 3 to 6 hp
B/D ratio:	36%

Designer:	Arthur Edmunds
Builder:	S2 Yachts
Years produced:	1975–1977
Sail area:	240 sq. ft.
Fuel tankage:	portable
Water tankage:	portable
Approx. trailering wgt.:	5,200 lbs.

Arthur Edmunds had his own design office for over 30 years, wrote the book *Designing Power and Sail* in 1998, and designed boats for Chris Craft and for Allied Boat Company (notably the Allied Princess 36 and Mistress 38). He fashioned this little vessel for S2 Yachts in 1975. She is a keel-centerboarder, as are her comps, and also like them, she is on the heavy side for a sailboat only 22 feet on deck—being yet another boat sometimes called a "23" because her LOA (not her LOD) is 22' 9", rounded to

23 feet. ***Best features:*** Headroom at 5' 0" is quite good for a 22-footer. Motion Index is also better than her comps—except for the highly ballasted Sailmaster 22, which is in a class by herself. She is definitely a cruiser, not a racer, so her PHRF of 261, while high, will not be of concern to most potential owners. ***Worst features:*** Her accommodation design and domed cabin may not appeal to everybody. That may be why her builders left her on the market for only three years.

Comps	LOD	Beam	MinDr	Displ	Bllst	SA/D	D/L	Avg. PHRF	Max. Speed	Motion Index	Space Index	No. of Berths	Head-room
ETAP 23 (22)	22' 0"	8' 2"	2' 3"	3,320	1,035	17.3	216	240	5.8	15.2	384	4	4' 5"
O'Day 23 Mk II (22)	22' 1"	8' 0"	2' 0"	3,500	900	16.3	211	240	6.0	16.1	390	5	5' 0"
S2 7.0 (22)	22' 3"	8' 0"	2' 2"	3,600	1,300	16.3	261	261	6.0	17.6	344	4	5' 0"
Sailmaster 22	22' 0"	7' 1"	2' 4"	3,650	1,600	15.5	263	288	5.4	22.8	297	2	4' 5"

Sailmaster 22
Early S&S fiberglass design

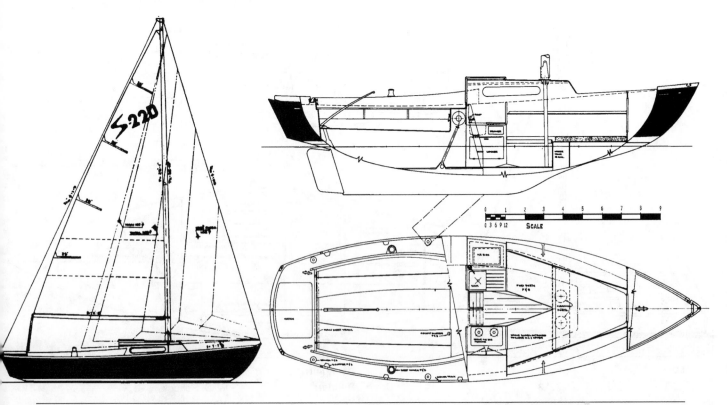

LOD:	22' 0"		**Designer:**	Sparkman & Stephens	
LOA:	22' 0"		**Builder:**	Werf Gusto, Holland	
LWL:	16' 6"		**Years produced:**	1961?–1965?	
Min./max. draft:	2' 4"/5' 0"		**Sail area:**	228 sq. ft.	
Bridge clearance:	29' 6"		**Fuel tankage:**	portable	
Power:	outboard 3 to 6 hp		**Water tankage:**	portable	
B/D ratio:	44%		**Approx. trailering wgt.:**	5,300 lbs.	

These boats, available either as an overnighter or as a day-sailer with little or no accommodations, were built to a high standard in Holland, first for importer Seafarer Fiberglass Yachts of New York City, then for Sailmaster Inc. of Annapolis, MD, and still later (about 1965), by Seafarer, by that time a manufacturer, operating out of a defunct supermarket in Huntington, Long Island, NY. Around that time Seafarer added a bustle at the stern, thereby magically increasing the length from 22' to 23', renamed the boat the Seafarer Kestrel, and offered the new, bigger

boat in a number of configurations (see pages 252 and 253). **Best features:** We like the big, comfortable cockpit and the space below devoted to accommodations for only two rather than for the usual four. We also like the classic style and elegance, including the beautifully varnished clear spruce spars and wood trim when the boats were new. **Worst features:** We wouldn't like the chores of sanding and varnishing all that wood and of maintaining the steel centerboard, which tends to corrode around its pivot point.

Comps	LOD	Beam	MinDr	Displ	Bllst	SA/D	D/L	Avg. PHRF	Max. Speed	Motion Index	Space Index	No. of Berths	Head-room
ETAP 23 (22)	22' 0"	8' 2"	2' 3"	3,320	1,035	17.3	216	240	5.8	15.2	384	4	4' 5"
O'Day 23 Mk II (22)	22' 1"	8' 0"	2' 0"	3,500	900	16.3	211	240	6.0	16.1	390	5	5' 0"
S2 7.0 (22)	22' 3"	8' 0"	2' 2"	3,600	1,300	16.3	261	261	6.0	17.6	344	4	5' 0"
Sailmaster 22	22' 0"	7' 1"	2' 4"	3,650	1,600	15.5	363	288	5.4	22.8	297	2	4' 5"

Santana 22
Gary Mull's 1965 design still survives

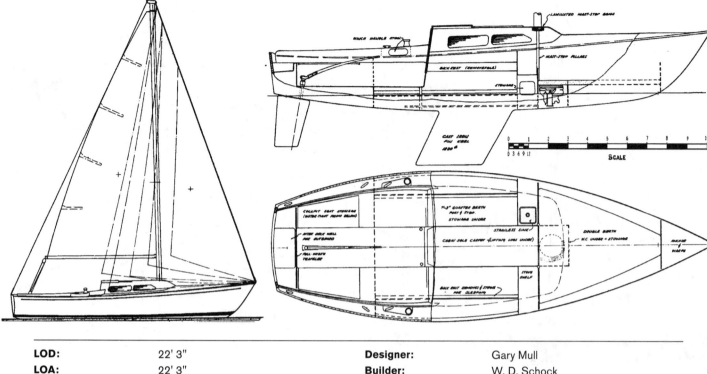

LOD:	22' 3"	**Designer:**	Gary Mull
LOA:	22' 3"	**Builder:**	W. D. Schock
LWL:	18' 9"	**Years produced:**	1966–present
Min./max. draft:	3' 6"	**Sail area:**	217 sq. ft.
Bridge clearance:	28' 6"	**Fuel tankage:**	portable
Power:	3 to 6 hp	**Water tankage:**	portable
B/D ratio:	47%	**Approx. trailering wgt.:**	4,000 lbs.

In 1965 Gary Mull sold the Santana 22, his first sailboat design, to W. D. Schock. The boat was successful and put Mull on the map as a fresh new talent in the racing sailboat game. She was removed from production in 1978 after 800 units were produced, but reinstated later. After more than 40 years, the "new Santana 22" is still on Schock's "current offerings" list. The dimensions and weights have changed a few inches and pounds here and there, but the new Santana 22 is close enough to the old version to race head-to-head in one-design regattas. ***Best features:***

Compared to her comps, the Santana may be considered old-fashioned, with her narrow beam and squared off fin-keel, spade-rudder underbody. But she is a wholesome design that many consider ageless—easy and fun to sail, forgiving, and still good-looking after all these years. A good support group of enthusiastic owners can be contacted on the Internet. ***Worst features:*** As a 1965 design, she is, after all, a bit old-fashioned. And compared with her comps, her deeper draft makes her harder to launch from a trailer.

Comps	LOD	Beam	MinDr	Displ	Bllst	SA/D	D/L	Avg. PHRF	Max. Speed	Motion Index	Space Index	No. of Berths	Head-room
Santana 22	22' 3"	7' 6"	3' 6"	2,600	1,220	18.4	142	246	5.8	13.8	266	4	3' 10"
Imperial 23 (22)	22' 2"	7' 6"	2' 9"	2,688	1,120	17.4	150	NA	6.0	13.6	301	4	4' 6"
Schock 23 (22)	22' 0"	8' 6"	2' 9"	2,800	1,100	21.5	142	198	6.1	11.6	394	4	4' 6"
Santana 2023 (22)	22' 0"	8' 6"	1' 2"	2,880	1,300	19.0	142	see text	6.1	11.9	395	4	4' 8"
S2 6.8 (22)	21' 9"	8' 0"	2' 0"	2,900	1,100	16.5	213	240	5.7	14.3	375	4	4' 3"

Santana 2023 (22)

A boat that comes in three flavors

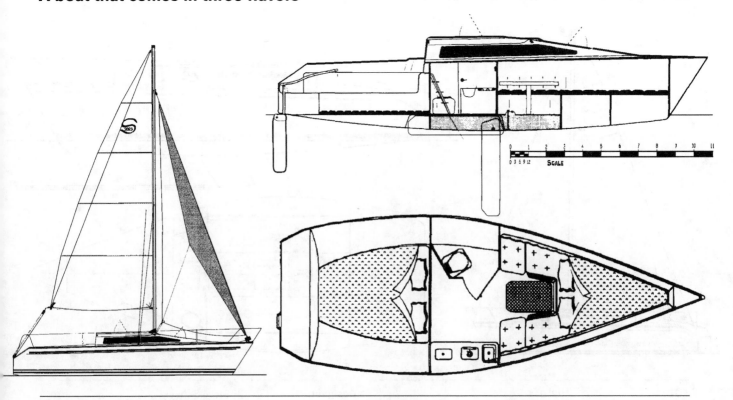

LOD:	22' 0"	**Designer:**	Steve Schock	
LOA:	23' 6"	**Builder:**	W. D. Schock	
LWL:	20' 7"	**Years produced:**	1994–2001	
Min./max. draft:	1' 2"/5' 4"	**Sail area:**	240 sq. ft.	
Bridge clearance:	31' 6"	**Fuel tankage:**	portable	
Power:	outboard 3 to 6 hp	**Water tankage:**	portable	
B/D ratio:	45%	**Approx. trailering wgt.:**	2,500 lbs.	

The Santana 2023 comes in three models: the A (PHRF = 224), which is called the standard cabin, the C (PHRF = 228), called the cruise cabin, and the R (PHRF = 174), the racing model. The one pictured here is a C. It has a cabin arranged for maximum accommodation. The A has what might be considered a typical cabin size. The R has a tall rig, and a sprit for an asymmetrical spinnaker. Of the five comps in this group (of which three are built by W. D. Schock), the Santana 2023 is the only boat using water ballast for stability. Note: Because the aft 20 inches of the hull are configured like a reverse transom, we are calling this boat a 22-footer on deck (LOD). *Best features:* It is said to be extremely easy to launch and rig the boat for sailing. *Worst features:* Judging from owner comments, Schock used plywood on the interior of the water ballast tanks on early boats, then turned to fiberglass starting in 1996. However, they continued to use a brittle caulking material for the joints around the top of the tank, which has often led to leaks. Owners have devised various fixes; none sounds easy to accomplish.

Comps	LOD	Beam	MinDr	Displ	Bllst	SA/D	D/L	Avg. PHRF	Max. Speed	Motion Index	Space Index	No. of Berths	Head-room
Santana 22	22' 3"	7' 6"	3' 6"	2,600	1,220	18.4	142	246	5.8	13.8	266	4	3' 10"
Imperial 23 (22)	22' 2"	7' 6"	2' 9"	2,688	1,120	17.4	150	NA	6.0	13.6	301	4	4' 6"
Schock 23 (22)	22' 0"	8' 6"	2' 9"	2,800	1,100	21.5	142	198	6.1	11.6	394	4	4' 6"
Santana 2023 (22)	22' 0"	8' 6"	1' 2"	2,880	1,300	19.0	142	see text	6.1	11.9	395	4	4' 8"
S2 6.8 (22)	21' 9"	8' 0"	2' 0"	2,900	1,100	16.5	213	240	5.7	14.3	375	4	4' 3"

Schock 23 (22)

A winged keel is standard on this one

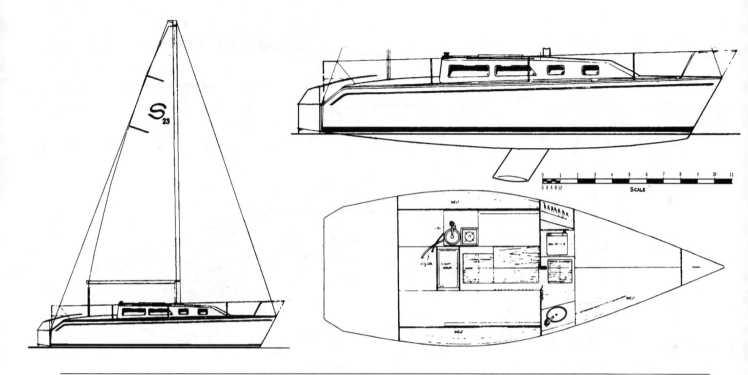

LOD:	22' 0"		**Designer:**	Steve Schock
LOA:	23' 4"		**Builder:**	W. D. Schock
LWL:	20' 7"		**Years produced:**	1988–1992
Min./max. draft:	2' 9"		**Sail area:**	267 sq. ft.
Bridge clearance:	31' 6"		**Fuel tankage:**	portable
Power:	outboard 3 to 6 hp		**Water tankage:**	portable
B/D ratio:	39%		**Approx. trailering wgt.:**	3,800 lbs.

The Schock 23 is the predecessor to Schock's Santana 2023 (22) (page 199), in which some components such as the stern configuration have been preserved (and are very similar to the stern on the Santana 23, designed for Schock in the late 1970s by Shad Turner). Note: The aft 20 inches of the hull are configured like a reverse transom, and therefore, in accordance with our treatment of reverse transoms (see pages 7 and 8), we are calling this boat a 22-footer on deck (LOD). *Best features:* The cockpit has deep, well-angled, comfortable backrests. Opening Lewmar ports give good ventilation, and an optional poptop increases headroom in the main cabin to 5' 11". The Schock is fitted with a bolt-on winged keel designed by Finnish engineer Reijo Salminen. Sailing a Schock 23 with a standard deep fin keel against an identical hull fitted with the shallower winged keel, the Schocks found that light-air windward performance was about equal, and the winged keel had the edge reaching and running. In heavier winds, the winged keel proved more effective than the standard fin on all points of sail. *Worst features:* Wings on a keel can pick up weed and jetsam, slowing the boat down.

Comps	LOD	Beam	MinDr	Displ	Bllst	SA/D	D/L	Avg. PHRF	Max. Speed	Motion Index	Space Index	No. of Berths	Head-room
Santana 22	22' 3"	7' 6"	3' 6"	2,600	1,220	18.4	142	246	5.8	13.8	266	4	3' 10"
Imperial 23 (22)	22' 2"	7' 6"	2' 9"	2,688	1,120	17.4	150	NA	6.0	13.6	301	4	4' 6"
Schock 23 (22)	22' 0"	8' 6"	2' 9"	2,800	1,100	21.5	142	198	6.1	11.6	394	4	4' 6"
Santana 2023 (22)	22' 0"	8' 6"	1' 2"	2,880	1,300	19.0	142	see text	6.1	11.9	395	4	4' 8"
S2 6.8 (22)	21' 9"	8' 0"	2' 0"	2,900	1,100	16.5	213	240	5.7	14.3	375	4	4' 3"

Seafarer 23 (22)
An enlargement of the Seafarer 22 (21)

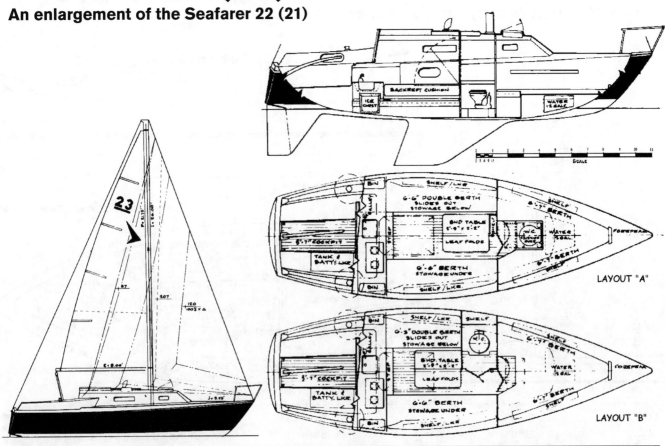

LOD:	22' 0"
LOA:	22' 5"
LWL:	18' 6"
Min./max. draft:	2' 4" shoal, 3' 3" deep
Bridge clearance:	28' 11"
Power:	outboard 3 to 6 hp
B/D ratio:	33%

Designer:	McCurdy & Rhodes
Builder:	Seafarer Fiberglass Yachts
Years produced:	1978–1984
Sail area:	207 sq. ft.
Fuel tankage:	portable
Water tankage:	12 gal.
Approx. trailering wgt.:	3,700 lbs.

Like her little sister, the Seafarer 22 (21) (see page 133), the Seafarer 23 (22) has two underbody options: a 2' 4" shoal keel, or a 3' 3" "high performance" keel. Our comments on the Seafarer 22 (21)'s underbody apply equally to the Seafarer 23 (22). In addition, the bigger boat has a choice of two layouts, as shown. One, Layout A, is a conventional arrangement for this size boat, with the head in the forward compartment, sandwiched between the two sides of the V-berth. If you have four people sleeping aboard, the two forward passengers will not appreciate the close proximity of any wee-hours visitors to the head from aft. The

other choice, Layout B, avoids that problem, but shrinks the elbow room in the main cabin. ***Best features:*** Except for the extra-high cockpit coaming, we like the looks of this boat a lot. We think that, at a glance, she looks like a much bigger vessel. ***Worst features:*** Normally a skeg-mounted rudder might result in greater ease of steering and handling compared with a freely suspended rudder. However, there are limits to the size of the skeg, which to our eye have been greatly exceeded on this boat. That is, we see too much wetted surface, which will simply slow the boat.

Comps	LOD	Beam	MinDr	Displ	Bllst	SA/D	D/L	Avg. PHRF	Max. Speed	Motion Index	Space Index	No. of Berths	Head-room
CS 22	21' 8"	8' 0"	2' 0"	2,460	1,150	17.0	205	249	5.6	12.4	341	4	4' 8"
Watkins 23XL	22' 3"	8' 0"	1' 3"	2,500	900	19.7	147	276	5.9	11.6	365	5	4' 10"
Seafarer 23 (22)	22' 0"	7' 7"	2' 4"	2,550	845	17.7	180	261	5.8	13.4	309	4	5' 1"

Seaward 22
One of Nick Hake's early small yacht designs

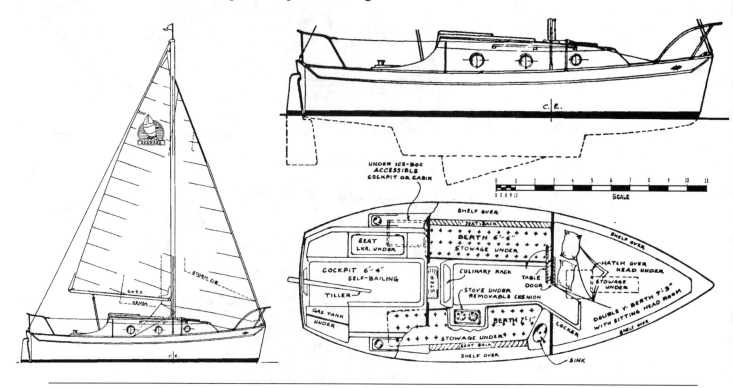

LOD:	21' 9"	**Designer:**	Nick Hake
LOA:	22' 2"	**Builder:**	Starboard Yachts, Hake Yachts
LWL:	20' 7"	**Years produced:**	1984–1988
Min./max. draft:	1' 11"/3' 5"	**Sail area:**	215 sq. ft.
Bridge clearance:	29' 0"	**Fuel tankage:**	portable
Power:	outboard 3 to 6 hp	**Water tankage:**	portable
B/D ratio:	34%	**Approx. trailering wgt.:**	3,100 lbs.

The Seaward 22 was first launched in 1984, and in 1989 magically became the Seaward 23 (see next page) by including a bowsprit in its length designation. The 22 has round ports while the 23 has better-looking rectangular ports, and there are many other differences as well. But the 23 by any other name is still a 22-footer on deck. **Best features:** To the builder's credit, the hardware is generally top quality and the finishing touches carefully applied. The icebox is accessible from both the cockpit and the cabin, a great convenience on a hot day when the helmsman wants

to reach for a cool one without bothering the crew below. **Worst features:** Although her performance parameters are mostly similar to her comps, she appears to suffer badly in the speed department compared to the Columbia 22, which has a PHRF rating a full 99 seconds lower, despite the fact that the Columbia is several hundred pounds heavier. In fact, measured against the 65 other boats in this guide in the 22-foot LOD range, the PHRF rating of the Seaward 22 (and 23) is worse than all but four other boats. We can't explain why.

Comps	LOD	Beam	MinDr	Displ	Bllst	SA/D	D/L	Avg. PHRF	Max. Speed	Motion Index	Space Index	No. of Berths	Head-room
Seaward 22	21' 9"	8' 4"	1' 11"	2,200	750	20.3	113	285	6.1	9.5	325	4	4' 6"
Hughes 22	21' 9"	7' 7"	1' 8"	2,200	825	20.8	132	282	5.9	11.2	314	6	5' 0"
Columbia 22	22' 0"	7' 9"	3' 2"	2,200	1,000	22.1	121	186	6.0	10.7	337	4	4' 7"

Seaward 23 (22)
An updated version of the Seaward 22

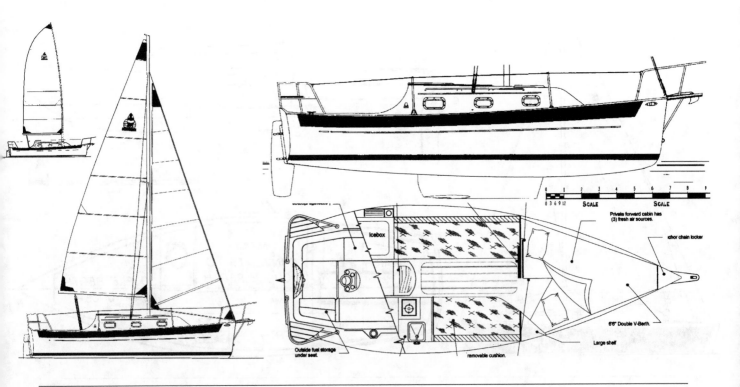

LOD:	21' 9"	**Designer:**	Nick Hake
LOA:	24' 6"	**Builder:**	Hake Yachts
LWL:	20' 7"	**Years produced:**	1989–2003
Min./max. draft:	2' 1"	**Sail area:**	240 sq. ft.
Bridge clearance:	30' 0"	**Fuel tankage:**	portable
Power:	outboard 6 to 8 hp	**Water tankage:**	portable
B/D ratio:	33%	**Approx. trailering wgt.:**	3,700 lbs.

The Seaward 23 (22) is a transformed version of the 22 reported on the previous page, though with the same waterline and the same basic hull structure. The centerboard on the 22 has been replaced with a very shallow fixed keel with wings, which, with a draft of just over two feet, is not likely to be very close-winded. There's a choice of rigs, either a fully battened cat rig with a big roach set on a freestanding carbon-fiber mast (inset), or a conventional sloop rig featuring a self-tacking jib. The sales brochure mentions a Yanmar diesel but doesn't give the size (which we assume is minimal) or say whether buyers can choose an outboard and omit the diesel. (We assume they can.) The sales brochure shows a wheel rather than the older 22's tiller; based on a cockpit configuration very similar to the older 22, we assume a tiller can be substituted (which we recommend doing for this size boat). *Best features:* The stern pulpit includes "catbird stern seats" on the quarters, for sightseeing while motoring along rivers. Hardware is upper-end quality. Other good features are the same as for the older 22. *Worst features:* Also the same as for the older 22.

Comps	LOD	Beam	MinDr	Displ	Bllst	SA/D	D/L	Avg. PHRF	Max. Speed	Motion Index	Space Index	No. of Berths	Head-room
Starwind 22	22' 0"	7' 9"	1' 11"	2,600	775	17.6	169	273	5.8	12.8	346	5	4' 9"
Pearson 22	22' 0"	7' 9"	3' 5"	2,600	1,000	18.4	183	246	5.8	13.3	298	4	4' 2"
Seaward 23 (22)	21' 9"	8' 4"	2' 1"	2,700	900	19.8	138	285	5.8	11.3	325	4	4' 8"
Bristol Caravel 22	22' 0"	7' 9"	2' 6"	2,850	1,150	16.4	172	288	5.8	14.1	322	4	4' 0"

South Coast 22
A boat designed by SCS's owner

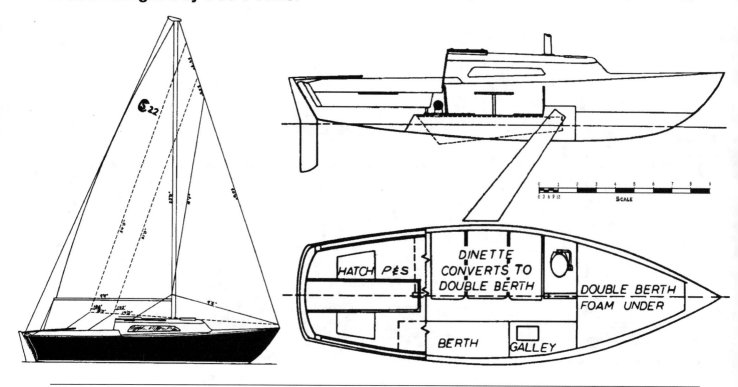

LOD:	22' 0"		**Designer:**	Hollis Metcalf
LOA:	22' 6"		**Builder:**	South Coast Seacraft
LWL:	17' 6"		**Years produced:**	1970–1973
Min./max. draft:	0' 10"/6' 9"		**Sail area:**	189 sq. ft.
Bridge clearance:	29' 0"		**Fuel tankage:**	portable
Power:	outboard 3 to 6 hp		**Water tankage:**	12 gal.
B/D ratio:	28%		**Approx. trailering wgt.:**	2,600 lbs.

Hollis Metcalf, owner of South Coast Seacraft, was a southern gentleman who sold a South Coast 23 kit to my wife and me in 1964 (see page 255). Metcalf, who had commissioned Carl Alberg to design the SC21 (see page 140), wanted to market a similar but more spacious and more easily trailerable version, and ended up designing the SC22 himself. The resulting boat was not a racer (note the high PHRF) but nevertheless was quite popular. ***Best features:*** The long, deep, heavily weighted board should help upwind performance and stability. Like her comps, the SC22 is relatively low-slung (limiting cabin space but improving sailing performance). Accommodations seem reasonably complete, with sleeping space for five—though we doubt five adults would want to cruise in such tight quarters. Though not shown on plans, a poptop with six-foot headroom was offered on later production. She has foam flotation. ***Worst features:*** The outboard rudder on a raked transom may lead to trouble if the outboard motor is not mounted well aft of the transom to avoid prop interference. But an outboard mounted that far back may be subject to prop cavitation. The SC22 may have dimensional stats similar to her comps, but her PHRF rating clearly shows she is not in the same league of racing performance as, say, the J/22.

Comps	LOD	Beam	MinDr	Displ	Bllst	SA/D	D/L	Avg. PHRF	Max. Speed	Motion Index	Space Index	No. of Berths	Head-room
J/22	21' 6"	8' 0"	3' 9"	1,790	700	24.7	117	180	5.8	8.4	389	4	4' 0"
South Coast 22	22' 0"	7' 1"	0' 10"	1,800	505	20.4	150	276	5.6	10.8	273	5	4' 3"
Grampian Classic 22	22' 4"	7' 0"	3' 9"	1,892	700	20.7	160	234	5.6	11.5	225	2	3' 5"

Spindrift 22

Jim Taylor draws a 22-footer

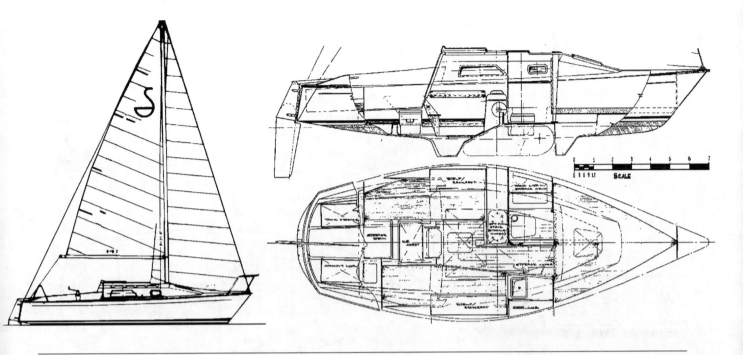

LOD:	21' 6"
LOA:	22' 10"
LWL:	19' 1"
Min./max. draft:	1' 8"/4' 8"
Bridge clearance:	30' 0"
Power:	outboard 3 to 6 hp
B/D ratio:	30%

Designer:	Jim Taylor
Builder:	Spectrum, Rebel, Spindrift
Years produced:	1982–1985
Sail area:	194 sq. ft.
Fuel tankage:	portable
Water tankage:	5 gal.
Approx. trailering wgt.:	2,800 lbs.

This boat started out as the Spectrum 22 for Spectrum Yacht Corp. of Largo, FL. The concept was to build a safe, forgiving boat for a family of four, fun to sail and with some elbow room in the interior. Jim Taylor's cozy and efficient layout on the original design is shown. When Spectrum left the scene, Rebel Industries bought the molds and revised the interior (without consulting the designer) and continued building the boat under the Starwind and then the Spindrift name. (But note: another Starwind 22, designed by Halsey Herreshoff, appeared around the same time, as shown on page 207; as did a Starwind 223, designed by Cortland Steck, as shown on page 208.) As might be expected, there is more than a passing resemblance between the Spectrum/Starwind/Spindrift 22 and designer Taylor's slightly smaller Precision 21 (page 122) and slightly larger Precision 23 (page 245). **Best features:** As with Jim Taylor's other designs, this one is wholesome and well-balanced, and fulfills her design concept nicely. **Worst features:** The variation in quality of workmanship and materials among several builders is noticeable.

Comps	LOD	Beam	MinDr	Displ	Bllst	SA/D	D/L	Avg. PHRF	Max. Speed	Motion Index	Space Index	No. of Berths	Head-room
Balboa 22	21' 7"	8' 0"	1' 3"	1,980	600	20.9	129	246	5.8	9.5	326	4	4' 4"
Dehler 22	22' 0"	8' 0"	1' 3"	1,980	880	25.1	140	225	5.8	9.7	344	4	4' 9"
Spindrft 22	21' 6"	8' 0"	1' 8"	1,990	600	19.6	128	252	5.9	9.5	345	4	4' 8"
Windrose 22/Laguna 22	21' 7"	8' 8"	2' 11"	2,280	900	19.0	148	246	5.8	10.9	337	4	4' 4"

Spirit 23 (22)
Sloop built in Tennessee, then Texas

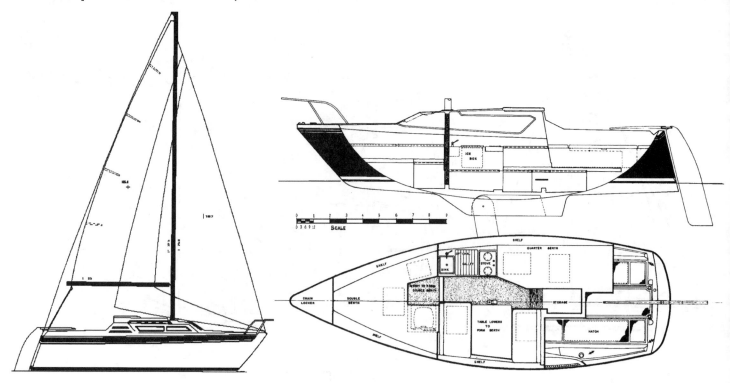

LOD:	22' 2"	**Designer:**	Robert Finch
LOA:	25' 3"	**Builder:**	North American Yachts, Spirit Yachts
LWL:	20' 0"	**Years produced:**	1975–1981
Min./max. draft:	2' 0"/5' 0"	**Sail area:**	215 sq. ft.
Bridge clearance:	31' 0"	**Fuel tankage:**	portable
Power:	outboard 3 to 6 hp	**Water tankage:**	portable
B/D ratio:	30%	**Approx. trailering wgt.:**	4,200 lbs.

The vessel shown here started out in 1975 as the North American 23, built by North American Yachts in Hendersonville, TN. But by 1978 she was being built in Austin, TX, as the Spirit 23, after a lawsuit was threatened by the builders of the North American 40, a Detroit firm totally separate from both North American Yachts and Glastron, the parent of Spirit Yachts, which built the Spirit 23 in Austin, TX. The Spirit line of sailboats was designed by Robert Finch, who also designed the Parker Dawson 26/Nauset 26 (page 364) and with Frank Butler had a hand in some early Coronado and Catalina Yacht designs including the ever-popular Catalina 27. The later Spirit 23s were available

with either a keel-centerboard arrangement (shown here) or a swept-back fin keel with an extra 315 lbs. of ballast, bigger displacement of 3,150 lbs., and a slightly bigger sailplan. There was also a choice of accommodations plan among later boats of either the dinette arrangement shown here, or a pair of settee berths. ***Best features:*** On later production, the settee berth arrangement included a starboard settee berth a full ten feet long, good for tall sailors (as long as they don't try to stand up in the 4' 9" high cabin—though an optional poptop could give 6' 1" headroom, according to the sales brochure). ***Worst features:*** A kick-up rudder was an option, not standard.

Comps	LOD	Beam	MinDr	Displ	Bllst	SA/D	D/L	Avg. PHRF	Max. Speed	Motion Index	Space Index	No. of Berths	Head-room
N.A. 23/Spirit 23 (22)	22' 2"	7' 11"	2' 0"	2,800	835	17.3	156	240	6.0	12.7	391	4	4' 9"
Rob Roy 23	22' 8"	6' 11"	1' 7"	2,800	900	20.7	135	201	6.1	14.3	228	2 or 3	4' 0"
Jeanneau Tonic 23 (22)	22' 5"	8' 2"	2' 3"	2,945	1,086	18.9	156	225	6.0	12.9	429	4	5' 7"
Hunter 23.5 (22)	21' 8"	8' 4"	1' 6"	3,000	1,000	18.2	136	240	6.2	12.3	471	6	4' 6"

Starwind 22

Near-clone of the Chrysler 22 (21)

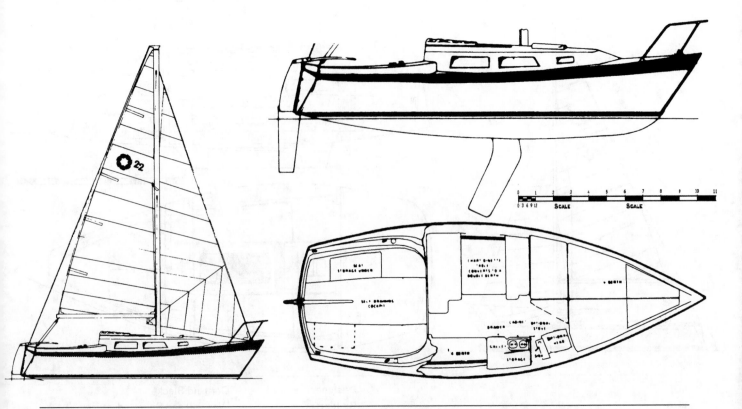

LOD:	22' 0"		**Designer:**	Halsey Herreshoff
LOA:	23' 6"		**Builder:**	Starwind Divison of Wellcraft
LWL:	19' 0"		**Years produced:**	1982–1984
Min./max. draft:	1' 11"/6' 0"		**Sail area:**	208 sq. ft.
Bridge clearance:	30' 3"		**Fuel tankage:**	portable
Power:	outboard 3 to 6 hp		**Water tankage:**	5 gal.
B/D ratio:	30%		**Approx. trailering wgt.:**	4,000 lbs.

The hull of the Starwind 22 appears to be a slightly modified clone of the Chrysler 22 (21), with the same waterline length and minimum draft, but with an extended stem and more angular reverse transom. Confusion about the Chrysler's displacement is mentioned in her writeup (page 92). To add to the confusion, the bigger, longer Starwind 22 shown here weighs 400 pounds less than the Chrysler. Go figure. In any case, the accommodations are close to identical, with a dinette opposite a sliding galley, and a head at one side of the forward cabin. On deck, the Chrysler's raised deck has been replaced on the Starwind by a trunk cabin with an optional poptop. The boat was produced for only three years before the Starwind Division of Wellcraft replaced her with the better-looking and better-performing Starwind 223 (page 208), designed by Cortland Steck. *Best features:* Headroom and Space Index are best of the comps. *Worst features:* No unusual special features were noted.

Comps	LOD	Beam	MinDr	Displ	Bllst	SA/D	D/L	Avg. PHRF	Max. Speed	Motion Index	Space Index	No. of Berths	Head-room
Starwind 22	22' 0"	7' 9"	1' 11"	2,600	775	17.6	169	273	5.8	12.8	346	5	4' 9"
Pearson 22	22' 0"	7' 9"	3' 5"	2,600	1,000	18.4	183	246	5.8	13.3	298	4	4' 2"
Seaward 23 (22)	21' 9"	8' 4"	2' 1"	2,700	900	19.8	138	285	5.8	11.3	325	4	4' 8"
Bristol Caravel 22	22' 0"	7' 9"	2' 6"	2,850	1,150	16.4	172	288	5.8	14.1	322	4	4' 0"

Starwind 223

Attractive and well-made small sloop

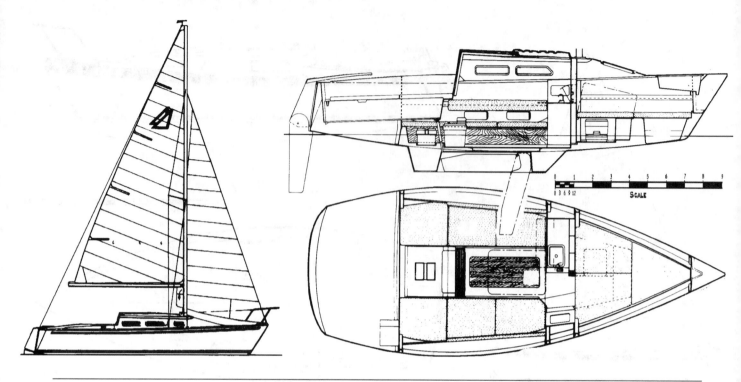

LOD:	22' 3"	**Designer:**	Cortland Steck
LOA:	23' 9"	**Builder:**	Wellcraft and Rebel Industries
LWL:	19' 4"	**Years produced:**	1982–1987
Min./max. draft:	1' 10"/5' 0"	**Sail area:**	219 sq. ft.
Bridge clearance:	31' 0"	**Fuel tankage:**	portable
Power:	outboard 3 to 6 hp	**Water tankage:**	portable
B/D ratio:	29%	**Approx. trailering wgt.:**	3,600 lbs.

This attractive design was produced first by the Starwind Division of Wellcraft (1982–1984) and later (1985–1987) by Rebel Industries. Although her layout below is somewhat conventional (how many ways can you configure a boat of this size?), she has plenty of nice features (see below) and not a lot of faults. **Best features:** She has the biggest beam and hence the highest Space Index of her comps. Marks of quality include a well-molded hull of mat, roving, and Coremat, with no chopped strand, a teak-and-holly cabin sole, cedar-lined hanging locker, anchor locker on deck, with a separate rope locker to help avoid tangle, a big Lexan translucent forward hatch for ventilation over the head, a sea hood over the main hatch to help provide watertight integrity, and a dinette table that attaches to either galley below or cockpit on deck. Settee and quarter berths are a generous 7' 9" long, and the wood-bottomed after cushions can be placed between the settees to make a cozy 6' 6" by 4' 4" double "honeymoon" berth. **Worst features:** The inboard chainplates make it less easy to go forward on deck, but provide a tighter sheeting angle for the jib, so to most sailors the extra performance upwind is worth the slight inconvenience.

Comps	LOD	Beam	MinDr	Displ	Bllst	SA/D	D/L	Avg. PHRF	Max. Speed	Motion Index	Space Index	No. of Berths	Head-room
Gloucester 22	21' 8"	8' 0"	1' 8"	2,400	800	19.3	165	186	5.8	11.8	324	4	4' 4"
Seafarer 22 (21)	21' 4"	7' 5"	2' 1"	2,400	1,010	18.5	174	270	5.7	13.1	289	4	4' 9"
Starwind 223	22' 3"	8' 6"	1' 10"	2,435	700	19.4	150	237	5.9	10.7	414	4	4' 10"
U.S. 22/Triton 22	21' 6"	7' 10"	2' 5"	2,450	950	17.8	138	279	6.0	11.6	321	5	4' 0"

U.S. 22/Triton 22

Brief production under Bayliner and Pearson

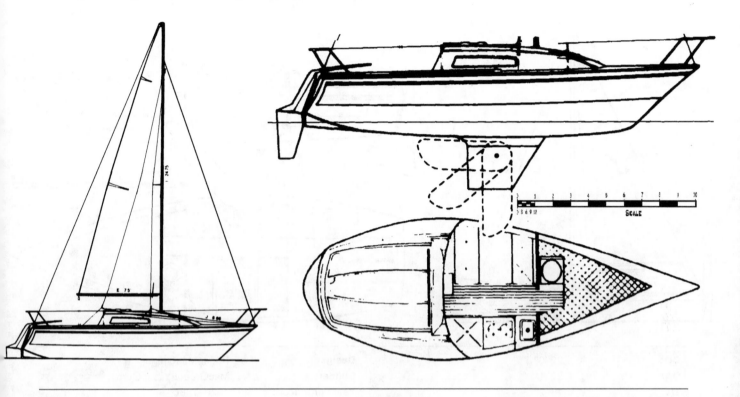

LOD:	21' 6"		Designer:	not identified by builder
LOA:	23' 0"		Builder:	U.S. Yachts, Triton Yachts
LWL:	19' 11"		Years produced:	1983–1985
Min./max. draft:	2' 5"/5' 9"		Sail area:	202 sq. ft.
Bridge clearance:	31' 3"		Fuel tankage:	portable
Power:	outboard 3 to 6 hp		Water tankage:	4 gal.
B/D ratio:	39%		Approx. trailering wgt.:	3,600 lbs.

The U.S. 22 came along around the time Pearson bought U.S. Yachts from Bayliner. The U.S. Yacht fleet then became the Triton Yacht fleet. See our write-up on U.S. 21/Triton 21 (page 144) for more details on the builders. The design origin of the U.S. 22 is somewhat obscure, but it is from the same racing/cruising traditions as the C&C and Gary Mull designs of the period. (One source claims Gary Mull actually did the design; he may be right.) The boat is available in either deep- or shoal-draft keel; ballast in each case is 950 lbs. **Best features:** The four-seater dinette is wide, extending to almost half the 7' 10" beam, and converts to a full-length double berth. The PHRF rating seems generous. Owners reporting on the Internet seem to think the boat is reasonably fast, well made, and generally very satisfactory. **Worst features:** Compared to comps, the draft is a little high, the ballast a little low, and the headroom low, too.

Comps	LOD	Beam	MinDr	Displ	Bllst	SA/D	D/L	Avg. PHRF	Max. Speed	Motion Index	Space Index	No. of Berths	Head-room
Gloucester 22	21' 8"	8' 0"	1' 8"	2,400	800	19.3	165	186	5.8	11.8	324	4	4' 4"
Seafarer 22 (21)	21' 4"	7' 5"	2' 1"	2,400	1,010	18.5	174	270	5.7	13.1	289	4	4' 9"
Starwind 223	22' 3"	8' 6"	1' 10"	2,435	700	19.4	150	237	5.9	10.7	414	4	4' 10"
U.S. 22/Triton 22	21' 6"	7' 10"	2' 5"	2,450	950	17.8	138	279	6.0	11.6	321	5	4' 0"

Venture 22 & 222
Low-cost water transportation for families

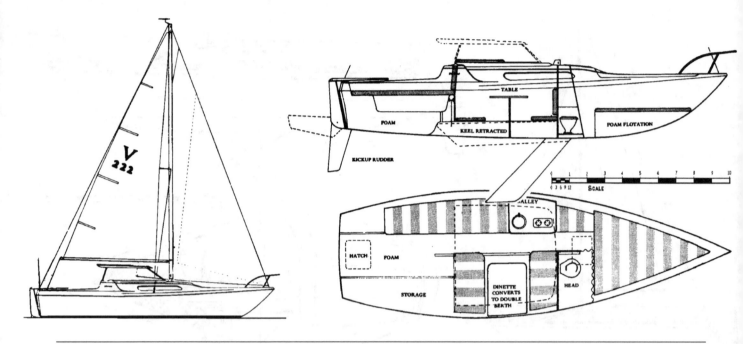

LOD:	22' 0"
LOA:	22' 11"
LWL:	18' 2"
Min./max. draft:	0' 11"/4' 0"
Bridge clearance:	27' 0"
Power:	outboard 3 to 6 hp
B/D ratio:	26%

Designer:	Roger MacGregor
Builder:	MacGregor Yacht Corp.
Years produced:	1970–1980
Sail area:	187 sq. ft.
Fuel tankage:	portable
Water tankage:	portable
Approx. trailering wgt.:	2,600 lbs.

Here is a vessel designed to satisfy the Great American public's desire for a simple, low-cost sailboat big enough to cruise a family of four (or five in a pinch), at least for a weekend. The hull walls are thin, the hardware is so-so, but the boat does not pretend to be a "yacht" (despite the word "yacht" in the name of the manufacturer), and the formula worked. As early as 1970 the company's ads said "There are more Ventures sold than any other cruising sailboat. The price is low. The trailer is your mooring. And . . . the wind is free." ***Best features:*** Very shallow draft plus a low-slung trailer, sold with the boat, that makes launching and retrieving as easy as it gets. A fold-down poptop and button-on canvas weather curtains provide interior space with 6' 1" headroom when at anchor or when sailing in a light breeze. Foam flotation under the cockpit and the forward V-berth make the boat unsinkable despite the weight of her 460 pound swing keel. And we like the dinette, which converts to a so-called "double" about 3' 4" wide and barely 6' long. ***Worst features:*** Did I mention cheap construction? Well, you can't have everything . . . .

Comps	LOD	Beam	MinDr	Displ	Bllst	SA/D	D/L	Avg. PHRF	Max. Speed	Motion Index	Space Index	No. of Berths	Head-room
Venture 22 & 222	22' 0"	7' 4"	0' 11"	1,800	475	20.2	134	258	5.7	10.1	279	5	4' 0"
MacGregor 22	22' 0"	7' 4"	1' 0"	1,800	500	19.2	108	258	5.9	9.6	263	5	4' 0"
Kells 22	22' 2"	7' 7"	0' 11"	1,890	525	19.2	142	NA	5.7	9.9	306	5	4' 6"

Watkins 23XL (22)

Can the Watkins hull be a clone of the Helsen 22?

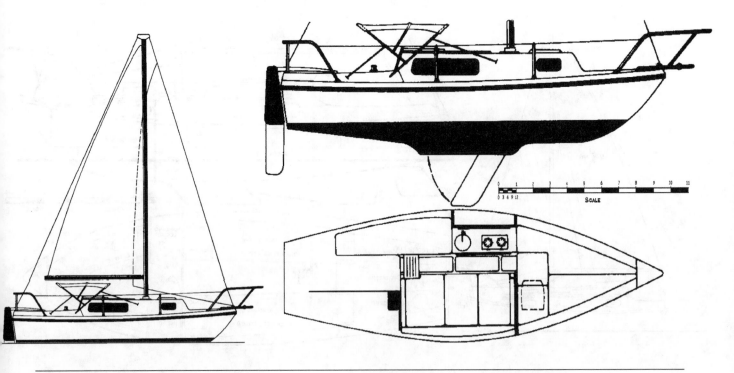

LOD:	22' 3"
LOA:	23' 0"
LWL:	19' 8"
Min./max. draft:	1' 3"/4' 6"
Bridge clearance:	30' 0"
Power:	outboard 3 to 6 hp
B/D ratio:	36%

Designer:	Watkins Brothers
Builder:	Watkins Yachts
Years produced:	1973–1980
Sail area:	199 sq. ft.
Fuel tankage:	portable
Water tankage:	15 gal.
Approx. trailering wgt.:	3,800 lbs.

Some say that the four Watson brothers of Clearwater, FL, obtained permission from their neighbor, designer-builder Jopie Helsen, owner of Helsen Yachts, to duplicate the hull of his Helsen 22, and that with some modifications, this hull became the first fiberglass boat they produced, the Watkins 23. If that happened, "some modifications" was an understatement. Virtually every dimension of the Watkins 23, from LWL, to LOA, to ballast and displacement, to draft, is bigger than the Helsen 22. True, the beam is the same eight feet, and the curve of the bow and the underbody bear a resemblance, but the sheerline, deck, and cabin house are all totally different. Furthermore, it appears in various sales brochures that two different deck molds were used at various times. **Best features:** You get basic sailing transportation for very little money. **Worst features:** Construction is mediocre, with equipment such as a galvanized boat trailer winch (which can quickly rust in salt water) mounted in the cabin to hoist the centerboard.

Comps	LOD	Beam	MinDr	Displ	Bllst	SA/D	D/L	Avg. PHRF	Max. Speed	Motion Index	Space Index	No. of Berths	Head-room
CS 22	21' 8"	8' 0"	2' 0"	2,460	1,150	17.0	205	249	5.6	12.4	341	4	4' 8"
Watkins 23XL	22' 3"	8' 0"	1' 3"	2,500	900	19.7	147	276	5.9	11.6	365	5	4' 10"
Seafarer 23 (22)	22' 0"	7' 7"	2' 4"	2,550	845	17.7	180	261	5.8	13.4	309	4	5' 1"

Westerly Nomad 22
Plastic toy boat on steroids

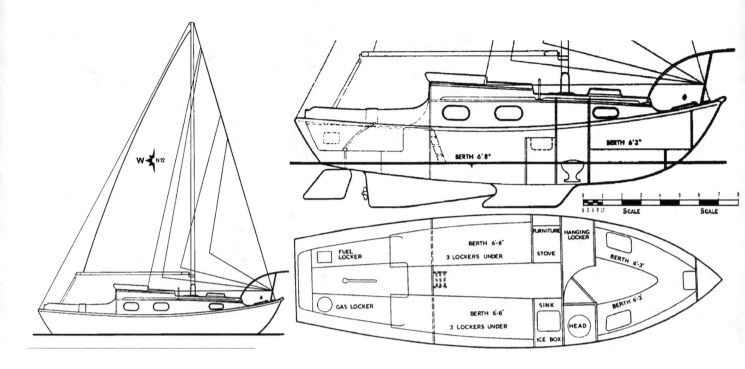

LOD:	22' 3"		**Designer:**	Denys Raynor
LOA:	22' 3"		**Builder:**	Westerly Marine
LWL:	18' 4"		**Years produced:**	1967–1969
Min./max. draft:	2' 3"		**Sail area:**	227 sq. ft.
Bridge clearance:	28' 0"		**Fuel tankage:**	varies
Power:	outboard 6 to 8 hp		**Water tankage:**	portable
B/D ratio:	26%		**Approx. trailering wgt.:**	5,500 lbs.

A total of 287 of these little twin-keel plastic boats were built. The Nomad was descended from the builder's first design, the Westerly 22, introduced in 1963. The first 22, 21' 6" long, had a simple, open plan layout and a gunter rig (with Bermudian rig optional). In 1967 came the introduction of the Nomad, which used virtually the same hull as the original 22, but extended the deck line, adding inside space. The Nomad could be bought with choice of engine: either a 6 to 10 hp outboard on a transom bracket, or a diesel inboard (Volvo Penta MD1) or a 6 hp Vire gasoline engine. (Note the small prop jutting out from a midship skeg between the twin keels.) ***Best features:*** She will sit on a half-tide mooring, thanks to her twin keels. A flatbed trailer will serve as a road conveyance. If a dodger is added, headroom becomes almost six feet. ***Worst features:*** Due to exceptionally large wetted surface, shallow twin keels, and smallish sail area, it will take a good while to get anywhere, especially if "anywhere" happens to be upwind. And if you plan to short-circuit your trip by motoring, get a tow car that can handle 5,500 pounds.

Comps	LOD	Beam	MinDr	Displ	Bllst	SA/D	D/L	Avg. PHRF	Max. Speed	Motion Index	Space Index	No. of Berths	Head-room
Alberg 22	22' 0"	7' 0"	3' 1"	3,200	1,500	17.4	349	282	5.4	20.7	274	4	4' 4"
Cape Dory Typhoon Sr 22	22' 5"	7' 5"	3' 1"	3,300	1,700	17.7	328	273	5.4	19.2	322	4	4' 8"
Ranger 23 (22)	22' 3"	7' 11"	3' 9"	3,400	1,500	18.7	190	216	6.0	15.8	318	4	4' 3"
Westerly Nomad 22	22' 3"	7' 5"	2' 3"	3,600	950	15.5	261	300	5.7	19.6	277	4	4' 7"

Windrose 22/Laguna 22

But for the deckhouse, a clone of the Balboa 22

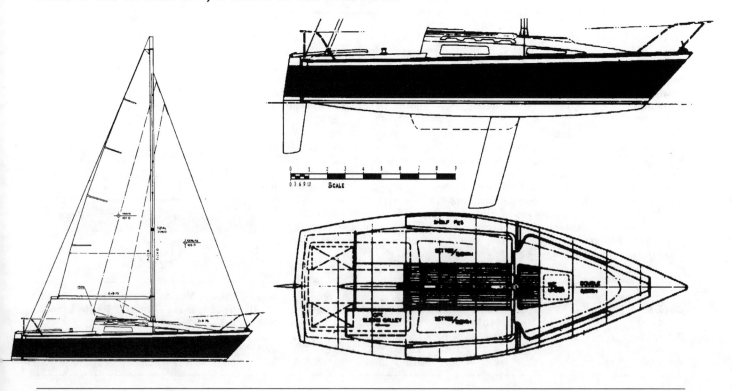

LOD:	21' 7"		Designer:	Shad Turner
LOA:	22' 7"		Builder:	Laguna Yachts
LWL:	19' 0"		Years produced:	1977–1987
Min./max. draft:	1' 3"/5' 6" swing, 2' 11" shoal		Sail area:	206 sq. ft.
Bridge clearance:	26' 6"		Fuel tankage:	portable
Power:	outboard 3 to 6 hp		Water tankage:	portable
B/D ratio:	39%		Approx. trailering wgt.:	3,200 lbs.

This boat and another from the same builder, called the Balboa 22 (see page 214), were almost the same boat. Their hulls were virtually identical and had the same ballast and displacement, but they had different deck molds. Both were available as either a shoal draft keelboat with a 2' 11" draft (easier to sail, less tender) or a swing-keel version with 1' 3" draft board up or 5' 6" draft keel down (better for upwind sailing, easier to stow on a trailer). Many skippers like to think of both the Windrose 22 and the Balboa 22 swing keel versions as very similar to both the Catalina 22 (page 157) and the Venture 22 (page 210). There is some merit in this appraisal, except that, while all four of the boats have roughly the same total displacement (about 1,800 to 2,300 pounds), the Windrose and Balboa have considerably more ballast and less structural materials. **Best features:** These were boats built for economy; used boat prices are lower than average. **Worst features:** Because the boats were built for economy, workmanship and quality is so-so at best.

Comps	LOD	Beam	MinDr	Displ	Bllst	SA/D	D/L	Avg. PHRF	Max. Speed	Motion Index	Space Index	No. of Berths	Head-room
Balboa 22	21' 7"	8' 0"	1' 3"	1,980	600	20.9	129	246	5.8	9.5	326	4	4' 4"
Dehler 22	22' 0"	8' 0"	1' 3"	1,980	880	25.1	140	225	5.8	9.7	344	4	4' 9"
Spindrft 22	21' 6"	8' 0"	1' 8"	1,990	600	19.6	128	252	5.9	9.5	345	4	4' 8"
Windrose 22/Laguna 22	21' 7"	8' 8"	2' 11"	2,280	900	19.0	148	246	5.8	10.9	337	4	4' 4"

Balboa 22

Balboa alias Windrose alias Laguna 22 . . .

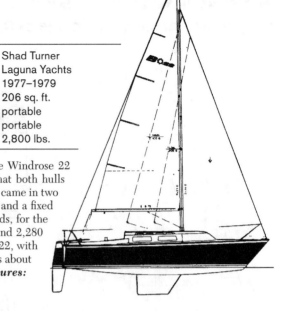

LOD:	21' 7"	**Designer:**	Shad Turner
LOA:	22' 7"	**Builder:**	Laguna Yachts
LWL:	19' 0"	**Years produced:**	1977–1979
Min./max. draft:	1' 3"/ 5' 6" swing, 2'11" shoal	**Sail area:**	206 sq. ft.
Bridge clearance:	31' 0"	**Fuel tankage:**	portable
Power:	outboard 3 to 6 hp	**Water tankage:**	portable
B/D ratio:	30%	**Approx. trailering wgt.:**	2,800 lbs.

The Balboa 22 was built by Laguna Yachts, the same company that built the Windrose 22 (page 213), also designed by Shad Turner. If you look closely, you will see that both hulls have identical dimensions, though the decks are somewhat different. Both hulls came in two choices of underbody: a swing-keel version (min and max drafts shown above) and a fixed fin-keel version with a draft of 2' 11". Ballast for the swing version is 600 pounds, for the fixed version is 900 pounds. Corresponding displacements are 1,980 (swing) and 2,280 (fixed). The Balboa 22 was only produced for three years, while the Windrose 22, with different deck mold, continued until the company ended production of all boats about 1987. **Best features:** Poptop gives six-foot headroom when erected. **Worst features:** Construction is below average—definitely not "yacht quality."

Comps	LOD	Beam	MinDr	Displ	Bllst	SA/D	D/L	Avg. PHRF	Max. Speed	Motion Index	Space Index	No. of Berths	Head- room
Balboa 22	21' 7"	8' 0"	1' 3"	1,980	600	20.9	129	246	5.8	9.5	326	4	4' 4"
Dehler 22	22' 0"	8' 0"	1' 3"	1,980	880	25.1	140	225	5.8	9.7	344	4	4' 9"
Spindrft 22	21' 6"	8' 0"	1' 8"	1,990	600	19.6	128	252	5.9	9.5	345	4	4' 8"
Windrose 22/Laguna 22	21' 7"	8' 0"	2' 11"	2,280	900	19.0	148	246	5.8	10.9	337	4	4' 4"

Kells 22

We don't know much about this one

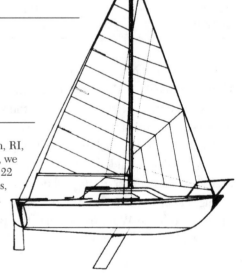

LOD:	22' 2"	**Designer:**	Paul A. Lindh
LOA:	22' 11"	**Builder:**	Kells Corp.
LWL:	18' 0"	**Years produced:**	1971–1980
Min./max. draft:	0' 11"/5' 0"	**Sail area:**	181 sq. ft.
Bridge clearance:	28' 0"	**Fuel tankage:**	portable
Power:	outboard 3 to 6 hp	**Water tankage:**	portable
B/D ratio:	28%	**Approx. trailering wgt.:**	2,600 lbs.

We don't know much about this design, which was produced by the Kells Corp. of Tiverton, RI, during the 1970s. By 1980 the company seems to have dropped out of sight. Unfortunately, we don't have an accommodations plan to show you. **Best features:** Like her comps, the Kells 22 should be easy to pull in and out at a ramp. She has good headroom compared to her comps, though it's sitting, not standing. And her specs indicate that she has more room below than her comps. **Worst features:** Due to her relatively high freeboard, we see her as not very graceful compared to her comps. Her 525-pound cast iron swing keel will have the same problems shared by other steel or iron swing-keelers: steady maintenance to keep rust at bay and the keel winch and cable operable, and danger of splitting the hull at the forward end of the trunk if the pendant parts and the keel crashes down uncontrolled.

Comps	LOD	Beam	MinDr	Displ	Bllst	SA/D	D/L	Avg. PHRF	Max. Speed	Motion Index	Space Index	No. of Berths	Head- room
Venture 222	22' 0"	7' 4"	0' 11"	1,800	475	20.2	134	258	5.7	10.1	279	5	4' 0"
MacGregor 22	22' 0"	7' 4"	1' 0"	1,800	500	19.2	108	258	5.9	9.6	263	5	4' 0"
Kells 22	22' 2"	7' 7"	0' 11"	1,850	525	19.2	142	NA	5.7	9.9	306	5	4' 6"

Old Boat or New?

A brand-new boat has its attractions, principal among them being the gleam and glitter that mark any object on which no other owner has left his fingerprints. In addition, it's sometimes easier to get financing and insurance. And if defects show up after the sale has been consummated, it's easiest to convince the builder to fix them without charge than to get action out of a former owner who, 99 times out of 100, will plead honest ignorance, usually sincerely.

But buying new has its disadvantages, too. A big depreciation in market price occurs the moment a new boat is sold, when it becomes "used," just like a new car. And the first owner must find and exterminate the "bugs" that infest practically any new boat.

Old boats are significantly less expensive than new, but have disadvantages of their own. For example, as boats get older, they require more maintenance, look less up-to-date, and command a lower market price when it comes time to sell.

Some companies won't insure boats more than 10 years old. If that happens, banks and finance companies won't loan money with the boat as collateral. The demand for such boats falls off, as do prices compared to more easily insured boats. But not all insurance companies discriminate against old boats. "Bundling" your homeowner, auto, and boat insurance so that the insurer gets some attractive business along with the nuisance items (such as looking for a company that is willing to underwrite your old sailboat) can help if you're having difficulty finding proper coverage.

What condition you're looking for—or are willing to settle for in order to get the most boat for the money—depends on how much work you are willing to do yourself. The worse the boat's condition, the lower the price. There just aren't that many handymen (or handywomen!) out there looking for a boat to fix up. The handyman specials often never get sold; they get carted to the dump instead, or are given to "fixers" like me free of charge.

The other side of the coin is that, very often, the asking price of a boat in better-than-average condition will be inflated out of proportion to the money needed to change an average boat into one in excellent condition. So, if you want to get the most for your money, look for a boat in average or not too bad condition, not a very good or excellent specimen.

—from Boating for Less, *Second Edition, 1991, by Steve Henkel, published by International Marine, Camden, Maine*

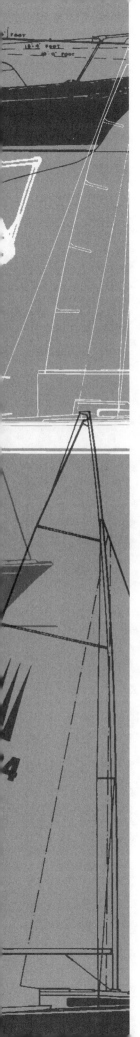

FIVE
Forty-Five Boats 23'

*3 vessels without accommodations plans appear at end of chapter

Aquarius/Balboa 23
Chubby sailer designed by a racing sailor

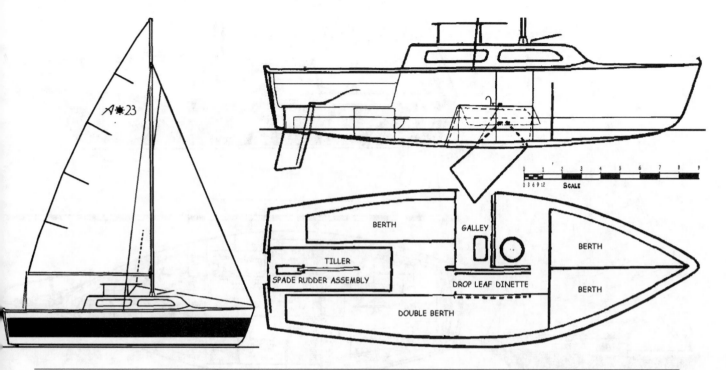

LOD:	22' 8"	**Designer:**	Peter Barrett/Stan Miller
LOA:	22' 8"	**Builder:**	Coastal Recreation
LWL:	21' 2"	**Years produced:**	1969–1980
Min./max. draft:	1' 1"/4' 7"	**Sail area:**	213 sq. ft.
Bridge clearance:	30' 6"	**Fuel tankage:**	portable
Power:	outboard 3 to 6 hp	**Water tankage:**	portable
B/D ratio:	36%	**Approx. trailering wgt.:**	3,300 lbs.

Peter Barrett (1935–2000) was one of America's most accomplished sailors, winning the U.S. Singlehanded Championship in 1962, a Silver Medal in the 1964 Olympics, and a Gold Medal in the 1968 Olympics, as well as winning many class championships. For some years he was an executive at North Sails, a world-class sailmaker. With co-designer Stan Miller, he designed only one series-built boat during his life, the Aquarius 23, having in mind at the time the comfort and safety of his wife and three small children. At various times the boat was offered with a masthead rig and/or a tall rig; the small standard rig is shown here. **Best features:** The centerboard totally retracts, making the boat easy to beach. The unusual spade rudder also retracts vertically into the cockpit for beaching. The so-called "double berth" is actually a single berth almost 14 feet long, thus accommodating very tall people—or two people sleeping head-to-head or toe-to-toe. Headroom is 4' 11" under the main hatch 4' 11" and 5' 11" with the poptop erected. **Worst features:** Because the freeboard is very high, partly to provide more than usual headroom for a 23-foot boat, she looks high and boxy.

Comps	LOD	Beam	MinDr	Displ	Bllst	SA/D	D/L	Avg. PHRF	Max. Speed	Motion Index	Space Index	No. of Berths	Head-room
Blazer 23	22' 6"	7' 10"	3' 11"	2,200	900	25.5	143	180	5.8	10.7	291	4	3' 8"
Aquarius/Balboa 23	22' 8"	7' 11"	1' 1"	2,280	815	19.7	107	282	6.2	10.3	416	5	4' 11"
Hunter 23	22' 9"	8' 0"	2' 3"	2,450	800	20.7	146	237	5.9	10.4	359	4	4' 7"
Precision 23	23' 5"	8' 6"	1' 11"	2,450	850	21.8	137	228	6.0	10.3	464	4	4' 6"
Paceship PY23 (22)	21' 7"	8' 0"	1' 9"	2,460	945	19.6	151	240	5.9	10.6	348	4	4' 6"

Bayfield 23/25 (23)
Don't let the name fool you

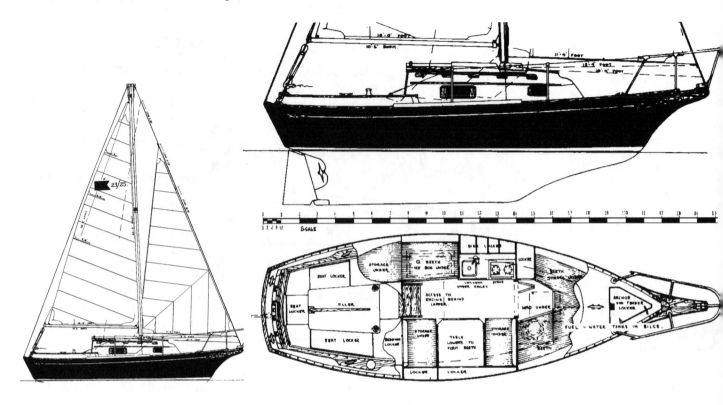

LOD:	23' 0"	**Designer:**	H. Ted Gozzard
LOA:	25' 0"	**Builder:**	Bayfield Boatyard
LWL:	19' 8"	**Years produced:**	1970–1988?
Min./max. draft:	2' 11"	**Sail area:**	240 sq. ft.
Bridge clearance:	33' 0"	**Fuel tankage:**	8 gal.
Power:	inbd. dsl. 7 to 10 hp	**Water tankage:**	8 gal.
B/D ratio:	41%	**Approx. trailering wgt.:**	5,300 lbs.

It's simple, really. The boat first came out as the Bayfield 25. Then someone pointed out that she was really only 23 feet on deck, and who did the marketers think they were trying to kid? The marketers agreed, but couldn't bear to admit the idea that the total boat from the tip of her bowsprit to the outer edge of her stern toerail was 25 feet. Thus she became the "23/25." Compared to other 23-footers, she won't win races (PHRF of 270) but she stands a chance of competing on liveaboard comfort with 5' 9" headroom and a Space Index of 400. **Best features:** Like her comp, the Morgan

22 (23) (page 239), the B23/25 has a two-person dinette (a little wider than the Morgan's) with a removable table that can be converted to a wide single berth. For those who like the so-called security of an inboard engine (which in our experience tends to break down as often as an outboard, and can be just as noisy and smelly, if not more so), the Bayfield is inboard-equipped. **Worst features:** We don't like to see the icebox under the port side quarter berth. It's so inconvenient to reach for a cold drink on a hot day. How about a big portable ice chest, instead?

Comps	LOD	Beam	MinDr	Displ	Bllst	SA/D	D/L	Avg. PHRF	Max. Speed	Motion Index	Space Index	No. of Berths	Head-room
Bayfield 23/25 (23)	23' 0"	8' 0"	2' 11"	3,500	1,300	16.7	205	270	5.9	15.8	400	4	5' 9"
Morgan 22 (23)	22' 10"	8' 0"	1' 10"	3,500	1,400	16.5	186	249	6.0	15.5	347	4	4' 6"
Montgomery 23	22' 7"	8' 0"	2' 5"	3,600	1,530	17.0	178	234	6.1	16.1	378	4	5' 4"

Blazer 23
Bruce Kirby adds berths to his popular Sonar

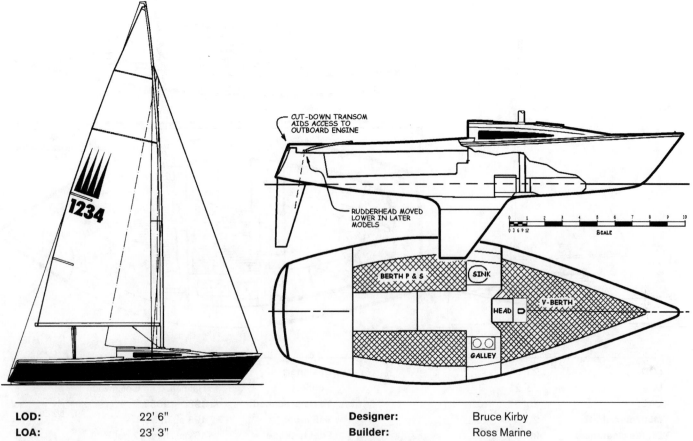

CUT-DOWN TRANSOM AIDS ACCESS TO OUTBOARD ENGINE

RUDDERHEAD MOVED LOWER IN LATER MODELS

SCALE

BERTH P & S | SINK | HEAD | V-BERTH | GALLEY

LOD:	22' 6"	Designer:	Bruce Kirby
LOA:	23' 3"	Builder:	Ross Marine
LWL:	19' 0"	Years produced:	1984–1989
Min./max. draft:	3' 11"	Sail area:	270 sq. ft.
Bridge clearance:	34' 0"	Fuel tankage:	portable
Power:	outboard 3 to 6 hp	Water tankage:	portable
B/D ratio:	41%	Approx. trailering wgt.:	3,200 lbs.

The Blazer 23, based on the popular one-design Sonar club racer but reconfigured to include weekend accommodations, was sometimes compared by her marketers to the J/24, despite some major differences between the two (such as an extra foot of waterline length on the J/24). A quick look at the specs shows both similarities and differences. (Specs for the J/24 are presented with her "real" comps on page 294.) *Best features:* The Blazer retains many of the specs of the Sonar, including relatively low displacement,

tall modern rig with plenty of sail, and low wetted surface, all of which are aimed at—and by and large achieve—exceptionally spritely performance in light and moderate air. Foam flotation for safety is also a plus. *Worst features:* Low profile and an extra-long cockpit result in a short, low cabin with significantly less accommodation space than the Blazer's comps. Due to her deep draft and deep, nonfolding rudder, using a hoist rather than a ramp for launching is a virtual necessity.

Comps	LOD	Beam	MinDr	Displ	Bllst	SA/D	D/L	Avg. PHRF	Max. Speed	Motion Index	Space Index	No. of Berths	Head- room
Blazer 23	22' 6"	7' 10"	3' 11"	2,200	900	25.5	143	180	5.8	10.7	291	4	3' 8"
Aquarius/Balboa 23	22' 8"	7' 11"	1' 1"	2,280	815	19.7	107	282	6.2	10.3	416	5	4' 11"
Hunter 23	22' 9"	8' 0"	2' 3"	2,450	800	20.7	146	237	5.9	11.4	359	4	4' 7"
Precision 23	23' 5"	8' 6"	1' 11"	2,450	850	21.8	137	228	6.0	10.3	464	4	4' 6"
Paceship PY23 (22)	21' 7"	8' 0"	1' 9"	2,460	945	19.6	151	240	5.9	11.6	348	4	4' 6"

Bluejacket Motorsailer 23
A "big-little" boat designed by William Garden

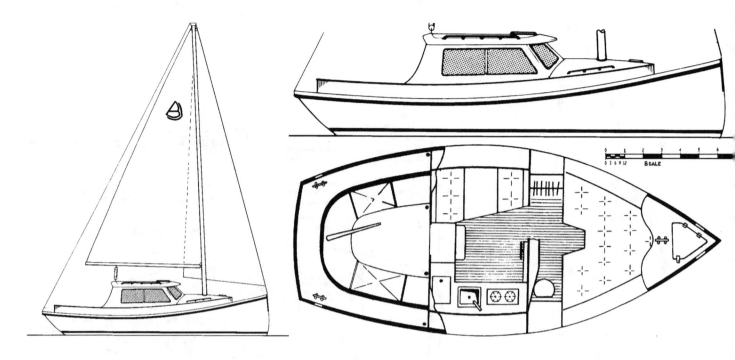

LOD:	23' 0"		Designer:	William Garden
LOA:	23' 2"		Builder:	Halman, then Collinwood
LWL:	20' 9"		Years produced:	1982–1988?
Min./max. draft:	2' 3"		Sail area:	196 sq. ft.
Bridge clearance:	30' 0"		Fuel tankage:	15 gal., later 12 gal.
Power:	inbd. Yanmar 15 to 18 hp		Water tankage:	24 gal., later 20 gal.
B/D ratio:	12%		Approx. trailering wgt.:	8,500 lbs.

This design started off as a graceful catboat, the *James W. Hart*. To gain space for accommodations, a keel was substituted for the cat's large centerboard, a small fin was added forward to aid in coming about after the board was removed, and a snug sloop rig was chosen for simplicity and ease of handling. Dual steering stations and 6' 2" headroom under the big-windowed pilothouse completed the transformation. **Best features:** The accommodations offer great comfort for two. The furniture is mostly single function so, for

example, you don't have to fold up your berth before you can have breakfast, or unfold the dinette (though the dinette does convert into a third berth if desired). There's an enclosed head and a built-in 3.3 cubic foot ice chest. A hydraulically operated steering wheel can be disconnected by turning a single valve, permitting use of a cockpit-mounted tiller. **Worst features:** The towing weight of around 8,500 lbs. (including 2,500 lbs. for stowed gear and the trailer itself) is a hefty load to pull, requiring a truck or SUV equivalent.

Comps	LOD	Beam	MinDr	Displ	Bllst	SA/D	D/L	Avg. PHRF	Max. Speed	Motion Index	Space Index	No. of Berths	Head- room
Pacific Seacraft Flicka 20	20' 0"	8' 0"	3' 3"	5,500	1,800	12.9	410	288	5.7	26.6	443	3 or 4	5' 11"
Bluejacket 23	23' 0"	10' 0"	2' 3"	6,000	700	9.5	300	NA	6.1	20.0	403	2	6' 2"
Herreshoff Prudence 23	22' 9"	8' 0"	3' 0"	6,800	1,600	16.4	394	NA	6.0	31.7	408	2	4' 9"
Falmouth Cutter (22)	22' 0"	8' 0"	3' 6"	7,400	2,500	15.0	365	NA	6.1	30.0	651	3	5' 11"

Cape Cod Marlin 23
Design descended from Nat Herreshoff

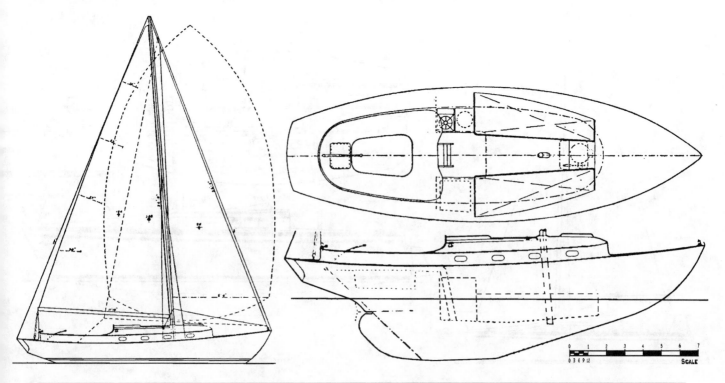

LOD:	23' 0"		**Designer:**	Sidney Herreshoff
LOA:	23' 0"		**Builder:**	Cape Cod Shipbuilding
LWL:	16' 11"		**Years produced:**	1957–present
Min./max. draft:	3' 3"		**Sail area:**	248 sq. ft.
Bridge clearance:	30' 0"		**Fuel tankage:**	portable
Power:	outboard, inboard Yanmar opt., 6 to 10 hp		**Water tankage:**	portable
B/D ratio:	31%		**Approx. trailering wgt.:**	4,800 lbs.

The famous Nat Herreshoff, "the Wizard of Bristol," in the early 1900s designed a racing class boat called the "12½," a name based on her waterline length. A slightly larger version, the Seawanhaka Fish Class, came in the 1920s. The Fish was 20' 9" long and 16' on the waterline. To produce the Marlin, one of Nat's sons, Sidney, enlarged the Fish design by pulling the stern out 2' 3" to provide for a permanent backstay, and modernizing the rig to include a masthead foretriangle. With the advent of fiberglass in the 1950s, Cape Cod Shipbuilding bought the design rights and began offering a fiberglass Marlin

in 1957—one of the earliest glass boats to hit the market. The boat is still made (to order) by Cape Cod Shipbuilding in Wareham, MA. In early 2009, her price was $65,000 plus sails. In addition, many buyers choose the Yanmar 10 hp diesel inboard engine, a $16,000 option. *Best features:* Versus the O'Day Tempest, she has more headroom and more elbow room. *Worst features:* Versus the two Pearson comps, she has less headroom and less elbow room. Also, the first Marlins are now over 50 years old. If you decide to buy a pre-owned one, look her over carefully first.

Comps	LOD	Beam	MinDr	Displ	Bllst	SA/D	D/L	Avg. PHRF	Max. Speed	Motion Index	Space Index	No. of Berths	Head-room
Pearson 23 Sloop	23' 0"	8' 0"	2' 4"	3,000	1,200	16.2	167	240	6.0	13.8	375	2	4' 8"
Pearson 23 Cat	23' 0"	8' 0"	4' 0"	3,000	1,200	16.2	167	240	6.0	13.8	375	2	4' 8"
O'Day Tempest 23	23' 2"	7' 8"	3' 9"	3,000	1,250	16.2	273	252	5.5	16.2	258	2	4' 0"
Cape Cod Marlin 23	23' 0"	7' 2"	3' 3"	3,200	1,400	18.3	295	264	5.5	19.0	288	2	4' 6"

Captiva 240 (23)
Rocket ship conversion to a cruiser

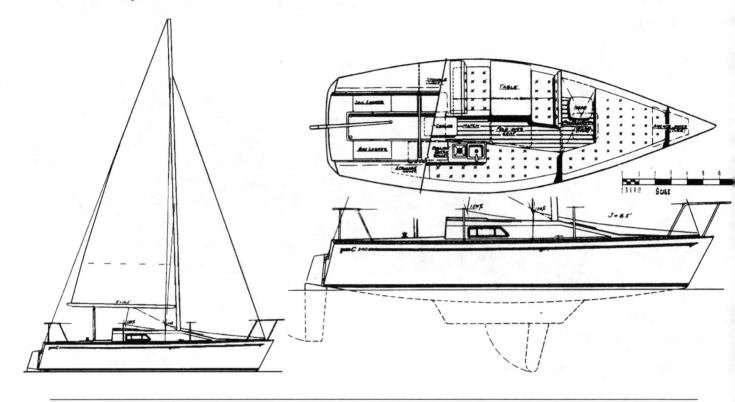

LOD:	23' 5"	**Designer:**	Rodgers & Scott
LOA:	25' 1"	**Builder:**	Captiva Yachts
LWL:	20' 6"	**Years produced:**	1986–1987
Min./max. draft:	2' 0"/4' 8"	**Sail area:**	258 sq. ft.
Bridge clearance:	34' 8"	**Fuel tankage:**	portable
Power:	outboard 3 to 6 hp	**Water tankage:**	portable
B/D ratio:	42%	**Approx. trailering wgt.:**	3,600 lbs.

O. H. Rodgers originally designed this craft as an all-out racing machine called the Rodgers 24, and Walt Scott modified it with a slightly different keel and rig for duty as a performance cruiser for Captiva Yachts of Oldsmar, FL (which unfortunately closed its doors shortly after the vessel was introduced to the market). She's relatively light in weight, especially considering she is equipped with pull-out galley, dining table, head, and sleeping accommodations for five below, and anchor locker, bow and stern pulpits and lifelines on deck. **Best features:** The biggest contrast between statistics of the three comps shown below is the difference in accommodations space, with the Captiva 240 leading the pack with a Space Index of 400. That is a result of the Captiva's combination of wider beam and relatively high topsides. Note also her cabin headroom of 5' 7". **Worst features:** The average PHRF rating of 213 may keep her from winning as many races as she otherwise might. Or maybe it won't. If you find a well-kept example, check her racing record.

Comps	LOD	Beam	MinDr	Displ	Bllst	SA/D	D/L	Avg. PHRF	Max. Speed	Motion Index	Space Index	No. of Berths	Head- room
Annapolis Weekender 24	24' 2"	6' 3"	3' 6"	2,300	1,120	20.0	176	276	5.7	15.5	236	4	4' 2"
Windrose 24	24' 0"	7' 10"	1' 6"	2,400	700	19.8	95	252	6.3	10.4	356	4	4' 4"
Captiva 240 (23)	23' 5"	8' 2"	2' 0"	2,400	1,000	23.0	124	213	6.1	10.3	400	5	5' 7"

Com-Pac 23
Long-running Hutchins vessel

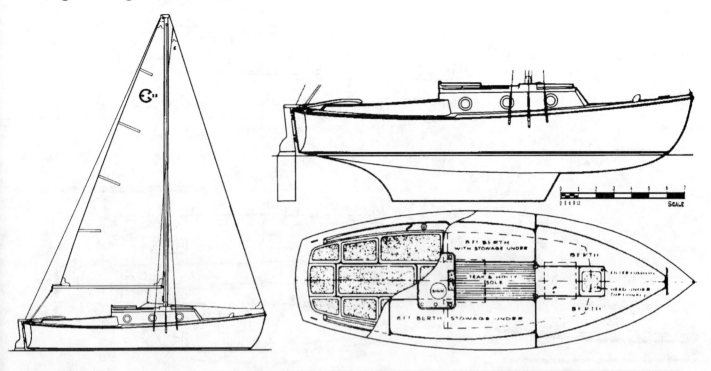

LOD:	22' 9"	**Designer:**	Clark Mills
LOA:	23' 10"	**Builder:**	Hutchins Company
LWL:	20' 2"	**Years produced:**	1979–present
Min./max. draft:	2' 3"	**Sail area:**	206 sq. ft.
Bridge clearance:	30' 0"	**Fuel tankage:**	portable
Power:	outboard or inboard 3 to 9 hp	**Water tankage:**	11 gal.
B/D ratio:	45%	**Approx. trailering wgt.:**	4,600 lbs.

Clark Mills designed this boat. He is also the designer of the Windmill, a popular racing sloop in the 1950s, and the Optimist Pram, the fiberglass successor to the International Optimist, which now has tens of thousands of copies sailing all over the world. The Com-Pac 23 shown here is the original version, but this venerable vessel (in production for 30 years) is now in its fourth iteration (called Mk IV). Along the way various changes have included a bowsprit (which moved the sail area center of effort forward, reducing weather helm), a small increase in ballast weight, an on-deck anchor locker, improvements in hardware including a

switch from round ports to rectangular ones, a PVC rubrail with stainless steel striker plate, a foil rudder blade in place of one made of flat plate, an optional 9 hp Yanmar inboard diesel engine, and others. (The company included the new bowsprit in the boat's length, changing it from 22' 9" to 23' 11"; we use LOD, not LOA, as a measure of length, so we exclude the bowsprit.) **Best features:** The finish is above average, with lots of teak below and a teak-and-holly sole. **Worst features:** The draft of the Com-Pac 23 at only 2' 3", with no centerboard, limits the boat's ability to sail close to the wind.

Comps	LOD	Beam	MinDr	Displ	Bllst	SA/D	D/L	Avg. PHRF	Max. Speed	Motion Index	Space Index	No. of Berths	Head-room
Com-Pac 23	22' 9"	7' 10"	2' 3"	3,000	1,340	19.2	163	260	6.0	13.9	329	4	4' 4"
Halcyon 23	22' 9"	7' 6"	3' 6"	3,100	1,100	16.9	213	NA	5.8	16.3	364	4	5' 5"
Coronado 23	22' 7"	7' 9"	2' 6"	3,100	1,350	17.9	171	270	6.0	14.9	341	4	4' 9"
Tanzer 22 (23)	22' 6"	7' 10"	2' 0"	3,100	1,500	16.7	180	240	6.0	14.9	295	4	4' 3"
San Juan 24 (23)	23' 4"	8' 0"	4' 0"	3,200	1,650	18.0	193	216	5.9	14.8	373	5	4' 6"

Coronado 23
Near clone to the Columbia 22

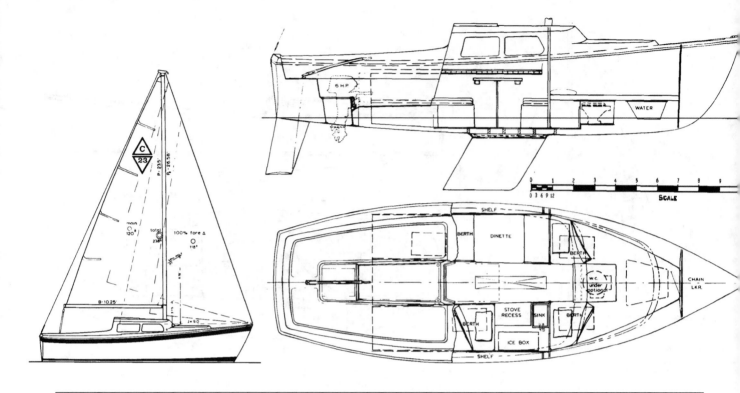

LOD:	22' 7"	
LOA:	22' 10"	
LWL:	20' 1"	
Min./max. draft:	3' 2" or 2' 6"/5' 0"	
Bridge clearance:	30' 4"	
Power:	outboard 3 to 6 hp	
B/D ratio:	31%	

Designer:	William Crealock
Builder:	Coronado Yachts
Years produced:	1969–1972
Sail area:	238 sq. ft.
Fuel tankage:	portable
Water tankage:	portable
Approx. trailering wgt.:	4,300 lbs.

Here is a boat that packs a lot of stuff into a limited space: four berths, a dinette, head, stove, icebox, and sink. There's also space in the cockpit for an outboard in a well, right at the feet of the helmsman. Furthermore, you have two choices of bottom configurations: a cast iron fin keel (as shown here) drawing 3' 2", or a keel/centerboard version with 250 lbs. of extra ballast and 2' 6" minimum draft, going to 5' 0" with the board down. For someone on a limited budget, this boat might be on their short list—or they might choose the almost identical Columbia 22 (with a different deck mold and a less extended bow) shown on page 161. Glancing at the accommodations plans of both vessels, one might conclude that they are identical until checking the dimensional specifications, which expose subtle differences. **Best features:** The placement of the outboard engine well under the tiller gives the helmsman very good access to the engine controls (although it reduces cockpit space somewhat). **Worst features:** Her PHRF seems to indicate a performance deficiency versus her comps.

Comps	LOD	Beam	MinDr	Displ	Bllst	SA/D	D/L	Avg. PHRF	Max. Speed	Motion Index	Space Index	No. of Berths	Head-room
Com-Pac 23	22' 9"	7' 10"	2' 3"	3,000	1,340	19.2	163	260	6.0	13.9	329	4	4' 4"
Halcyon 23	22' 9"	7' 6"	3' 6"	3,100	1,100	16.9	213	NA	5.8	16.3	364	4	5' 5"
Coronado 23	22' 7"	7' 9"	2' 6"	3,100	1,350	17.9	171	270	6.0	14.9	341	4	4' 9"
Tanzer 22 (23)	22' 6"	7' 10"	2' 0"	3,100	1,500	16.7	180	240	6.0	14.9	295	4	4' 3"
San Juan 24 (23)	23' 4"	8' 0"	4' 0"	3,200	1,650	18.0	193	216	5.9	14.8	373	5	4' 6"

Dehler 25 (23)

This boat launches on her own four-wheel trolley

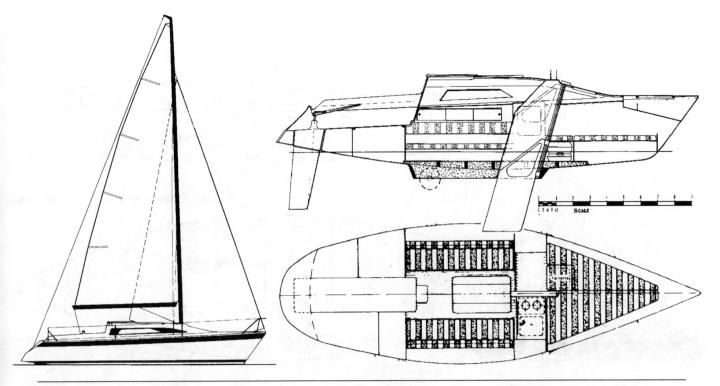

LOD:	23' 1"		**Designer:**	E. G. Van de Stadt
LOA:	24' 11"		**Builder:**	Dehler Yachtbau GmbH
LWL:	21' 10"		**Years produced:**	1985–1989?
Min./max. draft:	1' 4"/4' 3"		**Sail area:**	253 sq. ft.
Bridge clearance:	35' 0"		**Fuel tankage:**	portable
Power:	outboard 4 to 6 hp		**Water tankage:**	portable
B/D ratio:	51%		**Approx. trailering wgt.:**	4,000 lbs.

Here's something unusual: a water ballasted boat with an additional equal amount of lead ballast in a lifting keel—827 pounds in each form. That gives her a very high ballast-to-displacement ratio of 51%, and—unlike some other water ballasted boats—makes the Dehler suitably stiff. She is designed with trailering in mind, and consequently includes an automatic water ballast system, an easily removable rudder, well designed mast lowering equipment, and a specially built road trailer fitted with a four-wheeled "floating slip-way trolley." The heavy lifting keel is raised using a standard winch handle in a socket on deck just forward of the mast that operates a worm gear mechanism, which does the actual lifting. The boat was available either factory-finished or in various stages of construction for home finishing by using various kits and subassemblies offered as options at the factory. **Best features:** The Dehler is very well made and cleverly designed for easy launching and retrieval at a ramp. For example, a motor mount rides on tracks on her reverse transom for easily raising and lowering an outboard motor. She is also nicely finished. **Worst features:** Headroom is only 4' 9", making stays of more than a few days aboard a test of will. A canvas dodger may help in this department.

Comps	LOD	Beam	MinDr	Displ	Bllst	SA/D	D/L	Avg. PHRF	Max. Speed	Motion Index	Space Index	No. of Berths	Head-room
Merit 25 (24)	24' 0"	8' 0"	4' 0"	2,900	1,050	21.7	106	168	6.4	11.9	409	4	4' 1"
Seaward 25 (24)	24' 0"	8' 4"	2' 1"	3,100	1,100	17.7	114	270	6.4	11.7	483	5	5' 3"
Kirby 25	24' 7"	8' 9"	4' 2"	3,150	1,150	21.6	157	174	6.1	12.2	454	4	4' 6"
Dehler 25 (23)	23' 1"	8' 3"	1' 4"	3,245	1,654	20.1	139	186	6.3	13.2	382	4	4' 9"
Freedom 24	23' 9"	8' 3"	1' 10"	3,250	1,350	22.0	146	207	6.2	13.3	428	2	4' 7"

Ericson 23

This Bruce King design came in many choices

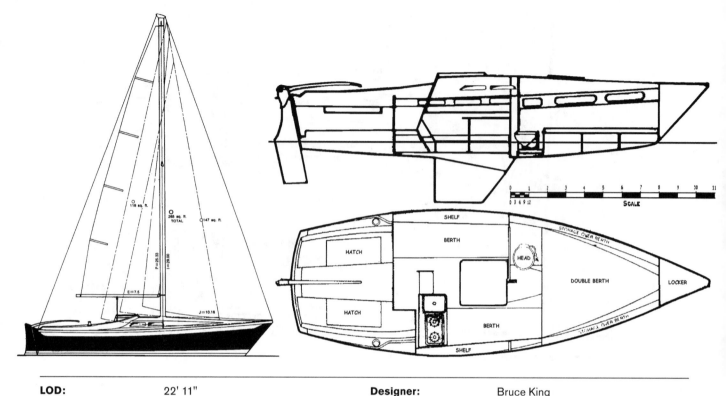

LOD:	22' 11"	**Designer:**	Bruce King
LOA:	23' 7"	**Builder:**	Ericson Yachts
LWL:	19' 6"	**Years produced:**	1968–1979
Min./max. draft:	3' 8" or 1' 11"/5' 11"	**Sail area:**	265 sq. ft.
Bridge clearance:	32' 9"	**Fuel tankage:**	portable
Power:	outboard 3 to 6 hp	**Water tankage:**	portable
B/D ratio:	39%	**Approx. trailering wgt.:**	4,800 lbs.

This trailerable microcruiser is available with either keel-centerboard (draft under two feet) or fin keel (draft under four feet) underbody, and with either a standard or tall rig. A keel-only Mk I version (1968–1970) was superceded by a Mk II (1974–1979) with choices including tall rig, keel, or centerboard. These variables affect her speed: PHRF for the Mk I runs from 222 to 267, avg. 252; Mk II keel runs from 216 to 234, avg. 225; Mk II c'board runs from 222 to 243, avg. 234. The Mk I came with an inboard rudder; the Mk II's was transom-hung. ***Best features:*** She has a head positioned for modesty, forward of the main half-bulkhead,

plus a table that folds up to the bulkhead, and space for both a small sink and a two-burner stove. Her relatively low PHRF (in the Mk II version) reflects performance superior to her peers. ***Worst features:*** A few boats have keel-stepped masts, which may make it difficult to rig when trailering at launching ramps; most feature a deck-stepped mast, which we'd prefer for handiness at ramps. The boat has been criticized for having small hatches and poor ventilation, though how serious a problem this might be would depend on the particular weather conditions where she is sailed.

Comps	LOD	Beam	MinDr	Displ	Bllst	SA/D	D/L	Avg. PHRF	Max. Speed	Motion Index	Space Index	No. of Berths	Head-room
O'Day 23 Mk I	23' 1"	7' 11"	2' 0"	3,100	1,250	18.4	173	234	6.0	14.3	418	5	4' 7"
Grampian 23	23' 3"	8' 0"	2' 4"	3,200	1,150	18.0	156	270	6.1	14.0	395	5	5' 4"
Ericson 23	22' 11"	7' 11"	1' 11"	3,200	1,250	19.5	193	see text	5.9	15.1	309	4	4' 3"

Gillmer 23
Unique sloop from 1960

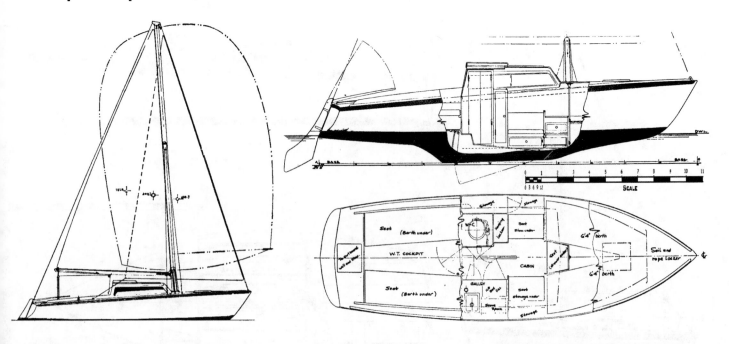

LOD:	22' 7"	**Designer:**	Thomas C. Gillmer
LOA:	25' 8"	**Builder:**	Henry Meneely/Holden
LWL:	21' 0"	**Years produced:**	1960–1962?
Min./max. draft:	1' 8"/3' 0"	**Sail area:**	242 sq. ft.
Bridge clearance:	31' 0"	**Fuel tankage:**	portable
Power:	outboard 3 to 6 hp	**Water tankage:**	portable
B/D ratio:	24%	**Approx. trailering wgt.:**	3,000 lbs.

The Gillmer 23 was reported in the January, 1960 issue of *Yachting* magazine as being a design "for the account of Henry T. Meneely who will have her built by Holden Laminated Plastics Co." We have found no evidence that any actual boats were built, but that doesn't mean that none were made. We would like to have seen how she looked in the round, so to speak, and how she sailed. She had several clever design features not often seen on more modern boats. ***Best features:*** Her stern freeboard slopes down to less than two feet, making it relatively easy to climb aboard from a dinghy. In addition to two berths in the cabin, there are two additional berths under the fiberglass seats in the cockpit. When these seats are tipped up, they form the sides of a canvas-topped shelter supported by the main boom, providing both privacy and protection from the weather. A high mast tabernacle makes easy work of raising and lowering (and stowing) the mast. Headroom below is more than a foot higher than her comps, and her Space Index is also proportionally greater. The layout below includes a head with stand-up access under the main hatch and hinged double doors, positioned for privacy. Stowage space is above average. ***Worst features:*** We could not find a Gillmer 23 in existence.

Comps	LOD	Beam	MinDr	Displ	Bllst	SA/D	D/L	Avg. PHRF	Max. Speed	Motion Index	Space Index	No. of Berths	Head-room
Venture of Newport (23)	22' 7"	7' 2"	1' 6"	2,000	600	21.5	120	255	5.9	10.2	312	5	4' 0"
Gillmer 23	22' 7"	7' 6"	1' 8"	2,068	500	23.9	100	NA	6.1	9.7	365	4	5' 0"
Clipper 23 (22)	22' 4"	7' 8"	2' 2"	2,100	550	21.6	142	258	5.8	10.6	351	5	4' 6"
Menger Oysterman 23	22' 6"	8' 0"	1' 8"	2,600	700	30.0	124	NA	6.2	10.4	312	4	4' 9"

Gloucester 23/LN 23
A boat with several names and several builders

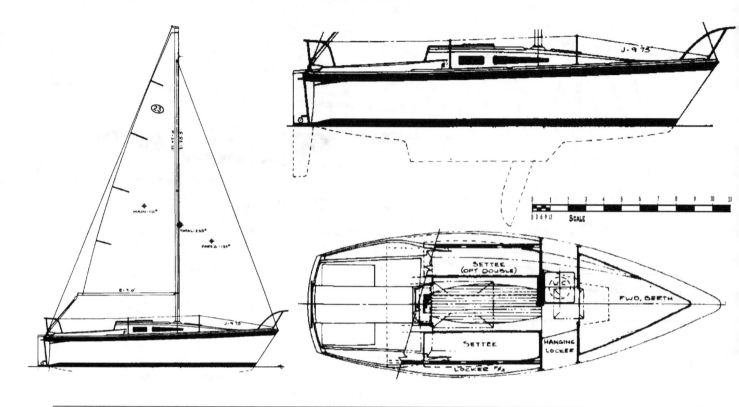

LOD:	22' 11"	**Designer:**	Stuart Windley	
LOA:	23' 4"	**Builder:**	Lockley-Newport Boats	
LWL:	20' 0"	**Years produced:**	1978–1984?	
Min./max. draft:	1' 11"/5' 6	**Sail area:**	235 sq. ft.	
Bridge clearance:	32' 6"	**Fuel tankage:**	portable	
Power:	outboard 3 to 6 hp	**Water tankage:**	10 gal.	
B/D ratio:	37%	**Approx. trailering wgt.:**	4,000 lbs.	

The Gloucester 23, also known as the Lockley Newport 23 and as the Classic 23, was built at one time by Gloucester Yachts, and later by Lockley-Newport Boats in Gloucester, VA, and still later at Classic Yachts in Chanute, KS. Like her sisters, the Gloucester 16 (page 33) and the Gloucester 19 (page 34), her molds were passed from one business entity to another, and construction was perhaps understandably what one might call "variable." ***Best features:***

There isn't much to get excited about with this boat, in our opinion. True, it's a matter of taste, but we feel that she is a plain Jane in a crowded field with many more attractive boats vying for attention—including her comps listed below. Sorry, but we can't conjure up any significant "best features" for her. ***Worst features:*** Her so-so construction and lack of amenities below top the list of things we feel work against her.

Comps	LOD	Beam	MinDr	Displ	Bllst	SA/D	D/L	Avg. PHRF	Max. Speed	Motion Index	Space Index	No. of Berths	Head-room
Santana Wavelength 24 (23)	22' 7"	9' 0"	4' 6"	2,500	1,100	25.0	133	162	6.0	9.6	400	4	4' 3"
Santana 23	22' 7"	8' 10"	0' 10"	2,600	1,130	24.0	132	171	6.1	10.2	427	4	4' 4"
San Juan 23	22' 7"	8' 0"	1' 1"	2,700	960	19.0	169	234	5.9	12.5	393	5	5' 0"
Gloucester 23/LN 23	22' 11"	8' 0"	1' 11"	2,700	1,000	19.4	151	270	6.0	12.4	411	4	5' 0"

Grampian 23
Basic sailboat transportation at a low price

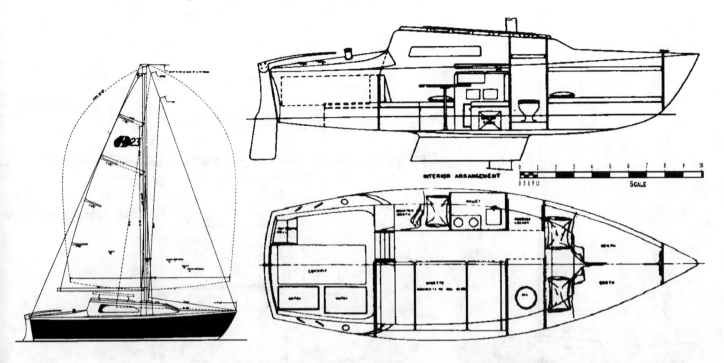

INTERIOR ARRANGEMENT

SCALE

LOD:	23' 3"	Designer:	Alex McGruer
LOA:	24' 9"	Builder:	Grampian Marine
LWL:	20' 11"	Years produced:	1972–1974
Min./max. draft:	2' 4"/5' 4"	Sail area:	244 sq. ft.
Bridge clearance:	32' 6"	Fuel tankage:	portable
Power:	outboard 3 to 6 hp	Water tankage:	portable
B/D ratio:	36%	Approx. trailering wgt.:	4,800 lbs.

The emphasis on this design appears to be to provide basic sailboat transportation at a low price. Beauty is not a selling point; her appearance is too slab-sided and top-heavy to qualify her as pretty. ***Best features:*** The raised poptop can be fitted with snap-on weather curtains and vinyl windows to make a serviceable convertible doghouse underway. Between the poptop hatch and a good-sized ventilation hatch forward, there should be plenty of air below. ***Worst features:*** The Grampian 23 is the slowest of her comps (despite her relatively long waterline), with a significantly higher PHRF rating. Construction is not

nearly as high in quality as either of her comps. Her cockpit is small and squeezed toward the stern, which tends to force the stern down and the bow up when the cockpit is loaded. One owner says that the cockpit is "about two feet short of perfect." Presumably, the original plan was to allot more space to accommodations, but the idea somehow didn't work, as seen by comparing the Grampian 23 to the O'Day 23 Mk I (page 240). The O'Day's layout nearly duplicates the Grampian's, but somehow ends up with a 6½-foot cockpit compared to the Grampian's 5½-foot arrangement.

Comps	LOD	Beam	MinDr	Displ	Bllst	SA/D	D/L	Avg. PHRF	Max. Speed	Motion Index	Space Index	No. of Berths	Head-room
O'Day 23 Mk I	23' 1"	7' 11"	2' 0"	3,100	1,250	18.4	173	234	6.0	14.3	418	5	4' 7"
Grampian 23	23' 3"	8' 0"	2' 4"	3,200	1,150	18.0	156	270	6.1	14.0	395	5	5' 4"
Ericson 23	22' 11"	7' 11"	1' 11"	3,200	1,250	19.5	193	see text	5.9	15.1	309	4	4' 3"

Halcyon 23
A small yacht from Britain

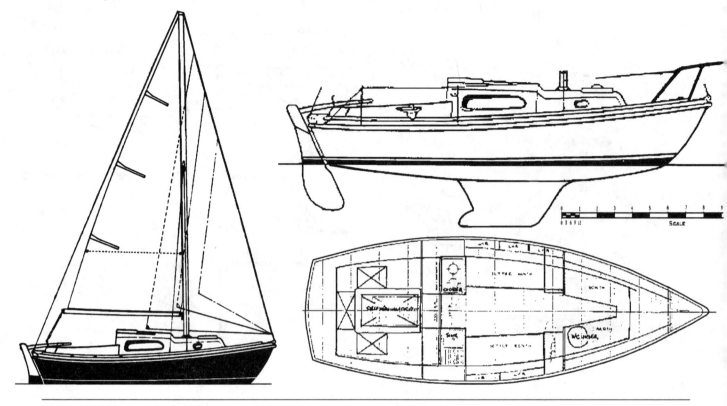

LOD:	22' 9"	**Designer:**	Alan Buchanan
LOA:	23' 4"	**Builder:**	Offshore Yachts Ltd.
LWL:	18' 8"	**Years produced:**	1965–1975
Min./max. draft:	3' 6"	**Sail area:**	225 sq. ft.
Bridge clearance:	33' 9"	**Fuel tankage:**	10 gal. (?)
Power:	inboard 5 hp	**Water tankage:**	20 gal. (?)
B/D ratio:	35%	**Approx. trailering wgt.:**	4,700 lbs.

Over four hundred of these little cruisers were built in England in the 1960s and 1970s, and a few were imported into the United States. They were available as kits in various stages of completion, or totally ready to sail with sink, head, pulpit and double lifelines, chart table, ice chest, and an inboard engine (gas or diesel of 5 hp). Two keel options, both of epoxy-coated iron, were offered: a fin with a bulb or twin bilge keels of a slightly lower draft for lying on the flat. *Best features:* The big-boat features offered as standard are impressive, especially the inboard engine. The ballast weight is shown here as 1,100 pounds, but 900 of these are mostly in

a bulb at the bottom of a fin keel, so ultimately her ability to stand up in a blow would likely be significantly greater than the boat's comps, all of which are centerboarders with inside ballast. *Worst features:* The basic boat came with a hand-start inboard engine, which sounds mighty inconvenient for all but the most hardened sail-right-into-the-slip sailors, who never use engines anyway. The outboard rudder is hung on the transom with no support or weed guards below the stock itself, leaving the rudder open to damage if it connects with a rocky bottom. Some do-it-yourself kits were badly finished. Let the boat buyer beware.

Comps	LOD	Beam	MinDr	Displ	Bllst	SA/D	D/L	Avg. PHRF	Max. Speed	Motion Index	Space Index	No. of Berths	Head-room
Com-Pac 23	22' 9"	7' 10"	2' 3"	3,000	1,340	19.2	163	260	6.0	13.9	329	4	4' 4"
Halcyon 23	22' 9"	7' 6"	3' 6"	3,100	1,100	16.9	213	NA	5.8	16.3	364	4	5' 5"
Coronado 23	22' 7"	7' 9"	2' 6"	3,100	1,350	17.9	171	270	6.0	14.9	341	4	4' 9"
Tanzer 22 (23)	22' 6"	7' 10"	2' 0"	3,100	1,500	16.7	180	240	6.0	14.9	295	4	4' 3"

Herreshoff Prudence 23
A traditional design by L. Francis Herreshoff

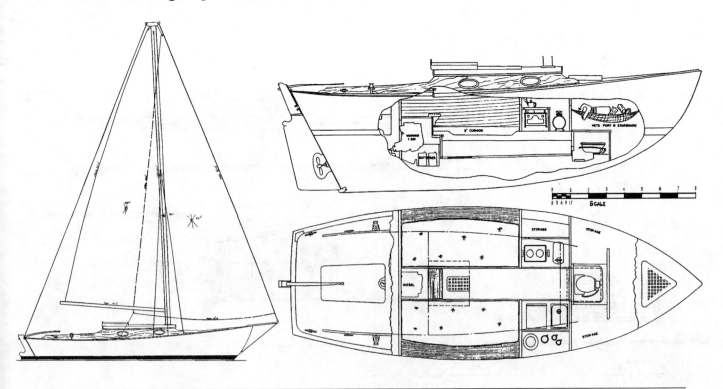

LOD:	22' 9"	**Designer:**	L. Francis Herreshoff
LOA:	26' 6"	**Builder:**	Middleton Marine
LWL:	19' 9"	**Years produced:**	1982–present
Min./max. draft:	3' 0"	**Sail area:**	315 sq. ft.
Bridge clearance:	33' 10"	**Fuel tankage:**	12 gal.
Power:	1GM inboard Yanmar	**Water tankage:**	20 gal.
B/D ratio:	24%	**Approx. trailering wgt.:**	9,800 lbs.

Since the 1980s, Middleton Marine of LaCrosse, FL, has been producing (to order) four different L. Francis Herreshoff designs in fiberglass: two sloops, the 23-foot Prudence and the 28-foot H28, and two ketches, the 36-foot Nereia, and the 37-foot Diddikai. All four of their offerings are available in various stages of kit assembly from hull-only, to ballast, bulkheads, and deck installed, to engine installed. The company also will produce finished yachts to order. **Best features:** The traditionalist will enjoy the design, originated in 1937. (The drawings—of the boat's wooden version—appear in the book, *Sensible Cruising Designs* by L. Francis Herreshoff, published in 1973 by International Marine Publishing.) As with any of her comps, the Prudence will satisfy the cruiser's need to explore distant places in relative comfort regardless of weather (short of a gale). **Worst features:** The headroom falls short of her comps by 14" or more—but if the galley were moved aft under the companionway, a dodger could be installed to provide reasonable standing headroom at the galley while preparing meals.

Comps	LOD	Beam	MinDr	Displ	Bllst	SA/D	D/L	Avg. PHRF	Max. Speed	Motion Index	Space Index	No. of Berths	Head-room
Pacific Seacraft Flicka 20	20' 0"	8' 0"	3' 3"	5,500	1,800	12.9	410	288	5.7	26.6	443	3 or 4	5' 11"
Bluejacket 23	23' 0"	10' 0"	2' 3"	6,000	700	9.5	300	NA	6.1	20.0	403	2	6' 2"
Herreshoff Prudence 23	22' 9"	8' 0"	3' 0"	6,800	1,600	16.4	394	NA	6.0	31.7	408	2	4' 9"
Falmouth Cutter (22)	22' 0"	8' 0"	3' 6"	7,400	2,500	15.0	365	NA	6.1	30.0	651	3	5' 11"

Hunter 23

Second Hunter in a series

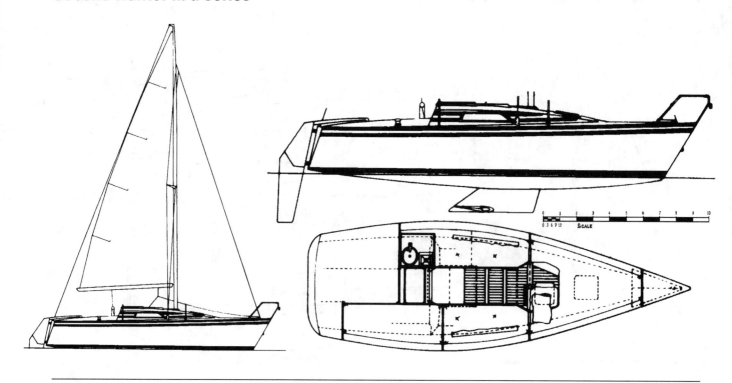

LOD:	22' 9"	**Designer:**	Hunter Design Team
LOA:	24' 8"	**Builder:**	Hunter Marine
LWL:	19' 7"	**Years produced:**	1985–1992
Min./max. draft:	2' 3"	**Sail area:**	235 sq. ft.
Bridge clearance:	33' 0"	**Fuel tankage:**	portable
Power:	outboard 3 to 6 hp	**Water tankage:**	6 gal.
B/D ratio:	33%	**Approx. trailering wgt.:**	3,700 lbs.

The Hunter 23 is second in this builder's series of boats of similar length. It started in 1981 with the Hunter 22 (page 176), and preceded the Hunter 23.5 (page 177). The "23" is the first of the series to offer a winged keel rather than the lead fin or iron keel-centerboard. (The succeeding "23.5" is a water-ballasted centerboarder.) The "23" also has a longer waterline (made possible partly by a reverse transom), lighter displacement, and a taller mast and greater sail area. She should be faster than her predecessor, and easier to trailer. **Best features:** Although the V-berth forward is only large enough for two children or one adult, owners may feel compensated by having the ability to convert the entire main cabin into a double bed (the full 8-foot width of the hull), by utilizing floorboards as supports and seatbacks as cushions. **Worst features:** Owners have reported leaking around the keel bolts and around the rudder gudgeons. Another source of annoyance has been the boat's tendency to sit down in the water by the port quarter, a result of putting batteries, water tank, and the transom-mounted outboard engine all in the aft quarter to port.

Comps	LOD	Beam	MinDr	Displ	Bllst	SA/D	D/L	Avg. PHRF	Max. Speed	Motion Index	Space Index	No. of Berths	Head- room
Blazer 23	22' 6"	7' 10"	3' 11"	2,200	900	25.5	143	180	5.8	10.7	291	4	3' 8"
Aquarius/Balboa 23	22' 8"	7' 11"	1' 1"	2,280	815	19.7	107	282	6.2	10.3	416	5	4' 11"
Hunter 23	22' 9"	8' 0"	2' 3"	2,450	800	20.7	146	237	5.9	10.4	359	4	4' 7"
Precision 23	23' 5"	8' 6"	1' 11"	2,450	850	21.8	137	228	6.0	10.3	464	4	4' 6"
Paceship PY23 (22)	21' 7"	8' 0"	1' 9"	2,460	945	19.6	151	240	5.9	11.6	348	4	4' 6"

Hunter 240 (23)
Water-ballasted hull from Hunter Design Team

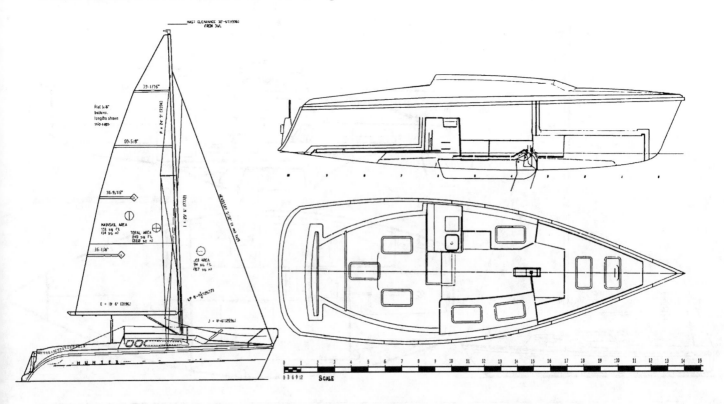

LOD:	23' 1"		Designer:	Hunter Design Team
LOA:	24' 4"		Builder:	Hunter Marine
LWL:	22' 1"		Years produced:	1997–present
Min./max. draft:	1' 6"/5' 6"		Sail area:	242 sq. ft.
Bridge clearance:	32' 6"		Fuel tankage:	portable
Power:	outboard 3 to 6 hp		Water tankage:	6.5 gal.
B/D ratio:	36%		Approx. trailering wgt.:	3,250 lbs.

It might seem that the Hunter 240 is a very different design from her two comps chosen here: modern rather than traditional, one mast rather than two, and so on. But most of her stats—even PHRF, which is a basic standard for comparison between boats—are very similar. There are differences, of course, the main one in our estimation being the water ballast under the floor of the Hunter rather than the lead under the floor of the other two boats. All have 1' 6" drafts with board up, and all have fairly light

boards (not so-called "lifting keels"). **Best features:** As with other Hunter trailer-sailers, the 240 has an innovative mast-raising system which makes rigging relatively fast and easy, and a custom trailer that fits the boat and eliminates some of the hassle of launching at a ramp. A movable table (not shown on the plan here) can be set up in the cockpit or the cabin. **Worst features:** Water ballast has never worked very well for any of the under 26-foot boats on which it has been tried, and the Hunter is no exception.

Comps	LOD	Beam	MinDr	Displ	Bllst	SA/D	D/L	Avg. PHRF	Max. Speed	Motion Index	Space Index	No. of Berths	Head-room
Sand Hen 24	23' 9"	8' 0"	1' 6"	3,500	1,500	19.1	137	NA	6.4	14.4	393	4	4' 9"
Hunter 240 (23)	23' 1"	8' 3"	1' 6"	3,600	1,300	16.5	148	255	6.3	14.6	416	4	4' 8"
Bahama Sandpiper 24	24' 0"	7' 11"	1' 6"	4,140	1,500	17.2	162	252	6.4	17.5	393	4	4' 9"

Irwin 23

Ted Irwin's smallest cruising design

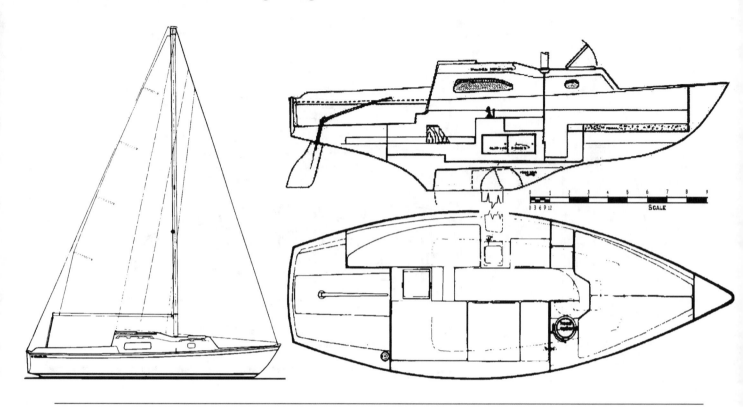

LOD:	23' 0"	**Designer:**	Ted Irwin
LOA:	23' 0"	**Builder:**	Irwin Yachts
LWL:	18' 6"	**Years produced:**	1968–1975
Min./max. draft:	2' 5"/5' 9"	**Sail area:**	255 sq. ft.
Bridge clearance:	31' 6"	**Fuel tankage:**	portable
Power:	outboard 3 to 6 hp	**Water tankage:**	portable
B/D ratio:	47%	**Approx. trailering wgt.:**	4,800 lbs.

Ted Irwin, who grew up in the Tampa Bay area of Florida, started in his teens to build boats of his own design. Later he designed a version of the Moth Class, which won the North American and world championships in its class. Along the way, he worked for Charlie Morgan, whose boats, such as the Morgan 24/25 reported on page 358, Irwin's designs tend to resemble. The Irwin 23 was the smallest boat commercially produced by Irwin, who ended up building hundreds of boats and dozens of models. ***Best features:***

Among her comps, the Irwin is probably the fastest boat, despite her PHRF rating and maximum theoretical speed being equal to both the Sovereign comps, which have no centerboard for going upwind efficiently, as does the Irwin. The Sovereigns also have higher topsides and a taller cabin, which may provide better headroom but contribute "top hamper" or windage that tends to slow the boat upwind. ***Worst features:*** Irwin's construction quality tended to be so-so at best.

Comps	LOD	Beam	MinDr	Displ	Bllst	SA/D	D/L	Avg. PHRF	Max. Speed	Motion Index	Space Index	No. of Berths	Head- room
Sovereign Antares (23)	23' 0"	8' 0"	2' 7"	3,000	1,200	16.3	254	252	5.8	17.0	389	4	5' 4"
Irwin 23	23' 0"	8' 0"	2' 5"	3,200	1,500	18.8	226	252	5.8	15.5	334	4	4' 9"
Sovereign 23	23' 0"	8' 0"	2' 4"	3,250	1,350	17.5	229	252	5.8	15.6	435	4	5' 7"
O'Day 240 (23)	22' 6"	8' 3"	2' 8"	3,600	1,200	17.0	178	231	6.1	15.2	438	4	5' 9"

Menger Oysterman 23
Character boat from the Chesapeake

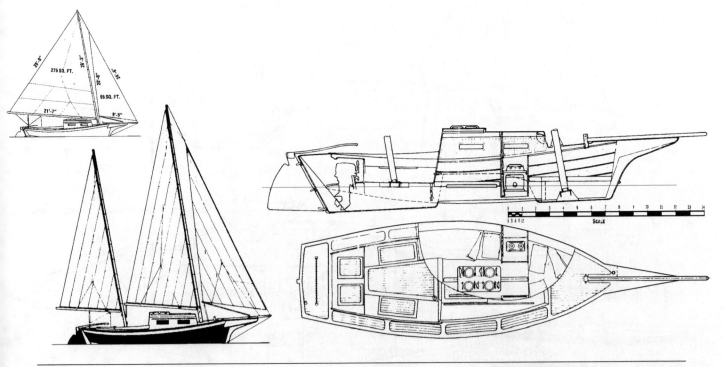

LOD:	22' 6"	**Designer:**	Bill Menger
LOA:	31' 1"	**Builder:**	Menger Boatworks
LWL:	21' 1"	**Years produced:**	1977–2000
Min./max. draft:	1' 8"/6' 0"	**Sail area:**	323 sq. ft. (ketch)
Bridge clearance:	32' 0"	**Fuel tankage:**	portable
Power:	outboard 4 to 6 hp	**Water tankage:**	12 gal. (optional)
B/D ratio:	27%	**Approx. trailering wgt.:**	4,000 lbs.

This little Chesapeake Bay skipjack is based on the lines of a Howard Chapelle design called Blue Crab. She could be bought from Menger Boatworks either as a ketch (favored by about 70% of buyers) or as a sloop. The ketch, with less sail area more spread out fore and aft, is easier to balance than the sloop when sailing in varying wind conditions. The sloop, on the other hand, is faster, simpler, and doesn't have a mast cluttering up the cockpit. Oddly, dimensions for this vessel seemed to vary more than most other designs, depending on the sales brochure. For example, in one place the ketch sail area is 309 square feet and in another it's 323 sq. ft. In one place the sloop area is 355 sq. ft. and

in another it's 370 sq. ft. Ballast is 600 lbs. in one place, 700 lbs. in another. It's a puzzlement. *Best features:* For someone looking for a character boat, this may be your cup of tea. The outboard engine is in a cockpit well, convenient to the helmsman. The jib is on a jib boom, making life easy for a singlehander tacking up a narrow channel or sailing downwind wing and wing. Those who have tried it claim you can sail upwind in two feet of water without excessive sideslip. *Worst features:* With a SA/D ratio of 30, she should be responsive in light air, while on the other hand she may be a bit tender in heavy air. But of course, you can always reef.

Comps	LOD	Beam	MinDr	Displ	Bllst	SA/D	D/L	Avg. PHRF	Max. Speed	Motion Index	Space Index	No. of Berths	Head-room
Venture of Newport (23)	22' 7"	7' 2"	1' 6"	2,000	600	21.5	120	255	5.9	10.2	312	5	4' 0"
Gillmer 23	22' 7"	7' 6"	1' 8"	2,068	500	23.9	100	NA	6.1	9.7	365	2	5' 0"
Clipper 23 (22)	22' 4"	7' 8"	2' 2"	2,100	550	21.6	142	258	5.8	10.6	351	5	4' 6"
Menger Oysterman 23	22' 6"	8' 0"	1' 8"	2,600	700	30.0	124	NA	6.2	10.4	312	4	4' 9"

Montgomery 23
A shippy little Lyle Hess design

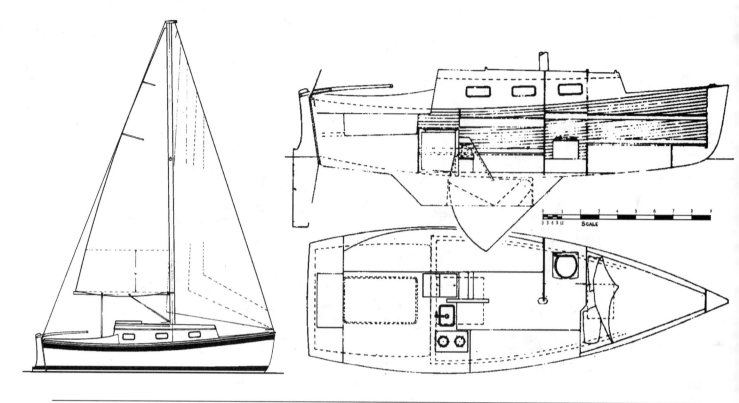

LOD:	22' 7"	**Designer:**	Lyle Hess
LOA:	23' 4"	**Builder:**	Montgomery Marine
LWL:	20' 10"	**Years produced:**	1979–1981
Min./max. draft:	2' 5"/4' 11"	**Sail area:**	249 sq. ft.
Bridge clearance:	33' 6"	**Fuel tankage:**	portable
Power:	outboard 3 to 6 hp	**Water tankage:**	12 gal.
B/D ratio:	43%	**Approx. trailering wgt.:**	5,400 lbs.

This is an unusual fiberglass boat, partly because her hull is lapstraked (that is, simulated overlapping planks are molded right into the hull), and partly because she has one of the tallest rigs (33' 6" bridge clearance) of all the 23-footers in this guide. (The Pearson 23 Cat is an exception.) The M23 was available either factory-finished or sold without the usual fiberglass interior liner for finishing by owner. If you're buying one of these boats used, check the finish to see if it is up to the factory standard (which was fairly high), or was homebuilt. In recent years a "new"

Montgomery 23 has been introduced by a company on the West Coast formed by Bob Eeg, formerly of Nor'Sea Yachts, but the new design is quite different from that of the model reported here. The new version, called the "Montgomery 23 Offshore Cutter," has a longer waterline of 22 feet, a heavier displacement of 4,600 pounds, an inboard 10 hp diesel as standard, bridge clearance of only 31 feet, and a different cabinhouse design. ***Best features:*** The boat looks admirably "shippy." ***Worst features:*** Her trailering weight of 5,400 pounds means a hefty truck is needed to tow her.

Comps	LOD	Beam	MinDr	Displ	Bllst	SA/D	D/L	Avg. PHRF	Max. Speed	Motion Index	Space Index	No. of Berths	Head-room
Bayfield 23	23' 0"	8' 0"	2' 11"	3,500	1,300	16.7	205	270	5.9	15.8	400	4	5' 9"
Morgan 22 (23)	22' 10"	8' 0"	1' 10"	3,500	1,400	16.5	186	249	6.0	15.5	347	4	4' 6"
Montgomery 23	22' 7"	8' 0"	2' 5"	3,600	1,530	17.0	178	234	6.1	16.1	378	4	5' 4"

Morgan 22 (23)
The smallest Charlie Morgan cruiser/racer

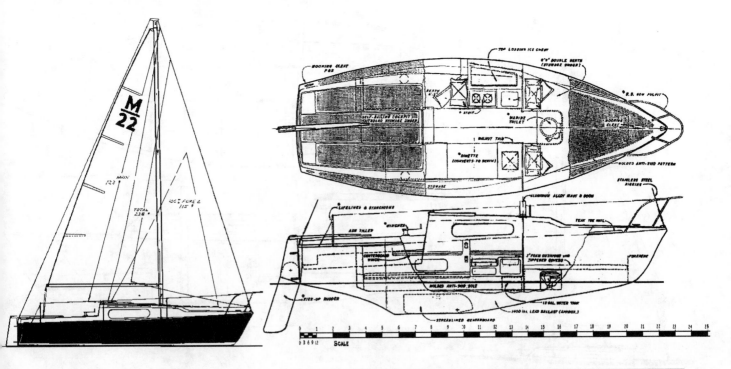

LOD:	22' 10"
LOA:	24' 10"
LWL:	20' 4"
Min./max. draft:	1' 10"/4' 11"
Bridge clearance:	30' 2"
Power:	outboard 3 to 6 hp
B/D ratio:	40%

Designer:	Charlie Morgan
Builder:	Morgan Yacht Corp.
Years produced:	1968–1976
Sail area:	238 sq. ft.
Fuel tankage:	portable
Water tankage:	portable
Approx. trailering wgt.:	5,300 lbs.

Our method of grouping comparable boats sometimes makes for strange bedfellows. That's the case here, where despite close similarities in LOD, beam, displacement, and ballast, the three "comp" boats are clearly different in appearance and in performance as well. The Morgan 22, Charlie Morgan's smallest racer-cruiser, compared to her comps is no match for space below, but on the other hand, we think she would be the clear winner in a round-the-buoys race against both the Bayfield and the Montgomery, despite the Montgomery's 15-seconds-per-mile lower PHRF rating. (Sometimes the ratings just don't seem fair.) **Best features:** She is fast, weatherly, and easy to handle—three good reasons for new sailors to choose her as their first cruising boat. Her two-person dinette with removable table that converts the dinette into a berth is comfortable and useful as a chart table. **Worst features:** Her centerboard control pendant is a Rube Goldberg affair, which needs periodic inspection and—almost always—eventual replacement.

Comps	LOD	Beam	MinDr	Displ	Bllst	SA/D	D/L	Avg. PHRF	Max. Speed	Motion Index	Space Index	No. of Berths	Head-room
Bayfield 23	23' 0"	8' 0"	2' 11"	3,500	1,300	16.7	205	270	5.9	15.8	400	4	5' 9"
Morgan 22 (23)	22' 10"	8' 0"	1' 10"	3,500	1,400	16.5	186	249	6.0	15.5	347	4	4' 6"
Montgomery 23	22' 7"	8' 0"	2' 5"	3,600	1,530	17.0	178	234	6.1	16.1	378	4	5' 4"

O'Day 23 Mk I
The whole cabin pops up on one version of this

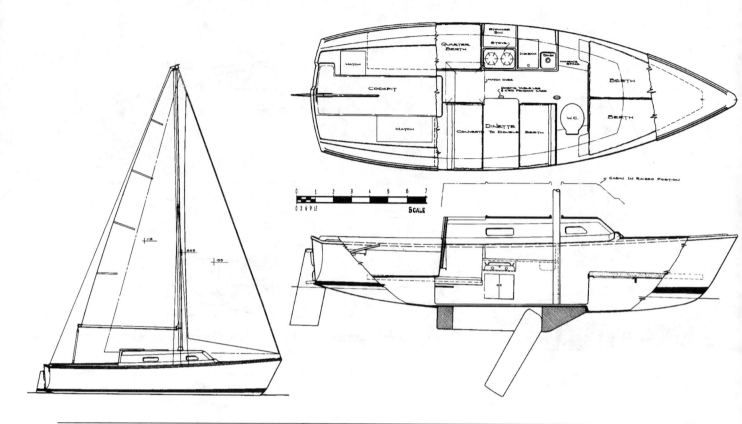

LOD:	23' 1"	**Designer:**	C. Raymond Hunt Assoc.	
LOA:	24' 1"	**Builder:**	O'Day Corp.	
LWL:	20' 0"	**Years produced:**	1970–1974	
Min./max. draft:	2' 0"/5' 5"	**Sail area:**	245 sq. ft.	
Bridge clearance:	31' 6"	**Fuel tankage:**	portable	
Power:	outboard 3 to 6 hp	**Water tankage:**	portable	
B/D ratio:	40%	**Approx. trailering wgt.:**	4,700 lbs.	

This vessel was produced in several versions—two types of poptops and a solid top—over five years, 1970 to 1974. A Mk II version (page 186) with no poptop (and other differences) followed in 1977. In the Mk I version, one of the poptop designs was a "convertible," that is, the whole cabin trunk roof lifted on struts (see phantom view). However, there were problems with sealing out rain and spray in the joint between cabin trunk and deck, and the through-the-deck mast. Consequently, the design was dropped in favor of an alternative poptop in which only the aft section lifted. This allowed the mast to be stepped in a tabernacle on the cabintop, making mast setup at a launching ramp much easier. ***Best features:*** Compared to her comps, the O'Day is in the middle on most dimensional parameters—not a bad place to be. The dinette layout conforms to the tastes of many 1970s sailors. ***Worst features:*** No significant negative features were noted by us, other than the "convertible" poptop idea.

Comps	LOD	Beam	MinDr	Displ	Bllst	SA/D	D/L	Avg. PHRF	Max. Speed	Motion Index	Space Index	No. of Berths	Head-room
O'Day 23 Mk I	23' 1"	7' 11"	2' 0"	3,100	1,250	18.4	173	234	6.0	14.3	418	5	4' 7"
Grampian 23	23' 3"	8' 0"	2' 4"	3,200	1,150	18.0	156	270	6.1	14.0	395	5	5' 4"
Ericson 23	22' 11"	7' 11"	3' 8"	3,200	1,250	19.5	193	see text	5.9	15.1	309	4	4' 3"

O'Day 240 (23)
One of O'Day's last commercial designs

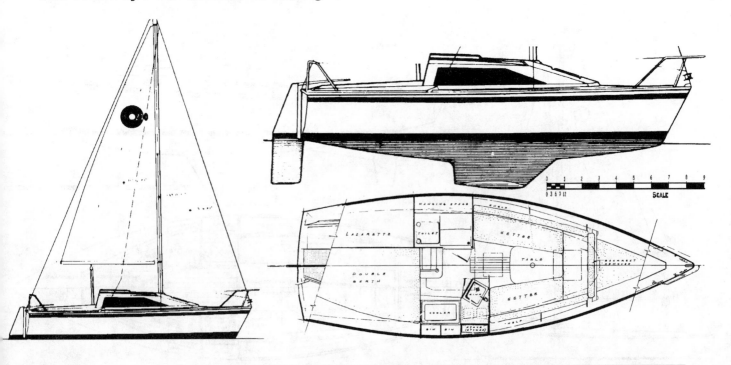

LOD:	22' 6"		**Designer:**	C. Raymond Hunt Assoc.
LOA:	24' 7"		**Builder:**	O'Day Corp.
LWL:	20' 11"		**Years produced:**	1988–1989
Min./max. draft:	2' 8"		**Sail area:**	249 sq. ft.
Bridge clearance:	32' 6"		**Fuel tankage:**	portable
Power:	outboard 3 to 6 hp		**Water tankage:**	12 gal.
B/D ratio:	33%		**Approx. trailering wgt.:**	5,400 lbs.

Every year *Sailing World* magazine runs a Boat of the Year contest in which they pick a new sailboat from each of several categories. In the quarter century since the contest began only five monohull sailboats of the type in this book—under 26 feet and with cruising accommodations—have been selected as winners. The O'Day 240 shown here was the 1989 winner—the same year that O'Day, to the regret of many, ended their long participation in the sailboat market. Among the judges' comments: the 240's heavy weight and her long waterline for her size will give her "punch and range that's often lacking in weekender/cruisers." They also liked her enclosed head, large cockpit locker, and working galley, admired her sleek look, and felt sail and engine controls were within easy reach. ***Best features:*** We second the Sailing World comments. We also note that compared to her comps, the 240 has the most headroom and the largest Space Index. Also, the boat's winged keel affords shallow draft for gunkholing while giving sailing performance in the same general range as a deeper fin. ***Worst features:*** Compared to her comps, the 240 has the lowest Motion Index.

Comps	LOD	Beam	MinDr	Displ	Bllst	SA/D	D/L	Avg. PHRF	Max. Speed	Motion Index	Space Index	No. of Berths	Head-room
Sovereign Antares (23)	23' 0"	8' 0"	2' 7"	3,000	1,200	16.3	254	252	5.8	17.0	389	4	5' 4"
Irwin 23	23' 0"	8' 0"	2' 5"	3,200	1,500	18.8	226	252	5.8	15.5	334	4	4' 9"
Sovereign 23	23' 0"	8' 0"	2' 4"	3,250	1,350	17.5	229	252	5.8	15.6	435	4	5' 7"
O'Day 240 (23)	22' 6"	8' 3"	2' 8"	3,600	1,200	17.0	178	231	6.1	15.2	438	4	5' 9"

O'Day Tempest 23
Overnighter by Philip L. Rhodes

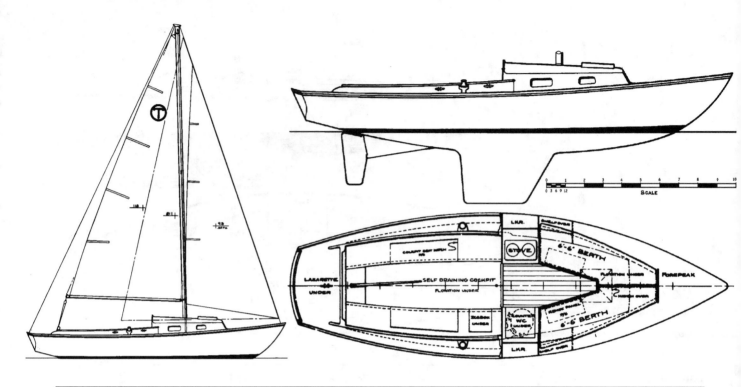

LOD:	23' 2"	**Designer:**	Philip L. Rhodes
LOA:	23' 2"	**Builder:**	O'Day Corp.
LWL:	17' 0"	**Years produced:**	1964–1973
Min./max. draft:	3' 9"	**Sail area:**	211 sq. ft.
Bridge clearance:	29' 0"	**Fuel tankage:**	portable
Power:	outboard 4 to 6 hp	**Water tankage:**	portable
B/D ratio:	42%	**Approx. trailering wgt.:**	4,600 lbs.

The O'Day Tempest 23 (not to be confused with the similarly named O'Day International Tempest, an open-cockpit racing machine) is a classic, attractive, and wholesome design for basic overnight cruising. ***Best features:*** Relatively long overhangs and low freeboard give this boat a sleek, graceful look typical of Philip Rhodes' designs. Flotation under cockpit sole and V-berth is a good safety feature. Her broader beam and deeper draft compared to the Cape Cod Marlin (page 223), a comp, help to make her more weatherly and stiff, despite the

Marlin's heavier but closer-to-the-surface ballast. On the other hand, the two Pearson comps surpass the Tempest in weatherliness and stiffness for the same reasons. ***Worst features:*** Her keel is iron rather than lead, requiring diligent maintenance to prevent deterioration from rust. Lack of a good place to put a portable cooler keeps her from qualifying as more than a basic overnighter, and overall space below is less than all her comps, partly due to her reduced headroom. She is known to sail slower than her PHRF rating.

Comps	LOD	Beam	MinDr	Displ	Bllst	SA/D	D/L	Avg. PHRF	Max. Speed	Motion Index	Space Index	No. of Berths	Head-room
Pearson 23 Sloop	23' 0"	8' 0"	2' 4"	3,000	1,200	16.2	167	240	6.0	13.8	375	2	4' 8"
Pearson 23 Cat	23' 0"	8' 0"	4' 0"	3,000	1,200	16.2	167	240	6.0	13.8	375	2	4' 8"
O'Day Tempest 23	23' 2"	7' 8"	3' 9"	3,000	1,250	16.2	273	252	5.5	16.2	258	2	4' 0"
Cape Cod Marlin 23	23' 0"	7' 2"	3' 3"	3,200	1,400	18.3	295	264	5.5	19.0	288	2	4' 6"

Pearson 23 Cat

Bill Shaw fat cat

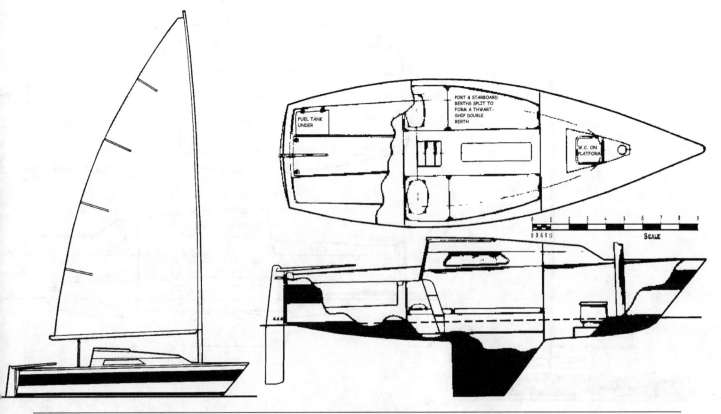

LOD:	23' 0"		**Designer:**	Bill Shaw
LOA:	23' 10"		**Builder:**	Pearson Yachts
LWL:	20' 0"		**Years produced:**	1983–1985
Min./max. draft:	4' 0"		**Sail area:**	210 sq. ft.
Bridge clearance:	36' 6"		**Fuel tankage:**	portable
Power:	outboard 3 to 6 hp		**Water tankage:**	portable
B/D ratio:	40%		**Approx. trailering wgt.:**	4,600 lbs.

This boat is one of Bill Shaw's few catboat designs. In a way it is a daring flight of fancy for Shaw, who was generally quite conservative in his designs. Not much was at risk, however, if the cat proved to not be very popular (which it wasn't; only 42 were built), since virtually the same molds and tooling were used to build the Pearson 23 sloop version (page 244). The Pearson sloop is a comp to the Pearson cat. The cat came with either a fin keel with external lead ballast, or a keel-centerboard combination (as did the sloop version on the next page). She also had an unstayed, spun-tapered aluminum mast with external sail track and stops. **Best features:** Part of the idea for the cat rig was its innate simplicity: only one sail to trim, and the ability to tack without adjusting any lines. One owner says, "It's hard to imagine a better singlehander's boat." **Worst features:** Some owners found the boom topping lift a nuisance to operate because of the pronounced roach in the mainsail, and replaced the lift with a rigid vang. The $7/8$" sailtrack tends to stick; some owners have tried Battcars, others installed something called Strongtrack, which slides over the existing track.

Comps	LOD	Beam	MinDr	Displ	Bllst	SA/D	D/L	Avg. PHRF	Max. Speed	Motion Index	Space Index	No. of Berths	Head-room
Pearson 23 Sloop	23' 0"	8' 0"	2' 4"	3,000	1,200	16.2	167	240	6.0	13.8	375	2	4' 8"
Pearson 23 Cat	23' 0"	8' 0"	4' 0"	3,000	1,200	16.2	167	240	6.0	13.8	375	2	4' 8"
O'Day Tempest 23	23' 2"	7' 8"	3' 9"	3,000	1,250	16.2	273	252	5.5	16.2	258	2	4' 0"
Cape Cod Marlin 23	23' 0"	7' 2"	3' 3"	3,200	1,400	18.3	295	264	5.5	19.0	288	2	4' 6"

Pearson 23 Sloop
Mate to the Pearson 23 Cat

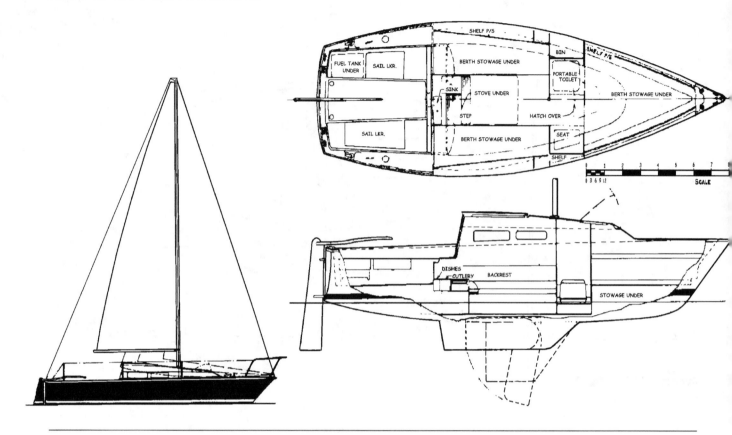

LOD:	23' 0"	**Designer:**	Bill Shaw
LOA:	23' 10"	**Builder:**	Pearson Yachts
LWL:	20' 0"	**Years produced:**	1983–1985
Min./max. draft:	2' 4"/5' 2" or 4' 0"	**Sail area:**	229 sq. ft.
Bridge clearance:	31' 0"	**Fuel tankage:**	portable
Power:	outboard 3 to 6 hp	**Water tankage:**	5 gal.
B/D ratio:	40%	**Approx. trailering wgt.:**	4,600 lbs.

This boat is the sloop version of the Pearson 23 catboat (page 243). Both versions used virtually the same hull molds and tooling, so we are including the Pearson cat as a comp to the Pearson sloop. The sloop came with either a fin keel with external lead ballast, or a keel-centerboard combination, as did the cat. (Both configurations are shown in phantom view in the profile drawing.) However, the sloop has a shorter mast (31 feet off the water instead of 36½ feet for the cat), about 10% more sail area (229 sq. ft. vs. 210 for the cat), and includes the performance benefits contributed by the slot effect inherent in the sloop and missing in the cat configuration. *Best features:* Quality construction and a wholesome design make her a good starter sailboat for cruising. *Worst features:* Not the easiest boat to launch from a trailer, whether fin-keeler or centerboarder.

Comps	LOD	Beam	MinDr	Displ	Bllst	SA/D	D/L	Avg. PHRF	Max. Speed	Motion Index	Space Index	No. of Berths	Head-room
Pearson 23 Sloop	23' 0"	8' 0"	2' 4"	3,000	1,200	16.2	167	240	6.0	13.8	375	2	4' 8"
Pearson 23 Cat	23' 0"	8' 0"	4' 0"	3,000	1,200	16.2	167	240	6.0	13.8	375	2	4' 8"
O'Day Tempest 23	23' 2"	7' 8"	3' 9"	3,000	1,250	16.2	273	252	5.5	16.2	258	2	4' 0"
Cape Cod Marlin 23	23' 0"	7' 2"	3' 3"	3,200	1,400	18.3	295	264	5.5	19.0	288	2	4' 6"

Precision 23
Wholesome traditional small cruiser

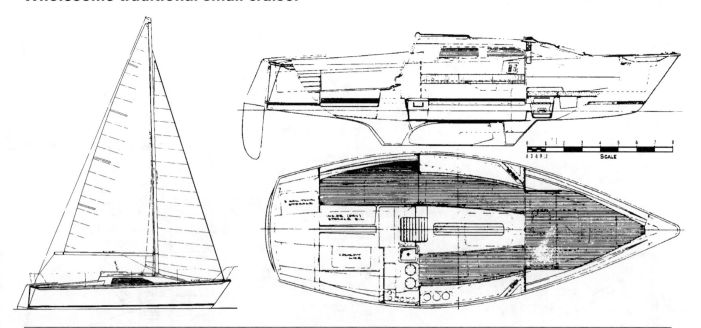

LOD:	23' 5"	**Designer:**	Jim Taylor
LOA:	24' 3"	**Builder:**	Precision Boatworks
LWL:	20' 0"	**Years produced:**	1985–present
Min./max. draft:	1' 11"/5' 4"	**Sail area:**	248 sq. ft.
Bridge clearance:	33' 4"	**Fuel tankage:**	portable
Power:	outboard 3 to 6 hp	**Water tankage:**	5 gal.
B/D ratio:	35%	**Approx. trailering wgt.:**	3,600 lbs.

Designer Jim Taylor says of the Precision 23, "Considered to be a maxi-trailerable, the Precision 23 far outstrips many boats in terms of true usable space, both on deck and below. Special emphasis has gone into giving the P23 her particularly bright and uncluttered interior. The bulkheads are intentionally trimmed back to avoid subdividing the visual space. Of special note, the typical intrusive mast compression support post has been eliminated by clever use of a rugged overhead support beam fiberglassed to the deck. The especially large companionway, multiple cabin ports and forward hatch contribute to the feeling of light and open space." In 1994, former Precision sales manager, the late Larry Norris, gave me his own description of the traditional, shoal-draft Precision 23 when I was writing a

review of the boat for *Practical Sailor*. He said that "the 23 has never been anything it wasn't originally intended to be: a trailerable sailboat of better than average cruising performance, but never a racing machine. It's too full forward and cut away aft to achieve really staggering downwind performance. But on the other hand, the boat will stay balanced in a blow with just a couple of fingers on the tiller." Our tests at the time bore out his assertions. **Best features:** Attractive traditional design, solid construction, adequately stable and weatherly, open and airy cabin with better-than-average space (note high Space Index below), good and caring customer service, and a well-satisfied and loyal owner group. **Worst features:** Nothing significant to report.

Comps	LOD	Beam	MinDr	Displ	Bllst	SA/D	D/L	Avg. PHRF	Max. Speed	Motion Index	Space Index	No. of Berths	Head-room
Blazer 23	22' 6"	7' 10"	3' 11"	2,200	900	25.5	143	180	5.8	10.7	291	4	3' 8"
Aquarius/Balboa 23	22' 8"	7' 11"	1' 1"	2,280	815	19.7	107	282	6.2	10.3	416	5	4' 11"
Hunter 23	22' 9"	8' 0"	2' 3"	2,450	800	20.7	146	237	5.9	11.4	359	4	4' 7"
Precision 23	23' 5"	8' 6"	1' 11"	2,450	850	21.8	137	228	6.0	10.3	464	4	4' 6"
Paceship PY23 (22)	21' 7"	8' 0"	1' 9"	2,460	945	19.6	151	240	5.9	11.6	348	4	4' 6"

Rob Roy 23
A pretty little Brewer character yawl

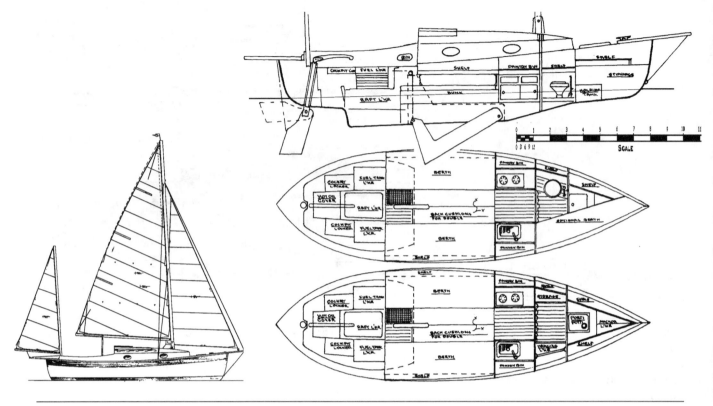

LOD:	22' 8"		**Designer:**	Ted Brewer
LOA:	27' 2"		**Builder:**	Marine Concepts
LWL:	21' 0"		**Years produced:**	1983–2000
Min./max. draft:	1' 7"/4' 8"		**Sail area:**	257 sq. ft.
Bridge clearance:	29' 6"		**Fuel tankage:**	portable
Power:	outboard 3 to 6 hp		**Water tankage:**	14 gal.
B/D ratio:	32%		**Approx. trailering wgt.:**	4,200 lbs.

There's nothing like a yawl rig to give character to a small sailboat. Add a canoe stern, comfortable accommodations for two (or three if you opt for a single berth forward squeezed in next to the head), reasonably good construction and finishing, and you have the makings of a classic small yacht. Ted Brewer, whose life has been spent designing comfortable cruising boats, has succeeded here in his efforts to create just such a boat; and Marine Concepts, which left the business in 2006, did a good job of building her. Rob Roy had a relatively long production run, from

1983 to 2000, with a hiatus from 1994 to 1997. ***Best features:*** She's a salty-looking boat, with practical features such as a tabernacle for the main mast, an unstayed mizzen, an L-shaped centerboard that frees up cabin space by keeping the board trunk small and out of the way, and an in-cockpit engine well. And of course, as a yawl she has the advantage of easily shortening sail when it comes on to blow. ***Worst features:*** She is not very fast or weatherly versus her comps, partly a result of her divided rig and oddly shaped centerboard, though she does fine on a reach.

Comps	LOD	Beam	MinDr	Displ	Bllst	SA/D	D/L	Avg. PHRF	Max. Speed	Motion Index	Space Index	No. of Berths	Head-room
N.A. 23/Spirit 23 (22)	22' 2"	7' 11"	2' 0"	2,800	835	17.3	156	240	6.0	12.7	391	4	4' 10"
Rob Roy 23	22' 8"	6' 11"	1' 7"	2,800	900	20.7	135	201	6.1	14.3	228	2 or 3	4' 0"
Jeanneau Tonic 23 (22)	22' 5"	8' 2"	2' 3"	2,945	1,086	18.9	156	225	6.0	12.9	429	4	5' 7"
Hunter 23.5 (22)	21' 8"	8' 4"	1' 6"	3,000	1,000	18.2	136	240	6.2	12.3	471	6	4' 6"

San Juan 23

A sailboat made in Auburn, Washington

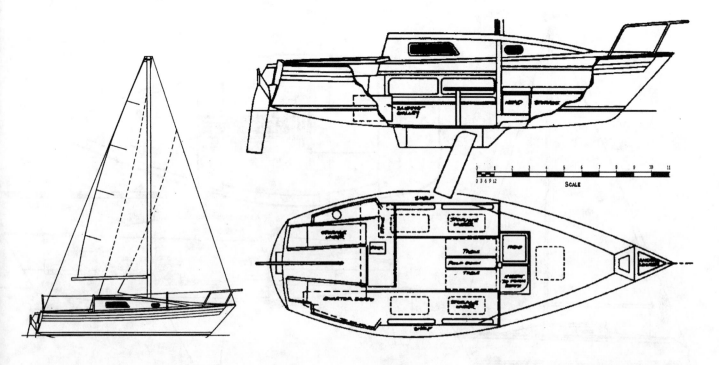

LOD:	22' 7"	**Designer:**	Don Clark
LOA:	24' 4"	**Builder:**	Clark Boat Company
LWL:	19' 3"	**Years produced:**	1976–1989
Min./max. draft:	1' 1"/4' 9"	**Sail area:**	238 sq. ft.
Bridge clearance:	31' 6"	**Fuel tankage:**	portable
Power:	outboard 3 to 6 hp	**Water tankage:**	9 gal.
B/D ratio:	36%	**Approx. trailering wgt.:**	4,000 lbs.

Don Clark, a small boat racing enthusiast with a family boatbuilding facility in Auburn, WA, designed the San Juan 23 and built her from 1976 until 1984, when the company closed its doors. In 1985 a different firm, San Juan Sailboats, acquired the molds and continued making the boats until about 1989. Two versions were made, the keel-centerboard design shown here, and a fin keel version with 4-foot draft, heavier displacement (1,100 pounds ballast, 3,000 pounds displacement) and slightly more sail area (256 sq. ft. versus 238 in the centerboard version). The centerboard version was introduced in 1976 and the keel version came a year later. More than 600 boats were built over the years. ***Best features:*** The layout below purportedly will sleep five, but the long, 11-foot berth to starboard wouldn't be comfortable for two six-footers. However, for extra-tall sailors, that berth is perfect. ***Worst features:*** Control of hull weight at the factory evidently was not a priority. Reportedly some boats weighed 1,000 pounds over the claimed weight of 3,000 pounds. Shoppers for used boats who plan to race might weigh before buying; the lighter boats are faster.

Comps	LOD	Beam	MinDr	Displ	Bllst	SA/D	D/L	Avg. PHRF	Max. Speed	Motion Index	Space Index	No. of Berths	Head-room
Santana Wavelength 24 (23)	22' 7"	9' 0"	4' 6"	2,500	1,100	25.0	133	162	6.0	9.6	400	4	4' 3"
Santana 23	22' 7"	8' 10"	0' 10"	2,600	1,130	24.0	132	171	6.1	10.2	427	4	4' 4"
San Juan 23	22' 7"	8' 0"	1' 1"	2,700	960	19.6	169	234	5.9	12.5	393	5	5' 0"
Gloucester 23/LN 23	22' 11"	8' 0"	1' 11"	2,700	1,000	19.4	151	270	6.0	12.4	411	4	5' 0"

Santana 23

Another racer-cruiser from the Schock stable

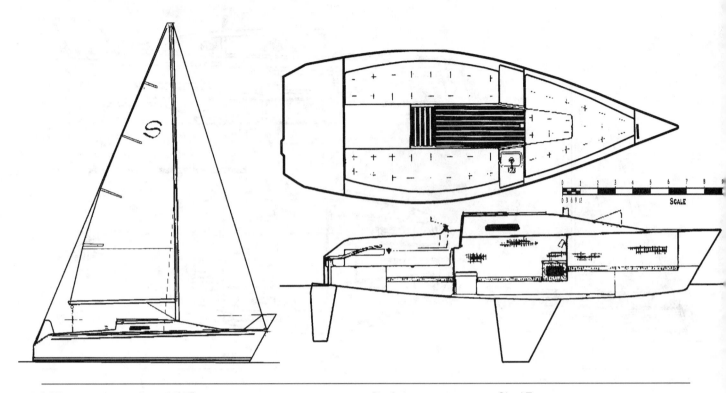

LOD:	22' 7"	**Designer:**	Shad Turner
LOA:	23' 4"	**Builder:**	W. D. Schock
LWL:	20' 7"	**Years produced:**	1978–1987
Min./max. draft:	(D) 0' 10"/5' 3"	**Sail area:**	284 sq. ft. (D), 273 sq. ft. (K)
Bridge clearance:	31' 6"	**Fuel tankage:**	portable
Power:	outboard 3 to 6 hp	**Water tankage:**	portable
B/D ratio:	43%	**Approx. trailering wgt.:**	3,900 lbs.

W. D. Schock, the Southern California sailboat builder, started building an International 14 racer right after World War II and never looked back. Over the years this family-run company introduced so many Santana-branded boats and Schock-branded boats that it can be easy for a casual observer to get confused. Even the Santana 23 (not to be confused with the Santana 22 or the Santana 25 reported elsewhere in this book) comes in two versions: the 23D (for daggerboard) with a vertically lifting keel and lifting outboard rudder, built from 1978 to 1984, and the 23K (for fixed keel)

pictured here, built from 1984 to 1987. A total of 144 of the former and 50 of the latter were built. ***Best features:*** A comparison of statistics with her comp, the San Juan 23, shows that the Santana 23 (either the K or D version), despite similar ballast and displacement figures, is (like the Wavelength 24) more of a serious racing boat. The Santana's PHRF, for example, is 63 seconds-per-mile faster than the San Juan 23. She also has the highest Space Index. ***Worst features:*** The hull is built light (weight excluding ballast is under 1,500 pounds), so you need to be careful to avoid damage.

Comps	LOD	Beam	MinDr	Displ	Bllst	SA/D	D/L	Avg. PHRF	Max. Speed	Motion Index	Space Index	No. of Berths	Head- room
Santana Wavelength 24 (23)	22' 7"	9' 0"	4' 6"	2,500	1,100	25.0	133	162	6.0	9.6	400	4	4' 3"
Santana 23	22' 7"	8' 10"	0' 10"	2,600	1,130	24.0	132	171	6.1	10.2	427	4	4' 4"
San Juan 23	22' 7"	8' 0"	1' 1"	2,700	960	19.6	169	234	5.9	12.5	393	5	5' 0"

Santana Wavelength 24 (23)
A Lindenberg design similar to the Santana 23

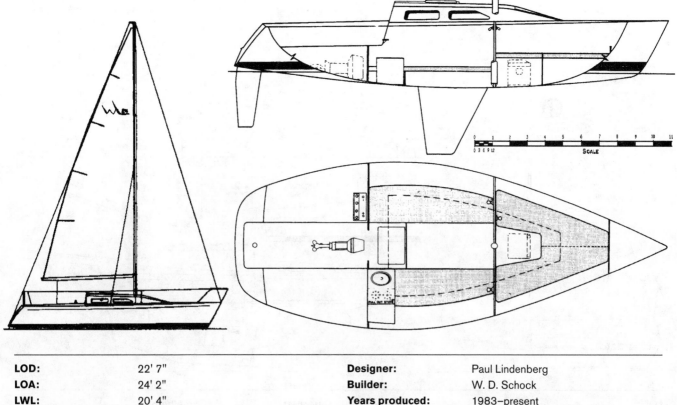

LOD:	22' 7"		**Designer:**	Paul Lindenberg
LOA:	24' 2"		**Builder:**	W. D. Schock
LWL:	20' 4"		**Years produced:**	1983–present
Min./max. draft:	4' 6"		**Sail area:**	288 sq. ft.
Bridge clearance:	34' 6"		**Fuel tankage:**	portable
Power:	outboard 3 to 6 hp		**Water tankage:**	portable
B/D ratio:	44%		**Approx. trailering wgt.:**	3,600 lbs.

Paul Lindenberg, a designer who specializes in lightweight racing sailboats, drew this vessel for W. D. Schock, and she was built from 1983 to 1992, and then recently reintroduced as a newly remodeled version. The new version has hammock-style bunks amidships which are lightweight, provide good support and comfort when racing, and give excellent access to the storage space under them. The boat appears to be remarkably similar to the Santana 23, a Shad Turner design for Schock, built from 1978 to 1987, which we have chosen as a comp. The Wavelength comes with either a winged or standard fin keel, and looks like she should go fast with either keel setup. **Best features:** An open transom, similar to the Santana 23's, provides good access to an outboard engine, and ensures adequate drainage of water slopping onto the cockpit sole. **Worst features:** If we were in the market for a racing boat of this size and were tempted by the Wavelength, we might opt instead for the near clone, the Santana 23D because of its extra nine inches of headroom, and its lifting keel, which makes launching from a trailer infinitely easier than dealing with a fin keel at the ramp.

Comps	LOD	Beam	MinDr	Displ	Bllst	SA/D	D/L	Avg. PHRF	Max. Speed	Motion Index	Space Index	No. of Berths	Head-room
Santana Wavelength 24 (23)	22' 7"	9' 0"	4' 6"	2,500	1,100	25.0	133	162	6.0	9.6	400	4	4' 3"
Santana 23	22' 7"	8' 10"	0' 10"	2,600	1,130	24.0	132	171	6.1	10.2	427	4	4' 4"
San Juan 23	22' 7"	8' 0"	1' 1"	2,700	960	19.6	169	234	5.9	12.5	393	5	5' 0"

Sea Sprite 22 (23)
Long-running design by Carl Alberg

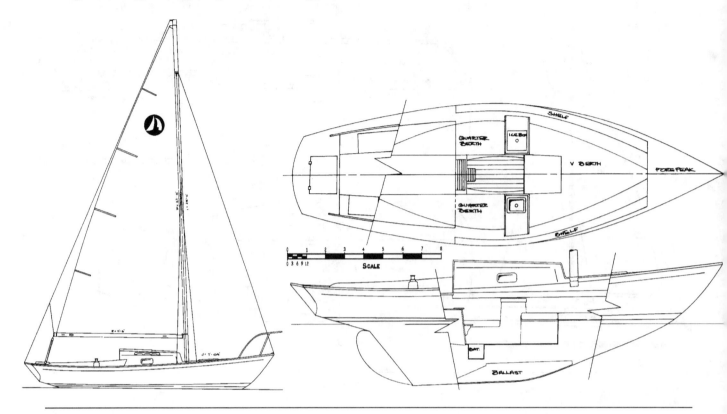

LOD:	22' 6"		**Designer:**	Carl Alberg
LOA:	22' 6"		**Builder:**	Sailstar, Ryder, et al.
LWL:	16' 3"		**Years produced:**	1958–1986
Min./max. draft:	3' 0"		**Sail area:**	247 sq. ft.
Bridge clearance:	32' 3"		**Fuel tankage:**	8 gal. (dsl., optional)
Power:	outboard or dsl. 7.5 hp		**Water tankage:**	9.5 gal.
B/D ratio:	44%		**Approx. trailering wgt.:**	4,900 lbs.

Carl Alberg designed many sailboats in the 22-foot and 23-foot size range, all of which looked similar. The Sea Sprite was one of the first, and is distinguished from the others (such as the South Coast 23, reported on page 255) by her relatively low silhouette and fractional rig. She was produced for 28 years by various builders, all of whom had their shops in Rhode Island and all of whom, to our knowledge, have since ceased building boats. These included American Boatbuilding, Wickford Shipyard, Sailstar, and C. E. Ryder Corp. A daysailer model with smaller cabin and longer cockpit was also offered by Sailstar. **Best features:** Depending on the builder, different features are offered. For example, Sailstar featured an outboard well in the open, giving better ventilation than Ryder's, which was hidden under a lazarette hatch. Ryder also encapsulated the lead ballast, whereas previous builders had used external, bolted on cast lead ballast. **Worst features:** The somewhat shallow draft of three feet detracts a bit from upwind performance, although reaching and running is unaffected.

Comps	LOD	Beam	MinDr	Displ	Bllst	SA/D	D/L	Avg. PHRF	Max. Speed	Motion Index	Space Index	No. of Berths	Head-room
Sea Sprite 22 (23)	22' 6"	7' 0"	3' 0"	3,350	1,475	17.6	349	264	5.4	21.3	257	4	4' 2"
Seafarer Kestrel Cruiser	23' 1"	7' 2"	2' 4"	3,700	1,400	15.7	351	270	5.5	22.1	319	4	4' 9"
Seafarer Kestrel Overnighter	23' 1"	7' 2"	2' 4"	3,700	1,400	15.7	351	270	5.5	22.1	319	2 or 4	4' 9"
South Coast 23	23' 0"	7' 3"	2' 10"	3,700	1,475	16.5	308	270	5.6	21.2	311	4	4' 5"

Seafarer Kestrel 23 Cruiser

A small S&S design for the traditional yachtsman

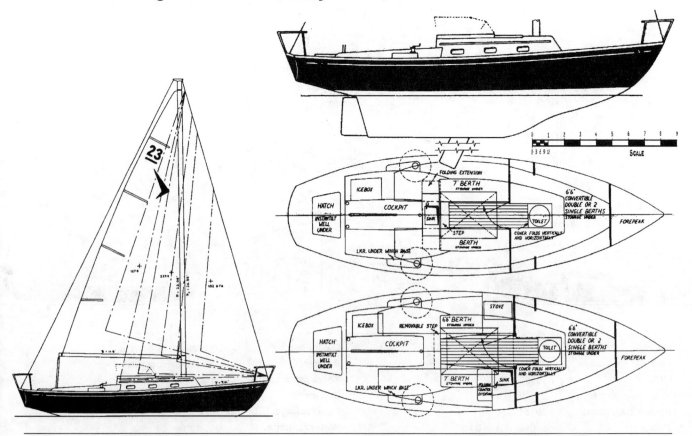

LOD:	23' 1"
LOA:	23' 1"
LWL:	16' 9"
Min./max. draft:	2' 4"/5' 0"
Bridge clearance:	29' 8"
Power:	outboard 3 to 6 hp
B/D ratio:	38%

Designer:	Sparkman & Stephens
Builder:	Seafarer Fiberglass Yachts
Years produced:	1967–1985
Sail area:	235 sq. ft.
Fuel tankage:	portable
Water tankage:	portable
Approx. trailering wgt.:	5,500 lbs.

The Seafarer Kestrel started out in 1967 with slightly smaller dimensions than those shown here: seven inches less LOD, three inches more LWL, one inch less beam, same minimum draft but a foot less draft with board down, seven square feet less sail area, 200 pounds less displacement, and 100 pounds less ballast—but with the same outward appearance. She was built first in Holland and imported, and later built at the Seafarer plant in Huntington, NY, in a building converted from an old supermarket. The Kestrel

was available in three different deck configurations and six accommodations plans, all using the same hull and rig. The cruiser layouts and profile are shown on this page, and the overnighter layouts and profile appear on the next page. **Best features:** We think the classic Sparkman & Stephens hull form is very striking. **Worst features:** Although the Dutch craftsmanship evident in the early hulls was top of the line, quality of the U.S.-built boats gradually eroded and cheapened over the years. Seafarer closed its doors in 1985.

Comps	LOD	Beam	MinDr	Displ	Bllst	SA/D	D/L	Avg. PHRF	Max. Speed	Motion Index	Space Index	No. of Berths	Head-room
Sea Sprite 22 (23)	22' 6"	7' 0"	3' 0"	3,350	1,475	17.6	349	264	5.4	21.3	257	4	4' 2"
Seafarer Kestrel 23 Cruiser	23' 1"	7' 2"	2' 4"	3,700	1,400	15.7	351	270	5.5	22.1	319	4	4' 9"
Seafarer Kestrel 23 Overnighter	23' 1"	7' 2"	2' 4"	3,700	1,400	15.7	351	270	5.5	22.1	319	2	4' 9"
South Coast 23	23' 0"	7' 3"	2' 10"	3,700	1,475	16.5	308	270	5.6	21.2	311	4	4' 5"

Seafarer Kestrel 23 Overnighter

. . . with the same hull as the Cruiser (previous page)

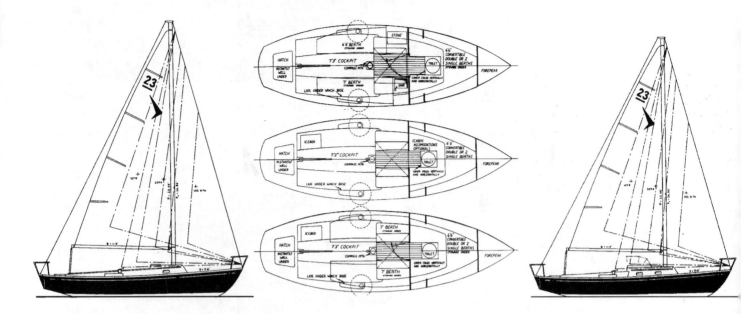

LOD:	23' 1"	**Designer:**	Sparkman & Stephens
LOA:	23' 1"	**Builder:**	Seafarer Fiberglass Yachts
LWL:	16' 9"	**Years produced:**	1967–1985
Min./max. draft:	2' 4"/5' 0"	**Sail area:**	235 sq. ft.
Bridge clearance:	29' 8"	**Fuel tankage:**	portable
Power:	outboard 3 to 6 hp	**Water tankage:**	portable
B/D ratio:	38%	**Approx. trailering wgt.:**	5,500 lbs.

Note: see comments for the Cruiser model on previous page. The two sailplans have identical hulls and rigs, but offer different cabin roof lengths, number of ports, and cabin arrangements as shown. At first glance, all these accommodations plans may appear to be identical. However, the top and bottom plans have four berths while the middle plan has only forward berths. The top plan has 6' 6" quarter berths aft of a stove and sink, while the bottom plan's quarter berths are 6 inches longer, and an icebox graces its cockpit. The middle plan actually comprises two plans: the one shown, plus another one not shown,

designed for owner completion, with nothing at all down below. ***Best features:*** As with the cruiser, the grace of the classic Sparkman & Stephens hull form will appeal to traditional sailors. The lazarette hatch has an "instantilt well" under it, permitting an outboard to be tilted up out of the water to reduce drag while sailing. (However, this design requires a long hull cutout to accommodate the lower unit of the engine when tilted, which introduces a drag of its own.) ***Worst features:*** As with the cruiser, quality of workmanship, while excellent in early production, eroded over the years.

Comps	LOD	Beam	MinDr	Displ	Bllst	SA/D	D/L	Avg. PHRF	Max. Speed	Motion Index	Space Index	No. of Berths	Head-room
Sea Sprite 22 (23)	22' 6"	7' 0"	3' 0"	3,350	1,475	17.6	349	264	5.4	21.3	257	4	4' 2"
Seafarer Kestrel 23 Cruiser	23' 1"	7' 2"	2' 4"	3,700	1,400	15.7	351	270	5.5	22.1	319	4	4' 9"
Seafarer Kestrel 23 Overnighter	23' 1"	7' 2"	2' 4"	3,700	1,400	15.7	351	270	5.5	22.1	319	2 or 4	4' 9"
South Coast 23	23' 0"	7' 3"	2' 10"	3,700	1,475	16.5	308	270	5.6	21.2	311	4	4' 5"

Seafarer 24C (23)
Centerboard version of the Seafarer 24K

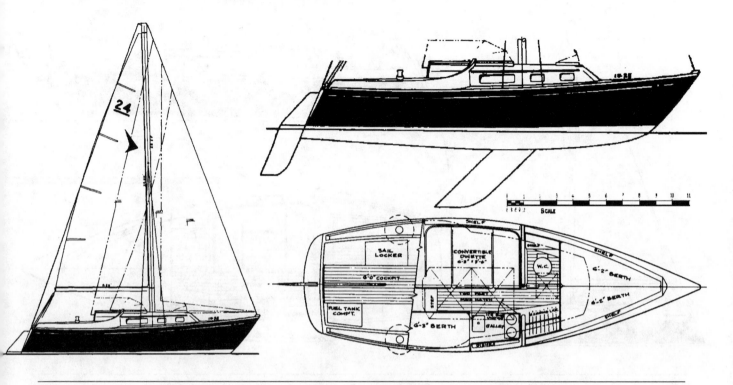

LOD:	22' 10"		**Designer:**	McCurdy & Rhodes
LOA:	26' 6"		**Builder:**	Seafarer Yachts
LWL:	20' 9"		**Years produced:**	1971–1976
Min./max. draft:	1' 9"/4' 6"		**Sail area:**	257 sq. ft.
Bridge clearance:	30' 5"		**Fuel tankage:**	portable
Power:	outboard 3 to 6 hp		**Water tankage:**	20 gal.
B/D ratio:	36%		**Approx. trailering wgt.:**	5,500 lbs.

As mentioned for her sistership, the Seafarer 24K (page 254), there are several versions of this design, including at least three different cabin layouts and two deck plans. See the latter vessel's page for details. Over the years the dimensions and weights of both keel and centerboard versions changed somewhat, according to various company sales brochures. ***Best features:*** The main advantage of the centerboard model is her ability to venture into shallow water and to launch more easily from a trailer. ***Worst features:***

The centerboard version has virtually the same ballast and displacement as the fixed keel design, but with ballast weight centered higher up: the board has only 207 lbs. of lead, which makes her significantly more tender than the keel boat in heavy air. A Seafarer brochure mentions that this version "has positive self-righting ability regardless of centerboard position." Maybe so, but since 85 percent of the ballast is only a foot below the LWL, righting moment is minimal. We'd not venture far out in heavy air.

Comps	LOD	Beam	MinDr	Displ	Bllst	SA/D	D/L	Avg. PHRF	Max. Speed	Motion Index	Space Index	No. of Berths	Head-room
Cal 24-2	24' 0"	7' 9"	4' 0"	3,700	1,400	18.3	235	228	5.9	18.0	420	4	4' 0"
Lapworth 24	24' 0"	7' 6"	4' 0"	3,850	2,050	19.1	215	249	6.0	19.0	378	4	5' 0"
Gladiator 24	24' 0"	7' 6"	4' 0"	3,850	2,050	17.1	215	249	6.0	19.0	359	4	4' 9"
Seafarer 24K (23)	22' 10"	7' 10"	3' 9"	3,910	1,400	16.6	195	240	6.1	17.8	372	5	4' 9"
Seafarer 24C (23)	22' 10"	7' 10"	1' 9"	3,920	1,407	16.5	196	243	6.1	17.3	372	5	4' 9"

Seafarer 24K (23)

"Mix-and-Match" design from McCurdy & Rhodes

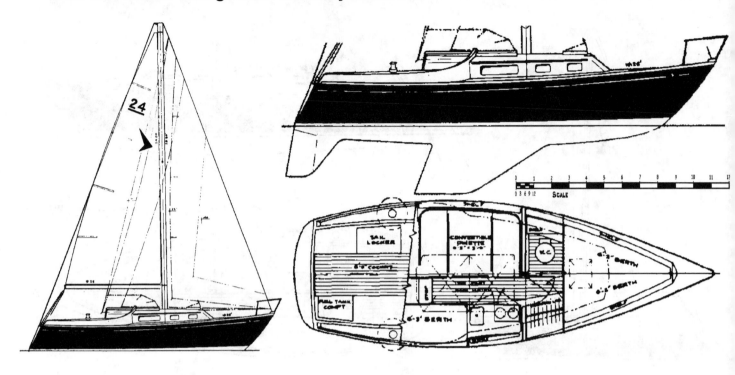

LOD:	22' 10"		**Designer:**	McCurdy & Rhodes
LOA:	24' 2"		**Builder:**	Seafarer Fiberglass Yachts
LWL:	20' 9"		**Years produced:**	1971–1976
Min./max. draft:	3' 9"		**Sail area:**	257 sq. ft.
Bridge clearance:	30' 5"		**Fuel tankage:**	portable
Power:	outboard 3 to 6 hp		**Water tankage:**	20 gal.
B/D ratio:	36%		**Approx. trailering wgt.:**	5,500 lbs.

There are several versions of this design, including at least three different cabin layouts and two deck plans. All choices could be mixed and matched. The version shown here has a fixed keel (3' 9" draft) and a traditional cabin house. An alternative is the Seafarer 24C, a centerboard version (page 253). An alternative to the cabin house (shown here) is the "Futura deck," in which the deck sweeps down towards the bow, giving (A) extra deck space forward and (B) 5' 10" headroom in the aft part of the cabin. Cabin layouts vary: a straight dinette (shown here) or a U-shaped dinette; more privacy in the head (with a door) or less; and other differences. Kits as well as finished boats were available. **Best features:** The companionway hatch is available in two locations rather than just one, to open up the interior. A dodger keeps the weather out. **Worst features:** The Futura deck is a little too rounded for secure footing when working on the foredeck in bumpy seas.

Comps	LOD	Beam	MinDr	Displ	Bllst	SA/D	D/L	Avg. PHRF	Max. Speed	Motion Index	Space Index	No. of Berths	Head-room
Cal 24-2	24' 0"	7' 9"	4' 0"	3,700	1,400	18.3	235	228	5.9	18.0	327	4	4' 0"
Lapworth 24	24' 0"	7' 6"	4' 0"	3,850	2,050	19.1	215	249	6.0	19.0	378	4	5' 0"
Gladiator 24	24' 0"	7' 6"	4' 0"	3,850	2,050	17.1	215	249	6.0	19.0	359	4	4' 9"
Seafarer 24K (23)	22' 10"	7' 10"	3' 9"	3,910	1,400	16.6	195	240	6.1	17.8	372	5	4' 9"
Seafarer 24C (23)	22' 10"	7' 10"	1' 9"	3,920	1,407	16.5	196	243	6.1	17.3	372	5	4' 9"

South Coast 23
The writer built one of these from a kit

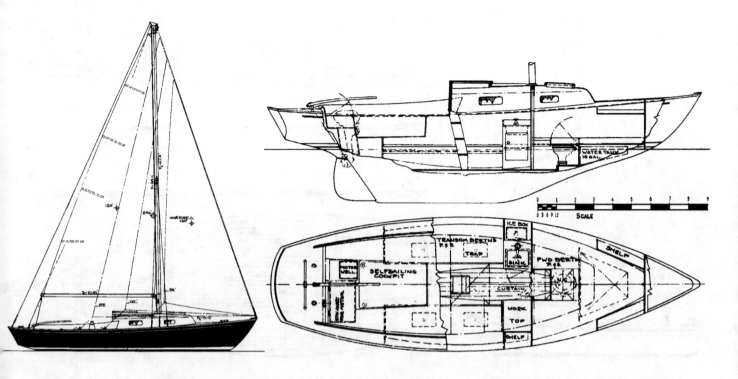

LOD:	23' 0"		**Designer:**	Carl Alberg
LOA:	23' 0"		**Builder:**	South Coast Seacraft
LWL:	17' 6"		**Years produced:**	1964–1973
Min./max. draft:	2' 10"		**Sail area:**	246 sq. ft.
Bridge clearance:	30' 9"		**Fuel tankage:**	portable
Power:	outboard 3 to 6 hp		**Water tankage:**	16 gal.
B/D ratio:	40%		**Approx. trailering wgt.:**	5,600 lbs.

Back in 1964, my wife and I bought a four-berth South Coast 23 kit boat, had it trucked from the factory in Shreveport, LA, to Darien, CT, and finished it off ourselves in nine months. My wife wrote up the story of how we did it for the January 1966 issue of *Yachting* magazine, and I wrote about converting our SC23 to a yawl in *Yachting*'s January 1971 issue, which was the start of my writing career. The boat made a reasonably good cruising vessel for a couple of relatively small stature. She was also available as a two-berth overnighter with a shorter cabin and as a four-berth model without the galley. **Best features:** Carl Alberg did a good job designing a graceful-looking hull with springy sheer and relatively low freeboard. A cockpit-mounted outboard motor well and a lazarette to store the motor when not in use were also good ideas. A 6 hp outboard with a high-thrust prop is all the power she needed, even in heavy air. **Worst features:** The boat's biggest fault is probably the shallow (2' 10") draft, which isn't quite enough to make the boat as close winded as she otherwise could be. We like to claim that's why we never won a race with her.

Comps	LOD	Beam	MinDr	Displ	Bllst	SA/D	D/L	Avg. PHRF	Max. Speed	Motion Index	Space Index	No. of Berths	Head-room
Sea Sprite 22 (23)	22' 6"	7' 0"	3' 0"	3,350	1,475	17.6	349	264	5.4	21.3	257	4	4' 2"
Seafarer Kestrel 23 Cruiser	23' 1"	7' 2"	2' 4"	3,700	1,400	15.7	351	270	5.5	22.1	319	4	4' 9"
Seafarer Kestrel 23 Overnighter	23' 1"	7' 2"	2' 4"	3,700	1,400	15.7	351	270	5.5	22.1	319	2 or 4	4' 9"
South Coast 23	23' 0"	7' 3"	2' 10"	3,700	1,475	16.5	308	270	5.6	21.2	311	4	4' 5"

Sovereign 23 & 24 (23)
Add a bowsprit, add a foot to LOD?

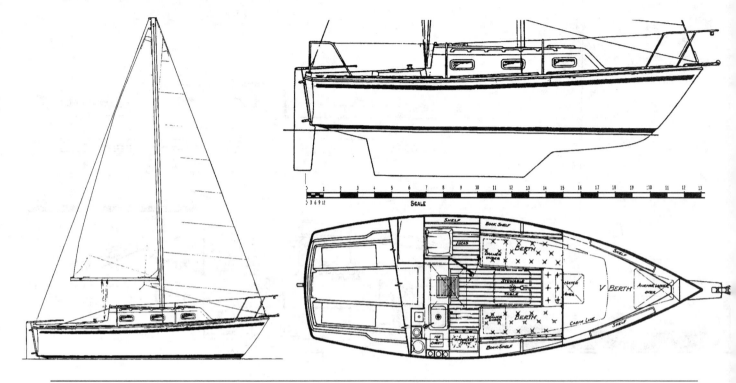

LOD:	23' 0"	**Designer:**	not specified by builder
LOA:	24' 6"	**Builder:**	Sovereign Yachts
LWL:	18' 6"	**Years produced:**	1979–1990
Min./max. draft:	2' 4"/3' 8"	**Sail area:**	240 sq. ft.
Bridge clearance:	30' 6"	**Fuel tankage:**	portable
Power:	outboard 3 to 6 hp	**Water tankage:**	portable
B/D ratio:	42%	**Approx. trailering wgt.:**	4,800 lbs.

Here's one of those boats that started life as a 23-footer, and a year or two later, without changing the hull, the marketers deemed that the boat had become a 24-footer, belatedly deciding to add the bowsprit as part of the length (which, of course, is not usual industry practice). The Sovereign Yacht Company of Largo, FL, offered the Sovereign 23 with a choice of two layouts. An A interior (shown here) provides a large open saloon area with no forward bulkhead, a fully enclosed head, and a galley centered around the companionway steps, under the main hatch. A more traditional B interior (not shown here) has the head

forward between the forward berths with a privacy door, more elbow room aft, and the galley still under the companionway hatch. The 23 was also available with either a shoal draft (2' 4") keel, shown here, or a "deep" (3' 8") keel, purportedly with the same ballast and displacement. **Best features:** Headroom and cabin space are very good for a 23-footer. **Worst features:** The statistics and specifications given in various Sovereign brochures are so inconsistent that we can't help but wonder about the accuracy of the company's claimed specifications. Be cautious before buying.

Comps	LOD	Beam	MinDr	Displ	Bllst	SA/D	D/L	Avg. PHRF	Max. Speed	Motion Index	Space Index	No. of Berths	Head- room
Sovereign Antares 24 (23)	23' 0"	8' 0"	2' 7"	3,000	1,200	16.3	254	252	5.8	17.0	389	4	5' 4"
Irwin 23	23' 0"	8' 0"	2' 5"	3,200	1,500	18.8	226	252	5.8	15.5	334	4	4' 9"
Sovereign 23	23' 0"	8' 0"	2' 4"	3,250	1,350	17.5	229	252	5.8	15.6	435	4	5' 7"
O'Day 240 (23)	22' 6"	8' 3"	2' 8"	3,600	1,200	17.0	178	231	6.1	15.2	438	4	5' 9"

Sovereign Antares 24 (23)
Another Sovereign with specification problems

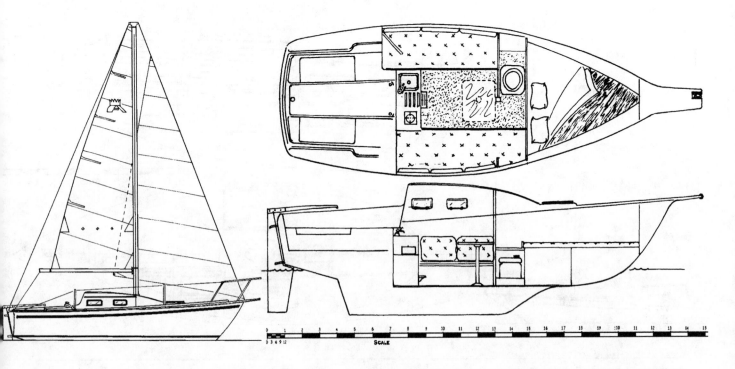

LOD:	23' 0"
LOA:	24' 8"
LWL:	18' 6"
Min./max. draft:	2' 7"
Bridge clearance:	30' 6"
Power:	outboard 4 to 6 hp
B/D ratio:	33%

Designer:	not specified by builder
Builder:	Sovereign Yachts
Years produced:	1986–1991
Sail area:	240 sq. ft.
Fuel tankage:	portable
Water tankage:	portable
Approx. trailering wgt.:	4,800 lbs.

The so-called 24-foot Antares hull, actually 23-feet long on deck, appears to be pulled out of the same mold as the older "traditional" Sovereign 23 (page 256), with a more streamlined deck. The 1986 Sovereign Yachts sales brochure indicates that the Antares is a much less expensive but still not *inexpensive*, no-frills version of the original Sovereign 23, with no fancy woodwork below and less hardware on deck (e.g., no genoa tracks and cars). **Best features:** Headroom and cabin space are both better than the Irwin, but not as good as the "traditional" Sovereign 23 or O'Day 240. In fact, unless a buyer wanted a wide deck for sunbathing at his dock or mooring, he would probably opt for the "traditional" 23's greater space below. **Worst features:** The keel is so shallow that we would worry about upwind performance. She certainly won't be competitive racing against, say, the Irwin 23 with her deep centerboard. There is no provision for an outboard well in the cockpit, so an outboard bracket bolted to the transom, inconveniently far from the helmsman, is all that is offered.

Comps	LOD	Beam	MinDr	Displ	Bllst	SA/D	D/L	Avg. PHRF	Max. Speed	Motion Index	Space Index	No. of Berths	Head-room
Sovereign Antares 24 (23)	23' 0"	8' 0"	2' 7"	3,000	1,200	16.3	254	252	5.8	17.0	389	4	5' 4"
Irwin 23	23' 0"	8' 0"	2' 5"	3,200	1,500	18.8	226	252	5.8	15.5	334	4	4' 9"
Sovereign 23	23' 0"	8' 0"	2' 4"	3,250	1,350	17.5	229	252	5.8	15.6	435	4	5' 7"
O'Day 240 (23)	22' 6"	8' 3"	2' 8"	3,600	1,200	17.0	178	231	6.1	15.2	438	4	5' 9"

Stone Horse 23

Classic cruising cutter by Sam Crocker

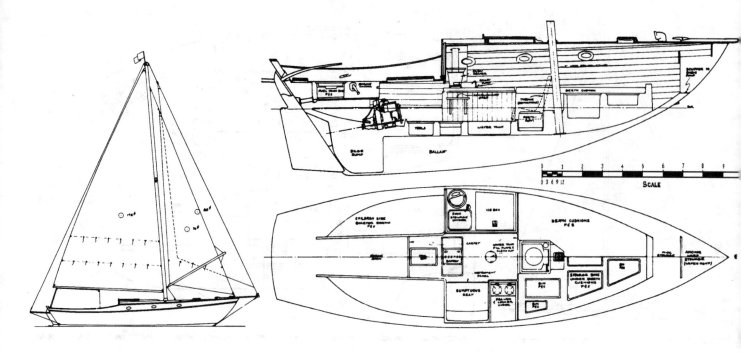

LOD:	23' 4"		Designer:	Sam Crocker
LOA:	27' 4"		Builder:	Edey & Duff
LWL:	18' 4"		Years produced:	1971–1994
Min./max. draft:	3' 6"		Sail area:	323 sq. ft.
Bridge clearance:	31' 0"		Fuel tankage:	portable
Power:	outboard or dsl. 3 to 8 hp		Water tankage:	portable
B/D ratio:	45%		Approx. trailering wgt.:	6,600 lbs.

The Stone Horse 23 (named after a shoal in Nantucket Sound) was designed some 75 years ago by New Englander Sam Crocker as a fine little cruising boat for two people. Although on deck she measures seven to ten inches shorter than her comps shown below, she is right in the thick of her comps' stats, except that she sleeps an honest two rather than four, if you discount the two "children's" quarter berths. She is cutter-rigged, giving her a wide choice of options in whatever wind speed and direction she finds herself. Her anchor can be rigged and

made ready on the short bowsprit on short notice. The jib can be equipped with roller furling and her forestaysail can be rigged with a jib boom on a traveler (not shown here) for easy singlehanded tacking in a narrow harbor. Given a couple of winches and jiffy reefing gear, she'd be an easy boat to handle. ***Best features:*** She's quite a pretty boat in a traditional way. ***Worst features:*** In heavy air she'll keep up with most boats her size and type, but in light air, despite her relatively high SA/D ratio, she's no speed demon.

Comps	LOD	Beam	MinDr	Displ	Bllst	SA/D	D/L	Avg. PHRF	Max. Speed	Motion Index	Space Index	No. of Berths	Head- room
Dolphin 24 (Pacific-Yankee)	24' 2"	7' 8"	2' 10"	4,250	1,750	18.1	277	246	5.8	21.1	406	4 to 5	4' 8"
Pearson Lark 24	24' 0"	8' 0"	4' 0"	4,300	1,500	16.7	303	246	5.8	20.5	456	4	4' 5"
Stone Horse 23	23' 4"	7' 1"	3' 6"	4,490	2,000	19.9	325	280	5.7	24.2	329	2	3' 9"
Dolphin 24 (O'Day)	24' 2"	7' 8"	2' 10"	4,500	1,440	17.1	293	246	5.8	22.3	370	4	4' 8"
Paceship Westwind 24	23' 11"	7' 11"	2' 2"	4,600	2,370	17.9	345	231	5.7	22.7	326	4	5' 6"

Tanzer 22 (23)
Popular Canadian 23-footer

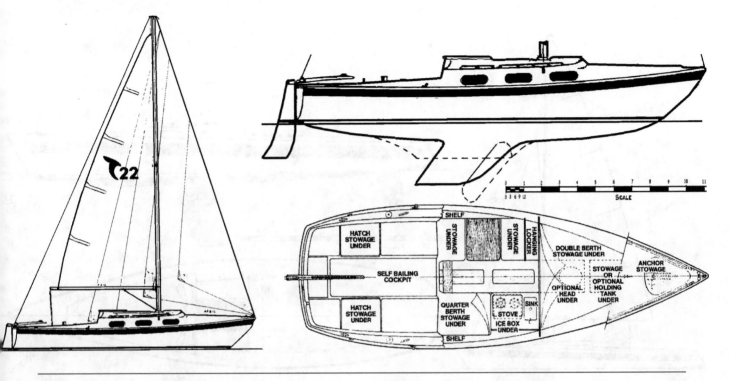

LOD:	22' 6"	**Designer:**	Johann Tanzer
LOA:	24' 7"	**Builder:**	Tanzer Yachts
LWL:	19' 9"	**Years produced:**	1970–1987
Min./max. draft:	swing: 2' 0", 4' 0"/fin: 3' 6"	**Sail area:**	222 sq. ft.
Bridge clearance:	29' 8"	**Fuel tankage:**	portable
Power:	outboard 3 to 6 hp	**Water tankage:**	portable
B/D ratio:	48%	**Approx. trailering wgt.:**	4,700 lbs.

Johann Tanzer designed this 22½-foot boat in 1970 and sold more than 2,200 copies over the following 17 years. Then (the story goes) his nervous banker closed down his otherwise healthy operation, sending him and his company into bankruptcy and ruin. She was available with either a swing keel (shown below in phantom view; draft 2' 0" keel up, 4' 0" keel down) or swept-back fin keel, which turned out to be the more popular choice. **Best features:** Although the boat has not been made for over 20 years, at the time of writing there is still a strong class association with an Internet presence, which promotes both one-design racing and

periodic cruising rendezvous. Despite her somewhat low SA/D ratio, the boat is relatively fast, as indicated by her PHRF rating compared to her comps. **Worst features:** The mainsheet is fixed to the cockpit sole just ahead of the tiller, which reduces the spaciousness of the otherwise big, wide cockpit. The side-opening icebox loses some of its cool every time the door is opened, and users risk being showered with food if the door is opened on starboard tack. Despite her beam near the top of her comp range, she registers the lowest Space Index as a result of her low headroom. The forward end of her V-berth is too narrow for two adults.

Comps	LOD	Beam	MinDr	Displ	Bllst	SA/D	D/L	Avg. PHRF	Max. Speed	Motion Index	Space Index	No. of Berths	Head-room
Com-Pac 23	22' 9"	7' 10"	2' 3"	3,000	1,340	19.2	163	260	6.0	13.9	329	4	4' 4"
Halcyon 23	22' 9"	7' 6"	3' 6"	3,100	1,100	16.9	213	NA	5.8	16.3	364	4	5' 5"
Coronado 23	22' 7"	7' 9"	2' 6"	3,100	1,350	17.9	171	270	6.0	14.9	341	4	4' 9"
Tanzer 22 (23)	22' 6"	7' 10"	2' 0"	3,100	1,500	16.7	180	240	6.0	14.9	295	4	4' 3"
San Juan 24 (23)	23' 4"	8' 0"	4' 0"	3,200	1,650	18.0	193	216	5.9	14.8	373	5	4' 6"

Wabbit 24 (23)
Lightweight creation by Tom Wylie

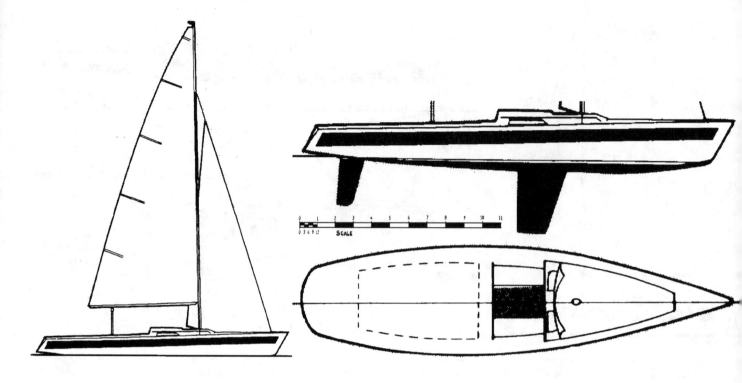

LOD:	23' 1"	Designer:	Tom Wylie
LOA:	23' 9"	Builder:	North Coast Yachts
LWL:	20' 0"	Years produced:	1981–1985?
Min./max. draft:	3' 6"	Sail area:	186 sq. ft.
Bridge clearance:	30' 0"	Fuel tankage:	portable
Power:	outboard 2 to 4 hp	Water tankage:	portable
B/D ratio:	50%	Approx. trailering wgt.:	2,000 lbs.

As the Wabbit 24 website points out, the Wabbit is "a long, lean, light, and very fast boat that could also function as a simple camping cruiser." Among all the 360 boats in this book, the Wabbit has the lowest D/L ratio (49)—except for a couple of odd boats with little or no ballast. Since any D/L under 100 makes the boat an ultralight, the Wabbit is the lightest of the light—carefully laminated of glass and foam sandwich. Is she fast? Well, her PHRF averages 150, more like that for a 30- to 36-foot racer-cruiser, so you can guess the answer. *Best features:* She's so fast it will make your head spin. *Worst features:* With such slight headroom and diminutive Space Index, you won't want to sleep aboard very often. Racers are urged to visit the Wabbit 24 website (www.wyliewabbit.org), which points out some weak spots and how to fix them. Viewers will be shown sketches of (1) a cabin top stiffener for mast compression reinforcement, (2) mast step lay-up reinforcement, (3) a partial bulkhead to support mast compression post, and (4) a new bulkhead. Bring your hammers and saws.

Comps	LOD	Beam	MinDr	Displ	Bllst	SA/D	D/L	Avg. PHRF	Max. Speed	Motion Index	Space Index	No. of Berths	Head-room
Wabbit 24 (23)	23' 1"	5' 7"	3' 6"	875	440	32.5	49	150	6.0	6.4	188	2	2' 8"
Ranger 23 (21) "Fun"	21' 4"	8' 0"	2' 4"	1,875	760	25.6	145	180	5.7	9.2	289	4	3' 10"
Moore 24 (23)	22' 9"	7' 2"	4' 1"	2,050	1,025	24.5	89	156	6.2	10.2	285	2	3' 6"

Moore 24 (23)
Ultralight from Santa Cruz

LOD:	22' 9"	**Designer:**	George Olson, Ron Moore
LOA:	23' 9"	**Builder:**	Moore Sailboats
LWL:	21' 9"	**Years produced:**	1972–1988
Min./max. draft:	4' 1"	**Sail area:**	247 sq. ft.
Bridge clearance:	30' 0"	**Fuel tankage:**	portable
Power:	outboard 2 to 4 hp	**Water tankage:**	portable
B/D ratio:	50%	**Approx. trailering wgt.:**	3,000 lbs.

The concept of the Moore 24 was originally conceived by George Olson (later the creator of the Santa Cruz 27, Olson 25, 29, and 30, and other superfast vessels). In the late sixties, Olson decided to create a boat to win a Trans-Pacific race being organized for boats under 30 feet. Starting with a keel from a beaten-up Cal 20, he created the ultralight *Grendal*, a 24-foot rocketship with under 6 feet of beam—a shape not unlike the Wabbit 24. The small-boat TransPac never happened, but *Grendal* won the Midget Ocean Racing Association season championship in 1970, among other honors. Then Olson, along with another Santa Cruz (CA) builder, Ron Moore and his brother John, modified *Grendal* to give her more beam by simply prying the sides apart with 2 × 4s. Soon George went on to other pursuits and Ron began building and selling the modified *Grendal* as the Moore 24. The boat continued to go through various transformations, such as raising the deck for better sitting headroom, moving the keel, and changing the sail plan. ***Best features:*** She's fast in heavy air; the high (50%) B/D ratio helps to keep the Moore 24 on her feet. ***Worst features:*** Due to her light weight and cramped cabin space, almost no one would want to buy this design as a cruising boat.

Comps	LOD	Beam	MinDr	Displ	Bllst	SA/D	D/L	Avg. PHRF	Max. Speed	Motion Index	Space Index	No. of Berths	Head-room
Wabbit 24 (23)	23' 1"	5' 7"	3' 6"	875	440	32.5	49	150	6.0	6.4	188	2	2' 8"
Ranger 23 (21) "Fun"	21' 4"	8' 0"	2' 4"	1,875	760	25.6	145	180	5.7	9.2	289	4	3' 10"
Moore 24 (23)	22' 9"	7' 2"	4' 1"	2,050	1,025	24.5	89	156	6.2	10.2	285	2	3' 6"

San Juan 24 (23)
Bruce Kirby racer/cruiser

LOD:	23' 4"	**Designer:**	Bruce Kirby
LOA:	24' 0"	**Builder:**	Clark Boats
LWL:	19' 6"	**Years produced:**	1973–1985
Min./max. draft:	4' 0"	**Sail area:**	245 sq. ft.
Bridge clearance:	32' 0"	**Fuel tankage:**	portable
Power:	outboard 3 to 6 hp	**Water tankage:**	portable
B/D ratio:	52%	**Approx. trailering wgt.:**	4,800 lbs.

Don Clark, designer of the San Juan 21 Mk I and II (pages 129 and 130) and owner of the Clark Boat Company of Kent, WA, went to Bruce Kirby for a hot new racer to be designed to the IOR Quarter Ton Rule. Clark imposed two important restrictions to broaden the market beyond the macho racer group: the boat could not draw more than 4' 0" or be wider than 8' 0", making the boat more useable in shoal waters and making trailering a little easier. ***Best features:*** The boat has been a success (and, at least so far, is the most popular quarter tonner ever), with over a thousand sailing. ***Worst features:*** Although she is fast and weatherly going upwind, dead downwind in heavy air under spinnaker she can be a little squirrelly, possibly a result of her narrow underbody aft.

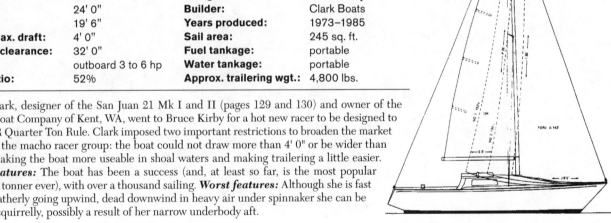

Comps	LOD	Beam	MinDr	Displ	Bllst	SA/D	D/L	Avg. PHRF	Max. Speed	Motion Index	Space Index	No. of Berths	Head-room
Com-Pac 23	22' 9"	7' 10"	2' 3"	3,000	1,340	19.2	163	260	6.0	13.9	329	4	4' 4"
Halcyon 23	22' 9"	7' 6"	3' 6"	3,100	1,100	16.9	213	NA	5.8	16.3	364	4	5' 5"
Coronado 23	22' 7"	7' 9"	2' 6"	3,100	1,350	17.9	171	270	6.0	14.9	341	4	4' 9"
Tanzer 22 (23)	22' 6"	7' 10"	2' 0"	3,100	1,500	16.7	180	240	6.0	14.9	295	4	4' 3"
San Juan 24 (23)	23' 4"	8' 0"	4' 0"	3,200	1,650	18.0	193	216	5.9	14.8	373	5	4' 6"

Venture of Newport (23)
Would architect Louis Sullivan approve?

LOD:	22' 7"	**Designer:**	Roger MacGregor
LOA:	27' 2"	**Builder:**	MacGregor Yachts
LWL:	19' 6"	**Years produced:**	1972–1982
Min./max. draft:	1' 6"/5' 6"	**Sail area:**	195 sq. ft.
Bridge clearance:	32' 0"	**Fuel tankage:**	portable
Power:	outboard 3 to 6 hp	**Water tankage:**	3 gal.
B/D ratio:	30%	**Approx. trailering wgt.:**	2,900 lbs.

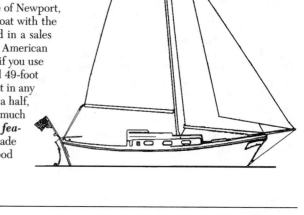

This vessel goes by a variety of names: Venture 23, MacGregor 23, Venture of Newport, and maybe others as well. All refer to the cutter-rigged, bowspritted sailboat with the springy sheer and raked mast pictured here. Her odd looks are explained in a sales brochure saying that she is "a modern replica of the famous English and American pilot cutters of the late 1800s." Well, not in our history book, but we guess if you use your imagination you might see some sort of connection between a typical 49-foot pilot cutter drawing eight feet of water, weighing 55 tons, and able to go out in any weather, and this Venture of Newport, a mere 23 feet, drawing a foot and a half, weighing one ton, and restricted to sailing in protected waters—but not much of one. **Best features:** Her springy sheer gives her a jaunty look. **Worst features:** She won't pass muster with sailors who aren't attracted to heavily made up women. Louis Sullivan said that form follows function, and here's a good example of where it doesn't.

Comps	LOD	Beam	MinDr	Displ	Bllst	SA/D	D/L	Avg. PHRF	Max. Speed	Motion Index	Space Index	No. of Berths	Head-room
Venture of Newport (23)	22' 7"	7' 2"	1' 6"	2,000	600	21.5	120	255	5.9	10.2	312	5	4' 0"
Gillmer 23	22' 7"	7' 6"	1' 8"	2,068	500	23.9	100	NA	6.1	9.7	365	2	5' 0"
Clipper 23 (22)	22' 4"	7' 8"	2' 2"	2,100	550	21.6	142	258	5.8	10.6	351	5	4' 6"
Menger Oysterman 23	22' 6"	8' 0"	1' 8"	2,600	700	30.0	124	NA	6.2	10.4	312	4	4' 9"

Little Details: Does a Boat's Color Matter?

Some people may not give color a second thought—but the color of the topsides and deck might make the difference between loving and hating your next boat.

My family and I have owned two black cruising sailboats, a blue one, and several white ones. And we'll probably never own another non-white boat again. Why?

First of all, dark colors are hot, since they absorb heat from the sun. Sleeping aboard our blue Tartan 27, I used to be awakened by the hot interior wall of my quarter berth, as the early morning sun's radiation became absorbed by the dark topside color outside. The fiberglass skin heated to well over 100 degrees Fahrenheit on a sunny day, on the inside. The outside was even hotter.

The deck of our South Coast 23 was colored a nifty-looking light tan, and was designed to prevent glare reflecting into the eyes of the crew back in the cockpit. But on a sunny day, particularly when the wind was light, the deck could be painfully hot to walk on barefoot. And who wants to wear shoes on a hot day on a hot boat in zero air?

Second of all, colors fade. Sure, builders talk about non-fading colors or special techniques (such as repainting every few years with Awlgrip or Imron), but in my experience, even non-fading colors fade, eventually.

Third, because of fading, colors are hard to match when a repair must be made. By the time a new fiberglass hull has been out of the mold a few months, or in sunny climates even a few weeks, it fades. For this reason, some manufacturers automatically paint their new hulls for easier color-matching later, rather than pigmenting the gel-coat. That's okay if the paint is as durable as the fiberglass gelcoat. Sometimes it is, and sometimes it isn't.

And fourth, white boats command higher resale prices, because more people prefer white boats than any other color, for the very reasons mentioned above. Higher demand translates to higher prices.

I recommend white.

—from Boating for Less, *Second Edition, 1991, by Steve Henkel,*
published by International Marine, Camden, Maine

SIX
Fifty-Three Boats 24'

*4 vessels without accommodations plans are grouped together at end of chapter

265

Allegra 24
Flicka 20's big sister

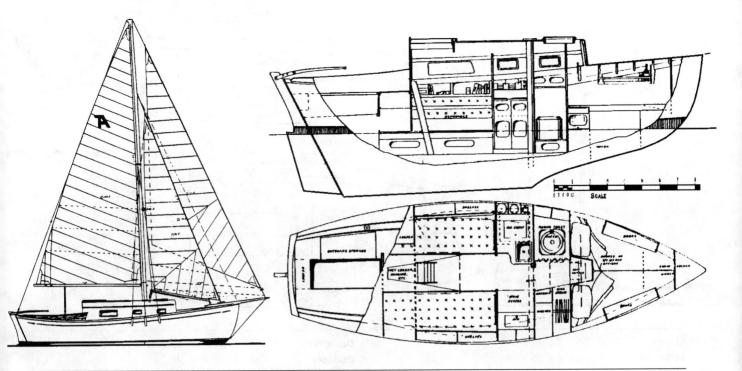

LOD:	23' 11"
LOA:	27' 0"
LWL:	20' 10"
Min./max. draft:	3' 5"
Bridge clearance:	34' 0"
Power:	outboard or inboard to 30 hp
B/D ratio:	32%

Designer:	Fred Bingham
Builder:	Fred Bingham and others
Years produced:	1983?–1990?
Sail area:	337 sq. ft.
Fuel tankage:	owner's choice
Water tankage:	owner's choice
Approx. trailering wgt.:	8,900 lbs.

Designer Fred Bingham is the father of Bruce Bingham, who conceived and built the Pacific Seacraft Flicka 20 (page 120). Father Fred started with the Flicka's hull and stretched it by four feet, without increasing the beam at all. The resulting extra space is most noticeable in the cabin. The head in the Allegra has its own compartment (as do all her comps) and the shortest berth is 6' 5" long. Kits and bare hulls were available on a custom basis; Fred Bingham organized a whole group of potential builders in Ventura, CA, Riviera Beach, FL, Noank, CT, and perhaps other locations as well, to receive orders on a custom basis. Power could be inboard or outboard; if an outboard engine is chosen, it must hang on a transom bracket, off center to miss the outboard rudder. **Best features:** The cutter rig, with the staysail on a boom and the jib on a roller furler, help to make the boat an easy singlehander. **Worst features:** Relative to her comps, the Allegra is a lighter, less beamy boat, better in the lighter air along coastal waters but perhaps not as satisfactory offshore when the going gets rough.

Comps	LOD	Beam	MinDr	Displ	Bllst	SA/D	D/L	Avg. PHRF	Max. Speed	Motion Index	Space Index	No. of Berths	Head-room
Allegra 24	23' 11"	8' 0"	3' 5"	6,200	2,000	16.0	306	NA	6.1	26.3	520	4	6' 1"
Eastward Ho 24	23' 8"	8' 8"	3' 10"	7,000	3,600	12.4	391	269	6.0	28.7	475	4	6' 4"
Blue Water 24	24' 0"	8' 7"	4' 1"	7,950	2,275	11.1	467	NA	5.9	33.2	418	4	6' 1"
Pacific Seacraft Dana 24	24' 0"	8' 7"	3' 10"	8,000	3,200	14.4	364	221	6.2	30.2	535	4	6' 1"
Aquarius Pilot Cutter 24	24' 0"	9' 0"	4' 0"	8,900	3,200	15.3	497	258	6.0	31.0	564	4	6' 3"

Allied Greenwich 24
A design that's not all things to all sailors

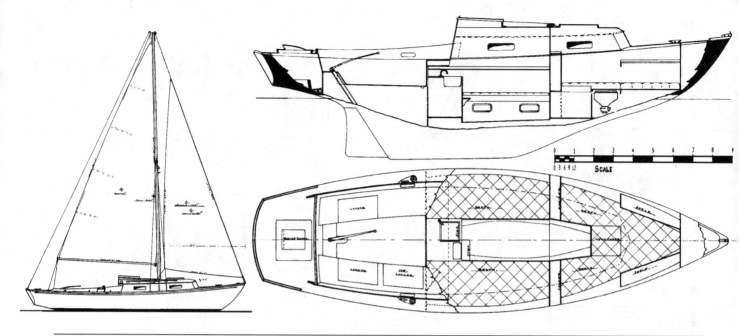

LOD:	24' 3"	**Designer:**	George Stadel
LOA:	24' 3"	**Builder:**	Allied Boats
LWL:	17' 5"	**Years produced:**	1968–1972
Min./max. draft:	3' 0"	**Sail area:**	264 sq. ft.
Bridge clearance:	30' 6"	**Fuel tankage:**	portable
Power:	outboard 3 to 6 hp	**Water tankage:**	15 gal.
B/D ratio:	39%	**Approx. trailering wgt.:**	5,700 lbs.

George Stadel's design for the Greenwich 24, the smallest sailboat ever produced by Allied Boats, was sold to the new Cape Dory Company in 1972, and after the design underwent some minor modifications, became the highly successful Cape Dory 25 (page 329). The Greenwich 24, billed by Allied as a "daysailer, coastal cruiser, racer, gunkholer with the kids," features relatively low freeboard, which gives her hull a sleek, traditional look. She has good ventilation, with a large forward hatch, main hatch, and an aft outboard engine hatch with integral cowl vent. **Best features:** Her relatively shallow 3-foot draft qualifies the Greenwich 24 as a "gunkholer" and "daysailer." Her icebox is accessible from both cockpit and cabin, a great convenience when weekending. **Worst features:** Although her

marketers intimated it, the boat is not all things to all sailors. Her draft is too shallow to let her be close winded, disqualifying her from being a satisfactory "racer." Her galley space is inadequate for more than a casual overnight. (Where, for example, is space for a two-burner stove?) With her narrow stern and longish counter overhang, any significant weight in the cockpit would make her stern-heavy to the point that the scuppers might let water in rather than drain out, and the open motorwell could scoop water underway, slowing the boat and gradually filling the motorwell. As one owner observed, "It did get rather exciting when the gas cans floated up and turned over as the well filled." (If the motor were removed, a flush plug could be inserted.)

Comps	LOD	Beam	MinDr	Displ	Bllst	SA/D	D/L	Avg. PHRF	Max. Speed	Motion Index	Space Index	No. of Berths	Head-room
Kenner Kittiwake 24	23' 7"	7' 5"	2' 10"	3,800	1,500	14.5	303	270	5.6	20.7	351	4	4' 6"
Allied Greenwich 24	24' 3"	7' 3"	3' 0"	3,825	1,500	17.3	323	273	5.6	21.6	304	4	4' 7"
Bridges Point 24	24' 0"	7' 9"	3' 5"	3,944	1,900	17.8	271	246	5.8	20.4	322	2, 3, 4	4' 5"

Annapolis Weekender 24
This design started life teaching sailing

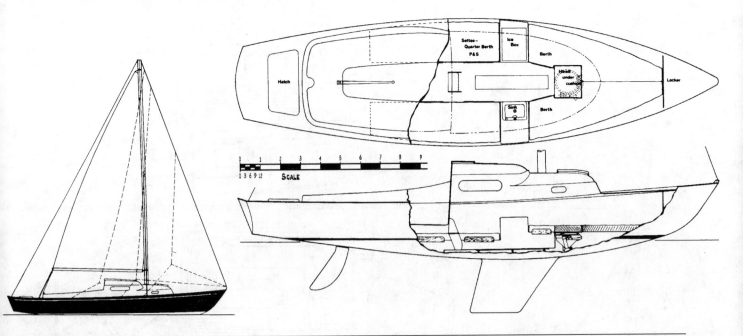

LOD:	24' 2"	**Designer:**	Sparkman & Stephens
LOA:	24' 2"	**Builder:**	Tidewater Boats
LWL:	18' 0"	**Years produced:**	1962–1977
Min./max. draft:	3' 6"	**Sail area:**	218 sq. ft.
Bridge clearance:	27' 0"	**Fuel tankage:**	portable
Power:	outboard 3 to 6 hp	**Water tankage:**	portable
B/D ratio:	49%	**Approx. trailering wgt.:**	3,300 lbs.

In 1961 Sparkman & Stephens designed the first version of this sloop, a daysailer called the Rainbow 24, to be a tough, easy-to-sail boat for the Annapolis Sailing School (which still uses them today to teach sailing). She was a safe, steady boat and purported to be "uncapsizable no matter what," instilling confidence in novice sailors. But even though the Rainbow had a roomy cockpit, its tiny cuddy did not lend itself to cruising. The builder came up with a solution for cruisers: the Weekender 24, a Rainbow with a longer, higher cabin, and a self-bailing cockpit, which the Rainbow lacked. **Best features:** With its relatively short mast (only

27 feet above the water), close to 50 percent ballast to displacement ratio, and a cast iron keel with its weight concentrated in a bulb at the bottom, the boat is about as stiff as she can be. If you carry too much sail in strong winds, and the boat heels excessively, she will develop a strong weather helm and simply round up into the wind—whether you like it or not. (New sailors might like this feature; others might not.) **Worst features:** With her relatively small sail area, she is not fast compared to, say, a J/24 or other modern boat, but if well-sailed might keep up with some of her contemporaries, such as an Ensign or Electra.

Comps	LOD	Beam	MinDr	Displ	Bllst	SA/D	D/L	Avg. PHRF	Max. Speed	Motion Index	Space Index	No. of Berths	Head-room
Shark 24	24' 0"	6' 10"	3' 2"	2,200	675	18.0	123	237	6.0	12.1	277	4	4' 0"
Annapolis Weekender 24	24' 2"	6' 3"	3' 6"	2,300	1,120	20.0	176	276	5.7	15.5	236	4	4' 2"
Windrose 24	24' 0"	7' 10"	1' 3"	2,400	700	19.8	95	252	6.3	10.4	356	4	4' 4"
Captiva 240 (23)	23' 5"	8' 2"	2' 0"	2,400	1,000	23.0	124	213	6.1	10.3	400	5	5' 7"

Aquarius Pilot Cutter 24
Traditional design with mix-and-match choices

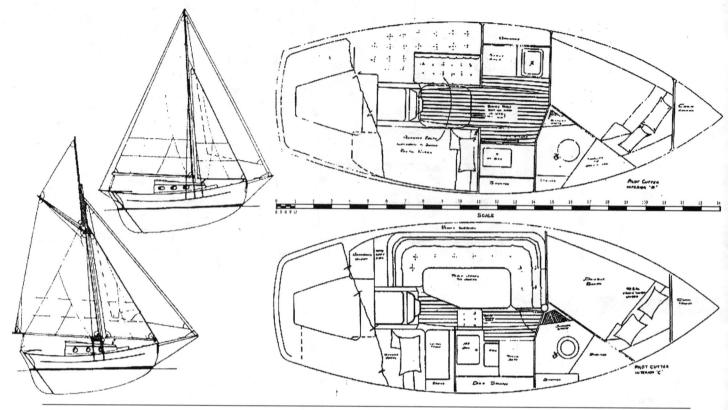

LOD:	24' 0"	Designer:	Frank Parish
LOA:	32' 0"	Builder:	Aquarius Yachts
LWL:	20' 0"	Years produced:	1978–1984
Min./max. draft:	4' 0"	Sail area:	410 sq. ft.
Bridge clearance:	37' 0"	Fuel tankage:	owner's choice
Power:	outboard or inboard 8 to 18 hp	Water tankage:	40 gal.
B/D ratio:	36%	Approx. trailering wgt.:	13,400 lbs.

This is a compact character boat conceived in the 1970s, but designed to look like something from the 1920s or 1930s, and having the same general characteristics: heavy scantlings, lots of bronze hardware (including the turnbuckles, chainplates, ten opening ports, even winches), and tanbark sails. Something like thirty-one of these boats were built, mostly the Marconi-rigged version; the gaff-rigged version was most likely intended for the light air prevalent along the East Coast. At least four interior layouts were offered (but because of space limitations, only two are shown here). Since these boats were built to order, no doubt the customer could have some other layout if he/she wanted. The standard engine was an 18-hp Volvo diesel, but a customer could mount an outboard bracket on the transom if desired. Some did. **Best features:** She has modern sail controls, with all lines leading aft to the cockpit. Lazyjacks are standard. Her Space Index at 564 tops the comps listed here. **Worst features:** Her displacement of 8,900 lbs. is more than any of her comps by over 10 percent and stretches the limit of practicality for a 24-foot boat, so her comps are probably all better performers in light air.

Comps	LOD	Beam	MinDr	Displ	Bllst	SA/D	D/L	Avg. PHRF	Max. Speed	Motion Index	Space Index	No. of Berths	Head-room
Allegra 24	23' 0"	8' 0"	3' 5"	6,200	2,000	16.0	306	NA	6.1	26.3	520	4	6' 7"
Eastward Ho 24	23' 8"	8' 8"	3' 10"	7,000	3,600	12.4	391	269	6.0	28.7	475	4	6' 4"
Blue Water 24	24' 0"	8' 7"	4' 1"	7,950	2,275	11.1	467	NA	5.9	33.2	418	4	6' 1"
Pacific Seacraft Dana 24	24' 2"	8' 7"	3' 10"	8,000	3,200	14.4	364	221	6.2	30.2	535	4	6' 1"
Aquarius Pilot Cutter 24	24' 0"	9' 0"	4' 0"	8,900	3,200	15.3	497	258	6.0	31.0	564	4	6' 3"

Atlantic City Cat 24

Drinks eight, sleeps six, feeds four

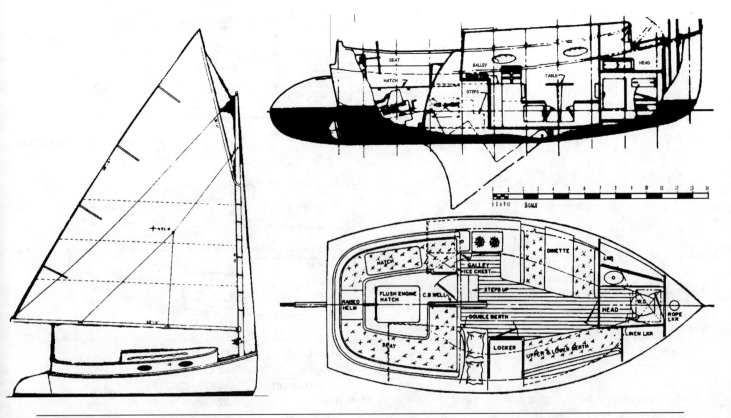

LOD:	24' 0"		**Designer:**	David P. Martin	
LOA:	28' 0"		**Builder:**	Mark-O Custom	
LWL:	22' 0"		**Years produced:**	1979–1989	
Min./max. draft:	2' 0"/5' 0"		**Sail area:**	452 sq. ft.	
Bridge clearance:	34' 0"		**Fuel tankage:**	20 gal.	
Power:	inboard BMW dsl 12 hp		**Water tankage:**	25 gal.	
B/D ratio:	28%		**Approx. trailering wgt.:**	12,000 lbs.	

If you've ever heard the sailor's description of a cozy cruiser, "drinks six, eats four, sleeps two," you'll appreciate that this boat is different: she drinks eight (if squeezed into the cockpit at anchor), eats four (at a dinette below, unless you go for trays on laps), and sleeps six (double berth under the starboard cockpit, upper and lower berths to starboard forward, and a dinette that converts to another double). We can't imagine who would want to sleep six in what amounts to a large walk-in closet, unless it's a family with four small kids. **Best features:** For the large, close-knit family that is totally committed to catboats, this might be a good choice; she certainly wins the Space Index sweepstakes with an index of 636, one of the biggest in this book. **Worst features:** Her sail area of 452 square feet, all in one big piece of cloth, can be hard to manage. Her centerboard shape, with its cutout forward to avoid cluttering up the cabin with a centerboard trunk, could be a problem too; ask some owners.

Comps	LOD	Beam	MinDr	Displ	Bllst	SA/D	D/L	Avg. PHRF	Max. Speed	Motion Index	Space Index	No. of Berths	Head-room
Nonsuch 22	22' 0"	8' 5"	3' 8"	5,000	1,880	16.7	258	245	6.1	21.2	454	2	6' 0"
Marshall 22	22' 2"	10' 2"	2' 0"	5,600	850	19.5	260	264	6.2	18.3	495	2 to 4	5' 2"
Menger Cat 23	22' 6"	10' 2"	2' 6"	6,500	850	20.0	299	NA	6.2	21.4	526	3	6' 0"
Atlantic City Cat 24	24' 0"	11' 0"	2' 0"	8,000	2,200	18.1	335	264	6.3	21.7	636	6	6' 2"

Bahama Sandpiper 24
Predecessor to Reuben Trane's Sand Hen 24

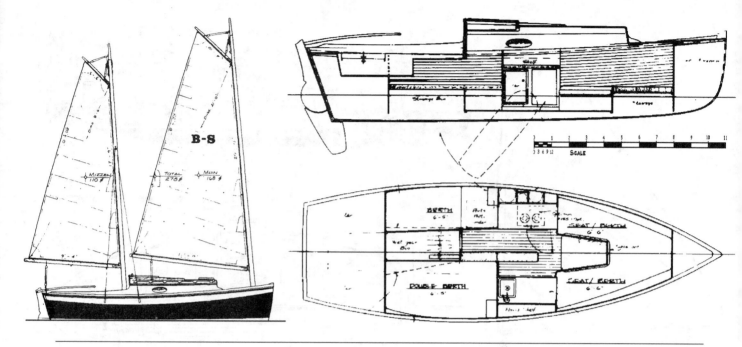

LOD:	24' 0"	**Designer:**	C. W. "Chuck" Paine
LOA:	24' 0"	**Builder:**	various
LWL:	22' 0"	**Years produced:**	1980?–1990?
Min./max. draft:	1' 6"/4' 0"	**Sail area:**	278 sq. ft.
Bridge clearance:	30' 6"	**Fuel tankage:**	portable
Power:	outboard 3 to 6 hp	**Water tankage:**	portable
B/D ratio:	36%	**Approx. trailering wgt.:**	6,200 lbs.

The Bahama Sandpiper was widely reported in the yachting press in 1980 when Bob Perry included her in his well-done book of sailing designs, *Sailing Designs Vol. II.* Not reported by Perry was the Sandpiper designer's choice of two rigs, either as the cat ketch shown here, or as a cutter. As reported by Perry, the mizzen is larger than in the revised design shown here, with the mizzen boom jutting 1' 8" further over the stern. We suspect the boat balances better under the revised rig. Other changes between the original and the version shown here include the mizzen mast stepped on deck (with shrouds added) rather than free-standing on the keel; a longer cabin trunk; improved leads for the sheets; and minor changes to the galley layout (drawers removed, no more built-in icebox). Stock plans were available from Chuck Paine and may still be today. Molded fiberglass hulls and decks were at one time also available for finishing by homebuilders, and by the mid-1980s Reuben Trane had purchased the molds and built a modified version that he called the Sand Hen 24 (page 308). **Best features:** There's nothing like a split rig to get our juices flowing; think of all the things you can do with it, like tacking up a narrow river singlehanded. **Worst features:** The Sandpiper is heavier than the Sand Hen; for cruising along shore, we'd go with the Sand Hen. All else being equal, lighter is likely to be faster.

Comps	LOD	Beam	MinDr	Displ	Bllst	SA/D	D/L	Avg. PHRF	Max. Speed	Motion Index	Space Index	No. of Berths	Head-room
Sand Hen 24	23' 9"	8' 0"	1' 6"	3,500	1,500	19.1	137	NA	6.4	14.4	393	4	4' 9"
Hunter 240 (23)	23' 1"	8' 3"	1' 6"	3,600	1,300	16.5	148	255	6.3	14.6	416	4	4' 8"
Bahama Sandpiper 24	24' 0"	7' 11"	1' 6"	4,140	1,500	17.2	162	252	6.4	17.5	393	4	4' 9"

Balboa 24

Another 24-footer from the Laguna family

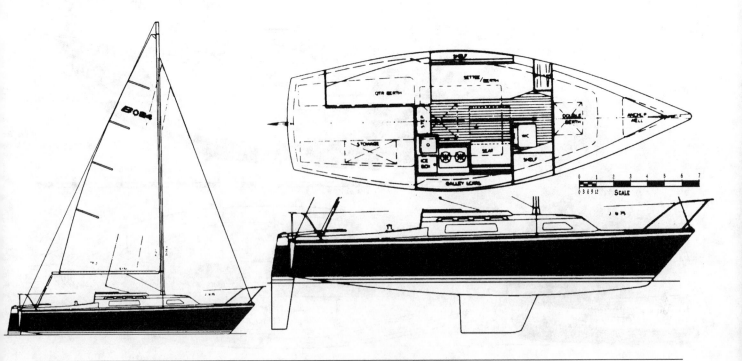

LOD:	23' 7"	**Designer:**	Shad Turner
LOA:	24' 9"	**Builder:**	Laguna Yachts
LWL:	20' 0"	**Years produced:**	1978–1987?
Min./max. draft:	2' 11"	**Sail area:**	220 sq. ft.
Bridge clearance:	26' 6"	**Fuel tankage:**	portable
Power:	outboard 3 to 6 hp	**Water tankage:**	portable
B/D ratio:	35%	**Approx. trailering wgt.:**	3,900 lbs.

The Balboa 24 closely resembles the Laguna 24 and Windrose 24 (page 315) made by the same company (Laguna Yachts) and drawn by the same designer (Shad Turner). The Balboa came in two versions, a ⅞ fractional rig version (shown here) and a masthead rig. We suppose there is very little difference between the two designs in terms of performance. The lower rig, with 26' 6" masthead clearance over the water and 220 square feet of sail may be slightly more stable in a blow, and the taller rig, 28' 0" off the water and with 251 square feet of sail may be slightly more powerful and able to accelerate faster in light air.

The Balboa is equipped with a poptop that expands the 3' 11" stooping headroom when raised. ***Best features:*** Comparing the Balboa to her comps is an interesting exercise. For example, why is the Balboa's PHRF rating only 12 seconds per mile higher than the J/24's? We have not sailed the Balboa 24, but assume that she is fast, even though her upwind performance and her PHRF rating may both be higher than the statistical evidence indicates, considering her shallow draft. ***Worst features:*** Headroom is even lower than the J/24's. Her keel appears to be too shallow for good upwind performance.

Comps	LOD	Beam	MinDr	Displ	Bllst	SA/D	D/L	Avg. PHRF	Max. Speed	Motion Index	Space Index	No. of Berths	Head- room
Balboa 24	23' 7"	8' 4"	2' 11"	2,600	900	18.6	145	186	6.0	11.2	365	4	3' 11"
J/24	24' 0"	8' 1"	4' 0"	2,750	945	21.3	153	174	6.0	10.8	372	4	4' 0"
Cal 24-1	24' 0"	8' 0"	2' 6"	2,800	1,000	20.9	156	228	6.0	12.7	295	4	4' 6"
Dufour 24	23' 8"	8' 2"	2' 5"	2,976	1,168	16.4	177	240	5.9	12.9	444	4	5' 4"

Blue Water 24

Is she a sloop or a cutter?

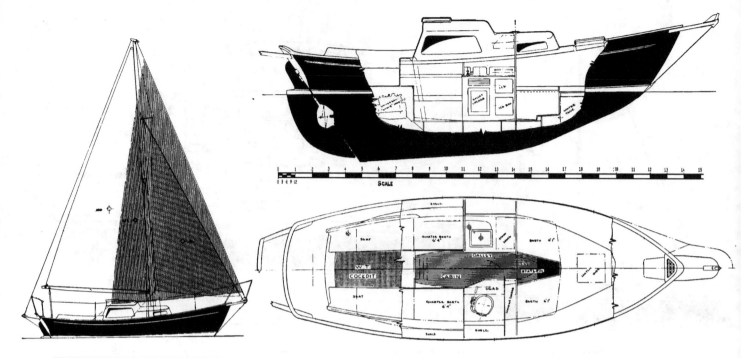

LOD:	24' 0"	**Designer:**	Thomas C. Gillmer
LOA:	27' 6"	**Builder:**	Blue Water Boats
LWL:	19' 8"	**Years produced:**	1961–1974?
Min./max. draft:	4' 1"	**Sail area:**	276 sq. ft.
Bridge clearance:	36' 0"	**Fuel tankage:**	12 gal.
Power:	inboard Atomic Four 30 hp	**Water tankage:**	20 gal.
B/D ratio:	29%	**Approx. trailering wgt.:**	11,700 lbs.

A syndicate in Annapolis, MD, calling themselves Blue Water Boats, commissioned Thomas Gillmer to design this perky small cruiser back in 1961, when they announced the boat would be supplied with "mildew-proofed Egyptian cotton working sails." Ah, how times have changed! The rig, incidently, shows a big masthead genoa as well as a 3/4 fractional rig with a diamond strut that looks as though it could poke a hole in the genny if it were trimmed in tight. It's not clear whether a buyer had to choose one sail or the other. In other words, is she a sloop or a cutter? The prominent doghouse provides clear headroom of 5' 7" under its roof, and 8 inches less forward under the trunk cabin.

Best features: The broad bowsprit with a pulpit extended over it gives good purchase for dealing with an anchor. We also like the big portlights in the doghouse, the better to check out one's neighbors in a cozy anchorage. **Worst features:** Among her comps, she has the lowest Space Index, though 418 is still a respectable number for a "little" 24-footer. Of the four comps listed below, the Blue Water 24 has by far the least enticing accommodations plan. For example, there appears to be no dining table, nor any place to put one. And the enclosed head compartment is located smack dab amidships, leaving only an 18-inch space to stand in front of the galley.

Comps	LOD	Beam	MinDr	Displ	Bllst	SA/D	D/L	Avg. PHRF	Max. Speed	Motion Index	Space Index	No. of Berths	Head-room
Eastward Ho 24	23' 8"	8' 8"	3' 10"	7,000	3,600	12.4	391	269	6.0	28.7	475	4	6' 4"
Blue Water 24	24' 0"	8' 7"	4' 1"	7,950	2,275	11.1	467	NA	5.9	33.2	418	4	6' 1"
Pacific Seacraft Dana 24	24' 2"	8' 7"	3' 10"	8,000	3,200	14.4	364	221	6.2	30.2	535	4	6' 1"
Aquarius Pilot Cutter 24	24' 0"	9' 0"	4' 0"	8,900	3,200	15.3	497	258	6.0	31.0	564	4	6' 3"

Bridges Point 24
The choices are many for this traditional design

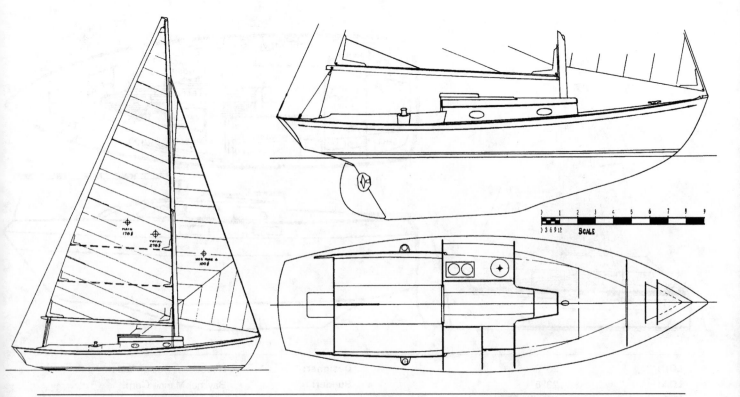

LOD:	24' 0"	**Designer:**	Joel White
LOA:	24' 0"	**Builder:**	Bridges Point Boat Yard
LWL:	18' 8"	**Years produced:**	1987–present
Min./max. draft:	3' 5"	**Sail area:**	278 sq. ft.
Bridge clearance:	33' 6"	**Fuel tankage:**	various
Power:	outboard or inboard 4 to 10 hp	**Water tankage:**	various
B/D ratio:	48%	**Approx. trailering wgt.:**	5,800 lbs.

The Bridges Point Boat Yard of Brooklin, ME, builds this pretty little sloop to order. She can be configured either as a cruiser or a daysailer. The cruiser has two different cabin lengths, a shorter one with a more traditional look, or a longer and higher one for those who want more room below. The daysailer has a longer cockpit and a much shorter cabin, and can either have a bulkhead and V-berths or be left open. The boat may also be purchased as a kit in various stages of completion. There is a choice of an outboard well for engines up to 10 hp

(though we think a Yamaha 6 hp with high thrust prop would do just fine), or gas or diesel inboard power. Other options, such as teak cabin, quarter berths, bridge deck, icebox, and so on, are also available. **Best features:** This boat features very high quality construction in the Maine boatyard tradition. If you buy new, you can have pretty much whatever kind of boat you want. **Worst features:** New or used, you'd better bring your checkbook with you—the one for the account with lots of disposable cash.

Comps	LOD	Beam	MinDr	Displ	Bllst	SA/D	D/L	Avg. PHRF	Max. Speed	Motion Index	Space Index	No. of Berths	Head-room
Kenner Kittiwake 24	23' 7"	7' 5"	2' 10"	3,800	1,500	14.5	303	270	5.6	20.7	351	4	4' 6"
Allied Greenwich 24	24' 3"	7' 3"	3' 0"	3,825	1,500	17.3	323	273	5.6	21.6	304	4	4' 7"
Bridges Point 24	24' 0"	7' 9"	3' 5"	3,944	1,900	17.8	271	246	5.8	20.4	322	2, 3, 4	4' 5"
Quickstep 24	23' 11"	7' 11"	3' 4"	4,000	1,300	16.4	260	258	5.8	19.1	341	5	4' 5"

Buccaneer 240/245 (24)
Floating apartment for coasting downwind

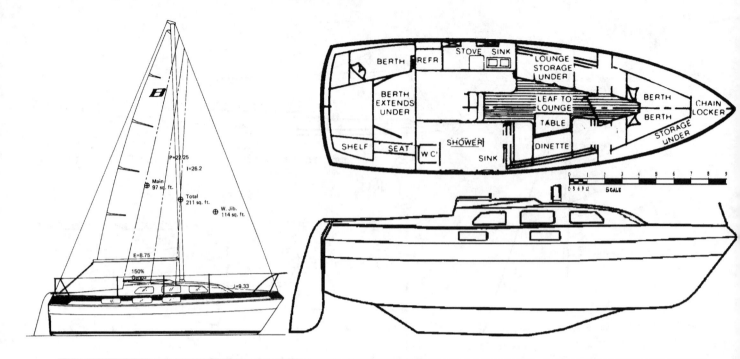

LOD:	23' 8"		**Designer:**	Buccaneer Design Team
LOA:	23' 8"		**Builder:**	Bayliner Marine Corp.
LWL:	20' 4"		**Years produced:**	1975–1979
Min./max. draft:	2' 6"		**Sail area:**	248 sq. ft.
Bridge clearance:	33' 10"		**Fuel tankage:**	portable
Power:	outboard 4 to 8 hp		**Water tankage:**	20 gal.
B/D ratio:	31%		**Approx. trailering wgt.:**	6,100 lbs.

William Garden, one of the most creative and admired yacht designers the world has ever known (and one of our personal favorites), was asked by Bayliner Marine in 1975 to design a 30-foot sloop for fiberglass production. He designed the Buccaneer 300 to a minimum weight for her length and cubic content. She had light ballast, great form stability, firm bilges, wide (ten feet) beam, and a 4-foot draft with 3,500 pounds of ballast—the minimum Garden considered possible without affecting the B300's good sailing qualities. The Buccaneer Design Team took it from there, scaling down the B300 in a way that unfortunately created a group of high, boxy looking "wedding cake" designs with keels too shallow and with too little ballast for good upwind performance. ***Best features:*** Very extensive accommodations, with double berth aft, V-berth forward, convertible dinette in a "lounge" area that doesn't need to be made up every morning, a huge "bathroom" with head, sink, and shower, galley with a "refrigerator" (actually, just an icebox?), stove, and two-basin sink. Oh, and there's 6-foot headroom too. ***Worst features:*** The penalty for the good living arrangements below is a boat that sails downwind satisfactorily, but is no good upwind.

Comps	LOD	Beam	MinDr	Displ	Bllst	SA/D	D/L	Avg. PHRF	Max. Speed	Motion Index	Space Index	No. of Berths	Head- room
Buccaneer 240/245 (24)	23' 8"	8' 0"	2' 6"	4,000	1,250	17.0	212	270	6.0	18.0	422	4	6' 0"
Tyler 24	24' 2"	7' 5"	2' 0"	4,000	1,650	16.2	223	NA	6.0	20.1	441	5	6' 0"
Cal T/4 (24)	24' 2"	8' 0"	4' 0"	4,000	2,000	16.3	193	234	6.1	17.5	353	4	5' 3"
Vivacity 24	23' 6"	8' 0"	2' 6"	4,300	1,700	15.4	215	NA	6.1	19.2	385	5	5' 7"

C&C 24

Boat with a famous name and a long production run

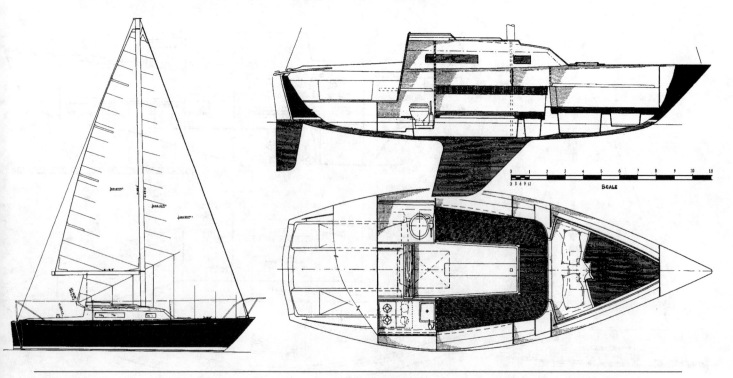

LOD:	23' 6"	**Designer:**	C&C Design Group	
LOA:	24' 0"	**Builder:**	C&C Yachts	
LWL:	19' 6"	**Years produced:**	1973–1984	
Min./max. draft:	4' 0"	**Sail area:**	252 sq. ft.	
Bridge clearance:	32' 6"	**Fuel tankage:**	portable	
Power:	outboard 4 to 6 hp	**Water tankage:**	portable	
B/D ratio:	33%	**Approx. trailering wgt.:**	4,800 lbs.	

During her 11-year production run, the C&C 24 (smallest boat in the C&C fleet) unsurprisingly went through some design changes in her accommodations plan. Early boats (1975 to about 1977, as shown here) had the head located aft to port and a small galley aft to starboard. On later boats, the head was moved forward to the traditional position between the V-berths, and the aft galley was expanded to fill the whole space around the companionway steps. **Best features:** Her wide beam helps to boost her Space Index to a level 10 percent above her nearest comps. The same wide beam plus her deeper draft (except for the Cal 24-3's optional deep fin keel) lend her an extra bit of stability going to weather. **Worst**

features: At least one owner mentioned that she tended to pound a little in choppy conditions. Two owners reported that the prop occasionally cavitated in waves. Still another owner observed that his fiancée did not like the head arrangement near the companionway in one of the early boats. The woman complained that a mere canvas curtain did not afford enough privacy, and that caused the owner to buy a larger boat. (Engaged sailors beware!) Some say the settee berths are too narrow. Several owners mentioned difficulty in replacing foggy plastic windows, which were factory-glued to the fiberglass. In the end they perservered, using new acrylic and 3M-5200, plus throughbolts.

Comps	LOD	Beam	MinDr	Displ	Bllst	SA/D	D/L	Avg. PHRF	Max. Speed	Motion Index	Space Index	No. of Berths	Head-room
C&C 24	23' 6"	8' 9"	4' 0"	3,200	1,050	18.6	193	222	5.9	13.0	443	4	5' 3"
S2 7.3 (24)	23' 6"	8' 0"	3' 0"	3,250	1,300	18.6	229	228	5.8	15.5	403	4	5' 0"
Cal 24-3	23' 9"	8' 0"	3' 4"	3,300	1,175	18.8	184	213	6.0	14.9	400	4 or 5	5' 0"
Mirage 24	23' 6"	8' 5"	4' 2"	3,700	1,500	15.0	204	225	6.0	15.4	370	4	4' 9"

Cal 24-1
First of a series of Cal 24 designs

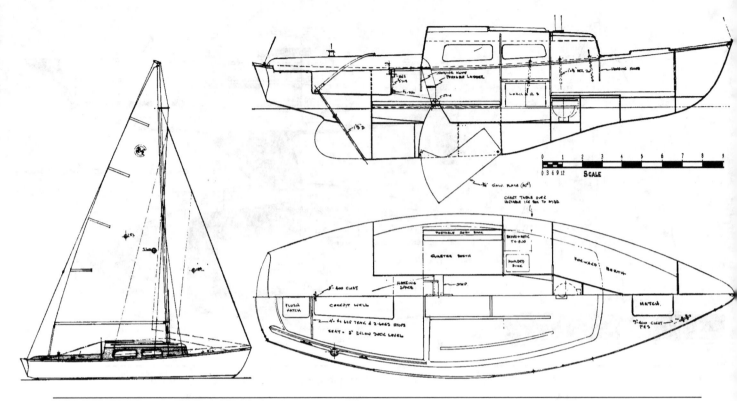

LOD:	24' 0"	**Designer:**	C. William Lapworth
LOA:	24' 0"	**Builder:**	Jensen Marine/Cal Boats
LWL:	20' 0"	**Years produced:**	1959–1968
Min./max. draft:	2' 6"/4' 6"	**Sail area:**	260 sq. ft.
Bridge clearance:	32' 6"	**Fuel tankage:**	portable
Power:	outboard 3 to 6 hp	**Water tankage:**	5 gal.
B/D ratio:	36%	**Approx. trailering wgt.:**	4,100 lbs.

Here is one of the earliest fiberglass designs, introduced in 1959. Bill Lapworth, a Southern Californian who designed all the Cal boats for Jensen Marine in the 1960s, was aiming for a light, competitive one-design boat and Midget Ocean Racing Club (MORC) racer. The boat was complete with stove, sink, and head, and was available either as a kit or complete and ready to sail. ***Best features:*** The hull is graceful, with springy sheer and relatively low freeboard, which minimizes undesirable windage. The ballast and displacement, and the SA/D and D/L ratios, are all quite similar to those of the J/24, so her sailing performance could be expected to be somewhat similar as well—except for the superior efficiency of the more modern J/24 underbody and rig, with her substantially bigger foretriangle area. That is, both boats have approximately 260 sq. ft. of sail, but the Cal foretriangle is only 108 square feet, versus the J/24 foretriangle of 125 square feet. ***Worst features:*** The beam of the Cal 24-1 is only 8 feet, making her Space Index the lowest among the comps. Plus, not all kit boats were finished to an acceptable standard of quality.

Comps	LOD	Beam	MinDr	Displ	Bllst	SA/D	D/L	Avg. PHRF	Max. Speed	Motion Index	Space Index	No. of Berths	Head-room
Balboa 24	23' 7"	8' 4"	2' 11"	2,600	900	18.6	145	186	6.0	11.2	365	4	3' 11"
J/24	24' 0"	8' 11"	4' 0"	2,750	945	21.3	153	174	6.0	10.8	372	4	4' 0"
Cal 24-I	24' 0"	8' 0"	2' 6"	2,800	1,000	20.9	156	228	6.0	12.7	295	4	4' 6"
Dufour 24	23' 8"	8' 2"	2' 5"	2,976	1,168	16.4	177	240	5.9	12.9	444	4	5' 4"

Cal 24-2

A racing 24-footer from Jensen Marine

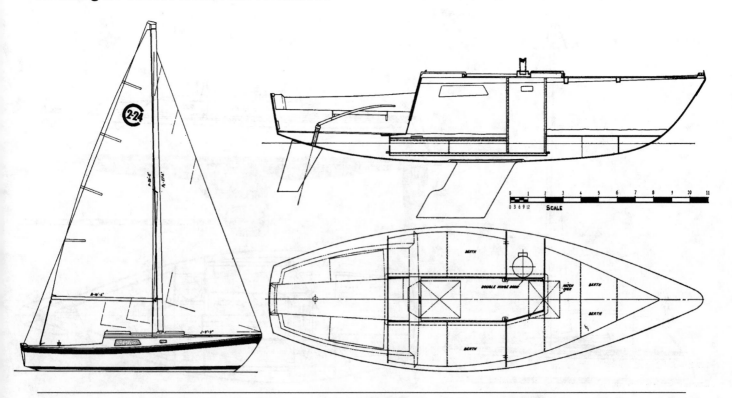

LOD:	24' 0"		**Designer:**	C. William Lapworth
LOA:	24' 0"		**Builder:**	Jensen Marine
LWL:	19' 2"		**Years produced:**	1968–1971
Min./max. draft:	4' 0"		**Sail area:**	274 sq. ft.
Bridge clearance:	34' 0"		**Fuel tankage:**	portable
Power:	outboard 4 to 8 hp		**Water tankage:**	portable
B/D ratio:	38%		**Approx. trailering wgt.:**	5,500 lbs.

The raised deck on the Cal 24-2 (sometimes called the Cal 2-24 by her marketers, and by others sometimes called the Cal 24 Mk II) provides an uncluttered foredeck, and though raised decks tend to increase headroom below, in this case they don't, as the headroom at 4' 0" is worst among the Cal's comps. Unlike her comps, the focus of the Cal 24-2's design was mainly on racing, and it shows in her PHRF rating, her lack of galley amenities, and her underbody form. Her fin keel and spade rudder give her a greater ability to manuever at the starting line and turn quickly

at marks, but prevent her from attaining the easy-steering straight-line stability of her more cruising-oriented long-keel comps. **Best features:** The Cal 24-2 has a presentable PHRF rating of 228, best of her comps and in line with her Cal 24-1 and Cal 24-3 sisters, as well as other boats as varied as the Neptune 24 (page 299) and even (somewhat suprisingly to us) the 8,000-pound Pacific Seacraft Dana 24 (page 303). **Worst features:** Along with her low headroom, the Cal 24-2 has the smallest Space Index of her comp group.

Comps	LOD	Beam	MinDr	Displ	Bllst	SA/D	D/L	Avg. PHRF	Max. Speed	Motion Index	Space Index	No. of Berths	Head-room
Cal 24-2	24' 0"	7' 9"	4' 0"	3,700	1,400	18.3	235	228	5.9	18.0	327	4	4' 0"
Lapworth 24	24' 0"	7' 6"	4' 0"	3,850	2,050	19.1	215	249	6.0	19.0	378	4	5' 0"
Gladiator 24	24' 0"	7' 6"	4' 0"	3,850	2,050	17.1	215	249	6.0	19.0	359	4	4' 9"
Seafarer 24K (23)	22' 10"	7' 10"	3' 9"	3,910	1,400	16.6	195	240	6.1	17.8	372	5	4' 9"
Seafarer 24C (23)	22' 10"	7' 10"	1' 9"	3,920	1,407	16.5	196	243	6.1	17.3	372	5	4' 9"

Cal 24-3
The final version of the Cal 24

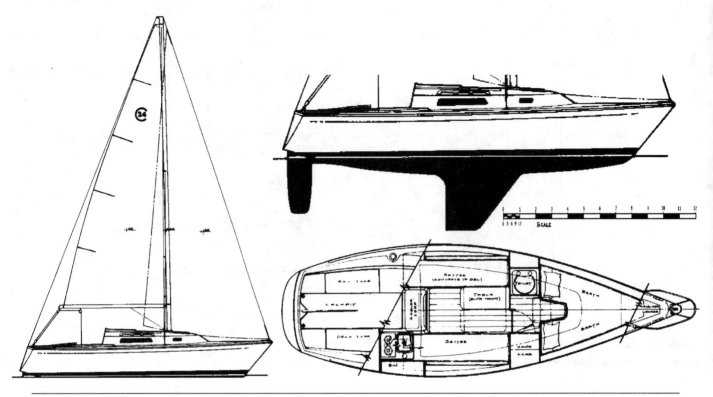

LOD:	23' 9"		**Designer:**	C. Raymond Hunt Assoc.
LOA:	24' 4"		**Builder:**	Cal Boats, Bangor Punta
LWL:	20' 0"		**Years produced:**	1984–1985
Min./max. draft:	3' 4"/4' 3"		**Sail area:**	260 sq. ft.
Bridge clearance:	33' 3"		**Fuel tankage:**	12 gal. optional
Power:	outboard 3 to 6 hp inboard opt.		**Water tankage:**	15 gal.
B/D ratio:	36%		**Approx. trailering wgt.:**	4,900 lbs.

The Cal people asked yacht designer C. Raymond Hunt Associates to come up with "a true blue-water sailboat that would be physically and legally trailerable without special permits." The result was a choice of drafts: 4' 3" for the blue-water-customer contingent, or 3' 4" for the trailer-boat folks. Well, both versions are trailerable, though not easily because of the draft. But then they didn't say the boat had to be easy to trailer, just *legal*. In general, the boat is in the mid- to upper-end in quality of construction, perhaps a cut above O'Day and on a par with Pearson, but below Pacific Seacraft. ***Best features:*** The iron bulb keel of the early Lapworth-designed Cal 24-2 was replaced by an external lead keel bolted to a stub in the Cal 24-3. Result: less maintenance, thinner section, lower center of gravity. Hardware is good quality throughout. The big main hatch is a plus. ***Worst features:*** As with most reverse-transom boats, the outboard bracket on the transom is hard to reach from the cockpit. Standard winches are too small for full-range sailing; Barient #19ST two-speed self-tailing winches were an extra cost option, but worth it. A boom vang, also an extra-cost option, is a necessity too.

Comps	LOD	Beam	MinDr	Displ	Bllst	SA/D	D/L	Avg. PHRF	Max. Speed	Motion Index	Space Index	No. of Berths	Head-room
C&C 24	23' 6"	8' 9"	4' 0"	3,200	1,050	18.6	193	222	5.9	13.0	443	4	5' 3"
S2 7.3 (24)	23' 6"	8' 0"	3' 0"	3,250	1,300	18.6	229	228	5.8	15.5	403	4	5' 0"
Cal 24-3	23' 9"	8' 0"	3' 4"	3,300	1,175	18.8	184	213	6.0	14.9	400	4 or 5	5' 0"
Mirage 24	23' 6"	8' 5"	4' 2"	3,700	1,500	15.0	204	225	6.0	15.4	370	4	4' 9"

Cal T/4 (24)

Quarter Tonner by Bill Lapworth

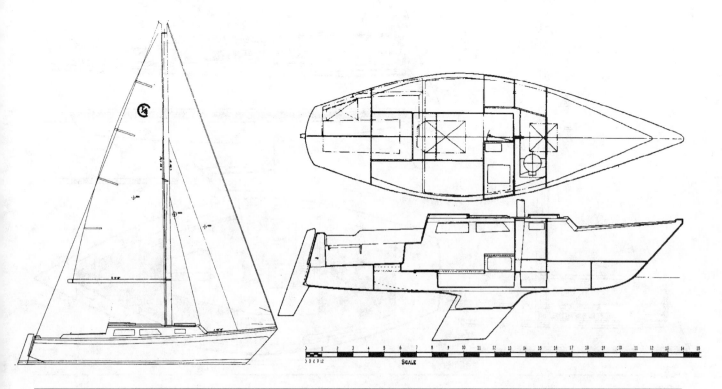

LOD:	24' 2"
LOA:	24' 2"
LWL:	21' 0"
Min./max. draft:	4' 0"
Bridge clearance:	32' 6"
Power:	outboard 3 to 6 hp
B/D ratio:	50%

Designer:	C. William Lapworth
Builder:	Cal Boats
Years produced:	1972–1973
Sail area:	256 sq. ft.
Fuel tankage:	portable
Water tankage:	portable
Approx. trailering wgt.:	6,100 lbs.

The boat was named the T/4 for her builder's intent that she do well in Quarter Ton racing. (We think she did fairly well in the few official Quarter Ton races staged in the 1970s and 1980s, but fell short of producing headlines.) *Best features:* With 4-foot deep fin keel, spade rudder, and 50 percent ballast to displacement ratio, she could run rings around the comps listed here. She has been described as an E-type Jag: robust, quick, agile, and fun. The high-aspect main is rigged far enough above the deck to give standing headroom for tall people standing up in the cockpit (more than 6' 6" clearance over the cockpit sole). *Worst features:* Compared with her comps, she has less headroom below, a lower Space Index, and perhaps lower directional stability (because of her relatively high aspect ratio keel).

Comps	LOD	Beam	MinDr	Displ	Bllst	SA/D	D/L	Avg. PHRF	Max. Speed	Motion Index	Space Index	No. of Berths	Head- room
Buccaneer 240/245 (24)	23' 8"	8' 0"	2' 6"	4,000	1,250	17.0	212	270	6.0	18.0	422	4	6' 0"
Tyler 24	24' 2"	7' 5"	2' 0"	4,000	1,650	16.2	223	NA	6.0	20.1	441	5	6' 0"
Cal T/4 (24)	24' 2"	8' 0"	4' 0"	4,000	2,000	16.3	193	234	6.1	17.5	353	4	5' 3"
Vivacity 24	23' 6"	8' 0"	2' 6"	4,300	1,700	15.4	215	NA	6.1	19.2	385	5	5' 7"

Capri 26 (24)

High, wide, and handsome, and drinks ten below

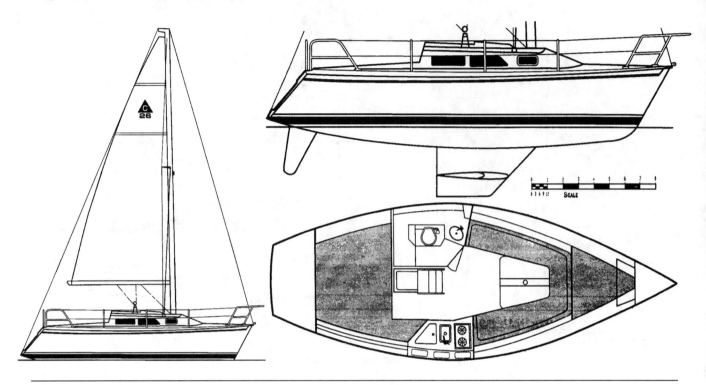

LOD:	23' 8"	**Designer:**	Catalina Design Team
LOA:	26' 2"	**Builder:**	Catalina Yachts
LWL:	22' 11"	**Years produced:**	1990–1997
Min./max. draft:	3' 5"/4' 10"	**Sail area:**	295 sq. ft.
Bridge clearance:	35' 0"	**Fuel tankage:**	10 gal.
Power:	inboard 2-cyl. dsl.	**Water tankage:**	25 gal.
B/D ratio:	36%	**Approx. trailering wgt.:**	7,125 lbs.

The Capri 26 (actually 23' 8" on deck because of her sharply raked transom) is full of big-boat features, which might make her desirable to the big-and-tall crowd. Headroom is over six feet, and the beam of almost ten feet allows a humungus double berth in the main cabin—good for a couple sailing without kids or guests, but maybe not so good for overnight parties of four or more. **Best features:** Cockpit seats are deep and comfortable. Ventilation includes five opening ports, including one in the cockpit well benefitting the aft berth. Galley includes a large insulated icebox, two-burner recessed stove, sink and pressure water system, and considerable storage space. The midships head is private and roomy. **Worst features:** The aft berth can feel somewhat constricted to those with claustrophobia. Racing the boat is a good possibility for those of competitive spirit, with her handicap of 210 and max speed of 6.4 due to her long waterline, but skippers should remember to stow all heavy gear ashore. Though the bow and stern areas might look tempting as stowage areas, for best boat speed they should be kept empty of any heavy gear—and there is no significant stowage area amidships, other than on the cabin sole under the table.

Comps	LOD	Beam	MinDr	Displ	Bllst	SA/D	D/L	Avg. PHRF	Max. Speed	Motion Index	Space Index	No. of Berths	Head-room
Capri 26 (24)	23' 8"	9' 0"	3' 5"	5,100	1,750	15.9	189	210	6.4	15.6	641	4	6' 1"
Cape Dory 25D (Mk II)	25' 0"	8' 0"	3' 6"	5,120	2,050	16.4	333	255	5.8	23.7	472	4	5' 11"
Rhodes Meridian 25	24' 9"	7' 0"	3' 3"	5,310	2,750	13.4	442	252	5.6	31.0	363	4	5' 8"
Contessa 26	25' 5.5"	7' 6"	4' 0"	5,400	2,300	15.8	260	246	6.1	24.8	447	4	5' 0"
Ericson 25 Mk I	24' 8"	8' 0"	2' 0"	5,400	2,500	13.8	267	234	6.1	23.3	457	4	5' 6"

Columbia Contender 24
A 24-footer with two names?

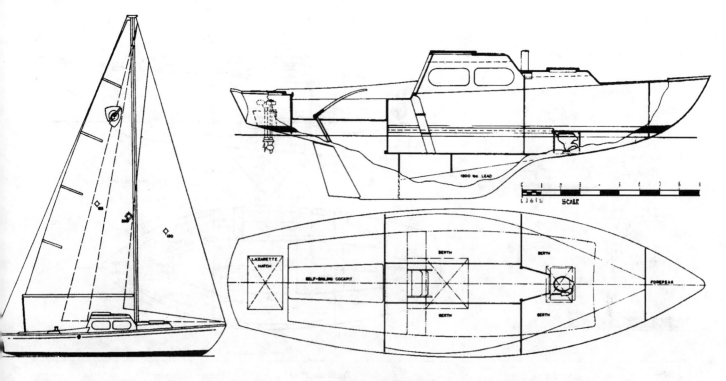

LOD:	24' 0"	**Designer:**	not specified by builder
LOA:	24' 0"	**Builder:**	Columbia Yachts
LWL:	18' 3"	**Years produced:**	1963–1967
Min./max. draft:	3' 3"	**Sail area:**	283 sq. ft.
Bridge clearance:	34' 0"	**Fuel tankage:**	portable
Power:	outboard 3 to 6 hp	**Water tankage:**	portable
B/D ratio:	44%	**Approx. trailering wgt.:**	5,450 lbs.

The Columbia Contender 24 shown here started out in 1963 as the Columbia 24, one of two 24-foot Columbia designs, the plain "24" having a trunk cabin with doghouse, and the other, the Challenger 24 (page 316), having a raised deck. In the table of comparable designs, there is a four-inch difference in LOD, a two-inch difference in beam, a one-inch difference in draft, and a 330-pound difference in displacement between the two Columbia 24 models, even though it is said that they shared the same hull made out of the same mold, and even though they are reported to have identical waterline lengths. We can't explain these anomalies, except to note that we have come across similar small variations in public reporting of statistical data on other boats, including some in this book. *Best features:* Although without amenities like a stove, icebox, or stowage space, this basic boat was quite inexpensive for her time, and no doubt drew many new sailors into yachting. *Worst features:* Although the outboard well is located conveniently close to the cockpit, it is in an unventilated area. Some owners have had trouble with the engine smothering in its own exhaust fumes, unless the hatch is removed or sufficient ventilation is established in some other way.

Comps	LOD	Beam	MinDr	Displ	Bllst	SA/D	D/L	Avg. PHRF	Max. Speed	Motion Index	Space Index	No. of Berths	Head-room
Islander Bahama 24	24' 0"	7' 10"	3' 5"	3,400	1,800	20.8	190	264	6.0	15.9	318	4	4' 6"
Columbia Contender 24	24' 0"	7' 10"	3' 3"	3,600	1,600	19.3	264	258	5.7	17.8	324	4	4' 9"
Columbia Challenger 24	24' 4"	8' 0"	3' 4"	3,930	1,800	18.4	301	258	5.7	19.0	360	4	4' 0"

Cornish Crabber 24
British gaff cutter revival

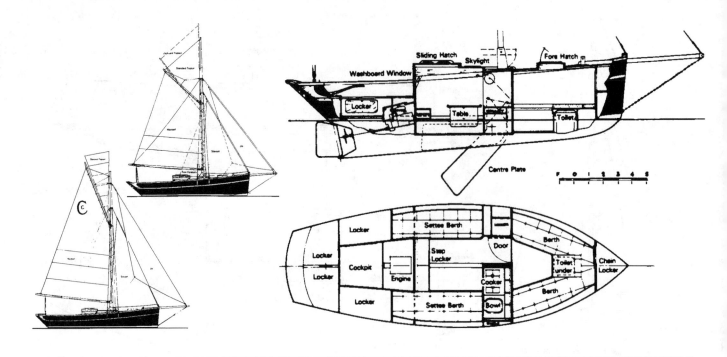

LOD:	24' 0"	**Designer:**	Roger Dongray
LOA:	29' 3"	**Builder:**	Britannia Yachts (importer)
LWL:	20' 3"	**Years produced:**	1974–present
Min./max. draft:	2' 5"/4' 8"	**Sail area:**	265 sq. ft.
Bridge clearance:	29' 0"	**Fuel tankage:**	portable
Power:	outboard 9 hp, inboard opt.	**Water tankage:**	portable
B/D ratio:	10%	**Approx. trailering wgt.:**	6,700 lbs.

The Cornish Crabber can be ordered in a variety of permutations. One choice is the rig: either (A) a gaff-headed mainsail with a standard topsail flying over it (top sailplan), which permits quick sail reduction when the wind pipes up, just by striking the topsail; or (B) the "Mark II," a rig with a larger main and a higher peaked gaff (bottom sailplan), which is more efficient to windward and in light air (but still not as efficient as a Marconi rig). The Mk II has 600 lbs. more displacement (compared to the base case of 4,600 lbs.) and a couple of inches difference in some dimensions (i.e., the Mk II sits 2 inches deeper in the water, making bridge clearance 2 inches less). Outboard power (8 hp recommended) or a 10 hp Yanmar diesel are also choices. ***Best features:*** As a character boat, the Cornish Crabber is hard to beat. But you have to like "pulling a lot of strings," that is, halyards, sheets, reef lines, and so on. ***Worst features:*** In light air the boat's weight is a bit too much for her sail area, with either rig. Not to put too fine an edge on it, in light air she's slow. (Note high PHRF.)

Comps	LOD	Beam	MinDr	Displ	Bllst	SA/D	D/L	Avg. PHRF	Max. Speed	Motion Index	Space Index	No. of Berths	Head-room
Cornish Crabber 24	24' 0"	8' 0"	2' 5"	4,600	600	17.6	247	360	6.0	19.3	415	4	4' 3"
Pacific Seacraft 25	26' 4"	8' 0"	3' 3"	4,750	1,750	12.8	229	NA	6.1	20.3	387	4	5' 0"
O'Day 26 (25)	25' 5"	8' 0"	2' 6"	4,800	1,850	15.7	213	234	6.2	19.8	484	5	5' 6"
Com-Pac 25	24' 7"	8' 6"	2' 6"	4,800	1,900	15.6	231	NA	6.1	18.4	509	5	5' 10"
Morgan 24/25	24' 11"	8' 0"	2' 9"	5,000	1,900	17.0	225	225	6.2	21.4	435	4	5' 8"

Dolphin 24 (O'Day)
Early cruiser designed to win races

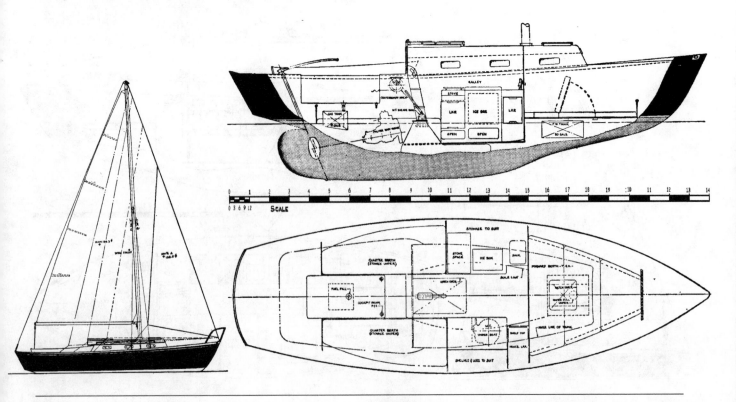

LOD:	24' 2"		**Designer:**	Sparkman & Stephens
LOA:	24' 2"		**Builder:**	Marscot Plastics Div., O'Day
LWL:	19' 0"		**Years produced:**	1960–1972
Min./max. draft:	2' 10"/5' 2"		**Sail area:**	291 sq. ft.
Bridge clearance:	33' 0"		**Fuel tankage:**	10 gal.
Power:	Palmer inboard 6 hp		**Water tankage:**	20 gal.
B/D ratio:	32%		**Approx. trailering wgt.:**	6,600 lbs.

Marscot Plastics was a pioneer in building plastic boats starting in the late 1940s. But by 1958 owner Palmer Scott decided to sell the business to O'Day, who formed the Marscot Plastic Division of George D. O'Day Associates. O'Day then contracted with Sparkman & Stephens to design a racer-cruiser modeled on a wooden yawl drawn by S&S designer Bill Shaw called the Shaw 24 and built in 1957. That design had won 27 consecutive races under MORC and other racing rules, and O'Day thought the Dolphin might do as well. Some Dolphins were sold as kits, and some have wooden deck houses and wooden spars. Most of the boats have a solid ⅜" thick bronze centerboard. Inboard power was standard in the form of a 6-hp Palmer Baby Huskie gasoline engine. A lighter Dolphin 24 (page 286) was built on the West Coast. *Best features:* The O'Day Dolphin is a heavily built vessel that sails well and has proven quite durable despite the passage of time—and she is still capable of winning races. There is an active and enthusiastic owner group. *Worst features:* With her wood trim and aging hardware, she can be a maintenance headache.

Comps	LOD	Beam	MinDr	Displ	Bllst	SA/D	D/L	Avg. PHRF	Max. Speed	Motion Index	Space Index	No. of Berths	Head-room
Dolphin 24 (Pacific/Yankee)	24' 2"	7' 8"	2' 10"	4,250	1,750	18.1	277	246	5.8	21.1	406	4 or 5	4' 8"
Pearson Lark 24	24' 0"	8' 0"	4' 0"	4,300	1,500	16.7	303	246	5.8	20.5	456	4	4' 5"
Stone Horse 23	23' 4"	7' 1"	3' 6"	4,490	2,000	19.9	325	280	5.7	24.2	329	2	3' 9"
Dolphin 24 (O'Day)	24' 2"	7' 8"	2' 10"	4,500	1,440	17.1	293	246	5.8	22.3	370	4	4' 8"
Paceship Westwind 24	23' 11"	7' 11"	2' 2"	4,600	2,370	17.9	345	231	5.7	22.7	326	4	5' 6"

Dolphin 24 (Pacific/Yankee)
A lighter and maybe faster version of the Dolphin

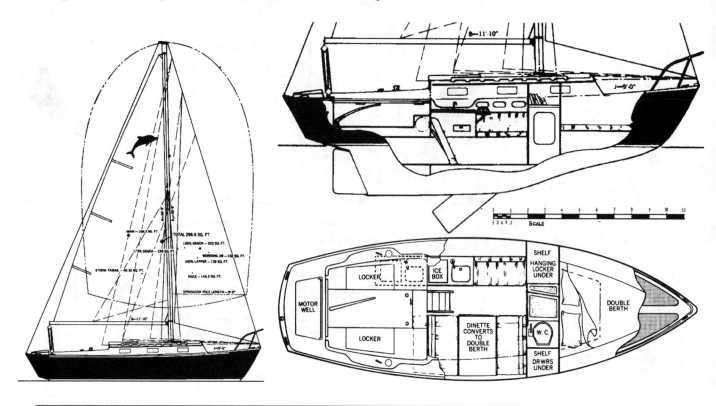

LOD:	24' 2"		**Designer:**	Sparkman & Stephens
LOA:	24' 2"		**Builder:**	Yankee Yachts, et al.
LWL:	19' 0"		**Years produced:**	1965–1977
Min./max. draft:	2' 10"/5' 2"		**Sail area:**	297 sq. ft.
Bridge clearance:	34' 0"		**Fuel tankage:**	portable
Power:	outboard 4 to 8 hp		**Water tankage:**	portable
B/D ratio:	41%		**Approx. trailering wgt.:**	6,300 lbs.

From 1965 until 1972, Yankee Yachts of Inglewood, CA, constructed a Dolphin somewhat different from the O'Day version (page 285). Yankee folded, and in 1976 and 1977 one of their former suppliers, who had inherited the Yankee molds, started up production again as Pacific Dolphin, Inc. These West Coast builders produced a boat that, compared to the O'Day version, was lighter overall by 250 lbs. despite 310 lbs. more ballast. Part of the difference in weight was in the centerboard, which instead of bronze was lead-ballasted fiberglass, and part was probably due to the substitution of an outboard well for the little Palmer 6-hp inboard engine in the original O'Day version. The rearrangement of the cabin furniture no doubt permitted some saving in weight as well. **Best features:** The relatively light weight West Coast Dolphin should be faster than her comps in light air. **Worst features:** The bridge deck has been lowered, increasing the possibility of green water finding its way into the cabin.

Comps	LOD	Beam	MinDr	Displ	Bllst	SA/D	D/L	Avg. PHRF	Max. Speed	Motion Index	Space Index	No. of Berths	Head-room
Dolphin 24 (Pacific/Yankee)	24' 2"	7' 8"	2' 10"	4,250	1,750	18.1	277	246	5.8	21.1	406	4 or 5	4' 8"
Pearson Lark 24	24' 0"	8' 0"	4' 0"	4,300	1,500	16.7	303	246	5.8	20.5	456	4	4' 5"
Stone Horse 23	23' 4"	7' 1"	3' 6"	4,490	2,000	19.9	325	280	5.7	24.2	329	2	3' 9"
Dolphin 24 (O'Day)	24' 2"	7' 8"	2' 10"	4,500	1,440	17.1	293	246	5.8	22.3	370	4	4' 8"
Paceship Westwind 24	23' 11"	7' 11"	2' 2"	4,600	2,370	17.9	345	231	5.7	22.7	326	4	5' 6"

Dufour 24
French import from the late 1970s

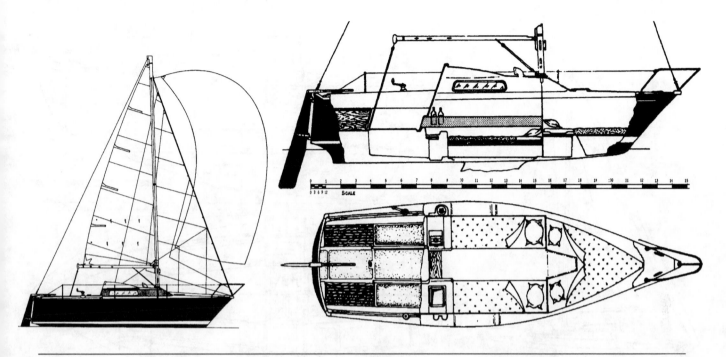

LOD:	23' 8"	**Designer:**	Michel Dufour
LOA:	26' 0"	**Builder:**	Dufour USA
LWL:	19' 7"	**Years produced:**	1977–1978
Min./max. draft:	2' 5"/3' 10"	**Sail area:**	212 sq. ft.
Bridge clearance:	31' 0"	**Fuel tankage:**	portable
Power:	outboard or inboard 4 to 8 hp	**Water tankage:**	portable
B/D ratio:	39%	**Approx. trailering wgt.:**	4,300 lbs.

This is a design with some unusual characteristics. You might expect a sleek, rounded hull from the French, á la Beneteau, but here you get high topsides, not an inch of springy sheer, and only a small spread of sail, oddly shifted forward. (It may be that the mast has been ooched forward to be positioned directly over the main bulkhead for support.) The hull design is apparently aimed at maximizing cabin space: a squared-off, slab-sided hull with the beam stretched wide all the way back to the transom; high topsides, and a bubble in the small coachroof to squeeze in extra inches of headroom and to aid in access to the cabin, since there is no companionway hatch. There are two keel options: shoal, with a draft of 2' 5" (too shallow for good upwind performance), and "deep fin" with a draft of 3' 10" **Best features:** Very deep cockpit coamings provide excellent back support. **Worst features:** The high, slab-sided topsides and small sail area make for unusually large "top hamper," which will tend to catch the wind and slide the boat sideways, especially in light air when the going is slow and the keel isn't moving fast enough to take a bite. The absence of a companionway hatch will make access to the cabin difficult for some. And where, you might ask, is the head? We don't see one, or a place for one. You could use a bucket in the 1970s, but not anymore.

Comps	LOD	Beam	MinDr	Displ	Bllst	SA/D	D/L	Avg. PHRF	Max. Speed	Motion Index	Space Index	No. of Berths	Head-room
Balboa 24	23' 7"	8' 4"	2' 11"	2,600	900	18.6	145	186	6.0	11.2	365	4	3' 11"
J/24	24' 0"	8' 11"	4' 0"	2,750	945	21.3	153	174	6.0	10.8	372	4	4' 0"
Cal 24-1	24' 0"	8' 0"	2' 6"	2,800	1,000	20.9	156	228	6.0	12.7	295	4	4' 6"
Dufour 24	23' 8"	8' 2"	2' 5"	2,960	1,168	16.4	177	240	5.9	12.9	444	4	5' 4"

Eastward Ho 24
A little yacht that looks good and sails well

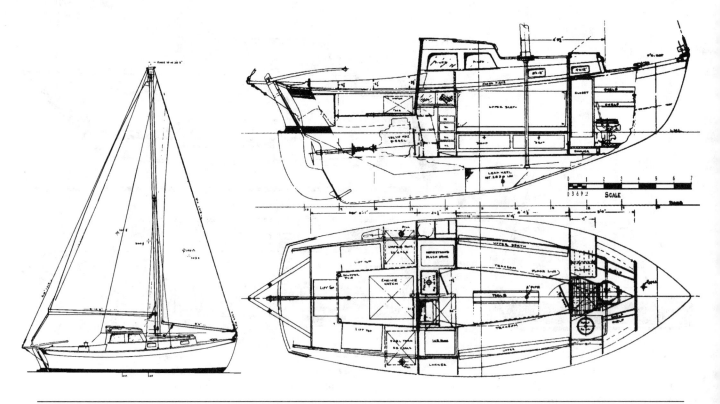

LOD:	23' 8"	**Designer:**	Eldredge McInnis
LOA:	25' 5"	**Builder:**	Portsmouth Yacht Co.
LWL:	20' 0"	**Years produced:**	1974–1981
Min./max. draft:	3' 10"	**Sail area:**	283 sq. ft.
Bridge clearance:	35' 0"	**Fuel tankage:**	22 gal.
Power:	gas or dsl. 22 to 30 hp	**Water tankage:**	22 gal.
B/D ratio:	51%	**Approx. trailering wgt.:**	10,400 lbs.

The Eastward Ho was available either as a sloop (shown here) or, with a bowsprit added, as a cutter. There was also a choice of motive power, including a Volvo MD-2 diesel (22 hp) or an Atomic Four (30 hp). The designer, Eldredge McInnis of Boston, MA, a firm started in 1926, tended to specialize in large yachts, especially motorsailers. (The firm closed in 1976 when Walter J. McInnis retired at age 83. Albert Eldredge had died in 1936 but was involved in sales, not design.) Even though she's less than 24 feet on deck, because of her displacement of 7,000 pounds she can use

the power to punch through waves. Typically, these boats were offered with a yacht finish, teak and holly sole, teak interior, fine jointer-work, and so on. ***Best features:*** This is a top-of-the-line yacht for her size range. She is durable, beautiful to look at, and a good sailer, especially when it breezes up. ***Worst features:*** When these boats come onto the market, which is rare, they typically command a premium price. That said, a 1978 model was recently listed on the Internet for $18,000, which, after all, is not a fortune for a really nice boat.

Comps	LOD	Beam	MinDr	Displ	Bllst	SA/D	D/L	Avg. PHRF	Max. Speed	Motion Index	Space Index	No. of Berths	Head- room
Eastward Ho 24	23' 8"	8' 8"	3' 10"	7,000	3,600	12.4	391	269	6.0	28.7	475	4	6' 4"
Blue Water 24	24' 0"	8' 7"	4' 1"	7,950	2,275	11.1	467	NA	5.9	33.2	418	4	6' 1"
Pacific Seacraft Dana 24	24' 2"	8' 7"	3' 10"	8,000	3,200	14.4	364	221	6.2	30.2	535	4	6' 1"
Aquarius Pilot Cutter 24	24' 0"	9' 0"	4' 0"	8,900	3,200	15.3	497	258	6.0	31.0	564	4	6' 3"

Elite 25 (24)

Like her comps, French boat, French style

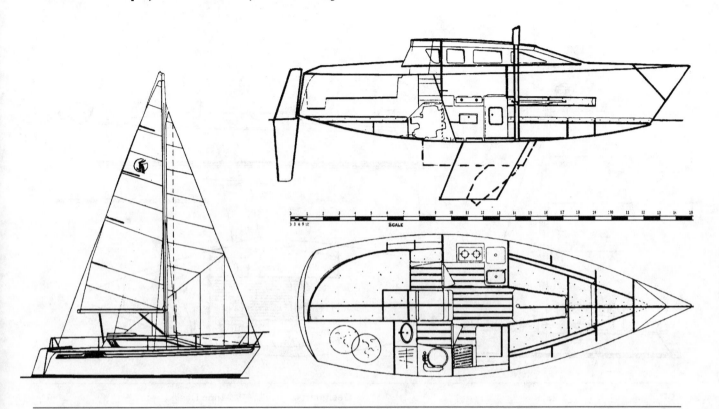

LOD:	24' 0"	**Designer:**	Joubert & Nivelt
LOA:	25' 10"	**Builder:**	Elite Yachts
LWL:	21' 6"	**Years produced:**	1983–1987
Min./max. draft:	2' 3"/5' 2"	**Sail area:**	252 sq. ft.
Bridge clearance:	34' 4"	**Fuel tankage:**	portable
Power:	outboard or inboard 6 to 10 hp	**Water tankage:**	20 gal.
B/D ratio:	41%	**Approx. trailering wgt.:**	6,400 lbs.

Elite Yachts de France of Fort Lauderdale, FL, imported these boats from Kirie Constructions Nautiques S.A., in La Rochelle, France. Joubert & Nivelt, French stylists who also designed the Ranger 23 "Fun" (page 125) and the Tanzer 25 Mk II (page 370) were behind the Elite 25 as well. Like the other three boats in this comp group (all, by the way, French in style and origin), the Elite 25 was available either as a fin keeler (4' 7" draft, 3,968 pounds displacement, 1,455 pounds ballast) or a keel-centerboarder (2' 3" draft board up, 5' 2" board down, 4,300 pounds displacement, 1,742 pounds ballast). ***Best features:*** The boats included good quality materials (aluminum ports and hatches, teak and holly cabin soles, varnished elm interiors, teak cockpit seats). PHRF of 201 signifies good speed versus comps. ***Worst features:*** Fabric cabin liners were not up to an otherwise good standard of quality.

Comps	LOD	Beam	MinDr	Displ	Bllst	SA/D	D/L	Avg. PHRF	Max. Speed	Motion Index	Space Index	No. of Berths	Head-room
Jeanneau Eolia 25	24' 7"	9' 2"	2' 7"	3,750	1,830	21.4	165	243	6.2	13.4	568	4	5' 8"
Dufour 1800 (25)	25' 1"	8' 10"	4' 3"	3,969	1,654	16.1	166	213	6.3	14.3	536	4	5' 6"
Kelt 7.60 (25)	24' 11"	9' 5"	4' 3"	4,189	1,765	17.5	157	204	6.4	13.7	577	4	5' 7"
Elite 25 (24)	24' 0"	8' 10"	2' 3"	4,300	1,742	15.2	193	201	6.2	15.9	527	4	6' 0"

Freedom 24
Bill Tripp, III, draws a trailerable racer-cruiser

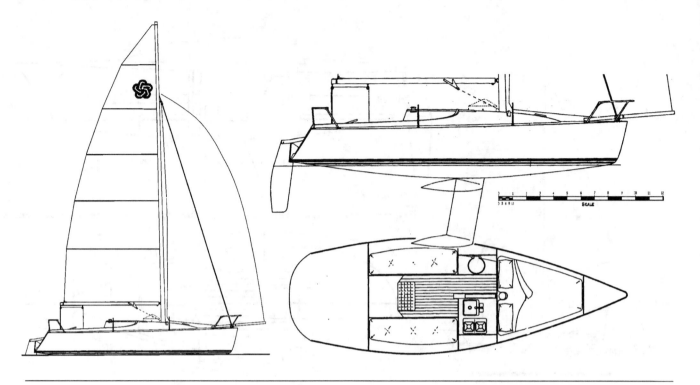

LOD:	23' 9"		**Designer:**	Tripp Design
LOA:	26' 11"		**Builder:**	Freedom Yachts
LWL:	21' 6"		**Years produced:**	1994–1996
Min./max. draft:	1' 10"/6' 0"		**Sail area:**	302 sq. ft.
Bridge clearance:	38' 6"		**Fuel tankage:**	portable
Power:	outboard 4 to 6 hp		**Water tankage:**	portable
B/D ratio:	42%		**Approx. trailering wgt.:**	4,600 lbs.

Freedom Yachts, a marketer of high quality sailboats, wanted to try selling a fast boat of high quality construction that was easy to trailer, launch, and sail, and with a good measure of comfort below. The design is by William H. Tripp, III, son of Bill Tripp, Jr., who designed the Bermuda 40 and the Block Island 40, among other popular craft. ***Best features:*** The jib, set on a roller furler, is self-tacking, and all controls are led to the cockpit for easy sailing. Foam flotation makes the boat unsinkable; the retractable rudder and lifting bulb keel (draft 6' down, 1' 10" up, with an intermediate position of 4' 5" for sailing in shallow water) eases launching from a ramp, given the right trailer and ramp. The finish inside and out is very good quality. ***Worst features:*** For the short period this boat was sold, her price was at the top end of her comps—but construction quality is also at or near the top end. Yet for some reason this boat did not sell well. Perhaps it was the small forward V-berth, big enough for kids but not adults, or her speed, indicated by her average PHRF of 207—quite a bit higher than most of her comps.

Comps	LOD	Beam	MinDr	Displ	Bllst	SA/D	D/L	Avg. PHRF	Max. Speed	Motion Index	Space Index	No. of Berths	Head-room
Merit 25 (24)	24' 0"	8' 0"	4' 0"	2,900	1,050	21.7	106	168	6.4	11.9	409	4	4' 1"
Seaward 25 (24)	24' 0"	8' 4"	2' 1"	3,100	1,100	17.7	114	270	6.4	11.7	483	5	5' 3"
Kirby 25	24' 7"	8' 9"	4' 2"	3,150	1,500	21.6	157	174	6.1	12.2	453	4	4' 6"
Dehler 25 (23)	23' 1"	8' 3"	1' 4"	3,245	1,654	20.1	139	186	6.3	13.2	412	4	4' 3"
Freedom 24	23' 9"	8' 3"	1' 10"	3,250	1,350	22.0	146	207	6.2	13.3	428	4	4' 7"

Freedom 25 (24)
Garry Hoyt said, "Why shouldn't it be different?"

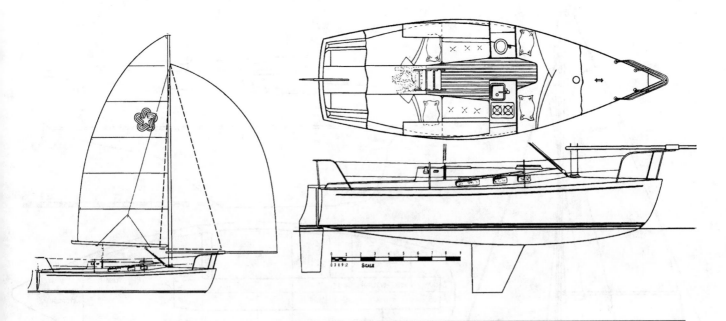

LOD:	24' 4"	**Designer:**	Garry Hoyt
LOA:	25' 8"	**Builder:**	Freedom Yachts
LWL:	20' 0"	**Years produced:**	1982–1984?
Min./max. draft:	4' 5"	**Sail area:**	260 sq. ft.
Bridge clearance:	33' 6"	**Fuel tankage:**	portable
Power:	outboard or inboard 4 to 9 hp	**Water tankage:**	10 gal.
B/D ratio:	29%	**Approx. trailering wgt.:**	5,350 lbs.

Garry Hoyt, main designer and marketer of the Freedom line of sailboats, is known as a free thinker when it comes to sailboat design. The Freedom 25, with her full-battened mainsail, small "staysail" jib, "gunmount" spinnaker handling gear, and unstayed mast, is a good example of the fruition of Hoyt's thinking. Hoyt says full-length battens have several advantages, the main one being ease of reefing. "A sailor wants a sail he can get up and get down quickly, a sail that is easy to handle, can be reefed easily, and provides acceptable performance." The fully battened sails are quieter too.

The little jib, which was an option on new boats, improves upwind performance in light air. The gunmount makes using a spinnaker a singlehanded job: one sailor can hoist, jibe, and douse the spinnaker without ever leaving the cockpit. The unstayed mast simplifies the rig and makes getting underway faster. **Best features:** Besides the above, the cockpit is deep and comfortable, with good back support. **Worst features:** The wing mast and sail sleeves on early boats didn't work out. Consequently, a conventional sailtrack on a round mast was used on most production.

Comps	LOD	Beam	MinDr	Displ	Bllst	SA/D	D/L	Avg. PHRF	Max. Speed	Motion Index	Space Index	No. of Berths	Head-room
Lancer 25	24' 8"	8' 0"	2' 4"	3,400	1,200	17.5	187	264	6.0	15.2	560	4 to 6	5' 10"
Freedom 25 (24)	24' 4"	8' 6"	4' 5"	3,500	1,025	18.0	195	186	6.0	14.3	532	4	4' 10"
Catalina 250	25' 0"	8' 6"	1' 8"	3,600	1,200	18.3	167	225	6.2	14.3	395	4	4' 3"
Hunter 25 Mk III	24' 6"	8' 5"	2' 0"	3,700	1,309	17.1	153	225	6.3	14.4	484	4	5' 4"
Santana 25	24' 7"	7' 10"	2' 7"	4,050	1,750	16.5	244	222	5.9	18.6	396	4	5' 2"

Gladiator 24
Lapworth 24 with a raised deck

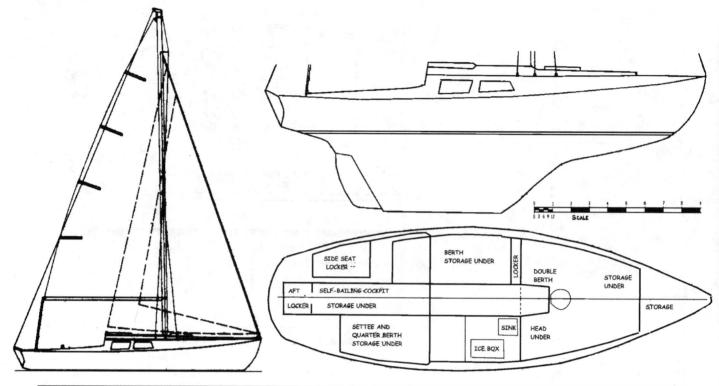

LOD:	24' 0"	**Designer:**	C. William Lapworth
LOA:	24' 0"	**Builder:**	Continental Plastics
LWL:	20' 0"	**Years produced:**	1958?–1966?
Min./max. draft:	4' 0"	**Sail area:**	263 sq. ft.
Bridge clearance:	33' 6"	**Fuel tankage:**	portable
Power:	outboard 3 to 6 hp	**Water tankage:**	10 gal.
B/D ratio:	53%	**Approx. trailering wgt.:**	5,700 lbs.

Somewhere around 1958 yacht designer William Lapworth drew two boats for the Continental Plastics Corporation of Costa Mesa, CA: the Lapworth 24 (or L24) and the Gladiator 24. The L24 (page 296) featured a longish trunk cabin and the Gladiator had a raised deck; otherwise both vessels looked very similar, with hulls of the same overall dimensions and exactly, or very nearly exactly, the same shape. Both were good on the race course, at least in heavy air, and with their relatively long and deep keels were weatherly and seaworthy. Both boats drew raves from California sailors. ***Best features:***

For her day—remember, fiberglass boats were being designed and built for the first time in the late 1950s—the Gladiator was right at the forefront of technology. ***Worst features:*** The keel, based on traditional 1950s knowledge of what worked on a sailboat, had a bit too much wetted surface to attain spectacular speeds, especially in light air. Lapworth figured out that a boat with a fin keel with a lot less wetted surface and somewhat less ballast would be better than the Gladiator or L24 as an all-round racing-cruising boat. The result was the Cal 24-2 (page 279).

Comps	LOD	Beam	MinDr	Displ	Bllst	SA/D	D/L	Avg. PHRF	Max. Speed	Motion Index	Space Index	No. of Berths	Head- room
Cal 24-2	24' 0"	7' 9"	4' 0"	3,700	1,400	18.3	235	228	5.9	18.0	327	4	4' 0"
Lapworth 24	24' 0"	7' 9"	4' 0"	3,850	2,050	19.1	215	249	6.0	19.0	378	4	5' 0"
Gladiator 24	24' 0"	7' 6"	4' 0"	3,850	2,050	17.1	215	249	6.0	19.0	359	4	4' 9"
Seafarer 24K (23)	22' 10"	7' 10"	3' 9"	3,910	1,400	16.6	195	240	6.1	17.8	372	5	4' 9"
Seafarer 24C (23)	22' 10"	7' 10"	1' 9"	3,920	1,407	16.5	196	243	6.1	17.3	372	5	4' 9"

Helms 24

A furniture maker from Irmo built this boat

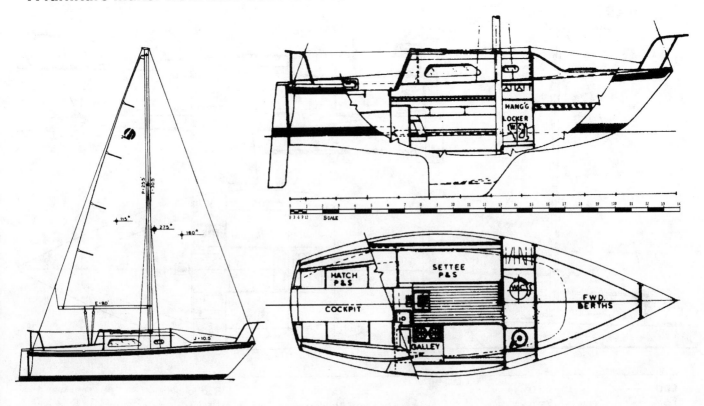

LOD:	23' 11"		Designer:	Stuart Windley
LOA:	23' 11"		Builder:	Helms Co.
LWL:	20' 10"		Years produced:	1976–1987
Min./max. draft:	3' 0"/4' 2"		Sail area:	275 sq. ft.
Bridge clearance:	34' 0"		Fuel tankage:	portable
Power:	outboard or inboard 4 to 8 hp		Water tankage:	15 gal.
B/D ratio:	33%		Approx. trailering wgt.:	6,300 lbs.

Jack A. Helms, a furniture maker in Irmo, SC, who also built Y-Flyers and Lightning sloops, decided to branch out into cruising sailboats, and the Helms 24 was one result. Among other models, he also produced the Helms 25, 27, 30, and 32. The Helms 24 is basically an outboard-powered boat, though a small Yanmar 1GM10 diesel was an option. She came in two models: shoal keel (3' 0" draft) or fin keel (4' 2" draft). The brochure says she sleeps five, with the port settee converting to a double. But even assuming the starboard settee extends aft under the stove for foot room, it's hard to imagine five full-sized humans sleeping aboard comfortably, especially with the kiddy-sized V-berth forward. **Best features:** With her wide beam and high sheer, her Space Index and headroom are much better than her comps. Her longer waterline and higher B/D ratio also help in the speed department, as indicated by her lower PHRF rating. **Worst features:** There may have been problems with leakage around the external lead keel seam. Check with other owners.

Comps	LOD	Beam	MinDr	Displ	Bllst	SA/D	D/L	Avg. PHRF	Max. Speed	Motion Index	Space Index	No. of Berths	Head-room
Quickstep 24	23' 11"	7' 11"	3' 4"	4,000	1,300	16.4	260	258	5.8	19.1	341	5	4' 5"
Helms 24	24' 0"	8' 11"	3' 0"	4,200	1,850	16.9	207	234	6.1	16.3	520	5	5' 8"
Pearson 24	23' 6"	8' 0"	4' 0"	4,300	1,800	17.2	303	252	5.8	20.7	375	4	4' 9"

J/24

World's most popular one-design keelboat

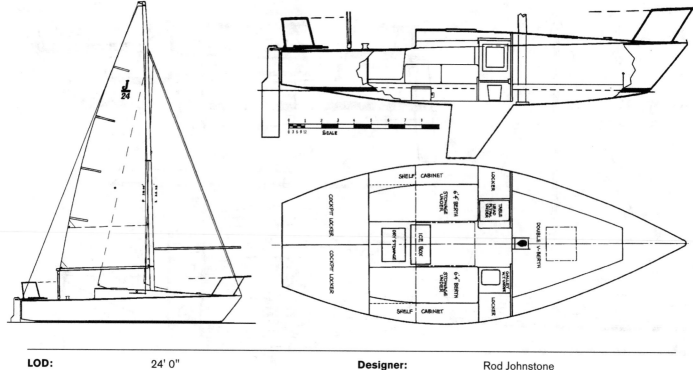

LOD:	24' 0"	**Designer:**	Rod Johnstone
LOA:	25' 0"	**Builder:**	J/Boats
LWL:	20' 0"	**Years produced:**	1977–present
Min./max. draft:	4' 0"	**Sail area:**	261 sq. ft.
Bridge clearance:	35' 6"	**Fuel tankage:**	portable
Power:	outboard 3 to 6 hp	**Water tankage:**	5 gal.
B/D ratio:	34%	**Approx. trailering wgt.:**	4,100 lbs.

With over 5,000 boats worldwide, the marketer's claim that the J/24 is the "world's most popular one-design keelboat" is probably true. We were attracted to the boat from the start, and in 1983 sold our Tartan 27 and had a J/24 built (#3333, *SuperPip3*), which our teenaged kids then raced (occasionally permitting us to join them) for several years at our local Noroton Yacht Club in Darien, CT. The boat is light and sails like a big dinghy. In anything over ten knots of air, "rail meat" is needed to keep the boat on her feet going upwind, but the ride can be thrilling. We cruised her occasionally, and once or twice trailered her to Newport for a week's

cruise of Narragansett Bay, where there was a public park with a launching crane available. But we wouldn't recommend the boat if cruising is your main aim. ***Best features:*** This is a great boat to race if you like to socialize and want to learn how to race well. ***Worst features:*** With her 4-foot draft, launching at any but the steepest launching ramps is out of the question. Luckily, most places where J/24s are raced have access to a crane. The J/24 has an eyebolt on the top of the keel for shackling to a crane hook. The crane can also be used to lift and set the mast, which steps not on deck but on the keel.

Comps	LOD	Beam	MinDr	Displ	Bllst	SA/D	D/L	Avg. PHRF	Max. Speed	Motion Index	Space Index	No. of Berths	Head-room
Balboa 24	23' 7"	8' 4"	2' 11"	2,600	900	18.6	145	186	6.0	11.2	365	4	3' 11"
J/24	24' 0"	8' 11"	4' 0"	2,750	945	21.3	153	174	6.0	10.8	372	4	4' 0"
Cal 24-1	24' 0"	8' 0"	2' 6"	2,800	1,000	20.9	156	228	6.0	12.7	295	4	4' 6"
Dufour 24	23' 8"	8' 2"	2' 5"	2,976	1,168	16.4	177	240	5.9	12.9	444	4	5' 4"

Kenner Kittiwake 24

A near clone of the South Coast 23

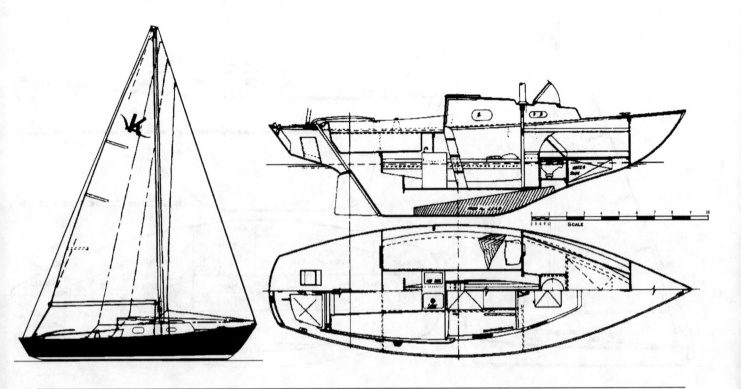

LOD:	23' 7"	**Designer:**	Carl Alberg (modified)
LOA:	23' 7"	**Builder:**	Kenner Boatworks, et al.
LWL:	17' 9"	**Years produced:**	1966–1978
Min./max. draft:	2' 10"	**Sail area:**	220 sq. ft.
Bridge clearance:	30' 9"	**Fuel tankage:**	portable
Power:	outboard 3 to 6 hp	**Water tankage:**	18 gal.
B/D ratio:	39%	**Approx. trailering wgt.:**	5,600 lbs.

In 1964, Carl Alberg drew plans for the South Coast 23 (page 255). Hollis Metcalf, proprietor of South Coast Seacraft, farmed out the molding to Kenner Boatworks, finishing the bare hulls at his own facility and marketing the boats countrywide. Not long afterward, the story goes, Kenner Boatworks "found a leftover boat" and refashioned it, by allegedly adding six inches to the stern overhang and raising a portion of the cabintop. (Whether they actually added six inches to the SC23's length we aren't sure, not having a boat to measure. A comparison of drawings of the two designs suggests that the two hulls may be the same length.) They then began marketing the design as the Kenner Kittiwake 24 (without referencing Alberg as the designer in ads) and produced boats from 1966 to 1971. Ray Greene took over production from about 1973 to 1975, and River City Sailcraft (believed to be related to Kenner Boatworks) built the boat from about 1976 to 1978. **Best features:** Same as for the South Coast 23. **Worst features:** Same as for the South Coast 23.

Comps	LOD	Beam	MinDr	Displ	Bllst	SA/D	D/L	Avg. PHRF	Max. Speed	Motion Index	Space Index	No. of Berths	Head-room
Kenner Kittiwake 24	23' 7"	7' 5"	2' 10"	3,800	1,500	14.5	303	270	5.6	20.7	351	4	4' 6"
Allied Greenwich 24	24' 3"	7' 3"	3' 0"	3,825	1,500	17.3	323	273	5.6	21.6	304	4	4' 7"
Bridges Point 24	24' 0"	7' 9"	3' 5"	3,944	1,900	17.8	271	246	5.8	20.4	322	2, 3, 4	4' 5"
Quickstep 24	23' 11"	7' 11"	3' 4"	4,000	1,300	16.4	260	258	5.8	19.1	341	5	4' 5"

Lapworth 24 (or L24)

Gladiator 24 with a cabin house

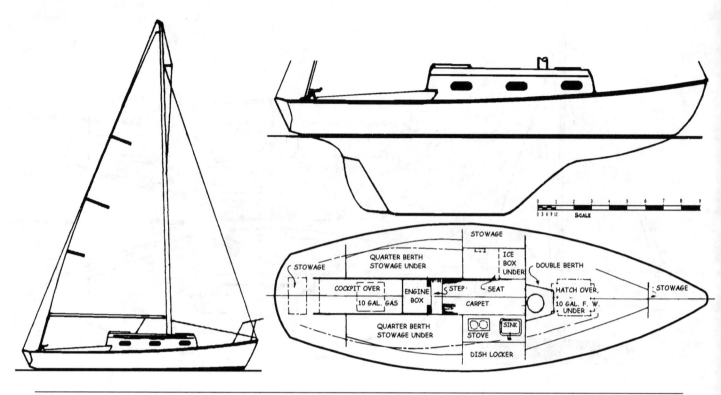

LOD:	24' 0"	**Designer:**	C. William Lapworth
LOA:	24' 0"	**Builder:**	Continental Plastics
LWL:	20' 0"	**Years produced:**	1958?–1966?
Min./max. draft:	4' 0"	**Sail area:**	298 sq. ft.
Bridge clearance:	33' 6"	**Fuel tankage:**	portable
Power:	outboard or inboard 4 to 9 hp	**Water tankage:**	10 gal.
B/D ratio:	53%	**Approx. trailering wgt.:**	5,700 lbs.

Sixteen-year-old Robin Lee Graham sailed *Dove*, a used L24 modified for ocean voyaging, starting in July, 1965, and getting most of the way around the world (from California westward to St. Thomas in the U.S. Virgin Islands) by November, 1968, before switching to an Allied Luders 33 to complete his circumnavigation in 1970. Graham subsequently wrote the book, *Dove*. An early ad for the L24 is headlined, "Three outstanding 24s," but strangely, no further mention is made of the other two, which are the Gladiator 24 (page 292), a raised-deck version with the same rig but slightly less sail area and

a slight shift in mast position, and the Spartan 24, a no-frills economy model based on the L24. The early L24 design was billed as displacing 4,350 pounds, but later somehow lost 500 pounds to end up at the weight shown here. ***Best features:*** The comparatively long deep keel on the L24 (and the Gladiator 24) versus her comps provides considerable directional stability (i.e., ability to keep sailing in one direction without needing to correct the course using the helm or sail trim). ***Worst features:*** Like all her comps except one, the L24's draft is too deep for convenient trailer-sailing.

Comps	LOD	Beam	MinDr	Displ	Bllst	SA/D	D/L	Avg. PHRF	Max. Speed	Motion Index	Space Index	No. of Berths	Head- room
Cal 24-2	24' 0"	7' 9"	4' 0"	3,700	1,400	18.3	235	228	5.9	18.0	420	4	4' 0"
Lapworth 24	24' 0"	7' 9"	4' 0"	3,850	2,050	19.1	215	249	6.0	19.0	378	4	5' 0"
Gladiator 24	24' 0"	7' 6"	4' 0"	3,850	2,050	17.1	215	249	6.0	19.0	359	4	4' 9"
Seafarer 24K (23)	22' 10"	7' 10"	3' 9"	3,910	1,400	16.6	195	240	6.1	17.8	372	5	4' 9"
Seafarer 24C (23)	22' 10"	7' 10"	1' 9"	3,920	1,407	16.5	196	243	6.1	17.3	372	5	4' 9"

Merit 25 (24)

Does this boat look like a J/24 to you?

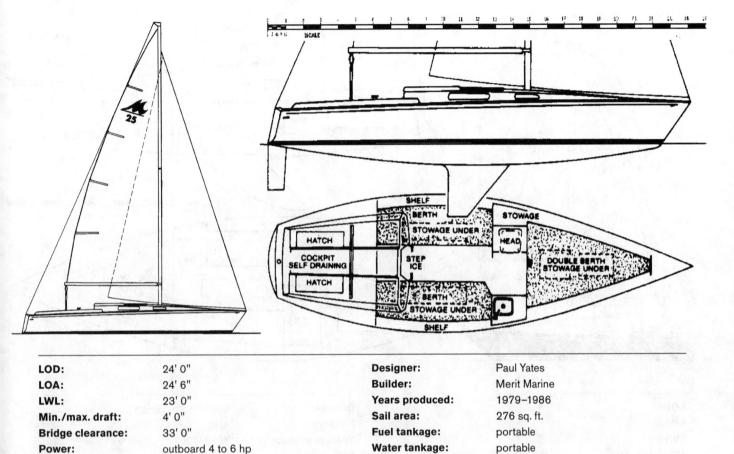

LOD:	24' 0"		**Designer:**	Paul Yates
LOA:	24' 6"		**Builder:**	Merit Marine
LWL:	23' 0"		**Years produced:**	1979–1986
Min./max. draft:	4' 0"		**Sail area:**	276 sq. ft.
Bridge clearance:	33' 0"		**Fuel tankage:**	portable
Power:	outboard 4 to 6 hp		**Water tankage:**	portable
B/D ratio:	36%		**Approx. trailering wgt.:**	4,500 lbs.

According to one unproven but not necessarily false story, a J/24 disappeared into designer/builder Paul Yates' garage in 1978, and some months later reappeared as the first Merit 25. The two designs are indeed similar in many ways. But the Merit is judged by many to be more comfortable, faster in light air, and less expensive—at least in the San Francisco Bay area, where she was spawned. *Best features:* She is fast and has won the MORC Internationals three times. The cockpit has backrests of a reasonable height for comfort. The cabin is well-organized for short cruises compared with other boats of the same ilk. She is easily trailered, though launching via hoist is infinitely easier than at a ramp. *Worst features:* Merit 25s that have been raced hard for a number of years sometimes develop an unusual structural problem: the keel begins to flex at the point of attachment to the hull, requiring a major reinforcement job. This happens primarily, if not exclusively, to post-1984 hulls in which the cabin soles have been lowered to give increased headroom—a design change that reduced the structural integrity of the hull in the area of the keel. **Note:** The actual waterline length is in question. If the LOA (in this case hull length) is 24' 6" as advertised, the waterline length can't be 20' 6" as the sales brochure states. Waterline is 23' 0" scaled from drawing.

Comps	LOD	Beam	MinDr	Displ	Bllst	SA/D	D/L	Avg. PHRF	Max. Speed	Motion Index	Space Index	No. of Berths	Head-room
Merit 25 (24)	24' 0"	8' 0"	4' 0"	2,900	1,050	21.7	106	168	6.4	11.9	409	4	4' 1"
Seaward 25 (24)	24' 0"	8' 4"	2' 1"	3,100	1,100	17.7	114	270	6.4	11.7	483	5	5' 3"
Kirby 25	24' 7"	8' 9"	4' 2"	3,150	1,150	21.6	157	174	6.1	12.2	454	4	4' 6"
Dehler 25 (23)	23' 1"	8' 3"	1' 4"	3,245	1,654	20.1	139	186	6.3	13.2	382	4	4' 9"
Freedom 24	23' 9"	8' 3"	1' 10"	3,250	1,350	22.0	146	207	6.2	13.3	428	4	4' 7"

Mirage 24
Early C&C racer has done well over the years

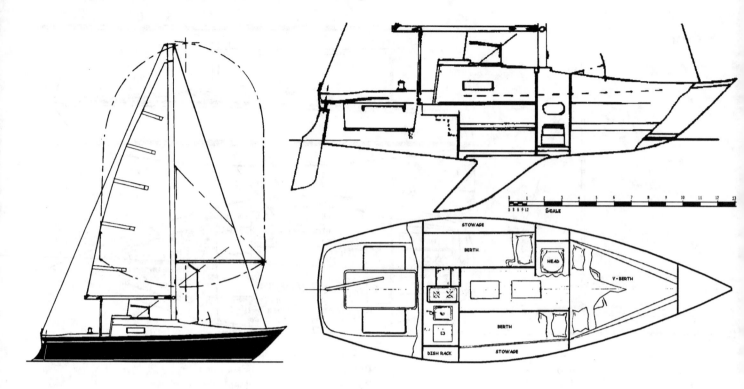

LOD:	23' 6"		**Designer:**	C&C Design Group
LOA:	25' 0"		**Builder:**	Mirage Yachts
LWL:	20' 0"		**Years produced:**	1972–1982?
Min./max. draft:	4' 2"		**Sail area:**	225 sq. ft.
Bridge clearance:	33' 0"		**Fuel tankage:**	portable
Power:	outboard 4 to 6 hp		**Water tankage:**	portable
B/D ratio:	41%		**Approx. trailering wgt.:**	5,500 lbs.

It appears that the Mirage 24, a C&C design, either started out as the "Northern Quarter Ton 24," or is almost a complete lookalike. The sailplans and layout shown here were used interchangeably for both boats in the sailing magazines of the 1970s, and the dimensions shown are probably those for both designs. (But caution: if you must have an absolutely certified correct dimension for this boat, you'll have to find an actual boat and measure her.) And be careful

of the mast. Three different mast lengths were apparently available, measuring 26' 6", 28' 0", and 29' 0". In any case, the boat has been quite successful in MORC and PHRF racing over the years. **Best features:** This is a boat designed to go fast in Quarter Ton racing, and she does. **Worst features:** Her ballast is higher than her comps, which leads us to assume that she could be faster in heavy air but slower in light air compared to her comps.

Comps	LOD	Beam	MinDr	Displ	Bllst	SA/D	D/L	Avg. PHRF	Max. Speed	Motion Index	Space Index	No. of Berths	Head-room
C&C 24	23' 6"	8' 9"	4' 0"	3,200	1,050	18.6	193	222	5.9	13.0	443	4	5' 3"
S2 7.3 (24)	23' 6"	8' 0"	3' 0"	3,250	1,300	18.6	229	228	5.8	15.5	403	4	5' 0"
Cal 24-3	23' 9"	8' 0"	3' 4"	3,300	1,175	18.8	184	213	6.0	14.9	400	4 or 5	5' 0"
Mirage 24	23' 6"	8' 5"	4' 2"	3,700	1,500	15.0	204	225	6.0	15.4	370	4	4' 9"

Neptune 24
Will this boat really accommodate six?

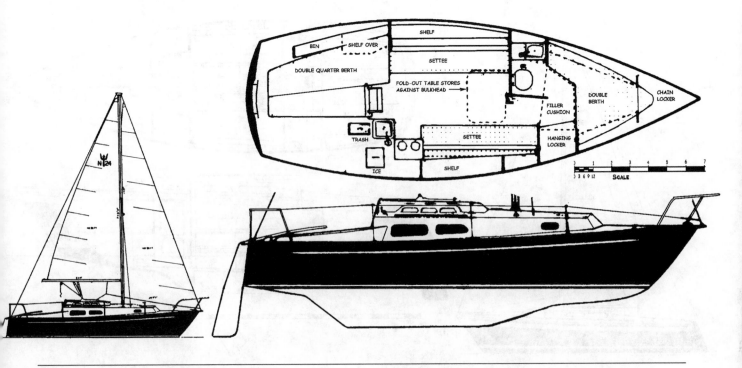

LOD:	24' 2"
LOA:	26' 9"
LWL:	21' 0"
Min./max. draft:	2' 0"/5' 0"
Bridge clearance:	30' 0"
Power:	outboard 3 to 6 hp
B/D ratio:	38%

Designer:	not specified by builder
Builder:	Capital Yachts
Years produced:	1975–1986
Sail area:	230 sq. ft.
Fuel tankage:	portable
Water tankage:	portable
Approx. trailering wgt.:	4,800 lbs.

Capital Yachts, Harbor City, CA, builders of the Newport, Neptune, and Gulf sailboat lines in the 1970s and 1980s, offered this commodious vessel in several configurations: shoal draft long keel (shown here) or deep fin keel (at 5-foot draft not easily trailerable or launchable without a crane), and standard rig or tall rig. Some owners of used boats report having boats with shoal keels and "bilge boards" or "daggerboard." We assume they mean a centerboard, apparently an option with the shoal keel. **Best features:** A poptop increases headroom to more than six feet, and a big forward hatch is a plus. Despite her beam being less than eight feet (note her comps feature beams of 8' 3" and 8' 4"), the Neptune 24's Space Index is best of the lot. That's due to the relatively high freeboard and bulbous trunk cabin, which increase interior space but at some sacrifice of external beauty. **Worst features:** Owners point out that two adults can't use the aft double (though, as the sales literature says somewhat enigmatically, "1½ people can"). The same is true for the forward V-berth, unless the filler cushion is put in place, which virtually eliminates head use. Other owner complaints include poor windward ability in the shoal draft version, lack of a door on the head, and a stove positioned too close to the side of the boat and to curtains.

Comps	LOD	Beam	MinDr	Displ	Bllst	SA/D	D/L	Avg. PHRF	Max. Speed	Motion Index	Space Index	No. of Berths	Head-room
Seaward 24	24' 4"	8' 3"	2' 0"	3,100	1,100	18.6	127	261	6.3	12.5	375	4 or 5	5' 0"
Ranger 24	23' 11"	8' 4"	4' 1"	3,150	1,200	17.8	176	216	6.0	13.6	429	4	5' 7"
Neptune 24	24' 2"	7' 11"	2' 0"	3,200	1,200	16.9	154	222	6.1	13.6	433	6	5' 6"

O'Day 25 (24)
Popular sloop from the peak of sailing boom times

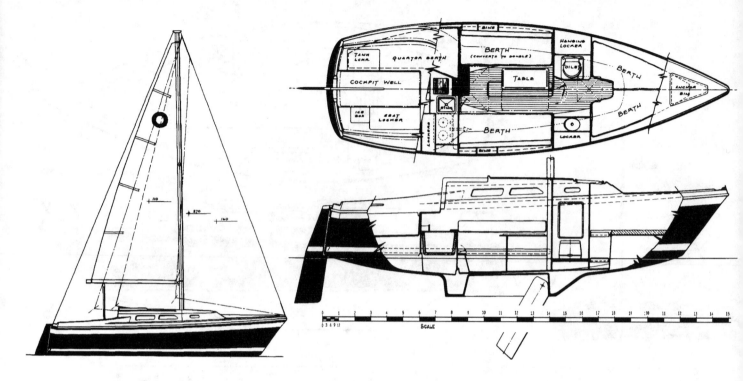

LOD:	24' 5"	**Designer:**	C. Raymond Hunt Assoc.
LOA:	26' 7"	**Builder:**	O'Day
LWL:	21' 0"	**Years produced:**	1975–1983
Min./max. draft:	2' 3"/6' 0"	**Sail area:**	270 sq. ft.
Bridge clearance:	33' 6"	**Fuel tankage:**	15 gal. (optional)
Power:	outboard or inboard 4 to 8 hp	**Water tankage:**	10 gal.
B/D ratio:	35%	**Approx. trailering wgt.:**	6,500 lbs.

The O'Day 25 (actually 24' 5" on deck) came in two variations: the keel-centerboarder shown here, and a deep fin keel version with 4' 6" draft, 20 square feet more sail area, two-foot higher mast, and 50 pounds less ballast. Outboard power on a stern bracket (or a small Atomic 2 gasoline engine of 7 hp) was the choice at one point; then diesels came in. Production of both types of O'Day 25s together totaled over 2,800 between 1975 and 1983,

right at the peak of the Golden Age of sailboat sales in this size range. **Best features:** Here is a nice-looking, good (though not superb) quality boat, with plenty of owners with whom to fraternize if you like to socialize. Just check Google to find the current O'Day owners' website. **Worst features:** The galley seems a bit skimpy to us, particularly when compared to, say, the La Paz 25 (page 353), a comp.

Comps	LOD	Beam	MinDr	Displ	Bllst	SA/D	D/L	Avg. PHRF	Max. Speed	Motion Index	Space Index	No. of Berths	Head- room
Watkins Seawolf 25	24' 11"	8' 0"	2' 6"	4,300	1,600	16.0	207	243	6.1	18.7	461	5	5' 11"
O'Day 25 (24)	24' 5"	8' 0"	2' 3"	4,400	1,525	16.1	212	234	6.1	19.1	508	5	5' 6"
Hunter 25 Mk II	25' 0"	8' 0"	2' 11"	4,400	1,800	15.3	239	225	6.0	19.6	430	5	5' 8"
La Paz 25	25' 7"	8' 0"	2' 0"	4,600	1,600	14.2	162	NA	6.5	18.6	411	5	6' 4"

Olson 25 (24)
Santa Cruz speedster: light, fast, strong

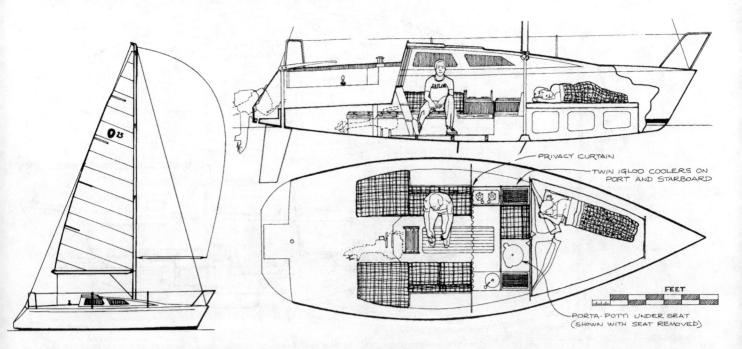

PRIVACY CURTAIN

TWIN IGLOO COOLERS ON PORT AND STARBOARD

FEET

PORTA-POTTI UNDER SEAT (SHOWN WITH SEAT REMOVED)

LOD:	23' 7"	**Designer:**	George Olson
LOA:	25' 0"	**Builder:**	Pacific Boats/Ericson Yachts
LWL:	21' 3"	**Years produced:**	1984–1989
Min./max. draft:	4' 6"	**Sail area:**	295 sq. ft.
Bridge clearance:	29' 6"	**Fuel tankage:**	portable
Power:	outboard 3 to 6 hp	**Water tankage:**	portable
B/D ratio:	45%	**Approx. trailering wgt.:**	4,300 lbs.

This boat was designed and built in Santa Cruz, CA, a hotbed of sailboat innovation tucked along the shore of Monterey Bay on the Pacific Ocean. George Olson, owner of Pacific Boats, wanted to create a boat that would go fast, rate well under MORC rules, look good, and be comfortable. It needed to be light in weight, but not necessarily in the extreme. When this boat came along in 1985, Santa Cruz was the center of ULDB activity. ULDB stands for Ultra Light Displacement Boat, meaning a D/L under 100. With a D/L of 135, the Olson 25 is more manageable in light air than she would have been as a strictly conceived ULDB. She was popular as a PHRF

and one-design racer, especially in the Monterey Bay area, but in the downward economy, which came shortly after her introduction, business suffered, and eventually Ericson began building her until that firm too went by the wayside. **Best features:** An open stern makes the transom-mounted outboard engine easier to manage. A nice finish below includes Bruynzeel plywood with satin finished regina mahogany veneer, and a teak and holly cabin sole. The companionway step can do double duty as a cocktail table. A bench seat athwartships between twin Igloo coolers is a unique and handy arrangement. **Worst features:** None identified.

Comps	LOD	Beam	MinDr	Displ	Bllst	SA/D	D/L	Avg. PHRF	Max. Speed	Motion Index	Space Index	No. of Berths	Head-room
Evelyn 25	24' 11"	8' 10"	4' 5"	2,600	1,100	24.8	117	147	6.2	9.8	422	4	4' 6"
Capri 25	24' 7"	9' 2"	4' 2"	2,785	900	22.3	177	171	5.9	10.7	414	4	4' 6"
Olson 25 (24)	23' 7"	9' 0"	4' 6"	2,900	1,300	23.2	135	159	6.2	10.7	428	4	4' 8"
Bombardier 7.6 (25)	25' 4"	8' 6"	4' 6"	3,300	985	24.4	129	168	6.4	12.5	375	5	4' 6"

Paceship Westwind 24
Ted Hood design for a Nova Scotia builder

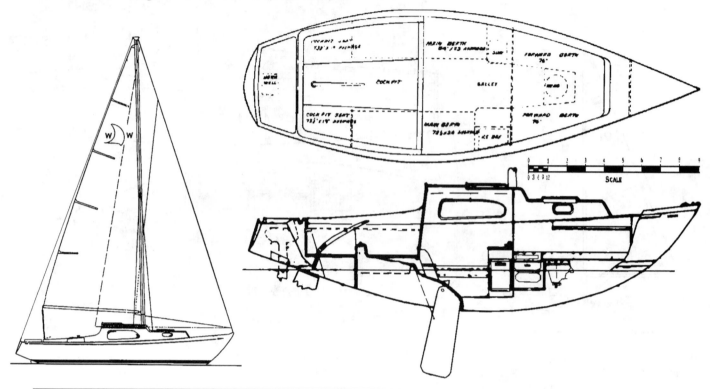

LOD:	23' 6"
LOA:	23' 11"
LWL:	18' 2"
Min./max. draft:	2' 2"/5' 6"
Bridge clearance:	35' 6"
Power:	outboard 3 to 6 hp
B/D ratio:	51%

Designer:	Ted Hood
Builder:	Paceship Yachts
Years produced:	1967–1977
Sail area:	311 sq. ft.
Fuel tankage:	portable
Water tankage:	12 gal.
Approx. trailering wgt.:	6,700 lbs.

Ted Hood founded Hood Sailmakers, which during the 1960s turned into the world's largest sailmaker. Also in the 1960s he began designing yachts, and eventually became a boatbuilder, founding Little Harbor Yachts. In 1967 he designed the deep-bellied whalelike hull you see here for Paceship Yachts of Mahone Bay, Nova Scotia. The design may look unconventional, but close inspection reveals some advantages. Above the waterline, the hull is quite conventional, but the lower midships section descends into a deep V down where ballast is most effective. (Note the relatively high ballast weight compared to the Westwind's comps, and her high D/L ratio, both of which should give her extra stability.) The hull depth also permits a lower cabin sole, which together with a doghouse in the cabintop yields the most headroom compared to her comps. **Best features:** In general, owners seem quite satisfied with their choice of boat. **Worst features:** Despite her good headroom, plus cabin sides which are very close to the gunwales (leaving very little room to walk forward), the boat has a lower Space Index than any of her comps.

Comps	LOD	Beam	MinDr	Displ	Bllst	SA/D	D/L	Avg. PHRF	Max. Speed	Motion Index	Space Index	No. of Berths	Head-room
Dolphin 24 (Pacific/Yankee)	24' 2"	7' 8"	2' 10"	4,250	1,750	18.1	277	246	5.8	21.1	406	4 or 5	4' 8"
Pearson Lark 24	24' 0"	8' 0"	4' 0"	4,300	1,500	16.7	303	246	5.8	20.5	456	4	4' 5"
Stone Horse 23	23' 4"	7' 1"	3' 6"	4,490	2,000	19.9	325	280	5.7	24.2	329	2	3' 9"
Dolphin 24 (O'Day)	24' 2"	7' 8"	2' 10"	4,500	1,440	17.1	293	246	5.8	22.3	370	4	4' 8"
Paceship Westwind 24	23' 6"	7' 11"	2' 2"	4,600	2,370	17.9	345	231	5.7	22.7	323	4	5' 6"

Pacific Seacraft Dana 24
Rock solid pocket cruiser from California

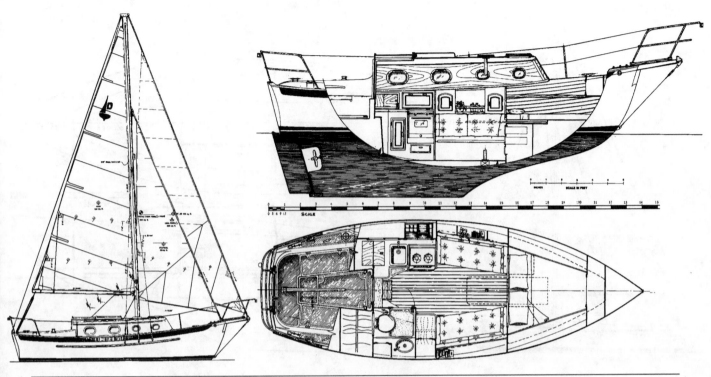

LOD:	24' 2"		**Designer:**	William Crealock
LOA:	27' 3"		**Builder:**	Pacific Seacraft
LWL:	21' 5"		**Years produced:**	1985–1999
Min./max. draft:	3' 10"		**Sail area:**	361 sq. ft.
Bridge clearance:	34' 0"		**Fuel tankage:**	portable
Power:	Yanmar diesel 18 hp		**Water tankage:**	portable
B/D ratio:	40%		**Approx. trailering wgt.:**	11,900 lbs.

This boat was designed to be a diminutive offshore passagemaker, to safely carry a single-hander or small family across a bay—or an ocean. The solid fiberglass laminate is one inch thick at the sheer and, it is claimed, gets thicker everywhere else. Her hull is heavy and her rig is on the modest side, as are the rigs of her comps, which all have SA/D ratios in the very low category. That's good for ocean sailing when the wind is blowing, but may cause consternation among the crew in areas where light air is the rule rather than the exception. The boat is elegantly finished, with heavy-duty rigging and quality hardware from Lewmar, Harken, and Schaefer. She is built to last. ***Best features:***

The layout below is very functional and has some clever special features. There is foot space for the settee berths under the V-berth, covered with cushions when not in use. During the day, bedding can be stored, hidden in the foot space. The dining table slides out from its hiding place in a slot under the V-berth, supported by the stainless steel mast strut when in use. The galley features everything you might need, including a gimballed stove with oven. Stowage space abounds, with both wet and dry hanging lockers, cabinets, drawers, and more, remarkable for this size boat. ***Worst features:*** Some light-air sailors may not like her low SA/D ratio.

Comps	LOD	Beam	MinDr	Displ	Bllst	SA/D	D/L	Avg. PHRF	Max. Speed	Motion Index	Space Index	No. of Berths	Head-room
Eastward Ho 24	23' 8"	8' 8"	3' 10"	7,000	3,600	12.4	391	269	6.0	28.7	475	4	6' 4"
Blue Water 24	24' 0"	8' 7"	4' 1"	7,950	2,275	11.1	467	NA	5.9	33.2	418	4	6' 1"
Pacific Seacraft Dana 24	24' 2"	8' 7"	3' 10"	8,000	3,200	14.4	364	221	6.2	30.2	535	4	6' 1"
Aquarius Pilot Cutter 24	24' 0"	9' 0"	4' 0"	8,900	3,200	15.3	497	258	6.0	31.0	564	4	6' 3"

Pearson 24

A short-lived replacement for the Pearson Lark

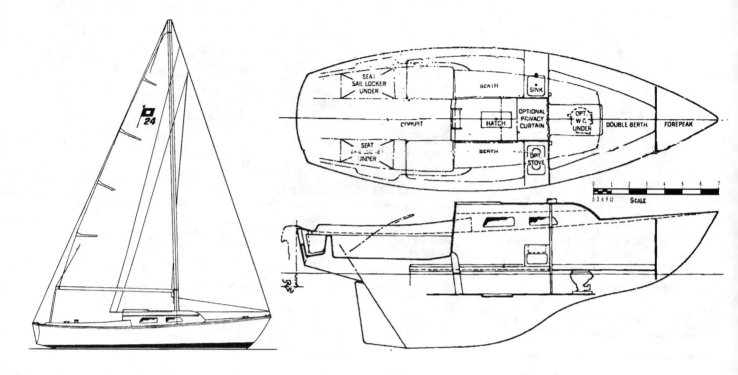

LOD:	23' 6"	**Designer:**	Bill Shaw
LOA:	23' 6"	**Builder:**	Pearson Yachts
LWL:	18' 6"	**Years produced:**	1968–1969
Min./max. draft:	4' 0"	**Sail area:**	285 sq. ft.
Bridge clearance:	31' 6"	**Fuel tankage:**	portable
Power:	outboard 4 to 6 hp	**Water tankage:**	15 gal.
B/D ratio:	42%	**Approx. trailering wgt.:**	6,400 lbs.

It is interesting to compare this boat with her near sistership, the Pearson Lark 24 (page 305). The Lark was phased out in 1968, the year that the Pearson 24 was introduced. The two boats were more similar than an initial glance might indicate. It looks to us as if the Pearson 24 design uses the same basic hull, but with six inches of the stern counter chopped off, and a new deck mold more in line with what the conservative customer base was looking for in the late 1960s. The traditional cabin house gives a 4-inch boost in headroom, but the Space Index is almost 20 percent lower than the Lark's. The rather unconventional

accommodations plan on the Lark was totally revamped on the P24 (to open up more space in the middle of the cabin) by moving the head forward into the V-berth area (requiring elimination of the Lark's hinged seatback facing aft), and eliminating the Lark's elaborate galley storage area. The elegant deck-loading icebox on the Lark is gone, with "provision for a portable ice chest" instead. The Pearson 24 was discontinued the year after she was introduced. We'd rather have kept the Lark. ***Best features:*** She's a good (but plain) cruising boat. ***Worst features:*** Her comps are probably both faster in light air.

Comps	LOD	Beam	MinDr	Displ	Bllst	SA/D	D/L	Avg. PHRF	Max. Speed	Motion Index	Space Index	No. of Berths	Head-room
Quickstep 24	23' 11"	7' 11"	3' 4"	4,000	1,300	16.4	260	258	5.8	19.1	341	5	4' 5"
Helms 24	24' 0"	8' 11"	4' 2"	4,200	1,850	16.9	207	234	6.1	16.3	520	5	5' 8"
Pearson 24	23' 6"	8' 0"	4' 0"	4,300	1,800	17.2	303	252	5.8	20.7	375	4	4' 9"

Pearson Lark 24
Cruising-oriented flush-decker by Bill Shaw

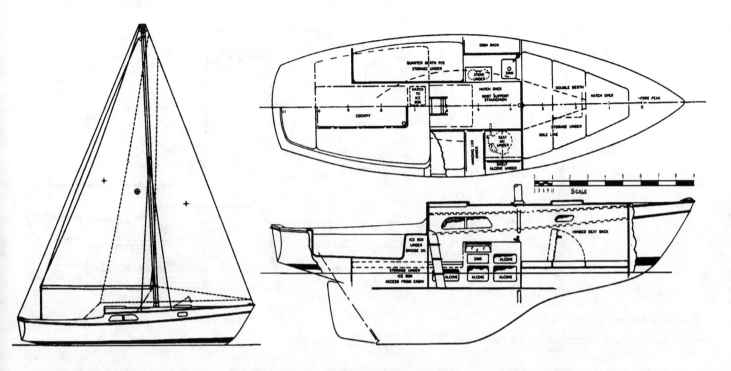

LOD:	24' 0"	**Designer:**	Bill Shaw
LOA:	24' 0"	**Builder:**	Pearson Yachts
LWL:	18' 6"	**Years produced:**	1966–1968
Min./max. draft:	4' 0"	**Sail area:**	276 sq. ft.
Bridge clearance:	31' 6"	**Fuel tankage:**	portable
Power:	outboard 4 to 6 hp	**Water tankage:**	15 gal.
B/D ratio:	35%	**Approx. trailering wgt.:**	6,400 lbs.

In 1985 I interviewed designer Bill Shaw, then executive vice president and chief designer for Pearson Yachts. He recalled the Lark being built "during a period when flush-deck types of boats were sort of popular. On the West Coast, they were very successful, and of course, in a small boat a flush deck gives you a tremendous amount of volume. . . . I've always been partial to that type of design." But, he said, "they're not as popular as I would like them to be. . . . The buyer likes change. . . but not radical ideas." The design was dropped after three or four years of low-volume production. Note that when he was with S&S, Shaw also did most of the design work on the racing-oriented Dolphin 24, a comp of the Lark, which was later produced by several builders. **Best features:** Just as designer Shaw said, on the Lark there's plenty of space below. Note her Space Index, 12 percent to 40 percent more than her comps. **Worst features:** Compared with her comps, the cruising oriented Lark has the highest PHRF rating, and the lowest Motion Index. You pays yer money and you takes yer choice.

Comps	LOD	Beam	MinDr	Displ	Bllst	SA/D	D/L	Avg. PHRF	Max. Speed	Motion Index	Space Index	No. of Berths	Head-room
Dolphin 24 (Pacific/Yankee)	24' 2"	7' 8"	2' 10"	4,250	1,750	18.1	277	246	5.8	21.1	406	4 or 5	4' 8"
Pearson Lark 24	24' 0"	8' 0"	4' 0"	4,300	1,500	16.7	303	246	5.8	20.5	456	4	4' 5"
Stone Horse 23	23' 4"	7' 1"	3' 6"	4,490	2,000	19.9	325	280	5.7	24.2	329	2	3' 9"
Dolphin 24 (O'Day)	24' 2"	7' 8"	2' 10"	4,500	1,440	17.1	293	246	5.8	22.3	370	4	4' 8"
Paceship Westwind 24	23' 11"	7' 11"	2' 2"	4,600	2,370	17.9	345	231	5.7	22.7	323	4	5' 6"

Quickstep 24
Nice design, good tracking, several builders

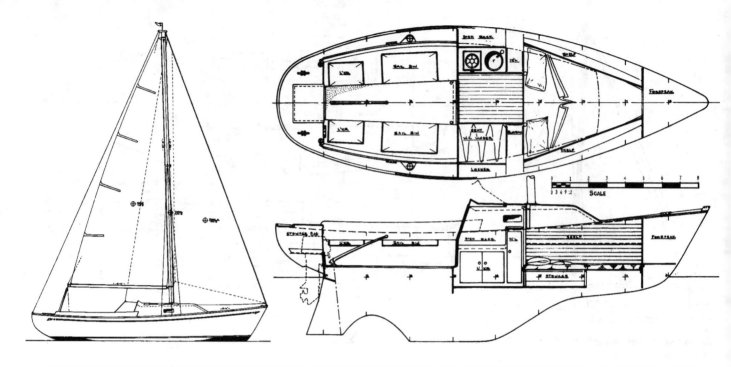

LOD:	23' 11"	**Designer:**	Ted Brewer	
LOA:	23' 11"	**Builder:**	various (see below)	
LWL:	19' 0"	**Years produced:**	1985–1991?	
Min./max. draft:	3' 4"	**Sail area:**	259 sq. ft.	
Bridge clearance:	31' 0"	**Fuel tankage:**	portable	
Power:	outboard 4 to 6 hp	**Water tankage:**	portable	
B/D ratio:	33%	**Approx. trailering wgt.:**	6,100 lbs.	

This good-looking vessel made the rounds among several builders. Ted Brewer's design was originally to be built in aluminum, but that plan didn't come to fruition. Stannard Boat Works of Newport, RI, had C. E. Ryder build a couple of dozen boats in fiberglass, and then sold the marketing rights to Gary Lannigan, who at the time was marketing director for Ryder. Lannigan had Ryder build some boats, but eventually left Ryder and switched production, first to The Anchorage, builder of the famous Dyer Dinks and Dhows, and later to Shannon Boat Company, and others. The boats were (with some exceptions) well built and well finished. Early accommodations were finished as shown here. Later production added quarter berths, which squeezed the galley space. ***Best features:*** With her longish keel and attached rudder, she wants to track a straight course and can be made to self-steer fairly easily, helping to make her a good singlehander. She is reported to handle a chop and a fresh breeze better than the average 24-footer. Her cockpit is large and comfortable. ***Worst features:*** Making a quick sharp turn may require an assist from the outboard (the other side of the coin from good tracking ability). Some owners (the ones with the quarter berths) complain of cramped accommodations.

Comps	LOD	Beam	MinDr	Displ	Bllst	SA/D	D/L	Avg. PHRF	Max. Speed	Motion Index	Space Index	No. of Berths	Head-room
Quickstep 24	23' 11"	7' 11"	3' 4"	4,000	1,300	16.4	260	258	5.8	19.1	341	5	4' 5"
Helms 24	24' 0"	8' 11"	4' 2"	4,200	1,850	16.9	207	234	6.1	16.3	520	5	5' 8"
Pearson 24	23' 6"	8' 0"	4' 0"	4,300	1,800	17.2	303	252	5.8	20.7	375	4	4' 9"

S2 7.3 (24)
One of a long line of boats named in meters

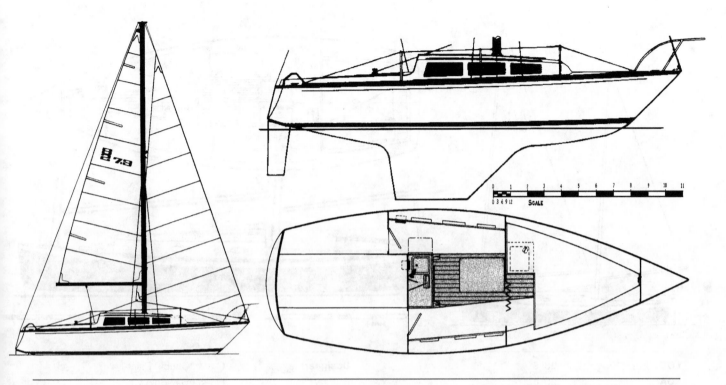

LOD:	23' 6"
LOA:	24' 0"
LWL:	18' 6"
Min./max. draft:	3' 0"/4' 0"
Bridge clearance:	34' 0"
Power:	outboard 3 to 6 hp
B/D ratio:	40%

Designer:	Arthur Edmonds
Builder:	S2 Yachts
Years produced:	1977–1987
Sail area:	255 sq. ft.
Fuel tankage:	portable
Water tankage:	15 gal.
Approx. trailering wgt.:	4,800 lbs.

Leon Slikkers, founder of S2 Yachts, started a boatbuilding company in the 1950s, sold it to AMF Corp. in 1969, and at first stayed on as president of the AMF Slickcraft Division. But he was dissatisfied, and in 1973 left AMF. The next year he started a new company, S2 Yachts (which one might imagine is short for "Slikkers second company"), and in 1975 came out with his first two sailboat models, the S2 7.0 (22 feet LOD, 23 LOA, designed by Arthur Edmonds; see page 196) and the 8.0 (26). The S2 7.3 came in 1977, followed by a whole slew of other sailboats up to 36 feet in length (11.0 meters, that is). An aside: we think the practice of naming boats by their length in meters rather than feet seems unnecessary—and perhaps misleading to buyers—similar to including appurtenances in the measurement, rather than just length on deck. **Best features:** Good space below for a 24-footer. **Worst features:** The old-fashioned keel design exposes so much wetted surface that we can't help but assume it slows her down in light air, compared with her comps.

Comps	LOD	Beam	MinDr	Displ	Bllst	SA/D	D/L	Avg. PHRF	Max. Speed	Motion Index	Space Index	No. of Berths	Head-room
C&C 24	23' 6"	8' 9"	4' 0"	3,200	1,050	18.6	193	222	5.9	13.0	443	4	5' 3"
S2 7.3 (24)	23' 6"	8' 0"	3' 0"	3,250	1,300	18.8	229	228	5.8	15.5	403	4	5' 0"
Cal 24-3	23' 9"	8' 0"	3' 4"	3,300	1,175	18.8	184	313	6.0	14.9	400	4 or 5	5' 0"
Mirage 24	23' 6"	8' 5"	4' 2"	3,700	1,500	15.0	204	225	6.0	15.4	370	4	4' 9"

Sand Hen 24

Reuben Trane's version of the Sandpiper 24

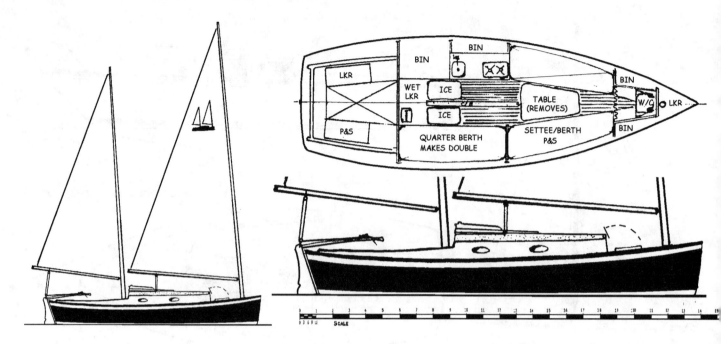

LOD:	23' 9"		**Designer:**	C. W. "Chuck" Paine
LOA:	25' 6"		**Builder:**	Florida Bay Boat Co.
LWL:	22' 6"		**Years produced:**	1986–1989?
Min./max. draft:	1' 6"/6' 0"		**Sail area:**	275 sq. ft.
Bridge clearance:	32' 0"		**Fuel tankage:**	portable
Power:	outboard 3 to 6 hp		**Water tankage:**	portable
B/D ratio:	43%		**Approx. trailering wgt.:**	5,300 lbs.

Most of the boats in the "Henhouse" of Reuben Trane, Florida Bay Boat Company's owner, were designed by Trane himself, the resident Hen expert, who also went by the name "Mon Poulet" and wrote his own advertising, filled with jokey but informative cartoons giving details and a sales pitch for each of his Hens. The Sand Hen, however, was designed by Chuck Paine in about 1980 as the Bahama Sandpiper 24 (page 272), and a set of molds was developed to sell bare hulls and decks as kit boats for do-it-yourselfers. Eventually Trane bought the molds, made some changes, mainly in the rig and interior plan, and commenced building the boat as a "beach cruiser." **Best features:** The boat shown here should make a great beach cruiser. With no shrouds to complicate the rigging, and lightweight spars (or maybe, these days, carbon fiber), getting from trailer to water and rigging the masts and sails would no doubt be an easy singlehanded job. Then you could short-tack down the narrow river (no jib to contend with), hook up the autopilot at the mouth of the river, and relax with your favorite beverage while the scenery rolls by. **Worst features:** It's hard to visualize where a conveniently located outboard engine could be mounted. Maybe a small inboard could be arranged?

Comps	LOD	Beam	MinDr	Displ	Bllst	SA/D	D/L	Avg. PHRF	Max. Speed	Motion Index	Space Index	No. of Berths	Head-room
Sand Hen 24	23' 9"	8' 0"	1' 6"	3,500	1,500	19.1	137	NA	6.4	14.4	393	4	4' 9"
Hunter 240 (23)	23' 1"	8' 3"	1' 6"	3,600	1,300	16.5	148	255	6.3	14.6	416	4	4' 8"
Bahama Sandpiper 24	24' 0"	7' 11"	1' 6"	4,140	1,500	17.2	162	252	6.4	17.5	393	4	4' 9"

Seaward 24
Nick Hake designs a seaworthy cruiser

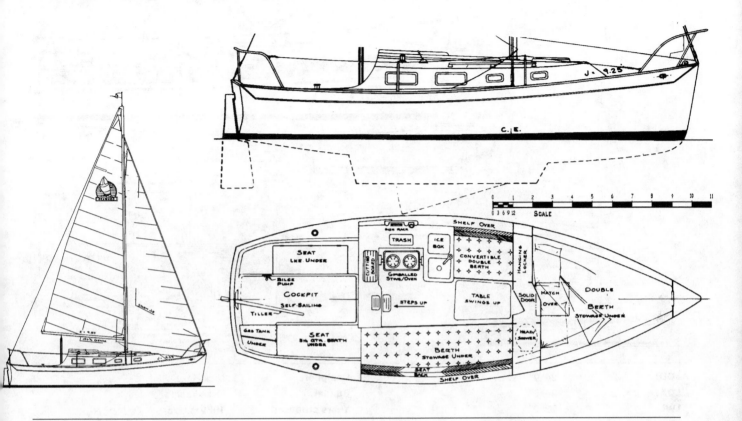

LOD:	24' 4"		**Designer:**	Nick Hake	
LOA:	24' 11"		**Builder:**	Hake Yachts	
LWL:	22' 2"		**Years produced:**	1984–1988	
Min./max. draft:	2' 0"/3' 6"		**Sail area:**	247 sq. ft.	
Bridge clearance:	32' 6"		**Fuel tankage:**	portable	
Power:	outboard 3 to 6 hp		**Water tankage:**	portable	
B/D ratio:	35%		**Approx. trailering wgt.:**	4,700 lbs.	

As with her comp, the Ranger 24 (page 317), it's hard not to forget that this is only a 24-footer. Like the Ranger, the accommodations plan of the Seaward 24 shows both a gimballed stove with oven and space for a refrigerator (though the same comment for the Ranger 24 applies: a refrigerator is somewhat impractical on an outboard powered sailboat because of the electrical drain on the batteries, which would require many hours of charging with the noise and smell of a running engine). ***Best features:*** Her relatively low freeboard and springy sheer give the Seaward 24 a sleek and salty look, as if she is ready for whatever challenges the sea might bring to her. She is well-built to boot, and with her generous sailplan and long waterline for her size has a better than even chance of satisfying the requirements of experienced sailors. ***Worst features:*** None noted.

Comps	LOD	Beam	MinDr	Displ	Bllst	SA/D	D/L	Avg. PHRF	Max. Speed	Motion Index	Space Index	No. of Berths	Head-room
Seaward 24	24' 4"	8' 3"	2' 0"	3,100	1,100	18.6	127	261	6.3	12.5	375	4 or 5	5' 0"
Ranger 24	23' 11"	8' 4"	4' 1"	3,150	1,200	17.6	176	216	6.0	13.6	429	4	5' 7"
Neptune 24	24' 2"	7' 11"	2' 0"	3,200	1,200	16.9	154	222	6.1	13.6	433	6	5' 6"

Seaward 25 (24)

A cruising boat with plenty of space for her size

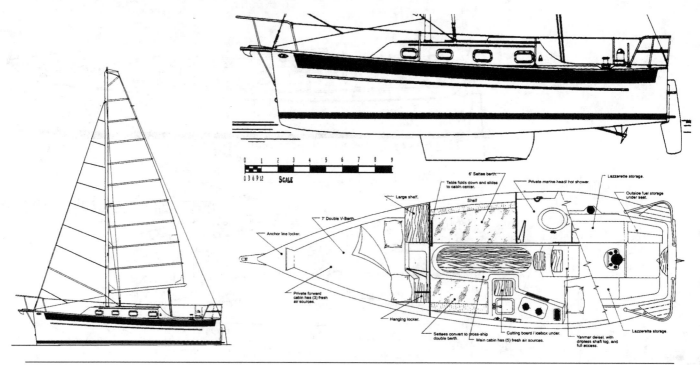

LOD:	24' 0"
LOA:	26' 9"
LWL:	23' 0"
Min./max. draft:	2' 1"
Bridge clearance:	30' 0"
Power:	outboard or inboard 4 to 12 hp
B/D ratio:	35%

Designer:	Nick Hake
Builder:	Hake Yachts
Years produced:	1989–2003
Sail area:	235 sq. ft.
Fuel tankage:	portable
Water tankage:	20 gal.
Approx. trailering wgt.:	4,700 lbs.

We admit that the list of comps in the table below is a hodgepodge of boats, even though the collection was compiled by grouping together all boats of similar length on deck with approximately the same displacement and ballast. But of the five choices, the Seaward 25 has by far the highest Space Index and the most headroom, as well as by far the worst PHRF rating. Maybe that's because all the comps except the Seaward 25 were designed to do well on the race course, whereas the Seaward design was aimed squarely at cruising comfort and space, with a mere passing wave at speed. (The inboard can always be turned on.) The design evolved over a period of time; the model shown

here is the last of a series of roughly 24-footers which were originally produced starting in 1984, and changed a bit every few years until the series was discontinued in 2003. Today Hake Yachts seems to be concentrating strictly on larger boats, where there is more money to be made. ***Best features:*** As can be seen by the numerous call-outs in the plan, the boat has several nice features, including a larger than usual galley area and a head with hot shower aft next to the companionway ladder. (Pressure hot and cold water is available for those who opted for the Yanmar 1GM10 or Westerbeke 20B diesel inboard.) Stern quarter seats are popular with the younger set. ***Worst features:*** None noted.

Comps	LOD	Beam	MinDr	Displ	Bllst	SA/D	D/L	Avg. PHRF	Max. Speed	Motion Index	Space Index	No. of Berths	Head-room
Merit 25 (24)	24' 0"	8' 0"	4' 0"	2,900	1,050	21.7	106	168	6.4	11.9	409	4	4' 1"
Seaward 25 (24)	24' 0"	8' 4"	2' 1"	3,100	1,100	17.7	114	270	6.4	11.7	483	5	5' 3"
Kirby 25	24' 7"	8' 9"	4' 2"	3,150	1,150	21.6	157	174	6.1	12.2	453	4	4' 6"
Dehler 25 (23)	23' 1"	8' 3"	1' 4"	3,245	1,654	20.1	139	186	6.3	13.2	412	4	4' 3"
Freedom 24	23' 9"	8' 3"	1' 10"	3,250	1,350	22.0	146	207	6.2	13.3	428	4	4' 7"

Seidelmann 25 (24)
Club racer-cruiser from a sailmaker-builder

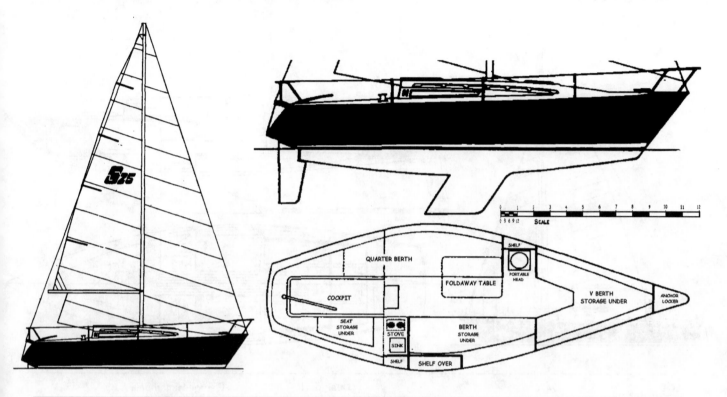

LOD:	24' 0"	**Designer:**	Bob Seidelmann
LOA:	24' 6"	**Builder:**	Seidelmann Yachts
LWL:	20' 0"	**Years produced:**	1977–1982
Min./max. draft:	3' 4"/4' 4"	**Sail area:**	282 sq. ft.
Bridge clearance:	36' 0"	**Fuel tankage:**	portable
Power:	outboard 4 to 10 hp	**Water tankage:**	10 gal.
B/D ratio:	48%	**Approx. trailering wgt.:**	6,700 lbs.

In the early 1960s racing sailor and designer J. Robert (Bob) Seidelmann, together with his father Joe, founded Seidelmann Sails. Bob co-designed the original Hunter 25 (page 344), Hunter's first sailboat, in 1973, started building his own sailboats in 1976 as "Seidelmann Yachts," and a year later launched the 24-footer (24' 6" LOA) shown here. Later he enlarged his range of production to sailboats from 24- to 37-feet long, and was also associated with the line of Pacemaker powerboats. Bob was recognized as one of the United States' top one-design sailors, winning championships in Lightnings, Comets, Dusters, and several other classes. **Best features:** The S25's wide beam gives good space down below (though not as much as her comps). **Worst features:** Some owners complain about poor construction. With its relatively narrow waterline and soft bilges, the boat is tender in heavy air unless there is plenty of "rail meat" on board.

Comps	LOD	Beam	MinDr	Displ	Bllst	SA/D	D/L	Avg. PHRF	Max. Speed	Motion Index	Space Index	No. of Berths	Head-room
Columbia 7.6 (25)	25' 1"	9' 2"	3' 6"	4,500	1,500	18.7	228	210	6.1	16.3	573	4	5' 8"
Cal 25 Mk II	25' 3"	9' 0"	3' 6"	4,500	2,000	18.5	189	219	6.3	16.1	558	5	5' 10"
Montego 25	25' 3"	9' 1"	3' 6"	4,550	1,800	17.1	236	216	6.1	16.9	557	4	5' 11"
Tanzer 25 Mk II	25' 3"	9' 7"	2' 11"	4,550	1,985	19.1	195	177	6.3	14.7	575	4	5' 9"
Seidelmann 25 (24)	24' 0"	9' 6"	3' 4"	4,600	2.200	16.3	257	216	6.0	16.5	549	4	5' 2"

Shark 24
Planing keel boat from the fifties

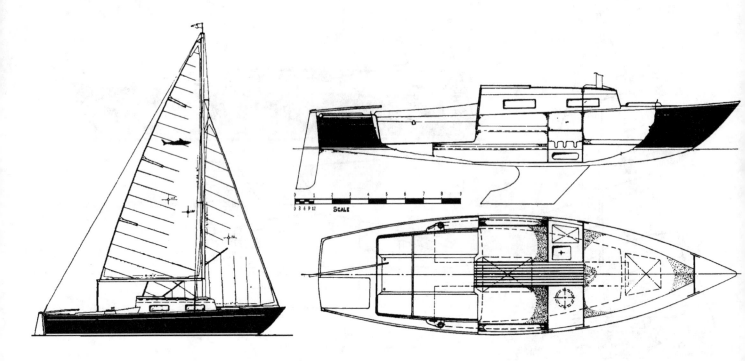

LOD:	24' 0"	**Designer:**	George Hinterhoeller
LOA:	25' 0"	**Builder:**	Hinterhoeller, Halman Mfg.
LWL:	20' 0"	**Years produced:**	1959–1985?
Min./max. draft:	3' 2"	**Sail area:**	190 sq. ft.
Bridge clearance:	30' 0"	**Fuel tankage:**	portable
Power:	outboard 3 to 6 hp	**Water tankage:**	portable
B/D ratio:	31%	**Approx. trailering wgt.:**	3,200 lbs.

The Shark was designed and built by George Hinterhoeller of Niagara-on-the-Lake, Ontario, who was later a successful builder of a variety of cruising boats such as the Nonsuch series (see page 185). To modern eyes the Shark is unusually long and skinny (though not in the extreme displayed, say, by the Wabbit, page 260), but in the 1950s when she was designed, long and skinny usually meant fast—reminiscent of the fast naval destroyers of World War II, which concluded only a few years earlier. Despite her narrow beam, she could plane, and on several races it is said that for long distances she made a good 10 mph (about 8.3 knots), beating competitors as large as 56 feet LOA. ***Best features:*** The boat's transom is cut out on the starboard side to accommodate an outboard engine. Although the engine can be tilted up when sailing, there is a slide-in panel that can close up the space when the engine is removed and stowed below, making the boat faster during races by keeping the ends light. ***Worst features:*** The iron fin keel needs frequent maintenance, especially in salt water, to keep corrosion at bay.

Comps	LOD	Beam	MinDr	Displ	Bllst	SA/D	D/L	Avg. PHRF	Max. Speed	Motion Index	Space Index	No. of Berths	Head-room
Shark 24	24' 0"	6' 10"	3' 2"	2,200	675	18.0	123	237	6.0	12.1	277	4	4' 0"
Annapolis Weekender 24	24' 2"	6' 3"	3' 6"	2,300	1,120	20.0	176	276	5.7	15.5	236	4	4' 2"
Windrose 24	24' 0"	7' 10"	1' 3"	2,400	700	19.8	95	252	6.3	10.4	356	4	4' 4"
Captiva 24 (23)	23' 5"	8' 2"	2' 0"	2,400	1,000	23.0	124	213	6.1	10.3	400	5	5' 7"

Tyler 24
Twin-keeler with six-foot headroom

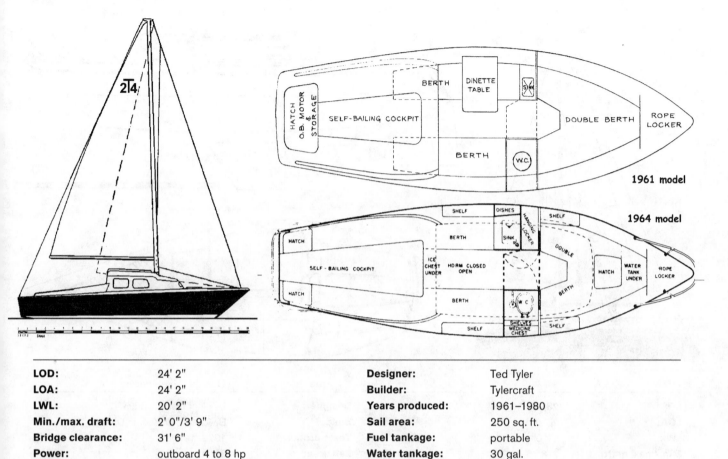

1961 model

1964 model

LOD:	24' 2"
LOA:	24' 2"
LWL:	20' 2"
Min./max. draft:	2' 0"/3' 9"
Bridge clearance:	31' 6"
Power:	outboard 4 to 8 hp
B/D ratio:	41%

Designer:	Ted Tyler
Builder:	Tylercraft
Years produced:	1961–1980
Sail area:	250 sq. ft.
Fuel tankage:	portable
Water tankage:	30 gal.
Approx. trailering wgt.:	6,100 lbs.

Tylercraft Inc. of Oakdale, Long Island, New York, started in the fiberglass boat business in 1960 with the Tyler 24 (shown here), and by 1967 was building not only the Tyler 24, but a Tyler 30 and a Tyler 40 as well. All were designed and produced by proprietor Ted Tyler. By 1971 the range of boats had changed; the 40-footer and 30-footer were no longer offered, and the catalog now included a T17, T24, T26, and T29. The T24 was available in three configurations: a daysailer weighing 3,650 pounds, a weekender sleeping 2 to 4 and weighing 3,890 pounds, and a racer accommodating 4 to 5 and weighing

4,030 pounds. Cabin layout varied from year to year; see layouts for two versions, one in 1961, the other in 1964. Apparently all the Tyler 24s were twin keelers, though there is some evidence that a T24 centerboarder drawing 2' 0" (board up) and 3' 9" (board down) was also available during some periods. (Information on the company, now long gone, and its products is difficult to find.)
Best and worst features: Not enough information to comment, except to note that the boat shown here has a good Space Index compared to her comps despite her narrower beam.

Comps	LOD	Beam	MinDr	Displ	Bllst	SA/D	D/L	Avg. PHRF	Max. Speed	Motion Index	Space Index	No. of Berths	Head- room
Buccaneer 240/245 (24)	23' 8"	8' 0"	2' 6"	4,000	1,250	17.0	212	270	6.0	18.0	422	4	6' 0"
Tyler 24	24' 2"	7' 5"	2' 0"	4,000	1,650	16.2	223	NA	6.0	20.1	441	5	6' 0"
Cal T/4 (24)	24' 2"	8' 0"	4' 0"	4,000	2,000	16.3	193	234	6.1	17.5	353	4	5' 3"
Vivacity 24	23' 6"	8' 0"	2' 6"	4,300	1,700	15.4	215	NA	6.1	19.2	385	5	5' 7"

U.S. 25/Triton 25 (24)
First Bayliner built her, then Pearson Yachts

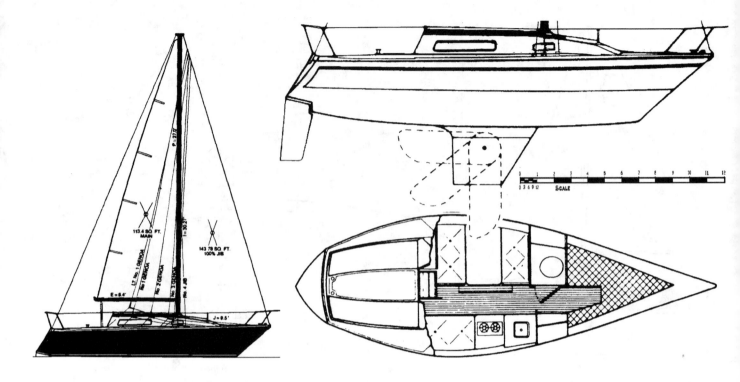

LOD:	23' 6"		**Designer:**	Bayliner Design Team
LOA:	25' 0"		**Builder:**	Bayliner, U.S. Yachts Division
LWL:	21' 5"		**Years produced:**	1978–1984
Min./max. draft:	2' 8"/5' 10"		**Sail area:**	250 sq. ft.
Bridge clearance:	33' 9"		**Fuel tankage:**	portable
Power:	outboard 4 to 8 hp		**Water tankage:**	4 gal.
B/D ratio:	33%		**Approx. trailering wgt.:**	5,600 lbs.

The United Sailing Yacht Division (U.S. Yachts) of Bayliner built the U.S. 25 until 1983. Then .Pearson bought the molds for some of the U.S. Yachts line and produced them for one year, 1984. Under Pearson, the line took on the name Triton (not to be confused with Pearson's very first fiberglass sailboat, the 29-foot Triton, introduced in 1959). The 25-footer was available with a swing keel (2' 8" up, 5' 10" down), a shoal draft fin keel (2' 8"), or a deep (4' 7") fin keel. A large foretriangle and a blade-like small mainsail gives the appearance of a fast racer, but in reality the boat does not stand out as a particularly fast boat. ***Best features:*** Construction was quite good—better than the "chopped strand" powerboats built by Bayliner in the early days. Trim included teak and holly sole and other niceties. ***Worst features:*** The pinched bow gives too little room for a full V-berth; use it for small kids only.

Comps	LOD	Beam	MinDr	Displ	Bllst	SA/D	D/L	Avg. PHRF	Max. Speed	Motion Index	Space Index	No. of Berths	Head-room
U.S. 25/Triton 25 (24)	23' 6"	8' 0"	2' 8"	3,750	1,250	17.0	170	216	6.2	16.0	451	5	5' 6"
Bremer 25	25' 0"	8' 0"	2' 6"	3,800	1,600	20.3	149	NA	6.4	15.7	509	4	6' 0"
Hunter 25 Mk I	24' 8"	8' 0"	2' 11"	3,850	1,800	11.7	210	222	6.0	17.1	404	5	5' 2"

Windrose 24
Shad Turner lightweight cruiser

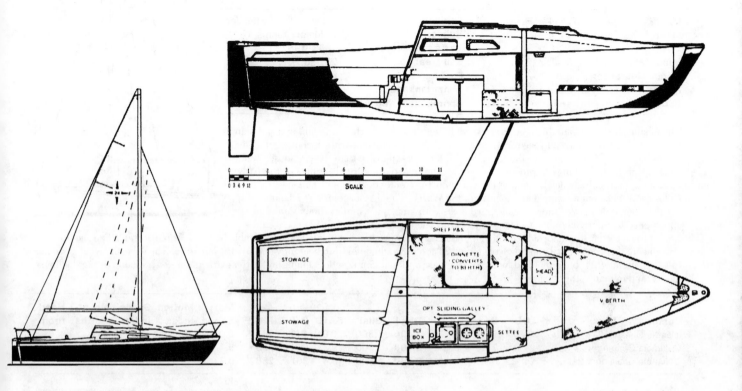

LOD:	24' 0"
LOA:	25' 0"
LWL:	21' 5"
Min./max. draft:	1' 3"/6' 4"
Bridge clearance:	32' 0"
Power:	outboard 3 to 6 hp
B/D ratio:	25%

Designer:	Shad Turner
Builder:	Laguna Yachts
Years produced:	1974–1983
Sail area:	222 sq. ft.
Fuel tankage:	portable
Water tankage:	portable
Approx. trailering wgt.:	3,600 lbs.

Shad Turner, who in the 1970s and 1980s also designed sailboats for W. D. Schock and Lancer, drew a whole series of boats for Laguna Yachts, including various Windroses, Lagunas, and Balboas. The result was usually, as in this case, a lightweight cruiser, not especially fast or stable, but designed for trailering and easy beaching for a picnic. ***Best features:*** Like her comps, the Windrose 24 has a modestly sized sailplan, in keeping with her low (25%) ballast-to-displacement ratio and swing keel of only 600 pounds.

She has a poptop, which the builder claimed in brochures gives 6' 2" headroom, but at least one owner measured and got 5' 10". Ah well, either is better than the 4' 4" stooping headroom without the poptop. ***Worst features:*** The rudder, which is not retractable when traversing rocky shoals with the board up, is therefore vulnerable to damage. The winch used to raise and lower the 600-pound keel needs frequent maintenance to prevent binding and seizing. Forward V-berth is only big enough for kids.

Comps	LOD	Beam	MinDr	Displ	Bllst	SA/D	D/L	Avg. PHRF	Max. Speed	Motion Index	Space Index	No. of Berths	Head-room
Shark 24	24' 0"	6' 10"	3' 2"	2,200	675	18.0	123	237	6.0	12.1	277	4	4' 0"
Annapolis Weekender 24	24' 2"	6' 3"	3' 6"	2,300	1,120	20.0	176	276	5.7	15.5	236	4	4' 2"
Windrose 24	24' 0"	7' 10"	1' 3"	2,400	700	19.8	95	252	6.3	10.4	356	4	4' 4"
Captiva 24 (23)	23' 5"	8' 2"	2' 0"	2,400	1,000	23.0	124	213	6.1	10.3	400	5	5' 7"

Columbia Challenger 24

Economical boat from the early 1960s

LOD:	24' 4"	**Designer:**	not specified by builder
LOA:	24' 4"	**Builder:**	Columbia Yachts
LWL:	18' 0"	**Years produced:**	1963–1967?
Min./max. draft:	3' 4"	**Sail area:**	287 sq. ft.
Bridge clearance:	32' 9"	**Fuel tankage:**	portable
Power:	outboard 3 to 6 hp	**Water tankage:**	portable
B/D ratio:	46%	**Approx. trailering wgt.:**	5,700 lbs.

The Challenger was Columbia's "economy model," with essentially the same hull and sail plan as the Columbia Contender 24 (page 283), but instead of a trunk cabin with doghouse, the Challenger has a raised deck. Back in 1963, she was $1,000 less expensive than the doghouse version "due to substantial savings in production cost," according to an ad of the time. In the early days, a company called Glas Laminates built not only the Contender 24 and Challenger 24 for Columbia Yachts, but also molded the hulls for the Wayfarer Yacht Corporation's Islander 24 and Islander Bahama 24 (shown below), two boats with amazingly similar dimensions and appearance to their Columbia Yachts counterparts. The most significant difference would appear to be the lapstrake topsides molded into the Wayfarer products, missing on the Columbia boats. ***Best features:*** When she was first introduced, this economical and relatively roomy 24-footer would be hard to beat for value. ***Worst features:*** The 4-berth layout is similar to the Contender 24, but simplified, with cooking gear optional. Some sailors might prefer the extra amenities available in the doghouse model (and in many other boats).

Comps	LOD	Beam	MinDr	Displ	Bllst	SA/D	D/L	Avg. PHRF	Max. Speed	Motion Index	Space Index	No. of Berths	Head-room
Islander Bahama 24	24' 0"	7' 10"	3' 5"	3,400	1,800	20.8	190	264	6.0	15.9	318	4	4' 6"
Columbia Contender 24	24' 0"	7' 10"	3' 3"	3,600	1,600	19.3	264	258	5.7	17.8	324	4	4' 9"
Columbia Challenger 24	24' 4"	8' 0"	3' 4"	3,930	1,800	18.4	301	258	5.7	19.0	360	4	4' 0"

Islander Bahama 24

Wayfarer also enters the fray in the early 1960s

LOD:	24' 0"	**Designer:**	Joseph H. McGlasson
LOA:	24' 0"	**Builder:**	Wayfarer Yacht Corp., et al.
LWL:	20' 0"	**Years produced:**	1961?–1970?
Min./max. draft:	3' 5"	**Sail area:**	294 sq. ft.
Bridge clearance:	32' 6"	**Fuel tankage:**	portable
Power:	outboard 3 to 6 hp	**Water tankage:**	portable
B/D ratio:	53%	**Approx. trailering wgt.:**	5,000 lbs.

Although the facts are somewhat murky, it seems likely that the Islander 24 and the Islander Bahama 24, two vessels with lapstrakes molded into their identical hulls but different deck layouts (one a trunk cabin with a doghouse, the other with a raised deck), were marketed first by McGlasson Marine, then by Wayfarer Yacht Corporation, and then by Islander Yachts, before the designs were taken over and marketed in slightly different form by Columbia Yachts. Except for the lapstrakes and a few other details, the Islander 24 is said to be almost an exact copy of the Columbia Contender 24 (page 283), and the Islander Bahama 24 is almost an exact copy of the Columbia Challenger 24 (above). ***Best features:*** See the notes for the Challenger 24. ***Worst features:*** Same comment.

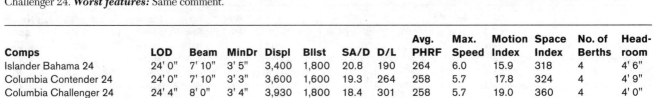

Comps	LOD	Beam	MinDr	Displ	Bllst	SA/D	D/L	Avg. PHRF	Max. Speed	Motion Index	Space Index	No. of Berths	Head-room
Islander Bahama 24	24' 0"	7' 10"	3' 5"	3,400	1,800	20.8	190	264	6.0	15.9	318	4	4' 6"
Columbia Contender 24	24' 0"	7' 10"	3' 3"	3,600	1,600	19.3	264	258	5.7	17.8	324	4	4' 9"
Columbia Challenger 24	24' 4"	8' 0"	3' 4"	3,930	1,800	18.4	301	258	5.7	19.0	360	4	4' 0"

Ranger 24
Ray Richards designed this cruiser-racer

LOD:	23' 11"	Designer:	Ray Richards
LOA:	24' 11"	Builder:	Ranger Fiberglass Boats
LWL:	20' 0"	Years produced:	1974–1978?
Min./max. draft:	4' 1"	Sail area:	335 sq. ft.
Bridge clearance:	32' 4"	Fuel tankage:	portable
Power:	outboard 3 to 6 hp	Water tankage:	portable
B/D ratio:	38%	Approx. trailering wgt.:	4,700 lbs.

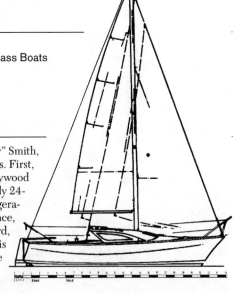

Designer Ray Richards of Seattle drew this quarter ton racer-cruiser for Howard "Smitty" Smith, owner of Ranger Fiberglass Boats of nearby Kent, WA. The boat is unusual in several ways. First, her topsides, though constructed of fiberglass, appear to be made of two panels of flat plywood bent to her sheer, giving her the look of a hard-chine plywood vessel. Second, though only 24-feet long, her sales brochure says that her sizable galley can accommodate "both a refrigerator and a gimballed range with oven." (We doubt many boats sold had either convenience, especially the refrigerator, which would require frequent charging of the batteries.) Third, she has full flotation, rare in a boat this size. **Best features:** Her outboard motor well is placed on her centerline, forward of the rudder in the cockpit, giving good access to the helmsman and, because the prop wash immediately impacts the rudderblade, good control at slow speeds around dock or mooring. **Worst features:** That "hard-chine" look will not appeal to everyone; it's not obvious why it is necessary.

Comps	LOD	Beam	MinDr	Displ	Bllst	SA/D	D/L	Avg. PHRF	Max. Speed	Motion Index	Space Index	No. of Berths	Head-room
Seaward 24	24' 4"	8' 3"	2' 0"	3,100	1,100	18.6	127	261	6.3	12.5	375	4 or 5	5' 0"
Ranger 24	23' 11"	8' 4"	4' 1"	3,150	1,200	17.8	176	216	6.0	13.6	429	4	5' 7"
Neptune 24	24' 2"	7' 11"	2' 0"	3,200	1,200	16.9	154	222	6.1	13.6	433	6	5' 6"

Vivacity 24
Heavy British import with twin keels

LOD:	23' 6"	Designer:	Alan Hill
LOA:	23' 6"	Builder:	Wells Yachts (importer)
LWL:	20' 9"	Years produced:	1968–1983?
Min./max. draft:	2' 6"/3' 8"	Sail area:	254 sq. ft.
Bridge clearance:	31' 0"	Fuel tankage:	portable
Power:	outbd. or inbd. 3 to 8 hp	Water tankage:	portable
B/D ratio:	40%	Approx. trailering wgt.:	5,800 lbs.

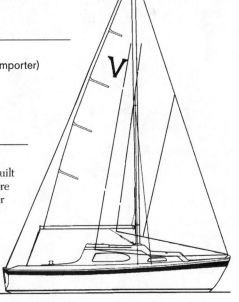

Designer Alan Hill drew the Vivacity 24 for Russell Marine in England in 1968. They were built in fin keel and bilge keel versions; the latter, designed to "stand on the hard," was by far the more popular. Although designed for outboard power, a few had inboard engines fitted. Like her comps, the Vivacity 24 is a relatively heavy and somewhat under-rigged coastal cruiser. **Best features:** The twin keeler sails and tracks well downwind. **Worst features:** Several owners say their Vivacity 24s are sluggish to windward and tend to pound in a chop. They also point out that their boats are under rigged for light air sailing conditions, and can benefit from additional light weather cruising chutes and foresails to keep them moving. But fully rigged in winds above 20 knots they can develop a nasty weather helm. Moral: reef at 15 knots.

Comps	LOD	Beam	MinDr	Displ	Bllst	SA/D	D/L	Avg. PHRF	Max. Speed	Motion Index	Space Index	No. of Berths	Head-room
Buccaneer 240/245 (24)	23' 8"	8' 0"	2' 6"	4,000	1,250	17.0	212	270	6.0	18.0	422	4	6' 0"
Tyler 24	24' 2"	7' 5"	2' 0"	4,000	1,650	16.2	223	NA	6.0	20.1	441	5	6' 0"
Cal T/4 (24)	24' 2"	8' 0"	4' 0"	4,000	2,000	16.3	193	234	6.1	17.5	353	4	5' 3"
Vivacity 24	23' 6"	8' 0"	2' 6"	4,300	1,700	15.4	215	NA	6.1	19.2	385	5	5' 7"

SEVEN
Sixty-Four Boats 25'

*7 vessels without accommodations plans are grouped together at end of chapter

Amphibi-Con 25
The "A/C 25" or "Amphibious Controversy" class

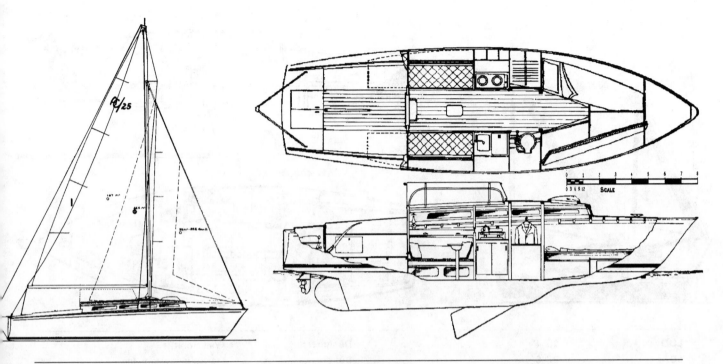

LOD:	25' 5"
LOA:	27' 0"
LWL:	21' 8"
Min./max. draft:	2' 5"/5' 0"
Bridge clearance:	33' 0"
Power:	outboard 6 to 10 hp
B/D ratio:	28%

Designer:	Hamlin and Butler
Builder:	Sailstar Boats
Years produced:	1964–1973?
Sail area:	278 sq. ft.
Fuel tankage:	portable
Water tankage:	20 gal.
Approx. trailering wgt.:	5,750 lbs.

The A/C 25 was originally conceived in 1954 by Maine designers Cy Hamlin and E. Farnham Butler as a lightweight trailerable racer-cruiser, built using glued strip construction. The vessel became available from Sailstar Boats in fiberglass in 1964, with practically no change in layout, either on deck or below, from the wood version shown here. (No drawings of the fiberglass version are available.) She was available as a kit, semi-finished, or fully found and ready to sail. The A/C 25 was the most popular boat in the Controversy series of boats built in wood by E. Farnham Butler's Mt. Desert Yacht Yard in Maine; his boats ranged from 15 to 37 feet on deck. ***Best features:*** The "convertible doghouse" is a unique feature, enabling the main cabin to be bathed in sun and fresh air in good weather, and to be fully enclosed in canvas when the weather turns nasty. A well in the lazarette for an outboard engine installation will appeal to those who find inboard engines too hard to deal with. ***Worst features:*** Among her comps, the A/C 25 is the lightest boat with the least ballast and close to the highest SA/D ratio, indicating that she will be among the liveliest in light air, but with her relatively low Motion Index, will tend to be jumpy in a seaway. We recall spending some time on one of these boats with another couple, and we found it to be comfortable, light, and airy.

Comps	LOD	Beam	MinDr	Displ	Bllst	SA/D	D/L	Avg. PHRF	Max. Speed	Motion Index	Space Index	No. of Berths	Head-room
Amphibi-Con 25	25' 5"	7' 9"	2' 5"	3,900	1,100	17.9	171	234	6.2	16.8	407	4	5' 8"
Catalina 25	25' 0"	8' 0"	2' 2"	4,150	1,500	16.7	170	225	6.3	17.8	464	5	5' 6"
Tanzer 7.5 (25)	24' 7"	8' 0"	2' 8"	4,150	1,950	15.9	178	201	6.3	17.6	529	4	5' 8"
Coronado 25 (cb version)	25' 0"	8' 0"	2' 6"	4,300	1,800	18.4	246	231	6.0	19.4	411	5	5' 8"

Beachcomber 25
Flat-bottomed beachable cat ketch with poptop

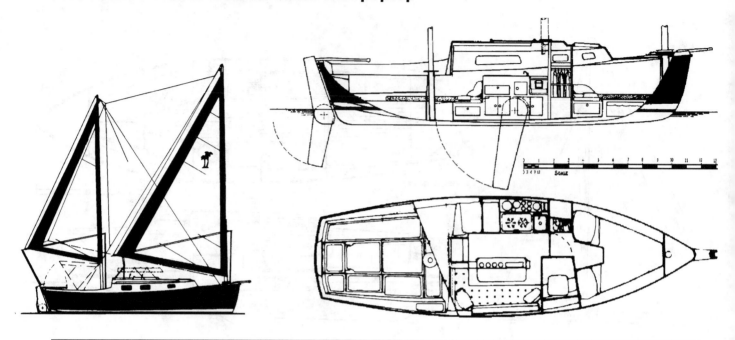

LOD:	25' 4"	Designer:	Walt Scott
LOA:	27' 6"	Builder:	Marine Innovators, Inc.
LWL:	23' 3"	Years produced:	1979–1981?
Min./max. draft:	1' 3"/5' 7"	Sail area:	275 sq. ft.
Bridge clearance:	31' 1"	Fuel tankage:	portable or 19 gal.
Power:	outboard or inboard, 6 to 10 hp	Water tankage:	20 gal.
B/D ratio:	26%	Approx. trailering wgt.:	7,500 lbs.

Cat ketches are themselves a bit unusual, especially when they are only 25 feet on deck. Add to that wishbone rigs on both masts (i.e., the rig typically used on windsurfing boards), and you have a vessel seldom seen. The Beachcomber 25 has tapered aluminum masts that can be rotated to wind up the sails like a pair of window shades. There are several advantages to such a rig: the foot of each sail acts like a vang, automatically building in sail efficiency when reaching and running; each sail may be easily reefed or furled, even by a single-hander; both sails are totally controlled from the cockpit; with the two-masted rig, extra sails may be set off the wind to increase

speed; and by flattening the mizzen and easing the main, the boat will lie in docile comfort at anchor (assuming the wind is steady and doesn't veer). **Best features:** The Beachcomber has a 1,400 pound grounding shoe and an extremely shallow, 15-inch draft, so she can be run up on a beach or mud flats—plus a high-efficiency centerboard for going to windward. The cabin is large and comfortable, with a poptop for tall sailors. **Worst features:** Learning the knack of sailing this type of craft may take a while; it's quite different from a standard sloop. The long grounding shoe acts like a long keel; increasing directional stability but reducing the ability to tack quickly.

Comps	LOD	Beam	MinDr	Displ	Bllst	SA/D	D/L	Avg. PHRF	Max. Speed	Motion Index	Space Index	No. of Berths	Head-room
Beneteau First 26 (25)	25' 5"	9' 2"	2' 9"	4,814	1,455	16.6	177	192	6.4	16.0	584	4	4' 3"
Ericson 25 Mk II	25' 5"	9' 3"	3' 11"	5,000	2,000	17.8	214	213	6.3	17.3	622	5	6' 1"
Kaiser 25	25' 4"	7' 10"	3' 7"	5,000	2,250	15.5	367	273	5.7	24.3	468	4	6' 2"
Westerly Tiger 25	25' 1"	8' 9"	4' 3"	5,264	2,240	12.5	226	225	6.3	19.7	447	5	5' 3"
Beachcomber 25	25' 4"	8' 0"	1' 3"	5,300	1,400	14.5	188	NA	6.5	20.8	510	5	5' 10"

Beneteau First 26 (25)
One of Beneteau's several 25-footers

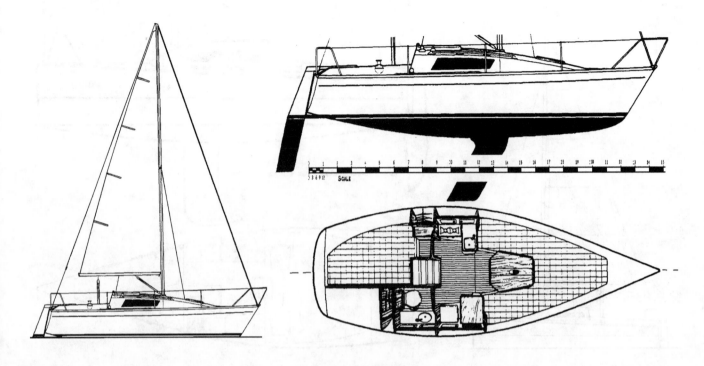

LOD:	25' 5"		Designer:	Group Finot
LOA:	26' 11"		Builder:	Beneteau
LWL:	23' 0"		Years produced:	1984–1991
Min./max. draft:	2' 9"/5' 9"/fin: 4' 3"		Sail area:	296 sq. ft.
Bridge clearance:	35' 6"		Fuel tankage:	10 gal.
Power:	various, diesel 10 hp		Water tankage:	52 gal.
B/D ratio:	30%		Approx. trailering wgt.:	6,900 lbs.

Beneteau has offered a number of boats in this size range over the years. This one, which is 26' 11" LOA but only 25' 5" LOD, comes with either a "pivoting retractable keel" (i.e., weighted centerboard) or a fixed keel with 4' 3" draft. The Beneteau brochure says the designer "played for space," and if the Space Index (584) is any indication, Jean-Marie Finot hit the jackpot on space versus most of the comps shown here, the Ericson 25 Mk II being the exception. The brochure also notes a stable, stiff hull and a generous sailplan. These parameters seem no more remarkable than any of her comps, except that her PHRF of 192 suggests a better potential for speed. **Best features:** The cabin layout is refreshingly unusual, with a dedicated space for a navigator's station, a head located aft, and a complete-looking galley (except for no icebox!). **Worst features:** The diesel engine, housed under the companionway ladder, will make the aft double berth hot in summer (but cozy in winter, if you like sailing among the icicles).

Comps	LOD	Beam	MinDr	Displ	Bllst	SA/D	D/L	Avg. PHRF	Max. Speed	Motion Index	Space Index	No. of Berths	Head-room
Beneteau First 26 (25)	25' 5"	9' 2"	2' 9"	4,814	1,455	16.6	177	192	6.4	16.0	584	4	4' 3"
Ericson 25 Mk II	25' 5"	9' 3"	3' 11"	5,000	2,000	17.8	214	213	6.3	17.3	622	5	6' 1"
Kaiser 25	25' 4"	7' 1"	3' 7"	5,000	2,250	15.5	367	273	5.7	24.3	468	4	6' 2"
Westerly Tiger 25	25' 1"	8' 9"	4' 3"	5,264	2,240	12.5	226	225	6.3	19.7	447	5	5' 3"
Beachcomber 25	25' 4"	8' 0"	1' 3"	5,300	1,400	14.5	188	NA	6.5	20.8	510	5	5' 10"

Bremer 25
Sport boat with surprising amenities

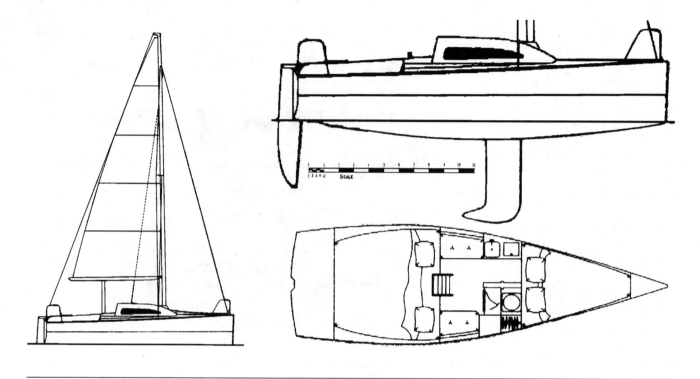

LOD:	25' 0"	**Designer:**	Mark Bremer
LOA:	26' 0"	**Builder:**	Bremer Marine
LWL:	22' 6"	**Years produced:**	1995–1998?
Min./max. draft:	2' 6"/6' 2"	**Sail area:**	309 sq. ft.
Bridge clearance:	40' 3"	**Fuel tankage:**	portable
Power:	outboard 4 to 6 hp	**Water tankage:**	3 gal.
B/D ratio:	42%	**Approx. trailering wgt.:**	5,300 lbs.

C. W. Hood Yachts of Marblehead, MA, built these boats from the board of Mark Bremer, a business consultant with an MBA who decided to try his hand at yacht design. The result is in some ways impressive. That is, how many 25-foot sleek-looking sport boats do you see with six-foot headroom? Or a double berth big enough to accommodate two full-sized adults? Or an enclosed stand-up head? Or a very deep keel with ballast of 1,600 pounds (42% B/D ratio) massed almost at its bottom? ***Best features:*** This boat has enough freeboard to make the cabin quite roomy. With her retractable keel, she shouldn't be too hard to launch and retrieve at a trailer ramp. And her trailer towing weight of just over 5,000 pounds is low enough to permit use of a variety of 20- to 30-year-old full-size cars equipped with towing packages to pull her over the road. ***Worst features:*** The forward berth would only be useful for two very small children or one small adult.

Comps	LOD	Beam	MinDr	Displ	Bllst	SA/D	D/L	Avg. PHRF	Max. Speed	Motion Index	Space Index	No. of Berths	Head-room
U.S. 25/Triton 25 (24)	23' 6"	8' 0"	2' 8"	3,750	1,250	17.0	170	216	6.2	16.0	451	5	5' 6"
Contest 25 OC	24' 8"	9' 0"	4' 11"	3,788	1,510	20.1	172	264	6.2	13.9	528	4	5' 4"
Bremer 25	25' 0"	8' 0"	2' 6"	3,800	1,600	20.3	149	NA	6.4	15.7	509	4	6' 0"
Hunter 25 Mk I	24' 8"	8' 0"	2' 11"	3,850	1,800	11.7	210	222	6.0	17.1	440	5	5' 2"

Bristol Corsair 24 (25)

Bristol Yachts' first "big" sailboat

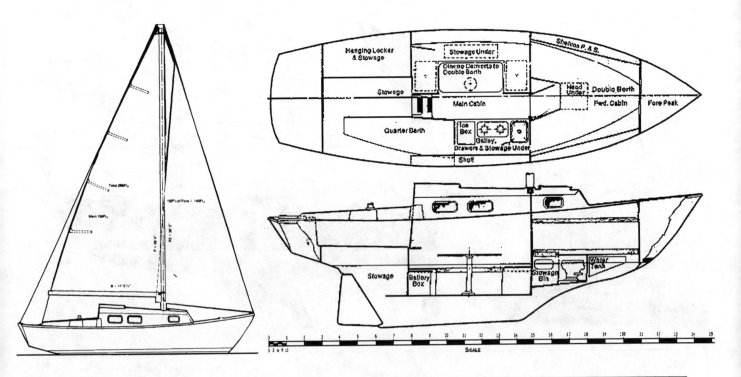

LOD:	24' 7"
LOA:	24' 7"
LWL:	18' 1"
Min./max. draft:	3' 5"
Bridge clearance:	33' 0"
Power:	outboard 6 to 10 hp
B/D ratio:	42%

Designer:	Paul Coble
Builder:	Bristol Yachts
Years produced:	1966–1983
Sail area:	296 sq. ft.
Fuel tankage:	portable
Water tankage:	12 gal.
Approx. trailering wgt.:	8,300 lbs.

Clint Pearson bought Sailstar Boats in Bristol, RI, after his old job disappeared when Pearson Yachts was bought by Grumman Allied Industries. Before long he had changed his new company's name to Bristol Yachts, and began expanding his line of boats. Among the first of the new designs (and in 1966 the largest) was the Corsair 24, designed by Newport, RI, designer and marine surveyor Paul Coble. A choice of two layouts was offered: either (1) the dinette arrangement shown, which accommodates five with the dinette converted to a double berth, or (2) a conventional layout with the same V-berth and

head location forward, but with port and starboard settee berths in the main cabin. Over 800 Corsairs were built. *Best features:* As with her two comps, the Corsair has virtually six feet of headroom in the cabin, unusual for a 25-foot sailboat. *Worst features:* As with her comps, the Corsair is not a boat you can plan to launch at a ramp for a casual afternoon sail, and then retrieve before cocktail hour. Not only is her 3' 5" draft not conducive to easy ramp launching, but on the trailer and equipped to sail away, the total weight is over 8,000 pounds, and requires a sizable towing vehicle rated to pull that big a load.

Comps	LOD	Beam	MinDr	Displ	Bllst	SA/D	D/L	Avg. PHRF	Max. Speed	Motion Index	Space Index	No. of Berths	Head-room
Parker Dawson 26 (25)	25' 3"	8' 0"	1' 8"	5,700	1,250	13.6	234	NA	6.3	23.2	497	5	5' 10"
Bristol Corsair 24 (25)	24' 7"	8' 0"	3' 5"	5,920	2,500	14.5	447	270	5.7	28.4	495	4 or 5	5' 11"
New Horizons 25	25' 3"	7' 9"	3' 0"	6,030	1,600	15.6	281	225	6.2	26.8	465	4	6' 2"

C&C 25

This C&C came in two versions, Mk I and Mk II

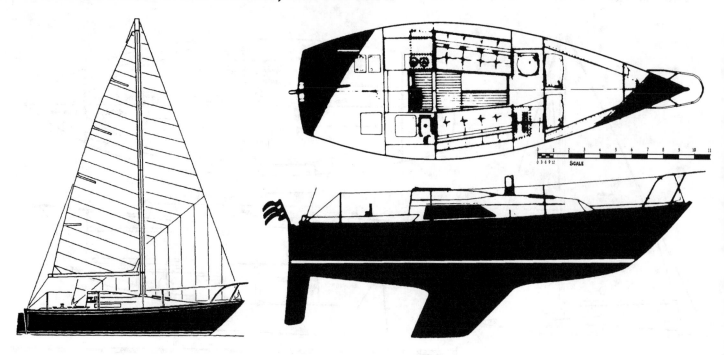

LOD:	25' 2"	**Designer:**	C&C Design Group
LOA:	25' 11"	**Builder:**	C&C Yachts
LWL:	20' 8"	**Years produced:**	1972–1984
Min./max. draft:	3' 10"/4' 3"	**Sail area:**	299 sq. ft.
Bridge clearance:	34' 10"	**Fuel tankage:**	portable
Power:	outboard 6 to 10 hp	**Water tankage:**	10 gal.
B/D ratio:	44%	**Approx. trailering wgt.:**	6,350 lbs.

The C&C 25 came out in 1972 as a capable racer-cruiser with more than average space below for a 25-footer. Eventually a Mk II version was introduced in the early 1980s, with the same hull and general accommodations plan, but tweaked for more speed. (The Mk I design is shown in the sail-plan, the Mk II is shown in the accommodations details.) The newer version replaced the forward-sloping cabin with a longer trunk cabin featuring a bubble at the after end that furnishes a few inches more headroom without appearing top-heavy; a reshaped keel (less raked, deeper by 5 inches) designed for higher pointing; 190 pounds less ballast; and other minor changes. The net result of the tweaking for speed was an average PHRF rating of 222 for both Mk I and Mk II, in other words no change at all. **Best features:** It is interesting to compare the racing oriented C&C with the comps shown here, chosen because of similar displacement, ballast, and D/L and SA/D ratios. The C&C comes out on top in Space Index and headroom (although the Mark 25 ends up with a lower PHRF rating; so much for perception of speed). **Worst features:** The galley seems squeezed up too close to the companionway ladder. Claustrophobic cooks beware.

Comps	LOD	Beam	MinDr	Displ	Bllst	SA/D	D/L	Avg. PHRF	Max. Speed	Motion Index	Space Index	No. of Berths	Head-room
Mark 25	24' 7"	9' 3"	3' 0"	4,130	1,779	20.3	230	216	6.0	15.3	495	4	5' 8"
South Coast Seacraft 25	25' 5"	8' 0"	3' 6"	4,200	1,800	19.1	218	231	6.1	18.4	379	5	5' 6"
C&C 25	25' 2"	8' 8"	3' 10"	4,250	1,880	18.2	215	222	6.1	16.5	555	4	5' 10"
North Star 500 (25)	24' 6"	9' 0"	5' 0"	4,300	1,710	17.7	231	228	6.0	16.3	472	4	4' 6"

Cal 25 Mk I

Good first boat for fixer-uppers

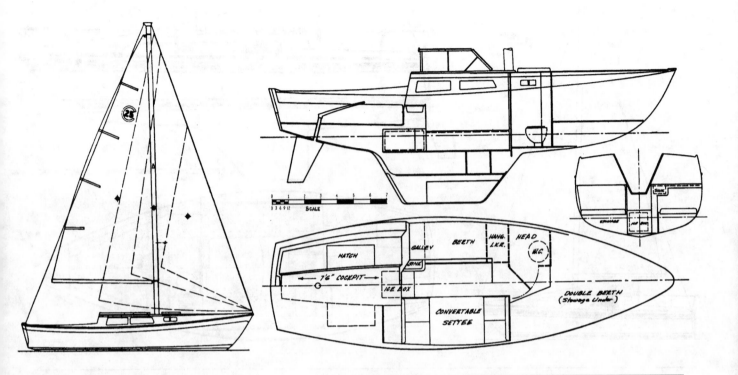

LOD:	25' 0"
LOA:	25' 0"
LWL:	20' 0"
Min./max. draft:	4' 0"
Bridge clearance:	34' 0"
Power:	outboard 5 to 8 hp
B/D ratio:	43%

Designer:	C. William Lapworth
Builder:	Cal Boats
Years produced:	1967–1979
Sail area:	287 sq. ft.
Fuel tankage:	portable
Water tankage:	15 gal.
Approx. trailering wgt.:	6,100 lbs.

The Cal 25 Mk I (not to be confused with the Mk II, a totally different design, reported on page 328) is stable in a blow, has a cockpit big enough to sail four and drink six, and will sleep a friendly group of four or even five souls. (One couple and their two young children completely rebuilt an old Cal 25 and then circumnavigated the world in her.) All Cal 25s are old, but they were very popular so lots of them are still around, and many are relatively inexpensive. If you decide to shop for one, be careful to examine the hull and deck closely for soft, spongy spots; check the deck beam under the mast; watch for leaking chain-plates, delaminating bulkheads, and bulkheads pulling away from the hull. Other problem points may be leaking portlights, worn rubrails, cracked rudder, bad electrical wiring, and mechanical problems with the main hatch. *Best features:* With a cast lead keel of 1,700 pounds, the Cal 25 Mk I is quite stiff in heavy air. It's a good first boat for folks who are handy with tools and want a boat that sails well and is forgiving. *Worst features:* The 4-foot draft means she is not convenient to launch on a ramp from a trailer, unless the ramp is steep and you can rig a tongue extension on the trailer.

Comps	LOD	Beam	MinDr	Displ	Bllst	SA/D	D/L	Avg. PHRF	Max. Speed	Motion Index	Space Index	No. of Berths	Head-room
Shaw Nutmeg 24 (25)	24' 6"	7' 7"	2' 9"	3,800	1,475	17.6	268	NA	5.8	19.3	319	4	4' 3"
Cape Dory 25 Mk I	24' 10"	7' 3"	3' 0"	3,850	1,500	17.2	295	255	5.7	21.1	372	4	5' 0"
Cal 25 Mk I	25' 0"	8' 0"	4' 0"	4,000	1,700	18.2	223	222	6.0	17.9	381	4 or 5	4' 6"

Cal 25 Mk II

Guess the designer: Hunt Assoc. or Lapworth?

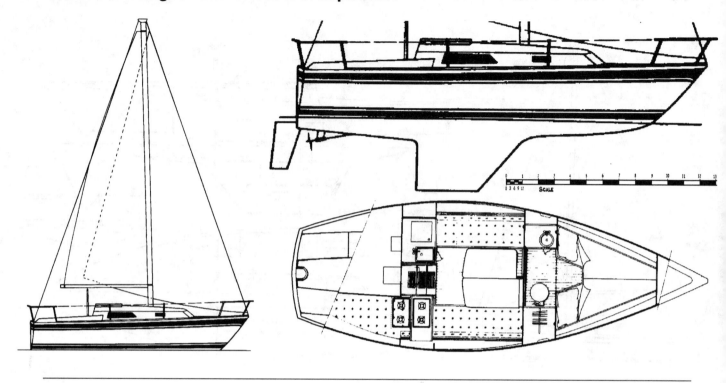

LOD:	25' 3"	**Designer:**	C. Raymond Hunt Assoc.
LOA:	25' 3"	**Builder:**	Cal Boats
LWL:	22' 0"	**Years produced:**	1978–1983
Min./max. draft:	3' 6"/4' 6"	**Sail area:**	315 sq. ft.
Bridge clearance:	37' 0"	**Fuel tankage:**	portable or 12.5 gal.
Power:	outboard or inboard, dsl. 11 hp	**Water tankage:**	22 gal.
B/D ratio:	44%	**Approx. trailering wgt.:**	6,600 lbs.

The plans of this boat look to us like a typical O'Day boat of the late 1970s, which leads us to assume that the designer in all probability was C. Raymond Hunt Associates, even though some of the yachting literature lists Bill Lapworth (1919–2006) as the designer. (They were probably confusing the Mk II with the Mk I.) In any case, the boat was available either with 3' 6" shoal draft or 4' 6" deep draft fin keel, and either with outboard or diesel inboard power. Production (1978 to 1983) was sandwiched between Lapworth's Cal 25 Mk I

(see page 327) and the Cal 24-3 designed by Hunt Associates (see page 280). Her stats are remarkably similar to almost all her comps; except for the Tanzer, her comps have PHRF ratings within 9 seconds per mile. There is a large Cal 25 Mk I racing group and fan club centered up and down the West Coast, but they spurn the Mk II, which is a totally different design (though with a similar average PHRF rating). **Best features:** The Cal 25 Mk II is a well built boat with good headroom and a relatively roomy head. **Worst features:** No significant problems.

Comps	LOD	Beam	MinDr	Displ	Bllst	SA/D	D/L	Avg. PHRF	Max. Speed	Motion Index	Space Index	No. of Berths	Head-room
Columbia 7.6 (25)	25' 1"	9' 2"	3' 6"	4,500	1,500	18.7	228	210	6.1	16.3	573	4	5' 8"
Cal 25 Mk II	25' 3"	9' 0"	3' 6"	4,500	2,000	18.5	189	219	6.3	16.1	558	5	5' 10"
Montego 25	25' 3"	9' 1"	3' 6"	4,550	1,800	17.1	236	216	6.1	16.9	557	4	5' 11"
Tanzer 25 Mk II	25' 3"	9' 7"	2' 11"	4,550	1,985	19.1	195	177	6.3	14.7	575	4	5' 9"
Seidelmann 25 (24)	24' 0"	9' 6"	3' 4"	4,600	2,200	16.3	257	216	6.0	16.5	549	4	5' 2"

Cape Dory 25 Mk I
Early Cape Dory offering by way of Allied Boat Co.

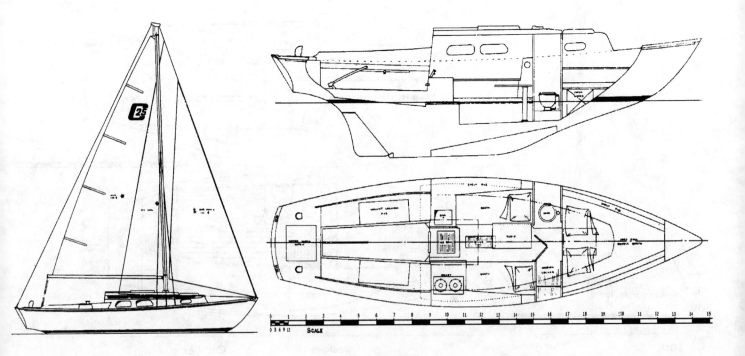

LOD:	24' 10"	**Designer:**	George Stadel
LOA:	24' 10"	**Builder:**	Cape Dory Yachts
LWL:	18' 0"	**Years produced:**	1972–1982
Min./max. draft:	3' 0"	**Sail area:**	264 sq. ft.
Bridge clearance:	31' 6"	**Fuel tankage:**	portable
Power:	outboard 4 to 8 hp	**Water tankage:**	portable
B/D ratio:	39%	**Approx. trailering wgt.:**	5,700 lbs.

This boat started life as the Allied Boat Company's Greenwich 24 (see page 268), but Allied sold the design and the molds to Cape Dory in 1972, when the company was beginning to add cruising boats (Carl Alberg's CD Typhoon 18 (19) in 1967, Ted Hood's CD 30 in 1971) to its daysailer offerings. Cape Dory modified the hull somewhat, raising the freeboard a bit to get more headroom (which added seven inches to her length on deck and the same amount to her waterline length), moving the head from between the forward V-berths to its own space on the port side, adding a hanging locker, enlarging the galley, and otherwise tweaking the design. ***Best features:*** These changes got rid of some of the "Worst features" we mentioned in the Greenwich 24 writeup, and if the manufacturer's specifications are to be believed, after all these additions were made, the boat's weight increased by a mere 25 pounds, with no change in ballast. Can you believe it? We don't. ***Worst features:*** Headroom is still too low, but this fault is corrected in the next incarnation, namely the CD 25D; see page 330.

Comps	LOD	Beam	MinDr	Displ	Bllst	SA/D	D/L	Avg. PHRF	Max. Speed	Motion Index	Space Index	No. of Berths	Headroom
Shaw Nutmeg 24 (25)	24' 6"	7' 7"	2' 9"	3,800	1,475	17.6	268	NA	5.8	19.3	319	4	4' 3"
Cape Dory 25 Mk I	24' 10"	7' 3"	3' 0"	3,850	1,500	17.2	295	255	5.7	21.1	372	4	5' 0"
Cal 25 Mk I	25' 0"	8' 0"	4' 0"	4,000	1,700	18.2	223	222	6.0	17.9	381	4 or 5	4' 6"

Cape Dory 25D (Mk II)
Replacement for the Cape Dory 25

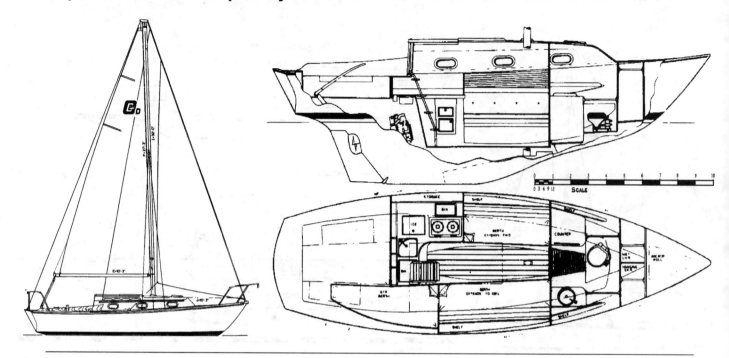

LOD:	25' 0"	**Designer:**	Carl Alberg
LOA:	25' 0"	**Builder:**	Cape Dory Yachts
LWL:	19' 0"	**Years produced:**	1981–1985
Min./max. draft:	3' 6"	**Sail area:**	304 sq. ft.
Bridge clearance:	35' 0"	**Fuel tankage:**	13 gal.
Power:	Yanmar 1GM dsl. 8 hp	**Water tankage:**	20 gal.
B/D ratio:	40%	**Approx. trailering wgt.:**	7,200 lbs.

Cape Dory Yachts decided to start from scratch on a new 25-footer after sales on their existing product, the CD 25, designed by George Stadel (see page 329) began to taper off. They hired Carl Alberg to come up with a bigger, heavier, more powerful boat capable of cruising two in comfort on extended cruises. Alberg eliminated the traditional forward V-berths and put in their place something not often seen in a boat this size: a head with vanity, wet and dry hanging lockers, and a really rare feature, a shower. Also included are an L-shaped galley, two settee berths amidships (with one convertible to a double), and a quarter berth

to starboard. Headroom is 5' 11", very good for a boat only 25 feet on deck. A single-cylinder 8-hp Yanmar is standard. ***Best features:*** In our opinion this boat might come close to the ideal boat for couples who want a cruising boat that can go offshore and has some elbow below, but still can be trailered hither and yon behind a big pickup truck. ***Worst features:*** The Cape Dory 25D wins the prize for the highest PHRF among her comps, though sailors who find this boat appealing probably won't do much racing anyway. For steering comfort, the tiller sprouting out of the cockpit sole is not the best.

Comps	LOD	Beam	MinDr	Displ	Bllst	SA/D	D/L	Avg. PHRF	Max. Speed	Motion Index	Space Index	No. of Berths	Head-room
Capri 26 (24)	23' 8"	9' 10"	3' 5"	5,100	1,750	15.9	189	210	6.4	15.6	641	4	6' 1"
Cape Dory 25D (Mk II)	25' 0"	8' 0"	3' 6"	5,120	2,050	16.4	333	255	5.8	23.7	472	4	5' 11"
Rhodes Meridian 25	24' 9"	7' 0"	3' 3"	5,310	2,750	13.4	442	252	5.6	31.0	363	4	5' 8"
Contessa 26	25' 5.5"	7' 6"	4' 0"	5,400	2,300	15.8	260	246	6.1	24.8	447	4	5' 0"
Ericson 25 Mk I	24' 8"	8' 0"	2' 0"	5,400	2,500	13.8	267	234	6.1	23.4	457	4	5' 6"

Capri 25

The Capri 25 is a Catalina 25 "Lite"

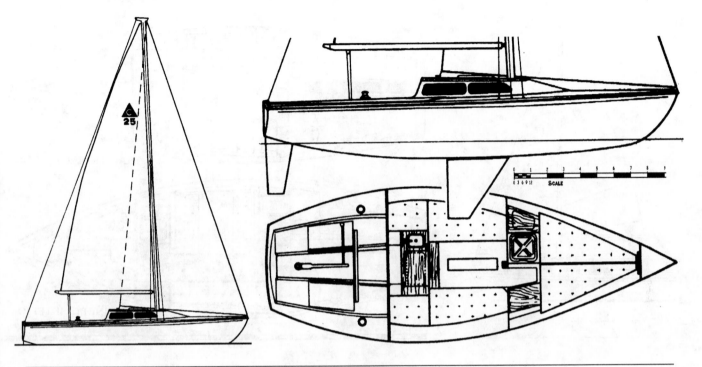

LOD:	24' 7"	**Designer:**	Frank Butler
LOA:	24' 7"	**Builder:**	Catalina Yachts
LWL:	19' 2"	**Years produced:**	1979–1989
Min./max. draft:	4' 2"	**Sail area:**	276 sq. ft.
Bridge clearance:	35' 6"	**Fuel tankage:**	portable
Power:	outboard 4 to 6 hp	**Water tankage:**	7.5 gal.
B/D ratio:	32%	**Approx. trailering wgt.:**	4,100 lbs.

The Capri 25 (by Catalina) is nothing like a Catalina 25 (page 332). The Capri is five inches shorter on deck, three feet shorter on the waterline, and weighs almost 1,400 pounds less than the Catalina, so we suppose you could call her a Catalina "Lite," especially since her towing weight is over a ton less, so you can use a smaller, lighter towing vehicle on the highway. Besides her lower weight, she has slightly more sail area and a sleeker fin keel, so she is also faster—way faster. In fact, her average PHRF rating is 171, which is, amazingly, 3 seconds per mile less than the legendary J/24, and a whopping 54 seconds less

than the Catalina 25. Needless to say, part of her weight loss is accomplished by the omission of cabin furniture and other niceties like the Catalina's on-deck anchor locker. Other weight saving is achieved by eliminating 600 pounds of ballast, and by using a then-new material, Coremat, to replace some of the hull and deck laminate. ***Best features:*** If you like round-the-buoys racing and/or socializing in a one-design fleet, this may be the boat for you. She has a bit more space below than a J/24, and six inches more head-room, but otherwise her character is in the same range. ***Worst features:*** Nothing significant noticed.

Comps	LOD	Beam	MinDr	Displ	Bllst	SA/D	D/L	Avg. PHRF	Max. Speed	Motion Index	Space Index	No. of Berths	Head-room
Evelyn 25	24' 11"	8' 10"	4' 5"	2,600	1,100	24.8	117	147	6.2	9.8	422	4	4' 6"
Capri 25	24' 7"	9' 2"	4' 2"	2,785	900	22.3	177	171	5.9	10.7	414	4	4' 6"
Olson 25	23' 7"	9' 0"	4' 6"	2,900	1,300	23.2	135	159	6.2	10.7	428	4	4' 8"
Bombardier 7.6 (25)	25' 4"	8' 6"	4' 6"	3,300	985	24.4	129	168	6.4	12.5	375	5	4' 6"

Catalina 25

Over 5,000 of these 25-footers were built

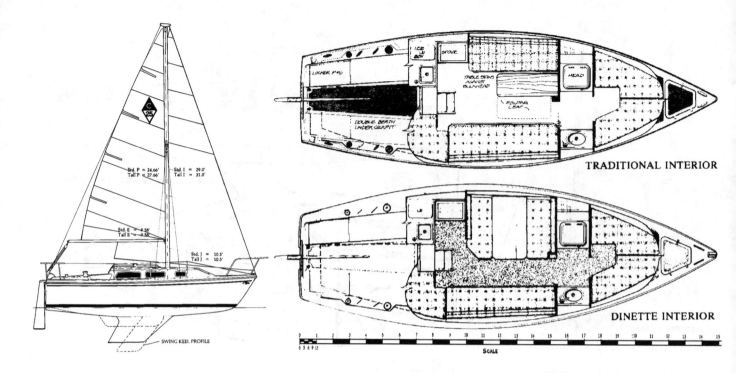

Std. P = 24.66'
Tall P = 27.66'
Std. I = 29.0'
Tall I = 31.0'

Std. E = 9.58'
Tall E = 9.58'

Std. J = 10.5'
Tall J = 10.5'

SWING KEEL PROFILE

TRADITIONAL INTERIOR

DINETTE INTERIOR

SCALE

LOD:	25' 0"	
LOA:	26' 6"	
LWL:	22' 2"	
Min./max. draft:	2' 2"/5' 0"/fin: 4' 0"	
Bridge clearance:	33' 6"	
Power:	outboard or inboard 4 to 8 hp	
B/D ratio:	36%	

Designer:	Frank Butler
Builder:	Catalina Yachts
Years produced:	1976–1987
Sail area:	270 sq. ft.
Fuel tankage:	portable
Water tankage:	varies 10 to 20 gal.
Approx. trailering wgt.:	6,250 lbs.

This is one of Catalina's most popular boats, with over 5,000 built from 1976 to 1987. There were plenty of choices: standard rig (shown here) or tall rig, three feet higher, with 7 percent more sail area; swing keel (2' 2" up, 5' 0" down) or fin keel (4' 0" draft, 400 pounds more ballast); traditional or dinette interior (see layout); outboard or inboard; available flip-top to increase cabin headroom from 5' 6" to 6' 6". (In 1987 a new, quite similar but by no means identical version was introduced, which continued in production through 1991. The new version offered a choice of either a 1,900 pound fin keel or a 1,750 pound wing keel.) ***Best features:*** One of the best things about owning a popular boat like the Catalina 25 is the automatic chance to make new friends among the thousands of existing C25 owners. Among the reasons for the boat's phenomenal popularity was her low first cost, whether new or used. ***Worst features:*** Construction quality over the years varied from poor to very good. Among mechanical problems, boats with swing keels tended to require more than average maintenance.

Comps	LOD	Beam	MinDr	Displ	Bllst	SA/D	D/L	Avg. PHRF	Max. Speed	Motion Index	Space Index	No. of Berths	Head-room
Amphibi-Con 25	25' 5"	7' 9"	2' 5"	3,900	1,100	17.9	171	234	6.2	16.8	407	4	5' 8"
Catalina 25	25' 0"	8' 0"	2' 2"	4,150	1,500	16.7	170	225	6.3	17.3	464	5	5' 6"
Tanzer 7.5 (25)	24' 7"	8' 0"	2' 8"	4,150	1,950	15.9	178	201	6.3	17.6	529	4	5' 8"
Coronado 25 (cb version)	25' 0"	8' 0"	2' 6"	4,300	1,800	18.4	246	231	6.0	19.4	411	5	5' 6"

Catalina 250

A choice between water ballast, fin, and wing keel

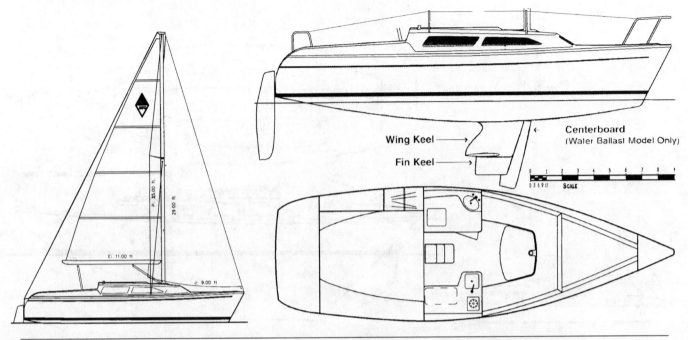

Wing Keel

Centerboard
(Water Ballast Model Only)

Fin Keel

SCALE

LOD:	25' 0"
LOA:	26' 11"
LWL:	21' 3"
Min./max. draft:	1' 8"/5' 9"
Bridge clearance:	33' 4"
Power:	outboard 6 to 8 hp
B/D ratio:	33%

Designer:	Catalina Design Team
Builder:	Catalina Yachts
Years produced:	1994–present
Sail area:	268 sq. ft.
Fuel tankage:	portable
Water tankage:	varies 5 to 12 gal.
Approx. trailering wgt.:	5,400 lbs.

This Catalina has been available as a wing keeler, a centerboarder (in the water ballast model only), and (until recently) a fin keeler. Over the years a number of changes have been made, some small, some big. For example, headroom increased from 4' 3" (as shown here) to 4' 8", and from 6' 4" to 7' 1" with a pop-top (now standard) in place. (In the wing keel model, headroom with the pop-top down is 5' 3", a whole foot more than with the water ballast model.) An optional tall rig is available, increasing sail area by 30 square feet and bridge clearance by three feet. A Mk II version recently appeared, combining these and other improvements in the new model. **Best features:** The wing keel model comes close to being an ideal combination of features and economy for new sailors just starting out and wanting to test the waters. **Worst features:** The water ballast version has some inherent weaknesses, for example, water is only one eleventh the density of lead, limiting its effectiveness as ballast; since shallow draft is paramount for easy ramp launching, the ballast cannot be as deep as with conventional lead ballast; and to attain enough total weight to be even partially effective, it must be spread out into the ends of the hull, which tends to slow the boat in waves. The bottom line is that water ballast makes for a slower, more tender boat compared to an identical design with a lead keel.

Comps	LOD	Beam	MinDr	Displ	Bllst	SA/D	D/L	Avg. PHRF	Max. Speed	Motion Index	Space Index	No. of Berths	Head-room
Lancer 25	24' 8"	8' 0"	2' 4"	3,400	1,200	17.5	187	264	6.0	15.2	560	4 to 6	5' 10"
Freedom 25 (24)	24' 4"	8' 6"	2' 6"	3,500	1,025	18.0	195	186	6.0	14.3	432	4	4' 10"
Catalina 250	25' 0"	8' 6"	1' 8"	3,600	1,200	18.3	167	225	6.2	14.3	395	4	4' 3"
Hunter 25 Mk III	24' 6"	8' 5"	2' 0"	3,700	1,309	17.1	153	225	6.3	14.4	484	4	5' 4"
Santana 25	24' 7"	7' 10"	2' 7"	4,050	1,750	16.5	244	225	6.9	18.6	396	4	5' 2"

Cheoy Lee Flyer Mk III 25

A Folkboat design imported from Hong Kong

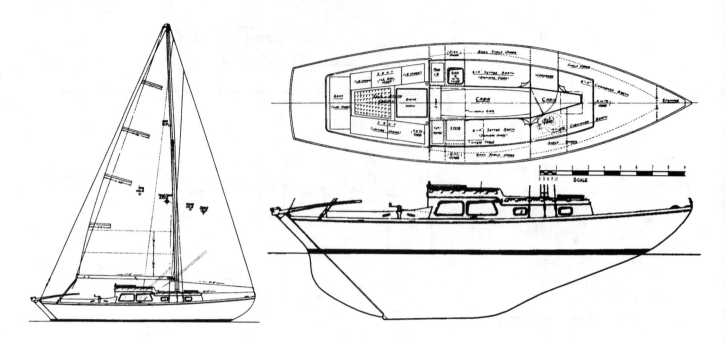

LOD:	25' 0"	**Designer:**	Arthur Robb (?) and others
LOA:	26' 2"	**Builder:**	Cheoy Lee Shipyard
LWL:	20' 0"	**Years produced:**	1966–1970
Min./max. draft:	3' 11"	**Sail area:**	310 sq. ft.
Bridge clearance:	33' 6"	**Fuel tankage:**	8 gal.
Power:	various, incl. 5 hp dsl.	**Water tankage:**	20 gal.
B/D ratio:	37%	**Approx. trailering wgt.:**	8,400 lbs.

Cheoy Lee Shipyard of Hong Kong built various versions of this Folkboat-type hull (note similarities to the Contessa 26 on page 337) between 1957 and 1970, some in wood, others in fiberglass. The Mk III vessel pictured here was available either with a teak hull and teak superstructure, or with a fiberglass hull and teak decks and cabinhouse. The Mk III is distinct from the Mk I and Mk II mainly because of her doghouse cabin, which was possibly the idea of British designer Arthur Robb, though Tord Sunden is generally credited with the basic hull design. In any case, the boat won accolades for her good performance on transpacific and transatlantic voyages. ***Best features:*** The Cheoy Lee artisans were well-known for their intricate teak carvings—dragons and such—with which they decorated the Flyer cabins, giving a luxurious effect. ***Worst features:*** Though the teak woodwork was masterful, the hardware was sometimes made from inferior grades of metal, and would corrode or wear quickly.

Comps	LOD	Beam	MinDr	Displ	Bllst	SA/D	D/L	Avg. PHRF	Max. Speed	Motion Index	Space Index	No. of Berths	Head-room
Parker Dawson 26 (25)	25' 3"	8' 0"	1' 8"	5,700	1,250	13.6	234	NA	6.3	23.2	497	5	5' 10"
South Coast Marine 25	25' 0"	8' 0"	2' 6"	5,700	1,750	15.3	275	NA	6.1	22.7	411	2 to 4	5' 0"
Bristol Corsair 24 (25)	24' 7"	8' 0"	3' 5"	5,920	2,500	14.5	447	270	5.7	28.4	495	4	5' 11"
Cheoy Lee Flyer Mk III 25	25' 0"	7' 2"	3' 11"	6,000	2,240	14.7	335	297	5.9	30.6	386	4	5' 4"
New Horizons 25	25' 3"	7' 9"	3' 0"	6,030	1,600	15.6	281	225	6.2	26.8	465	4	5' 2"

Columbia 7.6 (25)
"Widebody supercruiser" from Alan Payne

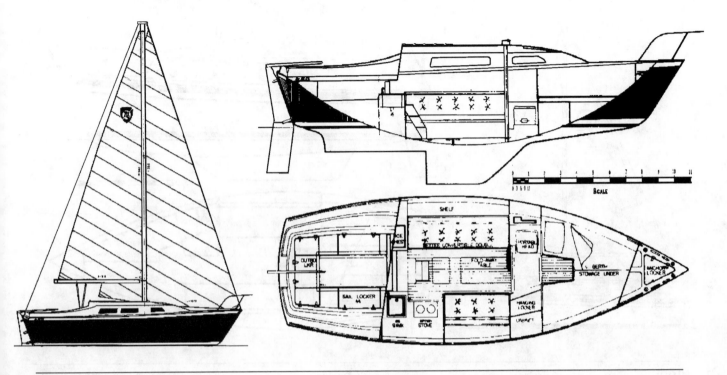

LOD:	25' 1"		**Designer:**	Alan Payne
LOA:	25' 9"		**Builder:**	Columbia Yachts, Aura Yachts
LWL:	20' 8"		**Years produced:**	1978–1986
Min./max. draft:	3' 6"		**Sail area:**	319 sq. ft.
Bridge clearance:	36' 6"		**Fuel tankage:**	portable
Power:	outboard, dsl. opt., 6 to 10 hp		**Water tankage:**	16 gal.
B/D ratio:	33%		**Approx. trailering wgt.:**	6,600 lbs.

The main claim to fame for Australian Alan Payne (1921–1995) was that he designed Australia's America's Cup entry boat in 1962 (Gretel) and 1970 (Gretel II), neither of which won, but were reasonably close to the winner. Later he designed some production sailboats, including the Columbia 7.6. A sales brochure calls her a "widebody supercruiser," but that seems an exaggeration; her "wide body" beam (9' 2") is exceeded by 20 other boats in this guide, and her Space Index (573) is respectable for her length but not extraordinary; check the Irwin 10/4

(page 347) for an example of a much roomier 25-footer. When Columbia ceased production, Aura Yachts of Canada took over production for a brief period, offering kits as well as finished boats. **Best features:** We see no special features that distinguish this vessel from her comps. **Worst features:** We would guess that the 7.6's stability may be slightly lower than her comps due to her lower ballast. Workmanship may vary considerably depending on the builder at any given time—especially among the individuals building kit boats.

Comps	LOD	Beam	MinDr	Displ	Bllst	SA/D	D/L	Avg. PHRF	Max. Speed	Motion Index	Space Index	No. of Berths	Head-room
Columbia 7.6 (25)	25' 1"	9' 2"	3' 6"	4,500	1,500	18.7	228	210	6.1	16.3	573	4	5' 8"
Cal 25 Mk II	25' 3"	9' 0"	3' 6"	4,500	2,000	18.5	189	219	6.3	16.1	558	5	5' 10"
Montego 25	25' 3"	9' 1"	3' 6"	4,550	1,800	17.1	236	216	6.1	16.9	557	4	5' 11"
Tanzer 25 Mk II	25' 3"	9' 7"	2' 11"	4,550	1,985	19.1	195	177	6.3	14.7	575	4	5' 9"
Seidelmann 25 (24)	24' 0"	9' 6"	3' 4"	4,600	2,200	16.3	257	216	6.0	16.5	549	4	5' 2"

Com-Pac 25

Lots of space for a trailerable 25-footer

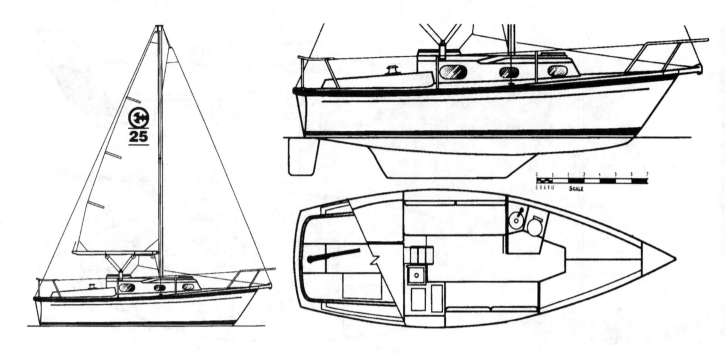

LOD:	24' 7"	**Designer:**	Hutchins Design Team
LOA:	28' 2"	**Builder:**	Hutchins Co.
LWL:	21' 0"	**Years produced:**	1995–present
Min./max. draft:	2' 6"	**Sail area:**	278 sq. ft.
Bridge clearance:	32' 9"	**Fuel tankage:**	optional
Power:	inboard or outboard 6 to 12 hp	**Water tankage:**	20 gal.
B/D ratio:	40%	**Approx. trailering wgt.:**	6,900 lbs.

The Com-Pac 25 offers accommodations for five, 5' 10" headroom, a big folding galley table that flips down from the bulkhead, and a private enclosed head. She has an 8' 6" beam, which is wider than her comps, but still road-legal in the United States. So all you need is a big enough tow vehicle (and that no longer means "any full-size car; try a big truck or van with a tow package and extra power). There are six bronze opening ports with screens for ventilation; and there's plenty of teak and teak veneer in the cabin. Options include a two-cylinder 12-horse-power freshwater cooled inboard diesel, and Edson wheel steering. **Best features:** Her Space Index and her head-room are both highest among her comps. **Worst features:** Her mainsail is less than 40 percent of her total sail area, which makes sail handling easier but limits overall power, especially sailing downwind. Inboard sheeting might improve the boat's windward performance, according to one reviewer.

Comps	LOD	Beam	MinDr	Displ	Bllst	SA/D	D/L	Avg. PHRF	Max. Speed	Motion Index	Space Index	No. of Berths	Head-room
Cornish Crabber 24	24' 0"	8' 0"	2' 5"	4,600	600	17.6	247	360	6.0	19.3	415	4	4' 3"
Pacific Seacraft 25	24' 6"	8' 0"	3' 3"	4,750	1,750	12.8	229	NA	6.1	20.3	387	4	5' 0"
O'Day 26 (25)	25' 4"	8' 0"	2' 6"	4,800	1,850	15.7	213	234	6.2	19.8	484	5	5' 6"
Com-Pac 25	24' 7"	8' 6"	2' 6"	4,800	1,900	15.6	231	NA	6.1	18.4	509	5	5' 10"
Morgan 24/25	24' 11"	8' 0"	2' 9"	5,000	1,900	17.0	225	225	6.2	21.4	435	4	5' 8"

Contessa 26 (25)
Folkboat design from England and Canada

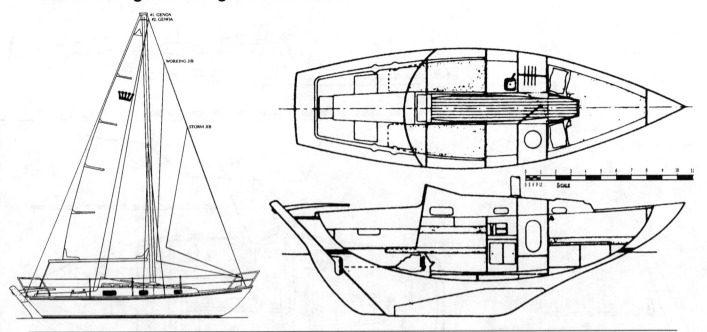

LOD:	25' 5.5"		**Designer:**	David Sadler
LOA:	27' 1"		**Builder:**	J. J. Taylor & Sons
LWL:	21' 0"		**Years produced:**	1965–1990
Min./max. draft:	4' 0"		**Sail area:**	304 sq. ft.
Bridge clearance:	33' 0"		**Fuel tankage:**	varies
Power:	inboard 6 to 10 hp		**Water tankage:**	varies
B/D ratio:	43%		**Approx. trailering wgt.:**	7,600 lbs.

The Scandinavian Folkboat concept (heavy displacement, long keel with highly raked attached outboard rudder, narrow hull, low freeboard, springy sheer) inspired this British design by David Sadler in collaboration with Contessa Yachts owner Jeremy Rodgers, based in Lymington, England. The boats proved very seaworthy in tough conditions, such as the OSTAR (Observer Singlehanded Transatlantic Race), the Fastnet Race, and a 27,000 mile round-the-world voyage by young Tania Abei. After building 350 boats in England in less than four years, the molds were shipped to Canada where J. J. Taylor & Sons began selling to the North American market. The boat was first known as the Contessa 26, and later, for legal reasons, as the J. J. Taylor 26. In 1983 many changes were made, such as lead in place of iron keel (increasing ballast by 300 lbs.); a lowered cabin sole to increase headroom; and addition of a midships hatch. There were many engine types over the years, such as 7 hp Vire, 6.6 hp Petter, 7 hp Faryman, 9 hp Yanmar. *Best features:* Good sea boat, very good tracking ability (good for windvane steering), good pointing ability. She also looks pretty. *Worst features:* Low coach roof and narrow beam give the cabin a closed-in feeling. There's no space to stand up under a companionway hatch, since there is no hatch; instead, a "bubble" facilitates entry to the cabin. Low freeboard gives a wet ride in rough conditions. Some boats need scuppers relocated.

Comps	LOD	Beam	MinDr	Displ	Bllst	SA/D	D/L	Avg. PHRF	Max. Speed	Motion Index	Space Index	No. of Berths	Head-room
Capri 26 (24)	23' 8"	9' 10"	3' 5"	5,100	1,750	15.9	189	210	6.4	15.6	641	4	6' 1"
Cape Dory 25D (Mk II)	25' 0"	8' 0"	3' 6"	5,120	2,050	16.4	333	255	5.8	23.7	472	4	5' 11"
Rhodes Meridian 25	24' 9"	7' 0"	3' 3"	5,310	2,750	13.4	442	252	5.6	31.0	363	4	5' 8"
Contessa 26 (25)	25' 5.5"	7' 6"	4' 0"	5,400	2,300	15.8	260	246	6.1	24.8	447	4	5' 0"
Ericson 25 Mk I	24' 8"	8' 0"	2' 0"	5,400	2,500	13.8	234	234	6.1	23.4	457	4	5' 6"

Coronado 25
Early fiberglass boat presaged Catalina success

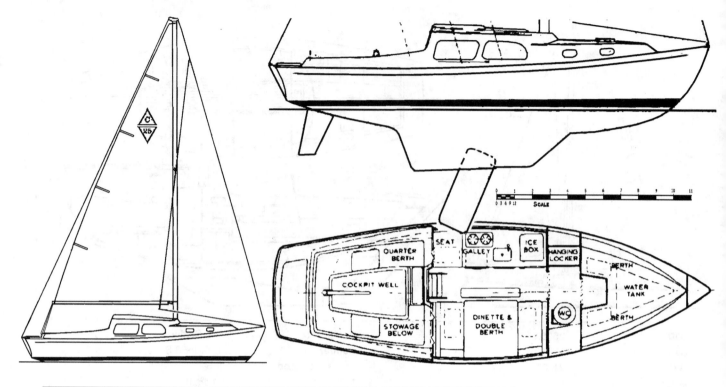

LOD:	25' 0"		**Designer:**	Frank Butler & Ed Edgars
LOA:	25' 0"		**Builder:**	Wesco & Coronado Yachts
LWL:	19' 10"		**Years produced:**	1965–1972
Min./max. draft:	2' 6"/7' 0"		**Sail area:**	304 sq. ft.
Bridge clearance:	34' 0"		**Fuel tankage:**	portable
Power:	outboard 6 to 10 hp		**Water tankage:**	portable
B/D ratio:	42%		**Approx. trailering wgt.:**	6,400 lbs.

This boat, conceived by Frank Butler (who went on later to own and run Catalina Yachts, one of the world's most successful boatbuilders) was in the vanguard of early fiberglass designs. The Coronado 25 was offered as either a centerboarder (2' 6" draft with board up, 7' 0" with it down) or as a fin keeler (3' 8" fixed draft). The centerboarder displaced 4,300 pounds with a ballast of 1,800 pounds; the fin keel model was considerably heavier at 4,950 pounds with 2,150 pounds of ballast—though the ballast and displacement figures varied somewhat over the years the boat was built. The listed sail area was also different for the two configurations: 273 square feet for the centerboard model, 309 square feet for keel model, though strangely, the rated area with 100 percent foretriangle was the same for either configuration. Despite the significant differences in weight, draft, and sail area, average PHRF ratings for both versions are in the 231 seconds per mile range. **Best features:** Heaviest among her comps, she also has the highest Motion Index. **Worst features:** Any boats of this model still sailing are at least 38 years old, and are therefore likely to require more than the usual maintenance.

Comps	LOD	Beam	MinDr	Displ	Bllst	SA/D	D/L	Avg. PHRF	Max. Speed	Motion Index	Space Index	No. of Berths	Head- room
Amphibi-Con 25	25' 5"	7' 9"	2' 5"	3,900	1,100	17.9	171	234	6.2	16.8	407	4	5' 8"
Catalina 25	25' 0"	8' 0"	2' 2"	4,150	1,500	16.7	170	225	6.3	17.3	464	5	5' 6"
Tanzer 7.5 (25)	24' 7"	8' 0"	2' 8"	4,150	1,950	15.9	178	201	6.3	17.6	529	4	5' 8"
Coronado 25 (cb version)	25' 0"	8' 0"	2' 6"	4,300	1,800	18.4	246	231	6.0	19.4	411	5	5' 6"

Dufour 1800 (25)

This one has a cabin table with four positions

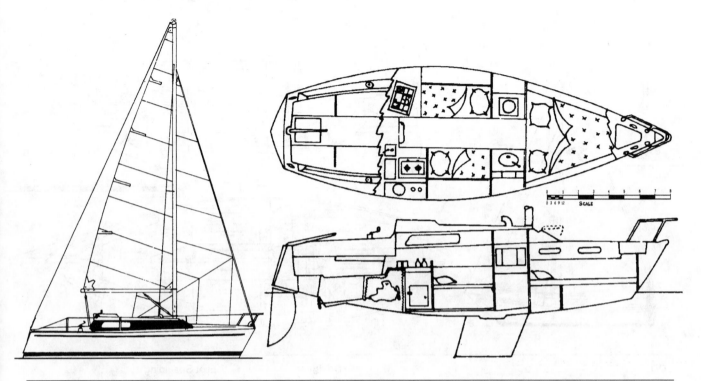

LOD:	25' 1"		**Designer:**	Dufour & Cordelle
LOA:	26' 1"		**Builder:**	Dufour Yachts
LWL:	22' 0"		**Years produced:**	1979–1983
Min./max. draft:	4' 3"		**Sail area:**	253 sq. ft.
Bridge clearance:	36' 6"		**Fuel tankage:**	portable
Power:	outboard or inboard 6 to 10 hp		**Water tankage:**	portable
B/D ratio:	42%		**Approx. trailering wgt.:**	5,800 lbs.

Michel Dufour, a French engineer with a love of sailing, founded a shipyard in La Rochelle, France, in 1964. The company is still in business. The Dufour 1800 (which refers to the boat's displacement, roughly 1,800 kilograms) was designed by the team of Laurent Cordelle and Michel Dufour, and introduced in 1979 as the successor to the Dufour 25, a vessel that never established a presence in the United States market. The 1800, which sold mostly in Europe but developed a following in Canada and to some extent in the United States, came with a choice of standard keel (shown here), deep keel, shallow keel, or lifting keel. An outboard well, in the cockpit on the boat's centerline just forward of the rudder, provides good steering control under power. An inboard was also available. *Best features:* The cabin table, which when not in use is stored beneath the starboard berth, is unusually clever in that it mounts in any of three different positions: (1) fore and aft attached to the main bulkhead; (2) athwartships attached to the seat backs on either side; or (3) in the cockpit, mounted on the bottom washboard. Down below, a half-size chart table to port, supported by the rear bulkhead, is also handy. *Worst features:* None noted.

Comps	LOD	Beam	MinDr	Displ	Bllst	SA/D	D/L	Avg. PHRF	Max. Speed	Motion Index	Space Index	No. of Berths	Head-room
Jeanneau Eolia 25	24' 7"	9' 2"	2' 7"	3,750	1,830	21.4	165	243	6.2	13.4	568	4	5' 8"
Dufour 1800 (25)	25' 1"	8' 10"	4' 3"	3,969	1,654	16.1	166	213	6.3	14.3	536	4	5' 6"
Kelt 7.60 (25)	24' 11"	9' 5"	4' 3"	4,189	1,765	17.5	157	204	6.4	13.7	577	4	5' 7"
Elite 25 (24)	24' 0"	8' 10"	2' 3"	4,300	1,742	15.2	193	201	6.2	15.9	527	4	6' 0"

Eastsail 25
Custom-built cruiser for offshore use

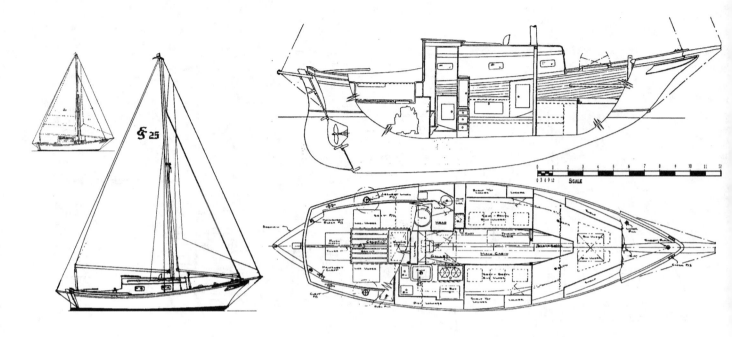

LOD:	25' 0"	**Designer:**	Eliot Spaulding
LOA:	29' 8"	**Builder:**	Eastsail Yachts
LWL:	20' 10"	**Years produced:**	1982–present
Min./max. draft:	3' 8"	**Sail area:**	400 sq. ft.
Bridge clearance:	34' 0"	**Fuel tankage:**	varies
Power:	outboard or inboard 10 to 20 hp	**Water tankage:**	varies
B/D ratio:	32%	**Approx. trailering wgt.:**	10,600 lbs.

The builders, Eastsail Yachts of Bow, New Hampshire, advertise this as a "rugged, trailerable, pocket cruiser of traditional lines carrying a full keel and full headroom, designed for the long voyage," that is, extended offshore cruising. That puts her squarely in the same oceangoing category with two of her comps, the Vertue and the Fisher. The Eastsail is what amounts to a custom boat, with the owner specifying rig, interior design, wood trim (teak, mahogany, or plain white paneling with minimal hardwood trim), number of berths, tankage, motor power (small inboard diesel or a four-stroke outboard mounted under the lazarette hatch),

traditional bronze or modern stainless steel hardware, and so on. An "All Weather" model (see inset in sailplan) raises the boom a bit to sneak a doghouse underneath it, adding a little to the masthead bridge clearance and 300 pounds to the displacement, but changing little else. ***Best features:*** If you're not quite ready to do a circumnavigation, but want to sail, say, regularly from Maine to Florida and back, this may be a better choice than the more purpose-built Vertue or Fisher. ***Worst features:*** The cabin house appears to be high enough to obstruct a clear view from the helmsman's position when seated.

Comps	LOD	Beam	MinDr	Displ	Bllst	SA/D	D/L	Avg. PHRF	Max. Speed	Motion Index	Space Index	No. of Berths	Head-room
New Moon 25	25' 0"	8' 6"	3' 8"	6,800	2,300	15.8	336	NA	6.1	27.3	532	4	6' 0"
Eastsail 25	25' 0"	8' 6"	3' 8"	7,200	2,300	17.2	355	NA	6.1	27.2	532	5	6' 0"
Vertue 25	25' 3"	7' 10"	4' 5"	9,220	4,400	14.2	414	NA	6.2	40.1	542	4	6' 2"
Fisher 25	25' 3"	9' 4"	3' 9"	10,000	4,500	7.2	482	NA	6.1	35.2	567	5	6' 0"

Ericson 25 Mk I
Nice small cruiser by Bruce King

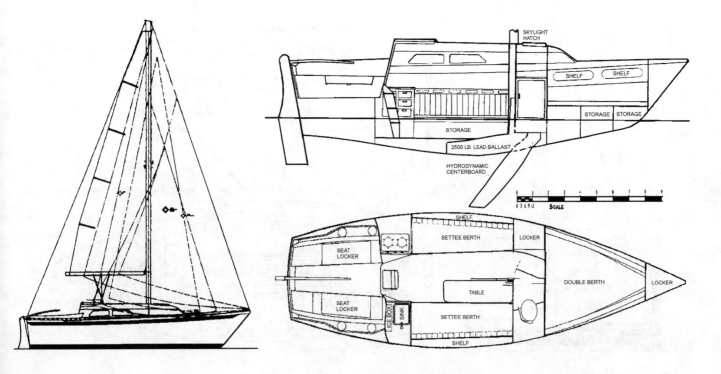

LOD:	24' 8"
LOA:	25' 5"
LWL:	20' 10"
Min./max. draft:	2' 0"/5' 0"
Bridge clearance:	35' 0"
Power:	outboard or inboard 6 to 10 hp
B/D ratio:	46%

Designer:	Bruce King
Builder:	Ericson Yachts
Years produced:	1972–1978
Sail area:	265 sq. ft.
Fuel tankage:	portable or 9 gal.
Water tankage:	9 gal.
Approx. trailering wgt.:	7,700 lbs.

When she came out in 1972, this vessel was seen as remarkably roomy for a 25-footer, as indeed she was. A slightly larger, slightly lighter fin-keel version with more sail area but a similar interior arrangement, the Ericson 25+ or Mk II (page 342), was introduced in 1978, the year the Mk I was discontinued. The Ericson 25 Mk I, like her successor, is well-finished and nicely laid out for comfortable alongshore cruising. She is also designed to race, with testing done in the Davidson Laboratory at Stevens Institute and a hull rated as a quarter-tonner. **Best features:** She cleverly combines a high aspect ratio centerboard with a trunk almost totally beneath the cabin sole, eliminating the nuisance of a protruding trunk splitting the cabin in two. Her sales brochure touts her easy trailerability, and shows a photo of the boat on a four-wheel trailer, her 7,700 pounds of load towed by a Cadillac sedan—something that today no ordinary car, including a Cadillac, could come close to doing. **Worst features:** We could not come up with any significant negative features.

Comps	LOD	Beam	MinDr	Displ	Bllst	SA/D	D/L	Avg. PHRF	Max. Speed	Motion Index	Space Index	No. of Berths	Head-room
Yankee 26	24' 6"	8' 8"	4' 6"	5,335	2,150	15.4	270	234	6.1	20.7	534	4	6' 0"
Contessa 26	25' 5.5"	7' 6"	4' 0"	5,400	2,300	15.8	260	246	6.1	24.8	202	4	5' 0"
Ericson 25 Mk I	24' 8"	8' 0"	2' 0"	5,400	2,500	13.8	267	234	6.1	23.4	457	4	5' 6"
South Coast Marine 25	25' 0"	8' 0"	2' 6"	5,700	1,750	15.3	275	NA	6.1	22.7	411	2 to 4	5' 0"
Cheoy Lee Flyer 25	25' 0"	7' 2"	3' 11"	6,000	2,240	14.7	335	297	5.9	30.6	386	4	5' 4"

Ericson 25+ or Mk II

A longer, roomier, taller Ericson 25

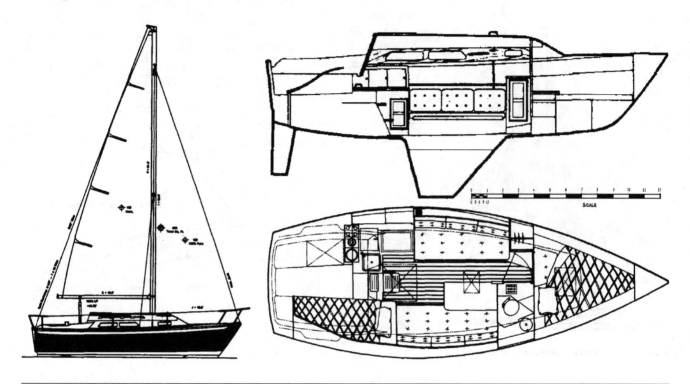

LOD:	25' 5"	**Designer:**	Bruce King
LOA:	25' 5"	**Builder:**	Ericson Yachts
LWL:	21' 10"	**Years produced:**	1978–1984
Min./max. draft:	3' 11"/4' 11"	**Sail area:**	325 sq. ft.
Bridge clearance:	40' 6"	**Fuel tankage:**	15 gal.
Power:	diesel or OMC 7 to 15 hp	**Water tankage:**	18 gal.
B/D ratio:	40%	**Approx. trailering wgt.:**	7,100 lbs.

Besides changing from a centerboarder to a fin keeler, the Mk II or 25+ version of the Ericson 25 adds a little length and beam, plus five feet of mast height and 23 percent of sail area to the Mk I (page 341). At the same time, displacement is reduced by 400 pounds and ballast is reduced by 500 pounds. No wonder that average PHRF on the Mk II is reduced from 234 on the Mk I to a mere 213. The layout below on the Mk II is roughly the same as on the Mk I, except a starboard-side quarterberth has been added and the galley components have been shifted

around a bit. Power options included a transom-hung outboard, a diesel inboard (7½ hp), or an OMC Saildrive (10 hp.). Keel options include either shoal draft (almost four feet) or deep draft (almost five feet). **Best features:** Fit and finish are good, as on the Mk I. With her wide beam, tall cabin, and relatively long waterline, the Mk II wins the elbow room prize with a Space Index of a whopping 622; only three other boats in this guide have a bigger Space Index. **Worst features:** As with the Ericson Mk I, we found no significant negative features.

Comps	LOD	Beam	MinDr	Displ	Bllst	SA/D	D/L	Avg. PHRF	Max. Speed	Motion Index	Space Index	No. of Berths	Head-room
Beneteau First 26 (25)	25' 5"	9' 2"	2' 9"	4,814	1,455	16.6	177	192	6.4	16.0	584	4	4' 3"
Ericson 25 Mk II	25' 5"	9' 3"	3' 11"	5,000	2,000	17.8	214	213	6.3	17.3	622	5	6' 1"
Kaiser 25	25' 4"	7' 10"	3' 7"	5,000	2,250	15.5	367	273	5.7	24.3	468	4	6' 2"
Westerly Tiger 25	25' 1"	8' 9"	4' 3"	5,264	2,240	12.5	226	225	6.3	19.7	447	5	5' 3"
Beachcomber 25	25' 4"	8' 0"	7' 3"	5,300	1,400	14.5	188	NA	6.5	20.8	510	5	5' 10"

Fisher 25
Two-story motorsailor from England

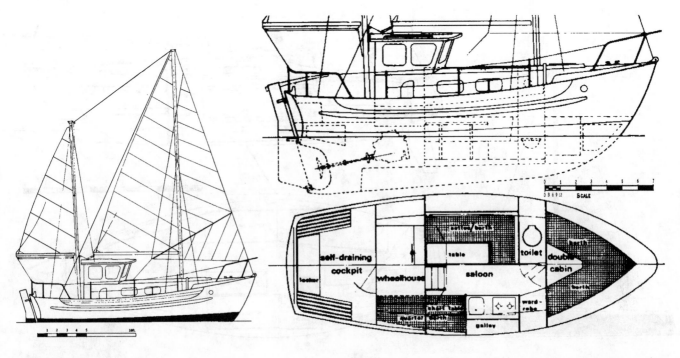

LOD:	24' 6"		**Designer:**	Gordon Wyatt & David Freeman
LOA:	25' 3"		**Builder:**	Fairways and Northshore Yacht Yards
LWL:	21' 0"		**Years produced:**	1975–present
Min./max. draft:	3' 9"		**Sail area:**	210 sq. ft.
Bridge clearance:	27' 6"		**Fuel tankage:**	50 gal.
Power:	inboard dsl. 20 to 30 hp		**Water tankage:**	50 gal.
B/D ratio:	48%		**Approx. trailering wgt.:**	15,200 lbs.

Northshore Yacht Yards in Itchenor, Sussex, England, (a company that bought the former builder, Fairways Fisher) builds this chubby 25-foot motorsailer. The design is now over 30 years old, and in those years more than 250 have been built. Options include either a sloop or the ketch rig shown here. She can be steered from a tiller in the aft cockpit, or from inside, in the comfort of the pilot house. ***Best features:*** Her Space Index is in the top 2 percent of the boats in this book, and her pilot house will be welcome in cold, clammy environs. ***Worst features:*** The sail area,

only 210 sq. ft. measured with 100 percent foretriangle, is tiny; it compares with boats in this guide of only around 23 feet and 3,000 pounds displacement, versus the Fisher's displacement of more than three times as much. Her SA/D ratio is 7.2, the lowest of all the boats in this guide. Consequently, don't count on the sails to move this boat in less than 10 knots of breeze. Sailing in sunny weather, there's poor visibility from the cockpit, and if it's hot, it would be nice if the pilot house were equipped with an air conditioner.

Comps	LOD	Beam	MinDr	Displ	Bllst	SA/D	D/L	Avg. PHRF	Max. Speed	Motion Index	Space Index	No. of Berths	Head-room
New Moon 25	25' 0"	8' 6"	3' 8"	6,800	2,300	15.8	336	NA	6.1	27.3	532	4	6' 0"
Eastsail 25	25' 0"	8' 6"	3' 8"	7,200	2,300	17.2	355	NA	6.1	27.2	532	5	6' 0"
Vertue 25	25' 3"	7' 10"	4' 5"	9,220	4,400	14.2	414	NA	6.2	40.1	542	4	6' 2"
Fisher 25	24' 6"	9' 4"	3' 9"	10,000	4,500	7.2	482	NA	6.1	35.2	567	5	6' 0"

Hunter 25 Mk I

The Mk I is the "wedge top," the Mk II is the "box top"

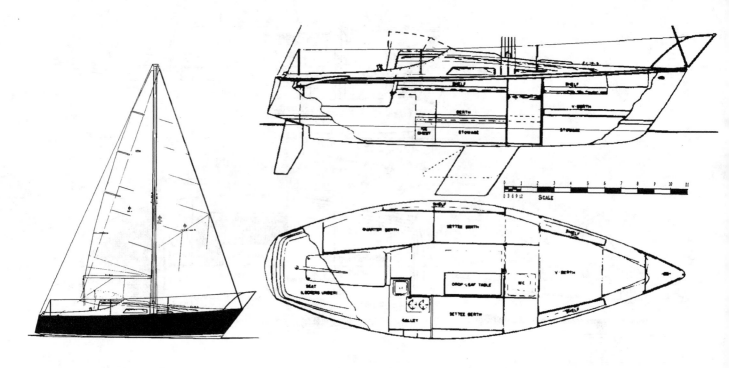

LOD:	24' 8"	**Designer:**	Cherubini & Seidelmann
LOA:	25' 0"	**Builder:**	Hunter Marine
LWL:	20' 2"	**Years produced:**	1972–1976
Min./max. draft:	2' 11"/3' 11"	**Sail area:**	180 sq. ft.
Bridge clearance:	34' 1"	**Fuel tankage:**	portable
Power:	outboard 4 to 8 hp	**Water tankage:**	15 gal.
B/D ratio:	47%	**Approx. trailering wgt.:**	5,700 lbs.

The Hunter 25 was the first sailboat design to be produced by Hunter. It was a success, and in 1977 was followed by the Hunter 25 Mark II, which retained the hull and layout below but sported a new and boxy deck with six inches more headroom. There were several pet names for the Mk I, with her low-domed cabintop and coaming going around the edge of the spray hood, including "bubble top" and "spitfire canopy." After the Mk II came along, the names that stuck were "wedge top" for the earlier design and "box top" for the later, taller cabin. Both models were offered with either 2' 11" shoal draft or 3' 11" "standard" draft fin keel. **Best features:** An optional spray hood over the companionway gives 6' 7" headroom over the galley area, and an optional pop-top extends full headroom throughout the cabin. **Worst features:** Compared to her comps, the Hunter 25 Mk I has less headroom and the lowest theoretical speed under power.

Comps	LOD	Beam	MinDr	Displ	Bllst	SA/D	D/L	Avg. PHRF	Max. Speed	Motion Index	Space Index	No. of Berths	Head-room
U.S. 25/Triton 25 (24)	23' 6"	8' 0"	2' 8"	3,750	1,250	17.0	170	216	6.2	16.0	451	5	5' 6"
Bremer 25	25' 0"	8' 0"	2' 6"	3,800	1,600	20.3	149	NA	6.4	15.7	509	4	6' 0"
Hunter 25 Mk I	24' 8"	8' 0"	2' 11"	3,850	1,800	11.7	210	222	6.0	17.1	440	5	5' 2"

Hunter 25 Mk II
Fast, roomy cruiser, shoal or deep draft

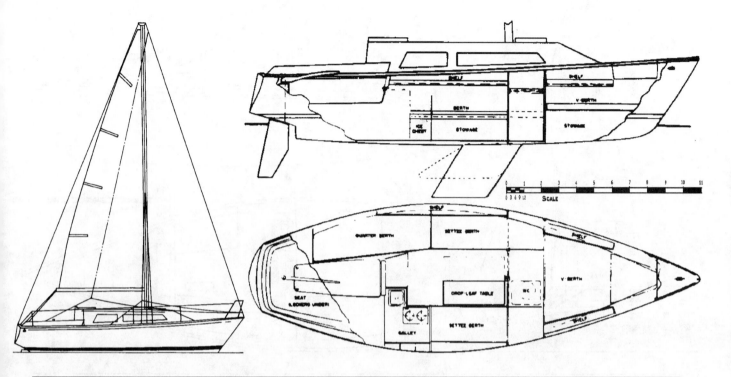

LOD:	24' 8"	**Designer:**	Seidelmann & Cherubini
LOA:	25' 0"	**Builder:**	Hunter Marine
LWL:	20' 2"	**Years produced:**	1977–1983
Min./max. draft:	2' 11"/3' 11"	**Sail area:**	256 sq. ft.
Bridge clearance:	34' 1"	**Fuel tankage:**	portable
Power:	outboard 6 to 10 hp	**Water tankage:**	15 gal.
B/D ratio:	41%	**Approx. trailering wgt.:**	5,500 lbs.

New Jersey designers Bob Seidelmann and John Cherubini were invited by Hunter Marine to act as a team in modifying the original Hunter 25 Mk I (1973–1976). They succeeded by raising freeboard and lengthening the coachroof for more space below, and adding a new hatch and anchor well. As a result, displacement increased by 550 pounds despite no increase at all in ballast (leading us to question the veracity of the weight numbers in the sales brochures). The new design (called a "box top" as opposed to a "wedge top" in the Mk I version,

referring of course to the shape of the cabin top) was offered in two keel configurations: a fin keel giving a draft just under four feet, and a winged keel for shoal draft of just under three feet, but with a loss of only three seconds per mile on average PHRF (228 vs. 225). **Best features:** Compared to her comps, the Hunter 25 in either deep fin or shoal draft version appears to be fast, if her PHRF numbers are an indicator (which we suspect they are). **Worst features:** Construction quality is average at best.

Comps	LOD	Beam	MinDr	Displ	Bllst	SA/D	D/L	Avg. PHRF	Max. Speed	Motion Index	Space Index	No. of Berths	Head-room
Watkins Seawolf 25	24' 11"	8' 0"	2' 6"	4,300	1,600	16.0	207	243	6.1	18.7	461	5	5' 11"
O'Day 25 (24)	24' 5"	8' 0"	2' 3"	4,400	1,525	16.1	212	234	6.1	18.7	508	5	5' 6"
Hunter 25 Mk II	24' 8"	8' 0"	2' 11"	4,400	1,800	15.3	239	225	6.0	19.6	430	5	5' 8"
La Paz 25	25' 1"	8' 0"	2' 0"	4,600	1,600	14.2	162	NA	6.5	18.6	519	6	6' 4"

Hunter 25 Mk III

Shoal draft upgrade of the Hunter 24 with a lead keel

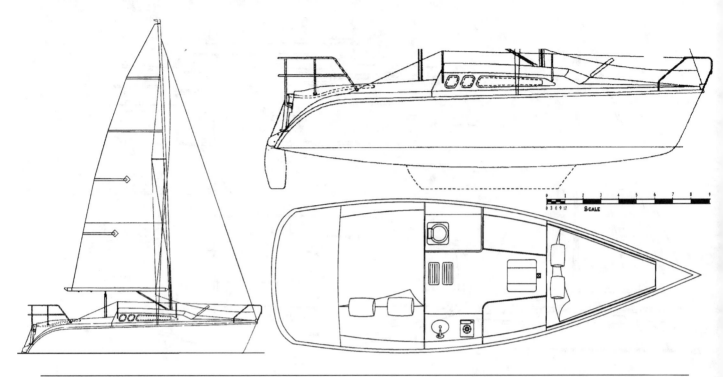

LOD:	24' 6"		**Designer:**	Glenn Henderson
LOA:	25' 1"		**Builder:**	Hunter Marine
LWL:	22' 1"		**Years produced:**	2006–present
Min./max. draft:	2' 0"		**Sail area:**	255 sq. ft.
Bridge clearance:	31' 8"		**Fuel tankage:**	portable
Power:	outboard 6 to 8 hp		**Water tankage:**	15 gal.
B/D ratio:	35%		**Approx. trailering wgt.:**	6,500 lbs.

The sales brochure explains that the Hunter 25 Mk III is "an upgraded version of our very successful Hunter 24" (i.e., 240), reported on page 235. In profile the two designs look almost identical (except, of course, for a small difference in length), but down below the H25 Mk III's accommodations are rearranged, with the head moved out into the middle of the boat on the larger model. One other major change: the water ballast version is no longer available, and instead a very shallow-draft lead keel has been substituted. *Best features:* The elevated seats on the stern quarters have proven to be very popular among boat buyers, giving an uninterrupted "catbird's seat" view of the scene without interference from the cabinhouse or other cockpit occupants. A mast-raising system—similar to the Catalina 250—makes life at the launching ramp easier. *Worst features:* Like the Lancer 25, the extremely shallow fixed keel (2' 0" draft compared with the Lancer's 2' 4") is not adequate to prevent noticeable sideslip while sailing upwind. The Hunter's other three comps have centerboards or keels of more useful dimensions.

Comps	LOD	Beam	MinDr	Displ	Bllst	SA/D	D/L	Avg. PHRF	Max. Speed	Motion Index	Space Index	No. of Berths	Head-room
Lancer 25	24' 8"	8' 0"	2' 4"	3,400	1,200	17.5	187	264	6.0	15.3	560	4 to 6	5' 10"
Freedom 25	24' 4"	8' 6"	4' 5"	3,500	1,025	18.0	195	186	6.0	14.3	432	4	4' 10"
Catalina 250	25' 0"	8' 6"	1' 8"	3,600	1,200	18.3	167	225	6.2	14.3	395	4	4' 3"
Hunter 25 Mk III	24' 6"	8' 5"	2' 0"	3,700	1,309	17.1	153	225	6.3	14.4	484	4	5' 4"
Santana 25	24' 7"	7' 10"	2' 7"	4,050	1,750	16.5	244	222	5.9	18.6	396	4	5' 2"

Irwin 10/4 (25)
Fat boat with plenty of space below

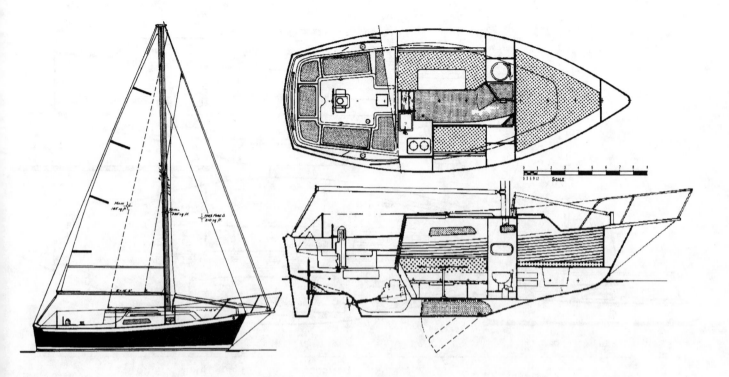

LOD:	25' 4"	**Designer:**	Ted Irwin
LOA:	29' 7"	**Builder:**	Irwin Yachts
LWL:	21' 10"	**Years produced:**	1975–1979
Min./max. draft:	2' 9"/6' 8"	**Sail area:**	395 sq. ft.
Bridge clearance:	39' 6"	**Fuel tankage:**	20 gal. (optional)
Power:	Atomic 2 or Yanmar 8 hp	**Water tankage:**	45 gal.
B/D ratio:	29%	**Approx. trailering wgt.:**	10,400 lbs.

This catboat hull with a cutter rig is called the 10/4 supposedly because she is ten feet, four inches wide. But she could also be called that because her Space Index—of 640, way beyond her comps—is so high that she could "drink ten, eat six, and sleep four" as the saying goes. **Best features:** Her layout below provides a feeling of spaciousness rare in a 25-footer. Her heavy displacement and wide beam makes her stable in a breeze. The icebox, on the port side, is accessible both from the cockpit (so those on deck don't have to bother the cook to get a cold drink) and also from below deck. **Worst features:** In light air she's slow. There was one of these in our home harbor, and I remember literally running rings around her in four or five knots with our (then) South Coast 23. Over 10 knots of breeze, she peps up.

Comps	LOD	Beam	MinDr	Displ	Bllst	SA/D	D/L	Avg. PHRF	Max. Speed	Motion Index	Space Index	No. of Berths	Head-room
Newman Friendship 25	25' 0"	8' 8"	4' 3"	7,000	2,000	18.9	337	NA	6.1	27.3	423	4	4' 8"
Irwin 10/4 (25)	25' 4"	10' 4"	2' 9"	7,000	2,000	17.3	300	234	6.3	20.9	640	4	5' 8"
Vancouver 25	25' 0"	8' 6"	4' 0"	7,000	3,200	16.6	307	NA	6.2	26.0	586	4	6' 1"

Irwin 25

Early design by Ted Irwin

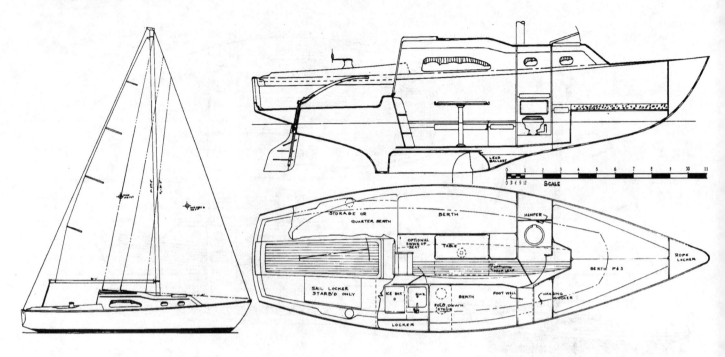

LOD:	25' 3"	**Designer:**	Ted Irwin
LOA:	25' 3"	**Builder:**	Irwin Yachts
LWL:	20' 6"	**Years produced:**	1968–1975
Min./max. draft:	2' 8"/6' 8"	**Sail area:**	302 sq. ft.
Bridge clearance:	34' 4"	**Fuel tankage:**	portable
Power:	outboard or inboard 4 to 8 hp	**Water tankage:**	25 gal.
B/D ratio:	44%	**Approx. trailering wgt.:**	7,300 lbs.

Ted Irwin grew up in St. Petersburg, FL, and as a kid sailed boats in Tampa Bay. As a young man, he worked briefly in the plant of Charlie Morgan's Morgan Yacht Corp. That experience may have rubbed off a bit on the design of his Irwin 25 (introduced in 1968), which to a great extent resembles the Morgan 24/25 (page 358) introduced in 1965. Both boats were popular club racers in the later 1960s and 1970s, but somehow the Morgan usually had the edge. The Irwin has the same displacement but a bit more ballast, a foot shorter waterline but a longer LOD as her overhangs are not as chopped off

as the Morgan's; she has many similarities below the waterline, including a high aspect ratio centerboard. Her Space Index is slightly greater, her headroom gains an inch due to her doghouse, and her PHRF is a scant three seconds per mile higher. She was available as a keel/centerboarder (as shown here) or with a full keel (4' 0" draft, 1825 lbs. ballast). She had a choice of layouts: settee berths and a portside quarter berth (as shown here) or a dinette arrangement. ***Best features:*** None notable. ***Worst features:*** Centerboards and pendants on these boats are prone to problems.

Comps	LOD	Beam	MinDr	Displ	Bllst	SA/D	D/L	Avg. PHRF	Max. Speed	Motion Index	Space Index	No. of Berths	Head-room
Walton 25	25' 3"	7' 3"	3' 10"	4,900	2,000	16.0	281	NA	6.0	24.9	392	4	5' 7"
Talman Katama 25	24' 8"	8' 0"	2' 6"	5,000	1,900	15.4	259	NA	6.1	22.1	363	4	4' 6"
Irwin 25	25' 3"	8' 0"	2' 8"	5,000	2,200	16.5	259	228	6.1	21.9	470	4 to 6	5' 9"
Yankee 26 (25)	24' 6"	8' 8"	4' 6"	5,335	2,150	15.4	270	234	6.1	20.7	534	4	6' 2"

Jeanneau Eolia 25
A French design with an unusual cabin plan

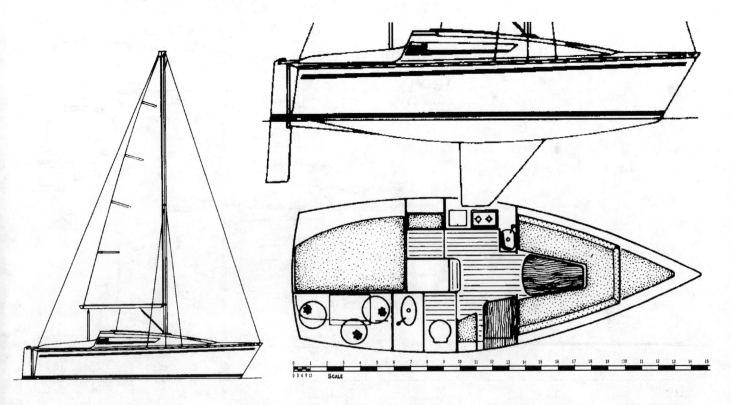

LOD:	24' 7"	Designer:	Philippe Briand
LOA:	25' 9"	Builder:	Jeanneau
LWL:	21' 8"	Years produced:	1983–1989
Min./max. draft:	2' 7"/5' 11"	Sail area:	241 sq. ft.
Bridge clearance:	34' 6"	Fuel tankage:	5 gal.
Power:	outboard or inboard 6 to 8 hp	Water tankage:	5 gal.
B/D ratio:	49%	Approx. trailering wgt.:	5,600 lbs.

The Jeanneau Eolia 25 was available either as a fin keeler (fixed draft 4' 9", shown here) or as a keel-centerboarder (draft 2' 7" board up, or 5' 11" board down). Although an outboard was an option, a high percentage of the boats sold have a raw-water-cooled Yanmar 1GM10 diesel of 7.5 hp. Either choice should power the Eolia 25 at hull speed. **Best features:** We think the layout is quite clever, with a double berth aft under the cockpit, an enclosed stand-up head in the highest location in the cabin, a modest-sized but practical nav station, and a U-shaped dining area seating up to 7 or 8 souls for that relaxing after-the-race beverage. The table slides down on the mast compression strut to form the center portion of a double berth. The arrangement below makes the cabin seem quite airy and pleasant, despite a too-small forward hatch and no opening ports. **Worst features:** We can't imagine why this boat has a PHRF rating 30 to 40 seconds a mile higher than her comps. We don't think she deserves such harsh treatment.

Comps	LOD	Beam	MinDr	Displ	Bllst	SA/D	D/L	Avg. PHRF	Max. Speed	Motion Index	Space Index	No. of Berths	Head-room
Jeanneau Eolia 25	24' 7"	9' 2"	2' 7"	3,750	1,830	21.4	165	243	6.2	13.4	568	4	5' 8"
Dufour 1800 (25)	25' 1"	8' 10"	4' 3"	3,969	1,654	16.1	166	213	6.3	14.3	536	4	5' 6"
Kelt 7.60 (25)	24' 11"	9' 5"	4' 3"	4,189	1,765	17.5	157	204	6.4	13.7	577	4	5' 7"
Elite 25 (24)	24' 0"	8' 10"	2' 3"	4,300	1,742	15.2	193	201	6.2	15.9	527	4	6' 0"

Kaiser 25

A traditional cruising sloop made in Delaware

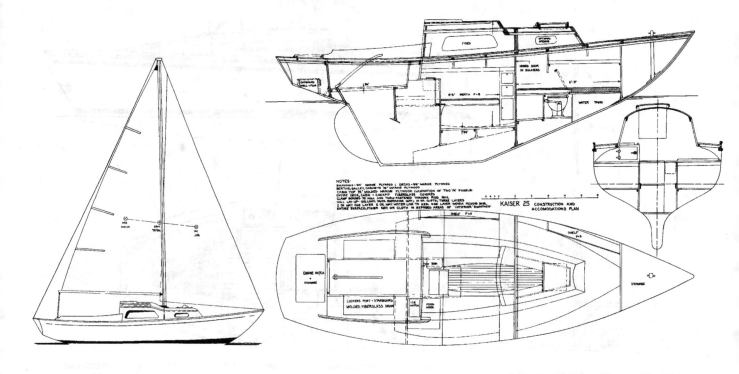

LOD:	25' 4"		**Designer:**	John Kaiser
LOA:	25' 4"		**Builder:**	John Kaiser Assoc.
LWL:	18' 3"		**Years produced:**	1962?–1964?
Min./max. draft:	3' 7"		**Sail area:**	284 sq. ft.
Bridge clearance:	30' 6"		**Fuel tankage:**	portable
Power:	outboard or inboard 6 hp		**Water tankage:**	20 gal.
B/D ratio:	45%		**Approx. trailering wgt.:**	7,100 lbs.

Designer-marketer John Kaiser of Greenville, Delaware, offered a number of fiberglass sailboats back in the early 1960s, including the cruiser shown here, built to his specifications by Plastic Fabricators, Inc. of Wilmington, Delaware. In his sales brochure, Kaiser says that "it is the intention of the designer to produce a small, able, and comfortable cruising-racing sloop of superior quality in every detail." The brochure also states that while the entire hull and deck is normally plastic, a superstructure (presumably meaning deck and cabin house) of wood is available at owner's option, and that various changes in the accommodations plan could also be made "at a slight extra cost." An outboard well with watertight plug was standard; inboard power was available at a cost, depending on make and model. ***Best features:*** This looks like a high-quality product for its day. ***Worst features:*** None discovered.

Comps	LOD	Beam	MinDr	Displ	Bllst	SA/D	D/L	Avg. PHRF	Max. Speed	Motion Index	Space Index	No. of Berths	Head-room
Beneteau First 26 (25)	25' 5"	9' 2"	2' 9"	4,814	1,455	16.6	177	192	6.4	16.0	584	4	4' 3"
Ericson 25 Mk II	25' 5"	9' 3"	3' 11"	5,000	2,000	17.8	214	213	6.3	17.3	622	5	6' 1"
Kaiser 25	25' 4"	7' 10"	3' 7"	5,000	2,250	15.5	367	273	5.7	24.3	468	4	6' 2"
Westerly Tiger 25	25' 1"	8' 9"	4' 3"	5,264	2,240	12.5	226	225	6.3	19.7	447	5	5' 3"
Beachcomber 25	25' 4"	8' 0"	1' 3"	5,300	1,400	14.5	188	NA	6.5	20.8	510	5	5' 10"

Kelt 7.60 (25)

French design built first in France, then in Canada

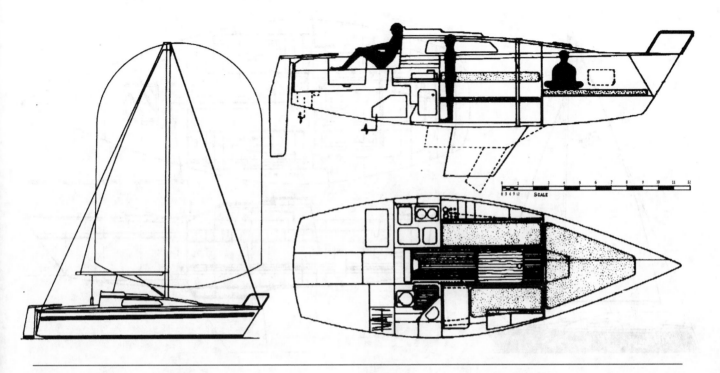

LOD:	24' 11"
LOA:	25' 5"
LWL:	22' 10"
Min./max. draft:	4' 3"
Bridge clearance:	31' 6"
Power:	outboard or inboard 6 to 10 hp
B/D ratio:	42%

Designer:	Jean Berret
Builder:	Kelt Marine
Years produced:	1980–1984?
Sail area:	285 sq. ft.
Fuel tankage:	portable
Water tankage:	portable
Approx. trailering wgt.:	6,300 lbs.

All four comps in the group with the Kelt 7.60 are French, and it shows in the style of all of them. In some ways the Kelt 7.60 (24' 11" = 7.60 meters) seems particularly similar to one comp, namely the Dufour 1800. Both boats originated in France and later found favor in Canada. The Kelt was even built, under license, in Ontario. Both have a good-sized chart table, a fin keel with 4' 3" draft, about 5' 6" cabin headroom, a keel-centerboard option, and an outboard well in the cockpit (though the well was not installed on every Kelt 7.60). The similarities between Kelt and Dufour seem to end there, however.

Both are beamy boats, but the Kelt is seven inches wider. The Dufour has a five-foot higher bridge clearance, 13 percent less sail area, and a midships head, whereas the Kelt's head is aft where the cabin height is higher, as in another of her comps, the Jeanneau Eolia. *Best features:* The Kelt wins the Space Index sweepstakes among her comps, bolstered by a combination of widest beam and relatively good headroom. Her small mainsail relative to her foretriangle, along with her low masthead, should make her easy to handle in heavy air despite her low D/L ratio. *Worst features:* None noted.

Comps	LOD	Beam	MinDr	Displ	Bllst	SA/D	D/L	Avg. PHRF	Max. Speed	Motion Index	Space Index	No. of Berths	Head-room
Jeanneau Eolia 25	24' 7"	9' 2"	2' 7"	3,750	1,830	21.4	165	243	6.2	13.4	568	4	5' 8"
Dufour 1800 (25)	25' 1"	8' 10"	4' 3"	3,969	1,654	16.1	166	213	6.3	14.3	536	4	5' 6"
Kelt 7.60 (25)	24' 11"	9' 5"	4' 3"	4,189	1,765	17.5	157	204	6.4	13.7	577	4	5' 7"
Elite 25 (24)	24' 0"	8' 10"	2' 3"	4,300	1,742	15.2	193	201	6.2	15.9	527	4	6' 0"

Kirby 25
A design meant "to beat the J/24s"

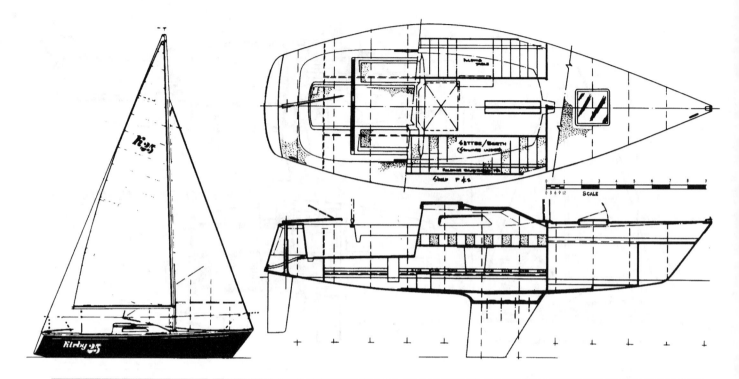

LOD:	24' 7"		**Designer:**	Bruce Kirby
LOA:	25' 2"		**Builder:**	Mirage Yachts
LWL:	20' 9"		**Years produced:**	1978–1983
Min./max. draft:	4' 2"		**Sail area:**	290 sq. ft.
Bridge clearance:	36' 6"		**Fuel tankage:**	portable
Power:	outboard 4 to 6 hp		**Water tankage:**	portable
B/D ratio:	37%		**Approx. trailering wgt.:**	4,700 lbs.

More than 200 of these popular PHRF and "half-ton rule" racers were built by Mirage Yachts in Montreal between 1978 and 1983, after Mirage owner Dick Steffin asked Bruce Kirby to "draw me a boat to beat the J/24s." This "hot" boat is generally seen as competitive and relatively inexpensive compared to the J/24 (page 294), and is suited to racers more than cruisers. ***Best features:*** Kirby 25s are spirited, fast, and agile, with a fractional rig and bendy mast, which permits precise control of sail shape. The boats are well-made, with neat and tidy liners that double as structural elements.

Worst features: The number of controls—particularly the running backstays, which need to be readjusted after every tack going upwind—may put off some inexperienced sailors and relaxed cruising types. Also, accommodations below are stripped out, as becomes a highly competitive racer. The ends of the boat, both bow and stern, are off limits to heavy cruising supplies; fast boats always keep the ends light. In fact, a portable ice chest, Coleman stove, and portable plastic wash tub may be all that some hard-nosed racers will permit on board.

Comps	LOD	Beam	MinDr	Displ	Bllst	SA/D	D/L	Avg. PHRF	Max. Speed	Motion Index	Space Index	No. of Berths	Head- room
Merit 25 (24)	24' 0"	8' 0"	4' 0"	2,900	1,050	21.7	106	168	6.4	11.9	409	4	4' 1"
Seaward 25 (24)	24' 0"	8' 4"	2' 1"	3,100	1,100	17.7	114	270	6.4	11.7	483	5	5' 3"
Kirby 25	24' 7"	8' 9"	4' 2"	3,150	1,150	21.6	157	174	6.1	12.2	453	4	4' 6"
Dehler 25 (23)	23' 1"	8' 3"	1' 4"	3,245	1,654	20.1	139	186	6.3	13.2	412	4	4' 3"
Freedom 24 (23)	22' 10"	8' 3"	1' 10"	3,250	1,350	22.0	146	207	6.2	13.3	419	4	4' 7"

La Paz 25
Lyle Hess trailerable motorsailor

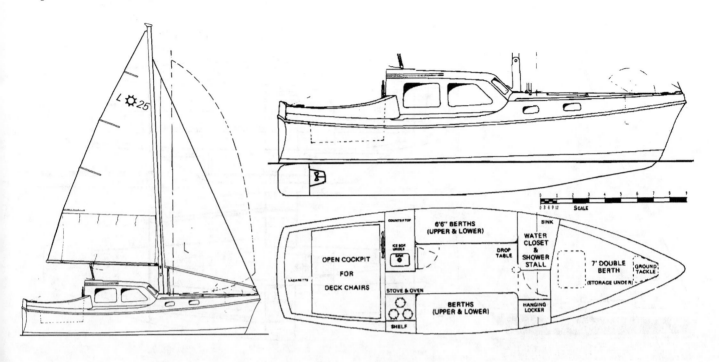

LOD:	25' 1"	**Designer:**	Lyle Hess
LOA:	25' 1"	**Builder:**	Coastal Recreation
LWL:	23' 4"	**Years produced:**	1974–1975
Min./max. draft:	2' 0"/2' 0"	**Sail area:**	245 sq. ft.
Bridge clearance:	32' 0"	**Fuel tankage:**	20 gal.
Power:	gas or dsl. 20 to 28 hp	**Water tankage:**	25 gal.
B/D ratio:	35%	**Approx. trailering wgt.:**	6,700 lbs.

You can almost imagine the client talking to the designer, laying out his needs: "I want a fast, shallow draft, trailerable motorsailer I can easily tow with my pickup to Mexico—say La Paz—to launch off the beach and cruise for a few weeks with my wife, occasionally inviting a couple of my grown children to join us for a few days, maybe even with grandkids. I need good standing headroom below, a place for comfortable deck chairs in a spacious cockpit, and a stall shower. Oh, and my wife is a gourmet cook who likes to bake bread, so we'll need space for a big stove with an oven. She'll spend a lot of time in the galley, so make it bright and airy down below." That's a lot to ask, but Lyle Hess made a valiant attempt to satisfy the customer's needs. About the only thing missing is an inside steering station for sailing in inclement weather. *Best features:* She beats her comps in the space department—especially on headroom—and also on maximum speed (important under power, which motorsailers usually do a lot.) *Worst features:* With no centerboard and only two feet of draft, one shouldn't expect good upwind performance.

Comps	LOD	Beam	MinDr	Displ	Bllst	SA/D	D/L	Avg. PHRF	Max. Speed	Motion Index	Space Index	No. of Berths	Head-room
Watkins Seawolf 25	24' 11"	8' 0"	2' 6"	4,300	1,600	16.0	207	243	6.1	18.7	461	5	5' 11"
O'Day 25 (24)	24' 5"	8' 0"	2' 3"	4,400	1,525	16.1	212	234	6.1	18.7	508	5	5' 6"
Hunter 25 Mk II	24' 8"	8' 0"	2' 11"	4,400	1,800	15.3	239	225	6.0	19.6	430	5	5' 8"
La Paz 25	25' 1"	8' 0"	2' 0"	4,600	1,600	14.2	162	NA	6.5	18.6	519	6	6' 4"

Lancer 25

Could oblivious crew fall into the keel cavity?

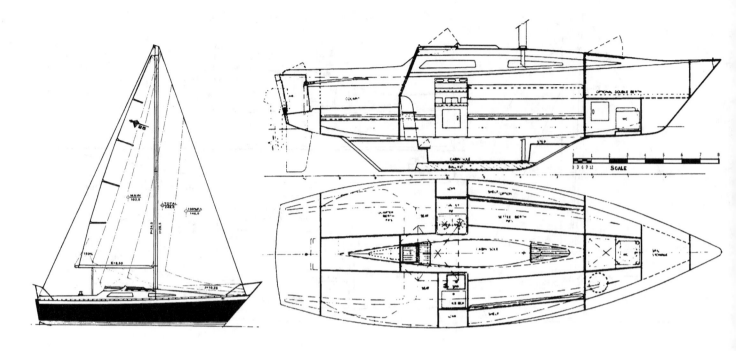

LOD:	24' 8"	**Designer:**	Shad Turner
LOA:	24' 8"	**Builder:**	Lancer Yachts
LWL:	20' 1"	**Years produced:**	1974–1985
Min./max. draft:	2' 4"	**Sail area:**	248 sq. ft.
Bridge clearance:	32' 0"	**Fuel tankage:**	portable
Power:	outboard 6 to 8 hp	**Water tankage:**	15 gal.
B/D ratio:	35%	**Approx. trailering wgt.:**	5,400 lbs.

The Lancer 25 has some features not commonly found in boats of this size, for example: berths for four with two quarter berths and two settee berths, all 6' 4" long, plus an optional mini-double V-berth forward over the head area— "mini" because the berth is only 6' 0" long; a standard bed ashore measures 6' 8". Also, the port side counter doubles as a nav work station when the stove is flipped to a counter-side-up position. Good standing headroom is achieved below, but only in part of the cabin (for details see below). **Best features:** The outstanding parameter of the Lancer versus her comps is her headroom, 5' 10", which is gained by lowering part of the cabin sole down into the extra-wide keel cavity (18" at its widest). The remainder of the cabin sole, including the portion on which you would rest your feet while sitting on either settee berth, looks to be about 18 inches higher. **Worst features:** We have not seen this boat close up, but wonder if absent-minded or oblivious crew might not be in danger of falling into the keel cavity when arising from a settee. Also, the Lancer's 2' 4" keel is not deep enough to permit efficient sailing to windward.

Comps	LOD	Beam	MinDr	Displ	Bllst	SA/D	D/L	Avg. PHRF	Max. Speed	Motion Index	Space Index	No. of Berths	Head-room
Lancer 25	24' 8"	8' 0"	2' 4"	3,400	1,200	17.5	187	264	6.0	15.2	560	4 to 6	5' 10"
Freedom 25 (24)	24' 4"	8' 6"	4' 5"	3,500	1,025	18.0	195	186	6.0	14.3	432	4	4' 10"
Catalina 250	25' 0"	8' 6"	1' 8"	3,600	1,200	18.3	167	225	6.2	14.3	395	4	4' 3"
Hunter 25 Mk III	24' 6"	8' 5"	2' 0"	3,700	1,309	17.1	153	225	6.3	14.4	484	4	5' 4"
Santana 25	24' 7"	7' 10"	2' 7"	4,050	1,750	16.5	244	222	5.9	18.6	396	4	5' 2"

MacGregor 25/Venture 25
Hundreds of these boats are old and worn, but fixable

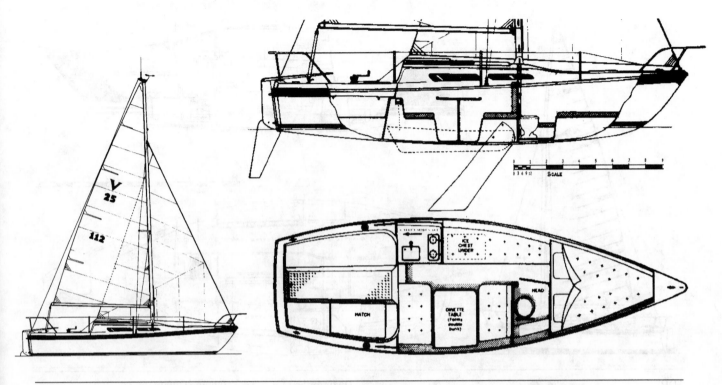

LOD:	25' 0"		**Designer:**	Roger MacGregor
LOA:	26' 4"		**Builder:**	MacGregor Yachts
LWL:	22' 10"		**Years produced:**	1973–1987
Min./max. draft:	1' 6"/5' 0"		**Sail area:**	303 sq. ft.
Bridge clearance:	32' 0"		**Fuel tankage:**	portable
Power:	outboard 3 to 6 hp		**Water tankage:**	portable
B/D ratio:	27%		**Approx. trailering wgt.:**	3,100 lbs.

This popular design started out as the Venture 25 in 1973, and in 1981 became the MacGregor 25, with no major changes to the design. Over the years there was a choice of two sailplans, either a three quarters fractional rig or a masthead rig. The fractional rig is shown here. The boat is lightly built and has ample sail area (note the higher SA/D versus comps) so she will have a good turn of speed if properly equipped and tuned. For example, many owners have thrown away the "worthless" stock rudder and purchased a nicely faired replacement rudder available on the Internet from an aftermarket supplier. *Best features:* There is a huge variety of these boats available

on the used market today, some in near-derelict mode, ready to be picked up for the asking. For someone with not much money, good do-it-yourself skills, some spare time and space, and a yen to try sailing, the MacGregor (or Venture) 25 should be on the list of possible acquisitions. *Worst features:* Since these boats are now old, with even the newest having been around for more than 20 years, wear and tear will have started to cause problems. Common complaints include rotting mast base and/or chainplates, swing keel problems including leaking around the pivot hole, and keel cable breakage. An Internet forum provides more information.

Comps	LOD	Beam	MinDr	Displ	Bllst	SA/D	D/L	Avg. PHRF	Max. Speed	Motion Index	Space Index	No. of Berths	Head-room
Terrapin 24 (25)	24' 6"	8' 0"	0' 9"	2,050	100	21.4	113	NA	6.0	9.2	379	5	5' 0"
MacGregor 25	25' 0"	7' 11"	1' 6"	2,200	600	28.7	83	234	6.4	9.0	402	5	4' 9"
Nimble 24 (25)	24' 7"	7' 10"	1' 4"	2,400	700	22.5	81	249	6.5	9.6	348	4	4' 6"

Mark 25

Tall, fat racer-cruiser designed by Cuthbertson

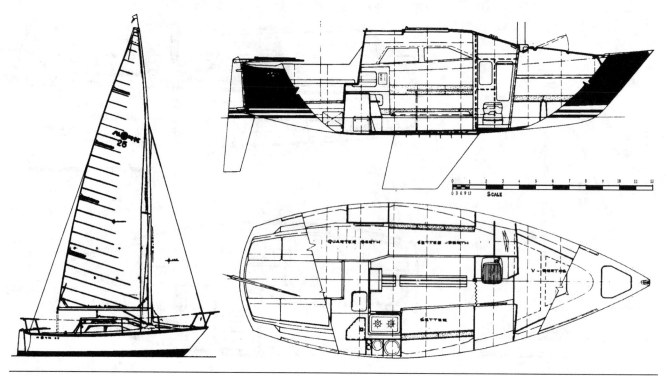

LOD:	24' 7"		**Designer:**	George Cuthbertson
LOA:	25' 4"		**Builder:**	Mark Yachts Ltd., others
LWL:	20' 0"		**Years produced:**	1984–1991
Min./max. draft:	3' 0"/4' 3"		**Sail area:**	330 sq. ft.
Bridge clearance:	43' 6"		**Fuel tankage:**	portable
Power:	outboard 6 to 10 hp		**Water tankage:**	portable
B/D ratio:	43%		**Approx. trailering wgt.:**	6,200 lbs.

Mark Yachts Ltd. of Old Saybrook, CT, induced George Cuthbertson of C&C fame to design this unusual "cat-sloop" rigged yacht. The design concept was to maximize cruising accommodations while maintaining performance similar to "day racers" like the J/24. (The scheme was only partially successful; as an indicator, the Mark 25's PHRF is about 216—6 seconds lower than the C&C 25—compared to the J/24's 174.) Various builders (including Ontario Yachts of Canada, Sumner Yachts, and Eli Laminates) apparently built the vessels at various times, and after Mark Yachts Ltd. disappeared, Sumner marketed the Mark 25 in 1990 and 1991. Two keel drafts were available, shoal (3' 0") and deep (4' 3"). The deep version gives a very noticeable improvement in performance. The big, high aspect-ratio rig is a distinctive feature, resulting in a bridge clearance of almost 44 feet (tallest of all the boats in this guide)—and the boat will sail respectably even without the tiny blade jib. **Best features:** The boat is easy to handle, well balanced and very maneuverable. The high trunk cabin and "bubble" in the deck at the mast, plus wide 9' 3" beam, help provide plenty of room below. A huge companionway hatch and sizable portlights give plenty of cabin light. **Worst features:** Deep cockpit seats are comfortable but limit visibility over the high cabin house.

Comps	LOD	Beam	MinDr	Displ	Bllst	SA/D	D/L	Avg. PHRF	Max. Speed	Motion Index	Space Index	No. of Berths	Head- room
Mark 25	24' 7"	9' 3"	3' 0"	4,130	1,779	20.3	230	216	6.0	15.3	495	4	5' 8"
South Coast Seacraft 25	25' 5"	8' 0"	3' 6"	4,200	1,800	19.1	218	231	6.1	18.4	379	5	5' 6"
C&C 25	25' 2"	8' 8"	3' 10"	4,250	1,880	18.2	215	222	6.1	16.5	555	4	5' 10"
North Star 500 (25)	24' 6"	9' 0"	5' 0"	4,300	1,710	17.7	231	228	6.0	16.3	472	4	4' 6"

Montego 25
Fast boat from a Florida builder

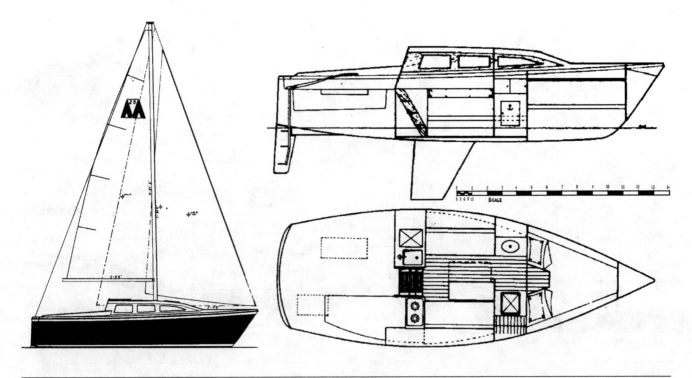

LOD:	25' 3"	**Designer:**	Jopie Helsen	
LOA:	25' 3"	**Builder:**	Universal Marine Corp.	
LWL:	20' 6"	**Years produced:**	1981–1984	
Min./max. draft:	3' 6"/4' 6"	**Sail area:**	305 sq. ft.	
Bridge clearance:	37' 3"	**Fuel tankage:**	portable	
Power:	outboard 4 to 10 hp	**Water tankage:**	20 gal.	
B/D ratio:	40%	**Approx. trailering wgt.:**	6,650 lbs.	

Designer Jopie Helsen owned a marina in St. Petersburg, FL, and designed boats on the side. This one may have been his best effort. She has a high Motion Index, good space down below, is relatively easy to singlehand, and properly sailed will give good performance on the race course. **Best features:** We used to race against a Montego 25 in our Morgan 24/25 (page 358), and although we won the season trophy once or twice based on the average of our scores, we were never able to beat the Montego,

either boat for boat or on corrected time. She is fast, we observed, in both light and heavy air. And despite having the most headroom among her comps, she manages to avoid having a top-heavy look on the water. A wide companionway hatch and opening ports keep her cabin light and airy. She was available with either a shoal (3' 6") draft or deep fin (4' 6"). Sailing performance is distinctly better with the deep keel option. **Worst features:** No significant faults observed.

Comps	LOD	Beam	MinDr	Displ	Bllst	SA/D	D/L	Avg. PHRF	Max. Speed	Motion Index	Space Index	No. of Berths	Head-room
Columbia 7.6 (25)	25' 1"	9' 2"	3' 6"	4,500	1,500	18.7	228	210	6.1	16.3	573	4	5' 8"
Cal 25 Mk II	25' 3"	9' 0"	3' 6"	4,500	2,000	18.5	189	219	6.3	16.1	558	5	5' 10"
Montego 25	25' 3"	9' 1"	3' 6"	4,550	1,800	17.1	236	216	6.1	16.9	557	4	5' 11"
Tanzer 25 Mk II	25' 3"	9' 7"	2' 11"	4,550	1,985	19.1	195	177	6.3	14.7	575	4	5' 9"
Seidelmann 25 (24)	24' 0"	9' 6"	3' 4"	4,600	2,200	16.3	257	216	6.0	16.5	549	4	5' 2"

Morgan 24/25 (25)
We used to win races with one of these

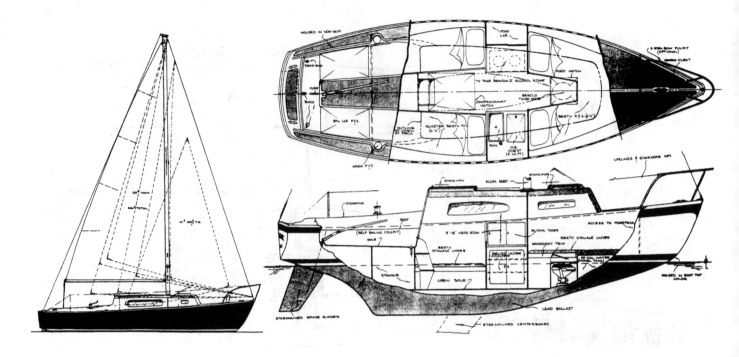

LOD:	24' 11"
LOA:	24' 11"
LWL:	21' 6"
Min./max. draft:	2' 9"/6' 6"
Bridge clearance:	34' 0"
Power:	outboard or inboard 6 to 9 hp
B/D ratio:	38%

Designer:	Charlie Morgan
Builder:	Morgan Yacht Corp.
Years produced:	1965–1976
Sail area:	310 sq. ft.
Fuel tankage:	portable
Water tankage:	portable
Approx. trailering wgt.:	7,100 lbs.

The Morgan 24/25 is so called because the final design at 24' 11" is virtually 25 feet long, but designer Morgan, who started out with a concept less than 24' 6" and expanded it to 24' 11" before actual production started, "never got around" to changing the name. After Gerber (the baby food people) bought his company, their marketing experts started calling it by its rightful name, the Morgan 25. In 1990 we moved from Connecticut to Florida and found a 1968 Morgan 25 "project boat" to fix up. (You can find the writeups of some of the improvement projects we

undertook in *Practical Sailor*, a publication we wrote for when Dan Spurr was editor.) We loved the boat, and won races with our local sailing club fleet in Sarasota, FL. **Best features:** The boat is fast, weatherly, and especially good in light air. She's also an easy singlehander and terrific weekender for two. Her hull is easily driven; our 6 hp Yamaha with a high-thrust prop easily drove her at hull speed. **Worst features:** There were problems with the centerboard pendant system, which involved a rod passing through a packing gland—a real Rube Goldberg affair.

Comps	LOD	Beam	MinDr	Displ	Bllst	SA/D	D/L	Avg. PHRF	Max. Speed	Motion Index	Space Index	No. of Berths	Head- room
Cornish Crabber 24	24' 0"	8' 0"	2' 5"	4,600	600	17.6	247	360	6.0	19.3	415	4	4' 3"
Pacific Seacraft 25	24' 6"	8' 0"	3' 3"	4,750	1,750	12.8	229	NA	6.1	20.3	387	4	5' 0"
O'Day 26 (25)	25' 5"	8' 0"	2' 6"	4,800	1,850	15.7	213	234	6.2	19.8	484	5	5' 6"
Com-Pac 25	24' 7"	8' 6"	2' 6"	4,800	1,900	15.6	231	NA	6.1	18.4	509	5	5' 10"
Morgan 24/25 (25)	24' 11"	8' 0"	2' 9"	5,000	1,900	17.0	225	225	6.2	21.4	435	4	5' 8"

New Horizons 25
S&S predecessor to the Tartan 27

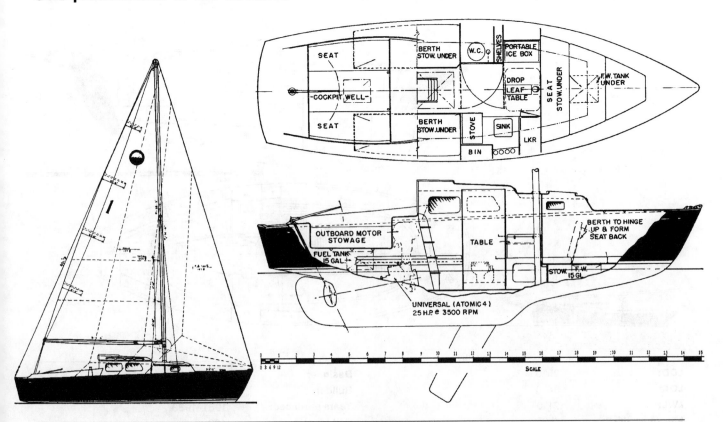

LOD:	25' 3"	**Designer:**	Sparkman & Stephens
LOA:	25' 3"	**Builder:**	Ray Greene & Co.
LWL:	21' 3"	**Years produced:**	1958–1966?
Min./max. draft:	3' 0"/7' 0"	**Sail area:**	324 sq. ft.
Bridge clearance:	35' 0"	**Fuel tankage:**	15 gal.
Power:	outboard or inboard 8 to 25 hp	**Water tankage:**	15 gal.
B/D ratio:	27%	**Approx. trailering wgt.:**	8,700 lbs.

This design by Sparkman & Stephens for Ray Greene & Co. of Toledo, OH, came with a Universal Atomic Four inboard engine as standard, though one option was to dispense with the inboard and use an outboard instead (as shown in phantom on the drawing). She initially had reverse sheer (as shown here) but in about 1960 the sheer was flattened somewhat for aesthetic reasons. An unusual feature was a dinghy designed for the boat, to be carried on stern davits. When the larger but similar-looking Tartan 27, another S&S design, was introduced in 1961 (3 years after the New

Horizons) for nearby Tartan (then known as Douglass & McLeod, in Grand River, OH), it quickly diverted customer interest from the Ray Greene boat, much to Greene's disgust. ***Best features:*** The good headroom (over six feet) is unusual for a 25-foot sailboat. We liked the idea of a dinghy in davits, too, but wonder whether it might have been ugly to look at. ***Worst features:*** We remember admiring the design of this boat when she first came out, but after owning a Tartan 27, we can see how prospective buyers would switch their allegiances to the Tartan.

Comps	LOD	Beam	MinDr	Displ	Bllst	SA/D	D/L	Avg. PHRF	Max. Speed	Motion Index	Space Index	No. of Berths	Head-room
Parker Dawson 26 (25)	25' 3"	8' 0"	1' 8"	5,700	1,250	13.6	234	NA	6.3	23.2	497	5	5' 10"
Bristol Corsair 24 (25)	24' 7"	8' 0"	3' 5"	5,920	2,500	14.5	447	270	5.7	28.4	495	4	5' 11"
New Horizons 25	25' 3"	7' 9"	3' 0"	6,030	1,600	15.6	281	225	6.2	26.8	465	4	6' 2"

Newman Friendship Sloop 25
19th-century "Down East" design in fiberglass

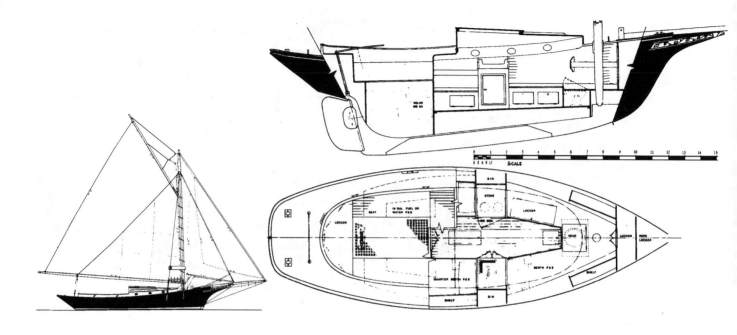

LOD:	25' 0"		**Designer:**	A. K. Carter
LOA:	34' 0"		**Builder:**	Jarvis Newman
LWL:	21' 0"		**Years produced:**	1981–1983
Min./max. draft:	4' 3"		**Sail area:**	432 sq. ft.
Bridge clearance:	25' 0"		**Fuel tankage:**	varies
Power:	Volvo MD6A dsl. 6 hp		**Water tankage:**	varies
B/D ratio:	29%		**Approx. trailering wgt.:**	10,400 lbs.

Jarvis Newman, a high-end boatbuilder in Southwest Harbor, ME, (home to several of the crème de la crème of boatbuilders: Hinckley, Morris Yachts, and others) took the lines of a Friendship sloop called the Pemaquid, built about 1914 by a fisherman named A. K. Carter at Bremen, ME. Newman built a fiberglass mold and began turning out hulls and decks for custom completion either by his own yard or by others (including some do-it-yourselfers). Some boats were finished to a more modern standard than others; some had deadeyes and lanyards instead of turnbuckles, most had varnished wooden spars and hardwood trim. ***Best features:*** She looks and sails like a Down East

Friendship, which is, of course, what she is. Typically, the finish on these Jarvis Newman boats, whether by professionals or amateurs finishing their own boats, is excellent. If you want to buy one used, Maine is the place to start looking. You'll find a Friendship Sloop Society on the Internet.

Worst features: Friendships (so named because one of the early designer-builders, Wilbur Morse, lived and worked in Friendship, ME) were designed for short-handed fishing on the banks off the Maine coast. They were good sea boats, but not fast in comparison with today's lower displacement, more efficiently rigged vessels. If you want to race, do it against other Friendships.

Comps	LOD	Beam	MinDr	Displ	Bllst	SA/D	D/L	Avg. PHRF	Max. Speed	Motion Index	Space Index	No. of Berths	Head-room
Newman Friendship Sloop 25	25' 0"	8' 8"	4' 3"	7,000	2,000	18.9	337	NA	6.1	27.3	423	4	4' 8"
Irwin 10/4 (25)	25' 4"	10' 4"	2' 9"	7,000	2,000	17.3	300	234	6.3	20.9	640	4	5' 8"
Vancouver 25	25' 0"	8' 6"	4' 0"	7,000	3,000	16.6	307	NA	6.2	26.0	586	4	6' 1"

Nimble 24/25 (25)
You can have a sloop or a yawl, trunk cabin or pilothouse

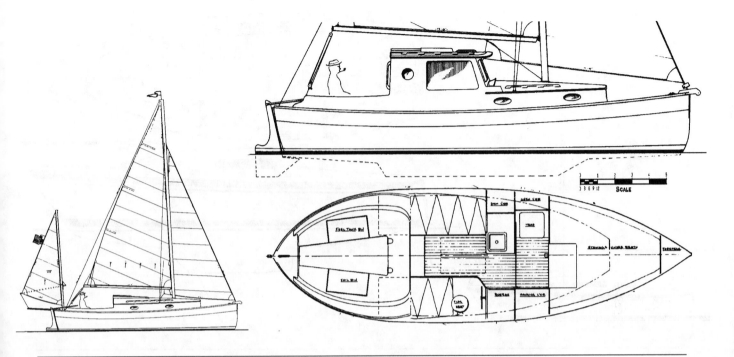

LOD:	24' 7"	**Designer:**	Ted Brewer
LOA:	27' 7"	**Builder:**	Nimble Boats
LWL:	23' 8"	**Years produced:**	1987–1993
Min./max. draft:	1' 4"/4' 2"	**Sail area:**	252 sq. ft.
Bridge clearance:	29' 6"	**Fuel tankage:**	portable
Power:	outboard 4 to 6 hp	**Water tankage:**	portable
B/D ratio:	29%	**Approx. trailering wgt.:**	3,600 lbs.

Ted Brewer has done a good job of creating a traditional-looking but trailerable character boat that has some good things going for it. One thing we especially liked is the optional mizzen mast with a 31-square foot sprit-rigged balancing sail. Mast and all can be pulled out like a weed and stored on deck when not in use—or the sail can just be furled in place by wrapping around its tiny mast. The yawl in the sailplan, also available as a sloop, was available either as a centerboarder (dimensions above) or as a shoal keeler with a 2' 6" draft (as shown in phantom lines in the profile drawing). A "tropical version" adds extra elliptical bronze ports and a solar vent. An "offshore version" adds a 200-pound lead shoe to the shoal-keeler. A "pilothouse version" (later lengthened slightly to become the "Arctic 25" and the "Kodiak 26") had a cabin layout identical to the standard version, but gained six feet of headroom under the house roof. *Best features:* The pilothouse has two steering stations, one in the cockpit with a tiller, and the other below with a wheel. She steers well even with the rudder in the "folded" position. She is well finished, with plenty of bronze hardware. *Worst features:* Her bottom is nearly flat and has hard bilges, so she tends to pound moderately in a chop.

Comps	LOD	Beam	MinDr	Displ	Bllst	SA/D	D/L	Avg. PHRF	Max. Speed	Motion Index	Space Index	No. of Berths	Head-room
Terrapin 24 (25)	24' 6"	8' 0"	0' 9"	2,050	100	21.4	113	NA	6.0	9.2	379	5	5' 0"
MacGregor 25	25' 0"	7' 11"	1' 6"	2,200	600	28.7	83	234	6.4	9.0	402	5	4' 9"
Nimble 24/25 (25)	24' 7"	7' 10"	1' 4"	2,400	700	22.5	81	249	6.5	9.6	348	4	4' 6"

O'Day 26 (25)
There goes a 26! Or is it a 25? Or a 24?

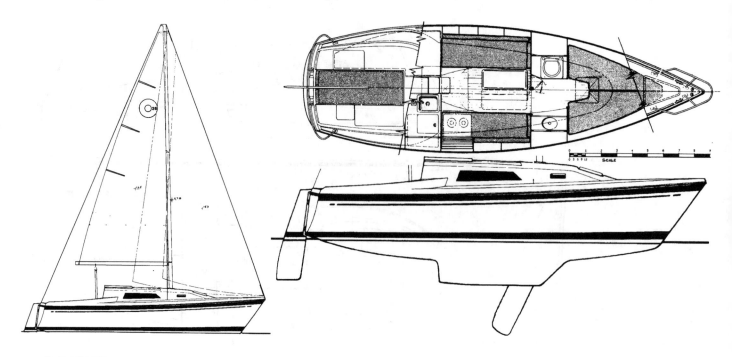

LOD:	25' 5"		**Designer:**	C. Raymond Hunt Assoc.
LOA:	27' 6"		**Builder:**	O'Day
LWL:	21' 7"		**Years produced:**	1984–1986
Min./max. draft:	2' 6"/6' 0"		**Sail area:**	280 sq. ft.
Bridge clearance:	33' 8"		**Fuel tankage:**	portable or 14 gal.
Power:	outboard or inboard 6 to 15 hp		**Water tankage:**	20 gal.
B/D ratio:	39%		**Approx. trailering wgt.:**	6,900 lbs.

The O'Day 26 resembles her near-sistership, the O'Day 25 (page 300) to an extent that makes it difficult to distinguish one from the other. Both give buyers a choice of inboard or outboard power. The cabin and cockpit layouts on both are almost identical, and feature the same 5' 6" headroom. The waterline on the "26" is eleven inches longer than on the "25"—and on both vessels the hull length is stretched five inches beyond the LOD by virtue of a reverse transom, so the LOD on the 26 is actually in the 25 range, and the 25, eleven inches shorter, is actually in the 24 range. In any case, according to O'Day, the design basis behind the O'Day 26 was "to maximize the idea of a boat suitable for coastwise ocean sailing and over-the-road transport by a pleasure vehicle without any special size permits." The result, O'Day says, is a boat that "has the right stuff for easy trailer sailing." We wonder about that, in view of the 6,900 lbs. trailering weight, requiring a specially equipped SUV with extra engine power. A 2008 Ford E-250 van with a 4.6 liter V8 won't do it, but add a 5.4 liter engine and it will. Is that still considered a "pleasure vehicle"? ***Best features:*** The O'Day 26 probably has a little more speed than her comps. ***Worst features:*** None noticed.

Comps	LOD	Beam	MinDr	Displ	Bllst	SA/D	D/L	Avg. PHRF	Max. Speed	Motion Index	Space Index	No. of Berths	Head-room
Cornish Crabber 24	24' 0"	8' 0"	2' 5"	4,600	600	17.6	247	360	6.0	19.3	415	4	4' 3"
Pacific Seacraft 25	24' 6"	8' 0"	3' 3"	4,750	1,750	12.8	229	NA	6.1	20.3	387	4	5' 0"
O'Day 26 (25)	25' 5"	8' 0"	2' 6"	4,800	1,850	15.7	213	234	6.2	19.8	484	5	5' 6"
Com-Pac 25	24' 7"	8' 6"	2' 6"	4,800	1,900	15.6	231	NA	6.1	18.4	509	5	5' 10"
Morgan 24 (25)	24' 11"	8' 0"	2' 9"	5,000	1,900	17.0	225	225	6.2	21.4	435	4	5' 8"

Pacific Seacraft 25
Double-ender reminiscent of Billy Atkin's Eric

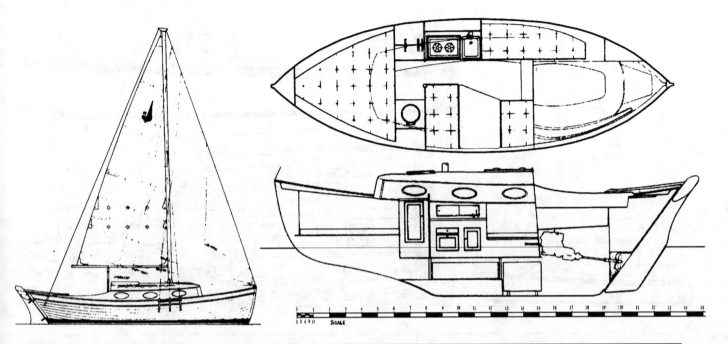

LOD:	24' 6"
LOA:	25' 11"
LWL:	21' 0"
Min./max. draft:	3' 3"
Bridge clearance:	30' 0"
Power:	Yanmar diesel 8 hp
B/D ratio:	37%

Designer:	Henry Mohrschladt
Builder:	Pacific Seacraft
Years produced:	1977–1981
Sail area:	226 sq. ft.
Fuel tankage:	16 gal.
Water tankage:	14 gal.
Approx. trailering wgt.:	6,800 lbs.

This double-ender is reminiscent of a miniaturized version of the Scandinavian redningskoites of yore, and the mid-1920s derivative designs of Colin Archer and William ("Billy") Atkin. She is the first design Henry Mohrschladt drew for his new company, Pacific Seacraft, of which he was president. (In 1988 *Fortune* magazine named Pacific Seacraft among recipients of the "top 100 U.S. quality products" award. Soon afterward, an offshore company came forward with a purchase offer and Pacific Seacraft was sold. In 2008 the company went bankrupt. The assets were purchased by the Brodie family, and moved to North Carolina,

where production continues.) Production of the 25 lasted only five years. Distinguishing characteristics include her lapstrake hull construction and her relatively tiny sailplan (SA/D is only 12.8; values below 16 are considered very low). ***Best features:*** We like her accommodations plan, perfect for one or two voyaging sailors. We enjoyed a similar arrangement in our Tartan 27. ***Worst features:*** Like her comp, the Cornish Crabber, the PS 25 lacks sufficient sail area to make her go well in light air. Because of her narrow ends and low freeboard, she also has a lower Space Index than any of her comps.

Comps	LOD	Beam	MinDr	Displ	Blst	SA/D	D/L	Avg. PHRF	Max. Speed	Motion Index	Space Index	No. of Berths	Head-room
Cornish Crabber 24	24' 0"	8' 0"	2' 5"	4,600	600	17.6	247	360	6.0	19.3	415	4	4' 3"
Pacific Seacraft 25	24' 6"	8' 0"	3' 3"	4,750	1,750	12.8	229	NA	6.1	20.3	387	4	5' 0"
O'Day 26 (25)	25' 5"	8' 0"	2' 6"	4,800	1,850	15.7	213	234	6.2	19.8	484	5	5' 6"
Com-Pac 25	24' 7"	8' 6"	2' 6"	4,800	1,900	15.6	231	NA	6.1	18.4	509	5	5' 10"
Morgan 24/25	24' 11"	8' 0"	2' 9"	5,000	1,900	17.0	225	225	6.2	21.4	435	4	5' 8"

Parker Dawson 26 (25)
Unique trailerable boat with a center cockpit

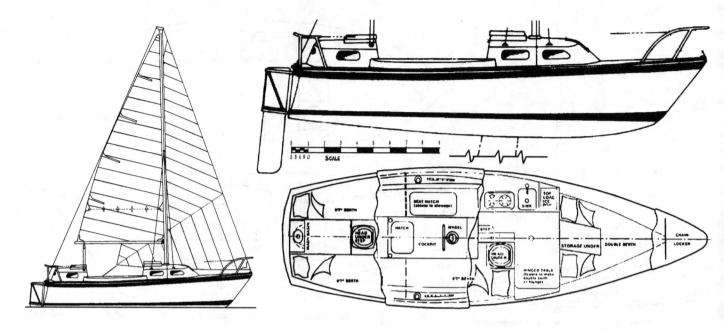

LOD:	25' 3"		**Designer:**	Bob Finch
LOA:	27' 1"		**Builder:**	Parker-Dawson et al.
LWL:	22' 2"		**Years produced:**	1972–1984
Min./max. draft:	1' 8"/5' 4"		**Sail area:**	271 sq. ft.
Bridge clearance:	32' 6"		**Fuel tankage:**	20 gal.
Power:	outboard or inboard 7 to 12 hp		**Water tankage:**	15 gal.
B/D ratio:	22%		**Approx. trailering wgt.:**	8,000 lbs.

This pocket cruiser is unique in several respects: (1) she has two separate cabins plus a center cockpit, which can be enclosed in canvas to serve as a third cabin; (2) a fixed-keel version with beefed-up rigging has crossed the Atlantic and a good part of the Pacific, indicating at least a smidgen of seaworthiness; and (3) she is trailerable and ramp-launchable despite her relatively heavy displacement for her size—provided your truck or SUV can handle 8,000 pound loads. A variety of options were available from various marketers (Midship Yachts, Dawson, Parker-Dawson, Nauset Marine, others) who offered at various times inboard diesel, inboard gas, and outboard power;

fixed shoal keel or swing keel; wheel or tiller steering; and sloop rig or ketch. **Best features:** The privacy that comes with two cabins and two heads is a great plus, especially if guests are aboard. **Worst features:** Speed is said to be so-so in light and medium air. Owners have complained about a lack of helm feel and drag on early models; later boats were given push-pull cable steering gear rather than the pull-pull variety, which evidently solved the problem. Rudder scabbards, originally of aluminum, were switched to fiberglass to eliminate rudder banging at moorings. And the swing keel can bang around in its trunk unless pinned in place, which owners sometimes forget to do.

Comps	LOD	Beam	MinDr	Displ	Bllst	SA/D	D/L	Avg. PHRF	Max. Speed	Motion Index	Space Index	No. of Berths	Head-room
Parker Dawson 26 (25)	25' 3"	8' 0"	1' 8"	5,700	1,250	13.6	234	NA	6.3	23.2	497	5	5' 10"
South Coast Marine 25	25' 0"	8' 0"	2' 6"	5,700	1,750	15.3	275	NA	6.1	22.7	411	2 to 4	5' 0"
Bristol Corsair 24 (25)	24' 7"	8' 0"	3' 5"	5,920	2,500	14.5	447	270	5.7	28.4	495	4	5' 11"
Cheoy Lee Flyer Mk III 25	25' 0"	7' 2"	3' 11"	6,000	2,240	14.7	335	297	5.9	30.6	386	4	5' 4"
New Horizons 25	25' 3"	7' 9"	3' 0"	6,030	1,600	15.6	281	225	6.2	26.8	465	4	5' 2"

Rhodes Meridian 25
Pretty masthead sloop by Philip Rhodes

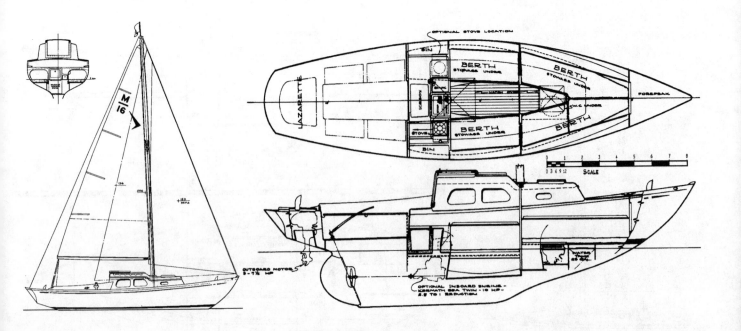

LOD:	24' 9"		**Designer:**	Philip L. Rhodes
LOA:	24' 9"		**Builder:**	Seafarer F'Glass Yachts
LWL:	17' 6"		**Years produced:**	1961–1967?
Min./max. draft:	3' 3"		**Sail area:**	277 sq. ft.
Bridge clearance:	30' 3"		**Fuel tankage:**	portable
Power:	outboard or inboard 6 to 10 hp		**Water tankage:**	24 gal.
B/D ratio:	52%		**Approx. trailering wgt.:**	7,500 lbs.

The first Meridians were imported from De Vries Lentsch, a well established Dutch yard. Later they were built at the Seafarer plant in Huntington, NY, on Long Island. Like many boats from the board of Philip Rhodes, she is pretty to look at, but because of her relatively narrow beam, slack bilges, and shallow ballast location, she is also relatively tender in a breeze, has a tendency to hobbyhorse in a chop, and has little elbow room below. *Best features:* The large windows in her doghouse help to allay any crew claustrophobia despite the narrow confines of the cabin. *Worst features:* The optional Kermath 10 hp Sea Twin inboard was mounted so low in the bilge that servicing (especially oil change) was extra difficult, and any casual bilge water that collects can corrode the crankcase and engine block. Also, the icebox sits immediately above the engine. As a consequence, despite three inches of insulation, the icebox's efficiency is badly compromised.

Comps	LOD	Beam	MinDr	Displ	Bllst	SA/D	D/L	Avg. PHRF	Max. Speed	Motion Index	Space Index	No. of Berths	Head-room
Capri 26 (24)	23' 8"	9' 10"	3' 5"	5,100	1,750	15.9	189	210	6.4	15.6	641	4	6' 1"
Cape Dory 25D (Mk II)	25' 0"	8' 0"	3' 6"	5,120	2,050	16.4	333	255	5.8	23.7	472	4	5' 11"
Rhodes Meridian 25	24' 9"	7' 0"	3' 3"	5,310	2,750	13.4	442	252	5.6	31.0	363	4	5' 8"
Contessa 26	25' 5.5"	7' 6"	4' 0"	5,400	2,300	15.8	260	246	6.1	24.8	447	4	5' 0"
Ericson 25 Mk I	24' 8"	8' 0"	2' 0"	5,400	2,500	13.8	267	234	6.1	23.4	457	4	5' 6"

Santana 25
A quarter-tonner designed by Shad Turner

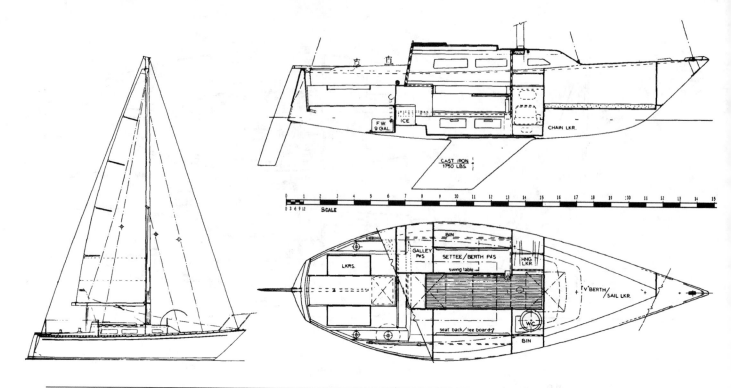

LOD:	24' 7"	**Designer:**	Shad Turner
LOA:	26' 4"	**Builder:**	W. D. Schock
LWL:	19' 6"	**Years produced:**	1972–1977?
Min./max. draft:	fin 4' 11"; swing 2' 7"/5' 6"	**Sail area:**	262 sq. ft.
Bridge clearance:	34' 6"	**Fuel tankage:**	portable
Power:	outboard 6 to 8 hp	**Water tankage:**	9 gal.
B/D ratio:	38%	**Approx. trailering wgt.:**	5,400 lbs.

Designer Shad Turner was only 32 when he designed the Santana 25, his first effort for the W. D. Schock Company. He had graduated from the University of Arizona and spent five years in the design game, two and a half of them in the office of W. I. B. Crealock, before drawing this quarter-ton racer-cruiser. She was available either as a keel boat (shown here) or with a swing keel more suitable for easy launching from a trailer (draft 2' 7" board up, 5' 6" board down). The swing keeler is also 450 pounds lighter than the fin keeler, weighing 3,600 pounds overall with ballast of 1,370 pounds (380 pounds less than the fin keel model), and has a slightly reduced sail area. *Best features:* Though headroom below is only 5' 2", it can be increased to 6' 2" in the area of the galley by raising the companionway hatch. *Worst features:* Space below is (along with the Catalina 250) at the low end of the range compared to her comps.

Comps	LOD	Beam	MinDr	Displ	Bllst	SA/D	D/L	Avg. PHRF	Max. Speed	Motion Index	Space Index	No. of Berths	Head- room
Catalina 250	25' 0"	8' 6"	1' 8"	3,600	1,200	18.3	167	225	6.2	14.3	395	4	4' 3"
Freedom 25	24' 4"	8' 6"	4' 5"	3,500	1,025	18.0	195	186	6.0	14.3	432	4	4' 10"
Lancer 25	24' 8"	8' 0"	2' 4"	3,400	1,200	17.5	187	264	6.0	15.3	560	4 to 6	5' 10"
Santana 25	24' 7"	7' 10"	2' 7"	4,050	1,750	16.5	244	222	5.9	18.6	396	4	5' 2"
Hunter 25 Mk III	24' 6"	8' 5"	2' 0"	3,700	1,309	17.1	153	225	6.3	14.4	484	4	5' 4"

Shaw Nutmeg 24 (25)
An independent Bill Shaw design

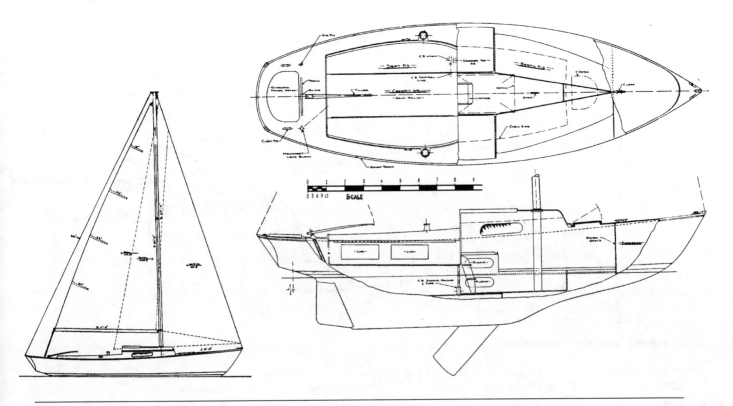

LOD:	24' 6"	Designer:	Bill Shaw
LOA:	24' 6"	Builder:	Tanzer Industries
LWL:	18' 6"	Years produced:	1964–1964
Min./max. draft:	2' 9"/5' 3"	Sail area:	268 sq. ft.
Bridge clearance:	30' 0"	Fuel tankage:	portable
Power:	outboard 4 to 6 hp	Water tankage:	portable
B/D ratio:	39%	Approx. trailering wgt.:	5,600 lbs.

This weekending sloop was conceived by Bill Shaw just before he joined Pearson Yachts as their in-house designer near the beginning of the fiberglass era. The design was farmed out to Tanzer Industries in Canada, and marketed by a yacht broker who was a friend of Shaw. Only a few Nutmegs were ever built, but by chance one was moored in my home harbor in Darien, CT, when my wife and I were in the market for a boat about that size, so we tested her out. We thought she was kind of roughly finished below, had no special attractions for us, and was above our price range, so we ended up buying a considerably cheaper South Coast 23 kit boat instead. **Best features:** The boat has low freeboard and a nice springy sheer, presenting a pretty picture to dockside observers. **Worst features:** Despite Bill Shaw's fame engendered by the success of his Shaw 24 in winning MORC races, the Nutmeg never measured up (though maybe it's just that she never got a chance to compete). In any case, for most folks she lacks sufficient cruising space below, and not enough boats were sold to permit organizing a one-design class for club racing.

Comps	LOD	Beam	MinDr	Displ	Bllst	SA/D	D/L	Avg. PHRF	Max. Speed	Motion Index	Space Index	No. of Berths	Head-room
Shaw Nutmeg 24 (25)	24' 6"	7' 7"	2' 9"	3,800	1,475	17.6	268	NA	5.8	19.3	319	4	4' 3"
Cape Dory 25 Mk I	24' 10"	7' 3"	3' 0"	3,850	1,500	17.2	295	255	5.7	21.1	372	4	5' 6"
Cal 25 Mk I	25' 0"	8' 0"	4' 0"	4,000	1,700	18.2	223	222	6.0	17.9	381	4 or 5	4' 6"

South Coast Seacraft 25

A cruiser that resembles the Cal 25

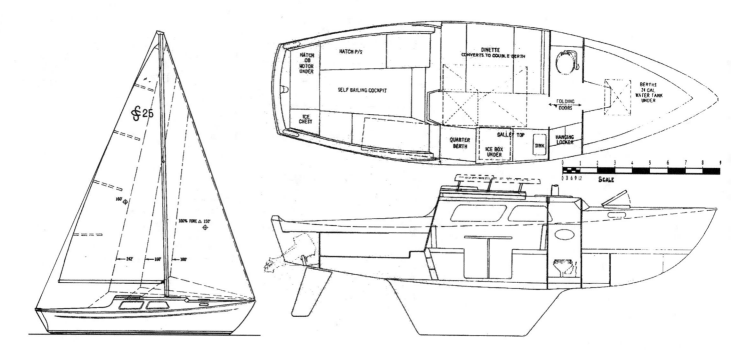

LOD:	25' 5"	**Designer:**	Warren Metcalf
LOA:	25' 5"	**Builder:**	South Coast Seacraft
LWL:	20' 6"	**Years produced:**	1970–1973
Min./max. draft:	3' 6"	**Sail area:**	310 sq. ft.
Bridge clearance:	34' 6"	**Fuel tankage:**	portable
Power:	outboard 6 to 10 hp	**Water tankage:**	24 gal.
B/D ratio:	43%	**Approx. trailering wgt.:**	5,800 lbs.

South Coast Seacraft owner Hollis Metcalf's son, Warren, was being groomed to take over his father's company, but the younger Metcalf died tragically in a diving accident when he was just finishing the design of his first vessel, the SC 25. It is interesting to observe that the hull and underbody of Warren Metcalf's SC 25 seem to closely resemble the popular Cal 25 (see page 327), at least in profile. In any case, Hollis was brokenhearted by his son's death, and sold the company in 1975 to three investors from Chicago. Production continued, but the company's finances declined and the plant closed in 1981. **Best features:** Headroom is an acceptable 5' 6", but with the poptop-type hatch in the elevated position, headroom increases to 6' 1", very good for a 25-footer. A supplemental ice chest in the stern quarter of the cockpit, presumably so the helmsperson doesn't have to bother the cook to pass up a cool beverage, is a clever touch. **Worst features:** The bridge deck appears to be shallow enough to permit water to pour down into the cabin if enough water from rain or waves sloshes into the cockpit.

Comps	LOD	Beam	MinDr	Displ	Blist	SA/D	D/L	Avg. PHRF	Max. Speed	Motion Index	Space Index	No. of Berths	Head-room
Mark 25	24' 7"	9' 3"	3' 0"	4,130	1,779	20.3	230	216	6.0	15.3	495	4	5' 8"
South Coast Seacraft 25	25' 5"	8' 0"	3' 6"	4,200	1,800	19.1	218	231	6.1	18.4	379	5	5' 6"
C&C 25	25' 2"	8' 8"	3' 10"	4,250	1,880	18.2	215	222	6.1	16.5	555	4	5' 10"
North Star 500 (25)	24' 6"	9' 0"	5' 0"	4,300	1,710	17.7	231	228	6.0	16.3	472	4	4' 6"

Tanzer 7.5 (25)
Johann Tanzer's design has self-tacking jib

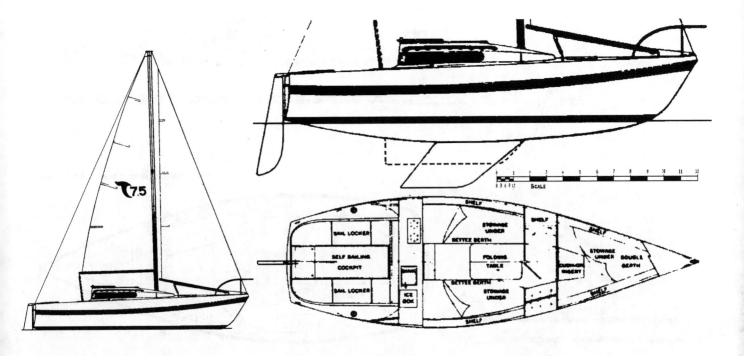

LOD:	24' 7"	Designer:	Johann Tanzer
LOA:	26' 0"	**Builder:**	Tanzer Yachts
LWL:	21' 10"	**Years produced:**	1977–1987
Min./max. draft:	2' 8"/4' 0"	**Sail area:**	256 sq. ft.
Bridge clearance:	32' 0"	**Fuel tankage:**	portable
Power:	outboard 4 to 8 hp	**Water tankage:**	10 gal.
B/D ratio:	47%	**Approx. trailering wgt.:**	6,250 lbs.

Designer/builder Johann Tanzer tried to put together a Boat for All Sailors. He started with a sleek hull with choice of fin keel (4' 0" draft, 1,600 lbs. of ballast, 3,800 lbs. displacement) for those who want more performance, or shoal draft (per stats below: 2' 8" draft, 1,950 lbs. ballast, 4,150 lbs. displacement), for those who sail in shallow-water areas. Then he took the unusual step of adding a self-tacking jib on a jib-boom, making the boat much easier to singlehand upwind, and offering some appeal to the family learning to sail, who might be bothered by "all those strings to pull," while also offering a conventional array of other foresails for better performance under specific conditions of wind and sea. Tanzer also tried to maximize space below by using a raised-deck configuration with a bubble-like cabin added on top, giving increased headroom as well as more storage space. (Space Index of 529 is significantly greater than the comps shown here.) **Best features:** Tanzer succeeded in most of the design ideas he tried to incorporate. **Worst features:** The shoal draft model doesn't do well upwind compared to conventional craft; adding a centerboard would have made her better.

Comps	LOD	Beam	MinDr	Displ	Bllst	SA/D	D/L	Avg. PHRF	Max. Speed	Motion Index	Space Index	No. of Berths	Head- room
Amphibi-Con 25	25' 5"	7' 9"	2' 5"	3,900	1,100	17.9	171	234	6.2	16.8	407	4	5' 8"
Catalina 25	25' 0"	8' 0"	2' 2"	4,150	1,500	16.7	170	225	6.3	17.8	464	5	5' 6"
Tanzer 7.5 (25)	24' 7"	8' 0"	2' 8"	4,150	1,950	15.9	178	201	6.3	17.6	529	4	5' 8"
Coronado 25 (cb version)	25' 0"	8' 0"	2' 6"	4,300	7,800	18.4	246	231	6.0	19.4	411	5	5' 6"

Tanzer 25 Mk II
The fast one among her comps

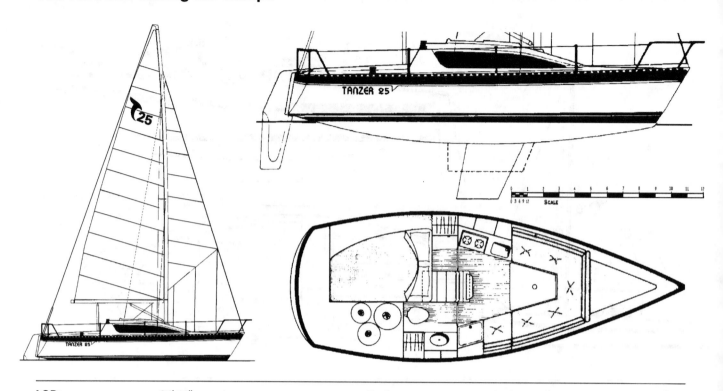

LOD:	24' 11"	**Designer:**	Joubert-Nivelt
LOA:	27' 1"	**Builder:**	Tanzer and various others
LWL:	21' 10"	**Years produced:**	1986–1992?
Min./max. draft:	2' 11"/4' 8"	**Sail area:**	328 sq. ft.
Bridge clearance:	39' 0"	**Fuel tankage:**	10 gal.
Power:	outboard or inboard 6 to10 hp	**Water tankage:**	12 gal.
B/D ratio:	44%	**Approx. trailering wgt.:**	5,600 lbs.

The original builder, Tanzer Industries Ltd., hired the French design team of Joubert-Nivelt to draw the Tanzer 25 Mk II, but produced only a few boats before going out of business in 1986. The assets were sold, first to an auction house, then to Canadian Yacht Builders, a firm that acquired the assets of a number of failed builders. Later on, several other builders and/or marketers were involved, among them Challenger Yachts of Canada and Mirage Yachts. Inevitably, the quality varied and specs changed slightly as the vessel's molds were moved from one builder to another, but the boats were quite popular and production continued through about 1992. **Best features:** Compared to her comps, the Tanzer 25 Mk II has a much lower PHRF rating. (The rating is presumably for the deep fin keel rather than the shoal keel, which was also offered.) A double berth aft under the cockpit, the enclosed head, separate wet and dry lockers, and U-shaped dinette in an open cabin layout all contributed to the boat's popularity. **Worst features:** Construction quality from different builders can vary. Investigate before buying.

Comps	LOD	Beam	MinDr	Displ	Bllst	SA/D	D/L	Avg. PHRF	Max. Speed	Motion Index	Space Index	No. of Berths	Head-room
Columbia 7.6 (25)	25' 1"	9' 2"	3' 6"	4,500	1,500	18.7	228	210	6.1	16.3	573	4	5' 8"
Cal 25 Mk II	25' 3"	9' 0"	3' 6"	4,500	2,000	18.5	189	219	6.3	16.1	558	5	5' 10"
Montego 25	25' 3"	9' 1"	3' 6"	4,500	1,800	17.1	236	216	6.1	16.9	557	4	5' 11"
Tanzer 25 Mk II	24' 11"	9' 7"	2' 11"	4,550	1,985	19.1	195	180	6.3	14.7	575	4	5' 9"
Seidelmann 25 (24)	24' 0"	9' 6"	3' 4"	4,600	2,200	16.3	257	216	6.0	16.5	549	4	5' 2"

Terrapin 24 (25)

Like its namesake, this craft is slow but comfortable

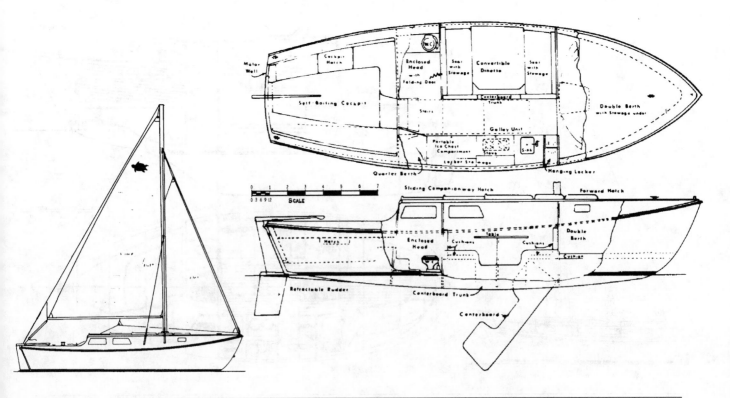

LOD:	24' 6"		**Designer:**	Dave Westphal
LOA:	25' 3"		**Builder:**	Friendship Mfg. Co.
LWL:	20' 1"		**Years produced:**	1973?–1977?
Min./max. draft:	0' 9"/5' 0"		**Sail area:**	216 sq. ft.
Bridge clearance:	28' 6"		**Fuel tankage:**	portable
Power:	outboard 3 to 6 hp		**Water tankage:**	portable
B/D ratio:	5%		**Approx. trailering wgt.:**	3,000 lbs.

The Florida designer of this ultra-shallow-draft boat had two things in mind: (1) easy trailering and launching from ramps, or even from beaches or low bulkheads, without immersing the trailer (says the sales literature, though how this can be accomplished, even using a fully-rollered trailer, with a boat weighing more than a ton, is not mentioned) and (2) cruising in relatively good comfort for this size vessel. To this end, the rig is on the short side (28' 6" bridge clearance, mast stepped on deck, for easy raising and striking), the draft is a mere nine inches, and

the towing weight is only 3,000 pounds. ***Best features:*** The companionway utilizes two rather than just one sliding hatch to open up the cabin to more light and air than would otherwise be available. The galley area, which runs along the starboard side amidships, is as spacious as one would want. ***Worst features:*** The boat apparently has no ballast other than the steel centerboard, which we assume weighs something like a hundred pounds. The flat bottom is likely to pound in a chop. The short, low-slung rig will be slower than average in light air.

Comps	LOD	Beam	MinDr	Displ	Bllst	SA/D	D/L	Avg. PHRF	Max. Speed	Motion Index	Space Index	No. of Berths	Head-room
Terrapin 24 (25)	24' 6"	8' 0"	0' 9"	2,050	100	21.4	113	NA	6.0	9.2	379	5	5' 0"
MacGregor 25	25' 0"	7' 11"	1' 6"	2,200	600	28.7	83	234	6.4	9.0	402	5	4' 9"
Nimble 24/25 (25)	24' 7"	7' 10"	1' 4"	2,400	700	22.5	81	249	6.5	9.6	348	4	4' 6"

Vancouver 25
Pint-sized long-distance cruiser

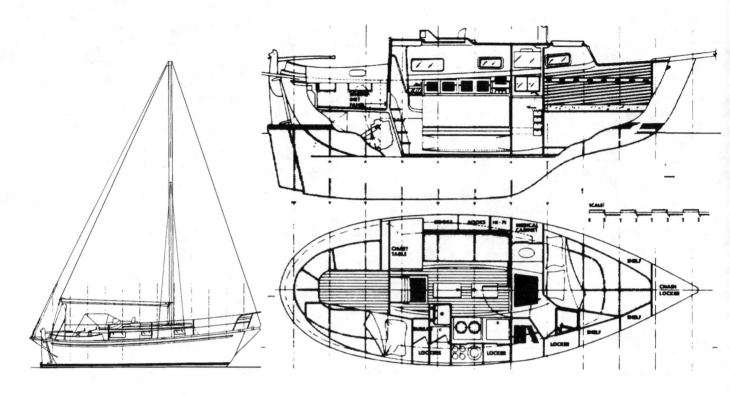

LOD:	25' 0"	**Designer:**	Bob Harris
LOA:	29' 2"	**Builder:**	Vancouver Yachts
LWL:	21' 8"	**Years produced:**	1983–1987
Min./max. draft:	4' 0"	**Sail area:**	380 sq. ft.
Bridge clearance:	36' 6"	**Fuel tankage:**	25 gal.
Power:	Yanmar dsl. 7.5 or 15 hp	**Water tankage:**	54 gal.
B/D ratio:	46%	**Approx. trailering wgt.:**	10,400 lbs.

Not many of these beefy Taiwan-built imports were made, perhaps because they weren't heavily advertised. But we can picture taking off from Seattle to cruise the Inside Passage to Alaska, or even doing a partial circumnavigation in one of these. *Best features:* Full cruising amenities are unusual in a boat this size: boom gallows, stern anchor roller chock on the boomkin, long companionway dodger, stand-up shower, large water and fuel tanks, big chart table, good ventilation, lots of storage space. Owners say she is extremely seakindly, and tracks her course well. Her outboard rudder makes mounting

a windvane (such as a Monitor) relatively convenient. Standard equipment is extensive and generally of high quality (e.g., two stainless steel water tanks, dorade vents, etc.). *Worst features:* Some of her through-hull fittings are difficult to access. Hull may be susceptible to some small-scale blistering. The 15 hp Yanmar is said to move the boat at only five knots, possibly indicating either insufficient horsepower or the wrong prop selection. The theoretical hull speed based on waterline length is 6.2 knots. The battenless mainsail, supposedly for easier reefing, doesn't make sense to us. We'd add 'em.

Comps	LOD	Beam	MinDr	Displ	Bllst	SA/D	D/L	Avg. PHRF	Max. Speed	Motion Index	Space Index	No. of Berths	Head-room
Newman Friendship Sloop 25	25' 0"	8' 8"	4' 3"	7,000	2,000	18.9	337	NA	6.1	27.3	423	4	4' 8"
Irwin 10/4 (25)	25' 4"	10' 4"	2' 9"	7,000	2,000	17.3	300	234	6.3	20.9	640	4	5' 8"
Vancouver 25	25' 0"	8' 6"	4' 0"	7,000	3,200	16.3	307	NA	6.2	26.0	586	4	6' 1"

Vertue II 25

An ocean sailer that exudes tradition

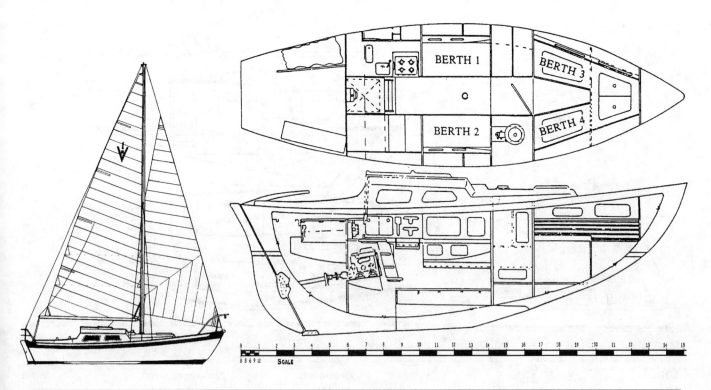

LOD:	25' 3"		**Designer:**	Laurent Giles Ltd.
LOA:	25' 8"		**Builder:**	Bossoms Boatyard Ltd.
LWL:	21' 6"		**Years produced:**	1958?–present
Min./max. draft:	4' 5"		**Sail area:**	391 sq. ft.
Bridge clearance:	38' 0"		**Fuel tankage:**	20 gal.
Power:	inboard 9 hp		**Water tankage:**	13 gal.
B/D ratio:	48%		**Approx. trailering wgt.:**	14,400 lbs.

Humphrey Barton crossed the Atlantic in a wood version of this design in 1950, and since then many sailors desiring to circumnavigate the world in a small yacht have chosen this boat. She is an update of an old design (1936), way overbuilt even after being reconceived in fiberglass. Therefore she is very heavy for a 25-footer, but that is to some sailors' liking. **Best features:** For long distance ocean sailing, there's nothing like having a well-proven and dependable boat. Her Motion Index (the higher the number, the greater the comfort) is the highest of all the boats in this guide. (The Fisher 25 is second highest.) Tall circumnavigators will like her 6' 2" standing headroom under the doghouse. Bossoms Boatyard, a quaint, cozy yard along the Thames only a couple of miles from Oxford, England, has the molds and, when we last checked, will furnish her either as a finished boat or as a kit for home completion by the customer. **Worst features:** If you want to trailer the Vertue, you'll need a huge truck to do the hauling; with trailer and stores she'll weigh about 14,400 pounds.

Comps	LOD	Beam	MinDr	Displ	Bllst	SA/D	D/L	Avg. PHRF	Max. Speed	Motion Index	Space Index	No. of Berths	Head-room
New Moon 25	25' 0"	8' 6"	3' 8"	6,800	2,300	15.8	336	NA	6.1	27.3	532	4	6' 0"
Eastsail 25	25' 0"	8' 6"	3' 8"	7,200	2,300	17.2	355	NA	6.1	27.2	532	5	6' 0"
Vertue II 25	25' 3"	7' 10"	4' 5"	9,220	4,400	14.2	414	NA	6.2	40.1	542	4	6' 2"
Fisher 25	24' 6"	9' 4"	3' 9"	10,000	4,500	7.2	482	NA	6.1	35.2	567	5	6' 0"

Walton 25

George B. Walton markets a Folkboat design

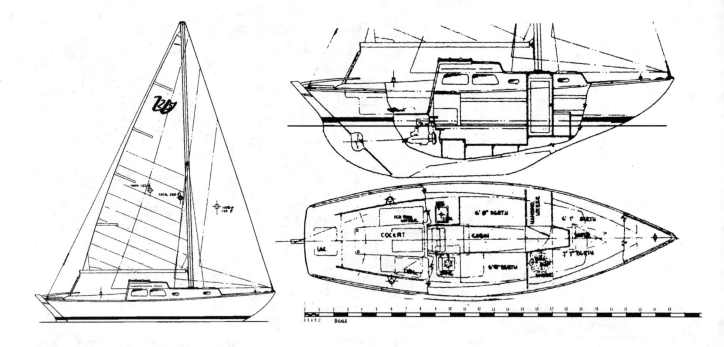

LOD:	25' 3"
LOA:	25' 9"
LWL:	19' 10"
Min./max. draft:	3' 10"
Bridge clearance:	31' 6"
Power:	inboard 6 to 9 hp
B/D ratio:	41%

Designer:	None specified
Builder:	George B. Walton (marketer)
Years produced:	1962?–1964?
Sail area:	288 sq. ft.
Fuel tankage:	varies
Water tankage:	varies
Approx. trailering wgt.:	7,000 lbs.

Here is another Scandinavian Folkboat (heavy displacement, long keel with highly raked attached outboard rudder, narrow hull, low freeboard, springy sheer) similar to the Contessa 26 (25) on page 337 but slightly smaller in size and weight. The boat was marketed by George B. Walton, Inc. of Annapolis, MD, in the early 1960s, but almost nothing remains in the literature about the boat. Even the scantily informative sales brochure is missing key data; we had to guess at ballast and displacement, based mainly on scaling down from the Contessa. The engine in the drawing

looks small; we assume it was similar to the Contessa's, maybe a 7 hp Vire, 6.6 hp Petter, 7 hp Faryman, or even a 9 hp Yanmar. We wish we had more information on this boat. ***Best features:*** Like other Folkboat designs, she is probably a good sea boat, has good tracking ability, and good pointing ability, and looks pretty. Her doghouse cabin gives good headroom for a 25-footer. ***Worst features:*** Low coach roof and narrow beam give the cabin a closed-in feeling. Low freeboard relative to comps may give a wet ride in rough conditions.

Comps	LOD	Beam	MinDr	Displ	Bllst	SA/D	D/L	Avg. PHRF	Max. Speed	Motion Index	Space Index	No. of Berths	Head-room
Walton 25	25' 3"	7' 3"	3' 10"	4,900	2,000	16.0	281	NA	6.0	24.9	392	4	5' 7"
Talman Katama 25	24' 8"	8' 0"	2' 6"	5,000	1,900	15.4	259	NA	6.1	22.1	363	4	4' 6"
Irwin 25	25' 3"	8' 0"	2' 8"	5,000	2,200	16.5	259	228	6.1	21.9	470	4 to 6	5' 9"
Yankee 26 (25)	24' 6"	8' 8"	4' 6"	5,335	2,150	15.4	270	234	6.1	20.7	534	4	6' 2"

Watkins Seawolf 25

Shallow draft keel boat from a Florida builder

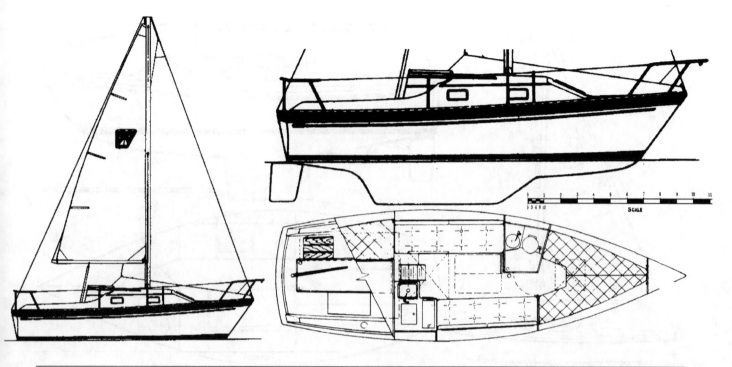

LOD:	24' 11"	**Designer:**	Watkins Design Team
LOA:	24' 11"	**Builder:**	Watkins Yachts
LWL:	21' 0"	**Years produced:**	1983–1989
Min./max. draft:	2' 6"/4' 0"	**Sail area:**	265 sq. ft.
Bridge clearance:	32' 9"	**Fuel tankage:**	portable
Power:	outboard or inboard 6 to 10 hp	**Water tankage:**	40 gal.
B/D ratio:	37%	**Approx. trailering wgt.:**	6,400 lbs.

One unconfirmed story is that the Watkins 25 started life as a Columbia T23 (page 162), although we don't see any physical resemblance whatsoever. The in-house Watkins design team supposedly then modified the design extensively, changing the transom from reverse to near-vertical, adding a new underbody, raising the gunwale six inches, adding a couple of feet to lengthen the deck, and totally redesigning the deck and trunk cabin. The story goes on to say that the W25 molds eventually ended up in the hands of Com-Pac Yachts, another builder in the Clearwater, FL, area, and with a reshaping of the forward

end of the deckhouse and some changes in trim became the Com-Pac 25 (see page 336). **Best features:** At 5' 11" the boat has the best headroom among her comps. Her extruded and perforated aluminum toe rail is handy for easy placement of genoa blocks and fenders. **Worst features:** The very shallow (2' 6") keel is convenient but prevents good upwind performance; a deep-keel version was available toward the end of the boat's production run but didn't attract many buyers. The rudder depth looks a bit low to us, and therefore might give control problems under adverse weather conditions.

Comps	LOD	Beam	MinDr	Displ	Bllst	SA/D	D/L	Avg. PHRF	Max. Speed	Motion Index	Space Index	No. of Berths	Head-room
Watkins Seawolf 25	24' 11"	8' 0"	2' 6"	4,300	1,600	16.0	207	243	6.1	18.7	461	5	5' 11"
O'Day 25 (24)	24' 5"	8' 0"	2' 3"	4,400	1,525	16.1	212	234	6.1	18.7	508	5	5' 6"
Hunter 25 Mk II	24' 8"	8' 0"	2' 11"	4,400	1,800	15.3	239	225	6.0	19.6	430	5	5' 8"
La Paz 25	25' 1"	8' 0"	2' 0"	4,600	1,600	14.2	162	NA	6.5	18.6	519	6	6' 4"

Westerly Tiger 25
A fin-keeler faster than the Westerly Centaur 26

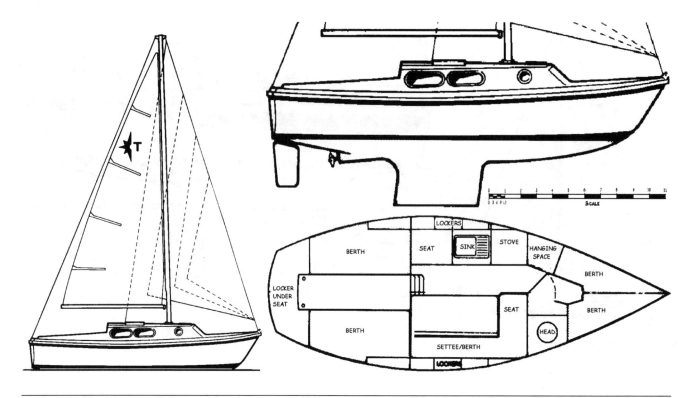

LOD:	25' 1"		**Designer:**	John A. Butler
LOA:	25' 1"		**Builder:**	Westerly Marine
LWL:	21' 10"		**Years produced:**	1969–1976
Min./max. draft:	4' 3"		**Sail area:**	237 sq. ft.
Bridge clearance:	35' 0"		**Fuel tankage:**	10 gal.
Power:	inboard 6 to 16 hp		**Water tankage:**	20 gal.
B/D ratio:	43%		**Approx. trailering wgt.:**	7,500 lbs.

The English-built Westerly Tiger is a stretched version of the 22-foot Laurent Giles–designed Westerly Cirrus. Her appearance is typical of small but heavily-built Westerly sailboats, except for the absence of the bow knuckle seen, for instance, on 26-foot Westerly Centaurs. With a single, deeper fin keel, the Tiger is faster and performs better than the bilge-keeled Centaur, which was introduced in the same year as the Tiger (1969), and was considerably more popular than the Tiger despite her performance shortcomings. The Tiger was phased out in 1976, replaced by the Westerly Pembroke, a fin-keeled version of the Centaur. ***Best features:*** Among her comps, the Tiger has the second-to-heaviest displacement, the most ballast, and a D/L ratio of 226, putting her in the heavy displacement category. Consequently, for sailors looking for good sailing characteristics in heavy weather and chop, this boat (and the Kaiser 25) are probably marginally better than their comps. ***Worst features:*** With an SA/D of 12.5, the boat is under rigged for light air versus her comps.

Comps	LOD	Beam	MinDr	Displ	Bllst	SA/D	D/L	Avg. PHRF	Max. Speed	Motion Index	Space Index	No. of Berths	Head-room
Beneteau First 26 (25)	25' 5"	9' 2"	2' 9"	4,484	1,455	16.6	177	192	6.4	16.0	584	4	4' 3"
Ericson 25 Mk II	25' 5"	9' 3"	3' 11"	5,000	2,000	17.8	214	213	6.3	17.3	622	5	6' 1"
Kaiser 25	25' 4"	7' 10"	3' 7"	5,000	2,250	15.5	367	273	5.7	24.3	468	4	6' 2"
Westerly Tiger 25	25' 1"	8' 9"	4' 3"	5,264	2,240	12.5	226	225	6.3	19.7	447	5	5' 3"
Beachcomber 25	25' 4"	8' 0"	1' 3"	5,300	1,400	14.5	188	NA	6.5	20.8	510	5	5' 10"

Yankee 26 (25)
An S&S design built on the West Coast

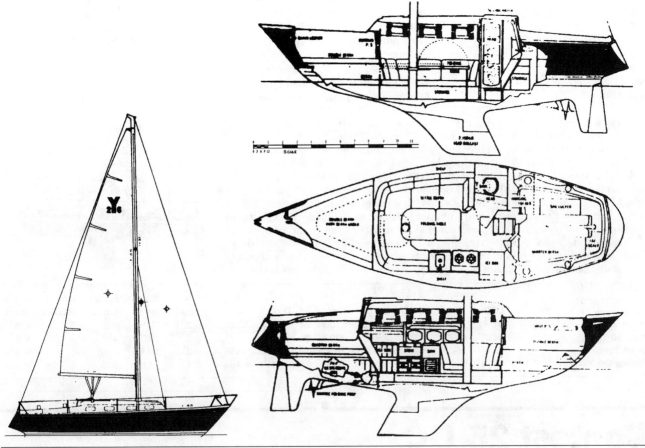

LOD:	24' 6"	**Designer:**	Sparkman & Stephens
LOA:	26' 0"	**Builder:**	Heritage Boat Works
LWL:	20' 8"	**Years produced:**	1972–1990
Min./max. draft:	4' 6"	**Sail area:**	294 sq. ft.
Bridge clearance:	36' 0"	**Fuel tankage:**	15 gal.
Power:	inboard BMW dsl. 8 hp	**Water tankage:**	15 gal.
B/D ratio:	40%	**Approx. trailering wgt.:**	7,500 lbs.

Yankee Yachts of Santa Ana, CA, engaged the eminent firm of Sparkman & Stephens to design for them a fast, attractive racer-cruiser, which the builder then produced from 1972 to 1975, at which time Yankee Yachts, saddled by a recession and rising oil prices, left the sailboat business. Heritage Yacht Company (1975–1982) acquired the tooling, and successor Heritage Boat Works of Hood River, Oregon, (1982–1990) continued production and sales until 1990. *Best features:*

The beamy S&S design is solid and commodious, with Space Index and headroom well above her comps. At the same time, PHRF at 234 is equal to or less than her comps, indicating a good turn of speed for this type of boat. No doubt her deep (4' 6") fixed keel and her relatively tall rig both contribute to her good performance. *Worst features:* Some owners report problems with severe gelcoat crazing, requiring extensive (and expensive) repair work to correct.

Comps	LOD	Beam	MinDr	Displ	Bllst	SA/D	D/L	Avg. PHRF	Max. Speed	Motion Index	Space Index	No. of Berths	Head- room
Walton 25	25' 3"	7' 3"	3' 10"	4,900	2,000	16.0	281	NA	6.0	24.9	392	4	5' 7"
Talman Katama 25	24' 8"	8' 0"	2' 6"	5,000	1,900	15.4	259	NA	6.1	22.1	363	4	4' 6"
Irwin 25	25' 3"	8' 0"	2' 8"	5,000	2,200	16.5	259	228	6.1	21.9	470	4 to 6	5' 9"
Yankee 26 (25)	24' 6"	8' 8"	4' 6"	5,335	2,150	15.4	270	234	6.1	20.7	534	4	6' 2"

Bombardier 7.6 (25)
A Canadian PHRF speedster from Ron Holland

LOD:	25' 4"	**Designer:**	Ron Holland
LOA:	26' 3"	**Builder:**	Bombardier Ltd., Canada
LWL:	22' 6"	**Years produced:**	1980–1983
Min./max. draft:	4' 6"	**Sail area:**	338 sq. ft.
Bridge clearance:	39' 0"	**Fuel tankage:**	portable
Power:	outboard 3 to 6 hp	**Water tankage:**	portable
B/D ratio:	30%	**Approx. trailering wgt.:**	4,900 lbs.

This fractional rig speedster with a PHRF handicap of 168 seems to be at least roughly in the same league as her comps, namely the Evelyn 25 (much lighter, considerably higher B/D ratio, and close to the same SA/D ratio, but should she be 21 seconds per mile faster than the Bombardier?); the Capri 25 (also lighter, but with a shorter waterline length, a shallower keel, and 3 seconds per mile slower on the PHRF scale); and the Olson 25 (a little lighter and beamier, but with a PHRF rating 9 seconds lower). Something like 163 Bombardier hulls were built. She sleeps five: two in a V-berth forward, two in a convertible dinette to port (with galley to starboard) and a quarter berth aft to starboard. ***Best features:*** She is quick and agile, and with her Ron Holland pedigree, she is apt to make the average around-the-buoys racer happy, while still serving the typical young sailing family as an overnight cruiser. ***Worst features:*** Her iron keel and thin hull may need more than the usual amount of maintenance to keep in first-class condition.

Comps	LOD	Beam	MinDr	Displ	Bllst	SA/D	D/L	Avg. PHRF	Max. Speed	Motion Index	Space Index	No. of Berths	Head- room
Evelyn 25	24' 11"	8' 10"	4' 5"	2,600	1,100	24.8	117	147	6.2	9.8	422	4	4' 6"
Capri 25	24' 7"	9' 2"	4' 2"	2,785	900	22.3	177	171	5.9	10.7	414	4	4' 6"
Olson 25	23' 7"	9' 0"	4' 6"	2,900	1,300	23.2	135	159	6.2	10.7	428	4	4' 8"
Bombardier 7.6 (25)	25' 4"	8' 6"	4' 6"	3,300	985	24.4	129	168	6.4	12.5	375	5	4' 6"

Contest 25 OC
A short-lived import from Holland

LOD:	24' 8"	**Designer:**	Jac de Ridder
LOA:	25' 0"	**Builder:**	Conyplex, Holland
LWL:	21' 5"	**Years produced:**	1982–1985
Min./max. draft:	4' 11"	**Sail area:**	306 sq. ft.
Bridge clearance:	38' 0"	**Fuel tankage:**	20 gal.
Power:	inboard Volvo Penta 7 hp	**Water tankage:**	26 gal.
B/D ratio:	40%	**Approx. trailering wgt.:**	5,600 lbs.

Conyplex, a builder in the Netherlands, began building the original Contest 25 designed by G. Luyten in 1959, and sales, totalling about 300 units, continued until 1969. A second version, designed by Dick Zaal, was introduced in 1974, and continued in production until 1980. In 1982 the Jac de Ridder design shown here, the Contest 25 OC (perhaps for "Offshore Cruiser"?) came along, but only about 30 were built before the U.S. small sailboat market evaporated in the recession of 1986. Conyplex is still in business today in Holland, but over the years since the 1980s has built only larger boats. ***Best features:*** The beam on the Contest is a foot wider than any of her comps, and her freeboard amidships is also relatively high, putting her Space Index above her comps. ***Worst features:*** The Contest's relatively deep draft (4' 11") and fixed fin limit her cruising ground to deep-water territory, and her high PHRF must have been a disappointment to prospective buyers.

Comps	LOD	Beam	MinDr	Displ	Bllst	SA/D	D/L	Avg. PHRF	Max. Speed	Motion Index	Space Index	No. of Berths	Head- room
U.S. 25/Triton 25 (24)	23' 6"	8' 0"	2' 8"	3,750	1,250	17.0	170	216	6.2	16.0	451	5	5' 6"
Contest 25 OC	24' 8"	9' 0"	4' 11"	3,788	1,510	20.1	172	264	6.2	13.9	528	4	5' 4"
Bremer 25	25' 0"	8' 0"	2' 6"	3,800	1,600	20.3	149	NA	6.4	15.7	509	2	6' 0"
Hunter 25 Mk I	24' 8"	8' 0"	2' 11"	3,850	1,800	11.7	210	222	6.0	17.1	440	5	5' 2"

Evelyn 25

High-tech lightweight from Formula Yachts

LOD:	24' 11"
LOA:	24' 11"
LWL:	21' 6"
Min./max. draft:	4' 5"
Bridge clearance:	34' 0"
Power:	outboard 3 to 6 hp
B/D ratio:	42%

Designer:	Bob Evelyn
Builder:	Formula Yachts
Years produced:	1985–1995
Sail area:	295 sq. ft.
Fuel tankage:	portable
Water tankage:	portable
Approx. trailering wgt.:	3,950 lbs.

This boat, built at designer-builder Bob Evelyn's high-tech facility in Groton, CT, was meant to be light. Like her three comp sisters, her D/L ratio doesn't fall low enough to be in the ultralight range (i.e., under 100), but she is lightest of the four, and also has the lightest weight, excluding ballast (1,500 lbs. versus the Olson's 1,600 lbs). Her hull, laid up by hand, uses a Divinycell core, unidirectional fiberglass, and carbon-fiber stiffening. Below she contains the usual V-berth forward and a pair of settee berths in the main cabin, along with a separate compartment for the head and a nav table that folds down from the main bulkhead. **Best features:** Hardware is top quality, including a keel-stepped mast from Hall Spars, Harken ball-bearing traveler, and dual-speed winches. **Worst features:** In 1985 the management at Formula Yachts predicted that the boat's PHRF rating would turn out to be in "the low 170s." Even after more than a decade of race course performance, the boat's performance has been in the range of 147—perhaps testifying to the owners' passion for racing.

Comps	LOD	Beam	MinDr	Displ	Bllst	SA/D	D/L	Avg. PHRF	Max. Speed	Motion Index	Space Index	No. of Berths	Head-room
Evelyn 25	24' 11"	8' 10"	4' 5"	2,600	1,100	24.8	117	147	6.2	9.8	422	4	4' 6"
Capri 25	24' 7"	9' 2"	4' 2"	2,785	900	22.3	177	171	5.9	10.7	414	4	4' 6"
Olson 25	23' 7"	9' 0"	4' 6"	2,900	1,300	23.2	135	159	6.2	10.7	428	4	4' 8"
Bombardier 7.6 (25)	25' 4"	8' 6"	4' 6"	3,300	985	24.4	129	168	6.4	12.5	375	5	4' 6"

New Moon 25

Eastsail's lower priced cruiser

LOD:	25' 0"
LOA:	25' 6"
LWL:	20' 10"
Min./max. draft:	3' 8"
Bridge clearance:	34' 0"
Power:	outboard 6 to 10 hp
B/D ratio:	34%

Designer:	Eliot Spaulding
Builder:	Eastsail Yachts
Years produced:	2006–present
Sail area:	355 sq. ft.
Fuel tankage:	portable
Water tankage:	50 gal.
Approx. trailering wgt.:	9,600 lbs.

The New Moon is offered by Eastsail Yachts of Bow, NH, as a more economical coastal cruising version of their Eastsail 25 (see page 340) designed for extended offshore cruising. As such, the vessel comes out of the same mold as the Eastsail 25, but a spoon bow replaces the clipper bow and bowsprit; she is sloop rather than cutter rigged (with a shorter main boom and shorter foot on the jib, but no change in masthead height), and is powered by a four stroke outboard gasoline engine housed under the lazarette hatch in a well, rather than by an inboard diesel under the cockpit. (A Mercury 9.9 hp four stroke is recommended; another good choice would be a Yamaha four stroke of the same horsepower.) Her cabin trim is also less spiffy, with reduced teak trim, giving her, in the words of her marketers, "a bright and airy interior . . . achieved by a combination of teak and white laminates styled in the Herreshoff theme." She also sports stainless hardware rather than more ornate bronze in some places. **Best features:** If you're looking for economy but would like some custom features (like adding a self-tending jib on a boom, for example), you might want to talk to Eastsail. **Worst features:** As in the offshore model, the cabin house appears to be high enough to obstruct a clear view from the helmsman's position when seated.

Comps	LOD	Beam	MinDr	Displ	Bllst	SA/D	D/L	Avg. PHRF	Max. Speed	Motion Index	Space Index	No. of Berths	Head-room
New Moon 25	25' 0"	8' 6"	3' 8"	6,800	2,300	15.8	336	NA	6.1	27.3	532	4	6' 0"
Eastsail 25	25' 0"	8' 6"	3' 8"	7,200	2,300	17.2	355	NA	6.1	27.2	532	5	6' 0"
Vertue II 25	25' 3"	7' 10"	4' 5"	9,220	4,400	14.2	414	NA	6.2	40.1	542	4	6' 2"
Fisher 25	24' 6"	9' 4"	3' 9"	10,000	4,500	7.2	482	NA	6.1	35.2	567	5	6' 0"

North Star 500 (25)
Quarter ton world champion in the early 1970s

LOD:	24' 6"	**Designer:**	Sparkman & Stephens
LOA:	24' 11"	**Builder:**	North Star Yachts Inc.
LWL:	13' 3"	**Years produced:**	1971–1973
Min./max. draft:	5' 0"	**Sail area:**	292 sq. ft.
Bridge clearance:	36' 0"	**Fuel tankage:**	8 gal.
Power:	inboard Atomic Four 25 hp	**Water tankage:**	13 gal.
B/D ratio:	40%	**Approx. trailering wgt.:**	6,400 lbs.

In 1969, U.S. Steel, anxious to take part in the boom in leisure market goods, bought Hughes Boatworks Ltd. of Centralia, Ontario, Canada, and began selling boats under the North Star Yachts brand name. In 1971, the company contracted with Sparkman & Stephens to design the North Star 500 (25) with the notion of competing in Quarter Ton races. The new design promptly won the quarter ton World Championship. However, production of the boat was discontinued in 1973, perhaps partly because she was a comparatively well built but expensive toy with a single purpose, namely to win quarter ton races. The recession of 1973–1974 also may have been a factor in her demise. ***Best features:*** She's a fast quarter tonner. ***Worst features:*** The North Star has the least headroom in her comp group, and the deepest draft, both of which limits her utility as a cruising boat. For example, one of her comps, the C&C 25 (page 326), which came out in 1972, has less draft, more headroom, and a lot more space below, and according to her PHRF rating, may be a faster boat.

Comps	LOD	Beam	MinDr	Displ	Bllst	SA/D	D/L	Avg. PHRF	Max. Speed	Motion Index	Space Index	No. of Berths	Head-room
Mark 25	24' 7"	9' 3"	3' 0"	4,130	1,779	20.3	230	216	6.0	15.3	495	4	5' 8"
South Coast Seacraft 25	25' 5"	8' 0"	3' 6"	4,200	1,800	19.1	218	231	6.1	18.4	379	5	5' 8"
C&C 25	24' 7"	8' 8"	3' 10"	4,250	1,880	18.2	215	222	6.1	16.5	555	4	5' 10"
North Star 500 (25)	24' 6"	9' 0"	5' 0"	4,300	1,710	17.7	231	228	6.0	16.3	472	4	4' 6"

South Coast Marine 25
A double ender with details left to the owner

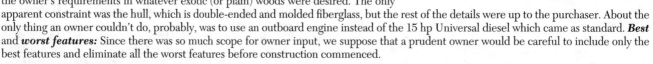

LOD:	25' 0"	**Designer:**	Phil Arnold
LOA:	31' 6"	**Builder:**	South Coast Marine
LWL:	21' 0"	**Years produced:**	1984?–1988?
Min./max. draft:	2' 6"/4' 0"	**Sail area:**	306 sq. ft.
Bridge clearance:	Varies	**Fuel tankage:**	NA
Power:	Universal diesel 15 hp	**Water tankage:**	NA
B/D ratio:	31%	**Approx. trailering wgt.:**	8,100 lbs.

Here is a boat that could be customized to owner's specifications in a major way: fixed keel or centerboard, gaff-rigged yawl or various other rigs, interior layout fitted to the owner's requirements in whatever exotic (or plain) woods were desired. The only apparent constraint was the hull, which is double-ended and molded fiberglass, but the rest of the details were up to the purchaser. About the only thing an owner couldn't do, probably, was to use an outboard engine instead of the 15 hp Universal diesel which came as standard. ***Best and worst features:*** Since there was so much scope for owner input, we suppose that a prudent owner would be careful to include only the best features and eliminate all the worst features before construction commenced.

Comps	LOD	Beam	MinDr	Displ	Bllst	SA/D	D/L	Avg. PHRF	Max. Speed	Motion Index	Space Index	No. of Berths	Head-room
Parker Dawson 26 (25)	25' 3"	8' 0"	1' 8"	5,700	1,250	13.6	234	NA	6.3	23.2	497	5	5' 10"
South Coast Marine 25	25' 0"	8' 0"	2' 6"	5,700	1,750	15.3	275	NA	6.1	22.7	411	2 to 4	5' 0"
Bristol Corsair 24 (25)	24' 7"	8' 0"	3' 5"	5,920	2,500	14.5	447	270	5.7	28.4	495	4	5' 11"
Cheoy Lee Flyer Mk III 25	25' 0"	7' 2"	3' 11"	6,000	2,240	14.7	335	297	5.9	30.6	386	4	5' 4"
New Horizons 25	25' 3"	7' 9"	3' 0"	6,030	1,600	15.6	281	225	6.2	26.8	465	4	5' 2"

Talman Katama 25

Does anybody else remember this boat?

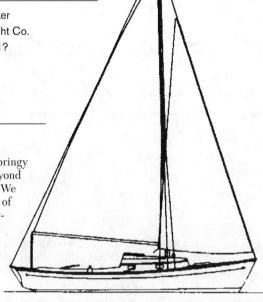

LOD:	24' 8"	Designer:	Robert Baker
LOA:	24' 8"	Builder:	Talman Yacht Co.
LWL:	20' 6"	Years produced:	1969–1971?
Min./max. draft:	2' 6"/5' 0"	Sail area:	282 sq. ft.
Bridge clearance:	32' 0"	Fuel tankage:	portable
Power:	6 to 10 hp	Water tankage:	portable
B/D ratio:	39%	Approx. trailering wgt.:	7,100 lbs.

Here is a light, handy centerboard boat that has lots going for it: nice profile, springy sheer, big cockpit, simple masthead rig with comfortable sail area . . . but beyond that, little trace remains in the annals of sailboats about the boat or its fate. We remember seeing one or two Katama specimens sailing around the western end of Long Island Sound in the early 1970s, but aside from a small ad in an old *Yachting* magazine, we know little else. Does anybody else remember this boat? ***Best features:*** She's a nice-looking boat with a good-sized cockpit big enough for a small party of, say, six mariners. ***Worst features:*** We don't have enough information to say anything negative, except to point out that her headroom isn't as good as that of any of her comps.

Comps	LOD	Beam	MinDr	Displ	Bllst	SA/D	D/L	Avg. PHRF	Max. Speed	Motion Index	Space Index	No. of Berths	Head-room
Walton 25	25' 3"	7' 3"	3' 10"	4,900	2,000	16.0	281	NA	6.0	24.9	392	4	5' 7"
Talman Katama 25	24' 8"	8' 0"	2' 6"	5,000	1,900	15.4	259	NA	6.1	22.1	363	4	4' 6"
Irwin 25	25' 3"	8' 0"	2' 8"	5,000	2,200	16.5	259	228	6.1	21.9	470	4 to 6	5' 9"
Yankee 26 (25)	24' 6"	8' 8"	4' 6"	5,335	2,150	15.4	270	234	6.1	20.7	534	4	6' 2"

EIGHT
What to Consider When Buying a Small Cruising Sailboat

Most cruising sailors are interested in boats that are, above all, lovely to look at (or at least cute), exhilarating to sail, and comfortable to live aboard (at least for a few nights at a time). Since different people have different tastes and different standards of comfort, beauty, and excitement, it follows that there can be no single "perfect" boat for everyone. Instead, each boat design is the result of many compromises, and this is particularly true of small cruising boats such as those in this guide. The designer of a pocket cruiser is asked, in effect, to pack three bushels of potatoes into a two-bushel container, and the ingenuity with which he/she does this has much to do with the boat's success.

Some sailboats in this volume are good cruisers but mediocre racers. Others do better at racing than cruising. Some have good comfort below but not on deck (or vice versa). Some are good for sailing in deep water but not shallow, or for long voyages but not brief day sails. In spite of these complications, for readers who can make informed choices, some of the stock fiberglass boats in this volume may be candidates to fulfill their dreams. Below are some criteria to help in formulating these choices.

CHECK PERFORMANCE IN VARIOUS CONDITIONS

How well will a particular design do in racing or cruising? For those planning to race in a specific geographic area, the best boat choice is likely to involve the types of boats that are already racing in that area—either one-design classes or cruising boats racing in PHRF. Most such boats will have LODs in the range of 18 feet and up. (Note how few of the boats in this book below the 18-foot range have been rated to race with PHRF fleets.) Sailors who could care less about racing can also check relative performance of various boats they are attracted to, by noting the comments on the reviews in this book, and by checking with any owners in local fleets.

LOOK AT SAILS AND RIG

If your local waters have light to moderate prevailing winds (e.g., in places like Long Island Sound, the breeze is often under 10 knots or so), boats with an SA/D ratio in the higher-than-average range (above 18 to 21) will do relatively well. So will boats with comparatively tall rigs.

Sailing in high-wind areas like San Francisco Bay is, of course, another matter—not that you can't sail a boat there if she has a high SA/D ratio; you'll just find it necessary to reef the main and use a smaller jib more often than you would in lighter winds.

How you plan to use your boat may affect your decision on what type of rig to favor. For example, a permanent backstay is usually preferable to just a headstay and a pair of aft-leading shrouds providing mast support. That three-stay arrangement limits forward movement of the main boom going downwind, and the shrouds are under more of a strain in hard conditions of wind and waves. On the other hand, a simple three-stay rig with no backstay makes rigging at a launching ramp easier and quicker, and permits a long main boom and/or a bigger mainsail roach.

At the other extreme, you'll the have the ultimate in belt-and-suspenders protection of the mast with a permanent backstay with forward, middle, and aft side shrouds as well as the usual forestay—eight wires in all (as typified by the South Coast 23 on page 255).

Here's another rigging issue: think twice about choosing a boat with the mainsheet led to the backstay rather than to a traveler bridging across the cockpit, or to a block and cam cleat fastened to the cockpit sole. The backstay arrangement is usually a lot less convenient to adjust. And a final note on rigging—you may want to consider the advantages of a yawl rig. They are outlined on page 116, in the write-up of the Nimble 20.

WHICH POWERPLANT: INBOARD OR OUTBOARD?

Sometimes a potential buyer will face a choice of either an inboard engine, a transom-hung outboard, or outboard in a well in the cockpit. There are a number of issues to consider here.

1. Maintenance is generally easier on an outboard, which can be easily removed and put on a test stand for best accessibility to all of its parts.

2. In general, inboards have the edge on quietness, smooth-running reliability, overall efficiency, fuel economy, and longevity, although there are exceptions.

3. If weight is an issue, outboards win hands-down over inboards. In most cases an outboard of the size appropriate for the boats listed here is light enough to be moved from transom or cockpit well to some deeper and more central point, while underway, to balance the boat better and increase speed under sail.

4. Propeller drag can be eliminated or minimized better with an outboard. It is also easier to clear weed, sea grass, and plastic bags from an outboard.

5. Cost, both when new and when being replaced, is far lower with an outboard.

6. Engine controls (throttle, choke, starter, etc.) are usually easier to reach on an inboard, though some outboards may have "cockpit control kits" that can be installed in the same location as inboard controls. And of course, outboards mounted in a cockpit well, or on the transom itself (such as on the Morgan 24/25, page 358) are easier to access than those mounted further aft on a transom bracket.

7. Fuel tankage is generally permanently installed for inboard engines and portable for outboards. That makes outboard tanks easier to fill from a gas station far from the water. On the other hand, portable tanks may clutter up the cockpit if there is no designated out-of-the-way area to stow them.

8. If an outboard engine is substituted, the space taken by an inboard engine, usually installed aft of the companionway ladder under the cockpit, can often be better utilized by making it possible to enlarge galley space.

9. The prop shaft of an inboard is generally tucked well under the hull, and consequently is seldom exposed to the air even in high, cresting seas. That avoids cavitation, loss of traction of the prop, and undesirable revving of the engine. Outboard propellers, especially those located far aft of the transom on brackets, often fall victim to cavitation in waves—or even, if the boat is small enough, when a crew member walks forward, for example, to stand by the anchor, sinking the bow and lifting the stern.

10. Steering in tight quarters, such as when maneuvering at a slip, is usually easier with an inboard, as the prop is generally positioned just forward of the rudder, and can be used to "kick" the stern to starboard or port with a short burst of power, using the rudder to redirect the prop wash to one side or the other. On the other hand, some outboards (though by no means all) are mounted so that they can be rotated 360 degrees, providing prop thrust in any direction the skipper desires. But to take advantage of this feature, the engine attachment, whether on a transom-mounted bracket, rudder-mounted (as on the Sea Pearl 21, page 136), or side-mounted (as on the Dovekie 21, page 96) must be very sturdy and solidly attached to the hull. It must also be located so that the engine head and its steering handle won't be limited in movement by surrounding impediments such as the rudder, tiller, or deck contours. The plans of the South Coast 23 (page 255) show an outboard that can't be fully rotated. The builder received complaints about this, and on later boats a notch was molded into the port side cockpit seat to enable 360-degree engine rotation.

WHEEL OR TILLER?

Catboats aren't the only small craft that occasionally sport wheels. Some pros and cons are:

1. You can lift up the tiller to a vertical position when in port or on the hook, giving more space in the cockpit.

2. Underway, however, a tiller generally takes up more space in the cockpit, especially when it is swept back and forth during a series of quick tacks. By contrast, the helmsman may sit or stand back aft behind a wheel, out of the way, during tacking maneuvers.

3. Some helmsmen find they get stiff necks facing left and then right for long stints of steering with a tiller. Positioned behind a wheel, however, the helmsman can comfortably look straight toward the bow as well as to either side.

4. The tiller is mechanically simpler than a wheel, so with a tiller you worry less about maintenance.

5. With a tiller, you can more readily feel the balance of a boat under sail (e.g., weather or lee helm), so you can sail the boat more efficiently.

6. With a tiller extension, you can sit up high on the coaming to steer, allowing you to more easily see the trim of the sails and the water ahead.

7. A wheel provides more mechanical advantage than a tiller when the helm is not balanced.

8. When underway, it's much easier to lock a wheel into a given position using a brake than to lock a tiller.

9. When at anchor in rough weather, you must make sure to secure the tiller with lines to the coamings or it'll bang back and forth. With a wheel, you can use the brake, if so equipped.

10. The position of a wheel may make it awkward to get to and from the helmsman's seat, as when crew is replaced at the helm.

11. A wheel with a binnacle makes steering to a compass course (or a GPS course if the instrument cluster is so equipped) much easier than with a tiller.

HULL SHAPE: BEAMY OR NARROW?

In general, a long narrow boat is faster and easier to steer than a short fat boat. The Wabbit 24 (23) (page 260), with a beam of 5' 7", is a good example of long and narrow. Less beam requires a deep keel with considerable ballast at the bottom—or equivalent weight elsewhere, such as "rail meat" in the form of heavy crew hanging off the side of the boat—to keep from excessive heeling (or even capsizing).

At the other end of the beamy-narrow spectrum is the Cape Cod Catboat hull form, originally devised so fishermen could haul in their nets from the sides or stern of the boat without causing excessive heel. The wide bilges provide good "form stability," but sacrifice balanced steering when the wind blows hard under full sail. In high winds with a short, steep chop and insufficient power (such as might be typical with a reefed main and an outboard engine), a catboat's blunt bow may fail to punch through the waves, forcing the helmsman to turn away from the wind rather than into it, when tacking.

The single big sail of a catboat may also cause a severe weather helm when beating or reaching in heavy air, requiring a reef in the main to relieve the strain on the helmsman's arm. That's one reason you see wheels in place of tillers on some small cats.

Beamy boats, as a rule, have more spacious cockpits and cabins than do narrow ones. For more on this see "Crew Space and Crew Comfort."

HULL SHAPE: DEEP OR SHALLOW DRAFT?

Under every sailboat is a structure to prevent sideslip under sail. The structure can vary in depth from a fraction of an inch to several feet. The choice is yours: shallow fixed keel, deep fixed keel, swing keel, centerboard, lifting keel, twin bilge keels, or twin bilge boards or leeboards.

Each choice comes with some negatives. A deep fixed keel is not designed for easy launching and retrieving of a boat on a trailer, and won't serve well in shoal cruising areas. A shallow fixed keel may be better for shoal areas but is likely to provide poor upwind sailing performance. A heavy swing keel, even if housed below the cabin sole, can bind in its trunk, needs a device (typically a winch) for raising and lowering, and can be a maintenance headache.

A centerboard trunk that intrudes into the cabin space can be a source of annoyance when moving around the cabin. If the trunk is open on top, slop may splash up and soak the cabin sole, especially when underway. (The solution to this, obviously, is to devise a slop-proof centerboard trunk cap.) Generally, centerboarders have ballast placed higher in the hull, and ballast lodged within the board itself isn't usually heavy enough to help stabilize the hull to any great extent. Both centerboards and swing keels pivot up and down on pins that also may wear and need maintenance. And stones, sand, and even seaweed can jam inside the trunks of both centerboards and swing keels, immobilizing them, usually when in the "up" position.

Lifting keels, which slide up and down in a trunk rather than pivoting fore and aft, are usually operated from an inconvenient position away from the cockpit, such as inside the cabin or on the cabin roof next to the mast. And the sheer weight of lifting keels and swing keels, which are usually heavier than one person can lift, make maintenance such as cleaning and painting more difficult. Twin bilge keels and twin bilge boards or leeboards contribute less stability because their ballast is typically located higher than fin or swing keels. Except for hinged leeboards, they also have the added wetted surface, and consequent drag, of two blades rather than one blade beneath the water.

Each choice comes with some positives, too. Deep fin keels are best of all in terms of efficient sailing upwind and greatest hull stability. Shallow fins, while less efficient, permit gunkholing (maneuvering in shallow water).

All of the designs equipped with pivoting or sliding blades naturally make launching and hauling at a ramp easier than fixed fins do. A centerboard is usually easy to raise and lower, and can be useful in balancing the rig for efficient sailing. Going downwind, the board can be raised all the way or almost all the way, cutting resistance and increasing speed.

Swing keels (which often have only two positions, full up and full down) provide better stability than centerboards because of their deeper center of ballast.

Lifting keels keep weight better centered between bow and stern, and can often concentrate the weight lower, compared to swing keels.

Bilge keels provide a stable base for a sailboat hull to settle into when aground at low tide, and consequently are popular in Europe, where tides can rise and fall far enough to leave harbors totally drained of water. At low tide the boats just "lie on the hard."

Bilge boards, such as those on the Bay Hen 21 (page 85) fold into side spaces in the hull, leaving the center of the cabin open for moving around.

Leeboards, as seen, for example, on the Dovekie 21 (page 96), are attached with hinges and pivots on the outside of the hull, freeing up even more cabin space for other uses. Leeboards, as opposed to bilge keels and bilge boards, limit the blade's wetted surface mostly to the leeward blade, since the weather blade is designed to flop out and up, and skims along the surface of the water.

HULL SHAPE: FREEBOARD HIGH OR LOW?

Low freeboard is desirable for those who want to board from a dinghy alongside or from a low slip or pier, or for swimmers boarding from the water. Fishermen trying to net a catch find low freeboard an asset. Low freeboard also helps to reduce windage, which can make steering more difficult, especially when the boat is moving slowly as when pulling into a slip. On the other hand, boats with low freeboard may limit headroom as well as elbow room in the cabin. High freeboard, of course, results in the opposite of these consequences. Designer Howard Chapelle wrote in 1936 that "many modern yachts have excessive height of side, many yachtsmen and some designers labor under the delusion that high freeboard is desirable in a seagoing yacht. However, the windage and weight of excessively high topsides are actually a grave handicap, producing a sluggish sailor and, usually, a wet boat."

Chapelle also makes the point that "great freeboard has the tendency to make the hull appear short and chunky and this is not conducive to grace and beauty in hull design."

Chapelle's observations on freeboard are still valid more than 70 years after they were written.

HULL SHAPE: OUTBOARD RUDDER OR UNDERHUNG RUDDER?

On the small boats in this volume, an outboard rudder has several advantages. A rudder hung on open hinges—so-called pintles and gudgeons—can easily be removed for maintenance, or for trailer traveling to minimize chance of damage on the road. At sea, it's easy to look over the transom to see if the outboard rudder has picked up any weed or other flotsam. And it's easy to pull or flip up an outboard rudder equipped with appropriate hinges when beaching the boat for lunch or a swim.

On the other hand, the prop on a transom-hung outboard engine may interfere with (and even chew up) an outboard rudder pushed hard over unless the engine is sufficiently offset from the vessel's centerline.

CREW SPACE AND CREW COMFORT: COCKPITS

The division between space in the cockpit and space down below is determined largely by the location of the aft cabin bulkhead, at least on aft-cockpit boats. A good example of a relatively small-cockpit big-cabin is on the Vertue II 25 (page 373); the footwell in the cockpit is less than three feet long. Long distance ocean cruisers are often fitted with small cockpits so a rogue wave won't swamp the cockpit with too much weight, and so it will drain away fast. But a Vertue cockpit is no place to hold a beer party for a dozen of your closest friends.

Sometimes comfortable cockpits with good back support are so deep that the cockpit sole is at or near the boat's waterline, as on, for instance, the Pearson Ensign 22 (page 191). If cockpit drains (that is, "scuppers") were installed in an attempt to make the cockpit self-bailing, the water would drain into the cockpit instead of out of it. On some boats with the cockpit sole only slightly above the waterline, rainwater will drain out when the boat is at her mooring, but may drain in when under sail and heeled. Sometimes the scupper hoses can be re-led to avoid this problem, but not always.

Too little back support, such as on the J/24 (page 294) can be tiring on a cruise, especially for people in middle age or beyond, when back problems often start to surface.

A bridge deck between cockpit and companionway is a good safety measure, acting as a dam in stormy weather to keep water from inundating the cabin. The South Coast 23 (page 255) and the Allegra 24 (page 267) are examples of boats with wide bridge decks. The Santana 2023 (22) (page 199) and the S2 6.8 (page 195) are examples of vessels with narrow bridge decks. A wide bridge deck holds more plates and cans when the cook serves lunch to the cockpit crew and is more comfortable as a place to sit, or even lie down athwartships in the cockpit.

If maximum privacy is desired, a center cockpit with an aft cabin as well as a forward cabin, such as the Parker Dawson 26 (25) (page 364) may be the answer. Note two heads in that vessel, unusual in a 25-footer.

CREW SPACE AND CREW COMFORT: CABINS

Boat salesmen often emphasize the number of berths, usually between two and six in the 14- to 25-foot size range. They say: the more the merrier. But in reality, the fewer the berths, the more space for stowage and elbow room. Most of the boats in this volume are four-sleepers, with a V-berth forward and two settee berths or quarter berths aft. But even then a family of four may have problems with comfort. Berths should not be less than 6' 2" long nor less than 21" average width. And headroom over berths should be at least 21". Unfortunately, many of the boats reported in this guide fail to meet these standards. How important that is to the sailor depends to some extent on individual body size and shape. But few V-berths on any boat qualify as comfortable for a pair of average-sized adults.

Enclosed heads are rare in the 14- to 25-foot size range, though some are reported here. For example, the Beneteau First 26 (25) (page 323) has a particularly spacious installation but unfortunately it falls short on standing headroom—a very common shortcoming of most of the boats reported here.

Today, the legal choice is either a permanent toilet with a holding tank and pump-out system, or a portable toilet, known as a porta-pottie. Porta-potties were introduced in the 1960s, but the early designs were smelly and awkward to empty, and sailboats typically were sold with permanent flow-through toilets until the 1970s, when federal anti-pollution laws were enacted. The advantage of a porta-potti is that it can often be stowed in some out-of-the-way location (such as under the cockpit), and slid out for use in the cabin (or even in the cockpit, if the boat is anchored in a secluded place and the crew doesn't mind). That leaves more elbow room down below for other activities, like cooking and eating dinner.

A permanent head is the choice among "big boat" cruisers, for convenience and comfort. But big boats can carry big holding tanks without sacrificing much relative space and without having to consider the extra weight involved. Thetford, a large, long-time manufacturer of marine toilets and Porta-Pottis (their trade name), may be able to advise interested readers on further particulars. On the Internet, go to www.thetford.com.

Sailboat galleys for the boats in this volume tend to be located near the companionway ladder, where air circulation can carry away cooking odors; there's often standing headroom (at least with the main hatch open) and the cook can be part of the conversation going on in the cockpit. Galleys tend to be L-shaped, U-shaped, or I-shaped, and individual cooks may have a personal preference of one arrangement over another. We can think of no overwhelming reason why one shape should be better than another. But in every case, a well-equipped galley should include a two-burner stove, a stainless steel sink (molded fiberglass will eventually lose its smoothness), and an icebox, either built in or portable.

In boats in the 25-foot or less range, the dining area, if present at all, tends to contain either a dinette or a saloon table.

Some prefer the dinette arrangement, in which the table is generally removable for cleaning and can be stored on a quarter berth or wherever space is available. A dinette table very often can be lowered to become the base for a comfortable (or narrow and less comfortable) double berth. Our preference is for a dinette arrangement because the table can typically double as a chart table or as an extension of a galley counter. Also, dinettes usually permit the crew to pass unobstructed through the saloon area without dismantling the furniture.

Others may prefer the less cluttered look of a centrally located saloon table. Designs vary, from one setup using folding leaves on a centerboard trunk (see Beachcomber 25 on page 322), to one with the table normally stowed on the main bulkhead and folded aft and down for use (see Helms 24 on page 293), or mounted centrally on one or more legs (see Beneteau First 26 on page 323).

All cabin tables should be edged with fiddles to prevent contents from sliding or rolling off the edge when the boat is heeled.

IT'S YOUR MOVE

The above choices are only a few among all the decisions that need to be made (or ignored) before deciding on your best boat.

One choice we haven't discussed here is style. As mentioned in the Introduction, there are an incredible number of individual types of vessels—with style sleek or tubby, traditional or modern, and sometimes just plain weird. Some sailors could care less about style. But if there is something to be said for the phrases "clothes make the man" or "by his books shall ye know him," or "by his fruits shall ye know him," then there may be something to the idea that "by his boat shall ye know him."

So, when choosing the best boat to fit your needs, have a care. Just maybe, by your boat shall they know you.

NINE
One Hundred Choices for the Best Small Cruiser

Fifteen Cruisers for a Family of Four

Montgomery 17* (46)
Com-Pac 19 (27)
Jeanneau Bahia 23 (20)* (106)
O'Day 22 (21) (118)
Jeanneau Tonic 23 (22) (180)
Precision 23 (245)
Dolphin 24 (O'Day) (285)
Freedom 25 (24) (291)
Seaward 25 (24) (310)
Irwin 10/4 (25) (347)
Cal 25 Mk I (327)
Catalina 25 (332)
Beneteau First 26 (25) (323)
Ericson 25 Mk I (341)
O'Day 26 (25) (362)

Fifteen Cruisers for Around-the-Buoys Racing

Capri 18 (25)
Cal 20 (89)
Santana 20 (131)
Ranger 22 (21) (124)
J/22 (179)
Catalina 22 Mk I (157)
Santana 22 (198)
Tanzer 22 (23) (259)
Blazer 23 (221)
J/24 (294)
Olson 25 (24) (301)
Shark 24 (312)
Morgan 24 (25) (358)
Montego 25 (357)
Capri 25 (331)

Fourteen Cruisers for Easy Ramp-Launching and Trailering

Peep Hen 14 (51)
West Wight Potter 15* (64)
Com-Pac Legacy 17 (69)
Montgomery 17* (46)
Precision 18 (17) (55)
West Wight Potter 19* (65)
Alerion Express Cat 19* (20)
ETAP 20 (98)
Jeanneau Bahia 23 (20)* (106)
Santana 21 (132)
S2 6.9 (21) (128)
Dehler 22* (167)
Sirius 22* (139)
Terrapin 24 (371)

Thirteen Single-Masted Character Boats

Marshall Sanderling 18 (40)
Blue Water Blackwatch 19 (21)
Menger 19 (43)
Skipper 20 (18) (57)
Bay Hen 21 (85)
Falmouth Cutter 22 (170)
Bluejacket Motorsailer 23 (222)
Stone Horse 23 (258)
Eastward Ho 24 (288)
Nimble 24/25 (361)
La Paz 25 (353)
Newman Friendship Sloop 25 (360)
Parker Dawson 26 (25) (364)

Thirteen Cruisers for a Couple

Corinthian 19 (20) (95)
Sirius 22* (139)
Beneteau First 235 (22) (152)
Ranger 23 (22) (193)
Nonsuch 22 (185)
Bayfield 23/25 (23) (220)
Capri 26 (24) (282)
Pearson Lark 24 (305)
Quickstep 24 (306)
Elite 25 (24) (289)
C&C 25 (326)
Cape Dory 25D (330)
Com-Pac 25 (336)

Twelve Bluewater Cruisers

West Wight Potter 15* (64)
Cape Dory Typhoon 18 (19) (23)
West Wight Potter 19* (65)
Golif 21 (99)
Freedom 21 (22) (171)
Allegra 24 (267)
Blue Water 24 (274)
Pacific Seacraft Dana 24 (303)
Vancouver 25 (372)
Vertue II 25 (373)
Contessa 26 (25) (337)
Cheoy Lee Flyer III (25) (334)

Thirteen High-End Cruisers

Cornish Crabber 17 (31)
Alerion Express Cat 19* (20)
Cornish Shrimper 19 (32)
Pacific Seacraft Flicka 20 (120)
Cornish Crabber 22 (164)
Dehler 22* (167)
ETAP 23 (22) (169)
Herreshoff Prudence 23 (233)
Dehler 25 (23) (227)
Bridges Point 24 (275)
Cornish Crabber 24 (284)
Eastsail 25 (340)
New Moon 25 (379)

Twelve Two-Masted Character Boats

Nimble 20 (21) (116)
Parker Dawson Poacher 21 (121)
Sea Pearl 21 (136)
Menger Oysterman 23 (237)
Rob Roy 23 (246)
South Coast Seacraft 23 (368)
Bahama Sandpiper 24 (272)
Sand Hen 24 (308)
Beachcomber 25 (322)
Nimble 24/25 (361)
Fisher 25 (343)
South Coast Marine 25 (380)

* = Seven boats appear in above lists twice.

Listed on the opposite page are one hundred choices for the "Best Small Cruiser." There are, of course, many more than one hundred choices for the "best" small cruising sailboat. In fact, there are 360 choices reported in this guide alone, and at least a few boats beyond those, on which we failed to find sufficient data to include here. In any case, as the saying goes, one man's meat is another man's poison. That is, a sailboat that one person does not like at all can be one that someone else likes very much.

One of the main reasons for this is that different boats are designed for different purposes: boats best for cruising in shallow bay waters versus deep ocean waters, for example. Styles vary to suit different tastes: traditional versus modern design, for example. Boats that do well in around-the-buoy racing may not be so well suited to cruising. A boat built to the highest standards of quality may not suit the pocketbook of the casual weekend trailer-sailor. And the range of choices goes on and on.

To help narrow the field of choices for the reader who is eager to find the right boat to buy, and doesn't have the patience to wade through all the facts and figures on all 360 boats presented in this guide, we have (somewhat arbitrarily) devised a hundred choices, broken into groups of a dozen or so. Are you looking for a single-masted character boat? We list thirteen of them here, from 18 to 25 feet on deck. Do you yen for a two-masted yawl or ketch? We list every one of the dozen covered in this guide. Do you prefer a custom-built boat or at least very high quality construction? We show thirteen "high-end" choices, though you could find others in these pages. We also list fifteen good cruising boats for a family of four, and another thirteen for a cruising couple without children or guests aboard. We choose fifteen round-the-buoys racers for your consideration, and a dozen blue water cruisers, including a 15-footer that has sailed from California to Hawaii (though some may not agree that such a feat qualifies such a boat for offshore work).

Although there isn't space to include photos of every boat in this book, or even the one-hundred choices listed as "best," we have dug up representative sample photos from our vast collection of boat sales brochures to include on the following pages. They are arranged in roughly alphabetical order. If you don't find a picture of the boat you're interested in, try searching Google. There's a huge cache of photos there.

Alerion Express Cat 19 (details on page 20) is a high-end cruiser designed, among other things, for easy trailering and ramp launching.

Bay Hen 21 (page 85) is a character boat that's easy to launch and trailer.

Beneteau First 235 (22) (page 152) is a good boat for a cruising couple.

Beneteau First 26 (25) (page 323) will nicely accommodate a family of four for cruising.

Blazer 23 (page 221) is a competitive racer. The author (trimming jib) is sailing here with other writers John Rousmaniere (steering) and Freeman Pittman, tech editor at *Sail* magazine.

Bluejacket Motorsailer 23 (page 222) is a character boat with great comfort for cruising two.

Bluejacket Motorsailer 23 interior (also see to left) is particularly comfortable when cruising in rainy weather.

Bridges Point 24 (page 275) is available either as a finished boat or a kit.

Cal 20 (page 89), produced from 1961 to 1977, is still raced in several fleets around the country.

Cape Dory Typhoon 18 (19) (page 23) has enough ballast to stand up well in a blow.

Cape Dory 25D (page 330) comes close to being the ideal trailerable cruising boat.

Capri 26 (24) (page 282) features a cabin big enough to "drink ten."

Capri 18 (page 25) was introduced in 1985 and is still being sold today.

Cheoy Lee Flyer III (25) (page 334) has a Folkboat style hull.

Catalina 22 Mk I (page 157) wins the all-time popularity prize for cruising boats.

Catalina 25 (page 332) came in a great variety of configurations.

Com-Pac 25 (page 336) has an unusual volume of interior space for her length.

Com-Pac 19 (page 27) was drawn by Island Packet designer Bob Johnson.

Cornish Crabber 17 (page 31) is elegantly finished on deck and below.

Cornish Crabber 22 (page 164) sports a gaff cutter rig.

Cornish Crabber 24 (page 284) is a well-built gaff-rigged character boat.

Cornish Shrimper 19 (page 32), a character boat, has an elegant finish, but is short on headroom.

Dehler 22 (page 167) has a number of high quality features.

Dehler 22 (page 167) has a dolly, a.k.a. "floating slipway trolley," that is an unusual aid for launching from ramps and tidal flats.

Dehler 25 (23) (page 227) also uses a "slipway trolley."

Dolphin 24 (O'Day) (page 285) was available either as a kit or as a finished boat.

Elite 25 (24) (page 289) is fitted out in France, and features the French style of careful interior design.

Eastsail 25 (page 340) is generally built to a customer's specifications with extended offshore cruising in mind.

ETAP 20 (page 98) is built to a high standard of quality and is unsinkable.

ETAP 23 (22) (page 169) like other ETAP boats, she is double-skinned in a foam sandwich for flotation.

Fisher 25 (page 343) provides a cozy cabin and inside steering station for inclement weather.

Freedom 25 (24) (page 291) has a full-battened mainsail and "gunmount" spinnaker handling gear.

Freedom 21 (22) (page 171) has a patented "gunmount" for handling a spinnaker.

Golif 21 (page 99) from France has an unusual cabin ventilation system.

J/22 (page 179) has many active one-design fleets.

Irwin 10/4 (25) (page 347), as the saying goes, can drink ten, eat six, and sleep four.

J/24 (page 294) is said to be the world's most popular one-design keelboat.

J/24 (page 294) a second view.

Jeanneau Bahia 23 (20) (page 106) features a clever cabin table design.

La Paz 25 (page 353) features an open cockpit for deck chairs and berths for six below.

Menger Oysterman 23 (page 237) is a character boat based on the Chesapeake Bay Skipjack.

Montgomery 15 (page 71) and **Montgomery 17** (page 46) both have molded lapstrake hulls.

Marshall Sanderling 18 (page 40) has been in production for almost fifty years, and continues to be popular.

Morgan 24/25 (25) (page 358) is fast and weatherly, especially in light air.

Newman Friendship Sloop 25 (page 360) conjures romantic memories of Maine fishermen.

Nimble 24/25 (25) (page 361) was produced in several configurations, including both a sloop and a yawl rig.

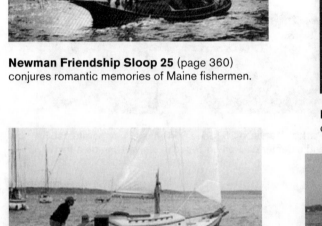

New Moon 25 (page 379) can be fitted out to the customer's specifications.

Nimble 24/25 (25) (page 361) is available as a pilothouse with six feet of headroom, great for cold weather cruising.

Nimble 20 (21) (page 116) features a yawl rig, rare in a boat so small.

Nonsuch 22 (page 185) was designed with the idea of elegant simplicity.

O'Day 26 (25) (page 362) is a near sistership to the O'Day 25.

Parker Dawson 26 (page 364) has two separate cabins, and a center cockpit enclosed in canvas can be a third.

Pacific Seacraft Flicka 20 (page 120) is generally considered a very high quality product, commanding a premium price in the used boat market.

Pearson Lark 24 (page 305) has a flush deck for maximum volume below.

Pacific Seacraft Dana 24 (page 303) is solidly built to cruise in a bay or an ocean.

Quickstep 24 (page 306) was built by several firms, giving a choice of several accommodations plans.

Rob Roy 23 (page 246) has the makings of a classic small yacht.

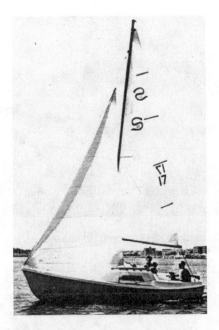

Santana 21 (page 132), with a D/L ratio of only 86, is classified as an ultralight.

Sand Hen 24 (page 308), with lightweight spars and no shrouds, should be easy to trailer and launch.

Santana 22 (page 198), an ageless design, is still popular after over 40 years.

Santana 20 (page 131) was a very early entry in the "sport boat" market and is still popular.

Sea Pearl 21 (page 136) is simple, light, and shallow draft, perfect for casual beach cruising.

Seaward 25 (24) (page 310) has a sleek and salty look and is well built.

Shark 24 (page 312) has done well in racing over the years.

Sirius 22 (21) (page 139) is roomy for her length.

South Coast 23 (page 255) was converted to a yawl from a sloop (see photo bottom left).

South Coast 23 (page 255) shown here was built from a kit.

Stone Horse 23 (page 258) is a classic designed over 75 years ago.

Tanzer 22 (23) (page 259) has a strong class association that promotes both one-design racing and cruising get-togethers (two views, left and right).

Vertue II 25 (page 373) is a no-nonsense heavy cruiser made for ocean passages.

Terrapin 24 (25) (page 371) is, like her namesake, slow but comfortable.

Vancouver 25 (page 372) is well equipped for extended cruising.

West Wight Potter 15 (page 64) has made some long distance cruises, including one from California to Hawaii.

West Wight Potter 19 (page 65) is still selling well after over thirty years of production.

TEN
Author's Gallery of Photos

I have been writing and illustrating most of my life. At age nine, in 1943, I traded a pencil drawing I had done of a World War II B-17 bomber to a third grade classmate for a die-cast toy boat, my first commercial transaction. In 1946, at age twelve, I won first prize in a state-wide Scholastic Arts contest for a pen-and-ink drawing. I went to college, trained as a mechanical engineer, found a job, and at night got an MBA.

My writing and drawing activities were almost exclusively extracurricular between 1955 and 1981, while I held day jobs at big corporations in Manhattan. However, in my spare time during this period, I wrote and illustrated a best-selling how-to book about bicycles titled *Bikes*.

During the same period, I developed, together with my wife Carol (the other half of the "we" in this book), a love for boats and sailing. Together in 1956 we bought our first boat, an eight-foot sailing dinghy, but soon tired of car-topping the boat to go sailing on the few navigable bodies of water in our area. Eventually we moved to Darien, Connecticut, on Long Island Sound, and began to devote more and more time to sailing.

In 1984, two partners and I launched *Sailor* magazine, a national bi-weekly periodical, concentrating on meaty stories about sailing people, boats, and gear. Besides being general manager of the enterprise, I also did considerable writing, some photography, and artwork. When *Sailor* ceased publication in 1986, I continued pursuing that career as a writer and illustrator of articles and books about yachting. Among my clients, for several of whom I became a contributing editor, were *Yachting* magazine

(where for a time I wrote the *Gadgets & Gilhickies* column as well as boat reviews); *Yacht Racing/Cruising* (now *Sailing World*), for which I did an illustrated column called Interesting Boats; *Sail* magazine; *Small Boat Journal*; *Motorboat* magazine; and *Woodenboat* magazine. My work has also appeared in *Video* magazine, *Oceans* magazine, *Boating Digest*, *Nautical Quarterly*, and other publications.

After we moved to Florida in 1991, I continued to write for *Practical Sailor, Powerboat Reports,* and a few other selected publications. I also wrote two more books, *Boating for Less* in 1987 and *Boat Trailers and Tow Vehicles* in 1991, both published by International Marine/McGraw-Hill.

We have owned a variety of boats, some thirty two in all, including (mainly for the kids) a Flipper, an Optimist, a Laser, a Laser II, two Blue Jays, two Fireballs, an International 420, and a variety of other small dinghies. Powerboats have included an over-powered 17-foot Boston Whaler and an old but still serviceable 22-foot Aquasport. Our cruising sailboats started with a 17-foot Picnic, which we found in a dump behind a bankrupt manufacturer and resuscitated, and continued with (in chronological order) a South Coast 23 designed by the eminent Carl Alberg (built from a kit), a Tartan 27 (maybe to be described in more detail in the next volume in this series?), a J/24 so we could participate more actively in round-the-buoys racing, a Hermann 17-foot catboat (when we became empty-nesters after the kids left us), and finally, a Morgan 24, after we moved to Sarasota County, on the Gulf Coast of Florida. See the following pages for more photos of our boating experiences.

Above: Our 1963 Picnic 17, soon after we brought her home from a dump. In this shot, I ponder the job ahead. It turned out that getting the deck to match up with the hull was a major problem.
Left: Our 1983 J/24, #3333, brand new and ready to be towed home.

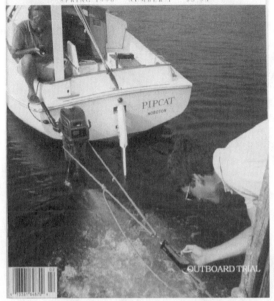

Author's boat *Pipcat* is the "cover girl" on the premier (and only) issue of a magazine tested by the folks at Taunton Press, publishers of *Fine Woodworking* magazine. Author's article was on outboard engine thrust.

Author's wife singlehands *Pipcat* on Long Island Sound.

Pipcat at anchor on a cruise. She is a 17-foot Hermann Cat, forerunner of the Cape Cod Cat 17. See page 22 for details.

Author sails a Menger Cat 17 with Bill Menger. A Marshall Sanderling 18 and a Molly Cat follow along in her wake. The occasion was a "Catboat Rendezvous" for a story written by the author that appeared in *Small Boat Journal* in July, 1988.

This Morgan 24/25 *Pipit*, owned by the author, was used as a "test platform" for analyzing sailing gear in *Practical Sailor*, a kind of *Consumer Reports* newsletter for sailors.

Author and wife aboard *Pipit*, cruising the Intracoastal Waterway in southwest Florida. For more on the Morgan 24/25 (25), see page 358.

Carol Henkel skippers a Nimble 24 yawl in a photoshoot for *Sail* magazine while the author (her husband) takes pictures.

Another shot of the Nimble 24 yawl, fitted out in the so-called tropical version.

The pilothouse version of the Nimble 24/25. See page 361 for details.

The author's J/24, *SuperPip3,* at her home pier.

Another shot of the *SuperPip3* getting ready to race in 1984. For more information, see page 294.

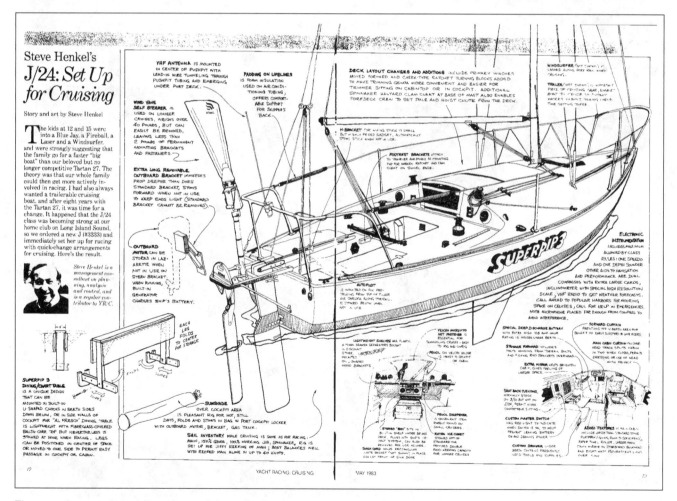

The same boat as the subject of one of the author's magazine columns, this one called "BOAT CLOSE-UP," which appeared in *Yacht Racing/Cruising* magazine in the May, 1983 issue.

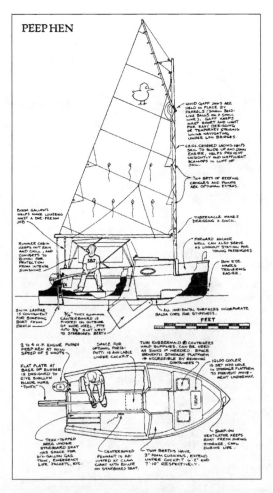

A sketch of the Peep Hen 14 for an article by the author, which appeared in the *Small Boat Journal* of June–July 1989.

Author tests a Peep Hen 14 in Miami in connection with the same article in *Small Boat Journal*.

The author testing the Peep Hen 14 for beachability. See page 51 for details.

Boat Check
Olson 25

Starting in 1970 with *Grendel*, a 24-foot ultra-light one-off that shook up the West Coast racing scene, George Olson has designed and built boats that are very light, very fast and very strong. The Olson 25 is the most recent addition to a successful line of ultra-light displacement racer/"cruisers" consisting of the popular Olson 30 (about 240 sold) and the Olson 40 (about 29 sold since introduction in September, 1982). The 25, however, is a departure from the thoroughbred ULDB approach that personifies its smokin' siblings.

"The 25 is not an ultra-light," says Bill McMurray, sales manager of Santa Cruz, California based Pacific Boats. "She's definitely light, but she's more of a dual purpose boat. It's a bit of a departure for us, but the MORC rule is becoming more and more popular on the West Coast. This boat is geared toward MORC, although it's not a hard-line approach."

A displacement to length ratio of 120.9 compared to the Olson 30's ratio of 77.3 backs up the thesis. "The 25 will be fast but pleasant to sail, says McMurray. "A few people have been a bit intimidated by the performance of the 30 and the 40 when it blows. The 25 will be more manageable."

The boat carries a masthead rig, which is encouraged by the MORC rule, but McMurray adds, "We're also exploring a fractional rig during the prototype stage. Recent rule changes in MORC mean the fractional rig is not as penalized. We're masthead believers, but we don't want to leave any stone unturned."

Highlights
● Interior has sleeping accommodations for four and comfortable seating for six, made possible by a clever arrangement where sections of the quarter bunks fold up as seat backs.
● Interior includes double-burner gimballed stove, sink w/pump, igloo cooler, portable toilet and privacy curtain.
● Hull construction is fiberglass stiffened with polyester foam core. Deck is vacuum-bagged ½" end-grain balsa and fiberglass sandwich.
● Two-spreader masthead rig allows use of low windage mast extrusion.

Details:
● Stanchion sockets are laminated into hull (a feature on all Olson designs) for strength, watertightness and durability.
● Structural supports under the cockpit floor double as a rack and clamp for outboard when stored below.
● Unique semi-open transom features built-in outboard bracket. Motor can be installed and removed while standing securely in the cockpit.
● Deck-to-hull joint has 2½-inch overlap and is bonded with Reid's Adhesive *and* bolted for long-term structural integrity.
● Mast is deck-stepped and hinged.
● Internal slab reefing hardware in boom is standard. Halyards are internal.
● Interior bulkheads are Brunzeel plywood with Regina mahogany veneer. Cabin sole is teak and holly.

Summary:
The Olson 25 is a significant broadening of approach for the company that helped establish Santa Cruz as the cradle of the ultra-light movement. A balanced combination of practical interior accommodations, spirited performance and manageability make this George Olson's most versatile design yet. ★

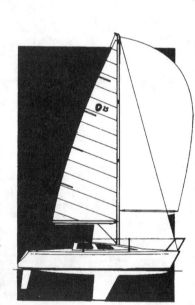

SAILOR

For the pilot issue of *Sailor* magazine in December, 1994, the author, by then editor-at-large for the magazine, worked onto a single page (page 301). The drawings of the Olson 25 for both the pilot issue of the magazine and this guide were other changes more in degree than in substance, the format designed for *Sailor* gradually transformed into the one used to

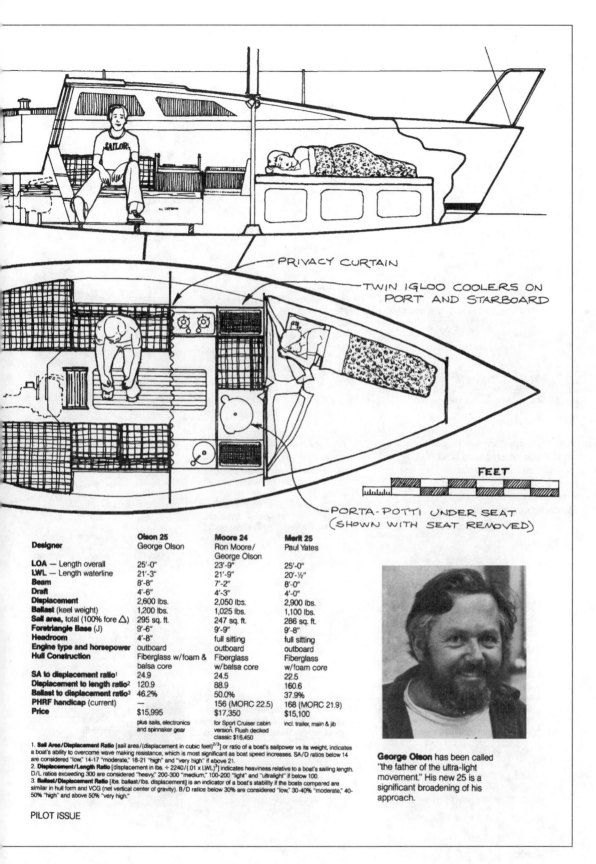

PRIVACY CURTAIN

TWIN IGLOO COOLERS ON PORT AND STARBOARD

FEET

PORTA-POTTI UNDER SEAT
(SHOWN WITH SEAT REMOVED)

Designer	Olson 25 George Olson	Moore 24 Ron Moore/ George Olson	Merit 25 Paul Yates
LOA — Length overall	25'-0"	23'-9"	25'-0"
LWL — Length waterline	21'-3"	21'-9"	20'-½"
Beam	8'-8"	7'-2"	8'-0"
Draft	4'-6"	4'-3"	4'-0"
Displacement	2,600 lbs.	2,050 lbs.	2,900 lbs.
Ballast (keel weight)	1,200 lbs.	1,025 lbs.	1,100 lbs.
Sail area, total (100% fore △)	295 sq. ft.	247 sq. ft.	286 sq. ft.
Foretriangle Base (J)	9'-6"	9'-9"	9'-8"
Headroom	4'-8"	full sitting	full sitting
Engine type and horsepower	outboard	outboard	outboard
Hull Construction	Fiberglass w/foam & balsa core	Fiberglass w/balsa core	Fiberglass w/foam core
SA to displacement ratio[1]	24.9	24.5	22.5
Displacement to length ratio[2]	120.9	88.9	160.6
Ballast to displacement ratio[3]	46.2%	50.0%	37.9%
PHRF handicap (current)	—	156 (MORC 22.5)	168 (MORC 21.9)
Price	$15,995	$17,350	$15,100
	plus sails, electronics and spinnaker gear	for Sport Cruiser cabin version. Flush decked classic $16,450	incl. trailer, main & jib

1. **Sail Area/Displacement Ratio** [sail area/(displacement in cubic feet)$^{2/3}$] or ratio of a boat's sailpower vs its weight, indicates a boat's ability to overcome wave making resistance, which is most significant as boat speed increases. SA/D ratios below 14 are considered "low," 14-17 "moderate," 18-21 "high" and "very high" if above 21.
2. **Displacement/Length Ratio** [displacement in lbs. ÷ 2240/(.01 x LWL)^3] indicates heaviness relative to a boat's sailing length. D/L ratios exceeding 300 are considered "heavy," 200-300 "medium," 100-200 "light" and "ultralight" if below 100.
3. **Ballast/Displacement Ratio** [lbs. ballast/lbs. displacement] is an indicator of a boat's stability if the boats compared are similar in hull form and VCG (net vertical center of gravity). B/D ratios below 30% are considered "low," 30-40% "moderate," 40-50% "high" and above 50% "very high."

PILOT ISSUE

George Olson has been called "the father of the ultra-light movement." His new 25 is a significant broadening of his approach.

together with editor Mark Smith to devise the "Boat Check" format shown here. With fewer words, a bigger sailplan, and report on boats in this guide. Note the similarities between the above reduced facsimile and the same subject compressed produced by the author.

An article in *Yachting* magazine appeared in January 1966, explaining how the author and his wife built *Pipit,* their South Coast 23 sloop. That article was written by Carol Henkel, the author's wife. In January, 1971 the author wrote another article in *Yachting*, telling how *Pipit* was converted to a yawl.

The South Coast 23 *Pipit* after conversion to a yawl.

Two more views of *Pipit* as a yawl. See details on page 255.

Index